BREWOOD

This view of the upper part of Dean Street, formerly known as Dean's End, is difficult to date with any accuracy, but may be as early as the 1870's. The road is paved and the footpaths cobbled, and there is no evidence of any gas street lighting, although a gas works began operation in the village in 1864. The shop doorway has now been bricked up and the bow window replaced with a flat window, but otherwise the scene has changed very little in the last century – even the tall chimney visible through the churchyard still exists. George Fox was a saddler and harness maker in 1869 until after the turn of the century. By the early 1970's the house was virtually derelict, but has since been restored.

BREWOOD

Some notes on the history of Brewood in Staffordshire,
with an account of the escape of Charles II
after the Battle of Worcester on 3rd September 1651.

David Horovitz

First published in 1988
ISBN 1 85421 011 4

second edition,
revised and enlarged,
with corrections, 1992.

Published by David Horovitz
Kiddemore Cottage,
Brewood, Stafford, ST19 9BH
in association with
The Self Publishing Association Ltd

ISBN 1 85421 175 7

Typeset by Images Design & Print Ltd, Hanley Swan, Worcs
Printed and Bound in Great Britain by Hartnolls Ltd, Bodmin, Cornwall

To Sylvia, Laura and Ben
without whom this work
would have been finished
in half the time.

"I say This only, . . . I know not how in any course of studies I could have better served . . . than by preserving the Memoirs of this Parish and the adjacent Parts, which before lay remote from common notice, and in a few years had been buried in unsearchable Oblivion. If the present Age be too immersed in Cares and Pleasures, to take any Relish or to make any Use of these discoveries, I then appeal to Posterity: for I believe the times will come when Persons of better inclination will arise, who will be glad to find any Collection of this nature; and will be ready to supply the Defects, and carry on the Continuation of it."

— The Reverend White Kennett, Vicar of Ambrosden, Oxfordshire, in "Parochial Antiquities . . . of Ambrosden, Burcester and other adjacent parts . . ." published in 1695.

CONTENTS

Photographs and Illustrations

Preface

In 1797, a correspondent writing to 'The Gentleman's Magazine' noted that "Brewood is a small market town in Staffordshire, situated on a gentle eminence . . . the situation of this town (or rather village) is rural, pleasant and retired, and is a proper place of retreat from the bustle of the large towns . . ." That description remains accurate some two centuries later, and perhaps explains why so many residents and visitors become captivated by its modest but seductive charms.

This book owes much to the work of many other authors, ranging from the Itinerary of Antonius written in the third century, via the irrepressible Dr Plot and his great 'The Natural History of Staffordshire' in 1686, to the incomparable 'Victoria History of the County of Stafford' of the present century. But a particular debt is due to those earlier historians of Brewood: the erudite John Hay, the benevolent William Parke and the sometimes eccentric James Hicks Smith, all of whom took great pains in the last century to gather and record material relating to the history of Brewood; to the industrious Thomas Cluett who published much of the local interest around the turn of the century; and not least to Mary Wakefield, who in more recent years compiled an invaluable record of many aspects of the village and its story. All shared an obvious affection for what the architectural historian Sir Nikolaus Pevsner described as "an engaging little town".

For willing co-operation in seeking out research material I am indebted to the staff at Shrewsbury Local Studies Library, Staffordshire Record Office, Shropshire Record Office and Wolverhampton, Stafford and Birmingham Public Libraries, but in particular to Cathy Bowden and Pauline Thomson of The William Salt Library, and to Clare Humphries and Sharon Pitt of Brewood Library, who have patiently and cheerfully rendered assistance well beyond the call of duty. My thanks are also due to David Bywater, John Haynes, Keith Fellows, Bob Meeson, Chris Welch, Dennis Morgan, Steven Wright, Suzanne Proudley, Bill Allsop, Frank Lowe, David Whitfield, Alex Chatwin, Eve Bell, and no less to all those others too numerous to name individually who have volunteered information and material. Mr P.R. de L. Giffard and Mr D.V. Fowkes offered a number of constructive observations on the text of the first edition, and Dr Margaret Gelling, doyenne of place-name scholars, has generously reviewed and corrected the two chapters relating to place-names in this edition, and given much other assistance, for which I record my appreciation. I am also glad of this opportunity to record formally my thanks to Mrs Annie Onion and Mrs Connie Bird who have been kind enough to share their memories of the Brewood area in the earliest years of the century. Many of the illustrations are taken from photographs collected over many years by Brewood Civic Society, which is to be commended for its foresight. I must also express my gratitude to those landowners who have allowed me to trudge around their fields and hedgerows seeking answers to the various riddles of the Brewood landscape, even if each excursion seemed to raise more questions than it solved. Finally, I am indebted to Tony Harold, founder of The Self Publishing Association, for his initiative and wise counsel, and to Wendy Semple, Stella Jeenes and Anita Hill for the infinite pains taken with the typesetting and illustrations.

W.G. Hoskins repeatedly emphasised of landscape history "everything is older than we think", and I have found it particularly rewarding to have unexpectedly located within the parish a prehistoric flint-working site and prehistoric finds at four other places; two unknown Roman roads; the possible site of a Roman fort; four unrecorded medieval moats; a vanished ironworking bloomery and the likely site of a blast furnace, as well as the location of a long-forgotten windmill and, though outside the parish, a curious unrecorded earthwork, possibly prehistoric, less than three miles from Brewood village. These discoveries are mentioned to show that there will always be secrets waiting to be revealed in our ancient landscape, and in the hope that others may be encouraged to undertake their own researches, exploration and publication, wherever they may be.

For this second edition an opportunity has been taken to incorporate additional material and make a number of corrections. Throughout, dimensions and areas are given, without apology, in traditional imperial measure. For all mistakes of fact or interpretation that remain, I am of course wholly responsible.

I would welcome any information from those who share an interest in Brewood and its environs which might correct inevitable errors or erroneous conclusions, or add to our knowledge of the history or prehistory of the area.

David Horovitz
Kiddemore Cottage,
Brewood
May 1992

1. Introduction

Some six miles from east to west and five miles from north to south, the parish of Brewood, still predominantly rural, is in the Cuttlestone hundred of south-west Staffordshire, lying alongside Shropshire,[1] and is one of the largest Staffordshire parishes. The curiously jagged county border forms the western boundary and the ancient Watling Street is the northern boundary for almost four miles.

The principal river is the Penk, which meanders northwards in the east of the parish and forms, with its tributary the Moat Brook, part of the southern boundary, but the parish is also a watershed, for streams on the north-west side flow westwards and eventually feed the Severn and the Irish Sea, while streams in the rest of the parish flow east and north and ultimately join the Humber and enter the North Sea.

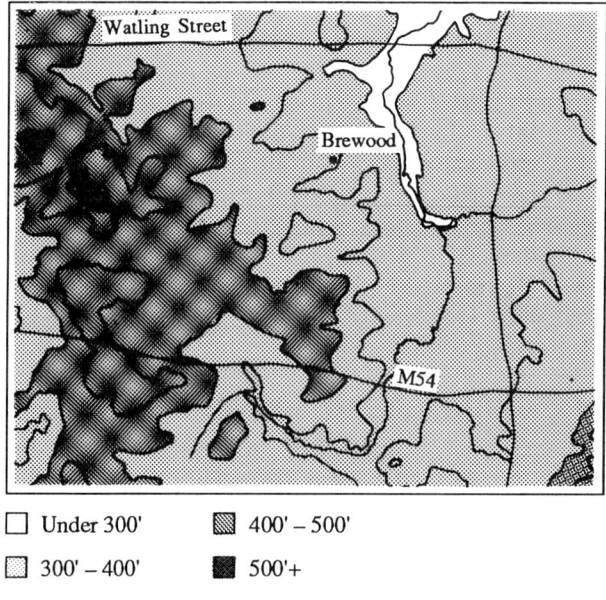

Contour map of the area around Brewood.

Undulating from below 300′ in the north-east to over 500′ on the western boundary north of Chillington, with the highest point at 513′ to the north of Boscobel sand beds, the land tends to be heavy in the north and west and lighter in the south and east. The main Stafford to Wolverhampton road runs north to south on the eastern side, and the M54 motorway crosses the southernmost part, almost parallel with Watling Street. The nearest towns are Stafford, some ten miles to the north, and Wolverhampton, some seven miles to the south.

Approached from every direction along leafy lanes, with many ancient ivy-clad oaks standing sentinel in the hedgerows,[2] Brewood village – geographically located at 52°40.5′, 2°10.2′ west – is concentrated mainly on the west side of a shallow valley, through which runs Chillington Brook, at a point where the land rises comparatively steeply on both sides. The hub of the village is Market Place and the dark sandstone parish church nearby at the top of the hill. Architecturally, the overall impression of the central village area, now protected as a Conservation Area, is Georgian, but many later façades conceal medieval internal timbering. The more recent part of the village is concentrated to the north-east, with a deep wooded cutting concealing the Shropshire Union Canal on the western edge.

Bishop's Wood, a compact and generally modern village, lies to the west of Brewood on the Shropshire border, and the larger and older village of Coven lies between Brewood and the eastern boundary of the parish.

Brewood from the south-east: an engraving from The Gentleman's Magazine of 1797.

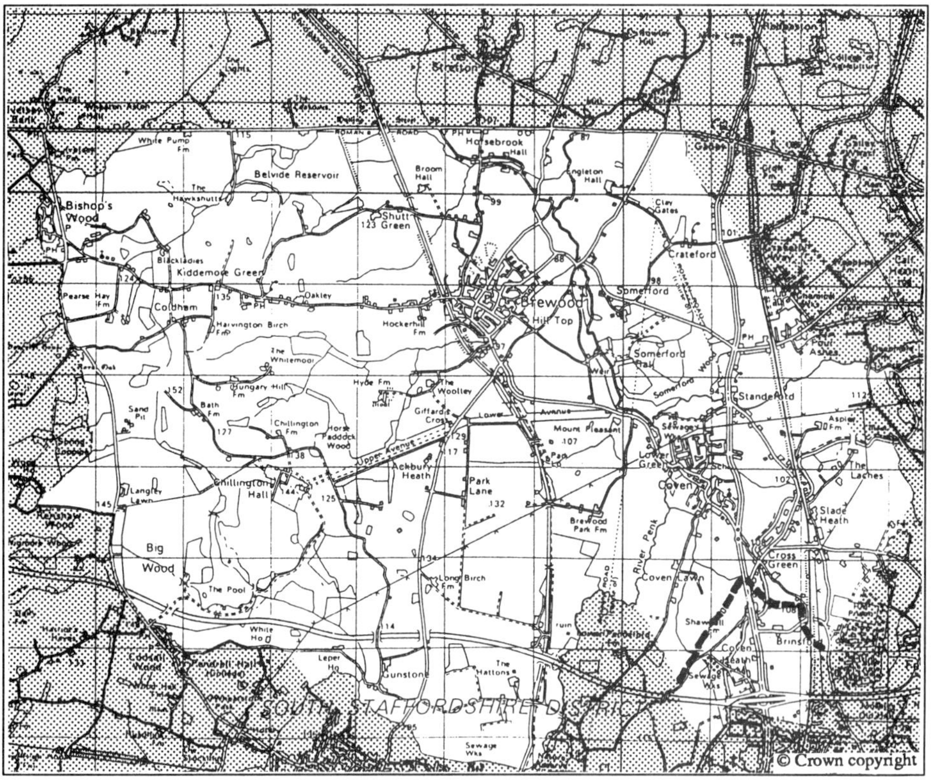

Brewood parish. The small piece at the south-east was added to the parish following boundary reorganisations in 1934. Scale approximately ¼" to one mile.

2. Geology

Brewood parish lies geologically on rocks of the triassic period of the Mesozoic era, that part to the west of a meandering line from Engleton to Long Birch being Lower red sandstone, with Lower Keuper to the east and a small area around the Laches lying on Upper Mottled sandstone.[3]

The land is predominantly Keuper Marl, with narrow alluvium deposits adjoining the River Penk and Deepmore Brook, which are in turn bounded by fluvio glacial gravels. A ribbon of Lower Keuper red and brown sandstone with pebbly layers runs through Gailey, Crateford and Somerford, widening to encompass Brewood Park, the Hattons and Pendeford. The eastern part of the parish, including Somerford and Coven, is boulder clay with unbedded sand and gravel.

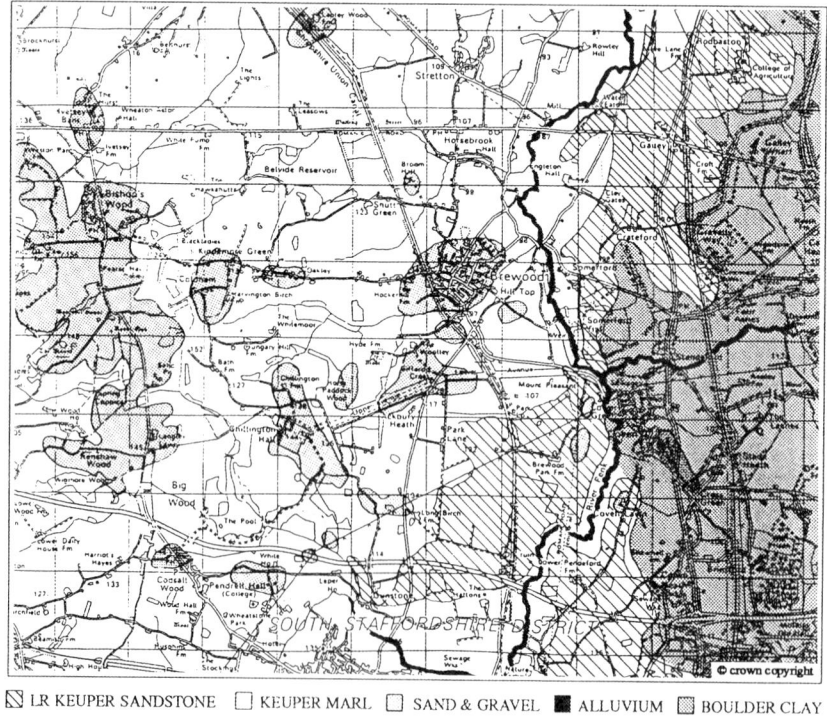

⊠ LR KEUPER SANDSTONE ☐ KEUPER MARL ☐ SAND & GRAVEL ■ ALLUVIUM ▨ BOULDER CLAY

Geological map of Brewood area.

The last glaciation reached its maximum southern extent at Wolverhampton between about 26,000 and 15,000 B.C. and has left deposits of clay, sand and gravel across the parish, principally from Bishop's Wood to Langley Lawn, and around Brewood village centre, Giffard's Cross, Chillington, the hill west of Long Birch, Harvington Birch, Broom Hall, the hill north-east of Bath Farm, and Brewood Park –

16

several pauses in the retreat of the ice-front, are prominent on the east of the parish around Boscobel. Glacial boulders, or erratics, are also to be found in various parts of the parish and in the village itself, with a group of particularly large boulders lying in the corner of a field south of Strangleford Birch Farm.[4] Others can be seen along Poplars Farm Way, Coven – the two tapering sandstone pillars are probably eighteenth or nineteenth century boundary markers – and a number have been used to mark the parish boundary near Codsall Wood. Most of the erratics are of grey granite, brought down in glaciers from North Wales, the Lake District or Scotland during various glacial periods.[5] They are frequently built into the corners and bases of walls and buildings as protection against vehicle damage.

Old marl pits scattered throughout the area attest to the extraction of marl to enrich the land over many centuries, and sandstone has long been used for building purposes from quarries within and close to the village. Sandstone slabs with footprints of prehistoric amphibious creatures, assigned to the rhynchocephalian reptile Rhynchosaurus, were found in the last century at the former Stradsfield Quarry.[6]

The sandstone which lies near the surface in and around the village explains why a number of earth tremors have been recorded in recent centuries. In his monumental work 'The Natural History of Staffordshire', published in 1686, Dr Robert Plot mentions an earthquake which occurred near Wolverhampton at about 11 a.m. on 25th December 1677 and adds

> Nov: 4, 1678, there happened another earthquake in this county, it was most dreadfull of any place I could hear of, about Brewood, whither it came with a noise, not like a clap, but a flat rumbleing distant Thunder, yet so great that it wakened people in their beds, at 11 a clock by the night, about what time it began, and continued till towards two in the morning; the earth moving very sensibly three times, at about ½ an hours distance, each motion from the other. The night following there happen'd another, but not so great, yet not without noise, as I suppose very few doe; if any, it must be where the fire damp kindles so deep in the earth, that the explosion cannot be heard through so dense a body as it may be thence to the superficies, though the convulsion may be sensible.[7]

Other tremors recorded on 4th November 1678; 21st November 1795;[8] at 4.15 am on 9th November 1852;[9] 6th October 1863;[10] at 1.35 pm on 25th March 1902;[11] 19th July 1984;[12] and at 2.45 pm on 2nd April 1990[13] were strongly felt in the area.

3. Prehistory

The first human inhabitants of the region were the nomadic hunters of the Upper Palaeolithic period who crossed the land bridge from mainland Europe in the warmer interglacial periods before the last ice age. Although the period lasted some 75,000 years, the total population of Britain probably averaged no more than two or three thousand, and few remains have been discovered, although two stone hand-axes from Drayton Bassett and Shenstone, both in the east of the county, have been dated from surrounding deposits to about 30,000 BC.[14]

Much more widespread are finds from the hunting and food-gathering Mesolithic people [12,000-4,500 BC] whose artifacts and habitation sites have been discovered at Cannock Wood, at Bourne Pool near Aldridge,[15] and at Boningale and Wrottesley Old Park on the Staffordshire-Shropshire border.[16] Although well outside Brewood parish, the latter site is of interest since it lies within the south-west corner of what was Brewood Forest. Flint finds, both tools and worked cores with associated waste, provide evidence of a major Mesolithic flint industry in the area which continued through the Neolithic period into the Bronze Age. Within the parish, a similar major site with flint tools and cores ranging from Mesolithic to Bronze Age date was discovered in 1990 on the south-east side of Stretton Bridge, and is doubtless only one of many similar sites along the Penk valley between Stretton Bridge and Cuttlestone Bridge. It is worth noting that flint occurs naturally in neither Staffordshire nor Shropshire, and was evidently transported considerable distances from the south and east.

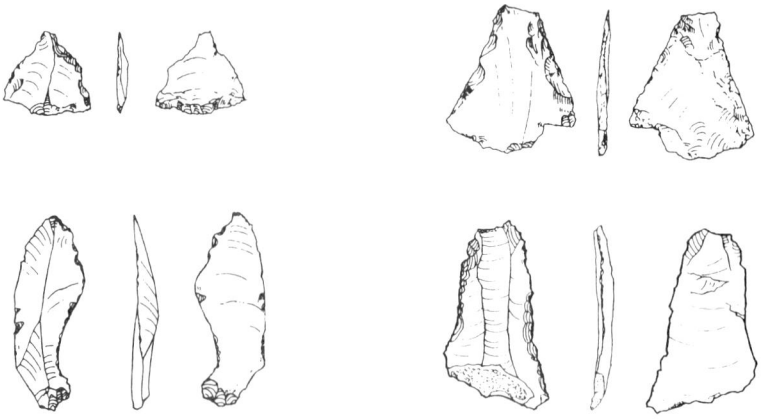

Mesolithic and Neolithic flints from Stretton Bridge. Two-thirds full size.

It was the Neolithic peoples who crossed the North Sea some 6,500 years ago who made the first real impact on this island, however, for whilst the earlier prehistoric settlers left few traces of their occupation and did little to transform the natural landscape, the pastoral Neolithic immigrants spread quickly, if thinly, throughout Britain, raising livestock, cultivating crops, manufacturing pottery and mining flint. Though small in stature, their organisational skills and capabilities are evidenced by their so-called causewayed camps and extraordinary megalithic monuments. From tumuli of the period there is evidence of the colonisation of most parts of Staffordshire, but the Neolithic people have given us much more than a few graves and primitive tools for, with the early metal-age peoples, they form a very large element in our ancestry, and as the first farmers they changed the physical landscape of a very substantial area of Britain. Within 2000 years they converted millions of acres of wildwood into farmland or heath, principally with stone axes produced at 'axe factories' in North Wales, the Lake District, and elsewhere. These axes, which may also have had a ritual significance, are often found far from their source of manufacture, and three have been discovered in the area: one at Weston Park,[17] one at Manor Farm, Shifnal, and one on the south side of Brook House, Featherstone.[18] Worked flints and cores of Neolithic date found near the river Penk south-east of Stretton Bridge in 1990[19] have already been mentioned. The only other recorded find in the parish which may be Neolithic is a flat, diamond-shaped perforated Neolithic hammer-head in fine-grained stone found at Langley Lawn in the 1970's.[20]

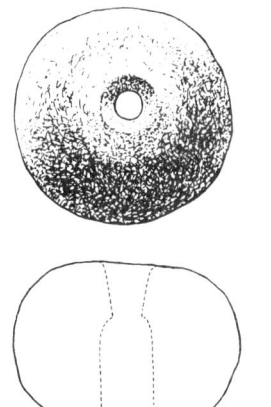

Perforated stone from Kiddemore Green, possibly a Mesolithic or Neolithic 'mace-head'. One-third scale.

A curiously perforated stone found to the south of Kiddemore Cottage at Kiddemore Green in 1983[21] may be a 'mace head' or hammer-stone of the same period, or even Mesolithic, but is a type of object found well into the Bronze Age, which began with the spread in about 2,500 BC of Germanic immigrants who smelted copper and tin to manufacture bronze tools and weapons. Cereals were cultivated, and cloth was woven from flax and wool. Conventional burial was gradually replaced by cremation, and many tumuli of the period have been identified in the region, mostly in north-east Staffordshire.

The Middle and Late Bronze Age is represented by palstaves – bronze axe heads designed to fit socketed wooden hafts – found scattered over the region, and Plot mentions a palstave found at Stretton,[22] and one found at The Laches,[23] on the eastern edge of the parish, in the seventeenth century. Another was found at Beacon Hill, near Congreve, in 1717, and one at Congreve itself shortly afterwards,[24] although the latter may be the same as the one found at Beacon Hill, and result from confused reporting.

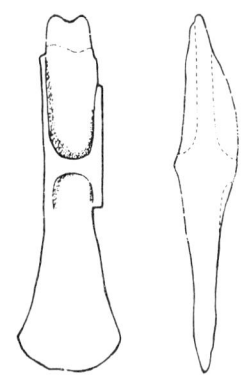

Unfortunately, the precise location of the finds is not recorded. In 1985 a shield pattern palstave of Middle Bronze Age date was found at Shaw Hall Farm, a similar palstave is known to have been found near Four Ashes, and a socketed bronze axe has been recorded from Water Eaton.[25]

Even though the knowledge of metal working was available, flint tools were still produced well into the Bronze Age, and a crudely flaked rectangular implement, 4½" long, with rounded ends, of white flint and with possible traces of secondary working,

Shield-pattern bronze palstave found to west of Shaw Hall Farm, Coven Heath, dating from the Middle Bronze Age. 5³/₈' long

found during the construction of the car-park to the north-west of St Dominic's School in 1985,[26] may, if indeed it has been worked by man, date from this period, and may have been deposited in spoil from the construction of the nearby canal.

A finely worked Bronze Age barbed and tanged arrowhead in cream-coloured flint was picked up after ploughing in recent years to the south of Watling Street west of the junction with Engleton Lane,[27] and a rectangular flat scraper in dark brown flint, probably of the same period,[28] has been found nearby to the north of Watling Street.

At Rowley Hill, two miles north of Brewood, is a tumulus, now almost obliterated by ploughing but recorded as being 65' in diameter and three feet high in 1907,[29] thought to date from the Bronze Age, and similar tumuli have been traced at Low Hill, Bushbury [where palstaves have also been found[30]], and Low Field, Four Ashes. The latter, believed to date from the early Bronze Age, were described by Plot as "The two lows on Calves-Heath, near the roadside that leads from Somerford to Four Crosses".[31]

On 20 April 1781, Thomas Whitgreave of Moseley, great-grandson of the Thomas Whitgreave involved in the escape of Charles II, recorded in his diary "This morning Mr. Walton, Mr. Hough and self walked to the Warren House upon Calf Heath to see two Roman Tumuli, which Mr Plot mentions in his History of Staffordshire."[32] By 1938 all traces of the tumuli – the only known prehistoric structures within the parish – had been obliterated by gravel workings, but the site, which is not known to have been excavated, and of which no description or illustration appears to have survived, lay between Four Ashes crossroads and Deepmore Farm.[33] Possibly associated with the site are a Bronze Age socketed bronze spear-head and two flint scrapers found south of Standeford Mill House in 1987,[34] and the palstave from Four Ashes.

Socketed spear-head from Standeford, Middle Bronze Age. 5 1/8" long

The Iron Age began with a wave of immigrants from the low countries in about 750 BC who settled in the southern half of England and introduced iron tools and implements. They were followed by other peoples from central Europe, principally those of the Hallstadt, La Tène and Belgæ cultures, known collectively as the Celts. These advanced warrior castes imposed themselves on natives who were already Celtic speaking, bringing with them innovations like the potter's wheel, the spoked iron-shod wheel, coinage, and crops such as emmer [the ancestor of modern wheat], rye and oats, which were cultivated with improved agricultural equipment, notably the mould-board plough which turned the earth. A number of regional cultures or tribes developed, each with its own name and with its territory dominated by formidable multiple-banked hill-forts, of which seven exist in Staffordshire, including Berry Ring near Stafford and Castle Ring on Cannock Chase. A multiple-ditched enclosure of Iron Age date has been revealed by aerial photography on the south side of Pave Lane, Newport; a possible prehistoric earthwork surrounding St Peter's church in Wolverhampton has been identified; and a hill-fort is recorded at Hilton in a Saxon charter, but its site is unknown.[35] Traces of banks and ditches – probably relatively recent – surround the prominent summit of Beacon Hill, near Congreve, but since the Roman place-name Pennocrucio is known to derive from a native Iron Age Celtic name, it is possible that Beacon Hill was a tribal base before the Roman occupation. Although no artifacts of prehistoric date have been recorded from Penn [a British name] it has been observed that the hill-top site above the church of Upper Penn would have provided an admirable defensive location for an Iron Age hill-fort, and there are unexplained terraces near the church. Is it possible that Brewood church overlies a modest hill-fort? It too has a British name and a possible prehistoric find has been recorded. The top end of Dean Street, curiously out of alignment with the southern part, and what is now Church Road, could conceivably follow the line of an early ditch surrounding a summit mound. The ground falls away steeply on the north to Sandy Lane, and even before quarrying for sand in the present century the land to the east of the churchyard dropped down steeply.

The resemblance of the great hill-forts of Staffordshire to the hill forts of the Welsh Marches supports the evidence that the whole of what is now Shropshire and the greater part of Cheshire and Staffordshire, including the Brewood area, as well as parts of Flintshire and Worcestershire, was the territory of the Cornovii, whose principal base was the hill fort strategically sited on the summit of the Wrekin, artificially steepened for extra defence, although the existence of a Civitas Letocetensium, or tribe of Letocetum, based at Wall, cannot be ruled out.

Little is known of the Cornovii: confusion has been caused by other tribes of the same name in Caithness and Cornwall, but academics have suggested that the name perhaps meant 'the people of the peninsula' or was linked to the Celtic religion and horned gods, both meanings being derived from the Latin 'corno' meaning horn. The geographic explanation does not fit the tribes in Caithness or Shropshire, and the latter theory seems perhaps slightly less unconvincing. It is doubtless no more than coincidence that the well-known Abbots Bromley horn dance, with its ancient origins [carbon dating has shown that some of the horns used in the dance are at least 900 years old] takes place within 17 miles of Brewood, and that excavations at the Roman posting station at Letocetum [Wall] have revealed what would seem to be a re-used first century shrine to a horned goddess, and ox skulls buried with the horns deliberately facing downwards.[36] Interestingly, the only two 'ancient' finds recorded from Barnfield sand beds when a thin layer of gravel was removed many years ago were a fossilised oyster shell – and the horn of a wild cow.[37]

From the sites and finds in the vicinity there is no doubt that Brewood was in an area of some importance in the later prehistoric period. Whilst there is no direct evidence that any prehistoric trackways passed through the Brewood area, it has been suggested that the central lowland area of Staffordshire was sufficiently free of dense woodland for regular trade-routes to have developed between the Severn and the Trent, and the prehistoric finds around Brewood may lie on the line of one such route. It has also been recognised that barrow burial was reserved for a special élite in Bronze Age society, and at least some of the local Bronze Age metal finds are perhaps more likely to be the remains of grave deposits associated with habitation sites than accidental losses, a likelihood reinforced by associated flint finds.

The lack of recorded prehistoric finds in Brewood itself – apart from the single implement from St Dominic's School – does not necessarily indicate an absence of prehistoric activity or settlement. Recorded discoveries will date from historic – i.e. relatively recent – times, but artifacts may have been found since prehistory and remained unrecorded, the area having been heavily cultivated for many hundreds, if not thousands, of years. A possible clue to an early discovery in Brewood may be the field name 'Gooldburynes', now unidentifiable but recorded in 1453[38] and meaning 'burial place where gold was found', recalling the Bronze Age gold torc or necklace found near Pattingham churchyard in 1700 and said to have weighed 3 lbs. 2 ozs., and a small gold ingot found in a field nearby in

1780.[39] There is some evidence that two Celtic gold staters [which could not have been Cornovian, for the Cornovii had no coinage] were found in recent years, one at Stretton – possibly near the Ivy House – and the other to the west of the Roman site of Pennocrucium. The first was an Ambiani, type 5, made in Gaul c.100-70 BC. No information is known of the second. Three adjoining fields shown on an estate plan of about 1727 on the north side of the junction of the lane to Hungry Hill Farm and the lane from Coldham to Chillington [where there is now a large pit, described on early Ordnance Survey maps as 'sandholes'], are each named Churchyard Leasow, and may be the 'Churchyordfeld' recorded in 1494,[40] perhaps indicating that bones were once found there, since the area has no apparent connection with the church.

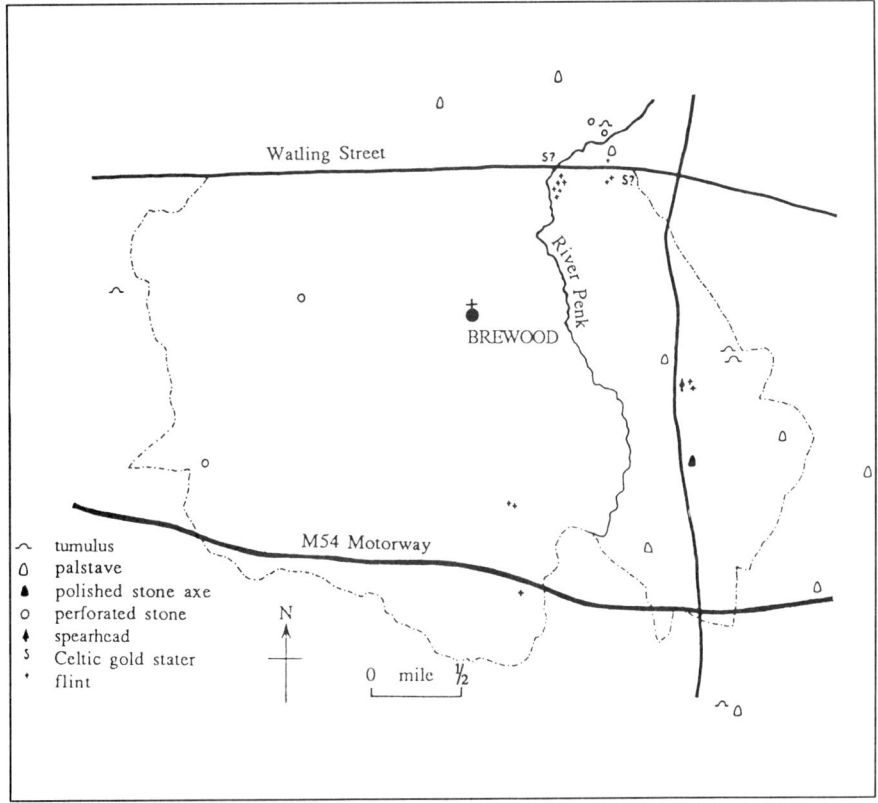

Prehistoric sites and finds in and around Brewood parish.

Intriguingly, etymologists have suggested that the name Cuttlestone, which survives in Cuttlestone Bridge[41] south west of Penkridge, but which may have been associated originally with the area where Watling Street crosses the River Penk,[42] may derive from 'Cuthwulf's Stone', perhaps a prehistoric megalith, now lost or destroyed, and that Ringhills,[43] in the

23

circle', conceivably with prehistoric connotations.[44] There is no apparent physical evidence to support the latter theory, although part of the hill is heavily wooded, which precludes complete investigation, and a worked flint found on the southern slopes of the hill in 1987 is of Bronze Age or Neolithic period.[45] Indeed, the nearby pine-topped hill[46] west of Port Lane near Long Birch is perhaps a more likely prehistoric site. There are small earthworks of unknown date [but perhaps connected with a windmill believed to have stood in the area at some date before the eighteenth century] on the summit, the elevated position with its steep southern slope and commanding views is the type of site which attracted prehistoric man, and several worked flints, possibly Mesolithic or Neolithic, were found on the southern flank in 1989 and 1992.[47]

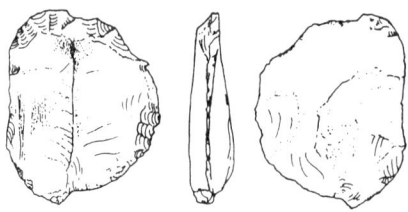

Neolithic flint scraper from southern slope of Ringhills, half-size.

4. The Romans

Although Julius Caesar led two expeditions to Britain in 55 BC and 54 BC, the first amounted to no more than a reconnaisance and the second resulted in no permanent settlement.

Nearly a century was to pass before a Roman force again set foot in Britain, when Claudius arrived with an army of conquest in 43 AD. But resistance was not overcome overnight, and it was another four years before Roman troops advanced into what is now Staffordshire. The campaign was led by the Governor, Ostorius Scapula, to push the frontier to the Severn and hold back the unpacified natives of the west. It seems that the coming of the Romans caused little upheaval in the region, since there is no record of any resistance to the newcomers by the Cornovii, and it was probably during this period that military engineers constructed the permanent highway known to us as Watling Street to link the south with Uriconium [Wroxeter]. It is possible that the route was ancient even at that time, for many Roman roads are known to follow much older lines, and Plot in 1686 recorded a number of mounds roughly on the line of Watling Street. Some of these mounds were almost certainly tumuli, such as the one at Rowley Hill.

Uriconium, later known as Viroconium, clearly derived its name from Uricon, or Caer Guricon, which may have been the Celtic name for the Wrekin or, more likely, for the hill fort on the summit, the name being transferred to the new Roman city when the subjugated Cornovii abandoned their former stronghold. It is uncertain why the name Uriconon [phonetically almost identical with the native name and the later Saxon Wroecan] was changed by the Romans to Viroconium: easier pronunciation is one possibility.

That Viroconium was the tribal capital of the local Cornovii after their subjugation by the Romans is known from several ancient sources, notably the geographer Ptolemy and the Antonine Itinerary [a Roman 'road-book' compiled in the early third century], and from one of the finest Roman inscriptions discovered in this country. Excavated in fragments near the forum building at Viroconium, the inscription, in elegant lettering of superb craftsmanship, records the dedication of the building to the Emperor Hadrian by the Civitas Cornoviorum, that is, the tribe of the Cornovii.

The Antonine Itinerary is also one of a number of ancient documentary sources identifying a Roman settlement, Pennocrucio [otherwise and more commonly Pennocrucium], between Uxacona and Letocetum. Letocetum has long been identified as Wall, near Lichfield, and Uxacona has been located at Redhill, east of Telford.

The probable existence of a large Roman site near Brewood had therefore long been recognised, for the Itinerary gives mileages between the places listed, Pennocrucium being 23 Roman miles from Viroconium and 12 Roman miles from Letocetum. The obvious etymological similarities led early historians to place Pennocrucium at Penkridge, and it was the perceptive Dr Plot who recognised what now seems obvious: that Penkridge is some distance from the Roman road.[48] He suggested that Stretton [Street-town] was a more likely site. Stebbing Shaw considered that the site lay to the west of the river at Stretton, mentioning Roman coins and other antiquities found after ploughing.[49] Unfortunately, further details of such finds are not given.

The possible site of Pennocrucium was also considered by a local nineteenth-century historian with a particular interest in the area, John Hay, who published 'Notes and Collections Relating to Brewood' in 1858 and 1860. He was not prepared to positively identify the Roman settlement, but felt that Stretton and Horsebrook "may fairly be presumed to have been originally . . . suburbs of the Roman station".[50]

Writing in 1881, James Hicks Smith, another historian with a special interest in Brewood, concluded: "On the assumption that any Roman fort or forts existed here, the site must have been the Great and Little Roughs, two pieces of woodland between the Hockerhill and Kiddemore, the one about ten, the other about twenty acres in extent, entrenched and intersected by ditches . . ." It is difficult to see what could have led to such a theory, since there is no apparent shred of evidence to link the two sites mentioned with the Romans, although the two irregularly-shaped areas of woodland are ditched and, in some places, also banked.[51]

Early in 1937 a workman digging gravel in a quarry at Engleton exposed ancient masonry and was fortunate to escape injury when it fell into the workings. The matter was drawn to the attention of Wolverhampton Archæological Society by Miss Dunkley of Brewood vicarage, and an initial examination of the site revealed fragments of Roman roofing tiles. Much interest was aroused by the possibility that the long sought posting station of Pennocrucium had finally been located. In fact, Pennocrucium had not been found, but the discovery was nevertheless of considerable interest and importance.

Carefully excavated between August and October by Diana Ashcroft and a team of helpers including pupils from Wolverhampton Grammar School under the supervision of Miss [later Dame] Kathleen Kenyon, the well-preserved remains of a substantial villa were revealed,[52] a type of building rare in the region. The only other known villas in Staffordshire are at Hales in the parish of Tyrley, and at Acton Trussell.[53]

Facing east some 500 yards south of Watling Street on the east bank of the Penk, Engleton villa, approximately 120' long and 72' wide, was built from squared blocks of red Bunter sandstone on gravel foundations. Diamond-shaped roofing tiles of two distinct types had been transported from the Ludlow area, and flooring tiles of limestone from either Wem or the south-east Midlands. Although the gravel workings had destroyed the southern part of the villa, the remains, which in many places stood several courses high, revealed a rectangular building with projecting end wings and a bath wing at the south west corner. The excavations have been the subject of more recent re-appraisal, but it is evident that alterations had been made at various periods, and during the first reconstruction the foundations of the new walls were built in hard blue stone – transported from some distance, for it is not found locally – which helped the excavators to identify the new work. In the fourth century the villa was converted into a tripartite one with a south wing and additional corridor which aligned the bath wing with the outside of the building. At the same time a front corridor and portico were added.

Large quantities of plaster fragments indicated that the interior of the villa had been decorated with brightly coloured plaster.

A boundary ditch which seems to have surrounded the site was thought to have been a substitute for the more usual walled farmyard, but an aerial photograph taken in 1978[54] shows what seems to be a square enclosure in the south-west corner of the field to the north of the villa site. This may be the walled farmyard, although the soil marks may have a more prosaic origin. No traces of outbuildings were discovered, but it is possible that they lie buried to the east of the villa.

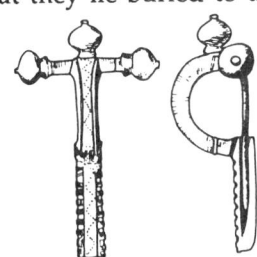

The finds from the excavations included a large crossbow brooch of the late third or fourth century, a fragment of a similar brooch, and an undatable pin with a ring head. Iron objects consisted of a ferrule, hook, staple, knife, linchpin, and some unidentifiable pieces, but no identifiable agricultural tools. Seven Roman coins were found, all dating from the second and third centuries. Amongst the finds, now held by Birmingham City Museum, is a human

Crossbow brooch, late third or fourth century, from Engleton villa. 2 7/8' long.

skull. Although not mentioned in the excavation report, contem-porary newspaper articles confirm that the skull was found during digging.

One curious discovery at the site which remains unexplained in the excavators' report was a small sandstone pillar with crudely moulded drum base, which lay at the bottom of a large pit, some 12' in diameter and 9' deep, cut through the hard floor of the courtyard slightly to the south of the main entrance. The pillar appeared to be a local copy of Roman work, and in recent years has been converted into a sundial which now stands in the garden at Engleton Hall Farm. It is doubtless no more than coincidence that a single well-turned sandstone pillar, some 3' high, has been found at the site of the Roman villa at Acton Scott, south of Church Stretton, and others are known to have been found elsewhere, including a villa near Bath.

Although there is evidence that some villas had their origins in iron-age farmsteads, the excavations at Engleton revealed no pre-Roman occupation. From datable pottery fragments the villa would appear to have been built no earlier than the late second century, but the remains could not be more accurately dated. The pottery sherds, coins and brooches indicate that the villa was occupied well into the fourth century, and the site then appears to have been completely abandoned.

The traditional image of Roman villas as Mediterranean-type shallow-roofed single storey buildings has been partially revised since the discovery of an apparently conventional villa at Winchester in 1987[55] which was 45′ high of two or three storeys, with a steeply inclined roof. The height could be determined from one gable wall which had collapsed outwards and was almost completely preserved. Similar buildings only occur in Britain and Gaul, and probably owe their basic design to late Iron Age structures. The excavations at Engleton revealed evidence of buttresses on four sides of one of the rooms, which may have been supports for a timber floor at a later period, and it is possible that the villa from the outside, with its sandstone walls and stone-tiled roof, resembled a Cotswold tithe barn with porticoed frontage.

During its life of perhaps 150 years, the villa, placed upstream to enjoy uncontaminated water, evidently enabled its privileged residents, perhaps local district or customs officers, to pass the long English winters in some comfort, with underfloor-heated north-wing, tepidarium and caldarium [warm room and hot room], and, for the truly hardy, an indoor cold plunge – notwithstanding the close proximity of the Penk.

A Saxon penny of Eadred [946-995 AD] and a silver halfpenny of Edward III found in the topsoil may indicate that long after the villa had fallen into ruin the site was used as a source of building stone and gravel – ironically, the very activity that led to its rediscovery.

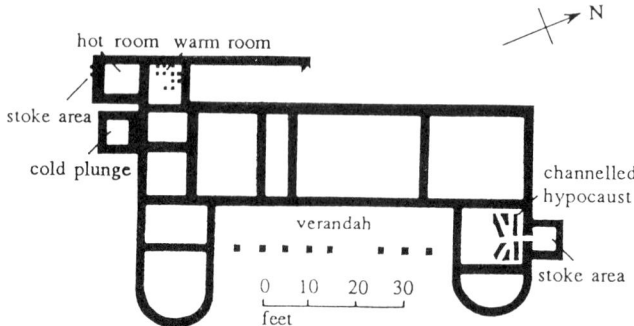

Suggested plan of Engleton villa in its first period. After Webster.

The remains of the villa were reburied at the conclusion of the excavations, and little is now visible, except the southern edge of the foundations, which have been colonised by rabbits.

It was not until 1946 that the mystery of Pennocrucium was finally solved. Aerial reconnaissance[56] showed cropmarks which formed a rectangular enclosure astride Watling Street, some 750 yards east of the Penk on a plateau to the west of the junction with Engleton Lane. Excavations two years later[57] confirmed the existence of a triple-ditched area 620' from east to west and 425' from north to south, giving a usable occupation area, allowing for probable ramparts and pallisades, of some 5 acres. The ditch profiles closely resembled those of the fourth century enclosure at Wall. Subsequent minor excavations[58] showed that the ditches enclosed a settlement of small wattle-and-daub buildings laid out in a rectangular street plan aligned with Watling Street, with possible cultivation plots and animal pens to the north and south. Entrance gates were identified in the centre of the east and west sides, and traces of cobbled side lanes within the enclosure included what may have been drains and gutters. Inside the central area of the settlement to the south of Watling Street a well was revealed some 3' in diameter, the upper part stone-lined and the lower part cut into solid rock. The high water table prevented complete excavation, but two coins were found dating from c.300 and c.375 AD. Various pits, gullies and occupation levels indicated that the settlement extended at least 110 yards east of the modern lane to Water Eaton.

Finds included a bronze dolphin brooch, many iron nails, a few fragments of greenish thick glass, and several baked clay weights, possibly used to weigh down thatched roofs. Nearly all the pottery found was of coarse ware, mainly undecorated black or grey, but several fragments of cream ware, Castor ware, amphorae, mortaria and Rhenish beakers were also found, together with various fragments of samian ware, some marked with the potter's stamp. The lower half of a rotary quern and a clay flue-tile were found on the site after ploughing in 1989, but it would be unsafe to conclude that hypocausts existed on the site from a single loose find.

The period of occupation was estimated as the last quarter of the first century to the early years of the fourth century, the settlement serving as a 'burgus' and staging post on the main route between the south and the military areas of north Wales and the north west. All that is visible today are traces of the boundary ditch on the west side of Engleton Lane, and a robber-ditch on the west side of the settlement, clearly marked by a dip in the hedgeline on the south side of Watling Street, which may mark the site of a surrounding wall, as existed at Wall.

The Latinised name Pennocrucio [based, unusually, on a British name meaning 'chief mound' or 'hill summit'/ 'tumulus on the hill', from the Celtic 'penno' meaning 'hill/ head/end' or, as an adjective, 'chief', and 'croco' or 'crug', meaning 'mound', with the native suffix '-io-'] is of interest, for until recently it perplexed philologists, who felt that the word was totally inappropriate for the modern topography of the Romano-British settlement. It was suggested that the name may originally have derived from a native hill fort on the higher ground to the south-west, or that it could signify a special assembly point for the

Cornovii tribe, or a place of some local importance. Alternatively, there may have been a great tumulus called 'the chief mound', now vanished, at the settlement site.

It must be added that at least one of the early Brewood historians concluded that the name Pennocrucio was connected with 'crucio', meaning 'cross', and decided, applying doubtful mathematics, that the Roman settlement was named after a stone cross which stood on the site, marking the point midway between Letocetum and Uxacona.[59]

It was in the 1980's that a Lichfield historian drew attention to what had been overlooked by the various place-name authorities, namely the tumulus at Rowley Hill some 1200 yards north of Watling Street on the crest of a shoulder of land rising steeply from the river Penk. The name Pennocrucio or Pennocrucium is therefore now taken to mean 'headland tumulus', after the Rowley Hill burial mound, incorporating the Celtic word 'crug', meaning either a tumulus, small pronounced hill, or larger hill with a distinctive summit.[60]

Pre-Roman settlement names occur very rarely in the Antonine Itinerary, but the name Pennocrucio undoubtedly derives from a native settlement, and perhaps the most interesting and plausible theory is that before the Roman invasion there was a large estate known as Pennocrucio with a principal settlement – possibly the modern village of Penkridge – within the Penkridge estates mentioned in Domesday Book 1,000 years later, and the Romans simply took the existing name for their new settlement.

The river Penk, formerly Penchrich [Pennocrucio], may have been so named because it flowed through a large area of the same name. The river almost certainly – and unusually – took its name from the area, and not the area from the river. It is perhaps worth noting that the name Cuttlestone, presumably once a place of some importance since it gave its name to the hundred, is now attached only to the bridge over the Penk a short distance north of Rowley Hill.[61] Is it possible that there could be a link between 'Cuthwulf's Stone', wherever it might have been, and the seemingly much venerated hill or tumulus after which the native British named a place at or near Pennocrucium?

In 1947 two Roman forts at Stretton Mill and Kinvaston, north of Watling Street, were partly excavated, having been identified from the air the previous year, and additional information has been obtained from later trenching and more recent aerial photographs.[62]

The rectangular Stretton Mill Fort[63] is a short distance to the north-west of Stretton Mill, the double ditches enclosing an area of about four acres, with gates in the north-west and south-east sides. Excavation showed that the ditches were V-shaped, the inner averaging some 12' wide and 6' deep, the outer slightly smaller. The subsoil was so sandy that the sides of the ditches had been lined with clay up to 2" thick. No rampart remains were found in position but hard subsoil lay just below the surface, and ploughing has probably destroyed the Roman levels. The only objects found were two pottery fragments which could only loosely be dated within the period 50 AD – 200 AD.

The fort at Kinvaston, to the south east of Kinvaston Hall Farm, was clearly very substantial, measuring 1475' by 575' and enclosing an area of no less than 26 acres. The double ditches on the north, east and south were of V-section, each about 16' wide and 7' deep, with gates in each side. There was a single ditch on the west, alongside the river. Like Stretton Mill fort, the ditch sides had been lined with clay some 2" thick. Apart from six corroded coins, three identified as Claudian, only a few fragments of samian and coarse red pottery and two metal objects, a bronze handle and a enamelled head-stud brooch, were found, and suggested that the fort was occupied in the third quarter of the first century. Although no traces of timber revetments were found, a large timber building was traced with its long axis at right angles to the eastern defences, and the presence of other wooden buildings was suggested by small lumps of daub in the trenches.

Double ditches at both Stretton Mill and Kinvaston forts show that they were not temporary marching camps, but substantial ramparted forts, created with prodigious labour and probably dating from Scapula's initial advance towards Wales in the mid first century. Both forts had been reduced in size, Kinvaston to 16 acres, as one type of garrison replaced another, possibly cavalry followed by infantry. Some idea of the capacity of the forts can be gained from the knowledge that the basic legion of 5300 men, split into 'cohorts' of infantry and 'alae' of cavalry, required some 50 acres, while an auxiliary cohort of 1000 would have required a five acre fort, and an alae of the same number would have occupied nine acres. Kinvaston fort alone could have accommodated 3000 infantry troops and 1000 cavalrymen, and it is possible that it was the fortress of half a legion, the remainder being based elsewhere.

Aerial photography has also revealed a double-ditched square fort of about 5 acres a short distance south-east of the settlement at Pennocrucium. Gates were located in the centre of each side, and ploughing has turned up light soil from the ramparts and gravelling from a central north-south road.[64]

Crop marks also show a small rectangular enclosure with single ditch between Kinvaston and Water Eaton, close to the Penk, and a square enclosure of about one acre with single ditch, probably a campaign camp, a short distance south of Kinvaston fort. What seems to be the corner of a large single-ditched enclosure has also been identified to the north of Water Eaton. Various other crop marks which await interpretation attest to very considerable Roman activity in the area.[65]

In addition to the major artery of Watling Street itself, there is evidence that a number of other roads radiated from Pennocrucium. A major road ran north-west to Chester, traceable for some miles by modern lanes past Stretton village; a section of road between Blythe Bridge and Leek was

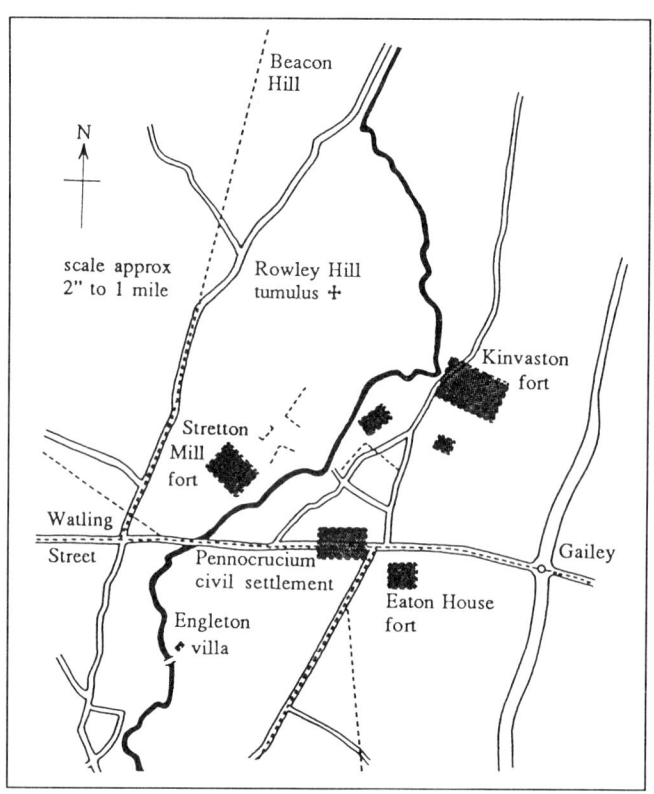

Roman sites, cropmarks and road to the north of Brewood. For clarity, modern buildings are not shown. Based on Oldfield 1981.

thought to continue to Pennocrucium, and in 1991 the lane running north from Watling Street at the Ivy House was identified as a Roman road running across Beacon Hill and through Whiston Mill, evidently a section of such a road;[66] and another road ran south from the civil settlement at Pennocrucium, turning south-west at Clay Gates and passing through Crateford and Standeford ['Stony-ford'] to Featherstone, where the route is then lost. Nineteenth century maps show an area called Stone Field between Standeford and Crateford.[67] Roman coins and brooches have been found to the south of Standeford Mill House,[68] close to the line of the road, which evidently ran, or was intended to run, to the Roman fort at Metchley, west of Edgbaston. The finds may indicate a permanent occupation site at the river crossing.

There is further evidence that another Roman road branched south at Clay Gates,[69] but no trace is detectable until after it has crossed the Penk, where its course is marked by a track to Brewood Park Farm. A slight rise in the Brewood to Coven road just to the east of the junction with the track

32

may mark the course of the agger. The line is lost beyond Upper Pendeford Farm, just outside the parish boundary,[70] but the road was clearly aligned with the Roman sites at Greensforge, near Swindon.

Taken in 1961, this view looking north over the area around Giffard's Cross, with Brewood village in the background, shows a short hedgerow and double line of cropmarks [arrowed] revealing the buried ditches of a Romano-British road from Pennocrucium running on a new alignment from Ackbury Heath, upper centre. Roman coins have been found in the fields between Giffard's Cross and the canal, which runs behind the bank of trees at the top of the photograph. The double line of trees running diagonally across the upper half of the photograph mark Chillington Upper and Lower Avenue, planted c.1727, crossing the curve of Port Lane. The lane running to the bottom left corner is Chillington Street, the former 'paved causeway', now an overgrown bridlepath, until the early part of the eighteenth century one of the main approaches to Chillington House, along which Elizabeth I and her retinue probably travelled on her visit to Chillington in 1575. The original width of Port Lane, with encroachments on which cottages were built, is clearly shown by old hedgelines. The building at centre right is Barn Cottages, traditionally said to be moated, although the water-filled depressions are in fact disused marl or gravel pits. The diagonal lines across the adjoining field are medieval ridge and furrow. The thin dark line sloping upwards from the upper right edge is the western boundary of the Bishop's Park, dating from 1200. The dark line running tot he centre of the trees in the foreground marks a grubbed-out hedge on the alignment of another Roman road which ran past Gunstone Farm, and is marked by the line of Heath House Lane, Codsall. Reproduced by kind permission of the Royal Commission on the Historical Monuments of England.

A Roman road is believed to have run from Somerford Bridge to Ackbury Heath. Roman coins and brooches have been found on the line of the road at Hill Top, north of the junction of Tinkers Lane and Sparrows End Lane, and on the west side of the road between the canal and Giffard's Cross.[71] At Ackbury Heath the road seems to have forked. Crop marks have revealed very clearly two parallel lines between Ackbury Heath and Chillington Street which mark the buried ditches of one branch.[72] The other branch is marked by hedgelines [some now destroyed] south of Ackbury. The line passes through Ladybirch Wood and runs to the east of and parallel with a length of lane north of Gunstone [now a no-through road], continued by a short hedgeline and lanes south of Codsall to Heath House Lane and across Wergs Road into Wrottesley Park. The route passes near Stoneleigh east of Codsall church, and across Histons Hill ['Uchestones' in the forteenth century], both names which may be of significance. Faint traces of the agger can be made out in fields to the south of the stream at Gunstone, and are more clearly shown in aerial photographs.

The other road branching slightly to the west from Ackbury is marked by a hedgeline adjoining Old Park Wood west of Long Birch; the alignment of Strawmoor Lane, Codsall; and old field boundaries which continue the line on the south of the Holyhead Road, where it must have run through or very close to the 'British Town' just inside the county at Wrottesley described by Plot, who claimed to have identified the lines of streets. The site was the subject of much speculation by early historians, but there is now considerable doubt whether the supposed remains seen by Plot were man-made. It is of interest, however, that a Mesolithic factory site lies within the area. A Roman brooch of early first century type has been found to the north-east of Bradshaw's Farm, and a broken Bronze Age celt to the south,[73] both within a short distance of the possible alignment, and a Romano-British site has been discovered at Pepperhill, just across the county boundary.[74] The destination of the road is uncertain, but it runs in the general direction of the extraordinary earthwork known as The Walls, probably of Iron Age date, at Chesterton, a name indicative of a Roman presence. It is possible that another Roman road running south-east through the northern part of Patshull Park is marked by the lane to the trigonometrical point north-east of Westbeech Farm.

It must not be forgotten that the typical straight alignments, perhaps properly classified as military or post roads, were merely an addition to the existing prehistoric network of tracks and paths which continued to be used during the Roman period. The Roman sites to the west and north of Brewood illustrate very clearly the use of the two different road systems, since only the Romano-British settlement of Pennocrucium itself, sitting astride Watling Street, is linked directly to one of the straight alignments. A roadless settlement, however, is as unlikely then as it would be now. Although no road has been traced linking Engleton villa to Watling Street or the settlement site, by tradition an ancient Celtic trackway passed the site from the east, alongside Engleton Hall Farm [the course is clearly marked on the First Edition of the 1" Ordnance Survey map], and the line of a footpath running north from Engleton villa to Watling Street is perhaps the ghost of a road of considerable antiquity.

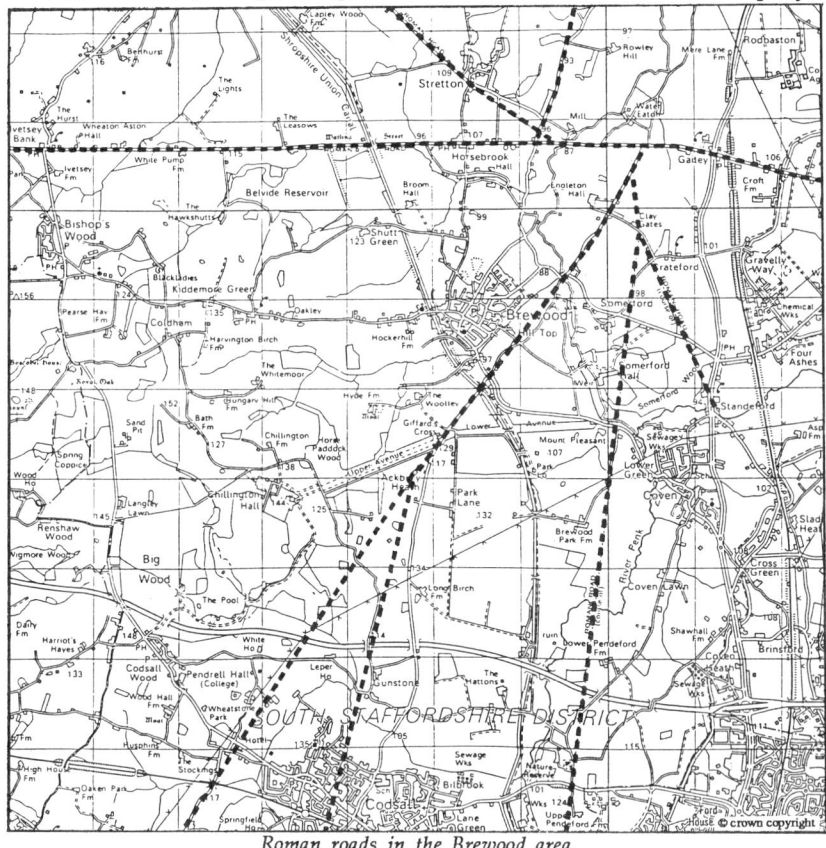

Roman roads in the Brewood area.

Other scattered finds of Roman material in Brewood include three Romano-British fibula brooches dating from early first century to mid second century found near Blackladies,[75] a fragment of samian ware found to the south of Kiddemore Green and a small piece of coarse red ware from fields between Long Birch and the motorway,[76] three brooches dating from the second and third centuries in the Engleton area, a small broken bronze statuette of a draped female figure found near Watling Street between the Penk and Engleton Lane,[77] and a Roman fibula brooch found west of The Bell public house alongside Watling Street, in addition to a large number of coin and brooch finds around the Roman sites and near the Roman roads. Curiously, no finds have been recorded from within Brewood village. Outside the parish, Roman material has also been found near Whiteladies and Whiteladies Farm,[78] with other finds in the Boscobel area,[79] and to the west of Wigmore Wood north-west of Codsall Wood, where a site which may have been a villa is now covered by the M54 motorway.[80] It is of interest that a section of the jagged county boundary nearby is aligned close to this site. An early Roman brooch and bronze coin of Constantine were found in spoil during the construction of the motorway at Tong,[81] and a number of Roman finds in Teddesley Park[82] suggests that more substantial remains may await discovery in that area. Samian sherds are also said to have been thrown up recently by moles in Penkridge churchyard.

The concentration of Roman sites in the north of the parish attests to considerable activity where Watling Street crossed the Penk, then possibly further west than the present bridge. The size of the forts at Stretton Mill and Kinvaston suggests that the area was used as a holding base for a large force to be drawn from when necessary to protect the forward troops, engineers, road builders and supply trains in the west and north-west, and to ensure by sheer strength of numbers the pacification of the local Cornovii. Thereafter, units would have been moved forward into Wales and the north, and Stretton Mill and Kinvaston forts could be reduced in size, leaving the area to enjoy some three and a half centuries of relatively peaceful Romanisation.

It is perhaps unsafe to speculate on the topography of the Brewood area during the Roman period, but the various Roman sites would have demanded very considerable quantities of wood and timber for the construction of buildings, bridges, palisades, wagons, and as fuel for the bakehouses, kitchens and villa hypocaust. Much of the nearby woodland may have been cleared for these purposes, but also to provide land for cultivation, with the additional military advantage that the possibility of surprise attack would be reduced. Indeed, there is the remote possibility that the various road and field alignments which are either parallel to or at right angles to the Roman road from Pennocrucium to Ackbury Heath mark the Roman division of territory known as 'centuriation', although evidence of this practice is admittedly very rare in England, and such evidence in Brewood would suggest the almost continuous cultivation of the areas in question for perhaps the last eighteen centuries, which seems most improbable.

Precise information about the way of life of the people of what is now Brewood during the Pax-Romano, which lasted for three and a half centuries – a dozen or more generations – is lacking, although there is ample evidence from other sources of a cultivated and sophisticated lifestyle, regulated by a well-ordered legal system and structured civil service.

There is no doubt that by the third century AD England not only had a much larger population than at the time of the Norman Conquest – perhaps as high as six million – but that the people lived in a much more organised and tamed landscape. The inference may be that the countryside around Brewood and the Roman sites was relatively clear of woodland, perhaps not too unlike the physical appearance as we know it today, but the picture would have changed very quickly after the Roman withdrawal, for forest and woodland soon re-establish on abandoned ground.

The Roman garrison nearby would have relied heavily on the native population for labour, provisions and services of every kind, and if there was no settlement in Brewood before the Roman conquest, it is tempting to imagine that a native community established itself there at some time during the occupation as a 'garrison town' to take advantage of the commercial opportunities without actually mixing with the invaders and moving into the civil settlement at Pennocrucium. Brewood may indeed have originated as a collection of licensed ale-houses and brothels, catering for the needs of the large numbers of off-duty military personnel and operating under official permit from the imperial authorities. Although any native settlement would have used Roman pottery and coins, day to day life may have been little affected by Roman ways, and a habitation site – which at this period would have consisted of little more than a clustered group of one-roomed huts – will have been in a constant state of expansion and retraction as buildings deteriorated, were abandoned and replaced. It is not uncommon for hamlets to 'creep' some distance over a period of time, and it is possible that if a settlement was in existence at this period – and the very name Brewood with its Celtic connections which may date back to the Iron Age, and the fact that the Romans adopted an existing Celtic name for their nearby settlement, make the existence of such a community more than probable – it did not lie precisely within the present village area. Indeed, it must not be overlooked that whilst no Roman material is known to have been found within the central village area, artifacts have been recorded from modern Hilltop, across which ran a Roman road, and which thus has a provable claim to Roman connections.

Finds to the west and south-west of Brewood indicate that there were probably permanent occupation sites in those areas, with others yet to be identified, and it is becoming increasingly evident that there was a much stronger Roman presence in and around Brewood than has hitherto been recognised. Our knowledge of the Roman settlement pattern locally is far from complete, and it would be surprising indeed if no further remains of Roman occupation come to light within Brewood parish.[83]

5. The Dark Ages

A question of particular interest is why the sites so carefully chosen and developed by the Romans were allowed to fall into decay, and in many cases disappear altogether.

On the grand scale there is Viroconium, where the fifth largest city in Roman Britain with a population of perhaps 60,000 almost completely disappeared while at the same time the town of Shrewsbury nearby grew from very small beginnings. The Roman forts and settlement at Pennocrucium and the Roman villa at Engleton are all but vanished to this day and, except for Watling Street, no trace is visible from the ground of the other Roman roads which radiated from the settlement. One reason may be the proximity of the sites to Watling Street itself, which we know from traces of Roman gravelling frequently exposed during roadworks has been used without serious interruption since Roman times.

In the hiatus after the Roman legions were withdrawn from Britain in the first half of the fifth century to help defend Rome against the advancing barbarians, Watling Street would have been the primary route used by invaders, refugees, or marauding bands, requiring or demanding food, supplies or other wants, and dwellings adjoining the highway might have expected some less-than-welcome visitors. The decendants of the native British, who were traditionally held to have despised the Roman invaders, notwithstanding – or perhaps as a result of – more than four centuries of Romanisation, would have been reluctant to remain near the danger zone, but not too far from an important trade and communication route.

The unbroken use of Roman roads may be one reason why, although many villages with ancient origins lie within a mile or so of such a road, very few indeed actually adjoin one. Brewood, Stretton, Penkridge, Lapley and Wheaton Aston are good examples of villages which have developed a short distance from a major Roman road, and it is significant that for very many miles in both directions Watling Street passes through very few ancient villages. Both Uxacona to the west and Letocetum to the east are now minor hamlets, the later inhabitants concentrating their settlements on sites a few miles away at Oakengates and Lichfield respectively. Indeed, the majority of known Romano-British villas, settlements and other minor occupation sites are, perhaps surprisingly, not located on or adjacent to known Roman roads, as illustrated locally by the various sites to the west and south-west of Brewood.

For the two centuries after the Romans withdrew from Britain, there is an almost complete absence of written history, and archæological evidence from the period is extremely scanty. We know that at the request of first the Romans, and later the Romano-British, various Germanic tribes, known collectively as the Ango-Saxons, arrived in Britain to assist in the defence of the country, but succeeding immigrants may have been less welcome, and eventually were seen as invaders themselves.

The group of tribes that advanced into Staffordshire by way of the Trent Valley and Leicestershire in the late sixth century was known as the Angles, who probably came from the area now known as Schleswig-Holstein. Excavated sites in the north of the county suggest from traces of Celtic influence that there was close contact between the invaders and the original inhabitants – as will be seen, the names Brewood and Bilbrook suggest contact between Welsh-speaking Celtic natives and the Anglo-Saxons – and there is little evidence that the invaders attempted to destroy or displace entirely the native British. Indeed, the Saxon settlement was sporadic, and seems to have involved only relatively modest numbers of immigrants: certainly far too few to sweep aside a Romano-British and Celtic population of up to six million.

The only tentative evidence of the period in Brewood is the name Engleton for the area around the Roman villa site, meaning 'the farmstead of the Angles', which is not necessarily contemporary – over a period of time the term 'Angles' came to refer to the Saxons generally, until by 1000AD the country as a whole was known as 'Englaland' – but may indicate the re-occupation of the site from a very early period. The suffix 'ton' continued in use long after the early stages of Saxon settlement, and examples in combination with personal names are numerous in the West Midlands, probably dating from the period of secondary Saxon settlement, that is, from the seventh century onwards. Saxon settlement at Engleton seems to be confirmed by a small bronze trapezoid plaque with typical Anglo-Saxon interlaced decoration found in recent years near the Penk, and

a Saxon penny of Eadred [946-955 AD] which was found in the topsoil when the Roman villa was excavated. The coin may mean that the site was used as a source of building stone as late as the tenth century, perhaps indicating that the area was sparsely inhabited between the fifth and the tenth centuries.

Another tribe of invaders which settled in the region was the pagan Mierce, or 'boundary folk', whose origins remain obscure, but who may have been responsible for introducing the cult of Woden to the region, as shown by place-name evidence: Wednesbury means 'Woden's Fortress' and Wednesfield 'Woden's Plain', while Weeford, 'a ford by the heathen temple', also indicates a sacred pagan site. It is now thought that such pagan names indicate the more remote areas where paganism was able to survive longest, rather than areas of early Anglo-Saxon intrusion. A possible connection with paganism in Brewood parish is the field name Bakelow, or Backlocks, at Hatton. In 1341 it was recorded as Bakelowfeld, and is thought to mean Bac(c)a's mound or hill.[84] Such personal names linked to the word 'low' are believed to mark the site of Anglo-Saxon pagan barrow burials dating from the early seventh century. The name Grenelowe, recorded in 1425, may have marked another tumulus.

It has been suggested that the boundary from which the Mierce, or Mercians, took their name was that between Anglo-Saxon and Celtic territory, a belt of high land between Cannock Chase and the Arden Forest, to the west of which stretched forests which bore Celtic names, such as Morfe, Kinver, and Brewood, and which, even in the eighth century, had not been divided between the Anglo-Saxon settlers. At least nine of the thirteen districts or settlements in the county which retained their Celtic names lie to the west of this boundary.[85] Against the 'march' of the Mercians lay the Celtic kingdom of Theyrnllwg, ancestor of the modern Powys, which is recorded as extending from Clwyd to Cannock Chase.

Within the greater kingdom of Mercia created by Penda between c. 630 and the middle of the seventh century a number of folk groups or tribal groups of uncertain ancestry have been identified, and later Anglo-Saxon charters mention the adjoining Tomsaetan and Pencersætan as two such groups. The Tomsaetan were named after the river Tame, and it seems highly probable that the Pencersætan occupied the Penk valley near Pennocrucium: place name evidence shows a concentration of habitative names of Old English origin in the Penk valley to the north and south of Penkridge, perhaps the centre of the Pencersætan, and although the extent of their territory remains uncertain, it may have extended as far as the Birmingham plateau, for a point on the southern boundary of Pencersaetan territory can be identified in a charter dated 849 of Coftune [Cofton Hackett] in Worcestershire.[86] To the west lay the tribal territory of the Wreocansætan, or people of the Wrekin.

An interesting possibility is that a large estate in the Brewood/Penkridge area preserved its identity from the Romano-British period, or earlier, until the Norman Conquest or later. An Anglian settlement with a major church [Penkridge] perhaps replaced the Roman settlement at Pennocrucium: a similar link has been persuasively suggested in the case of the Roman settlement at Letocetum, where a Roman or pre-Roman district based on that settlement remained intact and was eventually granted to the early Bishops.[87] It is uncertain whether estates near major Roman sites, such as Engleton near Pennocrucium, were created in Saxon times, or whether their origins lie in the lands or 'terretoria' which were attached to the Roman settlements, and the possible relationship between the Roman sites near Brewood and the local Anglo-Saxon estates remains a matter of speculation.

During the early part of the sixth century, two Celtic kingdoms remained in the west of the English plain, including Theyrnllwg, and a considerable Celtic population seems to have survived even beyond the eastern limits of these kingdoms: the existence of a Celtic Christian community as far east as Lichfield is suggested in the seventh century Welsh poem Marwnad Cynddylan or 'Elegy for Cynddlyan' which records a massacre c.655-658 of such a community by Morfael in alliance with Cynddylan of the Wroxeter region, who had previously campaigned with Penda against the Northumbrians, although it is probable that the traditions enshrined in the Elegy have little historical basis. However, the Mercians appear to have remained allies of the powerful Cornovii until the mid seventh century, by which time, after the arrival of missionaries from Northumbria in 653, the extensive Mercian kingdom had become Christian. Wulfhere, king of Mercia, already a Christian, accepted Chad as bishop of the Mercians and created various religious foundations in the county, including Lichfield Cathedral in 669. The close proximity of Lichfield to the pagan sites dedicated to Woden may mean that Chad deliberately placed his bishopric within an area of pagan religion, perhaps choosing Lichfield to commemorate its Celtic Christian martyrs, if indeed a massacre actually took place. The existence of a Celtic community in Brewood which may have been visited by Chad at this period is suggested by the dedication of the parish church to Chad, for it was the custom of the Celtic church to name its churches after their founders, and Chad is believed to have visited the West Midlands as a missionary before 665. On the death of Chad in 672 the ecclesiastical administration of Mercia was re-organised, with the diocese of Lichfield reduced in size. In 788, to satisfy the pride of Offa of Mercia,[88] the most powerful king of the period, who was the first to call himself 'King of the English' [the name England did not emerge until the tenth century] and who was irritated that his diocese should be subject to Canterbury, the see of Lichfield was raised to an archbishopric, but the change required the endorsement of both the Pope and Archbishop Jaenbert of Canterbury. The latter was reluctant to abandon Canterbury's supremacy and, in 803, on Offa's death, Lichfield was reduced to its former status. After the Conquest the bishop's seat was at Lichfield until 1075, at Chester from 1075 to 1102, at Coventry from 1102 to 1128 and jointly at Coventry and Lichfield from 1539. From 1228 to 1661 the official title was 'of Coventry and Lichfield', although the title 'Bishop of Chester' was occasionally used until the mid sixteenth century.[89]

If the parish church was not founded at the time of St Chad, Brewood may have been connected with the church by 822, when Bishop Athelwald instituted prebends [stipends granted from a portion of the revenues] of Lichfield Church, Brewood perhaps being one of them. The connection has been urged more definitely by earlier writers, but the evidence now seems elusive. It has also been claimed, on the most doubtful proof, that Brewood was part of the original endowment of the bishopric of Mercia by King Paeda, the first Christian king of Mercia, and son of Penda, who founded the Saxon kingdom of Mercia in about 626.[90] The possibility has been suggested by the recognition in twelfth century documents that Brewood was a portion of ancient church property. Various charters of Offa [c.780], when ruler of Mercia, confirm old possessions of the church and grant new.

The grants of new property are said to identify precisely the subject matter, but the charters of confirmation apparently use generalised descriptions. The absence of any specific gift of Brewood to the Church by Offa has been interpreted, perhaps less than objectively, as support for the view that it formed part of Paeda's original endowment. In fact the earliest specific reference to Brewood as part of the bishopric of Lichfield is the Domesday entry which records that it was held by the church before 1066. The next specific reference would seem to date from about 1176, when the prebend of Brewood was conferred on the newly-reconstituted Deanery of Lichfield,[91] but there is an indication that the prebend had existed for some time before then, for in 1125 William of Malmesbury wrote his 'Gesta Pontificum Anglorum,' which was revised between 1135 and 1140. He wrote of Lichfield: 'Athelwold in 822 appointed prebendaries and Huida became the first Provost or Dean,' and stated that there were 19 prebends given to 11 priests and 8 deacons, later increased to 22, including Brewood. There is evidence therefore that the prebend of Brewood existed some time before 1140, and it is not inconceivable that Brewood was amongst the original prebends.

There are few Christian Saxon remains in the region, but a number of round and rectangular shafted crosses exist, including a cross-shaft at Upper Penn which seems to be of eleventh century date, a fragmentary piece in Bushbury churchyard of the same period and a particularly fine example in St Peter's churchyard, Wolverhampton,[92] which has been dated to around 850, although it is possible that it is tenth century work in an earlier style. To the underside of the cap, the shaft is 14' high, and 22" in diameter at the top and 30" at the bottom. The measurements are significant for they are identical to those of the pillars of the forum at Viroconium. Furthermore, the fine-textured hard sandstone, unlike the coarse soft stone found near Wolverhampton, is similar to stone from Grinshill, near Shrewsbury, which was used by the Roman builders. It seems possible that the Wolverhampton shaft was a column pillaged from Viroconium and carved in Saxon times.[93] A plaster-cast of the shaft made in the last century is in the Victoria and Albert Museum, and records the exuberant carvings, now sadly eroded on the original due to inexcusable neglect by the civic authorities of one of the town's finest treasures.

While there are no churches in Staffordshire with definite pre-Norman fabric, many churches were destroyed in the Danish invasions of Staffordshire which began in 874. From their base at Repton the Danes conquered the whole of the surrounding area, but their southerly advance was eventually checked by the Saxons under King Alfred. By the Treaty of Wedmore, Danish authority was confined to an area known as the Danelaw, north of a line roughly from Chester to London and following in part the line of Watling Street. Thus Brewood found itself outside Danish control, and evidence gleaned from Domesday suggests that Danish influence in any part of Staffordshire remained minimal, although there are some traces in place-names, including Gunstone, 'the farmstead of Gunni', a Scandinavian personal name, the significance of which is uncertain.[94]

In the late ninth century the Danes renewed their attack on the area south of the Danelaw,[95] but were halted on their return north by Alfred's son, Edward the Elder, at a battle which took place on 6th August 910, probably at Tettenhall or Wednesfield, when the Merican and West Saxon army slaughtered many thousands of the enemy, including three Northumbrian kings. Edward's sister Ethelfreda played a prominent part in the recovery of the Danelaw, building a line of fortifications to defend the Danish invasion routes and to serve as bases for assaults against the Danes, including the fort at Stafford, built in 913, to cover the entry through Mercia. By 922 Edward, having control over most of England and the Danelaw, reorganised his Kingdom, and the old tribal divisions of Mercia were replaced by the creation of shires [i.e. 'shares'] or counties, administrative districts responsible for the maintenance of a defensive centre, which were subdivided into hundreds. That the hundreds of Staffordshire long pre-date Domesday is shown by the fact that in no case was an important manor the centre of a hundred in 1086.

So was born Staffordshire,[96] centred on the fort at Stafford. After some years of uneasy peace, the Danes rose in rebellion in 940, and records speak of great slaughter before the rebellion was put down. The area around Brewood was presumably peaceful when the Anglo-Saxon Great Council met at Penkridge in 958 under King Eadwig, but further Danish invasions occurred in 980, with the inhabitants of the Danelaw actively assisting the invaders. Tradition tells of a great massacre of the Danes near Tutbury in 1002, but when King Sweyn of Denmark led an invasion in 1013, the Mercian ealdorman refused to help repel the invaders, and for this Mercia, including Staffordshire, was severely ravaged in 1016 by Edmund Ironside. In the same year Mercia, and soon afterwards all of England, fell under the control of Canute. When the Vikings invaded England via the Humber estuary in 1066, Edwin, Earl of Mercia, attacked the invasion force but was heavily defeated at Fulford in Yorkshire, which probably explains his failure to join King Harold on his ill-fated march south to meet the Normans at Hastings. Had his surviving forces joined the King, English history may have taken a different course.

It is now recognised that the great majority of Anglo-Saxon settlements in the Midlands are located in river valleys on areas of glacial sands and gravels, where the lighter textured, tractable and free-draining soils deriving from the drift deposits were particularly heavily cultivated, while the heavy, badly drained soils based on clays tended only to be cleared and cultivated as the settlements expanded. Apart from good soil, an adequate water supply was also essential for settlement, and Brewood, lying on glacial deposits with numerous springs, meets both criteria. Several other early settlements or farmsteads within the parish similarly lie on islands of sand and gravel: Coven, Chillington, Harvington Birch, Bishop's Wood and Broom Hall. From the Domesday survey we know that there was an established and substantial community in Brewood [and others at Chillington and Coven] from late Saxon times at least, but apart from the Saxon finds from Engleton, the only other recorded material from the period within the parish is a gilt-on-bronze Saxon button-brooch with raised-line decoration dating from the ninth century found at Blackladies.[97]

Little is known of Saxon villages, except that they were usually little more than unplanned hamlets composed of houses linked by paths rather than streets and lacking continuous building lines or village greens, and there is no evidence of the nature of Saxon Brewood, although it is possible that traces may lie hidden in the topography of the village. While many roads, footpaths and hedges will date back to medieval times or even earlier, any such features which might have existed in Saxon times will be difficult to identify, although future research might well enable the development of the village to be determined with more certainty. The dearth of Saxon finds may be an indication both of sparse settlement in the area and, notwithstanding the Blackladies brooch, a relatively unsophisticated lifestyle. Wildwood and forest will have covered much of the area with scattered clearings supporting subsistence farming. For Brewood, in a region affected at one time or another by invasion, rebellion, ravages, pagan religion, and doubtless plague and famine, the period can with justification be described as the Dark Ages.

6. The Derivation of the name Brewood

Since time beyond memory the name Brewood has been pronounced locally as 'Brood', although it would perhaps be a mistake to place too much emphasis on the modern pronunciation, which may well have changed over the centuries, as has the pronunciation of most words in use for well over a thousand years. The not untypical variation in early spellings makes it difficult to determine the pronunciation at those periods, and indeed it is possible that there was no common pronunciation until comparatively recent times. The name was at one time thought to derive from an obsolete Welsh word 'bred-ych', meaning fear, terror or fright, as the modern 'braw' meaning terror or dismay, hence 'place of terror or danger', supposedly because the ruins of the Roman settlement at Pennocrucium were believed by the superstitious British to be haunted.[98]

The Iron Age Celts introduced the Indo-European language which was the ancestor of two distinct Celtic dialects, Brythonic and Goidelic. Goidelic survives in Irish, Scottish and Manx Gaelic, while Brythonic Celtic evolved into Welsh, Cornish and Breton. Philologists are cautious in ascribing a date to the arrival of Celtic-speaking tribes in Britain, but the general consensus is that the language reached these islands at some time between 2000 and 1200 BC, and was the language spoken throughout what is now England until the Celtic-speaking peoples were gradually absorbed into the new Germanic culture of the Angles, Saxons, Jutes and Danes, and slowly abandoned their British language.

Almost all Celtic place names derive from natural or man-made physical features, whereas the Saxons often incorporated personal names into place names and made much use of the formula 'settlement belonging to or associated with X', which the Romano-British did not. A possible example is Chillington, which almost certainly means 'settlement associated with Cilla'. The name Gunstone, meaning the farmstead associated with Gunni,[99] derives from a Norse name perhaps connected with the later Danish invasions of the early ninth century.

Old English is a Germanic language belonging to a different branch of the Indo-European family from the Celtic languages, and replaced Celtic in a large part of Britain from the fifth century onwards, introducing a vast number of Germanic Old English place names. Indeed, the great majority of present day place names are derived from the Old English language, of which modern English is a much modified descendant.

After the Norman Conquest, many place names were written down for the first time by Norman clerks, and since there was no established system of spelling English place-names, the clerks either wrote down what they heard from local speakers, or put down a version from the dictation of others who may not have been local people. Phonetic spelling is found especially in Domesday Book, and was invariably retained in later times, except perhaps in cases where the scribe had knowledge of an earlier version of the name from an Anglo-Saxon charter.

From the earliest records, Brewood is variously spelt as Breude [Domesday Book, 1086 – the earliest known reference to the name, from a period when the Anglo-Saxon equivelent of the letter W, derived from the runic alphabet and called Wynn, was often written by Norman scribes as U when it appeared in the middle of a word], Breoda [1193], Broude [c.1150], Breode [1151], Briwuda, Brewuda, Brewod(e) and Brewud(e) [c.1200], Brewde [1200], Bruwode [1245], Brehude [1290], Breuwode [1306], Brude [1462], Bruwood [1558], Bruyde [1561], Bre(e)wood(e) [1559] and Brewood.[100]

The name is without doubt a compound hybrid created from two words of different periods and origins.[101] The first element is derived from the Celtic 'bre', meaning 'hill' – perhaps a particularly impressive hill – the commonest of several Celtic names – the word provides the last element in the name Kinver, originally Cynibre, and is the root of the name Bredon, recorded as Briudun in 730 and Breodun in 772, 890 and 1086: very similar to the earliest spellings of Brewood. The second element in the name is 'wudu', the Old English word for 'wood'. Again, the word is a very common place-name element, although Brewood appears to be the only known example of the combination of 'wudu' with an earlier place-name or pre-English element. Brewood therefore means 'the wood by [or at] the hill called bre'. The forms Breoda and Breode may represent early shortenings of the name, forerunners of the modern pronunciation.

It is difficult to draw many conclusions from the name Brewood. It seems that at some time during the long period of Celtic occupation a hill in the area, presumably but not necessarily the one on which Brewood now stands, was known by the rather uninspired name 'Bre', 'the hill', although that cannot be taken as evidence of a habitation site or settlement. At some date after about 450 AD one of the Germanic tribes of invaders known collectively as the Anglo-Saxons reached the place and gave it the name by which it is now known. It seems possible that the local primitive-Welsh speaking Celts spoke of 'the hill', and the Germanic Anglo-Saxons, not realising that 'bre' was a common noun, took it for the name of the hill. Presumably a settlement already existed or was then founded on the site, and whilst we cannot know the precise date of Anglo-Saxon occupation, it may be possible to make tentative deductions from the place name. The word 'wood' is unlikely to have been applied to a place in the midst of thick forest, and it seems reasonable to assume therefore that the countryside around was relatively clear of woodland. Since the withdrawal of the Romans would have led to the gradual re-establishment of the wildwood and forest, it can perhaps be assumed that the name was probably given within a century or two of the Roman departure in the early fifth century, or well into the Anglo Saxon period when inroads had again been made into the wildwood, with clearings created for cultivation and grazing. The former supposition is perhaps more likely, the Saxon immigrants in the late sixth or early seventh century moving into an area long settled by the Celts, with whom they may have peacefully intermixed.

Whilst therefore there is no direct evidence for the existence of the settlement of Brewood before late Saxon times, there is circumstantial evidence, albeit slight, [including the dedication of the parish church to St Chad, possibly even by Chad himself about the mid-seventh century] that a habitation site known as Bre existed at or close to modern Brewood at a time when there was still Celtic influence in the area. The bipartite name Brewood can perhaps be taken as evidence of contact between Welsh- and English-speaking people, although it does not in itself provide proof of the survival of a Celtic community. It is possible however that the name may have passed from one linguistic community to another, and may provide clues about the date at which such change was made, and about the possible survival of a Welsh-speaking community. Until at least the early part of the sixth century, and perhaps as late as the latter part of the eighth century, a considerable Celtic population is believed to have inhabited the Western Midlands, and it is possible that the later name Brewood dates from about this period, perhaps applied to a site of much earlier origin, possibly even prehistoric. But although for those seeking positive proof of the age of Brewood, either as a name or as a settlement site, the Norman Conquest is, as often the case elsewhere, the earliest certain date a historian can offer, there is tentative evidence from local place-names that there has been continuous occupation in the area since at least the Roman period – the Roman settlement at Pennocrucium adopted an existing Celtic name, and the name Bilbrook is believed to have Celtic connections – and it is not inconceivable that Brewood was already an ancient settlement site when the Roman conquest began, with its origins in the Celtic Iron Age or earlier.

7. The Norman Conquest

In 1066 William, Duke of Normandy, became king after his victory at the Battle of Hastings, and his followers expected their customary rewards in the form of land and positions in church and state. William himself became the most important landowner in the country, inheriting the royal manors previously held by King Edward the Confessor, including Penkridge. Four of William's followers shared most of the remaining land in the county, and these tenants-in-chief of the king in turn sub-let many of their estates. Amongst those who accompanied William at the time of the Conquest was Corbuzzon, chamberlain to the King. At the time of Domesday he was probably dead, but his son, William Filius Corbucionis [or William Fitz Corbuson] is recorded as holding Chillington.

King William is known to have visited Staffordshire twice, and if the county had felt little impact from the Conquest, it had good reason to remember the visits of the king himself. In 1069 the county had joined a rebellion against him, encouraged by a landing of the Danes in the Humber. William marched north with his army and crushed the region with merciless severity at a battle fought at Stafford. But resistance in the area continued, and to impose his authority William and his forces returned the following year and ravaged a great swathe of country in Yorkshire, Cheshire, Derbyshire and Staffordshire, perhaps the most fearful genocide in the history of England. It was as a result of this campaign that William acquired the sobriquet 'Conquerer'. The King, in the words of a twelfth century writer, Ordericus Vitalis, confessed on his deathbed that he "fell on the English like a ravaging lion, commanded their houses and corn, with all their implements and chattels, to be burnt . . . and large herds of cattle and beasts to be butchered wherever they were found." The destruction was so fearful that, in the words of a contemporary writer, 'men, young and old, women and children wandered as far south as the Abbey of Evesham in quest of a morsel of bread', but we do not know whether the ravaging was deliberately intended to sudjugate the population, who probably had little interest or knowledge of the rebellion, or whether it was the result of William's troops scavenging for provisions and supplies, which in a poor county like Staffordshire would have had a disastrous effect on the local economy. To ensure that the disaffection was fully neutralised, William also arranged for a castle to be constructed in Stafford, probably at Broad Eye, near the river, in 1070, but it would seem to have been put to little use and cannot have been particularly substantial, since by 1086 it had seemingly fallen into ruin.[102]

The Anglo Saxon Chronicle records that in 1085, shortly before he left England for the last time in 1086, William the Conquerer sent commissioners out to all the counties, excluding the area north of the Tees and the middle Eden, with instructions to find out how many hundred hides there were in the shire, or what land and cattle the King himself had in the country, or what dues he ought to have in twelve months from the shire. Also, he had a record made of how much land his archbishops had, and his bishops and abbots and his earls . . . and what or how much everybody had who was occupying land in England, in land and cattle, and how much money it was worth. So very narrowly did he have it investigated that there was no single hide nor a yard of land nor indeed . . . one ox nor one cow nor one pig was there left out, and not put down in his record.[103]

The Domesday survey – the name had been adopted before 1180 – was an extraordinary logistical undertaking, describing in minute detail all levels of society in 1086. The exact purpose of the inquisition is not known but there is little doubt that the prime object was to facilitate the collection of taxes. It must also be noted that at Domesday the unit known as the hide was a fiscal hide, the precise nature of which is still uncertain but which bore little relationship to the hide of Bede's day. Furthermore, the listings given in Domesday may well be manorial holdings rather than villages. The chief landowners and their direct tenants are identified by name, and principal house-holders counted. For administrative reasons the listings were grouped into the pre-Conquest districts of hundreds. The reason why a hundred was so-called may perhaps be because it was rated at 100 hide tax units [Staffordshire with five hundreds had rather more than 500 hides], or because each hundred contained land for 100 families. 5-hide vills were characteristic of England south and west of the Danelaw, and Brewood is one such vill.

We cannot be sure of the precise manner in which the Domesday entry for Staffordshire was prepared, but some copies of the working papers or regional returns for other areas survive, which tell us that the King's Commissioners were required to answer a number of standardised questions about each place at the time of the death of King Edward [abbreviated in Domesday to 'T.R.E.'] and at the time of the return. One of the King's Commissioners was Walter Giffard, Justiciar of England. Surviving returns give some idea of the procedure adopted by the Commissioners. Sworn evidence was taken "from the Sheriff [Shire-reeve]; from all the barons and their Frenchmen; and from the whole hundred, the priests, the reeves, and six villagers from each village", and use was probably made of earlier written records. The Norman bureaucracy required a second group of Commissioners to go to areas not known to them to audit the recorded particulars.

The various returns were despatched to Winchester – then capital of England – collated, abridged and engrossed by a single scribe into one volume [since divided] covering the greater part of England, although some areas, including London, were for some reason not transcribed. The whole undertaking was completed in less than twelve months, although the transcription may have taken a little longer. The speed and efficiency with which the survey was carried out suggests that the collection of information in such a way was not new to the Anglo-Saxons. The book itself is written on both sides of parchment leaves measuring about 15" by 11", with place-names ruled through in red for emphasis.

The section relating to Staffordshire includes an unusual amount of local information, perhaps because the scribe who edited and engrossed the book at Winchester is thought to have been Sampson, or Sansone, listed with the clergy of Wolverhampton, and whilst elsewhere he relied on written returns alone, the Staffordshire entry may have included land known to him.

The entries relating to Brewood, Chillington and Coven, the first recorded reference to the place-name in each case, can be translated as follows:

IN COLVESTAN [CUTTLESTONE] HUNDRED
THE BISHOP OF CHESTER holds BREUDE. The Church held it T.R.E. There [are] 5h[ides]. There is land for 20 ploughs. In demesne are 3 ploughs and 8 serfs; and 24 villeins and 18 bordars with the priest have 14 ploughs. [There are] 2 mills rendering (de) 4s.; and [there are] 4a. of meadow. Wood[land] 1½ leagues in length and 1 league in breadth. T.R.E. it was worth £10. Now [it is worth] 100s.

THE LAND OF WILLIAM SON OF CORBUCION
IN CUTTLESTONE HUNDRED
The same W[illiam] holds CILLENTONE.[104] There are 3 h[ides]. There is land for 6 ploughs. In demesne is 1 plough and 9 serfs; and [there are] 13 villeins and 6 bordars with 5 ploughs. There [are] 2a. of meadow. Wood[land] 2 leagues in length and ½ league in breadth. It was worth £4; now [it is worth] 30s. The Bishop of Chester claims this land.

Jpſe. R. ten' in Cove. 1. hid. 7 Buered deeo. Alric tenut. 7 lib fuit. Tra. e. 11. car. In dnio. e una. 7 111. ſerui. 7 11. uilli 7 11. bord cu. 1. car. Ibi. 111. ac pa. Silua dimid leui lg. 7 una grent lat. In dnio regis. e h silua. Tra. ualet. xvi. solid.

[THE LAND OF ROBERT OF STAFFORD][105]
IN CUDULVESTAN [CUTTLESTONE] HUNDRED
The same R[obert] holds 1 [hide] in COVE and Buered [holds] of him. Alric held it and he was free. There is land for 2 ploughs. In demesne is 1 [plough] and 4 serfs; and [there are] 2 villeins and 2 bordars with 1 plough. There [are] 3a. of meadow. Wood[land] ½ league in length and 1 furlong in breadth. This wood[land] is in the King's demesne. The land is worth 16s.

A villein was an unfree tenant farmer or smallholder who held land in exchange for labour services.[106] Bordars were lesser tenants: one possibility is that they were peasants who were permitted to settle on the edge of the forest and were responsible for the great woodland clearances of this period. The theory fits the French meaning of the word, which seems to drop out of use by the thirteenth century, when the forest clearances came to an end. A serf was for all practical purposes a slave.

It is apparent that at the time of the survey Staffordshire was poor, primitive and sparsely populated, much of it woodland and waste. Indeed, until the discovery of mineral wealth, Staffordshire was one of the most backward counties in the country. Although one of the largest counties, the entry in Domesday is the shortest, with the exception of the small counties of Middlesex and Rutland. If the total taxation assessment of the county is taken as 550 hides or thereabouts, only Rutland, Cornwall and Chester had smaller assessments. Gloucestershire, a county of comparable size possessed approximately 2388 hides. Again, while 980 plough teams are recorded for Staffordshire, Shropshire had twice the number. At an estimated 120 acres per plough team, some 22000 acres in Staffordshire were arable, but the picture of agriculture in the county may be misleading since pasture land is almost totally ignored by Domesday.

Settlement was mainly in the south of the county and along the central river system, and the few towns were of little importance. South Staffordshire generally consisted of extensive areas of forest, small scattered hamlets and farmsteads, with subsistence agriculture the norm.

Cuttlestone hundred was one of the smallest of the five Staffordshire hundreds but it was also one of the most valuable in terms of taxable capacity and land value. Paradoxically, it was also one of the poorest, for reasons which remain unknown but which may be due, at least in part, to the ravages of 1016 and 1069-70, or perhaps simply because of shortages of capital and labour.

It is difficult to assess the population of Brewood, Chillington and Coven from the Domesday entries with any accuracy, since the returns do not give figures for individuals, but only for the number of those holding land in the various social classes that then existed. The recorded population of the parish was 87 [Brewood with 51, Chillington 28 and Coven 8], with a recorded Staffordshire population of 2866. Brewood parish therefore contributed 3% of the total county population, and Brewood vill alone 1.8%. Recent research has suggested that the size of an average household at the time of Domesday would have been about 5.5, and on that basis it is possible that there were approximately 280 people in Brewood, 155 in Chillington and 45 in Coven. The figures suggest that in the years immediately after the Conquest, Brewood was one of the larger communities in the region, and it is possible that only Stafford and Lichfield had greater populations,[107] but whether Brewood was a hamlet with the villein farmers clustered together in one group, or whether it took the form of a central nucleus with a number of outlying farmsteads is difficult to determine, although the latter is perhaps more likely.

The entries for Brewood and Chillington are of further interest since they are two of only eight vills held in religious hands [Brewood being held by the Bishop of Chester and Chillington claimed by him] in which a reduction in value is recorded: from ten pounds to 100s., and from four pounds to 30s respectively. It may however be misleading to rely on the former values, since jurors giving evidence to the Commissioners were relying on their memories of values twenty years earlier. Furthermore, the native language of the Commissioners was in many cases French, whilst the native language of those they interviewed was English and the returns were recorded in Latin. This, and the transcription of field returns, perhaps makes occasional errors inevitable. The reason for the reduction in value of Brewood and Chillington is unknown, and although it is tempting to speculate that it may be connected with King William's ravagings of 1069-70 – perhaps Watling Street was used by the King's army during one or both of the campaigns – there is no direct evidence to support such theory. Certainly in the case of Chillington, the number of actual ploughs coincides with the number of possible ploughs. The number of recorded ploughs suggests that Brewood had some 2040 acres of arable and Chillington 720. Although Brewood, Chillington and Coven are shown to have had 4, 2 and 3 acres of meadowland respectively, the significance is uncertain, for an acre varied from place to place between .88 and 3.3 modern acres.[108]

The basis of the Domesday valuation is not known but the plough, with its customary 8 oxen, clearly reflects the prosperity of the neighbourhood. On the assumption, which is unlikely, that each plough had a separate team, it can be calculated that there were perhaps 126 oxen in Brewood and some 48 in Chillington. Since the figures make no allowances for spare, ill or young beasts, however, the figures may give a crude approximation of the actual number of animals kept.

Woodland in the county in 1086 was much less evenly distributed than today, and south Staffordshire contained one of the larger areas of woodland, although none of the later recorded forests is identified by name. Brewood, Chillington and Coven all have areas of woodland recorded: Brewood ¾ mile by ½ mile [840 acres], Chillington 1 mile by ¼ mile [640 acres], and Coven ¼ mile by 220 yards [20 acres] and held by the King. The dimensions are difficult to interpret since the woods would have been irregular in shape.[109] It must also be remembered that in addition to the managed woodland mentioned in Domesday there were vast areas of uncultivated woodland which were not deemed worthy of recording by the Commissioners.

Mills were relatively uncommon in Staffordshire, with only 63 in the whole county, notwithstanding the numerous rivers and streams, but Brewood had two, one of which was probably at Engleton. The other may have been at Somerford or the Forge. All the mills recorded in Domesday were water-mills for grinding corn. Neither the windmill nor the fulling-mill for stamping cloth by water-driven hammers had yet made its appearance in England.

The reference to a priest at Brewood implies the existence of a church or chapel in or before 1086. Although some 40 churches are thought to have existed in Staffordshire at Domesday, only two are specifically mentioned. The social position of village clergy at the time of Domesday is uncertain, but they seem to have varied greatly in standing and wealth. The priest in Brewood is listed with the peasantry, which suggests that he was considered to be a member of the peasant community.

It is evident that most of the roads within the central village area were in existence from at least early medieval times, and whilst less apparent now, it seems that the original village may have been laid out in grid pattern, evidence of deliberate planning rather than haphazard development. Aligned in the same direction are Sandy Lane, lying in a wide cutting, the line of which is continued, particularly impressively, by a footpath to the north-west [formerly a lane[110] now interrupted by the Shropshire Union Canal] and hedgerows to the south of Lea Fields Farm, Shutt Green; Dean Street; Sparrows End Lane [and its continuation south-east beyond Tinkers Lane towards Somerford]; the sunken lane, now a bridlepath, from Brewood Hall to Hilltop; the east end of Deansfield Road; and the western end of Newport Street, which may formerly have continued in a straight line past the north of the church and on down the hill to The Pavement. Although the alignment of Dean Street does not continue past The Pavement, field boundaries to the south-east formerly marked the alignment, and although the deep cutting from The Pavement to the Port Lane crossroads suggests that the present road is of considerable age and may have followed that line from the earliest times, the road is conspicuously absent from William Yates map of Staffordshire, 1775, which, if accurate, indicates that the road dates from about the last quarter of the eighteenth century – it is shown on Robins and Sherriff's map of 1808.

Parallel with The Pavement are the southern part of Horsebrook Lane; Bargate Lane; Cresswell Lane; and field boundaries between Cresswell Farm and Shutt Green; Stafford Street; the southern part of Engleton Lane; Vicarage Road; and the footpath to the east of the church with the steps known as Jacob's Ladder.

The area bounded by Dean Street, Market Place, Sandy Lane and The Pavement has interesting contours, with a marked rectangular depression in the centre. The topography is easily explained: the depression is the result of quarrying during the first half of the present century.

Dirty Lane runs parallel with and at the back of Dean Street, evidently providing access to the tofts or gardens. Those tofts, or 'garthends', also continued, aligned almost north to south, to the south of the lane until about 1955. The curve of the lane to the west at its upper end echoes the curve in Kiddemore Green Road, with which it runs parallel. It is possible that the lane, a continuation of The Pavement, may originally have continued westwards at its southern end, on the north of and parallel to the stream, as marked by hedgelines which continue along the south of Little Hyde Rough and north of Big Hyde Rough, and perhaps pre-dates Dean Street, but such continuation seems to have been disused at a fairly early date: it is not marked on a plan of The Hyde estate made in 1704.

Of particular interest is the absence of habitation on the eastern side of the brook, which is almost devoid of housing except along Sparrows End Lane to the north, and at Hilltop on the east, although the area contains intriguing undulations. The reasons for the absence of development are unclear, but all ancient villages have undergone a constant process of change, and there is no reason to believe that Brewood has been immune from such changes. It is quite possible that the settlement pattern was in the past very different from the picture today.

If – which is far from certain – the present village layout has indeed resulted from deliberate planning, it might seem that the grid pattern has been based on the brook, which runs from the south west to the north east in what is clearly, from its straight line, an artificial channel. A stronger possibility is that the roads were aligned with the marked valley terrace. Alternatively, the church would have been one of the principal structures in a village planned in the Christian period, and the early planners might have been expected to have aligned the roads with the church, as is the case in many other ancient villages. Is it possible that the first church was sited elsewhere? One of the open fields of the manor was named Churchfeld,[111] recorded in 1364, and perhaps meant the field belonging to the church – or the field where a church once stood. But examples of churches relocating within a parish are extremely rare, and can almost certainly be discounted in the case of Brewood.

Perhaps most significant is the fact that almost every road in what is thought to be the oldest part of Brewood is either parallel with or at right angles to the Roman road which passed to the east of the village through the Hilltop-Port Lane crossroads on a north east- south west alignment. It is evident that roads and field boundaries [almost always historically informative] east and west of Hilltop are precisely aligned with the Roman road, and those alignments seem to extend to – and indeed well beyond – the village area.

If it is accepted that Brewood as we know it originated as a deliberately planned village – and Saxon settlement will probably have been an unplanned collection of insubstantial dwellings long since obliterated, even though the late Saxon population of Brewood was relatively substantial – the next problem is to determine the period in which it was planned. It is now recognised by landscape historians that many planned northern villages lie in an area which was badly affected by the ravagings of William the Conqueror in 1069-70, and that the planning of those villages perhaps dates from this period. William may have realised that while the devastation undoubtedly served as a salutary warning to those who survived, his revenues were correspondingly reduced by the loss of taxes from so many hamlets and villages. Newly planned villages created from old scattered and decimated settlements would be better placed to develop into stronger economic units, and since there is a strong inference in Domesday Book that Brewood may also have been affected by the ravaging of the Normans, it is possible that the nucleus of the modern village was laid out in the later part of the eleventh century, perhaps on the site of a settlement which was then ancient, with the landholdings and roads aligned with the Roman road to the east, still then identifiable either as a road or field boundary. On balance, however, it will be seen that it is perhaps more likely that the village layout has its origins in a slightly later period.

8. Medieval Brewood

The importance of Brewood in the centuries after the Norman conquest is shown by the visits of the early Kings when travelling through their kingdom, recorded by various warrants and charters dated there, although it would be unsafe to assume that the King was himself present at the actual date of every deed. A charter granted by Henry II to the Burgesses of Newport, Shropshire, is dated from 'Breuwood', probably after the King had travelled through Newport on his way south from Chester in September 1165.[112] It is well recorded that the King travelled extensively, seldom being in one place for long, and public charters, letters patent and close letters survive to confirm that King John had a temporary residence – "Camera regis nostra apud Breude", 'our chamber at Brewood' – and is known to have visited Brewood on Tuesday 4th April 1200, Friday 27th-Sunday 29th January 1206, and Saturday 18th August 1207,[113] on each occasion halting during a journey between Lichfield and Kinver. A warrant of King John in the Close Rolls acknowledges the payment of a sum of money at the King's Brewood residence by the Sheriff of Nottingham for which the Barons of the Exchequer are directed to give credit.[114] These are the first known documentary references to a royal residence at Brewood, but it must not be forgotten that William the Conqueror had land at Brewood from at least 1086, recorded in the Domesday entry for Coven.

Although the term 'camera regis' was normally applied to a royal court or palace, and although the historian Gough says, "In that great old city [of Brewood] King John kept his court", it is clear that the description 'city' is no more than literary licence, and a royal house may have been the residence of a noble, spiritual or temporal, at which the King rested on occasions during his travels, and was not necessarily his own property. There is no evidence that any noble had a property in Brewood,[115] but it is well recorded that the Bishop had his palace and throne at Lichfield, his castle at Eccleshall, and manor houses elsewhere, including Longdon and Brewood, where he also had a park. It is probable, therefore, that the 'camera regis' at Brewood was the Bishop's residence, requisitioned as necessary. The probability is strengthened by the existence of several documentary references to the Bishop's residence, but none to a separate royal residence.

The exact nature and location of the Bishop's residence, in existence from perhaps before the Conquest until at least 1473 and in recent times known locally as 'the Bishop's Palace', are not known, but traditionally it is believed to have occupied "the square formed by the east side of the Market Place and the north side of the churchyard",[116] although it must be said that there is no firm evidence to support the tradition. In a parliamentary survey dated 22nd March 1646 Thomas Foulk [Fowke] is recorded as holding under a lease dated 1618 inter alia "one pasture called the court, where the Manor House anciently stood. . .",[117] and Stebbing Shaw states that the house stood "in that piece of ground Eastward from the church, yet [i.e. still] called the court."[118] The name 'court' is of particular interest, for it has several meanings – regal, judicial and topographical – and although it cannot be known in what sense the word was originally used, it is not impossible that it was apposite in each sense: buildings forming a courtyard used as a royal residence and as a courthouse. Bill's Court, so-called in the last century after the old Brewood family of that name, was in the same area, and was perhaps the same site. It is also of interest that the Fleur-de-Lis public house stood in the same area – and the emblem was that of the Fowke family. In 1897 some low timber-built houses on the south side of Market Place on the site of The Dreadnought, said to be the remains of a larger building, were demolished, together with an ancient doorway, and although it has been suggested that they may have been connected with the Bishop's residence,[119] that is most unlikely. Some of the old oak from the houses is said to have been used as a fireplace lintel in the Old Smithy in Sandy Lane. In digging graves in the part of the churchyard to the north of the church annexed in 1825, "several very substantial foundations" are reported to have been found, and are said to have existed in 1864;[120] at another time during pipe-laying works in Sandy Lane more foundations were reported to have been detected, and in about 1920 substantial remains are said to have been unearthed when digging graves to the north and east of the churchyard.[121] If the reports are to be relied upon, it is possible that the remains may be connected with the Bishop's residence, in which case it would seem to have been of some considerable size, which would not be unexpected given the status of the Bishop who would be accustomed to a residence of some splendour. [The Bishops of Lichfield were as itinerant as the great barons, and judging by the witnesses to their charters, were surrounded by members of the local gentry, as well as their usual retinue of household officials: the Bishop of Worcester was said to have 100 horses in his travelling household.] The Bishop's residence may have been a relatively conventional hall house of one storey, but a more complex arrangement of buildings, perhaps incorporating a first-floor hall, seems more likely. Building stone was readily available in Brewood, but evidence from other sites of the period suggests that the construction was just as likely to have been of timber, equally abundant locally. Unfortunately, it is unclear where in Sandy Lane or the churchyard the foundations were found, or the nature, extent or alignment of the remains, and it is therefore uncertain whether the building or buildings were aligned with the present road layout. A careful study of the earliest known detailed large scale map of Brewood made in 1808 by Robins and Sherriff[122] reveals interesting property boundaries to the east of buildings on the north-east side of Market Place, which seem to continue the alignment of the east end of Newport Street, and are followed by the former alignment of the southern end of Vicarage Road. A parallel boundary ran in 1808 from the eastern corner of the old churchyard. Is it possible that the alignments are associated with the site of the Bishop's residence? It may be no more than coincidence that the north-western building-line of Market Place lies at right angles to these alignments.

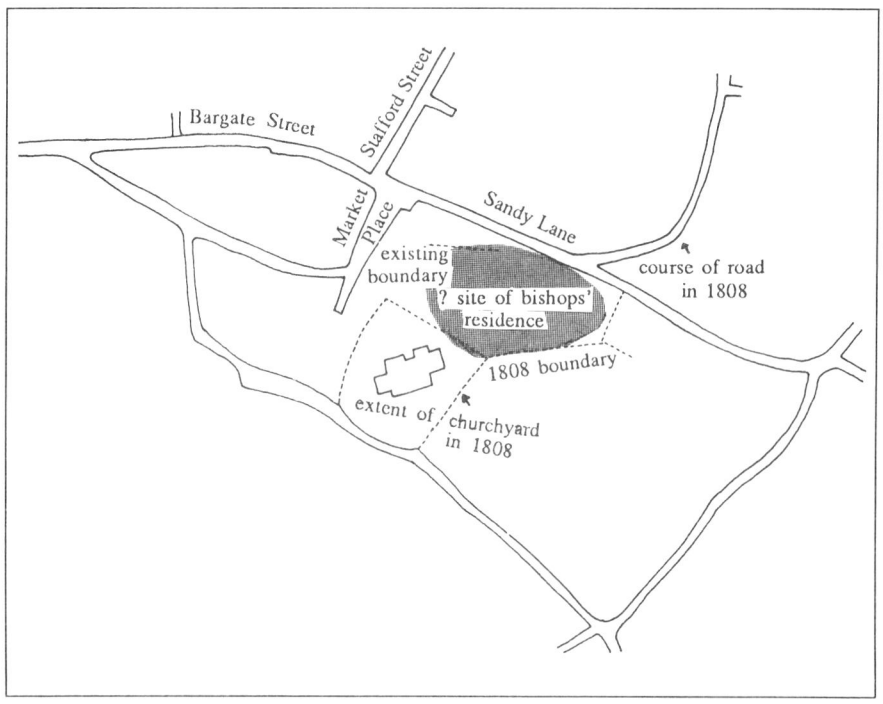

Plan based on survey of parish made in 1808 by Josiah Robins and James Sherriff, Staffordshire Record Office S90/375.

That the King was accommodated in the Bishop's residence is possibly strengthened by inferences to be drawn from a dispute which occurred after the death of the Bishop of Lichfield, Geoffrey de Muscamp, in 1208, when a long-simmering disagreement between the prebendaries of Lichfield and the monks of Coventry as to the right of election of a new Bishop was revived. At the same time, King John and the Pope were involved in a dispute as to the archbishopric of Canterbury. The monks of Coventry unilaterally appointed Joibert, their prior, to the bishopric of Lichfield, and forwarded their Deed of Election to Stephen Langton, named by the Pope to be Archbishop of Canterbury against the wishes of King John, who was so enraged that he seized not only the episcopal property of Joibert but also his private property. The church property he retained even after the election and consecration of William de Cornhull as Bishop of Lichfield in 1215, and the Bishop's Brewood residence may well have been appropriated and utilised as his own property.[123]

58

Lead papal bulla of Pope Innocent III or IV. Obverse illegible. 1 3/8" diameter.

The dispute between King John and the Pope is of further interest, for the Pope involved was Innocent III. A lead papal bulla, or seal, found in about 1985 on the north-eastern outskirts of the village,[124] is of the same Pope. It is perhaps fanciful to imagine that the bulla was attached to a document relating to the dispute and was lost by a clerk in the King's party en route to or from Lichfield via Watling Street.

On 28th July 1221, William de Cornhull, Bishop of Coventry and Lichfield, was granted the right to hold a market in his town of Brewood every Friday until the full age of Henry III [confirmed, together with the grant of a Monday market, in 1256], possibly to compensate for the revenues lost with the disafforestation of Brewood Forest in 1204, and there is further evidence of an episcopal residence at Brewood [presumably the same as in King John's time, although we cannot be certain] in an episcopate of Roger de Weseham, Bishop of Coventry and Lichfield, which records an ordination of the vicarage of Aston-juxta-Birmingham, dated at Brewood 23rd November 1254.[125] Bishop Weseham appears to have suffered from some type of paralysis, and resigned his bishopric at his manor of Brewood on 4th December 1256 having been granted a pension of 200 marks per annum. He died on Sunday 1st May 1257 at Brewood and was buried in Lichfield Cathedral the following Tuesday, the Archbishop of Dublin conducting the funeral service.

As observed earlier, the street plan of the village of Brewood and the layout of the surrounding fields appears to be based on a grid plan, the result of deliberate planning. It is known that the clergy were responsible for some of the earliest town planning in England, if the long-forgotten expertise of the Romans is discounted. Bury St Edmunds, for example, was laid out by the local Abbot between 1066 and 1086. Geographically closer, Stratford-upon-Avon was planned by the Bishop of Worcester, who owned the entire manor, after he had obtained the grant of a market in 1196, and it is likely that Roger de Clinton, Bishop of Lichfield from 1129 to 1148,[126] who is known to have been responsible for the first rebuilding of Lichfield Cathedral, the foundation of Buildwas Abbey, Farewell Nunnery near Lichfield, and probably Blackladies, confirmed the monastic foundations of Blithbury and Canwell, and laid out Lichfield in a rectangular street plan, with his successor completing his work by obaining a market and borough status.[127]

It is significant that the Bishop of Lichfield owned the entire manor of Brewood, [increased from the five hides held at Domesday by 80 acres of assarted land granted by Henry II in 1135 from the royal Forest], had a park nearby, was granted the right to hold a market in 1221, and the earliest parts of the parish church date from the same period. It is possible that the expansionist Roger de Clinton, before, during or after founding the Priory of Blackladies, laid out Brewood on a typical rectangular street plan at some time during the second quarter of the twelfth century – perhaps because it was mid-way between his cathedral at Lichfield and his abbey at Buildwas – his successors acquiring the valuable right of a market, the first step on the road to commercial growth and prosperity, at about the time the parish church was rebuilt.

Brewood from the south-east photographed on 25th July 1957. Behind the church spire is the Victorian School, demolished in 1966. Above it to the right is a curved row of nineteenth century cottages where the library now stands. The diagonal line across the top left corner is the Shropshire Union Canal. The houses of St Chad's Close now occupy the large open area lower right. The photograph shows how the lower part of Dirty Lane on the left may have been a continuation of The Pavement. The parallel strips of the tofts or gardens between Dean Street and Dirty Lane may have been laid out with a newly-planned village in the early twelfth century. Cambridge University Collection: copyright reserved.

Certainly there is evidence of a deliberate attempt by the Bishops to develop Brewood as an urban centre, for in or before 1280 they had created burgage tenure, a special form of free tenure associated with attempts to promote commercial expansion, under which land was held almost invariably by payment of money rent instead of manorial obligations, with freedom to sell or leave by will and burgesses enjoying privileges at the market and in payment of tolls, the tenement being at Woodhouse-end, a location which has not been indentified with certainty. The tenant was Richard le Mason, followed by Richard of Wolverhampton in about 1315, and later Thomas de la Hyde. With the tenement went 9 acres of land in 'Eskborrow' [Ackbury]. Medieval burgage plots commonly took on a characteristic shape – long and narrow, with one short side abutting on the market place or another principal street. The grouping of these burgages together, with roughly similar lengths, delineated the borough territory even when – as at Brewood – there were neither walls nor other physical

Brewood from the south-east, photographed on 25th July 1957. Brewood Hall is in the centre foreground. The square building slightly left of centre in the lower half of the photograph is the nonconformist chapel in Sandy Lane, rebuilt in 1842 and demolished in 1936. Cambridge University Collection: copyright reserved.

boundaries. Since burgage tenure is very unlikely to have been created before the grant of a market had been obtained, it seems safe to assume that in Brewood the first burgages appeared between 1221 and 1280. By 1298 there were 29 tenants of burgages,[128] and one of the common fields in the manor was called Burgage Field. As late as 1897 there are references to land known as Burgage End and The Burgage in the Deanery manor.

Technically, the legal privilege of burgage tenure meant borough status, but in the case of Brewood [and also Penkridge, where burgesses were established during the same period] the status was, not unusually, never formalised by charter. Nevertheless, Brewood can legitimately claim to be an ancient borough,[129] although the term 'borough' was an imprecise one, and in reality Brewood remained an ordinary agricultural community differing from its neighbours only in the legal privilege of burgage tenure. In all there were 22 boroughs in Staffordshire by 1364, a remarkable number for one of the poorest and most underdeveloped parts of England. Leicestershire, for example, had only three, and only five counties had more than Staffordshire. The reasons why the number of boroughs in Staffordshire was so large remains a mystery.[130]

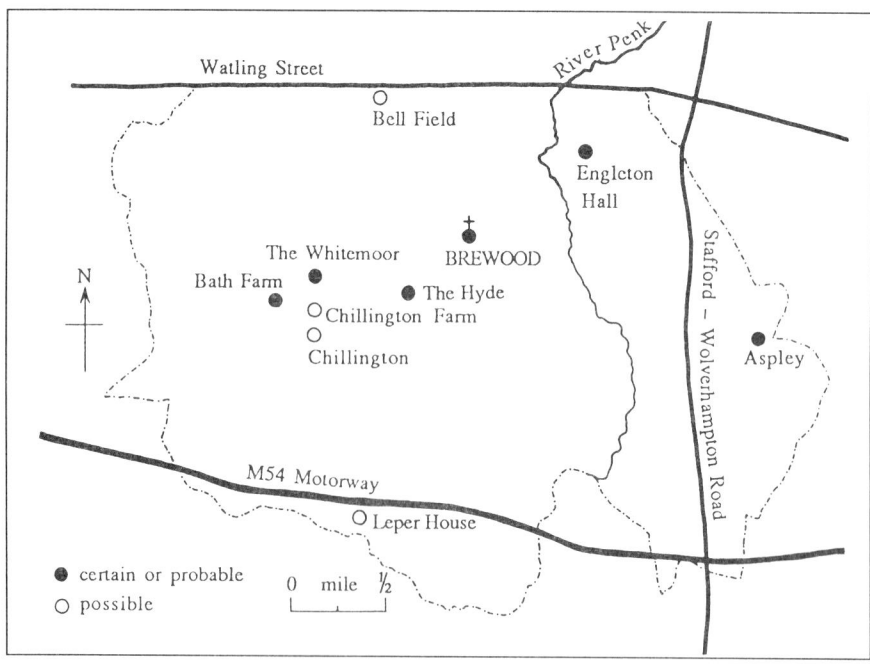

Moated sites in Brewood parish.

It is noticeable that in villages in many parts of the south and Midlands small roughly rectangular closes were created around the village, while the planned villages of the north, most apparently of Norman creation, had ribbon-like tofts running back from the dwellings. Brewood seems to follow the pattern found in northern England, and probably still preserves many of its hedged burgage plots, particularly on the west side of Dean Street,[131] and perhaps along Stafford Street. The Brewood landscape would have consisted of long hedgerows bordering the vast open-strip fields, small hedged fields on the outer edges of the village representing peripheral assarts, and a mosaic of tofts and closes enmeshing the village itself. In addition there were the lesser outlying settlements such as Hatton, Coven, Somerford, Gunstone, Horsebrook and Aspley, as well as the substantial hamlet of Chillington. The moated sites within the parish – at The Hyde, Engleton, Aspley, Whitemoor, and the un-named one south of Bath Farm – may be associated with areas of forest clearance in the fourteenth century.

By 1255 the Bishop held a view of frankpledge in the manor of Brewood and its members, jointly assessed at five hides, geldable [taxable]. On 2nd June 1259 the Bishop was granted by a charter issued at Woodstock by his uncle, Henry III, the right to hold an additional market each Monday, and an annual fair on the vigil, feast and morrow of the Nativity of the Virgin [7th, 8th and 9th September], an indication of increasing commercial activity in the village. By 1275 a vicarage had been ordained[132] and endowed with all the altar and mortuary dues and, with the exception of the Dean's land, the tithes of lamb and wool, the Dean being granted a pension payable by the Vicar of 10 marks [£6 13s 4d]. The advowson was held by the Deans of Lichfield until 1868, when it passed to the Bishop, who still holds it.

On Monday 10th October 1278, Edward I visited Brewood. The royal visit must have been particularly memorable for both hosts and visitors, since the King almost certainly witnessed a disastrous fire which seems to have been concentrated on the southern side of the village, for five days later he issued a mandate from Torton ordering

> Roger de Clifford, Justice of the Forest this side Trent . . . to cause Henry le Mercer of Brewood, Dean of Lichfield, to have four oaks in the hay of Caneleye within the forest of Kanek, and to cause Philip le Clerk to have four oaks and Amice the widow to have two oaks from the said hay, for the rebuilding of their houses that were lately burnt by mischance when the king was at Brewode, of the king's gift[133]

It is possible that other properties were destroyed, but the royal largesse may not have extended to the lowest classes. The mandate is of interest for the inference that the Dean normally resided in Brewood, and for the only known reference to Philip le Clerk, presumably the Vicar of Brewood, or possibly an ecclesiastic attached to the Dean with his own house at Brewood. The mandate also provides some indication of the close proximity of at least some of the more important residences at that period.

It was customary for the later Plantagenet Kings to hold assizes during their frequent perambulations around their kingdom, and on Monday 24th July 1279 Edward I was again at Brewood, en route from Woodstock to Northamptonshire, his retinue including Ralph Hengham, a Justice of the Kings Bench, who conducted the 'coram rege', or assize before the King, which was held during the visit, presumably in the great hall of the Bishop's residence.[134] This is the only known assize to have been held at Brewood.

The Bishop's manor of Brewood was surveyed in 1291 in connection with the concession made by King Edward I which gave the then Pope one tenth of the value of all church property in England [the Taxation of Pope Nicholas IV]. The survey records that the Bishop of Coventry and Lichfield had in 'Brewod', in the Deanery of Lichfield, about 30 free tenants and tenants of new lands, 29 tenants of burgesses, 62 neifs and 36 cottars. There were four caracutes of land, worth 30s yearly [a caracute being the Danish equivalent of a hide, which varied from place to place], rents of assize worth £21 yearly, view of frankpledge[135] worth 15s, pannage 15s, stock worth 60s, and pasturage and herbage worth 14s, and the Bishop received from the auxilliary vills 30s yearly. The perquisites of the court were 30s a year, and there were two mills – presumably the same as those mentioned in Domesday – worth 60s a year. [One of the mills, probably Somerford, had been rebuilt by the Bishop before 1288.] The total annual value of the manor was £38 4s and the tithes declared at £3 16s 4d. In the same survey, the prebendal stall of Brewood in Lichfield Cathedral was valued at 40 marks [£26 13s 4d] a year. The value of the entire manor at Domesday had been only £5, an indication of the rapid economic growth which had taken place over the preceding two centuries. By way of comparison, the total value of Brewood in 1391 was £64 17s 4d, and of Wolverhampton £54 13s 4d.

Included amongst the pleas before the Itinerant Justices on 7th January 1293 was a claim by Roger, Bishop of Coventry and Lichfield, to the 'free warren, fair, market, gallows and waif' in his several manors, including Brewood. Attached to the plea were warrants of King John dated 6th August 1214 and two other warrants, one of Richard II certifying John's warrant, the other a decision on the above pleas by Edward I dated 28th January 1377.[136]

By 1298 the Bishop had 147 tenants in Brewood, one of the largest numbers in any of his Staffordshire manors, an indication of the expanding population during this period.[137]

A confirmation of the advowson of Kyngeston to Rocester Abbey by Walter Langton, Bishop of Coventry and Lichfield and Lord Treasurer, is dated at Brewood 19th September 1305,[138] evidence that the episcopal residence was still in use, and in the survey 'Nomina Villarum' for Staffordshire made in 1315-16, a list drawn up following a promise by the knights and barons of parliament that a footsoldier would be provided from every village in the kingdom for the war against the Scots – the men were not in fact called-up – residences of the Bishop are listed at Longdon, Rugeley, Cannock, Eccleshall, Haywood, Lichfield and Brewood.[139] By 1321, however, a survey of the Bishop's holdings at Brewood shows that the capital messuage, with a garden and close, had been leased out for a rent of 18d, which seems to have been well below the market rent, for it was then estimated that an increase to 40d might be achieved. Further evidence of economic decline is apparent in the listing of underwood valued at 50 marks [£33 6s 8d] for which only 12s was obtained for underwood sold; a mill worth 4 marks [£2 13s 4d] for which £1 12s 8d was received; a fish pond worth 10s per annum but having no fish; and rent of Assize from freemen at 40s and rent of Assize from serfs estimated at £10, but only 20s was received from the freemen and 12s from the serfs.

In 1314 there is a reference to the twice yearly 'great court' held in Brewood, presumably the court leet, the criminal court of record for the district held before the lord or his steward, traditionally held at Easter and Michaelmas.

In 1326 Bishop Roger de Northburgh wrote a letter directing that a search be made for two nuns from Whiteladies, Elizabeth de la Zouche and Alice de Kellenhal, who had left the convent. In 1332 one of the missing nuns reappeared and made her confession before the Bishop in Brewood church, and was given absolution and re-admitted to the convent.

In the late thirteenth century the system of taxation based essentially on landholding was replaced with one related to each taxpayer's 'moveables', an indication that the landed classes were no longer the only wealthy group. The subsidies, levied to meet the demands of the Crown for additional revenue, particularly for military operations, started in 1290, and there were sixteen impositions between that date and 1332. The subsidy for 1327 relating to Brewood and the adjoining vills is of interest in several ways, particularly as a record of early occupations and locative surnames, but is of little value in calculating population figures, for it is known that for various reasons many people managed to evade the tax. The following is a translation of the Latin return:

Brewode cum Membris

From Roger le Heustere	4s		Walter Beublat	2s	
John son of Henry	3s	1d	William del Hethe	3s	6d
Wilmot le Colt	3s		William Godewyn	2s	
William son of Stephen	3s	10d	William Scot	3s	2d
Stephen de Grenhul	2s	3d	William Dobbe		18d
Adam Aylward	4s		Robert Hemery		2s
Robert Chichely	3s		Walter Gilbert		21d
Wiliam son of Robert	2s		John de Strangleford		12d
Jordan le Botiler	4s	6d	John son of William	2s	6d
From the Black Nuns	2s				

Chylynton

From Ada Gyffard	5s		Walter Othegrene	2s	
Henry de Erkebarwe		12d	Richard Othegrene		18d
Roger de Erkebarwe	2s		Hutred son of Richard	3s	
Robert de Chirchehous		18d	Adam son of Hutred	3s	
Thomas at walle	2s	6d	John on the Hethe	2s	6d
Richard le Budel	3s		Robert Edden		12d
John at walle	2s		John on the hull	2s	
William de Northhale	3s	3d	Robert de St. Peter	3s	
Edith Attenore	3s		John atte Nore	3s	6d
John le Penynton	3s		John son of Galfrid	2s	6d

Horsebrok

From Juliana de Bromhale	2s		William Colet	2s	
Wilmot de Crakeford	4s		John Isoten		18d
Robert preposito	5s		Richard son of Richard	5s	
William son of preposito	2s		William Skent	2s	6d
Felicia Skent	2s	6d			

Engleton

From Hugo de Engleton	3s		John de Hethe	2s	6d
Richard Jurdan	3s	3d	Nicholas le Heustere	2s	

Somerford

From William Jurdan	3s		William le Palmere	2s	
Richard Hert		12d	John Douce		12d
William Agas	4s		John Onthegrene	2s	6d

Hatton

From Henry in le Huyrne	3s	6d	Richard le Schirreue	2s	3d
From William de Schelfhul	2s		William Raven	2s	9d
Richard son of Robert	2s	6d			

Gunstun

From Hugo de Gunstun	2s	6d	Peter de Wabieleye	2s	
Matilda Cornett	7s	3d	Walter atte Siche	2s	
William le Newemon		18d	Wilmot le Mareschal	2s	
John atte forde	2s		Wilmot Silvott		18d
Roger de Brewode	2s	6d			

			Total	£9	8s	5d

Covene [listed separately]

From Roger Bercario	3s		Richard Stede	2s	
Walter Bercario		18d	John Prest	2s	

Robert son of Walter	12d	William Wilran	2s
Robert son of Johanis	12d	John Batten	10d
John Margery	3s	John le Smyth	2s
William son of Johanis	2s 6d	Jacobe le Colier	2s
Walter Polt	6d		

The subsidy assessment of 1334 is also of interest, for it reveals that only five places in Staffordshire had higher assessments than the £7 13s 8d levied on Brewood and its members, namely Stafford [£14 8s]; Lichfield [£13 6s 8d]; Newcastle [£10 16s 8d]; Brockton [£10 10s 2½d]; and Alstonfield [£8].[140]

In 1348 the parish was badly affected by the Black Death, perhaps the worst catastrophe to befall it in its long history, and the Poll Tax assessment of 1380-81 records 249 individuals over 14 in the parish at that date.

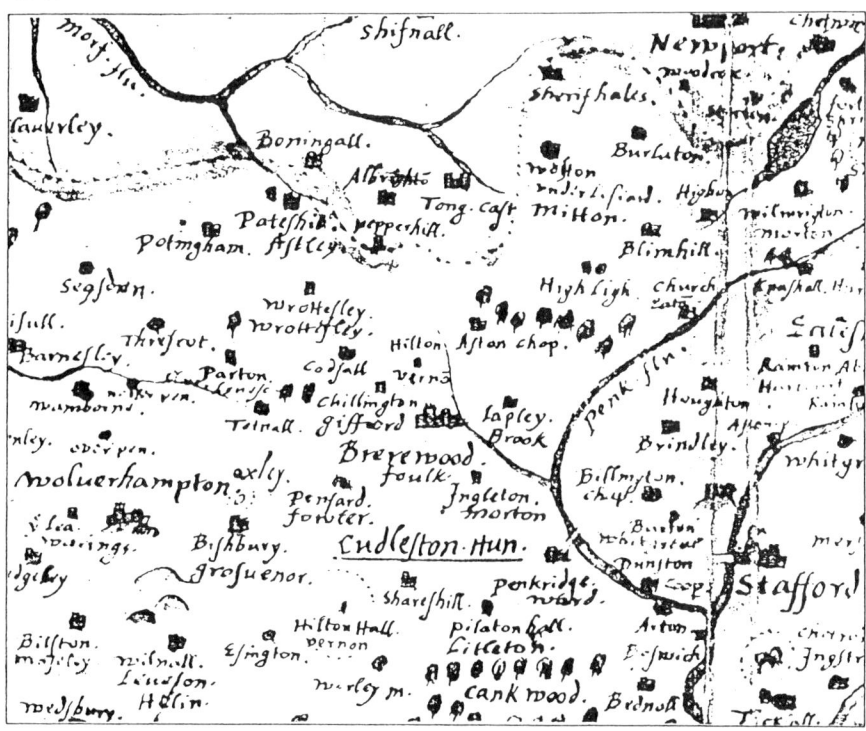

Extract from a manuscript map of Staffordshire drawn in 1599 by William Smith (?1550-1611), an antiquarian and herald at the College of Arms. North is to the right, and many places show the name of the principal landowner. Of particular interest is 'Hilton', north-east of Chillington. The place has not been identified, but since it is shown linked to the Vernons, it may be a duplication of Hilton [Hall], which appears lower left. Reproduction by kind permission of the Trustees of the William Salt Library, WSL 650/38B.

By letters patent dated some time between 1387 and 1390, Walter Skirlaw, Bishop of Lichfield, was confirmed in possession of his fair and market in

Brewood, and at about this time the hall-house incorporated into Smithy Cottages was built, together with the now demolished hall-house which stood nearby to the south.

By 1473 the manor-house ["porta manerii"] was being leased to the Vicar of Brewood, and a lease of pasture described as the site of the manor in 1538 indicates that it was no longer existing at that date. The hall house forming the structure of what is now The Swan public house and the timberwork of Sutherland House in Bargate Street may date from this period.

Various house and street names within Brewood village, including Dean Cottage, Dean's End [one house of this name at the lower end of Dean Street, another on the east side of the junction of Newport Street and School Road], Dean's Gate, The Deanery, Dean's Croft, Dean Street House, Dean's Hall Farm – all on the south side of the village – and Dean Street, Deansfield Road and Deansfield Close, attest to the early connection between Brewood and the Deans of Lichfield. A Dean of Lichfield is first recorded in about 1140, and the Deanery was originally endowed with lands and tithes from the Bishop's estates, but in about 1176 Bishop Peche found it necessary to re-endow the Deanery which had been "ruined during

Dean Street in about 1905. On the left is Old Smithy Cottages, now a single house which incorporates an open-hall house of about 1350. The internal roof timbers are still smoke-blackened from the central open fire which would have been used in the early life of the house. The nearest cottage in the range is a relatively recent addition, dating from the early 1600's. On the right is the end of the range of timbered cottages in The Pavement demolished in 1962.

the time of war", ie. the civil war of Stephen's reign. Included in the endowment was the prebend of Brewood. At about the same date the Deanery was also given half a 'wara' of land[141] and a dwellinghouse in Brewood. A piece of moor at Brewood was added by Roger de Hyde in 1222 and, as already noted, the Dean's house was destroyed by fire in 1278: perhaps the same residence as that granted a century earlier. A roll of receipts and expenses relating to the Deanery survives from 1333-4, and records the receipt of £40 from the farmer of the prebend of Brewood and Adbaston. There may have been problems with the farm at Brewood [Dean's Hall Farm?] as the Dean employed a messenger to take letters to the farmer and to the Vicar of Brewood and the Abbott of Lilleshall "touching the farm at Brewood". He also sent an official to inspect defects in the houses at Brewood.

Until extinguished by an Order in Council dated 27th August 1846, Brewood remained a peculiar of the Dean, exempt from Bishop's visitations, and the Dean was patron and rector of Brewood, prebend of Brewood and Adbaston, and lord of the Deanery manor in Brewood. Until at least the eighteenth century the Dean kept a triennial visitation, and it seems that he continued to appoint the vicar until the end of the last century.

Apart from formal administrative and ecclesiastical documents, there is little recorded information about matters affecting Brewood in the medieval period. There is, however, a record of a complaint to the King's Justices by Gillian, daughter of Herbert of Wyrley, alleging that on 1st August 1292 Robert of Derby, servant of the Dean of Lichfield

> upon the high road between Brewood and Somerford, came and assailed this Gillian with evil words against the peace, and against her will took from her and carried away a silver buckle to the value of eighteen pence, and six shillings and two pence sterling that were in a bladder, against the will of the aforesaid Gillian, and he still hath them; to the grievous damage of this Gillian of a hundred shillings; of which she prayeth remedy for God's sake and for the Queen's soul's sake.

The outcome of the matter is not known.

The Coroner's Rolls contain an interesting note of an inquest heard on 6th September 1330 before 12 named jurors of the liberty of Brewood

> that it happened at Brewode in a certain place called Hubbeleye [Hubbal] that a certain Nicholas, son of William Godwine, went from Brewode towards the White Nuns of Brewode, and being detained by instigation of the devil, drowned himself in a certain marlpit . . . William de la Withies first found him and raised the hue and cry . . .[142]

Suicide, despite the harshness of life during that period, was almost unknown and considered a great sin, for only God could decide when life was to end: anyone who took his own life was assumed to have been possessed by the devil, and for that reason could not be buried in consecrated ground. The report is of interest for the inference that the route from Brewood to Whiteladies may then have been via Hubbal to the north, and for early confirmation of the use of marl on the land. Several marl and gravel pits still lie clustered to the north of Whiteladies.[143]

From the time of Domesday, Brewood had managed to rebuild its shaky economy in the space of two centuries to the point where it had secured the patronage of the Bishop, had at least one building worthy of the royal description 'our chamber', had received at least six royal visits, enjoyed the benefits and status of two weekly markets and an annual three-day fair, was the location of a twice-yearly great court, had established burgage tenure, and had the wealth, materials and craftsmen to build or rebuild the church and a vicarage. It had secured release from the onerous obligations associated with the royal Forest, had been chosen by the Bishop as the site for one of his parks, and was clearly a place of some importance, for it is said to have been noted [as 'Briuerne'] in the Mappa Mundi, compiled by Gervase of Canterbury in about 1199.[144]

In other places those factors were sufficient to ensure continued growth into a town or even city. But history has shown that the thirteenth century was perhaps the high point of economic achievement in Brewood, although the reasons why the impetus of the previous two centuries failed to propel Brewood to greater prosperity are not readily apparent. The answer is probably a combination of many factors. Since the beginning of the fourteenth century England had been in economic stagnation, if not decline. The parish is known to have been hit by the Black Death, and the resulting labour shortages inevitably made a greater impact in the smaller rural villages, which relied so heavily on ploughmen and labourers to realise the potential of the hard-won land, some of which may have been abandoned before the workforce was decimated by plague. It is also evident that other places in the area were better placed geographically to attract trade. Brewood lies neither on a river, where a bridge would attract traffic, nor on a principal highway.

But whatever the combination of reasons which led to the failure of Brewood to achieve further economic growth, it is clear that by the first quarter of the fourteenth century the interest of the Bishops, who had been the driving force behind attempts at expansion, had waned, for episcopal visits to Brewood had ceased, and the Bishop's residence was leased out. The golden age of Brewood had come to an end.

9. The Poll Tax of 1380-1

Poll Taxes were first levied in 1377 and 1379, taking their name from the Middle English word 'polle', meaning a head, for the tax was in theory payable at a rate of one groat [4d] by all over the age of 14, although research suggests that many managed to evade registration. The 1377 Poll Tax returns for Brewood record 190 'heads', which should have produced £3 3s 4d, but for some reason the local Constables collecting the tax, William Colyns and John de Chetewyntte, declared a return of £4 13s 4d.[145] The Poll Tax of 1380-1 was the spark that ignited the Peasants Revolt of 1381 – in which the peasantry of Staffordshire were not involved – for the tax was three times higher than the levies of 1377 and 1379, varying between one groat for a serf and 60 groats for a nobleman. But anomalies were created by this graduation: in villages which included a nobleman, knight, squire or lawyer, the villeins might pay only one groat per head, whereas villages entirely occupied by villeins paid three groats – the equivalent of a weeks wages or the annual rent of an acre of land.

The Poll Tax return for 'Brewode, Chilynton, Horsebroke, Somerford, Engleton, Hatton, Dunston [Gunstone]' of 1380-1 still exists.[146] It contains 249 names, with 45 peasant households, and some 40 artificers and retail tradesman. 15 servants are recorded, 12 of them married, and all attached to households. None of the 35 labourers was attached to a household. The return is of considerable interest for the particulars it contains of the various trades and occupations within the parish in the fourteenth century – the number of female labourers and husbandmen is particularly noteworthy – and for the insight it provides from surnames to the proportion of those who had come to the parish from other areas, both nearby and further afield. The following is a translation from the original Latin:

William of Weston, labourer, Juliana his wife	2s	
William Parker, woodcutter, Edith his wife	2s	
John of Barre, smith, Denise his wife	2s	
Richard Parker, husbandman, Agnes his wife	2s	
John Braban, weaver, Joanna his wife	2s	
Henry Parker, chapman, Agnes his wife	2s	
Radulf Tailor, tailor, Edith his wife	2s	
John of Greenhill, husbandman, Felicia his wife	2s	
Richard Sawer, husbandman, Agnes his wife	2s	
William Glover, glovemaker, Amicia his wife	2s	
John Crouke, miller, Maltilda his wife	2s	
John son and his serf		12d
William Cartwright, wheelwright, Alice his wife	2s	4d
John their son and their serf		8d
Robert Cartwright, wheelwright		12d
Adam of Barre, labourer		12d

William Lily, labourer		12d
William Botiller, husbandman, Margaret his wife	2s	
Rose Botiller, serf, Ada Wobaston		12d
William Pickstock, labourer, Edith his wife	2s	
John of Gunstone, dyer, Alice his wife	2s	
John Otour, labourer, Joan his wife	2s	
Richard Wilkes, husbandman		12d
Joan Chillington, serf, John Crouke		12d
Agnes Chalener, labourer		12d
John, serf, John Millward		12d
Agnes Vicary, 'souster'		12d
Richard Sawer, junior, serf, Richard Sawer		12d
Agnes Sawer, serf, Richard Sawer		12d
Joan her serf		12d
Felicia Crow, labourer		12d
Margery Corbin, baker		12d
John Moldesley, shoemaker, Alice his wife	2s	
John Sadler, draper, Eleanor his wife	2s	
William Day, thatcher, Matilda his wife		20d
John Goose, salter, Alice his wife		20d
John Stuche, husbandman, Juliana his wife	2s	
John of Egg, thresher, Joan his wife	2s	
Felicia of Willon, labourer		12d
John Wymondsley, labourer, Marjorie his wife		20d
Marjorie Ousshe, widow		12d
Matilda Fisher, labourer		12d
Alice Avis, chapman		12d
Stephen Merryweather, baker, Maria his wife	2s	
John of the Heath, husbandman, Alice his wife	2s	
Ralph of Heath, labourer, Alice his wife	2s	
Philip Millward, miller, Maiota his serf		20d
Denise Merryweather, widow, Robert her serf	2s	
Robert Thatcher, cooper, Marjorie his wife	2s	
Roger Tailor, tailor, Eva his wife	2s	
John Barker, Alice his wife	2s	
John, serf, Roger Tailor		12d
John Mansel, tanner, Matilda his wife	2s	
John, servant, John Mansel		12d
Alice of the Hall, widow, Alice her daughter	2s	
Alice Dicouns, labourer		12d
Isolda Seuster, labourer		12d
Edith of Bothe, labourer		12d
Robert Huntgrim, labourer, Marjorie his wife	2s	
John Millward, serf, miller		12d
Richard Chapman, thresher		12d
Peter Walker, fuller		12d
Alice his wife		12d
William Walker, labourer		12d
Alice Bedemon, labourer		12d
William Bedemon, labourer		12d

William Bedemon junior, labourer		12d
Richard Palicer, labourer, John at the Cross, tailor	2s	
Nicholas Magson, husbandman		12d
Peter Colman, husbandman, Alice his wife	3s	
Thomas Barker, barker, Alice his wife	2s	
Richard of the Hyde, husbandman, Sybil his wife	2s	
William Barnville, barker, Alice his wife	2s	6d
John at the Ash, serf, John Longeley		12d
Henry Belot, salter, Petronilla his wife	2s	
Peter Bonker, husbandman, Agnes his wife	2s	
John Wyot, labourer		12d
William at Pyrie, husbandman, Ginster Agnes his wife	2s	
William at Pyrie senior, husbandman, Isabel his wife	2s	
Nicholas Newman, husbandman, Joan his wife	2s	
Richard at the Ford, Alice his wife	2s	
Richard Pulesdon, labourer, Felicia his wife	2s	
Thomas Sewalle, labourer, Juliana his wife	2s	
Hugh Brown, thresher, Agnes his wife	2s	
Agnes of Somerford, widow, Christine her serf	2s	
Elizabeth of Pyrie, widow		12d
Nicholas at Mere, husbandman, Felicia his wife	2s	
Richard Bond, husbandman, Edith his wife	2s	
Richard Bradeley, husbandman, Christine his wife	2s	
William Idriche, husbandman, Felicia his wife	2s	
Jeavon Cook, husbandman		12d
John Campion, husbandman, Denise his wife	2s	4d
William their serf		8d
Thomas Campion, husbandman, Marjorie his wife	2s	
John Longeley, husbandman, Clarice his wife	2s	
Henry Somerford, husbandman, Alice his wife	2s	
John Woodhamcot, husbandman, Alice his wife	2s	
Richard Aspley, husbandman, Agnes his wife	2s	4d
William of Parys, husbandman, Alice his wife	2s	
John Chaundeys, husbandman, Sybil his wife	2s	
Thomas of Bradeley, husbandman, Juliana his wife	2s	
John of Coven, husbandman, Helen his wife	2s	
Amicia Wilcox, widow, Robert Molle, labourer	2s	
John Wasteneys, tailor, Alice his wife	2s	
Alan Smith, smith, Agnes his wife	2s	
John Cox, husbandman, Helen his wife	2s	
Richard Isuton, labourer, John Henries, husbandman, Alice his wife	3s	
John son John Henries, husbandman, Felicia his wife	2s	
Adam Walker, husbandman	2s	
Joan his wife	2s	
William Crakeford, husbandman, Felicia his wife	2s	
William Thornby, tailor, Thomas Skut, thatcher	2s	
Richard Henries, Denise his wife	2s	
Thomas Hitchings, husbandman, Edith his wife	2s	
John Wanne, husbandman, Agnes his wife	2s	
Richard Jerkies, husbandman,		

Adam Wilkes, husbandman, Avicia his wife	3s	
Elizabeth Bate, ropemaker		12d
John Boket, salter, Joan his wife	2s	
William Bruynton, butcher, Maria wife	2s	
Ralph Salter, salter, Agnes wife	2s	
Ralph Hyde, husbandman, Joan his wife	2s	
Joan Simper, widow		12d
Richard of Pyrie, husbandman, Joan his wife	2s	
Marjorie Pyrie, widow		12d
William Wright, carpenter, Christine his wife	2s	
William Jenkins, labourer, Alice his wife	2s	
Thomas Walsall, labourer, Alice his wife	2s	
William Bobbington, labourer, John Pendeford, labourer	2s	
Hugh Wallhouse, carpenter, Helen his wife	2s	
William Challenor, blanket-maker, Amisia his wife	2s	
John Wallhouse, carpenter, Alice his wife	2s	
Peter Frenchman, labourer, Alice his wife	2s	
Thomas Beamois, husbandman, Isolada wife	2s	
Adam Bishop, husbandman, Agnes his wife	2s	
Roger French, husbandman, Edith his wife	2s	
Henry of Weston, labourer, Agnes his wife	2s	
Peter Porter, husbandman		12d
Richard Buffry, husbandman, Alice his wife	2s	
Henry Northall, husbandman, Agnes his wife	2s	
John Wright, carpenter, Benedicta his wife	2s	
John Daniel, tailor, Margaret his wife	2s	
Peter of Penynton, husbandman, Joan his wife	2s	
Adam Shepherd, husbandman, Agnes his wife	2s	
William Eyr, husbandman, Edith his wife	2s	
John Sabin, husbandman, Joan his wife	2s	
Petronilla Corbin, widow		12d
Alice of Walton, widow		12d
Juliana of Northall, Sybil Wore, labourer	2s	

Total from 249 taxpayers:	£12	9s	0d

For years after the Peasants Revolt money was raised by poll tax only from aliens. In 1513 a general poll tax was imposed, but raised less than a third of the expected £160,000. A poll tax in 1641 raised over £400,000, and during the reign of Charles II revenue was obtained in this way on several occasions, with the tax graded according to rank. For many years after 1688 poll taxes were used to finance the war with France. It had been abolished by the reign of William III, but in 1990 an annual poll tax was introduced amid much controversy to replace the domestic rating system which had been based on the hypothetical letting value of residential property. The tax proved so unpopular and difficult to administer that a new system of tax assessment was announced the following year.

10. Forest and Park

The concept of the Forest seems to have been introduced into England by the Normans, and William the Conqueror himself had 25. The word Forest, derived from 'forestum silvam', meaning the wood outside, i.e. outside the common law and subject to a special royal law whose object was the preservation of the King's hunting, was also introduced into our language by the Normans, and described an unenclosed area of land – not necessarily wooded – within which deer were protected by local bylaws. The word 'Forest' was thus a legal and not a geographical term, and carried a meaning entirely different from that of today. Occasionally the word chase was used by the Normans for an area reserved for hunting by one of the King's subjects.[147]

The date of the creation of Brewood Forest is not known – it is first mentioned by name in 1188[148] – but it is possible that it may have been one of the earliest of the King's Forests, since Domesday Book records that the King owned wooded land in Brewood parish in 1086: in the entry for Coven, Count Robert of Stafford is recorded as holding one hide, which Buered held under him. He also held a 20 acre wood half a league long and one furlong broad. But this wood, it is added, 'is in the King's Lordship'. The Domesday entry for Albrighton includes a reference to a wood there, also in the King's hands, capable of fattening 100 swine. That wood may have been part of what became known as Brewood Forest.[149] Further evidence is obtained from the Domesday entry for Codsall, recorded in the tenure of Chenvin, the King's thegn, who, it has been persuasively argued, was the same person as Richard the Forester. It is likely that Codsall was a holding within Brewood Forest and the seat of the Chief Forester.[150] In 1139 Pope Eugenius III confirmed the Bishop as lawful owner of Brewood "with its enclosed wood [haya] and forest,"[151] but it is unclear whether the word forest refers to a royal Forest.

Essentially, a Forest was a status symbol, and the King always ensured that he had at least twice as many as the total held by his nobles. The creation of new Forests was continued by Henry I, but had ceased by Magna Carta in 1215, when perhaps one-third of the country was subject to Forest law, and there were at least 134 Forests in England, and over 100 in Wales.

The creation of a Forest would not have altered either the existing physical landscape, the ownership of the land, or the use of the land: the only real change would have been the introduction of deer – usually fallow, introduced from the Continent in the 12th century and easier to keep in an enclosed area than the wilder red and roe deer – and the physical delineation of the Forest boundary by paling, banks or ditches. In addition a complex heirarchy of officials was established, with Forest bylaws enforced by Forest Courts, where the Justiciars of the Forest would periodically hear cases and which provided in the form of fines an important source of income. Routine cases were heard by the Court of Attachment which met every forty days, and more serious cases by the Swanimote. The Justices of the Forest would visit the area every four years or so to fix fines and punishments. Most of the cases seem to have fallen into two categories: the gentry who hunted deer for sport, and the poor who poached deer for food. There is no evidence to identify the location of the Court of Brewood Forest, but since the Chief Forester may have had his seat at Codsall, the Court was perhaps also located there.

A popular belief is that the courts inflicted barbaric sentences for even minor breaches of Forest law, but very few cases have been documented to support that view. In reality, the courts were more anxious to secure revenue, and fines were the invariable penalty, rarely so high as to deter wrongdoers, although 'trespass against the venison' – stealing the King's deer – could mean imprisonment. 'Trespass against the vert' was damage to vegetation by grazing or woodcutting, and was punishable by fine or confiscation of livestock. In theory, any dog living within a Forest was required to have one foot mutilated – known as 'expedition' – to prevent it chasing game, but in practice the requirement was avoided by payment of a regular fine, a legal fiction which amounted to a non-mutilation licence. Encroaching on Forest land, or 'assarting', was prohibited, but again seems to have been licensed or condoned by a token annual payment.[152] In that respect, it is of particular interest that most cases of assarting in England seem to have taken place in areas which were farmed in Roman times, leading to the conclusion that during the Dark Ages numerous forests developed on lands deserted by the Romano-British farmers. It is unclear whether this return of the woodland resulted from the traumas of the Roman withdrawal, from Saxon settlement, Viking raiding, the decimation of the population by plague, or from some other environmental cause, but Brewood was probably affected to a greater or lesser extent by all of those factors. If, as suggested earlier, Brewood was relatively clear of woodland during the Roman period, the return of the woodland during the intervening 700 years or so would fit this theory, and would account for the almost complete absence of evidence for Saxon occupation in or around Brewood. That the Norman kings tended to choose wooded and thinly populated areas for their Forests reinforces the theory. Furthermore, the landscape of winding lanes in the Brewood area attests to the gradual reclamation of a heavily wooded countryside over many centuries.

Regardless of the actual landowners, most Forests were also commons, and had ancient common-rights pre-dating the creation of Forest boundaries. The three parties having an interest in the Forest were the King, entitled to keep deer, appoint Forest officials, hold Forest Courts and share the fines; the landowners; and the commoners having various valuable rights such as pannage [the right to feed swine on beech-mast or acorns], estovers [rights to take timber for necessary repairs, e.g. hay-bote for fencing repairs, house-bote for repairs to dwellings], and common of turbary [the right to cut peat or turf for fuel]. Cows, pigs and oxen were grazed, but not sheep, which would have destroyed the pasture of the deer.

An indication of the realities of life within or close to the Forest is the name Woolley,[153] near The Hyde, which is recorded in 1199 as Wolveley, meaning the wood or glade of the wolves. Wolves were commonly found in England until the end of the thirteenth century[154] – and in some places much later still – and were hunted to keep down numbers rather than for sport or food. In 1281 a licence was granted to Peter Corbet to take wolves by man, dog or traps wherever they could be found in Staffordshire, Shropshire, Gloucestershire, Herefordshire or Worcestershire.[155]

It would be wrong to assume from the emphasis in surviving records that the Crown had a dominating influence in the Forests: in reality it was the commoners and landowners – who have, understandably, left few records – who were responsible for most of the grazing and Forestry management. Even the rights of the King were limited by local bylaws, and though the nobility may have been oppressed, English medieval Kings are generally acknowledged to have respected scrupulously the rights of their humbler subjects.

Unfortunately no perambulation survives to record the boundaries of Brewood Forest, but evidence from early records[156] suggests that it extended beyond Blymhill and Wheaton Aston to the north and perhaps as far south as the road from Tettenhall to Pattingham,[157] while references to Patshull [Pereshulla], Oaken [Aka] and Weston-under-Lizard among the Forest Pleas in the Pipe Rolls of 1187-8 shows that the western boundary extended well into Shropshire,[158] giving an area of well over 35 square miles. At the Shropshire Assizes of 1221,[159] Letitia, widow of William de Omfreeston, withdrew a suit against Walter de Beaumes [Beamish lies just west of Albrighton] for stopping up a road in Brewood to the injury of her free tenement in Umfreiston [Humphreston Hall, just north of Albrighton, where there are the remains of two moated sites]. Since the case was heard in Shropshire, and the road seems to have been very close to Albrighton, the reference to Brewood would appear to refer to Brewood Forest [presumably still known as such, even though it was then disafforested], an indication that the western boundary reached at least to the outskirts of Albrighton. In the Assize Rolls of 1271-2 Donington is described as "subt' Brewode", ie under Brewood Forest, and the nuns of both Blackladies and Whiteladies were known in formal documents as "of Brewood", indicating that both houses lay within Brewood Forest. On the east, the Forest is generally said to have extended to the Penk, which formed the western boundary of Cannock Forest between at least 1167 and 1301.[160] However, in 1286 the boundaries of Cannock Forest were defined by a jury ". . . by the sow to the river Pencriz (excluding Stafford), by that river to the bridge of Covene, near the park of Brewode, thence by the road to Pendeford, through the middle of Fossmore to Oxeford [Oxley] . . ." It seems reasonable to assume that Cannock Forest abutted Brewood Forest, in which case the boundary between the two south of Coven Bridge – Jackson's Bridge, also known as King's Bridge – was "the road to Pendeford." That road may have been Lawn Lane: it could not have been the Roman road passing through Brewood Park Farm, the southern part of which leading to Pendeford was still in use in the later eighteenth century – it is shown on Yates Map of Staffordshire of 1775 – for that road passes through Brewood Park, and Forest and Park could not share the same ground. Brewood parish therefore lay partly in Brewood Forest and partly in Cannock Forest. Indeed the area subject to Forest laws extended across the county from Fazeley Bridge on the Tame to the Shropshire Forests of Mount Gilbert [the Wrekin] and Morfe, sometimes known as Bridgnorth Forest.

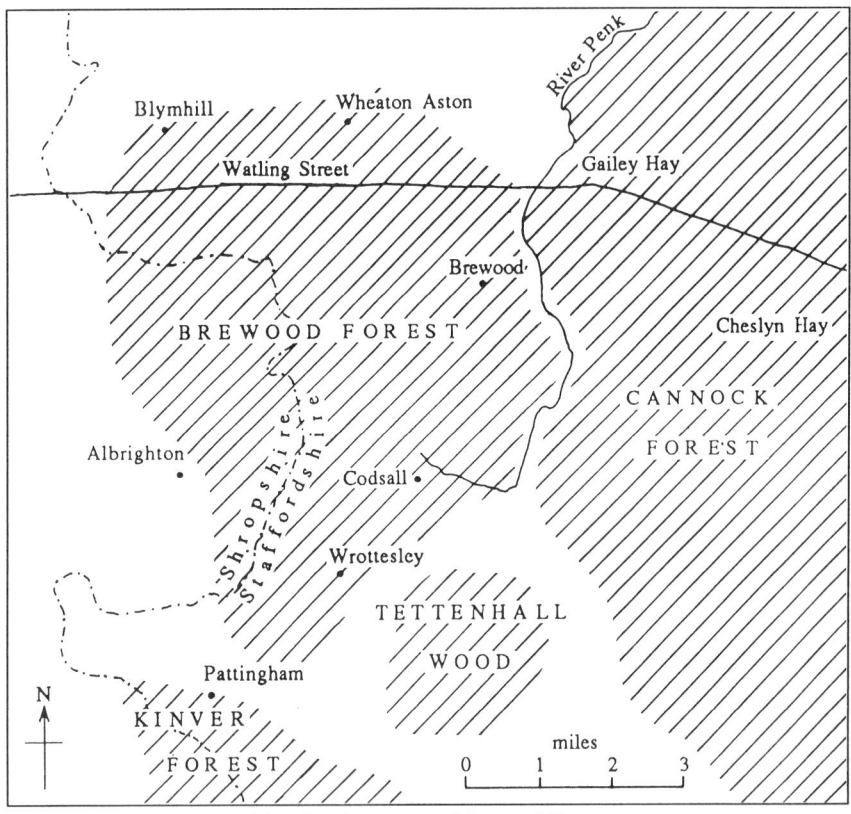

Map showing extent of Brewood Forest.

Forest law was so restrictive and unpopular that from the late twelfth century areas began to pay to be released from it or 'disafforested.' This suited King John who was in need of money to finance his military campaigns in Normandy and in 1199 "the knights dwelling around Brewood" purchased from the King their former Forest customs.[161]

A Charter of King John dated at Worcester 10th April 1200, just five days after the King was at Brewood, is in the following form:

> The King to Godfrey Fitz-Peter and Hugo de Nevill, greeting: We prohibit
> you from offering any impediment to the Lord Bishop of Coventry, who is
> enclosing a Park in his Wood of Brewood; for which park, containing two
> leagues in circumference . . . we have given him our Licence.[162]

Hugo de Nevill was then Chief Justice of England as well as Justice of the
Forest,[163] and the Charter seems to have been necessary to ensure that
problems did not arise from the proximity of the Bishop's "Wood of
Brewood" and the King's royal Forest of Brewood. The Charter
presumably resulted from representations made to the King while he was
in residence at his 'Camera Regis' at Brewood.

The next important document relating to Brewood Forest is the Charter
of Disafforestation bought by the inhabitants of the Forest dated at
Bruges [Bridgnorth] on 13th March 1204, which disafforests the King's
Forest at

> Browud, in respect of all things that to a Forest or Foresters belong.
> Therefore the said Forest and the men who dwelt therein are disafforested
> and their heirs for ever, and are acquitted as to the King and his heirs, in all
> matters hereunto belonging.[164]

For whatever reason, the Charter seems not to have been acted upon, for
immediately after another visit to Brewood from 27th to 29th January
1206, a mandate in the form of a Close Letter dated 4th February was
addressed by the King to the Justiciar of the Forests:

> The King to Hugo de Nevill, greetings:
> Know that we have given Licence to the Bishop of Coventry that he might
> make a saltatorium [a deer leap, so designed that deer could leap from the
> forest into the Bishop's Park, but not back again] in his park of Brewood,
> against the Forest; and therefore you are commanded to permit this
> much.[165]

The document is further evidence of the proximity of Brewood Forest and
the Bishop's park.

Additional evidence of the ineffectiveness of the Charter of
Disafforestation is contained in the proceedings of the Forest Assizes for
the Shropshire portion of Brewood Forest of March 1209, which record a
payment of 100 marks by the "knights and men who live in Brewood" [i.e.
the Forest] so that they and their heirs might be permanently
disafforested according to the terms of the King's Charter, with the
amount of the payment to be proportionately shared between those who
had exercised rights within Forest limits.[166] It seems particularly unjust
that the local people found it necessary to pay what must have been a
considerable sum to have the disafforestation properly enforced. The
payment is an indication of the substantial revenues that were paid to the

Forest Courts and of the difficulties created for the local people by the existence of the royal game preserves, but the payment pales into insignificance compared with the phenomenal sum of five thousand marks paid by the men of Devon to King John in 1204 for the disafforestation of the whole county, with the exception of Dartmoor and Exmoor. Even after the payment by the men of Brewood in 1209 it is unclear whether the disafforestation was thereafter properly observed in the locality: the stopping-up of the road in Brewood Forest which affected Umfreiston occurred in 1221, and in 1256 six thousand oaks were felled in Tong Wood, which was then said to have been recently taken out of Brewood Forest.[167] But release from the onerous obligations and restrictions of Forest Law undoubtedly led to an upsurge in the clearance and cultivation of marginal land which continued – apart from the years of decline in the late thirteenth and fourteenth centuries – to this day.

From the Pleas of Cannock Forest, which retained its Forest status until Elizabethan times, there is a thirteenth century reference to Brewood and its environs which is of particular interest and is therefore quoted at length:

It was presented that when the huntsmen of the King were hunting in the bailiwicke of Gaueleye [Gailey] 4 E. I [1275-76] they put up a stag with their dogs, and followed it as far as the Park at Brewode into a wood there, and John de la Wytemore came up with a bow and arrow and shot at it, and it fled out of the forest as far as the fish pond of the [Black] Nuns of Brewood[168], and the said John followed it, and dragged it out dead from the said fish pond; and John Giffard of Chillington came up and stated he had pursued the stag, and claimed the whole of it; and they skinned it and the said John took half of it and carried it to his house, and the Nuns of Brewode had the other half. As they are poor they are pardoned for the good of the King's soul, and although the said stag was taken outside the Forest, yet it was the "chasia" of the King, and put up by his dogs within the Forest, and taken in front of them against the assize. The Sheriff is ordered, therefore, to arrest the said John and John, who being convicted of the above were committed to prison. John de la Wytemore was fined 1 mark, and John de Chillington 20s.

And the same Bishop [Roger] has a saltatarium against the Forest, in his part of Brewode which adjoins the boundaries of the Forest. It is not known by what warrant. He, being infirm and weak, appeared by his attorney, Robert de Pype, at Lichfield. He said he was not bound to answer except to the King's Writ, nor without his peers, the Barons of England, and said he found his church in seisin of the woods with power to take venison, etc. The Bishop was commanded to appear before the King at the Parliament. Nothing was done, but later the Forest was taken into the King's hands, the Bishop showing no warrant. The Bishop subsequently took proceedings to recover, and produced Charters, and showed that his predecessor had been accustomed to hunt and take in the woods at will, beasts which came from the Forest of the King.

After further proceedings, the Bishop came before the King at Westminster, 18 Ed. I [1289-90] and gave up all his woods, etc., in Cannock Forest, and the King of his special favour conceded and granted again to the Bishop the same woods, to hold in free and perpetual alms as his free chase for ever, and so that it may be lawful for him to enclose his woods and make parks in them at his will, so long as he and his successors made in them no saltatories or used nets to capture the King's deer – and for this concession the Bishop gave to the King £1000.[169] [A phenomenal sum at that time.]

Records of royal hunts are very few. It seems unlikely that the early Kings would have had the time and opportunity to make frequent visits to their many Forests. The King's hunting was therefore usually conducted in his name by professional huntsmen, who would take deer according to the King's order. Thousands of such orders exist from the reign of Henry III alone.

By 1300 so many areas in the Midlands had claimed and been granted disafforestation that the Forests were greatly reduced and virtually limited to the 'haiae' or Hays, the enclosures or spaces within the Forest,[170] of which Pearse [or Priests] Hay, Wet Hay, Hag Hay, Ivetsey [Wulfgeat's hay] – all near Bishop's Wood – Harriot's Hayes and the former Cowhay, otherwise the Moor,[171] at Kiddemore Green are examples within Brewood Forest, but by the fourteenth century even the Hays were being disafforested and cultivated.

If the royal Forest of Brewood was shortlived, however, the Bishop's Park had a much longer history.

Deer parks were created by the larger landowners on their own land, and owed their origin to the Norman passion for venison. Licences to empark were required from the King before a park could be enclosed, the word 'park' originally meaning 'an enclosure'. Once established in England the number of parks rapidly increased, and the heyday of the medieval park was probably the 14th century when it is estimated that there were over 3,000 in England alone. About 100 such parks have been identified in medieval Staffordshire, the earliest created at nearby Stretton in 1175.[172]

Parks gradually began to be created by the lesser landowners, with most nobles and Bishops each possessing several. Apart from deer, the medieval park also provided a sanctuary and breeding ground for rabbits, which were introduced from the Continent in the early 13th century and, like venison, were considered a special delicacy.

Medieval parks were always fairly densely wooded, not only to provide timber, but also because deer are primarily woodland animals. One difference between a park and a Forest was that a park essentially provided meat for the table – venison and rabbits – and timber, while a Forest was an area of open country protected by law as a sporting reserve, primarily to be used for hunting. Other differences were that parks had perimeter fences to retain the deer, and were wholly private property, not having any special laws or administration. Parks were sometimes used for sport, but that was not their main function.

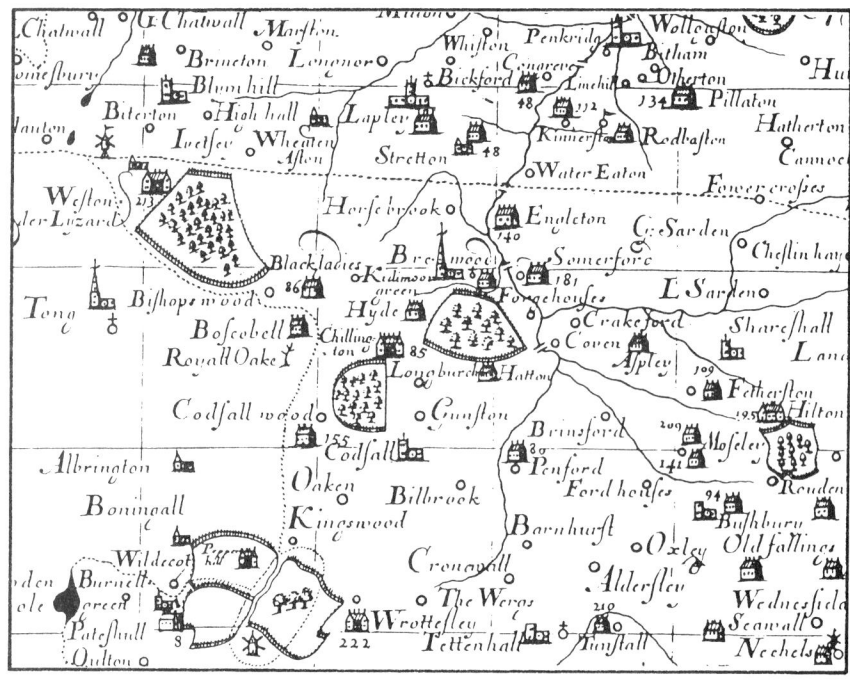

Extract from the map of Staffordshire published in 1682 by Dr. Robert Plot, almost certainly based on surveys by Gregory King, showing the fenced parks at Chillington and Brewood Park.

A park had been created at Chillington by 1287, when John Giffard was summoned for illegally detaining two oxen there,[173] with 5 more acres enclosed as parkland in 1511, the site now commemorated by Old Park Wood, half a mile south of Chillington Hall, and in 1650 the pastures at Chillington included New Park, the Old Park, and the Common Park, but the origins of Brewood Park date to 1200, when King John, after a visit to Brewood on 4th April, granted a licence to the bishop to enclose a park two leagues in circumference within the woodland of the manor.[174] It was relatively large – 893 acres and 21 poles, divided into three parts, when surveyed in 1646[175] – compared with the average of about 200 acres, and was unusual in that it had no perimeter bank.[176] It is noticeable that most parks were situated some distance from the principal residence, and both Chillington Park and Brewood Park fall into this category, the latter lying on the western side of the Penk about half a mile from Brewood village. The northern boundary is said to have followed the line of Chillington Lower Avenue, but a half-timbered cottage formerly known as

Park Cottage [now The White House], north of The Lower Avenue on what is now the Coven Road, suggests that the boundary may have been further north, perhaps Coven Road itself, a possibility reinforced by the fact that most parks were eliptical or rectangular with rounded corners, and Yates map of 1775 shows Park Lane curving eastwards towards Coven, echoing the southern curve of Park Lane. On the other hand, the double ditches which run along the centre of the Lower Avenue may have enclosed the park pale, and the Avenue may have adopted the line of the older park boundary: the survey of 1646 mentions "the trees in the Pale Row," which

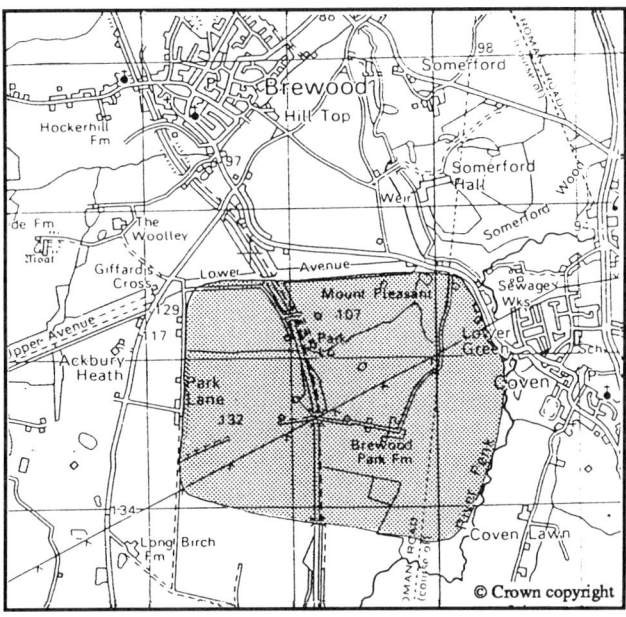

Brewood Park. The northern and eastern boundaries are conjectural.

may have been what is now called the Lower Avenue. Indeed, there is the intriguing possibility that the Lower Avenue may mark the course of a Roman road connecting the fork of the Roman road at Giffard's Cross with the Roman river crossing south of Somerford. The west side of Brewood Park is marked by Park Lane, recorded as Parklone in 1338[177] and having a straight alignment close to the Romano-British Port Lane [suggesting, misleadingly, the possibility of much older origins, but nevertheless having hedgerows perhaps 800 years old], and the south was a straight line parallel to the Avenue, marked by hedgerows and footpaths running from the end of Park Lane to Chillington Brook, now difficult to trace [but which seems to have run south from The Forge Pool, then south-east, turning south to join the river Penk south-east of Brewood Park Farm[178]], which is said to have formed the eastern boundary.[179]

On 26th July 1213, during a vacancy in the bishopric of Coventry and

83

Lichfield, King John permitted the Archbishop of Dublin[180] to take 30 stags in 'Brewud Park', but since the authority was addressed to the custodian of the vacant see, it may be inferred that the Bishop's Park was to supply the order. In 1243 a mandate was issued permitting Hugo of Arden to have 15 does from the Park, and on 8th August 1245 a Warrant was issued at Bridgnorth, "To the Keeper of the Bishopric of Chester to allow William Luvel, the King's huntsman, to take 10 bucks for the King's use out of the park at Bruwode, and to carry them to Chester for the King's use",[181] and another mandate is recorded in the same year for delivery of 4 fallow bucks and 8 fallow does from the Park.

The saltatorium or deer-leap in Brewood Park licenced 'against the Forest' in 1206 was reported to be to the injury of Cannock Forest in 1286, and in same year the pleas of Cannock Forest contain a record that

> on the Thursday before Easter ten years earlier a buck was driven from the Park of Browde and followed by a greyhound, which caught it in the fields of Coven, within [Cannock] Forest, and one Hugh de Pendeford came up, who is now dead, and took the greyhound away and retained it without warrant. And John de Pendeford, who was at that time a verderer of the Forest, came up and caused the buck to be skinned and carried away to his house at Pendeford, and shortly afterwards he sold all his lands and other goods he had within the county, and went beyond the sea and has never returned . . .[182]

In 1298 the King sent a commission to investigate deer-stealing from the Parks at Haywood and Brewood.[183] In 1322 the Park and a pasture were valued at 100s, but no rent was received because of the tenant's right of turbary.[184] In 1324 the jury of Cuttlestone Hundred found that William of Stretton and his brother Thomas, chaplain, were "common malefactors, going about in the society of other malefactors armed to fairs and markets, to the great terror of the people," and that they had beaten John Balle and another at Penkridge, and with others had broken into the Bishop's Park at Brewood when the see was vacant and had taken beasts from it. Both brothers admitted their guilt and were fined 4 marks after providing 6 sureties each for good behaviour.[185] In 1478 the herbage and pannage of the park was valued at £10, and in 1485 23s 4d was spent repairing the Park palings. Bishop Rowland Lee, at the request of Thomas Cromwell, appointed Ralph Sadleyer as Keeper of the Park and Bailiff of the Manor in 1534, but by the following year he had been replaced by Thomas Giffard who was paid £5 0s 8d as Bailiff and Custodian of the Park.

In the Staffordshire Quarter Sessions Rolls is an Indictment against

> Walter Smetenham late of Hylton in the par. of Wolverhampton yeom. and Edward Tomlynson late of the same, with many other malefactors, for breaking into the close and park of John Gyffard esq. called 'Brewood Park' enclosed with wooden stakes being an ancient park and one used from time immemorial for the care, breeding and nourishing of deer, 2 Sept.

1593, and for chasing the deer and taking and slaying a doe contrary to Statute [of] 12 Jan 1562.[186]

It seems likely that the Park was leased along with the manor to the Giffards from an early date: Thomas Giffard refers to the deer park in his will dated 1559, and makes specific provision for his widow to have two deer each year.[187]

In 1609 the Park was leased to John Giffard, and by 1647 Peter Giffard was leasing it for £8, two bucks and two does per annum, but the Commissioners for Sequestration calculated the market rent to be £134 13s 1½d. In assessing the value of the woodland they suggested that local iron-working would provide a ready demand for the timber, and also claimed that "a great part of Brewood Park will bear good corn and may be much improved by ploughing". In 1637 Archbishop Laud was reporting to the King that Bishop Wright of Lichfield had ignored the prohibition on the cutting of timber on the episcopal estates and had been "making waste of the poor woods there remaining." Ten years later it was alleged that in two years the same Bishop had cut and sold timber at Brewood worth over £130.[188] In 1648 Peter Giffard was farming the Park for the Parliamentary Committee which administered the county during the Civil War: only two brace of deer were left in the park, part of which had been sown with corn and another 100 acres prepared for ploughing. He cut down 110 trees for timber, valued at £300, almost two thirds of which was used to repair the Park pales, "in these distracted times . . . so pulled down and stolen", and disposed of the rest to friends and neighbours. In the previous two years 50 cords of wood had been cut and taken to his house for his own use.[189] Large quantities of charcoal were supplied to the ironworks at Brewood Forge and Coven Furnace and bark was sold to Francis Spooner, a tanner of Brewood, for £5 10s. Oak bark was used in vast quantities by the tanners who soaked it in pits to release tannin, in which hides were steeped as part of the tanning process. In 1651 the Park was leased to Sir Robert King, and George Allatt's Park, being part of Brewood Park, is recorded in 1654, so called because the tenants were Allatt and others.

Brewood Park, now divided into curiously geometric fields, presumably dating from the period when disparking occurred in the seventeenth or eighteenth century, is still remembered in the names of Brewood Park Farm and Park Lodge, the latter perhaps the site of the Keeper's Lodge, or 'custodis domus' mentioned several times in old accounts of the Royal Receivers, including a brief note in 1321 recording under the heading 'Keeper's House' the purchase of "DC clalath [clay-lathes] bought for vjd. [6d.]" These were split lathes used in the construction of wattle-and-daub panels or partitions in half-timbered houses, and provide evidence of the type of building on the site at that time. The Lodge, with timbering of about 1600 exposed on the eastern side, is typically situated near the highest part of Brewood Park so that the keeper or parker [the origin of the surname], who was responsible for culling and feeding the animals and maintaining the hedges and paling, could easily oversee the whole Park. In 1932 it was the home of Albert Biddle, rat-catcher. To the north of the Lodge and east of Chillington Bridge over the Shropshire Union Canal are the overgrown remains of a rectangular enclosure, some 60′ from east to west and 90′ from north to south, of random sandstone, the walls some two feet thick and 6′ high with flat capstones. Within and around the derelict walls are early Victorian bricks and large sandstone blocks, with a 7′ tall square-section pillar in the north-east corner. The ruins are those of an L-shaped complex of farm buildings, in use until recent years.

One meadow at Brewood Park Farm is said to have been known as Hangman's Field, and, it has been suggested, may have been the site of a gallows or 'forches', recalling the Bishop's claim before the Itinerant Justices on 7th January 1293 for various rights, including gallows, in his several manors including Brewood, but the field is probably that in the south-west corner of the Park shown as Hanging Flat on the 1838 Tithe Map. The Old English word 'hangende' means a slope, and 'flat' was a local word for a furlong, hence 'sloping furlong.'

In addition to the Forest and Park, there were various 'coney burrows' in the parish where rabbits were encouraged to breed in artificial warrens. The rabbit was re-introduced into Britain in about 1100, and for centuries the word was applied only to the baby animal; the adult was known as a coney. In medieval times the rabbit was a delicacy, and was also valued for its soft fur. Unlike the modern rabbit, it could not dig its own burrow. It was encouraged to breed in warrens or coneyburrows, and artificial mounds [now known as pillow mounds] were often constructed for that purpose, sometimes provided with a system of artificial tunnels. A charter of free warren in Brewood was granted by Henry III to Bishop Roger de Mouland in 1293,[190] and Sir John Giffard and his heirs received a similar grant in 1319, but free warren at that period meant rights to hunt smaller game – hare, rabbit and fox. It later came to be associated with rabbits in the same way that Forests were associated with deer. A field called 'Conyborovgh' is shown on a Chillington estate map of about 1727 between Gunstone and the Leper House,[191] and Hicks-Smith's '1680 map of Brewood' compiled in 1880 shows 'the coney burrows' to the north of Deansfield Road, commemorated in the name Coneybere Gardens.[192] In 1661 John Giffard of Blackladies was leasing a 'warren of connies' at Bishop's Wood from his father, Peter Giffard of Chillington, and the warrener William Lloyd of Bishop's Wood listed in the Catholic Returns of 1706 was probably connected with this same warren, which may be the one recorded in 1724 on the waste land at Bishop's Wood, leased by the Giffards to John Blakemore. In 1781 there was also a warren at Calf Heath near Four Ashes.

11. Plague and Pestilence

The population of England at the beginning of the fourteenth century probably numbered around seven million. Most villages were little more than a handful of dwellings – modern research suggests that they were probably reasonably substantial buildings rather than flimsy hovels – infested with rats, fleas and mice, whose occupants wore the same threadbare clothing for months on end, and whose bodies crawled with vermin. The vast majority of the population lived in this way, and most of the rest lived in towns which, at their worst, were even more insanitary than the villages. The people did not live in squalor from choice, but they possessed neither the means to avoid it nor the knowledge of its consequences. It is perhaps hardly surprising that some 40% of the population died before they were 20, and most of the rest before they reached 50.

Living standards had been slowly improving, but now began a period of climatic change and economic stagnation, if not decline: the situation in Brewood is apparent from the theoretical values and the income actually received as recorded in the survey of the Bishop's holdings in 1321. In the more remote areas marginal land was abandoned, with a dramatic decline in arable farming.

Bubonic plague,[193] which seems to have originated in northern India, swept at various times along the trading routes into Europe, carried by the black or house rat. It was caused by an internal parasite of the rat, transmitted to humans by the rat flea. Epidemics of plague were only possible in areas with a huge rat population, and by 1348 rats were so common that it was inevitable that plague would spread to England. It was preceded by several decades of hardship and pestilence. In the late 13th century there had been a series of disastrous harvests, and in 1315-1317 a great famine had affected the whole of northern Europe which was so severe that some historians believe it had a greater effect on the economy than the plague. Those problems were compounded by outbreaks of sheep murrain in 1317-19 followed by an outbreak of cattle disease. In 1325-6 there was an acute drought, and in the Midlands records from 1310 to 1320 show an increased death-rate, holdings being surrendered, and crops left unharvested. It is said that in 1341 the nuns of Whiteladies had their income greatly reduced as a result of 'a Murrain among their sheep on their farm at Montford', and floods which destroyed their crops.

Plague seems to have entered the country via Weymouth or Southampton and spread rapidly during the mild winter of 1348-9. Port towns were naturally the first affected, but fleas in the clothing of travellers quickly spread the disease throughout the country before it died out the following autumn.

Many contemporary accounts tell how the disease took its highest toll of the poor, who were inevitably more exposed to rats and their fleas. Once infected, the victim could expect a quick but painful death. Bubonic plague caused swelling and internal bleeding around the lymph glands, and had a mortality rate of perhaps 70%. The pneumonic form of the disease was transmitted between humans through the air, and brought death within four days, with 100% mortality. Other epidemics paled by comparison, even to a population familiar with the horrors of tuberculosis, smallpox, diptheria, typhus, dysentry, measles, and other fatal diseases.

Estimates of the level of mortality vary widely, but perhaps one in five of the population died, with a higher proportion in the crowded cities and ports. It is possible that more than two centuries elapsed before the population level of 1348 was regained.

Records show that plague stripped many areas of their workforce, and in 1351 Edward III remitted the taxes of Roger de Elmrugge who held land in Staffordshire, as 'on account of the deadly pestilence lately in those parts the lands are so much deteriorated in value that he will not be able to answer the whole farm without loss'.

The twice-weekly market in Brewood will have attracted bands of itinerant merchants, making the village particularly vulnerable to the pestilence. Wolverhampton was devastated by plague in 1349, and it may have been from there that the disease spread to Brewood.[194] Evidence of the mortality is contained in the 'Answers of the Custodian or Receiver of Rents of the Bishop of Lichfield's Tenants' in the Manor of Brewood. The list for 1360 of "the names of the tenants of irrigated land, accustomed to pay stuck [possibly an irrigation or market tax], and who had died in the late pestilence"[195] confirms that rents of Assize of Freemen and Natives of Brewood Manor had been 'in decasu' – falling off – and identifies twenty such tenants who, when other men, women and children who must also have perished are added, must have represented a considerable proportion of so small a place at that time. The list gives first the names of the dead tenants and secondly those who held their land in 1360:

John Parkes	John Dyerson
John Ochel	John Ochant
William at the Pool	Richard Wele
Walter Thurstans	John Collyns
John the Smith	Henry the Dey
William Stuck (senior)	William Stuck (Clerk)
William Silnot }	Nicholas the Parker
William Dobbin }	
William Raven	William of Mytton
Thomas Henderson	John Dobbin
Richard the Hinde	John Edrych of Hatton
William Godwyn }	
William at the Mere }	

William [illegible]	}	remains in the hands of
Richard o' the Green	}	the lord for default of
Henry Rowley	}	of tenancy
Richard Schirman	}	
Henry the Hayward	}	
Nicholas of Crateford	}	
Adam of Northcott	}	

Parkes, Pool and Mere were evidently places in the Bishop's demesne. A shearman was a person who finished woollen cloth by shearing the nap, and a dey was a dairyman. Parker, Hinde and Hayward were clearly officials of the park, and William Stuck (clerk) was the priest: mortality among the clergy was heavier than the laity, for by the very nature of their calling priests were exposed to contagion. 'Northcott' is Northicote, near Bushbury, and William Godwyn is probably the man of the same name whose son drowned himself in a marl-pit on the road to Whiteladies in 1330.

The population of Brewood immediately prior to the outbreak is not known,[196] but in 1298 the Bishop alone had 147 tenants at Brewood.[197] Assuming that the figure includes both married couples and single people, using a multiplier of 2.5 to calculate total family figures suggests that there may have been about 370 tenants and dependants of the Bishop. It is impossible to calculate the number of other people within the parish, but if it is assumed that the Bishop's tenants comprised 50% of all the tenants, we are left with a figure of 740. It may not be unsafe to say that at the end of the thirteenth century the population numbered around 750.

The Poll Tax Return for Brewood in 1377 lists 280 taxable inhabitants.[198] The Poll Tax Assessment of 1380-1 for "Brewode, Chilynton, Horsebroke, Engletone, Hatton, and Dunston [Gunstone]" records 249 adults with an additional 29 in Coven, and using the above multiplier of 2.5 suggests a population of about 700. Given these estimates, and the named dead tenants of the Bishop, it seems possible that some 10% of the population died in the epidemic, but it will be clear that the crudity of the calculations and the figures on which they are based reduces them virtually to guesswork.

The devastation caused by the plague exacerbated the general economic decline and resulted in considerable social and economic upheavals, replacing the earlier land shortage by an acute labour shortage. Wages almost doubled between 1340 and 1360, despite legislative attempts as early as 1349 to peg them, and during this period some landlords tried to reimpose feudal labour services. Resentment at these measures and the Poll Tax assessment contributed significantly to the Peasants Revolt of 1381.

Plague and other epidemics persisted, with outbreaks in 1361-3, 1368-71, 1374-5, 1390 and 1400, and it was this repeated mortality which reduced the population of the country at the end of the century to perhaps a little over two million, a figure which was probably little higher one hundred years later.

Stebbing Shaw records[199] that plague began in Wolverhampton on 28th July 1579, in 1593 more than eleven hundred people died from plague in Lichfield alone and in 1596-8 an epidemic spread throughout Staffordshire. The effects are evidenced in Brewood by the burial entries in the parish registers. The average annual number of burials between 1575 and 1595 is 22, but in 1597 42 people died – 13 in February alone – with the mortality rate doubtless increased by the exceptionally bad harvests of 1596 and 1597. In 1610 an outbreak was so virulent in Stafford that the Quarter Sessions were abandoned.

In the register of burials for Brewood parish in 1623 are the following poignant entries:

Nov 9	William Mathewes, of Kerrimore Green
Nov 25	Joyce Mathewes, of Kerrimore Green
Nov 27	John Mathewes, of Kerrimore Green
Nov 29	Ellenor Mathewes, of Kerrimore Green
Dec 4	Frances Mathewes, of Kerrimore Green

There is no indication of what calamity or misfortune may have caused the deaths of the five people, presumably from the same house and family. A search of the registers does however reveal further information:

William Mathewes, husbandman married = [not known - presumably
baptised 1/10/1579　　　　　　　　　　　from outside the parish,
　　　　　　　　　　　　　　　　　　　where the marriage took
　　　　　　　　　　　　　　　　　　　place, since there is no
　　　　　　　　　　　　　　　　　　　record of a marriage in
　　　　　　　　　　　　　　　　　　　the Brewood registers]

William	Richard	Elnor	Frances	John	Joyce
baptised	baptised	baptised	baptised	baptised	baptised
10/3/1609	17/6/1611	29/1/1612	16/6/1616	24/1/1618	11/3/1623

When Elnor Mathewes was baptised in 1612, she was described as the daughter of William Mathewes of Brewood, and it seems that the family moved to Kiddemore Green between that date and the tragedy in 1623.

If it was William the son whose death is recorded, then the five who died were aged 16, 2, 7, 13 and 9, and it can only be assumed that they were the victims of illness. It takes little imagination to visualise the scene at the graveyard at Brewood church as the grief-stricken parents attended five times in the space of four weeks to bury five of their children. Since there are no further entries relating to the family in the registers, it seems that the survivors moved away from the area, perhaps to the mother's home parish, to start a new life away from the scene of the tragedy.

An epidemic may have caused the death of the eight people buried in

Brewood within 22 days in January 1633. On Christmas Day 1646 Parliament ordered a collection throughout London and Westminster to be used in part for 'the distressed and infected inhabitants by the plague in the town of Stafford.' In the Constables' Accounts for Brewood it is recorded in 1665 that 12s 6d was paid to the High Constable "for infected persons that were in Cheslin Hay", and as late as 1720 the Brewood Churchwardens' Accounts contain an entry: "For a form of prayer about the plague . . . 2s 6d." The word plague was however by this date applied to any epidemic, and the reference does not refer to plague proper.

On 18th December 1763 the parish register records the burial of John, Thomas and Sarah, the children of John and Esther Boydon of Park Lane, who had all died of smallpox.

Brewood did not escape the terrible cholera outbreak in the district in 1849, for in September seven people died, all, significantly, from the workhouse.[200] In October 1897 a serious epidemic of measles and several cases of scarlet fever occurred and the local Medical Officer of Health was sufficiently concerned to close the National School for three weeks.

12. Lawlessness in Brewood, 1400 – 1600

In the early fifteenth century Staffordshire was an area of lawlessness and disorder. In 1407 there were constant attacks on the King's estates, the houses of his tenants were broken into, the roads around Stafford and Lichfield were swarming with marauders, and women and old men were attacked and assaulted.[201] One of the King's officers was stabbed through the heart when collecting taxes, and the anarchy became so serious that the Sheriff fled into Derbyshire. In 1414 Henry V came in person to Lichfield where he stayed for two months hearing cases of lawlessness.[202] The first few cases that follow are typical of the type of incident occurring throughout the county during the period. Perhaps the most surprising aspect is the number of high-born malefactors.

The Coroner's Rolls record an inquest held in 1408 on John Geffery of Brewood.[203] The jury found that he had been unlawfully killed by Mathew ap Madoc who had struck him on the head with a bludgeon, and that Thomas Bille, John Ferre and John Pyre were present aiding and abetting Mathew.

The slow but inexorable progress of the law is revealed by a subsequent Indictment five years later alleging that John del Pirye of Gunston, yeoman, Thomas Byle of Penford, yeoman, and John Gyffard of Chillington, armiger [holding a coat of arms] had broken into the house of William Kent, the bailiff of Brewood, in 1408, and had unlawfully killed John Jeffrey, the servant of William, and that Thomas Gyffard of Chillington, squire, had knowingly received them at Chillington.

The saga continues[204] with the surrender to the court in 1414 of John del Pirye of Gunston, constable of the vill of Albrighton, indicted for permitting the escape of Edward Taillour of Tonge, tailor, and of John his son – both of whom were in custody for a robbery – and as an accessory to the death of John Geffery of Brewood, murdered at Brewood by one Mathew ap Madoc in 1408. John produced a general pardon dated 20th January 1413.

In 1415 a further Indictment was issued alleging that John Gyffard of Chillington, gentleman, and others had unlawfully killed Edmund Clerk [a clergyman] of Stretton at Wolverhampton, and that Thomas Dyle of Pendeford, yeoman, and John Gyffard of Chillington, armiger, had broken into the house of William, the bailiff of Brewood, and unlawfully killed John Geffery, William's servant.

An endorsement to the Indictment records that John Gyffard and Thomas Dyle surrendered and produced Letters Patent of the King dated 25th January 1415 pardoning them for all treasons, felonies, etc., perpetuated before 8th December 1413. The pardon may have been a reward for service to the crown by Thomas Giffard, who is said to have accompanied the king in his French campaign until forced by ill-health to return to England, but the possible involvement of John Giffard in the murder of John Geffery at Brewood, and the part played by his father, Thomas Giffard, must forever remain a mystery.

An Indictment issued in 1413[205] alleged that Henry Deykyn of Tetynhale, yoman, and Edmund Stretton of Stretton, yoman, had feloniously killed Nowell del Hay of Horsebroke in 1408.

Dekyn seems to have achieved some notoriety, for he was further indicted for feloniously killing John de Burton at Boterhale the previous year. Unfortunately, the outcome of the case is not known.

A further indictment the same year against John Gyffard of Chillington, gentleman, and Henry Wyghtwyke, of Tettenhall, yeoman, alleged they had murdered Edmund clerk of Stretton at Wolverhampton in 1411. Again, the involvement of John Giffard is unclear and there is no record of the outcome of the case, but presumably Giffard eventually produced to the court his General Pardon granted in 1415.

In 1413 there is an Indictment[206] alleging that John Endover, Prior of Greseley in Derbyshire, and Nicholas de Creyton, chaplain, had abducted Matilda de Hortone, a nun in the convent priory of Brewode, at Brewode, [presumably Blackladies] and had robbed her of a gold ring worth 6s 8d, and other goods worth 20s. From records of the following year we learn that Nicholas de Creyton had surrendered to the court and been acquitted by a jury. There is no record of any further action against the Prior of Greseley.

In 1413 an Indictment was issued against Ralph Marchynton, of Carwalle [Caverswall], gentleman, Robert Erdeswyke,[207] and Thomas Gyffard of Chillington who, with 100 others, had assembled illegally armed to kill Thomas Bykley, chaplain six years earlier, had broken into the park of Bromshulf [Bramshall], searching for Thomas Bykley, and had taken his brother John Bykley, who had been forced to reveal the whereabouts of his brother. What had provoked the trio of illustrious gentry to raise an armed force to seek out and kill a clergyman [if indeed the charge was well founded] is not known, since the records contain no further reference to the incident, but it is curious that the Giffard family had previously been implicated in the death of a clergyman.

An interesting curiosity is a record dated 1414 of the forfeiture from the vill of Brewode of the value of a "Pirystre" [?peartree] which had caused the death of Isabella de Erkbarrowe [Ackbury], "accidentally killed, as shown by the Rolls of Richard Leveson, one of the Coroners". In the Middle Ages it was not unusual for the value of an object which had caused an accidental death to be forfeited to the crown in expiation for the soul of the person who had died, a concept known as deodand, literally 'a thing given to God.'[208]

Records survive from the fifteenth century of a number of minor disputes of a mundane nature involving Brewood people, mainly allegations of cattle trespass. In 1422, for example, Richard Knyghtley sued William Wooley, yeoman, William Webbe, husbandman, and John Powker [all of Brewood], William Bromhale, John Roke, William Penford, William Harryes, and John Brom [all of Horsebrook, husbandmen], for depasturing their cattle on his grass at "Bromhaste" [Broomhall], and in 1426 Richard Peshale of Patshull sued Thomas Taillour and John Ferron, both husbandmen, Henry Northale, barker, John Colyns and Richard Nicholas [both yeomen, all of Brewood] for the recovery of 6 oxen, 16 steers and 6 cows, worth £10, which were being unlawfully detained.[209]

From a later period is an Indictment from the Quarter Sessions Rolls dated 4th October 1586, when William Smyth, Constable of Brewood

> . . . presented that Edward Cooke of Brewood, Thomas Storye and [blank] Hamlet of [Wheaton] Aston and Richard Turner of Weston Hewes played dice with [o]thers in the house of the said Edward on the day of the Nativity of the Blessed Virgin St Mary last past and upon the morrow after, and that the said constable forbidding them the same they waylaid him and abused him and did shut the doors against him. And that the like unlawful games was there on the Sunday next following and that there was two . . . of dice and four pair of cards used all at one time.[210]

The case does not mean that dice and cards were unlawful, but it was an offence to gamble on Sundays, and the matter may have been viewed more gravely in Brewood since the church was dedicated to the Nativity of the Blessed Virgin, and the date was of particular religious significance.

The Hamlets seem to have been compulsive gamblers, not above using the legal process themselves to intimidate the local enforcement officer, for in the same records is an Indictment against

> . . . John Hamlet, Thomas Hamlet, William Hamlette, brethren, common gamblers [who had] sundry times sythen the first day of March last past frequented the house of John Border of Aston late alehousekeeper and there played for money at tables and cards eight shillings a game with other persons against the will of the said Border threatening him that if [he] would not suffer them to play there, they would make him repent it, and that they would make him spend 40s with other cruel words. Some of them there playing the other gave ai[d] to their 'brether' whereby they have deceived some that played with them 20 marks; some of the said Hamlets being heretofore presented for the like offence by one Bryndley then Constable then procured a warrant of the peace from Westminster against the said Constable to his great charges; if the like be now suffered no constable dare present them thereafter.[211]

An interesting insight into corruption in Elizabeth's reign is obtained from the Quarter Sessions Rolls of 4th October 1586.[212] Thomas Archer of Nottingham, deputising for Richard Dawes, Clerk of the Market to the Royal Household, was indicted for sitting at Penkridge on 3rd December

1585, "under pretence to execute his office" and accepting 2s. from the Constable of Penkridge "by way of composition for the allowing of the weights and measures of the said town and for other weights and measures in the said Constablewick; without reviewing or reforming any at all". Henry Gee, servant to Thomas Wallis, Dawe's deputy, likewise allegedly demanded money on the same day from "other constables in the . . . hundred using great threatenings unto them if they would not . . . pay". Archer and Gee were further accused that on 7th February 1586 they again sat at Penkridge where Archer improperly claimed "fees due to his office" for the approval of weights and measures by "great threatenings unto them that would not . . . pay" by which menaces he obtained various sums from 18 Constables in the hundred, including 2s from William Smythe, Constable of Brewood and 15d from Roger Bysshop, Constable of Coven.

In the following year, an Inquisition at view of Frankpledge was held in Brewood on 19th April before Roger Eccleshall, Steward of the Manor and a jury of 14 named villagers into claims that "Barnard Turner of Brewood lab. stole a white wether sheep, price 12d of Ric. Pole at Brewood 18 Feb 1587; Mathew Talbot of Brewood lab. stole a goose price 8d of Robt. Warner of Brewood 22 Jan 1587."[213] The outcome of the cases is not known, but sheep stealing at that time was a particularly serious offence.

In the Quarter Sessions Rolls for 1601[214] there is a Presentment endorsed true bill – that is, the facts were established to the satisfaction of the Grand Jury – against "Robt. Bisshopp late of Brewood lab. for escaping from Ric. Duncalfe constable of Brewood, to whose custody he had been committed by Roger Fowke esq J.P. for felony 14 Oct [1601]". There is no further information on the case, but Richard Duncalfe himself, "late constable of Brewood," was subsequently indicted to appear at the Quarter Sessions to answer charges "touching certain trespasses and other misdeeds". The Indictment is endorsed with a memorandum that Duncalfe could not be found in the bailiwick.

In the Quarter Sessions Rolls for 1602[215] is a record of the outlawing of "John Blakemeare of Brewood, badger" for failing to appear before the Court. A badger was a person who bought commodities, especially corn, in one place and sold them in another. Outlawing was a serious matter, since it meant that the outlaw could not claim the benefit or protection of the law, and his property could be taken with impunity.

13. Beggars, Vagabonds and Poverty

In the Middle Ages poverty was largely due to an under-developed economy in which famine and pestilence recurred and begging was endemic. The situation was greatly aggravated in the early sixteenth century by economic as well as religious upheavals: rising prices, resulting in part from the debasement of the coinage during the reigns of Henry VIII and Edward VI were blamed on the mania for sheep farming and the enclosure of common land. Of less importance as a cause of poverty in Tudor times was the dissolution of the monastries. By 1536 they were not wealthy and could offer very little assistance to the needy. Tales of hordes of displaced monks and nuns attempting to earn their keep in the outside world are unproven, but many servants and dependants whose services were not required by the new owners of the monastic lands must have swollen the numbers of the destitute.

Poverty was also appearing in the other more advanced countries of Europe in the sixteenth century, and poor relief became a matter of pressing concern to the Government. Roads swarmed with the uprooted and homeless, vagrants and vagabonds, destitute and orphaned children, gypsies, rogues and the wandering idle, as well as the able-bodied who, it was felt, should provide for themselves. But the concern of the government was not induced so much by compassion as the fear of disaffection which might be spread by vagrants. The property-owning classes were particularly alarmed by the growth of the problem, and reaction was often brutal: persistent vagrants were burned through the ear, and in 1591, 71 vagabonds were so burned in two months in Middlesex alone. But this duty became distasteful to the authorities, and the more common punishment was whipping 'until their backs be bloody'. Every village and town was required to provide a whipping-post, and it was the duty of the Constable, after stripping the victim to the waist and securing his wrists to the iron clasps on either side of the post, to carry out the punishment. In Brewood, the whipping-post was probably attached to the stocks which stood at High Green, or was perhaps one of the posts of the Market Cross in Market Square. Even a century later females were not exempt from whipping, as an entry dating from 1688 in the Brewood Constables' Accounts reveals: "For whipping Mary Hollygreen 1s 0d." Women were not usually whipped in public during the eighteenth century, and in 1791 the whipping of female vagrants was forbidden by law.

The problem of vagrancy reached crisis point in the period 1594 to 1597, all years of successive bad harvests, great scarcity and distress. In 1597 Parliament debated the whole issue of poor relief, and introduced a compulsory poor rate. The Justices of the Peace were to appoint from two to four Overseers of the Poor in every parish. They had power to levy the

96

poor rate and bind poor children as apprentices. The Quarter Sessions were empowered to have workhouses built, to set the able-bodied to work, and to provide for the infirm. The Privy Council ensured by persistent pressure that the system was put into effect throughout the land. In 1601, all the poor laws were redrawn, and the maintenance of the 'impotent poor' and the setting to work of the able-bodied in workhouses was the responsibility of the Parish Guardian or Overseer.

It is difficult to say whether the problem of the poor in Brewood was any greater than in other villages in the region,[216] but the early registers of burials bear sombre testimony to the number of unidentified itinerant vagrants who died in the parish. The picture of destitute children wandering the countryside seems particularly distressing. One reason for the seemingly high number of beggars might be the proximity of Brewood to Watling Street, the principal highway across central England. An analysis of the entries in the burial registers suggest that from 1570 to 1644, some 2.5% of all burials in Brewood were of homeless vagabonds. While it is impossible to calculate how many destitute travellers passed through Brewood during the same period, it must have been very many times the number of recorded burials. The following burial entries are taken from the parish registers between 1570 and 1644, with one entry from 1653:

1571 Dec 13	And d[aughter] of a poor woman
1571 [Feb]	A poore child
1590 Nov 22	A poore woman
1591 July 31	A poore boy overwhelmed with hay
1592 April 3	A poore woman called Anne Digbye
1593 Mar 24	A poore childe
1593 Sept 17	A poore woman
1594 May 15	A poore child
1594 Dec -	A poore child
1595 Oct 30	A poore child
1595 [Nov/Dec]	A beggar boye
1596 Nov 15	A beggar woman
1597 July -	A poore child
1597 Aug 1	A beggar's child
1598 Jan -	Three poore folkes
1598 Nov -	A poore woman
1599 Jan 27	Richard Smith, a poore man
1601 Mar 8	A poore childe
1608 July 13	A poore childe from Horsbroke
1611 July 29	A traveler from John Benion's, of the stregh [?]
1617 Mar 1	Winny, whose surname we knowe not

1618 Mar 5	A certaine poor man dyinge in the cross
1618 Sept 30	Yevan, a poore wandering boy
1619 Mar 23	Margaret, a poore wandering wench, dying in the crosse
1620 Aug 1	Edward Smith, a poore child dying in the church porch
1623 May 22	A certaine poore childe dying in the church porch
1623 Oct 19	A poore man dying in Thomas Johnsonne his barne, whose name we know not
1624 Sept 27	A poore wandering boy, whose name is unknowne, dying at Sommerford
1624 Nov 6	A poore woman (whose name is not known otherwise then Bridget)
1625 Feb 13	A poore child, dying at Harrises, of Coldone
1625 June 26	Thomas Pooler, a poor wandring boy
1625 Sept 26	A poore wandring man
1625 Oct 23	A poore wandering woman
1625 Nov 30	A poor wandring man, unknowne
1626 June 11	A poore child
1626 Aug 16	A poore child, unknowne by name
1626 Sept 15	A poore child which came from London
1629 May 17	A poore child, whose name is unknowne
1642 Feb 5	A poore child
1644 Feb 5	A poore travelling man
1653 Dec 10	Jonathan, a beggar

It is noticeable that the number of burials is particularly high in the 1590's, which coincides with a succession of bad harvests during the early years of the decade, forcing up the price of corn and bringing 'savage dearth' to the area,[217] aggravated by an epidemic which spread throughout Staffordshire in 1596-8.

The parish registers record intermittently the burial of numerous un-named 'vagrants' and 'strangers' well into the eighteenth century. Possibly associated with a vagrant who died in the parish is the name Dead Woman's Grave for a field in the north corner of the junction of Shutt Green Lane and the track to Birk's Barn Farm.[218] The word grave may be derived from the Old English 'græfe', meaning copse or thicket, and does not necessarily relate to a burial place. The woman whose body was presumably found there may have been one of the many un-named vagrants listed in the register of burials. It is not known whether the field name Liermore, meaning marshland where a grave was found, recorded in 1567,[219] is connected with Dead Woman's Grave.

The Brewood registers of baptism also include some curious and poignant entries:

1608 Oct 2	Richard, son of Thomas Rock, of the Woodes and Lanes.
1617 Oct 19	A certaine child named Yevan, which was born in the house of Thomas Floyd, whose father and mother we know not
1617 Nov 23	A certain child called Ann, whose father and mother we know not; the child was borne in the house of Thomas of Thomas Floyde [see above], of Coven
1618 April 13	A poore childe named Thomas, born in John Northal's barne
1619 Mar 21	Humphrie, s[on] of Edward Tannet, born in the South Church Porch
1626 Sept 29	Thomas Davisonne, borne in the church porch

From the Quarter Sessions Rolls of 1605 there is an undated Petition of "Ric. Reade of Acton Trussell: that Joan Purchall of Brewood; a beggar, be ordered to take and support a child which she left outside his house." The Petition is endorsed: "no order taken in court thereupon."

It was the responsibility of the Overseers of the poor to pay out dole to the destitute and meet the expense of removing paupers from the parish. A stranger who might become a charge on the parish would be presented before the local magistrate, who would attempt to establish the stranger's home parish or any place where he or she had previously lived for sufficient time to acquire entitlement to poor relief, or 'settlement'. A removal order would be issued by the magistrate requiring the Overseer to escort the stranger to the parish border in the direction of the nearest settlement parish. The Overseers also contributed to the maintenance of the local workhouse. The Poor Relief Act of 1601 provided that the impotent [able-bodied] poor should be housed in "convenient houses of habitation or dwelling", and permitted more than one family to be placed in one cottage or house. Those who refused to enter the workhouse after the Act of 1722 were to lose all entitlement to poor relief. The Poor Relief Act of 1662 permitted the division of parishes into townships, and four Overseers for Brewood were elected annually in vestry, one for each of the four 'quarters' or 'liberties' of Brewood town, and Kiddemore Green; Chillington, Hattons and Gunstone; Somerford, Engleton and Horsebrook; and Coven, each keeping their own accounts, until the last century, when six Overseers were elected annually in vestry with one set of accounts. It appears that not all Overseers were concientious in performing their duties for in the seventeenth century the parishioners of Brewood petitioned the justices, claiming that Henry Finch, Overseer, had not accounted for all the money recovered for the poor. The accounts cover the period from 1662 to 1756, and are almost complete. Generally the entries are of little interest, being in the main records of numerous payments of a few shillings to named individuals 'in want' or 'in need', or for shoes, a shirt, 'cloaths', coal, thatching, etc.

During the same period pauper children were often apprenticed within the parish, either voluntarily or compulsorily, as evidenced by entries in the register of burials in 1719, "Sept 29 – Ann Moore parish apprentice," and in 1769, "Dec 15 – Joseph, son of William Ingram, parish apprentice to Robert Barbor Esq." [of Somerford].

The cost of poor relief grew steadily from the early seventeenth century, especially from the 1770s. For Brewood parish, £347 3s 0d. was spent in the year ended Easter 1776; an average of £462 0s 3d for the years ended Easter 1783, 1784 and 1785; and £1,275 17s 7d in the year ended Easter 1803, an increase over 27 years of no less than 367.5%. The national increase over the same period was 266.6%.[220]

In an effort to make the system more efficient and to reduce rates, responsibility for the administration of the poor law [except for the actual collection of the rates] was in 1834 taken from the parishes to elected Boards of Guardians of the Poor serving a 'Union' of parishes. This Board was responsible for building and administering a 'Union Workhouse' in the principal village or town, to which surrounding parishes sent their poor. The Brewood parish workhouse was formerly in Kiddemore Green Road between the Churchfields and Hockerhill. The precise location is uncertain – possibly it was the house at the eastern end of the cottages known as St Mary's Row – but it was still in existence in 1867,[221] although it is unclear whether it was the workhouse mentioned in the parish registers in 1738. At the end of the eighteenth century the workhouse was moved to premises at Bargate, and in 1818 Robert Parke is recorded as "governor of the house of industry, Bargate Street". In 1837 it became the workhouse for the Penkridge Union created in September of the previous year, with a capacity of 150, and between 1838 and 1842 the building was enlarged to house 200 inmates. It was further enlarged in 1865.[222] The Guardians of the Penkridge Union held their meetings at the Lion Hotel, and recipients of relief were required to make their way to the Lion from the scattered parishes of the Union to collect their benefit.

The Poor Law Union had a duty to feed and shelter the homeless, but often applied the principal that no pauper should be fed or housed better than the poorest wage-earner – and some wages were pitifully low. In the workhouse husband and wife, parent and child were separated, and fed the bare minimum to keep them alive. The law requiring the provision of married quarters for elderly couples was generally ignored, and husbands and wives who had lived a lifetime together spent their last years apart. Many of the inmates were set to menial work such as fraying hemp, for the purchase of which there are many entries in the Brewood parish accounts, and by 1851 there was a school at the workhouse, but after 1870 destitute children were permitted to attend local Board Schools. They were easily distinguishable from other pupils: girls had their hair cropped, boys' heads were shaved, and both wore drab uniforms.

In March 1872 the occupants of Brewood workhouse were moved to a new workhouse at Cannock. By 1874 the premises were unoccupied, and in 1878 the building was sold by tender to Major Monckton for £900 and the proceeds added to the Workhouse Charity. The property was then occupied for some years as a private residence by Miss Monckton. The long two-storey brick building with projecting wings and five-sided porch was used as a Dominican convent from 1920, and large extensions added to the rear in 1956. The property now houses a private school for girls.

Records survive from the early seventeenth century of many charitable donations and bequests to the poor of money and income from land, both within and outside the parish, including land at Dealf Hayes [Bloxwich], Essington, Great Wyrley, and Brinsford. These 'doles' were distributed at various times of the year, as specified by the donors, but Good Friday and St Thomas's Day [21st December] were most commonly chosen, the latter presumably to ease the burden of the poor during the long winter months. Doles were also distributed at Christmas, Midsummer and the Feast of St James [25th July], and payments given for the great bell of the church to be rung between 8 am and 9 am on Good Friday and 25th July.[223]

Other records of interest relating to the relief of distress are two briefs in aid of the parish for collection throughout England and Wales and Berwick-upon-Tweed: these were an early form of national disaster appeal before the days of property insurance, when the risk of fire was so much greater, and were read from the pulpit in parish churches around the country. One brief was granted on 2nd August 1783, to be made on 1st September for, amongst other purposes, the benefit of Andrew Cherington, whose bakehouse in Brewood – which seems to have been on the north side of the village – had been burnt down on 1st May 1783. [The other party was a widow from Preston [Vale], near Penkridge, whose house had burnt down. The total loss of both parties was given as £833 13s 6d] The other brief was granted on 3rd December 1816, to be made on 15th February 1817, "For a sudden and terrible fire broke out in the Park Lane, in the parish of Brewood, in the dwelling-house of Francis Pigott, Yeoman", the damage totalling £334 6s 0d.[224] No briefs are mentioned in the Brewood parish registers, but many are listed in the registers for Codsall in the latter half of the seventeenth century, which include a reference to 13s 4d collected on 24th January 1681 "upon a letter of request from Horsebroke in the parish of Brewood upon ye behalf of Will. Harris, Jo: Fletcher, Marie Thornton." No reason for the appeal is given.

14. Recusancy and Royalty

The Reformation of the church in England began in the reign of Henry VIII, due in part to his desire for a male heir to avoid succession claims at his death. When his first marriage produced no son, Henry challenged the papal dispensation permitting the marriage, his wife having previously been married to his brother, and with the assistance of Thomas Cranmer, an archbishop who accepted him as God's representative on earth, and Thomas Cromwell, a ruthless and efficient administrator, Henry obtained his divorce and remarried. A series of enactments severed the English church from Rome and made Henry Supreme Head of the Church of England. Although prominent dissidents were executed, over the country as a whole resistance was slight.

The dissolution of the monasteries, which saw the destruction of the nunneries of both Blackladies and Whiteladies, sealed the break with Rome, and the sale of monastic property filled the king's coffers, depleted by unsuccessful military ventures in Europe.

By the end of Henry's reign the reformation had reached everyone everywhere. For the Giffards it was a time of mixed feelings, for while Sir John Giffard prospered in the King's household and his family managed to acquire, as well as the nunnery of Blackladies, other monastic property in Derbyshire, he must have realised that his religious beliefs were not compatible with those of his King and that it could only be a matter of time before the family would come into conflict with the crown.

The death of Henry VIII and the short reign of the boy-King Edward VI enabled the Reformation to proceed apace, but the attempt after Edward's death to put Lady Jane Grey on the throne was a disatrous fiasco, and Henry's daughter Mary was made Queen. Mary, an intransigent Catholic, began to reverse the Reformation process with great zeal, attempting to restore the system prevailing even before Henry came to power. The leading reformers were imprisoned, over 300 executed and many scholars, clergy and prominent gentry fled abroad. But by the end of her reign, Mary had been unable to reverse the dissolution of the religious orders and her purge of the Protestants had evoked much sympathy among the general population for the bravery of the victims.

When Elizabeth I took the throne – nominally as a Catholic – on the death of Mary in 1558, the country was still at war with France, and she proceeded cautiously in religious matters. The doctrines of the Church of England were initially deliberately vague so that any Christian could interpret them as his conscience dictated. The Queen, however, was soon declared 'Supreme Governor, civil and ecclesiastical', and an Act of Uniformity ordered the use of the revised Prayer Book of Edward VI, prohibited the use of any other public worship, and required everybody to attend church. It was inevitable that there would be confrontation between the crown and many Catholics in the country, including the Giffards of Chillington, for opposition to official religious policy now began in earnest, and Catholics became known as recusants for their refusal to conform.

Elizabeth had been anxious to avoid a break with Rome but in 1570 the Pope declared Elizabeth excommunicated and deposed, a heretic and a bastard, and her subjects were absolved from their allegiance and encouraged to rebel.

In England Catholics were in a dilemma: either they were traitors or they disobeyed their church. Elizabeth had genuine sympathy: "The Queen would not have any of their consciences unnecessarily sifted, to know what affection they had to the old religion". She did, however, require their allegiance and recognition of her sovereignty, and it was for withholding such allegiance that Catholics were executed and seen as traitors.

Legislation against Catholics became more severe as the conflict increased, and in 1569 took place the last great English rising in arms for the Catholic faith, the Rebellion in the North. It was suppressed and the Catholic peers, Norfolk and Northumberland, executed. Nevertheless, the 1570's saw a marked Catholic revival, the result of large numbers of English students attending the Catholic colleges which had been established in Europe. It was at about this time that the sons of John Giffard were sent abroad for their education, in at least two cases with meagre funds. Several letters from them to friends in England were intercepted by the Queen's agents, and are now in the State Papers: a letter dated 5th August 1580, addressed to John Giffard but with the signature obliterated, complains "of hard usage in forbidding my brother Edward to speak to me, and in turning us both out into the world in a state of poverty"; on 21st September 1580, George Giffard wrote home from Paris, en route to Pont-a-mousson, in Lorraine; and on 12th October 1580, Richard Giffard wrote to George, apparently then back in England, from Amiens.

The Government became greatly alarmed at the success of the Jesuits, fearing that an invasion from Catholic Spain might receive encouragement from Catholics in England, and in 1581 it became high treason to leave the Church of England and convert to Catholicism. Anyone participating in mass was liable to fine and imprisonment, and a fine was imposed for failure to attend church. It was this last provision that provided an effective financial weapon to use against Catholic families, for they were liable to pay £260 a year or have two-thirds of their lands temporarily confiscated.

Thomas Bentham, Bishop of Lichfield, had found Staffordshire a particularly troublesome part of his diocese during Elizabeth's persecution of the Catholics.[225] Most of the clergy were conforming in 1559, but Bentham found it necessary in 1565 to stress the use of the Book of Common Prayer. Altars were to be replaced by tables, and churches were to be cleared of 'all sepulchres which were used on Good Friday, hand bells, and all manner of idols which be laid up in secret places in . . . church where Latin service was used'. But it was not only some of the clergy who were reluctant to conform: many of the population were hostile to the new ways, church attendances fell, and government agents reported that large numbers of people in Staffordshire 'are generally evil inclined towards religion and forbear coming to church and participating of the sacraments, using also very broad speeches in alehouses and elsewhere'. Concern was also mounting about the number of dedicated Jesuit missionaries who were infiltrating the country.

It may have been a concern to view the situation in Staffordshire at first hand and to assert her authority which persuaded Elizabeth to undertake a royal progress through the county in 1575.[226] Travelling to Kenilworth, she proceeded to Lichfield and via Chartley Castle to Stafford Castle, where she stayed on 8th August. The citizens of Stafford made great preparations for her visit: houses were repainted, the streets gravelled and the cross repaired. Nevertheless, the Queen noticed the general air of decay in the town, and having asked the reason, was told that 'capping' and removing the assizes from the town were the main cause. Elizabeth promised to renew the statute relating to capping, and to re-establish the assizes.[227] Both promises were kept. From Stafford Elizabeth set out for Sudeley Castle in Gloucestershire, and stayed one night, Tuesday 9th August,[228] at Chillington House, evidently passing through Penkridge en route, for in the parish register for 1575 is the entry: "This year Elizabeth, Queen of England, travelled through the county of Stafford and town of Penkridge, making a journey to the house of John Giffard, Esquire." But what should have been a signal honour for Giffard, Chillington and Brewood ended ignominiously, and it is perhaps understandable that what should have been an event well remembered in local folklore became a subject hardly fit for discussion, to the extent that nineteenth century histories of the village otherwise rich in detail hardly touch on the matter – evidently out of deference to the sensitivities of the Giffard family[229] – and an otherwise admirable history of Brewood published as recently as 1959 does not even mention the royal visit.[230]

We have no record of what passed during the visit of the Queen and her retinue, but by family tradition the Queen took leave of her host with the words: "Gentle John, we thank you for your hospitality."[231] We do know that whilst in Staffordshire, the Queen had learnt that many of the Roman Catholics of the county had stopped attending their parish churches, and within three days of the Queen leaving Chillington, warrants were issued from Sudeley against several prominent Catholics from the Midlands, including John Giffard, "for refusing to come to the churche".

Elizabeth's personal involvement in the matter is unknown, but it is recorded that she herself occasionally committed to prison the recusants who were denounced to her in the course of her progresses: after visiting Rookwood House at Euston in Norfolk in 1578, "Young Rookwood . . . [was] commytted for obstinate papistrie", even though it was said that Elizabeth had shortly before thanked him for his hospitality and extended her hand for him to kiss.[232]

On 17th August, "John Gifforth" was summoned with others before a Council of Lords and Bishops at Worcester, and admitted he did not attend church, pleading that his conscience forbade attendance. The hearing was adjourned for two days, and then it was ordered "That John Gifford be committed to the Buishop of Rochester . . . save as he was licensed to repair home to his howse, being as he alleadged, by reason of her Majesties late being there, out of order and unfurnished . . ."

The reference to Chillington being 'out of order and unfurnished' as a direct result of Elizabeth's stay is strikingly curious. The inference may be that the Queen's visit was so disastrous that her officials felt justified in stripping the house, and that John Giffard was powerless to intervene, but if that was indeed what happened it seems to be almost without precedent or parallel.[233] It is perhaps more likely that prudent hosts removed all furnishings prior to a Royal visit, and that John Giffard had taken his valuables elsewhere, possibly to Blackladies, for he must have realised that his sovereign would have little sympathy for his religious beliefs. That possibility is reinforced by a footnote in a letter Sir Amias Paulet, custodian of Mary Queen of Scots, sent to Sir Francis Walsingham ten years later on 3rd October 1585: "I had almost forgotten to advertyse to you that the howse [i.e. Chillington] is verye well furnished".

At a further Council held at Windsor on 13th November 1575, John Giffard

> promised to repaire to his Parishe Churche at same times upon the Sondaies and Holy daies, but the same being one and-a-half mile from his howse he could not do it alwaies, their Lordshipps to be advertised from Mr Deane of Coventrie and Lichefeld being parson there, of such Sondaies and hollidaies as he should not be there, that then he and his familie shold be present at the Common Praier in the Chapel belonging to his howse, was suffered to go home.

It seems that John Giffard's attendance at church failed to satisfy the Council, for in 1580 he was held in the Marshalsea prison and suffered several further periods of arrest and imprisonment. In the records of the Privy Council there is an entry for 3rd March 1585 that

> John Giffard of Chillington in the Countie of Stafford, Esquire, upon commandment of the lords of her Majesties most honourable Privy Counsel for the matter of recusancy restrained to remain in or about London, upon his humble suite for recovery of his health being much impaired, as also for other his necessary business, is enlarged and licensed at his pleasure to repair to the Welles at Newman Regis, or to the Bath, as

also to his house at Chillington for his necessary business or else where as his occasions in any place shall serve to make his abode with his household so as the said John Giffard do not remain at his said house at Chillington nor at any place within the county of Stafford above one month at one time so long as the Queen of Scots is or does remain in any part of the Shire nor until she be clearly removed out of that countie provided allways that the said John Gifford shall not depart out of this realm to any place beyond the seas nor any other Realm without her majesties licence first obtained.

From the Quarter Sessions Rolls of 1584 we learn of an Indictment against many individuals, including "Rick. Mourton late of Engleton in that par. of Brewood, gent, . . . over 16 years on 15 Ap. [1583] For not resorting to their parish churches, or other usual places of worship, between 15 Ap. [1583] and 16 Mar [1584]".[234]

By 1588, the threat of a Spanish invasion had united the nation, and John Giffard was amongst those who put their country before their religion and took the oath of allegiance.[235] His name is included in a list dated 1592 of these recusants at liberty upon a bond.[236]

The Quarter Sessions Rolls also record a Certificate to the Justices issued on 12th June 1593 by "Thos. Grove vicar and George Bee constable that in accordance with the statute of 35 Eliz for restraining recusants to certain places of abode, John Gyffard of Chillington in the par. of Brewood has given notice of his repair to his 'mansion house' at Chillington". In 1604 Brewood was said to harbour "very many recusants", including John Giffard and his wife, and among those charged to appear before the Quarter Sessions for recusancy were the Brewood families of Yates, Woolley, Smythes, Rock and Hill.[237]

Little is known of John Giffard's successor, Walter, but he too was a recusant, defending his tenants, allowing their cattle into his grounds to protect them from the searchers, maintaining a chapel and chaplain, and encouraging two of his daughters to go to France and become nuns. Altogether, about 15 members of the Giffards of Chillington and Blackladies managed to reach the Continent to become priests or nuns.

One result of the persecution of the Catholics was the creation of built-in hiding places in Catholic houses during the period when Moseley Hall and Boscobel House were built respectively by Henry Pitt in about 1600 and John Giffard shortly afterwards. Unless hiding places formed part of the original construction there was a great risk of detection, but it seems likely that the hiding places in Boscobel at least were constructed within the existing building.[238] Recusants could not leave the country without the permission of the Government, and amongst the State Papers is a grant of safe conduct dated 25th June 1624 to "John Gifford of Boscobel, Co. Salop", to go with his wife and four daughters into France. There is not a little irony that the religious persecution of, amongst many others, the Giffards, resulted in the creation of hiding places which played such an important part in the escape of a future King.

106

In March 1624 John Brent of Chillington was prosecuted by the Mayor of Evesham and taken to Oxford, charged with offering scandalous speeches against Queen Elizabeth and the Church of England. It would seem that he was well-known to the authorities as an 'obstinate papist' of forty years standing, and indeed had been detained at the time of the Gunpowder Plot in 1605, although his alleged involvement is not known, and he was later freed. It was claimed that he acted as courier, delivering letters between recusants who were his friends. His objections to the Church of England were apparently that its ministers were 'Parliament ministers, not called of God', and could not perform miracles.[239]

Parish returns of 1641 show that there were 86 recusants in Brewood at that date.[240] In a volume of returns of the Commissioners for Sequestration during the interregnum is a record that "Thomas Stanton of Brewood, sequestrated for Popish recusancy the 25th day of March 1647, and so remaynes." He was doubtless related to William Stanton of Hatton, one of whose sheep was killed for the King's supper while Charles II was hiding at Boscobel, and whose horse was to have been used to carry Charles to Moseley.

Peter Giffard, Walter's son, successfully petitioned for relief from recusancy exactions over and above the £180 per annum for which he had been compounded in 1634, but he was imprisoned for taking up arms for the King early in the Civil War, and his lands forfeited when he became involved in further action against Parliament in 1648. By 1660, however, his estates had been recovered.

In the records of the Commissioners for Sequestration is a return of 'malignants' in the parish of Brewood who had been sequestered but allowed into composition for their estates, with the following names: Mr Walhouse, 1643; Anthony Hatton; John Hatton; John Huddlestone; Robert Stebbing; Jeffrey Rotiss; and John Wells.[241]

80 recusants were recorded in the parish in 1657.[242]

A curious entry from the Constables' Accounts of Brewood in 1666 relates to a burial at Whiteladies. Dated 24th June, it records a charge of one shilling "Bestowed in ale upon some neighbours, that were raised in the night to go to Chillington to meet a company of strange horsemen which went to Whiteladies with a funeral, not then knowing their occasion". Night burial was a custom from Puritan times, when it was made an offence for those not of the established church to bury their dead during the day with their customary religious service. Some Catholics appear to have continued the custom of night burial in the area long after it ceased to be necessary.

The Constables' Accounts also contain interesting entries in 1678, when the Popish Plot caused widespread alarm, with various references to "Papishes" and "Papishes' estate", and for "going by command to search for priests". On Christmas day, the Constable and John Leadbetter escorted a "Papish" priest to Stafford Gaol, paying the turnkey 4d for receiving the priest, and hiring a horse to carry him for 8d, evidence that business was conducted as normal on Christmas day at this period.

In 1668 Bonaventure Giffard, a member of the Wolverhampton branch of the family, was appointed as the first Roman Catholic Bishop [known as Vicar Apostolic] for the Midlands.

Towards the end of the seventeenth century anxiety increased at the prospect of a Roman Catholic inheriting the throne, and suspicion of Papists became particularly marked in the area. In November 1688 William of Orange arrived in England to accept the throne, but rumours continued to spread, and on the night of 12th December the story circulated that the Irish were burning Birmingham and that fires had been started in many other local towns. At Stafford, a mob was encouraged by troops to pull down the Roman Catholic chapel and break into the gaol to release the prisoners, while in Wolverhampton books and furniture from the Jesuit's place of worship were burnt on High Green, and one man was killed. Although we have no information as to the situation in Brewood at the time, there must have been considerable apprehension that anti-Catholic feelings might have been directed towards an area long known to be an active centre of Catholicism.

In 1706 there were at least 189 Catholics in Brewood, but that figure included children.[243]

A list of Roman Catholics who refused to take the Oath of Supremacy to George I after the riots and rebellion in Scotland in 1715[244] included the following names:

Richard Loyd, of Kerrymore Green, weaver
Richard Pendrell, of Hubbard [sic] Grange, in the county of Salop, gent.
Thomas How, of Boscobel, in the county of salop, gent
Joseph Leese, of Kerrymore Green, in the parish of Brewood
Frances Dale, of Chillington, Spinster
Creswell Wilkes, of Brewood forge, widow
Edward Bawford, of Brewood, gent.
Thomas Gifford, of Chillington, equire

It is said that the Giffards were amongst those families who "spilt their wine more than their blood" for the Stuart cause during the Jacobite rebellion.

On 6th April 1716, George I approved a Deed of Immunity in favour of those families who were instrumental in the escape of Charles II escape after the Battle of Worcester. A petition had been presented by 33 individuals, including 8 Penderels and 3 Giffards, claiming that their ancestors were exempted from penalties for being Papists, but that the matter had not been legally formalised. The Deed of Indemnity provided that: "If any of them should be prosecuted on account of their being Papists, they should be at liberty to apply to his majestye for his further directions thereon. Whereof all persons whomsoever it may concern are to take notice of this mark of his majesty's royal favour in regard to the fidelity and services of the said familys of the Crown".[245]

In 1767 there were 389 Catholics in Brewood parish,[246] and in 1780 there were 399, a very high proportion of just over 3000 for the whole of Staffordshire.

By the Relief Acts of 1778 and 1791, Roman Catholics were for the first time since 1559 allowed to practice their religion without incurring penalties. By 1851, Thomas Giffard of Chillington had "adopted liberal views", and then had only three or four tenants of "the Romish persuasion". He married a Protestant, and his children were educated in the faith of the Church of England. His brother, Walter Peter Giffard, who succeeded to the estate in 1861, was the first non-Catholic Giffard for many generations.

There have been five Roman Catholic chapels closely connected with Brewood: Blackladies, Chillington, Long Birch and, although outside the parish, Boscobel and Whiteladies. Blackladies chapel was open for public worship by 1791, the priest visiting from Chillington, and by 1834 was served by two priests. It was demolished in about 1872. The chapel at Chillington, which may have adjoined the gatehouse of the old Tudor house, was used regularly from at least 1721, and was a focal point for the residence of a considerable area, including 'Chillington Town', a village of 30 houses according to Gregory King's notebook of 1680. The chapel was demolished in about 1786 during the enlargement of the Hall. One curiosity from the register of Catholic marriages at the chapel is the record of wedding services which took place on 2nd and 4th March 1727/8 at the unusual hour of 7.00 am. Another entry in the registers mentions the delivery of one of the Giffard children by a male midwife. The chapel at Long Birch was used for public worship from at least 1779, with its own priest-in-charge. It was enlarged after the Vicar Apostolic left in 1804, and closed in 1844 when the Roman Catholic church of St Mary's opened in the village. Until 1844, Whiteladies was used as a burial place for Roman Catholics, the most celebrated being Joan Penderel, associated with the escape of Charles II after the Battle of Worcester.

15. The Muster Rolls

In 1516, Charles of Burgundy inherited the Spanish Dominions, and in 1519 succeeded his grandfather, Maximillian, as Holy Roman Emperor. Thus began a lifelong rivalry with Francis I of France which kept Catholic Europe too preoccupied to interfere in Henry VIII's dispute with Rome: in 1537 the Pope tried to start a Crusade against Henry, but the Pope's representative was refused entry both to France and imperial territory.

The situation changed dramatically in June 1538 when Charles and Francis ostensibly buried their differences and declared their friendship. There was a flurry of alarm and apprehension in England, and Henry began a costly programme building fortifications and ships. The Shire levies were mustered, an exercise which involved the registration of all able-bodied men, probably between the ages of 15 and 60, and Sir John Giffard and his son Thomas were both on the Commission for the General Muster. Sir John is recorded as possessing horses and harness complete for 7 men, and his son as having the same for 4 men. As the largest number returned for any single individual in Staffordshire was 10 [by Lord Stafford], the Giffards appear to have occupied at this date one of the most important positions in the county.[247] The Muster Roll for the Cuttlestone Hundred of Staffordshire[248] includes entries for "Brewoed", Chillington, Engleton, Horsebrook, Gunstone, Somerford and Coven. The entries for Brewood and Chillington, recording 46 men and 29 men respectively, are set out for interest. The other entries show that there were 2 men on the Roll in Engleton, 12 in Horsebrook, 6 in Gunstone, 13 in Somerford, and 21 in Coven, giving a total for the parish of 129. The figures are of interest in showing the relative population density of various parts of the parish in the early part of the sixteenth century.

"Brewoed"

Thes persons next foloing be abull men with bowes and have harnes and artilarie[249] as foloith their names:

In primis, Ric. Stiche
Item, Thomas Smyth
Item, John Bickeford harnes[250] for a man
Item, Thomas Smyth, thakker a bowe
Item, Ralph Hawkyns a bowe and x arrowes
Item, Thomas Peace a bowe
Item, Homfrey Hondeford a bowe
Item, Edward Schermon a bowe and x arrowes
Item, William Rocke
Item, Thomas Matson a bowe
Item, Thomas Molton

Thes persons next folloing be abull men with bills and have harnes and artilarie as foloith their names:

In primis. Ric. Ratthbon a bill
Item, Fraunces Stedeman a salet a bill and a pair of splentes[251]
Item, Roger Mason a horse and a gesturne
Item, William Corbyn
Item, Thomas Cartwryght a jakke[252] a salet and a bill[253]
Item, Ric Derne
Item, Thomas Weggewod
Item, John Styche
Item, James Sidebotham a sallet
Item, Thomas Jurdan
Item, Oliver Blakemeyr a bill
Item, Rondull Duncalfe a bill
Item, Robert Turner
Item, Thomas Colyns a bill and a stondert
Item, John Bristowe
Item, William Colyns a salet a bill and a peir of splentes
Item, John Hickman
Item, Ric. Colyns junior a gesturne a peir of splentes and a gorget
Item, Robert Grene
Item, Laurens Trant a peir of splentes
Item, Robert [sic]
Item, John Northall a salet and a bill
Item, John Prestwood
Item, Thomas Turnar
Item, Ric. Marshe a bille

Thes persons next foloing have harnes as hereafter ensuith their names:

In primis, Roger Fowke gent. harnes for a mon
In primis, Roger Eccleshall a bill
Item, Robert Byll a sallette a bill and a peir of splentes
Item, William Barkar a bille
Item, Thomas Harres a sallett
Item, Robert Liptroppe a bowe
Item, Thomas Johnson a jacke and a peir of splentes
Item, George Webbe, a bill
Item, Thomas Hynke a bill
Item, Robert Peace a bill

Chillington
Thes persons next foloing be abull men with bowes and have harnes and artilarie as foloitl. their names:

In primis, Roger Schorde
Item, John Jate harnes for a mon

Item, Thomas Turner
Item, Mathew Parker a bowe and a schieff of arrows
Item, William Bowedon a peir of splentes

Thes persons next foloing be abull men with bills and have harnes and artilarie as foloith their names:

In primis, John Lane esquyer horse and harnes for i j men
Item, Harre Fowke
Item, John Schert a bill
Item, Thomas Allat
Item, Ric. Walloes a gesturne and a salet
Item, Thomas Corbett a bowe and arrow
Item, Ric. Corbett
Item, John Smith senior a salet and a bill
Item, Ric. Stokes
Item, Thomas Addams
Item, Thomas Carryngton harnes for a man
Item, Ric. Poys
Item, William Smyth a salet and a bill
Item, John Corbyn
Item, Thomas Corbyn
Item, Homfrey Warde
Item, Ric. Hyncke
Item John Smyth of Hollyfaste a jacke and a salet
Item, Homfrey White a bill
Item, Robert Gought a bill

These foloing have harnes as hereafter ensuith their names:

In primis, Nicholas Colle a bill
Item, Ric. Carles
Item, William Carles a bill
Item, Homfrey Holwey a gesturne and a stondyert

Further musters were called from time to time, and the Quarter Sessions Rolls contain two entries connected with Brewood, an Indictment against Edward Barrett and Francis Sandye, for absence from the musters at Stafford presented by Richard Duncalfe, Constable of Brewood, c.1600[254], and an Indictment against 'Ric Longsley of Brewood yeom, Geoffrey Duffeilde of the same yeom, Francis Saunders of the same yeom, John Clymer of the same yeom, . . . To answer touching certain sevarl contempts by absenting themselves from the muster, and other misdeeds,' in 1601.[255]

One of the earliest fragments of the Constables' Accounts of Brewood is dated November 1604, and indicates that the parish held its own store of arms and armour:

"There remayneth of the parish armour, in Jhon [sic] Fletcher's hands, of Horsebrooke, Two Corslets, two pykes, two swords, one gyrdle."[256]

112

16. The Civil War

When, after the short Parliament of 1640, Charles I found it necessary to resist the Scottish Covenanters, who had objected to his bishops and the Prayer Book, a muster of the army was ordered, consisting of two elements: the rough trainbands, and pressed men. For Brewood-cum-membris, Edward Bourne, John Dill, John Swayne and William Groves were listed in the trained band of 1st June 1640, and Edward Lloyd, John Jeninges, and William Witt were included in the 'impressed bond'.[257] Charles' army reached Berwick, where the King negotiated a settlement with the Scots forces, but both sides probably realised that it was no more than a temporary truce.

For several years Charles and parliament had been moving inexorably towards confrontation, but although there is evidence of discontent among some of the prominent families of Staffordshire with the policies of the King, particularly on matters relating to taxation and monopolies, there was no great enthusiasm to take up arms when civil war broke out on 22nd August 1642. The Sheriff of Stafford, in an attempt to restrain potential agitators and keep the county neutral, issued a declaration on 15th November that "riots and unlawful assemblies have been made and committed . . . by certain persons in arrays and warlike manner", and a force was raised with officers sympathic to both causes to deal with any disturbances, Thomas Fowke and Thomas Whitgreave being appointed Captains of the Foot for Cuttlestone Hundred.

The choice of sides taken by activists was sometimes determined by religion, with Presbyterians and persecuted Puritans supporting parliament and Catholics assumed to support the King or remain neutral, to the extent that to avoid sequestration a Catholic was required to prove that he was not a royalist, whereas a non-Catholic had to have guilt proved against him. The Protestant landowners who fought for the King included John Lane, then of The Hyde, better known as Colonel Lane who assisted in the escape of Charles II after the battle of Worcester, and brother of Jane Lane, who was also involved in the King's escape. The Roman Catholic landowners who took up arms for the King included Peter Giffard of Chillington, his eldest son Walter Giffard of Marston, and three younger sons.[258] Roman Catholic landowners who did not take up arms for the King, and whose estates were sequestered, included John Giffard of Whiteladies. Sequestered property was either rented out or sold to provide revenue for continuing the war, but in 1644 the principle was established that 'delinquents' could compound – pay a large lump sum – for its return. The Fowkes of Brewood were royalists, but the Moretons of Engleton supported the parliamentary cause. The great bulk of the people, however, took no part in the struggle, and the fighting was confined to the professional soldiers and fanatics on each side. As the historian Lord

Clarendon observed, "the number of those who desired to sit still was greater than of those who desired to engage in either party".

There was some excitement, but no widespread support for his cause, when Charles crossed central Staffordshire with his forces early in September 1642 en route from Nottingham to Shrewsbury, but some of the more radical local royalists had ridden to Nottingham to join the King's army, among them Peter Giffard of Chillington and his sons. By the end of the year the royalists were in control of Stafford, Lichfield and Dudley, from where they were able to harry parliamentary forces and supply lines in the area.

On 31st December 1642 the counties of Warwick and Stafford were associated under the Lords Lieutenant and the Committees, and with this Ordinance the Civil War in Staffordshire began proper.

At Brewood, Peter Giffard had fortified and garrisoned the old Tudor house at Chillington, and the principal military activity in the parish seems to have centred on the house. It is likely that the villagers of Brewood suffered the same fate as those in other places as control passed from one side to the other: paying taxes to whichever side was in control of the area, and even sometimes to both sides.

The only engagement of any magnitude in the county during the war was the battle of Hopton Heath, north-east of Stafford, on 19th March 1643, when an attack on Stafford by parliamentary forces was forestalled by royalists reinforced by troops who had been permitted to surrender and leave the Close of Lichfield Cathedral early in 1643. Notwithstanding the death of the royalist commander, the Earl of Northampton, the superior royalist cavalry, which included John Lane of Brewood as one of its officers, caused the parliamentary forces to retire.

Due to carelessness on the part of the night-watch, the royalist garrison at Stafford was breached by a parliamentary force which entered the town undetected during the night of 16th May, "the people in this town being quiet in their beds", as Sir William Brereton, a prominent parliamentarian who fought at Hopton Heath, recorded. The town was taken almost without bloodshed with many prisoners, and the strategy was repeated at Wolverhampton a week later. For the rest of the war Stafford stayed in parliamentary hands, and was the meeting place of the Committee which administered the county on behalf of parliament, to which Committee were appointed as members on 7th June 1643 "Thomas Fulke [Fowke] of Brewood and Thomas Whitgreave, esquires, Captains of the foot in the Hundred of Cuttleston".

From the Order Book of the Stafford Committee and other contemporary records we have a somewhat disjointed but nevertheless informative impression of various matters affecting Brewood and its inhabitants. For example in January 1643 Thomas Woolrich of Brewood Park, a "Convict Recusant" whose property had been sequestered, petitioned for relief, which was granted in view of his "age and the imbecillity of his person" in return for a payment of £6.

On 27th March 1643 special Commissioners of Sequestration who were the sole judges of whether a person came within the definition of a 'delinquent' were ordered to be appointed. Pleas of neutrality were rejected by the parliamentary administrators: all estates were sequestrated unless the owner was known to be sympathetic to parliament and had given material assistance. A series of Ordinances required local committees to collect weekly pay for their troops. Staffordshire was assessed at £212 a week plus £5 for Lichfield, compared with £562 for Warwickshire and Coventry and £1800 for Devon, an indication of the relative poverty of the county.[259]

It is known that the royalist generals Lord Northampton the younger and Sir Henry Hastings were at Chillington shortly afterwards, for they wrote a joint letter from there to Prince Rupert on 27th March commending Wolverhampton as a place likely to help him, Stafford being unsuitable "the countrey being poore and provision for men and horse all spent".[260]

On 2nd July 1643 Charles I wrote to Colonel Leveson, Governor of Dudley Castle, commanding him to send warrants to the inhabitants of Seisdon and Cuttlestone hundreds for reasonable supply and provisions; to seize for the use of the garrison the estates and profits of all rebels; and to protect and defend loyal subjects.[261]

A diary kept by Mr Burghall, vicar of Acton in Cheshire and a staunch parliamentarian, contains the following entry for Thursday 10th August 1643: "Sir Wm Brereton being then at Stafford went with the forces he had there, against Mr Giffards House at Chillington, which was garrisoned with 3 great pieces of ordinance, & one set of drakes. They besieged the House and playing hard upon it two days altogether, upon Friday the Besieged yielded, being sore battered and not able to hold out any longer, so the house was surrendered upon fair Quarter being given them. They took prisoners Mr Giffard and his two sons, a seminary priest and above 60 others, and carried them to Stafford: Arms for 200 men, great stores of annunition and this with the loss of one man and a boy. And so Sir Wm Brereton returned in the afternoon to Nantwich."[262]

When the estates of Sir Walter Wrottesley were sequestrated and the rents assigned to the Parliamentary Committee at Stafford for the payment of parliamentary troops, an affidavit in mitigation was filed on his behalf: ". . . that [he] did voluntarily advance for the service of the state . . . and delivered to severall of the Commitee of Stafford, and other theire capteynes and officers, vizt – in sommer 1643, Fourteene horses at Threescore and six pounds, Twenty six beastes; at Threescore and Five poundes, Forty and Five sheepe at Thirteene pounds, and the lay money of the parke at Fifteene pounds, for the supply of the Garrison of Chillington . . ."[263]

Chillington was recaptured by Colonel Leveson for the royalists in September, and the King wrote to him on 25th September: "Whereas you have, with the forces under your command, taken Chillington House, in our county of Stafford, from those who rebelliously kept it against us, which being a place of much importance for our service in those parts," he is desired "to place a sufficient number of souldiers there in the garrison under such a commander as you shalt conceive fitt".[264]

The parish register records the burial of "a soldier" on 18th October 1643.

Early in December, 1643, parliamentary forces from Tong Castle and Lapley are said to have attacked a royalist party taking 30 loads of wheat from Weston-under-Lizard to Chillington. The engagement is reported to have involved over 200 troops, with the parliamentary force routed and pursued to Lapley Hall, then known as Lapley House, which was held by a parliamentary garrison of 70 men,[265] under the Governor, Captain Smith.

On 11th December 1643 the Stafford Order Book records details of an authority for Captain Stone to give a reward "as what he in his discretion shall think fitt" to Richard Blest, a soldier under Captain Wagstaffe, who was wounded at Chillington. The incident in which the injury occurred may be connected with the thwarted attack on the Chillington grain train.

On 21st December 1643, Captain Heveningham, commanding the royalist garrison at Chillington, led his forces from there "at about 12 of the clocke at night", and marched to Lapley, where his night raid successfully overcame the parliamentary defenders. It is recorded that the assault was assisted by a 'traitor' at Lapley identified as "Master Collier, servant to Squire Peters". "Twelve musketteirs kept garrison in the church adjoining, who hearing the house already taken, yielded themselves prisoners, and were, with their fellowes, sent all prisoners to Chillington which also was lately a [parliamentary] garrison, till Colonel Leveson [the royalist Governor of Dudley Castle, which was used as a base from which troops could be withdrawn to support other garrisons in South Staffordshire] took it by assault, and all the rebels in it prisoner."[266]

News of the loss of Lapley House quickly reached the parliamentary forces at Stafford, who next day despatched 400 troops with artillery to re-take the house. After arriving at Lapley but before their intention could be accomplished, word arrived that Colonel Leveson and 100 mounted troops were on their way to relieve the house, so they abandoned their plans, fired the barns which were full of corn, and retreated in darkness towards Stafford. They were soon overtaken by Colonel Leveson's party and lost some of their number in the fighting, with others taken prisoner. A cannon captured by the royalists was taken back to Lapley to protect the new royalist garrison at Lapley House.[267]

It is possible that the troops at Lapley were under the control of William Carless, for the Grant of Arms to Carless records that after mustering a troop and then a regiment of cavalry during the Civil War, he undertook the management of Lapley House and Tong Castle. He is believed to have been Governor of Tong Castle in 1645.[268]

On 26th December 1643 the parish register records the burial of "a soldier that came from Stafford". The man, whose name is not recorded, may have been amongst those sent to recover Lapley House and captured by Leveson.

From the Stafford Order Book we learn of a warrant issued on 11th January 1644 against Saunders Minion "for giving Intelligence to the Enemie at Chillington," but four days later his release from prison is ordered since "nothing doth appear against him." Doubtless the parliamentarians had been seeking scapegoats for their ignominious rout at Lapley.[269]

The same source records an order on 11th February 1644 permitting the wife of Walter Gifford to live with her mother-in-law at Chillington with her children and two maids without interference by parliamentary forces "so long as she or they shall not act or give or send intelligence."

On about 1st March 1644 "Col Rugeley led a force from Stafford against the garrison at Chillington House, which had recently scored a victory over the neighbouring Parliamentary garrison at Lapley."

The parliamentary forces seem at this time to have been apprehensive about their position, for on 4th March it was "ordered that no Papist be permitted to come within four miles of Stafford,"[270] and on 9th March an order was given for the removal of Peter Giffard and other prisoners from Stafford to Eccleshall Castle.

That the parliamentary troops in the area may have been undisciplined is evidenced by an entry in the Stafford Order Book on 20th March, permitting Mr Mason of Brewood "to search for any of his goods that have been taken away by any of our souldiers, and to take the same where he findeth them. Mr Lane is desired to take two musquetiers to assist him."

On the same date a further entry records a bargain struck with Walter Giffard, whereby for quarterly payments of £260 and the weekly pay and other duties of the local troops, he would be permitted to enjoy his estates for the following year, and would be given his liberty for £100 in hand, to live at Chillington and "not to act anything against the Parliament, and so long he shall remain in quiet."

For reasons which remain unclear, Mathew Moreton of Engleton was imprisoned by the Committee at Stafford in May 1644, and ordered to pay £100 within a week.[271] There is some mystery about this incident, for the Moretons of Engleton were parliamentarians, and indeed Moreton was himself a member of the Stafford Committee.[272]

An order from parliament dated 24th May 1644 assigns the rents and profits of Brewood-cum-membris to Sir William Brereton to maintain the garrison at Eccleshall, contrary to the decision of the Stafford Committee, which appealed to parliament and prayed that the revenues of Brewood might still be at the disposal of the Committee. The last Minute on this subject is dated 23rd July 1644, but the result of the appeal is not given and is not now known.

The parish register records the burial of "John Wourt, slain at Bromehall by a Soldier" on 1st June 1644. The name Wourt does not appear anywhere in the Brewood parish registers before this date, and he was presumably therefore not a local man.

On 12th June Isaak Tonkes of Brewood [a dealer who supplied the Foley ironworks with wood and perhaps ironstone] advanced to the Committee a grey mare valued at £3.

On 17th June the Stafford Order Book records an order "that the garrisons at Chillington and Lapley shalbee demolished and made unfitt for the like service herafter and this to bee donne with all convenient speede and Captayne Foxall captayne Port or one of them are intreated and intrusted to see itt effectually doone". This suggests that Colonel Rugeley's attack in March had succeeded in recapturing Chillington for parliament.

For whatever reason, the order was not put into immediate effect, for on 15th July is the entry "That Chillington house be remembered to be forthwith demolished according to the former order," and a subsequent entry gives the precise time and date of the destruction of the house: "22nd July 1644 : That [deleted '200'] all the horse and foote that can be spared shall go with theyr companies to morrow at foure of the clock to demolish Chillington House."

An order was made on 7th August "that Anthony Cadman who was taken prisoner by Sir Wm. Breretons forces and sent to Stafford" should be forthwith released on undertakings by his mother and Edward Birch of Coven "that he will never beare Armes any more against the King and Parliament." It is not known where Cadman, who may have been a juvenile, was captured.

An entry from the Order Book on 29th August records that at some time before that date Colonel Leigh and Captain Philip Jackson had been based at Chillington.

On 17th October the detention was ordered by the Committee of Edward Tonks of Brewood, the sub-tenant of Mrs Humfreys, until he paid the Treasurer £15 6s 8d, representing six month's arrears of "the Deanes Rent".

The local records are then silent until 6th March 1645, when a licence was issued by the Stafford Committee for Mrs Giffard, wife of Walter Giffard, to keep two cows at Chillington. On the following day all those having failed to pay their tithes to Isaack Tonkes of Brewood, including John Webb, Edward Webb and Thomas Harris of Horsebrook, were ordered to do so forthwith or appear before the Committee on 10th March, but on 18th March Tonkes was claiming that he had been unable to serve the order, and the Committee accordingly ordered all arrears to be paid by the Webbs and Harriss before 1st April 1645.

On 13th March, Thomas Fowke, "a delinquent," was permitted to enjoy [i.e. keep] his estate and have protection for himself and his goods in return for £15 already paid and two horses valued at £7 and £28, to be delivered on 13th April.

On 14th April 1645 the Stafford Committee agreed that Peter Giffard should be released from prison to live at Chillington in return for a payment of £165 in hand and three further payments of £65 on the following quarter days, and an undertaking not to act against parliament. A gentlemanly bargain was also recorded: if it became necessary to imprison Peter Giffard again, he would be refunded with £100 unless it could be shown that he had "acted against the Parliament."

14th April 1645: "Ordered in the behalfe of Mr Giffard that if in case he the said Mr Giffard shall free Mr Foley from any demaund to be made for such monies as he hath payed to this garrison of Stafford being the price of certen charcole carried this last yeare by Mr Giffard from Chillington to an Ironworke of the said Mr Folyes at Brewood That the said Mr Giffard shall be allowed the charges of cutting cording coling and carrying the said coles from the said committee if the same be otherwise discharged by the said Mr Foley." This entry from the Stafford Committee Order Book relates to the ironworks known as Brewood Park Forge or Brewood Upper Forge and Coven Furnace leased at the time by Walter Giffard to Thomas Foley and subsequently in 1669 to Philip Foley of Stourbridge. It is unclear whether the Giffards, staunch royalists, willingly supplied material for the benefit of the parliamentary forces, or simply acquiesced in the removal of charcoal produced at Chillington, but it has been suggested that the family were among those who adopted a pragmatic approach to the parliamentary Committee so that they could continue to exploit their assets.[273]

After capturing Wolverhampton for parliament in May 1643, Sir William Brereton returned to Stafford with "some cannon bulletts from Mr Folies forges; and the moulds which made these bulletts".[274] There were Foley forges at Stourbridge and to the south and west of Wolverhampton, but the reference may be to Brewood Forge or Coven Furnace, since both lie between Wolverhampton and Stafford. Accounts of the escape of Charles II after the battle of Worcester record that it was the workmen from Brewood Forge who chased John Penderel and Lord Wilmot as they were making for Brinsford from Boscobel.

On Thursday 15th May King Charles stayed at the Grosvenor's house at Bushbury, and the following day continued to Tong, en route to Chetwynd Hall, but seemingly did not enter Brewood parish, taking the road through Codsall and via Wrottesley to Albrighton. For most of that week royalist troops were quartered in the area.

From a diary kept by Captain Symmonds, a royalist officer, it appears that in May 1645, "Mr Giffard's house at Chillington which had been a rebel garrison, is now deserted by themselves." [Stebbing-Shaw records: "Satterday, May 17th 1645 R[ebels]. Mr Gifford's house at Chillington, three miles from Wolverhampton. Now slighted by themselves".][275]

There is evidence that Brewood church was at some stage one of twelve military posts in the region garrisoned or fortified by the royalists, which might explain the gap in the parish registers from 1645 to 1655, for in about 1644, Sir Walter Wrottesley of Wrottesley, when charged with supporting the royalist cause, declared that he was compelled to take the King's side since his house was surrounded by royal garrisons at Chillington, Brewood church, Lapley House, Lapley church, Lichfield, Rushall, Wolverhampton church, Leveson Hall at Wolverhampton, Dudley Castle, Patshull Hall, Lilleshall and Tong.[276] There is no evidence to suggest that earthworks or fortifications were erected around Brewood church, as was the case at Lapley church, where a ditch was dug around three sides of the building, but later filled in under a parliamentary mandate issued by Cromwell on 19th March 1645 ordering the inhabitants of adjacent hamlets to forthwith pull down the works and fortifications, and requiring every Constable in the hamlets to send six men every day until the work was completed.

It seems that Boscobel House was the scene of a skirmish and may have been besieged during the war, for in 1646 there is a record of a royalist who "served the King in the war and had been in Boscobel House at its surrender."

On June 14th 1645 Charles watched Cromwell's forces defeat the royalist army at the battle of Naseby, and eventually, after journeying around the country, threw himself upon the protection of the Scottish army, which then moved north to Newcastle. After negotiations, Charles was released by the Scots to parliamentary commissioners, and gradually the royalist garrisons surrendered. When the royalist garrison at Lichfield marched out on 10th July 1645 the war in Staffordshire was over and within the county troops were disbanded by October 1646.

Lodged eventually by the army at Hampton Court, Charles escaped to the Isle of Wight in 1648 and, as he expected, war erupted again, with a full scale invasion from Scotland and royalist risings in Wales, Essex and Kent. These were soon put down by Cromwell, but amongst those who had taken up arms for the King was Peter Giffard, then 67 years old. In a return made to the Committee for Compounding Estates in 1648 are the names of Peter Giffard of Chillington, "Papist in arms", and George, Thomas, John, Edward, and Walter Giffard, Papists, "all in arms".

Searches were made of districts suspected of harbouring royalist sympathisers, and it is said that a surprise raid on 'Boscobel Woods' revealed 200 men undergoing military exercises under Colonel Dud Dudley. He was captured with most of his recruits and taken to Hartlebury Castle and from there to Worcester. Although condemned to death, he escaped and lived to see the Restoration. It is not inconceivable that among the recruits were some of those subsequently involved in the escape of Charles II after the battle of Worcester.

After the defeat of the Scottish army at Preston on 17th-19th August 1648, Charles was recaptured and the army demanded his death. A special commission tried the King on a charge of tyranny, and he was beheaded on 30th January 1649.

Although in 1649 Peter Giffard was farming Brewood Park for the Parliamentary Committee, and it is recorded that about 35 trees were needed to repair the Park pales, "in these distracted times . . . so pulled down and stolen," an indication of the situation within the parish at this time, a return to the Committee for Compounding Estates suggests that when he was 69, Giffard was still in arms for the King, and the State Papers record that he was a prisoner on 28th March 1650, with a warrant recording the payment of a reward of £6 to the soldier who had apprehended him.

From the proceedings of the Committee for Compounding it appears that by 22nd September 1652, all Peter Giffard's lands had been forfeited, and most of them leased or sold.

The Churchwardens' Accounts for Brewood contain a much torn and almost illegible sheet dating from 1653. The words "maimed soldiers" can just be made out. In 1656 and for several succeeding years there are also entries for regular quarterly payments of £1 3s 4d for maimed soldiers.

It appears that after the Restoration steps were taken to identify parliamentary activists from the time of the Civil War, perhaps to settle old scores, for in the State Papers is

A list [dated 1662] of all such persons (as were then presented by the constables) that live in their several parishes and constablewikes and have borne armes and been in actual service against His Majestie and also his most royall father of blessed memory as followeth, viz:
Item: presented by Edward Tomlinson Constable of Brewood
        John BRADSHAW
        John ROWLEY
        Richard HAYWARD
        Thomas EVANS[277]

There is no record of any subsequent action against the four individuals.

17. Charles II and Brewood

Although the two local houses in which King Charles II is known to have stayed during his escape from Worcester are outside the parish – Boscobel by a few yards into Shropshire on the west, Moseley Hall a short distance across the south-eastern border – Charles almost certainly passed through the parish, for he is known to have stopped at Pendeford Mill on his journey from Boscobel to Moseley, and his guides and protectors were all closely associated with Brewood.

The story starts on 30th January 1649 when, after more than six years of Civil War, Charles I was beheaded at Whitehall. Six days after his father's execution, Charles Stuart, then 18 years old, was proclaimed King in his absence by the Scottish parliament in Edinburgh, but England was declared a Commonwealth, and a new government was installed which ruled the country for eleven years.

The King's elder son had fled to France and later Holland during the Civil War. In the summer of 1650, soon after his 20th birthday, he was persuaded by representatives from Scotland to take the first steps to recover his father's crown. He sailed from Holland and landed in Scotland on 16th June, gathering an army of sympathisers to defeat Oliver Cromwell's commonwealth forces. But his Scottish supporters were routed by parliamentary troops at Dunbar on 3rd September, Edinburgh was captured for parliament, and it was a hollow gesture when Charles was crowned King at Scone on 1st January 1651. At the ceremony, Charles swore to uphold the Covenants of 1638 and 1643, treaties with the Scottish parliament which upheld the establishment of Presbyterianism in England and Ireland, but took care not to antagonise the Catholics, a policy which was later to prove invaluable in his hour of need.

Charles moved south with his surviving forces, under the command of two rival Scottish soldiers of fortune, David Leslie and John Middleton, hoping that popular support would swell his army and enable him to regain his father's crown. But Charles had misjudged the sympathy of the people for his cause. While he had considerable support in England, the people had no liking for the Scots, English Presbyterians had little enthusiasm for the King's Catholic associates, and at Shrewsbury, Charles was met with closed gates. Continuing south without much opposition, Charles reached Worcester on 22nd August,[278] but his army of 16,000 was smaller than it had been when he had left Scotland. In the meantime, Lord Derby's royalist forces had been scattered at Wigan, but Lord Derby and Colonel Roscarrock had escaped to join Charles at Worcester, seeking refuge on the way at Boscobel House, an isolated lodge set on high ground in woods on the Shropshire-Staffordshire border.

Cromwell soon arrived at Worcester with 30,000 troops, and after some preliminary skirmishes, battle proper commenced on the afternoon of 3rd September. By dusk it was clear that the royalist forces were beaten, due in part to the reluctance of General Leslie to engage the enemy with his Scots cavalry.[279] Charles realised there was nothing more he could do, and with Lord Wilmot, Lord Derby, several other officers and a body of Scottish cavalry, rode away to the north.

The story of Charles' escape has come down to us from many different sources, all of which were published many years afterwards, and all of which differ to a greater or lesser extent. It is therefore impossible to be certain of the precise sequence of events which occurred after Charles fled north from Worcester, but the following version has been compiled from what seem to be the most credible sources.[280]

Before reaching Barbon's Bridge, half a mile out of Worcester, Charles stopped to confer with his commanders, and although he would have preferred to try to make for London, he was advised to ride for Scotland. Lord Talbot knew the area and was asked to lead the party, but Talbot produced a local man, Richard Walker, to act as guide. It was dark by the time the party reached Kinver Heath, and Walker was uncertain of the route. The party halted, and Charles conferred with Lord Derby, who mentioned his recent refuge at Boscobel House, and the strong Catholic following in the area – perhaps knowing of the arrest of Dud Dudley who was caught drilling recruits for the royalist cause during the Civil War. Charles quickly agreed to make for the house, and one of Charles' party, Charles Giffard, the fifth son of Peter Giffard of Chillington, acted as guide, accompanied by a servant, Francis Yates. The party, by now reduced in number to about 60, General Leslie and the Scottish cavalry having taken the more direct route northwards towards Newport, rode on north, stopping for refreshment at a house near Wordsley church just north of Stourbridge. As the party continued its journey, it was decided that instead of proceeding directly to Boscobel, Charles would be taken to Whiteladies, a substantial house built against the ruins of a former Augustinian Nunnery, some half mile south-west of Boscobel. The plan was to mislead any pursuers and to limit the number of people knowing the intended destination of the King.

There is no evidence to indicate the route taken to Whiteladies from Wordsley, but the party evidently took to the lanes north of Himley, skirting Wombourne and leaving Wolverhampton to the east, and a disused lane near Pattingham [perhaps the bridlepath from Norton via Meer Oak to Wrottesley now known as Deer's Leap] was, until the early years of the present century, known as King Charles Lane.[281]

Nearing Whiteladies, most of Charles' party rode away to join 3,000 Scottish cavalry near Tong Castle, leaving Lord Wilmot, Lord Derby, Charles Giffard and Francis Yates with Charles. After depositing Charles and Lord Wilmot at Whiteladies at about 3 am, the rest of the party, guided by Charles Giffard, left to join the retreating Scottish forces at Newport, but most were captured by parliamentary troops and taken to an inn at Bunbury in Cheshire. Lord Buckingham was among the few who escaped.

Whiteladies was owned by Dorothy, the wife of John Giffard, her second husband, but had been sequestered before the battle of Worcester. She had been allowed to reside there with her married daughter Frances Cotton [who was away from the house when Charles arrived], Mrs Anne Andrew, who was possibly the housekeeper, Edward and Bartholomew Martin, and various other people, until a purchaser could be found.

Charles was admitted to the house through the two-storey timbered gatehouse by George Penderel, then over 60 years of age and one of the five brothers who were to figure prominently in the events of the next few days. Refreshed with bread and cheese after the long ride, Charles removed his buff coat and red sash. He had given his George to Colonel Blague[282] and his gold to his servants on reaching the house. Bartholomew Martin, a boy, was sent to fetch William Penderel, the eldest of the brothers, from Boscobel, where he was warden with his wife. A third brother, Richard Penderel, who lived at Hubbal Grange, a house about half a mile west of Whiteladies, was also sent for, and John Penderel, who was "a kind of woodsward" at Whiteladies, was woken. George Penderel left at dawn to visit Robert Beard [or Bird] of the Talbot Inn at Tong, "an Honest Subject", to see if he knew of any royalist or commonwealth troops in the area, and returned to report that there had been no sightings of any strangers.

According to his own account dictated some thirty years later to Samuel Pepys, Charles was again advised to make for Scotland, but he was still intent on reaching London, and decided that his best chance was to travel on foot disguised as a countryman. To this end, he dressed in

> a very greasy old gray steeple turned hat, with the brims turned up, without lining or hat-band, the swett apprearing two inches deep through it round the band-place; a green cloth jump-coat, threadbare, even to the threads being worn white; and breeches of the same, with long knees downe to the garter; with old swetty leather doublet, a pair of white flannell-stockings next his leggs, their tops being cutt off to prevent their being discover'd; and upon them, a paire of old green yarne stockings, all worne, and dearned at the knees, with their feet cutt off. His shoes were old, all slasht for the ease of his feet . . . He had an old course shirt, patched both at the neck and hands, of that very course sort which . . . go by the name of nogging-shirts. His handkerchief was a very old one, torne and very

course . . . he had no gloves, but a long thorn-stick, not very strong, but crooked three or four severall ways, in his hands; his hair cutt short up to his ears, and hands coloured, . . . refusing to have any gloves.

The breeches, doublet and coat were provided by Richard Penderel, Humphrey Penderel provided the hat, and Edward Martin, a tenant at Whiteladies, the shirt. A band was given by George Penderel and shoes were supplied by William Creswell, a neighbour of the Penderel's. Charles' hair had already been cut with a knife by Lord Wilmot. The King's clothing was buried outside the house [Charles says thrown into a privy] and recovered some weeks later. In his new disguise, Charles, carrying a wood-bill to assume the appearance of a woodman, left the house with Richard Penderel, having been urged to make haste since parliamentary troops known to be quartered at Codsall[283] would doubtless soon be searching for fugitives.

Charles and Richard took refuge in a part of Renshaw Wood nearby known as Spring Coppice.[284] The rest of his party had earlier left Whiteladies to seek safety as best they could, Lord Wilmot having been guided by John Penderel to the house of John Huntbach at Brinsford, to go at night to Moseley Hall, the home of Thomas Whitgreave, which was known by the Penderels to have hiding places.

Accompanied by Richard Penderel, Charles remained in Spring Coppice throughout the day. William Penderel returned to his home, and Humphrey and George kept guard. Within an hour of the King leaving Whiteladies, parliamentary troops arrived, seeking information about the King or his troops, and were told that a party of horsemen, possibly including the King, had passed the house three hours earlier. They left at once in pursuit. Rain fell while Charles and Richard remained in the wood, and Charles later recollected that they were without food and drink, although another account says "a Mess of Milk, Eggs and Sugar in a black earthen cup" was brought by Margaret, the wife of Francis Yate or Yates of Langley Lawn, [brother-in-law of the Penderels, and not the Francis Yates who guided the King to Whiteladies from Worcester], who also provided a blanket which Charles threw over his shoulders. Charles exchanged his wood-bill for Francis Yates' lighter broom-hook, and was coached by Richard during the day in the distinctive countryman's way of speech and walking. At about 5 pm Charles and Richard left the wood and apparently visited Richard's house, Hubbal Grange,[285] but it is unclear whether Charles actually entered the house. Charles' own narrative, probably not entirely reliable in view of the years that had passed, states that he was given bread and cheese at one of the Penderel's houses, but he did not go in. Other versions relate that Charles entered and met 'Old Goodwife Penderel', otherwise 'Dame Joan', Richard's mother;[286] was given a meal; sat Nan, Richard's young daughter, on his knee; and left for Wales with Richard, having improved his disguise and chosen the alias William Jones should they be questioned. The intention was to walk to a house owned by a Mr Wolfe at Madeley, some nine miles west of Boscobel, near the river Severn. Wolfe was a Catholic, and Richard knew that his house contained hiding places.[287]

As Charles and Richard Penderel crossed the bridge at Evelith Mill, some three miles from their destination, at about 9 pm, they were challenged by the miller and forced to flee down a muddy lane and hide behind a hedge. There was a new moon on 5th September and there would have been almost no moonlight that night and for several nights afterwards.[288] Charles is said to have been guided by the sound of Richard Penderel's leather breeches.

Reaching Madeley in the early hours of Friday, 5th September, Charles learned at Wolfe's house that the Severn crossings were being carefully watched by parliamentary forces. Wolfe's house had already been searched by troops seeking escaping royalists, and the hiding places discovered. The house was no longer a safe refuge, and Charles was obliged to spend the rest of the day hiding in a barn at Madeley, where Mrs Wolfe is said to have stained his hands and face with walnut juice "of a reeky [smokey] colour." Since it appeared to be impossible to cross the Severn undetected, he decided to return that night to Boscobel, where he hoped to hear news of Lord Wilmot and perhaps try again to reach London. Meanwhile, Wilmot had moved from Moseley to Bentley Hall, the home of Colonel John Lane, formerly of The Hyde.

Returning from Madeley – possibly guided by Mr Wolfe's maid for the first mile or so – Charles and Richard made a detour and forded the stream near Evelith Mill to avoid disturbing the miller, reaching Boscobel in a state of some exhaustion in the early hours of Saturday, 6th September.

Richard cautiously approached the house alone to ensure that it was safe, and found that Colonel William Carless,[289] a royalist officer who had fought at Worcester and is said to have seen the last man killed there, was taking refuge, having spent the previous two days at the house of David Jones of Tong Heath, and been taken to Boscobel by Elizabeth Burgesse.[290] Carless is said to have been born at Broom Hall and was known to the Penderels. Richard and Carless left the house and escorted Charles back from the wood where he had been waiting. Charles was given bread and cheese and 'a Posset of thin milk and small beer', and William Penderel's wife removed his stockings and treated his blistered feet.

At 9 am Charles and Carless left the house and sought refuge in the branches of a large pollarded oak tree in the woods 150 yards to the south. Charles described the tree as "a greate Oake that had been Lop't some 3 or 4 Yeares before, and being growne out again very Bushy and Thick, could nott be seene through". Carless had seemingly hidden in the tree previously, and William Penderel's ladder was used to gain access to the upper branches.

William passed up two pillows for their comfort, and during the day Charles and Carless ate bread and cheese and drank 'small beer' which had been provided by Joane, William Penderel's wife. Both William and Joane stayed nearby on the pretext of gathering wood. Charles in his account says that whilst in the tree, he and Carless could "see soldiers going up and downe in the thickest of the Wood, searching for persons escaped, we seeing them now and again peeping out of the Woods". The two of them remained hidden in the tree for the rest of the day, and Charles, having had very little sleep since his flight from Worcester, slept part of the time with his head in Carless's lap. Their stay in the tree must have been particularly uncomfortable, and on their return to the house at dusk, Charles is said to have declared that he would risk remaining at the house rather than endure the discomfort, albeit with increased safety, in the tree.

While Charles and Carless were hiding in the oak, the Penderel brothers had kept watch and attempted to go about their usual business so that no suspicion fell on them and so that they could pick up the latest information as to the situation in the neighbourhood. Humphrey Penderel, the fifth brother, visited Shifnal, some four miles away, to pay 20s militia tax to Captain Broadway[291] of the commonwealth army, and overheard soldiers discussing the search at Whiteladies. Humphrey, recognised as living nearby, was detained and questioned and is said to have been told that a reward of £1,000 had been offered for information leading to the capture of the King. He revealed nothing and was released.[292] At the same time John Penderel, who had left Whiteladies on Thursday with Lord Wilmot, returned from Mr Huntbach's house at Brinsford where he had left Wilmot. Richard Penderel had ridden to Wolverhampton to buy provisions and speak to Mr George Mainwaring, who was known to Colonel Carless, to discuss the possibility of hiding two royalists. Mainwaring, who, like Carless, had been a royalist governor of Tong Castle during the Civil War,[293] promised to talk to Mr Whitgreave of Moseley.

Charles' own account is silent about events after leaving the safety of the oak and becomes, perhaps not surprisingly, a little confused, suggesting that he left for Moseley on Saturday evening, but from other evidence it seems that Charles expressed a wish to eat mutton, and Colonel Carless left the house and returned with a sheep, [the property of a tenant, William Staunton or Stanton of Hatton, who subsequently refused payment], which was killed. Charles helped to fry mutton collops in the kitchen. [Some versions say that this incident took place the following day]. That night, Charles slept on "a little pallet . . . put in the secret place", with the Penderel brothers standing watch. Charles rose early on the Sunday, and spent some time in meditation and prayers. The rest of the day he spent in or near the house and part of it in a "pretty Arbor in Boscobel garden, which grew upon a Mount and wherein there was a Stone Table and Seats about it". The only alarm was caused when Charles suffered a violent nose-bleed, but he explained that they occurred quite frequently, and were a matter of no concern. It is possible that the various accounts have played down Charles' despair at his situation at this time, but it is likely that he was in a state of physical and mental exhaustion, having slept but little since Worcester, knowing that he was in the hands of strangers and that capture would mean almost certain death.

John Penderel left to go to Moseley to seek the help of Lord Wilmot, presumably because Charles was unable to decide on his next move, but when Penderel arrived at Moseley, Wilmot had left for Bentley Hall, some five miles away. Penderel told Whitgreave and father Huddlestone, a Catholic priest who lived at Moseley, that Charles was "much dejected, having no hopes or prospect of redress".

Penderel was taken by Whitgreave and Huddlestone to Bentley. The house was owned by Colonel Lane [formerly of The Hyde], and Lord Wilmot had intended to travel to Bristol with the Colonel's sister, Mistress Jane Lane, who had a pass to travel with a servant. The plans were now changed, and Wilmot returned to Moseley to await the arrival of Charles.

Late on the Sunday evening, 7th September, four days after his defeat at Worcester, Charles took his leave of Carless and left Boscobel for the last time, accompanied by the five Penderel brothers and [according to some accounts] their brother-in-law Francis Yates. It was decided that Charles should ride most of the way to Moseley, explained in the later accounts by the fact that his feet were still bruised from the walk to and from Madeley, to the extent that rolls of paper had been placed between his toes to reduce the discomfort, but it is likely that Charles was so emotionally exhausted that he was incapable of walking. A horse could not be found; John Penderel went to borrow Mr Stanton's, but it had been lent out elsewhere, and he therefore decided to use the old mill horse from his brother Humphrey's mill at Whiteladies.

The horse was fetched and fitted with a worn saddle, and with Humphrey Penderel leading it by the bridle, the party started its journey, the Penderels armed with staves and possibly pistols.[294] There is no doubt that a great risk was taken, for several men and an old horse would have raised suspicion and been easy to intercept. Travelling on foot would have been far safer. Shortly after they left, commonwealth troops arrived and searched Boscobel and Whiteladies, but found nothing suspicious and left.

It is not known what route Charles and his party took from Boscobel, but local tradition, unsupported by evidence, says that they called at

Grange Farm, at Coven, and passed along Cow Lane, which ran eastwards on the north side of the farm.

In 1660, the year of the Restoration, several tracts relating the story of the King's escape were published. One in particular, "An Exact Narrative and Relation of his Most Sacred Majesties Escape from Worcester on the third of September 1651. Till his Arrivall at Paris", by Thomas Blount, concentrated almost exclusively on the first week of Charles' flight and his stay at Whiteladies and Boscobel, and from the dialect used and the local knowledge of people and places, it is likely that it was based on local enquiries and interviews with those involved, including the Penderels. In the narrative are some clues to the route which may have been taken by Charles from Boscobel to Moseley, a subject that seems to have received little previous research.

When Lord Wilmot, seemingly undisguised,[295] was taken by John Penderel to Brinsford, en route to Moseley, it appears that they used a lane, now a farm track to the Whitemoor,[296] past Hungry Hill, occupied by John Shores, and continued to a property occupied by John Climpson. The location of that property is uncertain, but a Chillington estate map of about 1727 shows fields near Whitemoor then occupied by John Clemson, who may have been a descendant of John Climpson, names being spelt variously at that time. [The Chillington Catholic registers record William Clemson of Hungry Hill the same year]. Wilmot and Penderel then seem to have continued along the track, following a line now marked by the edge of Wyrley Lane Plantation and Horse Paddock Wood, which led along field boundaries in an easterly curve to the south of The Hyde [then occupied by Mr Reynolds] to join Chillington Street south of Ackbury Heath. From there they crossed to Park Lane, which at that time turned east at the northern end into what is now the Coven road, which did not then lead west to Brewood. Passing Brewood Forge, they are said to have been chased by the 'Brewood forgemen', who were by tradition strongly anti-royalist. The chase was apparently abandoned after one Richard Dalton indicated that it was 'Colonel Crompton' [a staunch parliamentarian and Member of Parliament on three occasions between 1614 and 1629] they were pursuing. At Coven they spotted a party of horsemen, which forced them to hide in a dry pit, and then moved on towards the house of John Huntbach at Brinsford. It seems that John Penderel left Wilmot in the care of William Walker of Covenbrook,[297] a poor and elderly neighbour of Thomas Whitgreave and a former priest who held occasional services for Catholics in the Whiteladies area, and sheltered the horses in John Evans barn, before continuing to Huntbach's house and Moseley.

For Charles and the Penderel brothers, the obvious route from Boscobel to Moseley would have been south via Langley Lawn, at that time a trackway through the woods, and east from Codsall Wood, along the lane past the Leper House and on through Gunstone to Hatton. That route had the disadvantage that it passed close to the parliamentary troops quartered at Codsall. [Some writers have suggested that Brick-Kiln Lane, which adjoins the north side of Chillington Park, may have been used. This is unlikely, since it does not appear to pre-date the eighteenth century.] Alternatively it is possible that the Penderels escorted Charles along the same route as that taken by Wilmot, but turned south-east around the southern side of Brewood Park, the palings of which had been repaired two years earlier by Peter Giffard, and skirted north of Long Birch and The Hattons. That route would have taken them close to Chillington House – probably still ruinous from the Civil War – and Long Birch, both Catholic houses, and it is not inconceivable that one or both contained secret refuges designed to conceal Catholic priests or others escaping religious persecution.[298] The Penderels might have thought it safer to take a route that was never far from a sympathetic house in case it was necessary to seek refuge from parliamentary patrols. On the other hand, the sympathies of the two houses would have been known to the authorities, and there would have been obvious dangers in attempting to conceal the King at either house – although the same risk had attached to both Whiteladies and Boscobel. Blount's account simply indicates that muddy byways between Boscobel and Moseley were used by the party for security, which may mean that minor footpaths were chosen for the journey, although it is probable that most lanes in the area were no more than muddy byways.

By whatever route, the party soon reached Pendeford Mill, possibly the mill long since vanished but then on the east bank of the Penk directly east of The Old Hattons, or, perhaps more likely, Old Mill Farm at Coven Heath, and not to be confused with the later mill further south near Pendeford Hall.[299]

On reaching the Mill, Charles dismounted and continued his journey to Moseley on foot across Coven Heath, arriving in the early hours of 8th September. At Moseley, Charles, having called back the Penderels to thank them for their assistance – "My troubles make me forget myself; I thank you all" – was greeted in the darkness by Whitgreave and Huddlestone. Lord Wilmot was waiting inside the house.

Mr Iune Lane and King

The King was taken to the fireside where his sore feet were bathed and food and clean clothing brought. Then Charles slept for the first time since Worcester in a proper bed. For the rest of the day Charles rested, while three pupils of Father Huddlestone, the resident priest, kept watch, and horses were brought from Bentley Hall.[300]

On the following day, Tuesday 9th September, Charles was forced to hide in the secret chamber when troops, including

130

'Southall the Priest Catcher', arrived looking for him, but they eventually left without searching the house. Charles left Moseley late in the evening, disguised as 'William Jackson', a serving man to Jane Lane of Bentley Hall.

On the same Tuesday, a party of parliamentary troops from Cheshire descended on Whiteladies and surrounded the house. George Giffard was interrogated, but refused to admit that the King had stayed at the house, although he said a party of royalists had called briefly the previous Wednesday. It appears that information had been extracted from captives at Bunbury, perhaps from the ill-fated Francis Yates, but George Penderel's story was accepted by the parliamentary soldiers, although it is said that they caused great damage to the house, ripping out panelling in their search for the King and engaging in wanton vandalism when their search revealed nothing.

The escape route of Charles II after the battle of Worcester. Charles' flight began on 3rd September 1651, and he reached France on 16th October.

On Wednesday, 10th September, Wilmot, who had been at Bentley since the previous Friday, left to lodge with Sir Clement Fisher at Packington Hall, the King having left at dawn riding before Jane Lane as her servant with Mary Petre [Jane Lane's sister, sometimes referred to as Withy Petre, the result of a misreading of a manuscript of John Huntbach by Stebbing Shaw, where the abbreviation Willm was mistaken for Withy, an error repeated by many later historians] and her husband, and a royalist officer named Henry Lascalles. During the journey to Long Marston, where they stayed with John Tomes, the party rode through a troop of parliamentary cavalry near Stratford-on-Avon, after which the Petre's took their leave. The following day's journey took the King to Cirencester, via Chipping Campden, and on Friday 12th September the party travelled through Sodbury and Bristol to George North's house at Abbots Leigh, where they stayed for three days, trying unsuccessfully to find a ship to give them passage from Bristol. On Tuesday 16th September the King, Jane Lane and Lascalles travelled to Castle Cary en route to Colonel Francis Wyndham's house at Trent, where they arrived on the evening of the following day, to be greeted by Wyndham and Wilmot. During the next few days attempts were made without success to arrange a ship from Weymouth, Lyme or some other local port. On Monday 22nd September the King rode with Juliana Coningsby and others, pretending to be a runaway marriage party, to Charmouth, where they stayed at an inn, waiting for Captain Limbry to take them to a boat at Lyme. Limbry having failed to show up [for reasons which remain unclear], the party moved to Bridport the following day, where a suspicious ostler caused them to flee and escape pursuers by taking a side road to Broad Windsor, where they lodged at an inn accomodating 40 soldiers. On Wednesday 24th September the royal party returned to Trent, and further attempts were made to find a vessel from some port in Hampshire or Sussex. Several royalists were enlisted to help, and a Colonel Gounter in Sussex was approached.

The Kings escape m the Sea Adventure

On Monday 6th October the King's party was guided to Heale House, near Salisbury, and the following day the King visited Stonehenge, returning that evening to Heale House. The same day Wilmot visited Colonel Gounter, who tried unsuccessfully on the Wednesday to find a boat at Emsworth. The next few days were spent in a luckless search for a vessel. A French merchant, Francis Mancell, was then approached by Gounter, and he arranged for Captain Tattersall to take the King and Wilmot from Shoreham to a Normandy port. The King left Heale House on Monday 13th October, and was taken to the house of Thomas Symonds, Gounter's brother-in-law, at Hambledon. The next day the royal party rode to Brighelmstone [Brighton] by way of Howton, Bramber and Beeding, and stayed overnight at the George Inn. At two o'clock in the morning of Wednesday 15th October, the King and Wilmot were taken by Gounter to Shoreham, and at eight o'clock boarded the brig 'Surprise', which first sailed towards the Isle of Wight to throw off suspicion, and then turned south. After a scare from a sloop which turned out to be French, the boat reached Fécamp at mid-morning on the following day, Thursday 16th October.

After landing in France Charles and Wilmot had difficulty in hiring horses, doubtless due to their unkempt appearance, and it was not until the following day that they obtained horses and rode to Rouen, where they were put up at an inn only after an English Merchant had vouched for them. Dr Earle, the King's old tutor and chaplain, was the first to visit the inn to see the King, but failed at first to recognise his old pupil. A coach was hired and Charles and Wilmot entered Paris late in the evening to 20th October, having been met on the outskirts of the city by a welcoming party including Charles' mother Queen Henrietta Maria and his brother James, Duke of York.

Meanwhile in England rumours of the King's whereabouts since the battle of Worcester abounded. The Council of State had concluded on 13th October that "there are strong probabilities that Charles Stuart and the Duke of Buckingham were in or about Staffordshire some days after the victory at Worcester, and probably they may still be in those parts under disguise," and issued a warrant authorising Captain John Ley to search for them and deliver them to the Governor of Stafford or any other Justice of the Peace.

On 22nd October a newspaper, 'The Scout', quoted a report that the King had arrived in Holland, but felt it more likely that he had sailed from the Thames to France or Flanders on 14th October. On 28th October the 'Weekly Intelligencer' retracted its earlier claim that Charles had landed in Holland, and on the following day 'A Perfect Account' reported that a ship bound for Holland had recently been lost with all hands, and might have had Charles on board. A pamphlet published at about the same time giving the text of the Earl of Derby's speech from the scaffold on 15th October suggested that Charles, disguised as a seaman, had taken a boat to the Hague from Gravesend on 4th October.

News of the King's escape to France reached England on 30th October. Many different versions had been published towards the end of October, the most widely accepted based on a dispatch from Paris dated 23rd October. The story, briefly, was that on the day following the battle of Worcester, Charles, accompanied by Wilmot and the Duke of Buckingham, visited an isolated house in Cheshire for food, and travelled to the Lancashire border where they hid in a hollow tree. They walked all that night, and hid in a wood the following day. On 6th September they were told by a shepherd of a lady who would help them, and that lady took them, disguised as servants, to Bristol, from where they left for London, arriving about 20th September.

The escape of Charles II is particularly remarkable when it is remembered that he was well above average height, and a very substantial reward of one thousand pounds – more than the average workman would earn in a lifetime – had been offered for information leading to his capture. Many people, some very poor, were involved in the King's escape, but not one is known to have revealed information to the commonwealth authorities, even knowing of the likely fate awaiting those rendering assistance to Charles, as shown by the summary punishment which befell Lord Derby, who escorted the King to Whiteladies and was later captured and executed at Bolton on 16th October, and Francis Yates of Langley Lawn[301] who accompanied the King on his journey from Worcester to Whiteladies, and was later apprehended and hanged at Oxford. Sir Roger L'Estrange published in 'The Royal Observator' in 1681-5 a "List of persons who were instrumental in preserving the life of King Charles II, prior to his arrival at Bentley Hall, the seat of the Lanes". There are 49 names given in the list, and in Thomas Blount's 'Boscobel', published in 1660, 23 men and women who assisted Charles in his flight at Whiteladies, Madeley, Boscobel, Moseley and Bentley are identified.

The story of Charles' escape as recounted by Blount is generally accepted as the most reliable account, but contains only the first part of the story, that is until Charles reached Bentley Hall. In August 1660 Charles endorsed the book and urged all those involved in the escape to provide information to Blount. But in 1662, for reasons which remain unclear, Charles denounced the book as having "divers errors and mistakes . . . and not . . . a true and perfect narrative." To compound the volte face, Blount himself, a royalist Roman Catholic lawyer and legal writer, denied that he was the author of the book,[302] a puzzle that has never been satisfactorily explained. It is also of interest that when Charles related the story of his escape to Samuel Pepys – admittedly in very abbreviated form – on the boat carrying him back to England in 1660, he made no mention of hiding in a tree, an incident he might have been expected to remember well, although the despatch from Paris on 23rd October contains many similarities to the generally accepted version of the escape, including a reference to Charles hiding in a hollow tree. It was not until 1680, nearly 30 years after the event, during which time he would inevitably have become aware of the various printed versions of his escape, that Charles dictated a detailed account to Pepys, and first mentions the Boscobel Oak. It would be a courageous historian, however, who chose to cast doubt on the historical veracity of an established part of English folklore and one of the most dramatic episodes of English history.

Nine and a half years after his arrival in France, Charles II returned to England at the wish of the people on his thirtieth birthday, 29th May

1660 – thereafter known as Oak Apple Day. At the Restoration, Charles remembered those who had assisted him in his hour of peril, and is known to have intended an Order of Knighthood as a reward to those who had been instrumental in his escape. Recipients were to be called Knights of the Royal Oak, and entitled to wear a ribbon with a silver medallion depicting Charles in the Boscobel Oak, but the King was advised that the idea should be abandoned 'lest it might open those wounds afresh, which at that time were thought most prudent to be healed'. The fact that Charles proposed to levy a substantial 'membership fee' on those joining the order may also have influenced Charles' advisers. The names of the thirteen intended knights, with the income from their estates, included:

Walter Giffard	£1500	0	0
Colonel John Lane	£700	0	0
Thomas Whitgreave	£600	0	0

The name of Walter Giffard, Charles Giffard's younger brother, is of particular interest, for he is scarcely mentioned in the various versions of the escape. It seems possible that for whatever reason, the complete story of the escape remains untold, perhaps not entirely surprisingly, for after the troubled years of the Civil War, many people may have wondered how long the peace would last. As late as 1683 a group of Cromwell's old supporters attempted to assassinate the King on his way to the races at Newmarket. If the monarchy were to be toppled again, those who had assisted Charles might have reason to fear retribution, and the illiteracy of Francis Yates and the Penderel brothers may not be the only reason why we do not have their first hand accounts of the escape.

Charles intended on his return to England to include Boscobel, Moseley and Worcester in his first tour of the kingdom, but it became necessary to cancel the trip, and the King never returned to the local houses.

For their loyalty the Penderel brothers, Charles Giffard, Huddleston, Carless and Whitgreave were granted the privilege of exemption from the Test Act and other measures against recusants, and the immunity was extended to their descendants by George I and George II. On 6th April 1716 a Deed of Protection was given by George I to the descendants of those families who were instrumental in the escape. The Deed followed a petition by 33 individuals, including 8 Penderels and 3 Giffards, claiming that their ancestors were exempted from penalties for being papists, but that the matter had not been formalised and provided that "If any one of them should be prosecuted on account of their being Papists, they should be at liberty to apply to his Majestye for his further directions thereon, whereof all persons whomsoever it may concern are to take notice of this work of his majestye's royal favour in regard to the fidelity and services of the said familys of the crown".

Charles Giffard lived to enjoy a very eventful life. After his capture by parliamentary troops he managed to escape from the inn at Bunbury and eventually made his way to Holland. Six years later he is known to have been a prisoner in Shrewsbury Castle on trial for assisting in Charles' escape, but somehow came through unscathed. He petitioned Charles repeatedly for a pension after the Restoration, was involved in a variety of unsuccessful ventures, imprisoned several times for debt, was eventually granted a pension by the King, took a sinecure appointment which he later gave up, and probably died in or soon after 1691.

The Grant of Arms awarded by Charles II to Colonel Carless.

Colonel Carless eventually escaped to France after leaving Boscobel,[303] and at the Restoration was taken into the King's service, given a grant of wine, one-third of the London straw-tax, and a coat-of-arms.[304] He died in 1689 in London, and was buried on 28th May in Brewood churchyard, where he now lies to the north-east of the church in an unmarked grave. His burial is recorded in the parish registers: "Corinall William Carelesse, of Broumhall".

Under Letters Patent dated 24th July 1675, various rents were settled by Charles II on Sir Walter Wrottesley, Richard Congreve and John Giffard as trustees to pay Richard Penderel and William Penderel and their heirs for ever £100 each per annum; to Humphrey, John[305] and George Penderel and their heirs for ever 100 marks per annum jointly; and to Elizabeth Yates and her heirs £50 per annum. Francis Yates died in 1660, his will having been witnessed by Richard Penderel and Edward Martin, and left goods valued at over £69. In 1686, James II granted an annuity of £100 per annum to Nicholas Yates, only child of Francis and Margaret Yates of 'Long Lawn', near Boscobel, deceased, as reward for assistance given to the late King by the said Francis and Margaret.

Richard Penderel died in 1671 and was buried in the churchyard of St Giles-in-the-Fields, where his monument may still be seen. John lived at Beamish Hall, Albrighton, after the Restoration, and died in 1680; Humphrey is said to have died in 1687 or 1688 and been buried at Bloxwich,[306] but was in fact still drawing a pension in 1692, and William continued to live at Boscobel until his death in 1700. It appears that most of the Penderel brothers died in comparative wealth, bequeathing in some cases lands to their families, mainly in Kiddemore Green. Jane Lane made her way to France with her brother in December 1651, both disguised as peasants, and became a member of the court in exile. After the Restoration she was granted a pension of £1000 and married Sir Clement Fisher. She died in 1689.

Two entries in the parish records show the considerable local affection for

Charles II. In 1663 the Churchwardens' Accounts contain the entry: "To ye ringer on May ye 29th for ringing in honour of his blessed majesty's most gracious restoration . . . 3s", and a quaint but touching entry in the registers, presumably made by the Vicar, William Emery, dated 6th February 1684, reads: "King Charles the Second died aboute a Leaven of the clock in the foure noone, in the yeare 1684." These are the only references to a monarch in the registers – even the visit of Queen Elizabeth I to the parish in 1575 went unrecorded.

18. The Giffards

The Giffards of Chillington[307] – the name is pronounced with a soft G – are descended from Osborn de Bolebec, Seigneur or Lord of Longueville in Normandy, whose eldest son, Walter Giffard, Compte de Longueville-sur-Scie, came over with William the Conqueror[308] and was rewarded with over one hundred English manors. During Norman and Plantagenet times many members of the family held high office in church and state. Walter Giffard himself[309] was Justiciar of England, Earl of Buckingham, and one of the King's commissioners who took evidence used in the compilation of Domesday Book. His younger son, William, was Bishop of Winchester and Chancellor under the first three Norman Kings.

Walter Giffard the elder had two younger brothers, and it is probable that the Giffards of Chillington are descended from Berenger, one of the brothers, who was granted the barony of Fonthill in Wiltshire. A later Walter Giffard, younger brother of the third Lord Fonthill and grandson of Berenger, in 1166 held from Godfrey de Scudamore one knight's fee in Wiltshire. The arms of three stirrups and leathers born by the Giffards of Chillington were the arms of the Scudamores and may have been derived from them.[310] Although the precise relationship is uncertain, Walter Giffard of Fonthill was either a brother or father of Peter Giffard, the first of the family to own Chillington.

In Domesday Book, Cillentone [Chillington] is shown as held by William Fitz Corbucion, and it was his grandson, Peter Corbeson of Studley, who granted Chillington to Peter Giffard, the nephew of his wife, for 25 marks and a metal charger. The deed, which still exists, is undated, but is about 1178. This same Giffard accompanied Richard fitz Gilbert, Earl of Clare, popularly known as Strongbow, in his Irish campaign of 1172, and was rewarded with estates including Tachmelin. Little is known about the early Giffards of Chillington, but Peter Giffard the third is known to have seen service in Wales, and his successor, William, was loyal to the King during Simon de Montfort's rebellion in 1264-5, and was temporarily dispossessed of Chillington when the barons were in control of Staffordshire. The estate was during this period held by Robert Chenney, a Shropshire knight. John Giffard was next to head the house. Trained in the law, he became embroiled in various legal battles against claimants for parts of the Giffard estates. His main opponent was the Bishop of Lichfield, but all claims were successfully defended. The second Sir John Giffard also remained loyal to the crown. When the barons, including most of the other branches of the Giffards, took up arms against the Dispensers, he remained loyal to Edward II, fighting for the King in Scotland, and was one of the Commissioners of Array for Staffordshire.

Later in the fourteenth century Sir Edmund Giffard served in France in the retinue of Ralph, Earl of Stafford. Edmund's successor, John Giffard the fourth, defended attempts by Sir Adam de Peshall to claim Whiston manor, acquired in 1379. The dispute reached the assizes, and was resolved by Giffard exchanging the manor for land and rents in Stretton.

The first Thomas Giffard was Sheriff of Staffordshire in 1409 and accompanied Henry V during the invasion of France, but was apparently forced by illness to return to England.

Robert Giffard succeeded in 1420, and in old age married his second wife, Cassandra, who bore him a son and heir who was about 20 years old when his father died in 1486, leaving all his estate settled on his young wife. As she lived until 1537, the son, John Giffard, was over 70 before he succeeded to Chillington.

Sir John Giffard prospered under Henry VIII, holding a succession of offices in the King's household and serving as Sheriff of Staffordshire five times. He was appointed Ranger of the Seven Hays of the Forest of Cank, accompanied the King in his military expedition to France in 1513, and was also present at the Field of the Cloth of Gold seven years later. In 1514 he arranged the marriage of his son Thomas to the daughter of Sir John Montgomery, who held considerable estates in Derbyshire, and he himself married Sir John's widow, his first wife having died at an early age. From the considerable wealth secured by these marriages, the Giffards purchased several of the dissolved monastic properties in Derbyshire, Shropshire and Staffordshire, including Whiteladies and Blackladies, where younger branches of the family subsequently lived. Sir John died in 1556 at the age of 90, having fathered no less than 18 children, and his son, who had 17 children, was Sheriff of Staffordshire in 1530 and 1554 and represented the county in parliament in 1553-5, died four years later, leaving his son, another John Giffard, in succession.

John Giffard, who had 14 children, served as Sheriff of the county in 1573, but subsequently suffered considerably for his Catholic beliefs. The start of his downfall seems to have been the brief visit to Chillington by Queen Elizabeth I in 1575. Thereafter he suffered various periods of imprisonment before the threat of a Spanish invasion at the time of the Armada united the country, and he took the oath of allegiance, although even then his estates were not returned to him and he continued to be penalised.

Little is known about his son and successor, Walter, but he too was a devout Catholic. A younger brother, Gilbert, achieved everlasting notoriety as a Jesuit priest who was also a double agent, betraying his Jesuit friends and Mary, Queen of Scots. After involvement in the Babington conspiracy, he fled to France and died miserably in a French prison.

During the Civil War, Peter Giffard, Walter's son, fortified and garrisoned the Tudor house and, at the age of 61, rode with his sons to join the King's army at Nottingham. Chillington House was soon captured, changed hands several times, and Peter Giffard spent most of the war as a prisoner at Stafford and Eccleshall. He took up arms again for the King in 1648, and his lands were forfeited as a result, but he lived on to see most of them restored. All his sons had fought for the King and one of his brothers, Andrew, had been killed in a skirmish near Wolverhampton. His youngest son, Charles Giffard, was instrumental in the escape of Charles II after the battle of Worcester, conducting the King first to Whiteladies and then to Boscobel, both Giffard properties.

After the restoration of Charles II, permanent pensions were granted to those who had assisted in the escape of the King, and Peter's grandson, John, was appointed one of the three Trustees in the Letters Patent dated 24th July 1675 recording the pensions.

Three generations of Giffards succeeded Peter the royalist, but on the death in 1718 of Thomas Giffard, his great-grandson, without a male heir, the estate passed to a second cousin, Peter Giffard of Blackladies, descended from a younger son of Peter the royalist. Chillington passed to his son and grandson, both named Thomas. The remodelling of the estate was carried out by Thomas Giffard the elder in the early 1770's, but the building of a new house was interrupted for ten years when he died in 1776 aged 41, his son Thomas being only 12. After a spirited life as a young man, Thomas the younger married in 1788 and under the steadying influence of his wife, Charlotte, completed the rebuilding of Chillington Hall to designs by Sir John Soane. Thomas was succeeded in 1823 by his son, Thomas William, who had seven sons and five daughters. The fifth daughter became the second wife of the notorious 'Mad Jack' Mytton,[311] some of whose eccentric exploits are said to have taken place at Chillington. Thomas William's brother, Walter Peter, succeeded to the estate in 1861, the first non-Catholic Giffard at Chillington for many generations. The present owner, whose father Thomas succeeded to the estate in 1926, maintains in his names – Peter Richard de Longueville Giffard – a direct link with his ancester Peter Giffard, from whom the estate has passed in continuous descent in the male line for over 800 years, and the Compte de Longueville, who came over with William the Conqueror over 900 years ago.

19. The Manors

The word 'manor' signifies an area or estate over which a feudal lord exercised a series of rights, privileges and jurisdictions in relation to other inhabitants, and was the basic unit of land management in rural Britain until at least the eighteenth century. Within the manor would usually be some ancient demesne, which might became the lord's freehold; land attached to the manor but not demesne, which would become copyland; and land occupied by freeholders. The lord of the manor's demesne land was cultivated by peasant farmers who also worked their own plots, held from the lord in return both for labour on his land and other services or money payments. The peasants or serfs – of which there were several classes – were not free to leave the lord's land, and although some were little more than slaves and could be bought and sold, the lord was in theory not entitled to kill or maim them. In practice, however, all peasants were at the mercy of the lord.

From the twelfth century onwards many labour services were commuted into money payments as rents. The Black Death in 1348-49, which saw shortages of labour, high wages and low rents, meant that restrictions on the movement of serfs became unrealistic and unenforceable. Landlords subsequently attempted to reimpose labour service, but discontent culminated in the Peasants Revolt in 1381. Although the rising was suppressed, serfdom disappeared for largely economic reasons in the fifteenth century, replaced by yeoman farmers, who worked their own land, and wage labourers. In most places the manor died away during the agricultural revolution, and the manorial courts decayed, their powers transferred to the royal courts, although they retained limited powers until 1925.

The privileges of lordship included fines for manorial offences, including trespass by animals, failure to attend the manorial court, and breach of the assize of ale. Between 2s and 4s was charged for marriages within the manor and more for marriages outside, with up to 5s payable to leave the manor. Some 4% of the income of the Bishop of Lichfield was made up of tax from unfree tenants and payments for the right to feed swine on the lord's land.[312] The payment of 'heriot', a charge made on the death of a tenant, was a particularly heavy burden on the dead man's family.

The early manors within Brewood parish were those of Brewood, Aspley, Broom Hall, Chillington, Coven, Engleton, Gunstone, Hatton, Hyde, Somerford, and Deanery Manor.

The lordship of the manor of Brewood was held by the church of Lichfield from a very early date, and certainly from before the Conquest. In 1086 it was held by the Bishop as five hides, and the area was increased in about

1155 when Henry II granted the Bishop 80 acres of assarted land at Brewood, taken after 1135 from the royal Forest. In 1285 the manor was assessed in Pope Nicholas's Taxation at £38 4s, and included court income of 15s, with the same amount from view of frankpledge. The Bishop also received from the auxiliary vills, or outlying hamlets, 30s yearly, and there were two mills worth 60s annually. In 1293 the Bishop was also claiming 'infangtheof', the right to hang thieves found with the goods on them – it meant in fact the right to have a private gallows, and the chattels of the hanged thief – and 'waif', the right to straying animals or abandoned goods in the manor. A survey of the manor in 1361 recorded that 29 'customary natives' ploughed for the lord three days a year or paid 3d each day in lieu. The same tenants paid 1d each on the Feast of St Mark for a custom called Carriage of Salt. Another customary payment of frithsilver, literally 'peace-money', was payable on the same feastday, and a custom called Take of Pigs at the Feast of St Martin. A tallage called stuck, or stoc, possibly a form of market or irrigation tax, was also recorded, payable by tenants of the irrigated land. A fixed payment of 10s 4d for frithsilver, was made in 1473. At the same date, each brewer in Brewood and Horsebrook was paying 1d for toll of ale.[313] In the valuation of the Bishop's estates in 1534, Brewood manor and court was listed with a net worth of £58 2s 11d.

Although the Bishop's park was surveyed in 1647, the boundaries of the manor could not be identified, since the Giffard family had enjoyed 'unity of possession' of the manor of Chillington and other land in Chillington, Brewood, Hatton and Broom Hall 'many ages', and the Bishop's land could not be distinguished. We have no information as to the precise location of the manor house, but traditionally it stood on the south-west of Market Place, near what is now Church Road, with the manor barn said to have been on the north side of Bargate Street between Dawscroft and Bargate Lane.

At a view of frankpledge and courts leet and baron held on 9th March 1723, a jury of twelve named 'homagers' of Brewood held that

> . . . the said Mannor of Brewood is bounded in some places with the lands of . . . Peter Giffard Called Hattons then next on one Side with his lands belonging to the Lordship of Gunston, and afterwards with the Lordship of Chillington . . . and that certain Lands Called Langley Lawn and a Lane leading down towards [?]unnington Grounds Ranshaw or Ravenshaw Wood Ferney Fields, the old coppice adjoining to Boskabell are parcel of the said of the said Mannor of Chillington and that Certain Grounds adjoining to the said old Coppice are called Peirce Hay or Priests Hay which are part of the Mannor of Brewood and are holden of the same and thence the said Manor includes Bishop's Wood, and that the said Mannor of Brewood from thence reaches along the Mear Lane and thence passing on the further Side of Charter's Mires leaving the same on the Right hand to the Gate at Nunmore and going between Nunmore and Ivitsea Land

(lying in Blimhill parish) downwards to a certain place called Stinking Lake and from thence along the Road Called Wattling Street to Hawbrooke's Well and up the Marsh to a Rivulett called Marsh Brook and from thence up Part of the little Moor to or overagainst a Gate in Water Eaton Ground, and from thence to a Parcel of Ground called Brewood Fields, thence to the outside of Muchall's Rough, and to the Roadway leading from Somerford towards Calf Heath, and taking in Chandler's Land adjoining to Hag Hay and from thence to the River and down the same to Stantiford Bridge and thence down the Water Course to the Kemble including the same and on that Side of the River to Lows Bridge and from thence to the said Lands called Hatton's where they began to mention the boundary. . .[314]

The manor remained with the Bishop of Lichfield until 1853, when it passed with the park to the Giffard family, who still own such rights as survive.

The name Aspley, in Coven, means 'the wood with aspen trees'. It was a manor by 1507, the overlordship held by Simon Harcourt and the manor by Thomas Ellyngbrigg. The manor house was what is now Aspley farmhouse, which was formerly moated on three sides. Just over the parish boundary to the north-east of Lower Laches Farm is another moated site, which seems destined to be obliterated by the Western Orbital Motorway.

Brinsford – 'the ford of Brun' – partly in Brewood [since the boundary reorganisation of 1934] and partly in Featherstone, may have been an early manor, and was held in the early thirteenth century by Bertram de Burgo. By the eighteenth century it seems to have been joined with Coven, held by Thomas Lane of Bentley, later passing to the Monckton family.

Broom Hall,[315] meaning 'the hollow where brushwood grew', was probably part of the Bishop's manor of Brewood, and is recorded as Bromhale in about 1150. In about 1151 Walter Durdant, Bishop of Lichfield, granted to Ralph, his steward, certain lands at Broomhall, together with the right to try prisoners by fire and water [ordeal], and to hang thieves, in return for the supply of candles to the value of 4s a year for the high altar of Lichfield Cathedral. From about 1157 to a date between 1317 and 1473 the overlordship was granted to the Dean and Chapter of Lichfield, but then reverted to the Bishop and descended as part of the Liberty of Brewood until at least 1605.

The Carless family were tenants of lands at Broom Hall from at least 1556, and William Carless of Boscobel fame is said to have been born there in about 1620, although the parish registers record no baptismal entry. The Carless family remained at Broom Hall until 1724, when Peter Giffard as landlord won an action for ejectment.

From Domesday we learn that Chillington, recorded as Cillentone, possibly meaning 'the farmstead by the spring' or, more likely, 'the farmstead of Cilla', [and incorrectly placed in Warwickshire] was 3 hides held by William, son of Corbucion, but was claimed by the Bishop of Coventry and Lichfield, who by 1182 was holding the lordship. By 1279 a three-weekly court was being held, and a single court paper of 1306 survives. Peter Curbucion, who was probably William's son, was holding the manor at some time during the twelfth century, and his son Peter granted the manor to his wife's nephew Peter Giffard at a date between 1175 and 1182 to hold as half a knight's fee.[316] The grant was confirmed by Peter's son William. The manor has descended in the Giffard family to the present day. A perambulation of the manor survives from 1568.[317]

Coven, which perhaps means 'the place at the coves' or 'the closed-in place', was held by Ailric before the Conquest and by Robert de Stafford at Domesday, which contains the first recorded reference to the name. The family of de Coven, several of them knights, later held it, sometimes calling themselves de Penford. The manor lay partly within Cannock Forest which extended to the bridge which crosses the Penk. The overlordship descended in the Stafford family until at least 1605.

The Coven family occupied a hall at Coven at some time shortly after 1331. A 'hall house', with the owner unidentified, was taxable for 5 hearths in 1666, and may have been in existence in 1738, but no house known as Coven Hall now exists, and its precise location is unknown.

A court leet[318] and court baron[319] were held in the manor, and records survive from 1520 to 1630.

There was a fishpond in the vill in 1307, and there is a reference to an 'old fishpond' in 1322.

Coven is sometimes shown as 'Cotton' on early printed maps, almost certainly the result of an early transcription error repeated by subsequent cartographers.

From its name, 'farmstead of the Angles', and its Roman connections, Engleton is undoubtedly of considerable age. Traditionally, an ancient Celtic road is supposed to have run west from Claygates to the site of the Roman villa by the Penk before turning south and across the river to Brewood: certainly the sunken lane leading down to the river has every appearance of considerable age. Another ancient lane is said to have run north from the west side of the villa.

The name is recorded as Engleton as early as c.1206. By 1242 it was held by the Bishop, and was still so held until at least 1724. A lost village site at Engleton was probably deserted at some date between 1327 and 1539.[320] Thomas de Lovers held a fishery in Engleton in 1346, and when the Bishop leased the mill to Robert Knightley in 1467, a fishery in the mill-pond was included. In 1724 Fowke Hussey and Matthew Ducie each had a fishery adjoining their lands at Engleton, Matthew Ducie paying a rent of 10d to the lord of Brewood. In later times Engleton had its own headborough or constable appointed at the court leet, and in 1860 was still a separate township for the maintenance of its roads.

The name Gunstone derives from 'the farmstead of Gunni', of whom we have no information, and is recorded as Gunestone in 1240. The overlordship of Gunstone as a member of Brewood was held by the Bishop between at least 1477 and 1576.

Hatton means 'the farmstead on the heath', and is recorded as Hadton and Hattun in 1227. The overlordship of the manor of Hatton, a member of Brewood, was held by the Bishop between at least 1428 and 1477. A deserted village at Hatton is thought to have been abandoned between 1524 and 1666.[321] The lost village of Pendeford may have lain at what is now Lower Pendeford Farm, or at or near the site of Pendeford Hall, both sites lying just outside the parish boundary.[322]

The name Hyde, which is found in various parts of the country,[323] seems to derive from a hide of land detached from the principal manor by feudal sub-tenancy. Where the lord did not reserve the customary tenant service, the sub-tenancies were treated as new manors until reabsorbed in the principal manor. The Hyde, as a member of Brewood, is recorded in 1199, and the overlordship was held by the Bishop before 1292 until at least 1605. In 1295 the annual manorial service was the presentation of a rose to the Bishop and two appearances at his court at Brewood.[324] The place-name Hilton appears in the approximate location of Hyde in early printed maps, and there are occasional documentary references to the name in the seventeenth and eighteenth centuries. It seems possible that the moated site to the south of Bath Farm may have been originally occupied by the Hilton family.[325]

The name Somerford denotes 'a ford usable only in summer', and is mentioned in about 1275. It was within the manor of Brewood by 1126, and was held by the Bishop until 1761. In about 1314 Robert de Somerford held the manor by the intriguing service of finding a man with a horse worth half a mark and with a sack of hemp to follow the lord for 40 days when there was war in Wales; by attendance at the lord's three-weekly courts; by presentation of a tithing man at the twice-yearly great courts of Brewood; and by a rent of 40s a year.

A grant of 1222 exists of a moor at Brewood from Roger de Hyde to the Deanery of Lichfield, and an estate in Brewood which belonged to the Deans of Lichfield was known as the Deanery Manor by 1628, and remained with the Deans until 1868, when ownership became rested in the Ecclesiastical Commissioners.[326] In 1927 the remaining 117 acres of Deanery land were sold to Mr T.A.W. Giffard. The estate included the prebend of Brewood in Lichfield Cathedral by episcopal grant c.1176, and the Dean of Lichfield still retains the prebend.

20. Churches

The church of St Mary and St Chad

The church of St Mary and St Chad – by far the oldest building in Brewood parish – dates from at least the thirteenth century, although a priest is listed in the village in the Domesday survey of 1086, which implies that a church existed in the village from at least the eleventh century. There is evidence that Chad, who trained as a priest at Lindisfarne under Scottish teachers in the Celtic tradition of the early church, spent some time as a missionary in the west and north-west Midlands before 665 AD. It was the custom of the Celtic church to name churches after their founders, and almost all of the 30 or so ancient dedications to St Chad still extant are in the same region. It is not inconceivable that Chad visited Brewood in about the mid seventh century to preach to a Saxon community and founded the church at that date. In that respect it is of interest that circular or sub-circular raised churchyards are notable in Shropshire villages with Celtic connections.

Churches are only mentioned twice for Staffordshire in the Domesday survey, but about 40, including Brewood, are thought to have existed.[327] The prebend of Brewood probably dates from the mid-twelfth century, created by Roger de Clinton, Bishop of Lichfield.[328] Until the building of churches at Coven and Bishop's Wood in the middle of the last century, Brewood church served the entire parish. It is said that Lichfield, Buildwas and Brewood are the only churches in the country dedicated to St Mary and St Chad.

Brewood church, redrawn from a water colour of 1859 by Mrs Rebecca Moore and Miss Hinckes, who painted views of the interior and exterior of every parish church in Staffordshire. By kind permission of the Dean and Chapter of Lichfield Cathedral.

The present sandstone building, dedicated to the Blessed Virgin, but with its feast on the first Sunday after St Matthew's day [21st September], is not precisely aligned to the east, but by tradition towards the point at which the sun rose on the morning of St Matthew's day. The building consists of an aisled nave,[329] 78ft by 64ft, dating from about 1375, chancel, west tower, and spire, but the many reconstructions make it difficult to trace its history with any certainty. Although towers are common on Stafforshire churches, spires are less usual. The unusually wide south aisle may attest to the large processions which took place at an early date, perhaps during the time of the Bishop's residence in Brewood. The arches of an arcade of five bays are supported by tall octagonal pillars. The pinnacled tower and inset octagonal spire probably date from the early sixteenth century, and alterations were made to the building in the eighteenth century with a complete restoration, generally of thirteenth century style, in 1878-80 by G.E. Street at a cost of £6,124.

The chancel, the oldest part of the building, dating from about 1220 – it is surely significant that the Bishop's right to hold a market dates from 1221 – has been little altered, except for the east wall, which has been rebuilt. Both north and south walls contain lancet windows, and the north wall has a blocked doorway which led to a vestry, possibly added in the fourteenth century.

In the sixteenth century, or perhaps earlier, the walls of the north aisle were raised, buttresses added, and larger windows inserted.

There is evidence that during the Civil War the church was one of twelve military posts in the region garrisoned or fortified by the royalists, but further details are not known.

In his restoration, Street installed cross-gables on the south side of the nave which are thought to have existed originally, creating a narrow outer aisle with piers and arches in continuous mouldings, and a stepped lancet tripartite window under each gable. The square tower, some six feet thick at the base, and 169ft spire are Perpendicular in style with double buttresses and pinnacles at the corners, crenellated parapet [rebuilt in 1934], and four grotesque gargoyles, one on each wall, with a two-light opening on each face at the belfry stage. A Perpendicular window is above a four-centred arch in the west doorway. On the left side of the doorway is a benchmark set at a height of 364.3ft. The 4' square sundial on the south wall was installed in 1812, and the church clock, now electrified, was made in 1833 by William Hay of Darlington Street, Wolverhampton. The clock faces, 6'4" in diameter, in octagonal frames, were regilded in 1934. There was seemingly an earlier clock, for there are references in the Churchwardens' Accounts in 1656 to repairs to a clock, apparently made by John Baddeley of Tong, a well-known local maker. In 1772 the top of the spire was repaired at a cost of £40, and the weathercock may date from that time, for it appears in an engraving of 1799. It was regilded in 1934. The spire was rebuilt in the 1820's from the central tier of windows, and repointed in 1890 and 1921. Soon after the repointing of 1890 it was struck by lightning, and again in 1925, when the weathercock was badly damaged and the upper stonework loosened.

In the eighteenth century, the east wall of the chancel was rebuilt in brick and a Venetian window inserted, with galleries built in both aisles, at the west end and across the chancel arch.

There formerly existed a wooden south porch with shingled roof, perhaps dating from the 1520's, for on 10th December 1521 the Will of Dean Collingwood was proved in the Chapter House at Lichfield.[330] Amongst various legacies was £2 left to the prebend church of Brewood for building a porch. The Churchwardens' Accounts contain many early entries covering repairs, and the parish registers record both births and deaths occurring in the porch in the sixteenth and seventeenth centuries: it was evidently used as temporary shelter by beggars and the homeless. A stone porch with tiled roof existed on the north. Both porches were demolished towards the end of the eighteenth century after a vestry meeting on 16th March 1777 when the north and south doors were ordered to be stopped, and an entrance made at the west door. New windows were also ordered for the aisles, in 'much-the-cheapest style'. There is a tradition that the first workman to climb on the roof to start the work descended in 'much-the-cheapest' manner, by falling and sustaining serious injury.

Brewood church from the south-east in 1845, from a drawing in the church.

Extensive alterations to the interior took place in 1827-30. New pews were installed, with two family pews in the north-west corner of the nave. The north and south galleries were rebuilt, and the east gallery demolished. The carved oak chancel screen and choir stalls were broken up and dispersed about the parish and a new font installed, the old one ending up in a garden in Coven.

The restoration by Street saw the east wall of the chancel rebuilt in stone with three graded lancet windows. The north vestry was removed and the upper part of the south aisle rebuilt. The building was refloored and reroofed [in memel wood], the galleries and plaster ceilings removed, the tower arch opened up, and the box pews replaced by rush-seated chairs, which were themselves replaced in 1902 by the present oak pews. In the same year a rectangular polychrome achievement on canvas, 6' 7" in width, with the royal arms of William and Mary, formerly above the chancel arch, which had been removed during the 1879 restoration and consigned to a lumber room, was restored and placed on the north wall inside the tower. The choir stalls date from 1887 and the pulpit from 1879. In 1901 heating was installed. The organ, by Binns, was installed in 1911 at a cost of £684 and enlarged in 1952.[331]

A restoration in 1904 removed the partition forming a vestry behind the altar [restoring the chancel to its full length], altered the floor levels and removed iron railings from the Giffard tombs, referred to in Victorian times as "... the beautiful altar-tombs fenced with coarse iron as if to resist an army ..."[332] In 1911 a Codsall sandstone reredos, designed by the prolific ecclesiastical architect W.D. Caroë and carved by N. Hitch in the form of Jesus breaking the bread, with three saints on either side, was installed in memory of Richard Holt Briscoe of Chillington.[333] A similar reredos in metal is said to be in St Margaret's Church, Westminster.

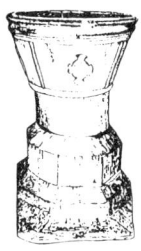

The 1911 works also included the creation of a vestry partitioned off at the west end of the north aisle. Electricity was connected to the church in 1927, gas lighting having been installed in 1864. In about 1927 the late sixteenth century font bowl[334] with simple carved roundels at each quarter forming debased maltese crosses was brought back to the church from the garden of The Beeches in Coven, where it had been built into a rockery, having lain in a farmyard for many years.

Late sixteenth-century font, which disappeared from the church during restorations in 1827-30, and was returned in about 1927, having been found in a garden at Coven.

During extensive repairs to the chancel by the Church Commisssioners in 1958, an aperture on the south side of the church at the corner of the tower and the nave revealed a crypt which had apparently been filled with rubble and sand in 1878. The infilling had settled to reveal limewashed vaulting.

The stained glass in the two lancet windows is by Bryans, one incorporating his 'signature' of a hound. Other windows commemorate the Reverend Jeremiah Smith [d.1884]; Charlotte Simpson [d.1875]; Rebecca Smith [d.1879]; James Hicks Smith [d.1881]; Maria Smith [d.1884]; Charles and Sarah Docker [d.1893 and 1887]; Mariana Wrottesley [d.1892]; Eliza Vile [d.1894]; The Reverend Edward Wrottesley [d.1901]; Sophia Briscoe [d.1910]; Mary Ann Hicks Smith [d.1911]; Frederick J Keeling [d.1911]; Charlotte Armstrong [d.1912]; and the Reverend Charles Dunkley. In about 1680 Gregory King recorded a shield of arms in the east window of the south side showing Giffard impaling Blount: Robert Giffard married Isabella Blount in about 1420.

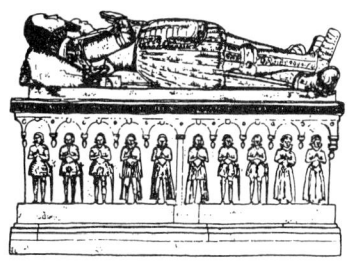

In the chancel, which is 64ft long and 30ft wide, are four magnificent alabaster altar tombs with traces of colouring. The oldest is of Sir John Giffard [d.1556], recumbent in mail and plate armour, and his two wives Jane [Hoorde] and Elizabeth [Gresley].[335] Around the tomb are their 18 children. The second has three similar recumbent effigies, with an inscription to Sir Thomas Giffard [d.1560] and his two wives Dorothy [Mongomery] and Ursula [Throckmorton]

Altar tomb of Sir John Giffard, who died in 1612, and his wife Joyce.

149

and their 17 children; a third of Sir John Giffard [d.1612] in Milan armour, inlaid with gold, and his wife Joyce [Leveson] with their 14 children, and a fourth of Walter Giffard [d.1632] and his wife Philippa [White], who died in 1636.

In the south aisle of the chancel is an incised floor slab [discovered under the south aisle during the restorations in 1878[336]] to Richard Lane [d.1518] and his wife, and at the west end of the south aisle is a delightful two-tiered polychrome alabaster wall monument to Edward Moreton [d.1630], his wife and children, and above to Mathew Moreton [d.1669], his wife and children. The monument was restored in 1838, when the dates in the upper tier were inserted, having previously been blank.[337] The tablet shows the husband and wife kneeling opposite each other. The sons kneel below their father and the daughters below their mother. Edward Moreton is commemorated by a floor slab nearby.

Tablets in the south aisle include those of Thomas Fowke [d.1652], Phineas Fowke [d.1710], and members of the Holland family. There are a number of other memorials of interest, including a brass plate to Joan Leveson, who died in 1572, which is reputed to have disappeared from the church in 1772, and been found in 1863 built into the house of the stationmaster at Four Ashes.[338]

Polychrome alabaster wall monument to Edward Moreton, who died in 1630, and Mathew Moreton, who died in 1669, and their wives and children.

Other tablets commemorate Jane Viscountess Galway [d.1788]; the Right Reverend Charles Berington, Roman Catholic Vicar Apostolic of the Midland District [d.1798]; John Parrot [d.1802]; John Turner [d.1824] and his wife; The Hon Edward Monckton [d.1832]; his widow [d.1834] and their children, 1814-78; Mary Countess of Cork and Orrery [d.1840]; the Reverend A.B. Haden, Vicar of Brewood [d.1863] and his wife; the Reverend William Rushton [d.1875]; and the Reverend Henry Kempston [d.1881] both of Brewood Grammar School; William Parke [d.1876]; and the Reverend William Wall [d.1899]. It is said that many of the old memorial tablets were taken away and destroyed in the early nineteenth century, and others were buried in the nave. There may be some connection with stories of fragments of inscribed stone having been found near the fishpond at Dean's Hall Farm some years ago. On the west wall of the chancel is a plaque commemorating Colonel Carless,[339] with a translation of his grant of arms.

Vertical grooves in various places around the exterior walls of the church a few feet above the ground were by tradition caused by bowmen sharpening their arrows before practice after morning service each Sunday in accordance with royal decree in early times. These grooves are not uncommonly found on medieval buildings and other monuments, such as Newport Butter Cross, but their origin has never been satisfactorily explained. Close examination suggests that some at least may be comparatively recent.

A medieval encaustic pictorial tile,[340] said to show Judas Iscariot throwing away the pieces of silver, was found during digging in the churchyard in 1908 to the west of the church, and may originally have been on the floor of the chancel.

The earliest of the church plate is a silver-gilt chalice and paten cover, dated 1634, with a silver-gilt paten of 1705 and a silver paten of 1718. The pulpit and lectern date from the restoration of 1879. Early furniture within the church includes an oak altar table in the vestry with plain bulbous legs, dating from about 1600, which was in use at the altar until Street's restoration, and a credence table dating from the second quarter of the seventeenth century. Several oak wainscot and side chairs are of the same date, and a larger wainscot chair appears to have been made up at a later date around an older panel. Two oak chests, one with carved panels, another smaller and planked, are seventeenth century. A small oak bench is probably Carolean.

The registers date from 1562, with gaps 1602-08 and 1645-55. They were obviously commenced in accordance with the Act passed on 9th March 1562 providing for a register to be maintained of births, marriages and deaths, but the originals have been lost, having been copied from 1562 to 1602 in the same hand. This was the result of an Act of 1603 requiring all registers to be recopied on parchment, most registers having been kept on less durable paper. The Act also provided that "for the safe keeping of the said book, the churchwardens, at the charge of the parish, shall provide one sure coffer with three locks and keys, whereof the one to remain with the minister and the other two with the churchwardens severally, so that neither the minister without the two churchwardens nor the churchwardens without the minister, shall at any time take that book out of the said coffer.". The iron-bound oak chest near the pulpit, 7'4" long, 2'4" high

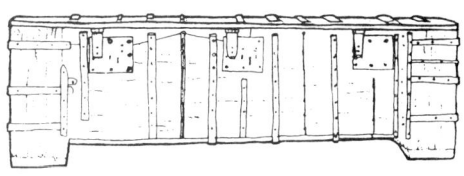

Iron-bound chest, Brewood church.

and 1'9" wide, is of earlier date – perhaps even thirteenth century, contemporary with the rebuilding of the church – but may have been fitted with its three locks at that period. The locks at the left and centre have at some stage been replaced. The wooden repair fillets may date from the seventeenth century: it seems possible that the locks were forced during the Civil War

151

period, when the church was a royalist garrison. At an early date – perhaps when made – the chest was fitted with iron rings at each end to enable it to be carried slung from a pole. The gap in the registers from 1602 to 1608 may be due to the incumbent at that time, who was described as "no preacher, a notable swearer and a drunkard".[341] The gap from 1645 to 1655 is probably explained by the turmoil of the Civil War.

The Parish Magazine was started in January 1874.

At the time of the Dissolution, the value of church property in Brewood was:

Glebe land	£3
Tithes of grain	£19
Rents	£3
Wool and lamb	£5
Total	£30

In May 1553 an inventory was taken of all church vestments, etc., by the King's Commissioners, 'Thomas Gyffard, Knyte, Walter Wrottesley and Edward Lyttleton Esquires'. The inventory included two suites of vestments, one blue bordered with green, the other tawney branched with flowers and one cope of the same; four vestments with albes, one green, one tawney, one dornick, one bordered green; one blue embroidered velvet cope; eight towels; two silver chalices with patens; four small brass candlesticks; one pair of organs; one brass pyx; three corporals with cases; one gilt cross with part of the staff copper; two brass crosses; one coverlet; one painted sepulchre cloth; two paxes; four bells; one sanctus bell; three sacring bells; one painted linen cross cloth; and one brass censer.

Vicars of Brewood[342] [list incomplete]:

1086	[unidentified][343]
1150-52	Robert
1194	Barnard de Brewood
[pre-1242]	Henry [Chaplain][344]
1275	[Sir] Robert de Twyford [Chaplain][345]
1278	[?] Philip le Clerk
c.1280	Peter de Brewode [346]
1294	Richard Roulesham/Rinlesham
1304	William de Pecco/Pek
1319	Robert, son of Adam de Brewode
1347	John de Brengworthe
1361	William Stuche
1361	Robert de Assheburn[347]
1371	Robert de Pulton[348]
1386	Richard Stone[349]

c.1470	William Robenet
c.1474	John Straker
1539	Henry Fleming[350]
1553	[Sir] Richard Wharton[351]
1571	Thomas Grove
1602	Roger Turner[352]
c.1615	Edward Palmer/Pasmore[353]
?1623	Augustin Lindsell
1629	William Lindsell [became Bishop of Hereford 1633]
1630	George Osney
1634	William Chandler[354]
1646	John Dolman[355]
1663	Charles Bagnold
1664	Richard Emery
1696	William Junks[356]
1715	Charles Dugard
1729	John Moss[357]
1737	William Budworth
1746	Richard Fenton[358]
	Henry Inge
1760	Richard Fowler[359]
1762	Thomas Feilde
1767	Thomas Muchall
1804	Baptist John Proby
1830	Alexander Bunn Haden
1863	Edward John Wrottesley
1901	Charles Dunkley
1928	Leslie Knights-Smith
1934	Charles B. Broughton-Thompson
1951	Sydney D. Austerberry
1960	Cyril V. Bishop
1964	Rolf Schottelvig
1982	John Ridyard
1990	Trevor Green

The churchyard has been much enlarged. In 1825 it was extended by the addition of land on the east side, taken out of a field called Bill's Court given by Mr T.W. Giffard. On the north side it formerly extended only as far as a line of lime trees [increased in number from 6 to 18 to celebrate the Coronation in 1937], where there was a wall and a roadway, open to carriages only on Sundays, called the Dean's Walk. A roadway on the north side of the church led north-west to what is now Church Road and south-east to The Pavement. In 1864 School Road was created on garden and croft land after the old vicarage and some old cottages had been demolished, which reduced the size of the churchyard to the west. 790 square yards of land for the new road were given by Mr Corser, and 993 square yards given by by Mr Haden to increase the churchyard to the north. The new churchyard wall in School Road was built at a cost of £358. The churchyard extension followed several years of controversy, including the circulation of printed notices published by a local resident objecting to the possibility of closing and locking the churchyard, a proposal apparently urged by the Vicar.

In 1877 two yew trees were recorded in the churchyard, a third having been blown down in the great gale of 14th October in that year. In May 1879 the churchyard was further enlarged by the addition of 587 square yards on the west side, and a further extension was made in April 1948, the ground given by Mr T.A.W. Giffard. A footpath joins Dean Street and Sandy Lane on the east edge of the churchyard, with blue brick steps known locally as Jacob's Ladder leading down into Sandy Lane. The steps seem to have been constructed between 1808 and 1838 – probably when the churchyard was enlarged in 1825. The name Jacob's Ladder dates from at least 1905, and is probably much older. The churchyard boundary on the east is a high red brick wall on sandstone plinth which runs north from Dean House until the ground begins to fall towards Sandy Lane. The ground behind the wall drops away steeply, the area to the south-east now partly occupied by the houses of St Chad's Close having been quarried for sand from c.1920 until about 1950, but on the south and west the churchyard is several feet above the adjoining road level, and indicates that the church lies on a pronounced mound which may not be a completely natural formation.

Near the south-east of the church is a sandstone coffin, 7ft 7in long and 2ft 7in wide at the head tapering to 1ft 11in at the foot, with a slight indentation for the top of the head and a central hole for the draining of body fluids, which was apparently dug out of the churchyard many years ago and would appear to be medieval. Stone coffins were normally used only for important burials, and the drain hole suggests that the coffin may at one time have stood within the church. It would be fanciful to suggest that the coffin may be connected with the death of Bishop Weseham at Brewood on 1st May 1257.

The earliest surviving legible gravestone would appear to be that of John Harper, who died on 21st March 1695.

In an unmarked grave [by tradition under the yews at the north-west end of the church] lies Colonel William Carless [or Carlos], who joined Charles II in the oak at Boscobel after both had fled from the battle of Worcester. Towards the end of the nineteenth century the grave was said to have been marked by a flat tombstone bearing the name Carless, but the stone had disappeared by 1897.[360] At the foot of a yew tree close to a holly near the north-west corner of the church is a small sandstone memorial stone with an arched top containing a carved sprig of oak leaves and the inscription 'Near here lieth/the remains of/Col William Carless/whom the King did call/Carlos/he died May 28 1689'. The lettering seems to be of eighteenth century style with the wording based on the old tombstone of Joan Penderel at Whiteladies, but the weathering on the stone shows that it is relatively recent. In fact it was erected at the instigation of Mrs Mary Wakefield in about 1939. Several other later members of the Carless family are buried near the north-west corner of the church, including Thomas Carless, who died in 1852, his tombstone insisting 'not Careless as heretofore written'.

Near the east wall of the churchyard is the grave of John Taylor, the Brewood sculptor who was born at Uplands, in Tinkers Lane, and who fell from scaffolding and died in 1887 at the age of 31. He worked on the Albert Memorial, Lichfield Cathedral, and Wolverhampton Art Gallery. A gravestone carved by him as a youth in the form of a cross covered by wreaths of flowers stands near the south door of the church. William Parke, the Brewood-born bookseller from Wolverhampton, is also buried in the churchyard. His tomb, with protective ironwork, lies near the south-east corner of the chancel. He retained strong connections with the village all his life, and was a friend of Dickens, Harrison Ainsworth and other eminent writers of the day.

A war memorial in Clipsham stone designed by W. Caroë in the shape of an 18' cross with angular stem on graded steps was erected in 1921 on the west side of the churchyard, and now records the village dead of both World Wars. It is fitting that their names should be given here:

1914-1918			1939-1945
B. Asprey	A. Farmer	G. Parkes	H. Barnes
G. Beech	W.H.Green	R.G.Perkin	E.G.Bell
P. Bentley	G. Haynes	C. Stanley	E. Cadwallader
E.E.Bickley	W. Haycock	E.C. Smith	R.C. Nash
J. Bill	A. Kerry	J.J. Stones	W. Rhodes
H. Bradbury	A. Lewis	S. Sargeant	L.H. Green
P. Bradley	E.A. Lewis	T. Till	A.G. Jell
G.H. Bridgwater	C. Moorhouse	C. Wakelam	M.A.Langley,DSC,RN
E.T. Cluett	A. Moorhouse	T. Wall	R.T.F. Saunders
R.L. Caunter	W. Nichols	W.H. Ward	
G.H. Davies	G. Newman		
E.J. Donlan	M.M. & B.G.W.Pearce		

A vicarage had been ordained and endowed in Brewood by 1275,[361] but the site is not known. In 1304 is a record of the augmentation of the manse of the vicarage of Brewood with a little pig or 3d per annum, and the following year William de Pecco, Vicar of Brewood, acquired from John de Horsebrok, one of the Vicars Choral of Lichfield, a piece of land in Brewood adjoining the vicarage manse on the west, in exchange for a piece of the ground of the vicarage next to the steps of the churchyard, which adjoined his land on the north and was fenced off from it. Because William's bakehouse was on John's land, William and his successors were to pay an annual rent of 3d for it. That rent was still being paid by the Vicar in 1650.[362] An old vicarage house,[363] which stood west of the

Brewood church and the old vicarage house, demolished in 1864, from an undated drawing in Brewood church.

churchyard, fronting an avenue of chestnut trees called Dean's Walk, was demolished in 1864 when the new vicarage house, built by the Vicar, A.B. Haden, as a private house called Elmsley, was purchased. The Rev. Haden had earlier built Deansfield House for his private use in 1833, and lived there until he moved to Elmsley in 1860. The old vicarage house was apparently gabled and built in the early eighteenth century, when Queen Anne's Bounty encouraged the rebuilding of parsonages: a grant from the Bounty was made to Brewood between 1718 and 1728. The building is shown in a sketch that hangs within the church. The foundations of the house indicated that the site had been occupied by a smaller building, probably a priest's house, with a parlour, kitchen, and two bedrooms. The Valor Ecclesiasticus survey records neither glebe nor manse among the holdings of the Vicar of Brewood, but the 'Survey of the Prebend, Parsonage, and Manor of Brewood' made in 1649 states: "there is a little vicarage house at Brewood with a small back side; there is no glebe belonging to the vicarage except the churchyard". In 1746 accumulated gifts made to supplement the Vicar's stipend were used to purchase just over 3 acres of glebe land in Walsall. In 1864 the only glebe land within the parish was a small garden and orchard attached to the vicarage house. When the trees in the garden were dug out in about 1865, some human bones were found, and five years earlier, when the foundations of the National School were excavated, two adult skeletons were found in adjoining land less than two feet from the surface, apparently buried without coffins.[364]

156

St Mary's Roman Catholic church

The Roman Catholic church of St Mary, built of local coursed rubble sandstone, is of late thirteenth century style, built in 1843-44 for a cost of £1,345 to a design by the prolific Victorian architect Augustus Welby Pugin, famous for his work on the rebuilt Houses of Parliament in 1834 at the age of 22, who donated three of the stained glass windows. The land for the church and churchyard was given by the Giffard family, and the church was formally opened on 22nd June 1844 by Cardinal Wiseman. The building has a five-bay aisled nave, chancel, north vestry, south porch, and short octagonal spire above the square west tower. Several of the windows have commemorative stained glass, the west one commemorating the First World War. In the Lady Chapel is a stone altar moved there after redecorations in 1887, with a polychrome wooden image of the Virgin and Child known as Our Lady of Brewood or The Madonna of Brewood in a shrine built in 1931.

By tradition the statue, reputedly of pre-reformation origin, was kept in the chapel at Whiteladies until the building was ransacked and set on fire by parliamentary soldiers hunting for Charles II on 9th September 1651 after the battle of Worcester. During the attack, the statue is said to have been pierced by a sword above the right knee, and at the back is a hole supposedly caused by a musket ball.

The scar was said to weep continually, even though the statue is dry with age, and the moisture was seemingly used by local Catholics to effect remarkable cures. From Whiteladies the statue was taken to the Catholic chapel at Blackladies where it stood at the altar. It was brought from Blackladies in 1844 when the new church was completed.[365]

A small sandstone pillar stoup some 33" high with latticework decoration of twelfth century style stands outside the south porch and is also reputed to have come from Whiteladies. There is a lych-gate at the entrance to the churchyard. North-east of the church is a rectangular single-storey stone building formerly used as a church hall, and to the north-west of the church the priest's house and school, both of brick and built in the 1840's, also to designs by Pugin. The presbytery

garden has a place in botanical history, for it was here that a new microscopic fungi in bladder senna was first found in the last century by the Rev. Philip G.M. Rhodes of Oscott College. The fungi was named *Diaporthe oncostoma* Fckl. var. *coluteae* grove.

St Paul's church, Coven

The church of St Paul at Coven was consecrated in February 1857, having been built on land given by George Monckton of Stretton, who also donated £1000 towards the building costs. The stone used in the construction was from Stradsfield quarry and was given by Mr T.W. Giffard. The church is cruciform in thirteenth century style, designed by E. Banks, with chancel, nave, transepts, south porch and vestry, and an octagonal turret and small spire at the south-west angle.

Church of St John the Baptist, Bishop's Wood

The church of St John the Baptist at Bishop's Wood is a cruciform building of local red sandstone in Early English style to a design by G.T. Robinson, with a shallow chancel, north vestry, and a south porch with square tower surmounted by a delicate spire. The church was opened on 16th June 1850 and consecrated on 10th June 1851. The one bell is dated 1858.

To the east of the church, and of about the same date, are the old school, now converted to a house, which retains large lancet windows on the south side, and the old schoolhouse.

21. Chillington

The name Chillington, first recorded in Domesday Book as Cillentone and wrongly listed in Warwickshire, is believed to mean the farmstead associated with Cilla, about whom we have no information of any kind, but who is presumed to have been a Saxon occupier or owner of land in the area. Recent research, however, has shown that there is a slight possibility that the first element in the name derives from the old English 'cille', meaning a spring, hence 'the settlement by the spring'.[366]

In 1086 it was held as 5 hides of the King by William, son of Corbucion, one of the few Saxon tenants permitted to retain lands after the Conquest. Peter Corbucion, believed to be William's son, held the manor in the twelfth century, and his son, also Peter, conveyed it to his wife's nephew, Peter Giffard, at some time between 1175 and 1182. By 1297 Sir John Giffard held property in the vills of Chillington and La Hyde which included a capital messuage, probably at Chillington, with a garden and curtilage attached, a caracute of land [the Danish equivalent of a hide, i.e. approximately 120 acres] with 40 acres growing wheat and the same of rye, 12 acres of woodland and some pasture.

Apart from a short period during the rebellion of Simon de Montfort in the 1260's when the family were dispossessed, the Giffard's have held the Chillington estate to the present day.

Of the earliest house – or, more properly, houses, for there may have been a succession – we are almost completely ignorant, and the large-scale landscaping in more recent centuries has probably destroyed any archæological evidence of early occupation. From at least Norman times, any house at Chillington would undoubtedly have been fairly substantial, reflecting the wealth and status of the Giffard family.[367] The cellars at Chillington contain a corner of old sandstone walling which may date from the twelfth century, but appears to be mainly Tudor, incorporating a number of tall rectangular windows with stone mullions, now below ground level. A sandstone pavement was exposed outside the house some years ago during drain laying, evidence that the ground level around the Georgian house has been raised by several feet.[368]

A park has existed at Chillington since at least 1287,[369] and in 1511 it was extended by the enclosure of five acres of arable land.[370]

The earliest building of which we have any knowledge is the old Tudor house, built mainly of stone[371] but at least partly of close timbering with brick infilling,[372] probably begun in the late 1530's by Sir John Giffard. That knowledge is derived from four main sources. The first two are estate plans of c.1727 and 1761 which both include small drawings of the old house [probably fairly

Chillington House, redrawn from a Chillington estate map c.1723. SRO D590/363.

159

accurately, since other buildings on the plans are known to be faithfully represented], principally a gatehouse facing east, said to have contained the chaplain's apartments, of three storeys and with two flanking towers, possibly polygonal, and a range of buildings forming a square courtyard to the rear. The gatehouse had the arms of the Giffard family carved over the entrance, with the inscription "The arms of Sir John Gyffard, Knt. In the year of our Lord mvxlviii and the first yere of King Edward the sixt. J.G."[373] The building adjoining the south side of the gatehouse, possibly the chapel, appears to have been topped by a large cross, perhaps common to all the Giffard houses. The hall was apparently on the east side of the mansion, from which a grand staircase ascended to the great gallery, and an oriel window recorded in 1663 contained armorial glass commemorating many of the Giffard marriage alliances.[374] Painted on the south wall of the courtyard were the Giffard crests of an archer and a panther's head.

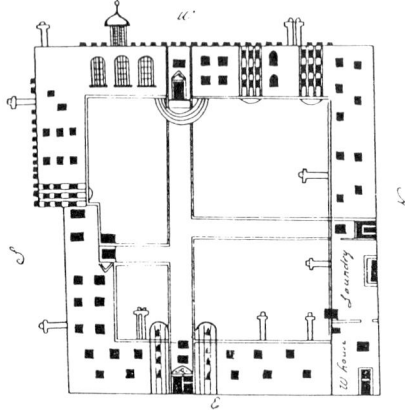

The fourth source is a plan on an account of a theft from the house. The account is undated, but probably eighteenth century.

The third source of information on the old house is correspondence from Sir Amias Paulet, custodian of Mary Queen of Scots during her imprisonment at Chartley, who wrote to Sir Francis Walsingham on 3rd October 1585 in response to enquiries about the suitability of Chillington as a possible place of confinement for the Queen:

A remarkable view of Chillington House, redrawn from a curious contemporary report of the route supposedly taken by thieves who used an old gate as a ladder to enter a window of the wash-house to steal 182 yards of cloth, and left through the gatehouse. The thieves were not caught. The wash-house and laundry appear in an odd combination of plan and elevation, and at least part of the buildings appear to have been crenellated. The document is undated, but appears to be c.1700. SRO D590/571d.

I understand that the howse is well seated and is furnished with many fayre lodgings, so as this Queen may be very well placed, with a great chamber, gallery, cabinet, and lodging for her gentlewomen,[375] as likewise the Govenor and his gentlemen may be lodged in consimilar sort, a fayre orchard, and garden walled about, great store of woodd, Cankwood no far off for coale, and sea coale may be had with little change. Two or three parks at hand, good pasturage adjoyninge to the howse besyde the dove howse and other like commodityes . . . I had almost forgotten to advertyse to you that the howse is verye well furnished.

This latter reference is of interest, for it was only five years previously that John Giffard, after receiving Queen Elizabeth and being subsequently called before the Privy Council for recusancy, had declared that the house was 'out of order and unfurnished' as a result of the Queen's visit. Evidently, despite his periods of imprisonment, Giffard had managed to refurnish his house. But Sir Amias was careful to detail the drawbacks if the Queen were to be accommodated:

> ... the howse being straight to lodge both these families, the brewehowse and brewing vessels so little as will brewe but one toone [tun] at a tyme, which is much less than sufficient, and no common brewehowse in any towne adjoyning or in any other place of this Shire that I can heare of: stable roome lesse than enought for XX geldings which may be enlarged to the numbre of 8 or 10, by means of a stall, and to a far greater nomber by the helpe of the barnes, whereof there are 3 or 4, yf they were not full of corne: hay in the howse 20 loads, or thereabouts, a small store for so many horses, as must followe this familye, and little hay to be had in these parts for money.

In a subsequent letter, Sir Amias provides revealing details of the religious persuasions of prominent families in the region, and highlights the security problems which would arise if the house was used to accommodate the Queen:

> Touching the state of the countrey, and the neighbours adjoyninge I have taken care to informe myself by the means of some men of credit in these parts, and do fynd that the gentlemen of calling and countenaunce and best affected in religion as Sir Walter Aston, Mr Bagot and Mr Greisley and a fewe such like, have their dwellings distant from Mr Giffords howse some X miles, some XII, and the nearest IX, only Mr Littleton[376] a very honest religious gentleman, as I heare, dwellinge within 3 or 4 miles or thereabouts. Mr Gifford having two brethren nere neighbours to his howse, the one of them ritche, and of good credit in the Shire and both of them backward in religion [these would be the Giffards of Blackladies and Whiteladies: the rich one from Whiteladies], so as the sayd howse seemeth to be barren of good neighbours. The strength of the howse deserveth little better comendation, the windowes of the one syde lying open upon the fielde, and the windowes of the other syde where this Queen should be lodged lying open upon the garden, which is environned with a wall of no great height than as a man may reache to the topp, only the third court which serveth for woodd and fewell is walled about, so as yf yt be meant that this Queen should make any long abode there, I must neede say for my discharge that the sayd howse is not of sufficient strengthe for so waightye a charge.

Needless to say, Chillington was turned down, and the Queen was rehoused at Chartley, despite protestations from its owner, the Earl of Essex, who urged that Chillington was a more suitable place of confinement. The only wonder is that Chillington should have been considered at all, given its lack of defences, demonstrated all too clearly by the number of times it changed hands during the Civil War – and that after 'fortifications' had been made. Although the plan of 1761 includes a stretch of water which, it has been suggested, could have formed part of a moat, a feature one might expect given the status of the family and the building, Sir Amias would most certainly have mentioned any moat in his report, and there are no references to a moat in any Civil War documentation. The stretch of water may simply have been a garden feature.

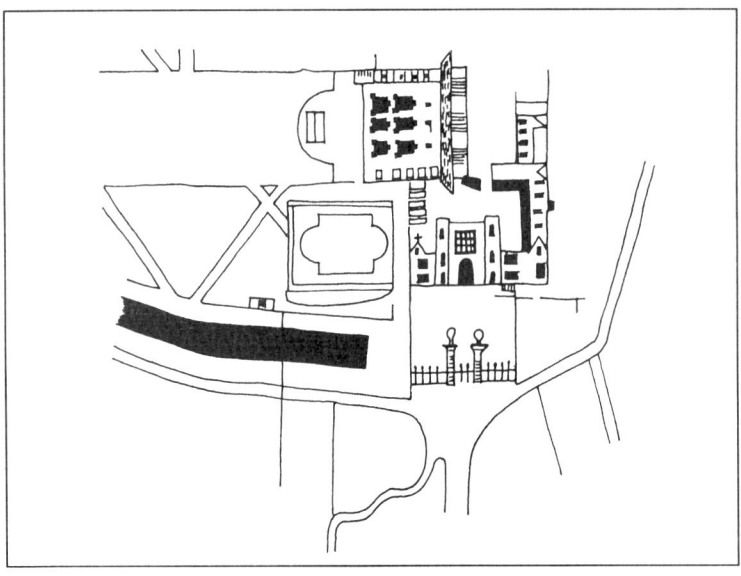

Chillington House, redrawn from a Chillington estate map of 1761. SRO D590/371.

The link between Mary Queen of Scots, Sir Amias Paulet, Sir Francis Walsingham and Chillington may well have been Gilbert Giffard, son of Sir John Giffard. While many old families have their black sheep, few have produced one so infamous for his treachery as Gilbert Giffard. After studying at the Catholic Colleges of Douai, Rheims and Rome [and expelled from the latter], he became a Roman Catholic priest and in 1583 began working as a spy for Sir Francis Walsingham. At Rheims he had met John Savage, later to be associated with Babington, a Roman Catholic who was planning to assassinate Queen Elizabeth. Obtaining from France an introduction to Mary Queen of Scots, Giffard visited Chartley and managed to gain the confidence of Mary, who entrusted him to carry her secret letters, hidden in barrels of beer supplied by a brewer in Burton. Paulet knew that Giffard was a government spy, and although initially suspicious, soon trusted him. It may have been Giffard who then suggested to Walsingham or the Earl of Essex – for reasons at which we can only guess – that Chillington would prove a suitable place of confinement for Mary, and it is of interest that on 3rd March 1585 the Privy Council ordered Sir John Giffard not to remain at his house at Chillington 'nor at any place within the county of Stafford above one month at one time so long as the Queen of Scots is or does remain in any part of the Shire . . .' In fact Sir John seems to have been appalled by the actions of his son, and there is no evidence that he was concerned in any way in the intrigues involving Mary.

As well as copying Mary's letters for Walsingham, Gilbert Giffard was simultaneously sending copies to France. Regularly visiting London and Paris, he became well acquainted with Babington and his co-conspirators, and encouraged them to pursue their plot, at the same time advising Walsingham of developments and also reporting secretly to the Spanish ambassador in Paris. Giffard continued to retain the trust of his various masters, and it was he who carried the fatal letters approving the plot to assassinate Queen Elizabeth from Mary to Babington – the evidence used to bring Mary to the executioner's block.[377]

As a footnote, a brief reference to the Tudor house at Chillington in Erdeswicke's 'History of Staffordshire' reads, in full: "the old house, temp Henry VIII, was remarkable for the various forms of windows and chimnies". This reference is seemingly taken from Plot, who, when writing of Tixall Hall near Shugborough in 1686, says

> . . . it is remarkable also that the windows of the house, tho' very numerous, are scarce two alike; and so 'tis at Chillington . . . It is observable that the tunnells of the chimneys in both these houses are very numerous, the Hall Chimney at Chilington having no less than 8 tunnells to one hearth; the fretwork of the tunnells also in both these seats: whence 'tis easy to collect that the beauty of the structure in those days (which seems to me to be temp. H.8) did not consist, as now, in uniformity; but in the greatest variety the Artist could possibly show.[378]

The earliest approaches to Chillington were along Chillington Street – formerly described as a 'paved causeway', and presumably used by Elizabeth and her entourage during her visit in 1575, but now an overgrown bridlepath – and via a lane [now marked in its southern part by the Staffordshire Way long-distance footpath which joins Port Lane a short distance north of Long Birch] which curved north west towards the house.

During the Civil War the house is known to have been fortified and garrisoned, and was besieged by both parliamentary and royalist forces at one time or another. The nature of the fortifications is unknown, but there is no evidence of any earthworks such as were constructed around Lapley church. In an action commenced in 1724 by Peter Giffard to regain possession of Broomhall from the Carless family, a witness, William Lewis, gave evidence that he remembered the "late unhappy wars in England", when Mr Giffard's family was driven out of Chillington, and Chillington Hall was garrisoned: "The house was battered by cannon, and much broken and torn; and for many years the doors stood open, the walls being in ruins and the house uninhabited". Since those events had occurred some eighty years earlier, the witness must have been of considerable age and enjoyed a remarkable memory.

In 1650 the pastures at Chillington included the New Park, the Old Park, and the Common Park.

The Tudor house at Chillington is known to have been partly demolished by Peter Giffard, who succeeded his brother in 1718. The present three-storey brick range on the south side of the quadrangle, with a staircase block constructed between it and the hall, and service courtyard and stable range, date from the same period. It is said that at least part of the new house was built on oak piling which has since decayed and caused structural problems. The red brick south wing, with stone dressings, has lead rainwater heads with the initials P.G.B. [Peter and Barbara Giffard], dated 1724. The architect and builder is thought to have been Francis Smith of Warwick [1672 - 1738], who was born at Wergs, the son of a bricklayer. There are eight regularly spaced windows, each with segmental heads, keystones and aprons to each storey. Internally, several of the rooms are oak panelled, and the fine staircase has turned balusters, carved strings, and moulded undersides to the heads and risers, with the walls of the staircase hall ornamented with decorative plaster-work of the same date. The kitchen, which originally had open fireplaces on two opposite walls, is open to the full height of the service wing. West of the house is the garden laid out by Peter Giffard which contains a stone screen which once led to a bowling alley. The fine wrought iron gates, which may be by Bakewell, incorporate the initials of Peter Giffard in the cresting. Within the former bowling alley is a large stone acorn on a plinth which commemorates the poet Cowper, who visited Chillington on a number of occasions. To the north is an impressive double farmyard including animal houses, granary and barn, designed on model lines in the early eighteenth century and perhaps remodelled later in the century by Lancelot 'Capability' Brown. An octagonal brick dovecote surmounted by a glazed lantern light by the stables dates from about 1730.

Between 1756 and his early death twenty years later, Thomas Giffard made substantial alterations to the park, employing 'Capability' Brown and James Paine, who had recently worked together at nearby Weston Park. The alterations included the obliteration of Chillington village, then known as Chillington Town, which was concentrated to the south of the house, in the early 1760's: it is unclear what arrangements were made to rehouse the dispossessed villagers. A roughly triangular lake of some 66 acres was created from three pools three-quarters of a mile south-west of the house, with a dam at its lower end, and many trees were planted.[379] From overgrown ruins which remain it seems that a complex arrangement of pools and sluices was created to the east of the dam. Field names suggest that the pools were stews or fishponds. A canal or private navigation from the south-east corner of the lake to the Hall was used to transport fuel and building materials, and near the west end is a sandstone bridge with single

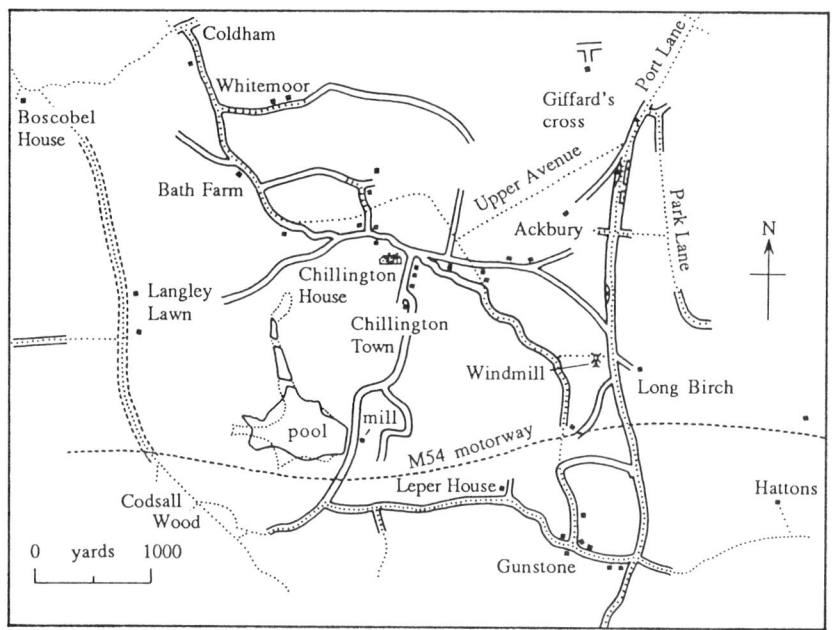

Map of Chillington area based on estate maps of the 1720's. "Chillington Town" was obliterated during the landscaping of the parkland in the 1760's, when three pools were linked to form a large lake. Existing roads are marked by dotted lines. With acknowledgements to Staffordshir Record Office D590/363a-b.

segmented arch, designed by Paine. The bridge is of interest for the arched courses of stonework, carved classical profile heads within roundels in the spandrels, and iron balustrade. A bridge designed by Brown is believed to have formerly existed at the other end of the canal. A sham bridge or causeway with five blind arches similar to Paine's bridge crosses the northern arm of the lake. Dating from about 1772[380] are a summerhouse in the form of a classical temple on the east bank, with a Roman Doric portico of local sandstone. A brick and stucco Gothic temple with central ogee-headed doorway and four-storey polygonal flanking turrets, one of which was decorated internally with contemporary plasterwork, was for reasons of safety almost completely demolished in 1975 having been badly

The Ionic temple, Chillington park, c.1771.

damaged by a falling tree in 1910. Only the foundations now remain. The resemblance of the building to Speedwell Castle may not be entirely coincidental. The so-called Ionic temple, which disguises a gamekeeper's cottage behind it, dates from 1785-6,[381] lies on the site of an earlier cottage, and may have been designed by Adam.[382] It has five bays with plain Ionic columns carrying an attic. The dome has been reconstructed in

165

glass-fibre. The gamekeeper's cottage had, until recently, a room with a barred window in an adjoining building said to have been used to hold poachers. The tree-lined Upper Avenue, over a mile long, from the house to Giffards's Cross, was created by Peter Giffard in about 1727,[383] and was perhaps designed to connect with the Lower Avenue, which may have existed from at least 1643: a parliamentary survey of that date refers to "the Trees in the Pale Row."[384] The road which runs alongside Upper Avenue existed in 1775, and may be contemporary with the Avenue itself.

An estate plan of about 1727 carries the endorsement: 'Planted in the Old Park 304 Elmes 205 Sycomores[385] in the year 1727.' The high brick walls around the northern half of the park probably date from the same period, and in themselves represent a phenomenal amount of materials and labour. An earth-covered brick conical ice house [said to have been used until the 1930's] near the south east end of the canal probably dates from the eighteenth century.

It is clear from surviving plans that much thought was given to the major rebuilding of the house by Thomas Giffard towards the end of the eighteenth century. Two designs were prepared by Robert Adam. One dated 1772 is for a mansion on a new site, probably near the lake, and the other incorporated the wing built in 1724. On coming of age in 1785, Thomas Giffard the younger organised designs for a new hall. From 1786, Sir John Soane was employed to prepare drawings, and his first designs were for a completely new house, later modified to include Peter Giffard's buildings of 1724, and the remaining Tudor buildings were largely demolished.

The Hon. John Byng, who visited Chillington Park on 1st July 1792 seems to have had a somewhat jaundiced impression of Chillington – perhaps the result of the indifferent meal he was served at the Red Lion in Brewood – for he recorded in his journal that "the house [is] now under repair, . . . an ugly, starving thing, – unquestion'd and unmolested," and found little to his liking in the park, taking "a drive betwixt a forced-up canal, and the old stream . . . Crossing a little, ugly bridge," presumably Paine's bridge. He also condemned the large number of trees felled or marked to be felled, with no trees planted to replace them.[386]

The present Hall consists of a long rectangle with the 1724 range forming its south end. It had originally been intended to give the new pink brickwork a stucco finish but, perhaps to lessen the contrast between new stucco and the brickwork of the older wing, it was never applied.

Chillington Hall from the north-east.

The principal east-facing two-storey front has a central Ionic portico of brown-banded Tunstall stone. To conceal the east end of the earlier and

166

higher range, the two end pavilions have an additional storey, which may have been a modification of the original design. The domed saloon is entered through the portico and a vestibule with Ionic columns. It was originally intended to be used as a chapel, and probably incorporates the walls of the Tudor great hall. The only source of light is a clerestory in the eliptical dome. A stone chimney-piece, dated 1547, and bearing shields of arms and an archer drawing a bow at a panther, seems to be based on panels which were formerly over the doorway of the Tudor hall. Again, the original design of the room has been modified, being asymmetrical and only three-quarters of the size originally proposed. Some of the interior work was completed by Thomas William Giffard, who succeeded in 1823, and the window on the staircase wall contains heraldic glass of about 1830 designed by John Freeth of Birmingham. A billiard room was added to the house in 1911, and the garden screen leading to the bowling alley restored in the same year.[387] In recent years much restoration work has been undertaken on both the Hall and the various other structures on the estate.[388]

By 1851 the park was open to the public during the summer, and proved very popular, with fêtes held regularly, attended by people from all over the Midlands.[389] The pool was noted for its 'beautiful fleet of vessels . . . from large yachts to the smallest of skiffs', and contem-porary illustrations confirm that sailing vessels of considerable size were indeed in use. Unfortunately, the visitors failed to respect the privilege extended to them by the Giffards – some of the festivities are said to have degenerated into 'nocturnal orgies and Bacchanalian jubilees' – and vandalism forced the family to close the park to the public.[390]

In 1971 Chillington Park, with the Upper and Lower Avenue, was designated a Conservation Area. The M54 motorway, constructed in 1983 after much local opposition, passes through the southernmost part of the park. Despite cuttings and landscaped artificial embankments, the effect of the traffic is not isolated completely from the tranquil centuries-old parkland.[391]

22. Giffard's Cross

Giffard's Cross, at the junction of Chillington Upper Avenue and Port Lane, traditionally commemorates an extraordinary rescue which occurred on the spot in the early years of the reign of Henry VIII, when the head of the house of Chillington was John Giffard. At that time it was not unusual for great families to keep private menageries of exotic animals, and a friend had given John Giffard a panther. One morning the animal escaped. The alarm was raised and John Giffard, armed with a bow and accompanied by his son, chased the beast towards a group of cottages on the crest of a hill about a mile away from the house. Urged on by cries of terror from the cottages, they saw the panther crouching ready to spring upon a woman with babe in arms. Fitting an arrow into his bow, John Giffard quickly took aim and, encouraged by his son's words "take breath, pull strong", managed to kill the panther in mid-leap. The woman and child escaped unhurt, and word of the deed soon spread. Two crests were awarded to the family as a result of the exploit – an archer in the act of drawing his bow, and a panther's head, with the motto 'Prenez haleine, tirez fort': 'take breath and pull strong'. The spot where the rescue took place was marked by an oak cross, known ever since as Giffard's Cross. Accounts of the incident published in the early part of this century go so far as to claim that John Giffard shot the panther while standing at the door of the hall, a mere mile away from the animal.

In the medieval period monumental crosses of all types were very common and served a variety of purposes: for divine protection at places where disasters had happened or might occur, such as bridges or fords; to denote boundaries of parishes or townships, or places where events like markets or preaching would take place; to commemorate an incident or exploit; or to mark and protect routeways.

Within Brewood parish, Cross Green on the eastern side may take its name from a cross which stood on the old Stafford to Wolverhampton road;[392] a Whytecrosse is mentioned in 1348 and 1390;[393] Crakeford crosse is recorded in 1493;[394] the name Nicholas Crosse appears in 1509;[395] and one of the open fields was called Cross Field,[396] although it is possible that it was so named because it lay across the direction of adjoining fields. Wayside crosses were not uncommon in England, for a popular treatise of 1496, 'Dives et Pauper', states: "For this reason be Crosses by the waye, that when folks passynge see the Crosses, they shold thinke on Hym that deyed on the Crosse and worshypp Hym above all thyngs." Crosses were later associated with Catholicism, and in 1571 the Archbishop of York issued instructions for the Rogationtide or 'Cross-week' perambulations, requiring the ministers to refrain from 'wearing any surplice, carrying of banners or handbells or staying at crosses or such like Popish ceremonies.'

It is not inconceivable that the disastrous visit of Queen Elizabeth I to Chillington House in 1575 was in part due to the Queen's ire at the prominent display of the 'Popish' symbol of Giffard's Cross, for the royal entourage would inevitably have passed the cross en route from Stafford via Penkridge to Chillington.

Many older crosses are broken, usually the result of Protestant fanaticism and an Act of 1643 which ordered that crosses be defaced and superstitious monuments destroyed, and wooden crosses in particular seem to be a rarity. Indeed, there is an illuminating observation in the journal of the Hon. John Byng, who records that on Sunday 1st July 1792, when returning from Chillington Park, he travelled ". . . up the avenue, at the top of which is a wooden cross! The first I ever saw, or heard of, in this country."[397]

It is of interest that the Catholic chapels of the old Tudor mansions at Chillington and Blackladies are shown in early drawings surmounted by a large cross, presumably of wood, with the upright flared towards the base and with the arm ends budded. There is no doubt that Giffard's Cross itself, of oak and some six feet high [with another two feet below ground] with botonné or trefoil terminations both to the post and the lap-jointed and pegged 3' 7" crosspiece, much weathered and decayed, is of considerable age, and may indeed be contemporary with the construction of the Tudor house between about 1537 and 1547. Formerly standing in the garden of the lodge at the junction of the Upper and Lower Avenue at Chillington, and replaced in 1984 by a full-size replica, the original is now under cover at the rear of Chillington Hall.[398]

Intriguingly, the Poll Tax Assessment of 1380-81 mentions Johannes Atte Crosse [John at the Cross] living within the parish. Sadly, it is not possible to say where that cross was located: it may have been the market cross, which is known to have had ancient origins, or perhaps there was a cross at Giffard's Cross as early as the fourteenth century. Alternatively, 'Johannes' may have lived at one of the other crosses recorded in the parish or elsewhere.

Historical evidence which might support the panther rescue legend is interesting. Although a panther's head crest was granted to John Giffard on 28th May 1513, it was not until ten years later on 17th July 1523 that the crest of an armoured demi-archer was granted. In the saloon at Chillington Hall is a chimney-piece of white unweathered stone, clearly not local, dated 1547, which it is said may incorporate in restored form original carved panels illustrating an archer aiming his bow at what could be a panther, with the Latin motto of the Giffards. It has been suggested that

169

the panels were formerly above the doorway of the Tudor hall. There is a record dated 23rd September 1663 of the Giffard arms of stirrups and panthers head 'cut in stone over the great door, at the entrance unto the hall', but the archer and panther are recorded 'painted [sic] upon the south wall in the great Court.' 'Gyffarde's Crosse' itself is recorded at least as early as 1569,[399] and a Chillington estate map c.1727 suggests that it formerly stood in the centre of Port Lane, which was then a very wide roadway and almost certainly dates back to at least the Romano-British, and perhaps even the Celtic, period. It is possible that the line of the road was moved very slightly to the east when the Upper Avenue was created in about 1727, with the cross left in its original position.

However, the long existence of the cross and the grant of panther's head and archer crests cannot be taken as proof of the rescue. There is no documentary or other evidence of a menagerie or panther at the old Tudor house at Chillington, and news of an animal as exotic as a panther and an extraordinary rescue would inevitably have spread rapidly in a rural backwater like Brewood, and been passed down from generation to generation. It is almost inconceivable that more than three centuries would pass before the first recorded reference to the incident, but the legend seems indeed not to have appeared in print until Victorian times, more than 300 years after the exploit is supposed to have occurred. The indefatigable antiquarian Dr Plot, always keen to record any unusual anecdote, makes no mention of the story, and Stebbing-Shaw, the great Staffordshire historian, was apparently unaware of the legend, even though he knew of the cross, for he says of Chillington: ". . . at the bottom of the long avenue in front of the house stands a large wooden cross, similar to what are frequently seen in Catholic countries", but he makes no mention of the legend. Most telling of all, however, are early histories of Brewood published in 1858 and 1860 which, although containing all kinds of information relating, however remotely, to Brewood and its environs, make no mention of any legend associated with the ancient wooden cross, and indeed suggest that the crest is that of a tiger's head, adding: "No trace whatever can now be found in the College of Arms of the reason of the two grants of Crests, remarkable and recent as they are." In fact, there is some uncertainty whether the crest is a leopard's head or that of a panther or tiger. A heraldic visitation of Staffordshire made by Glover in 1583 records the crest of 'une teste de Panthaire' granted in 1513 to the Giffards of Chillington, with leopards heads and a demi-archer included in the Giffard standard, but other reference works mention a tiger's head.[400]

Perhaps Stebbing-Shaw's observation provides a clue to the true origins of the cross. It may have been erected after members of the staunchly Catholic family, who are known to have visited the Continent, had observed roadside crosses in the Catholic countries, and placed their own cross on the skyline at a point where Port Lane is visible from Chillington Hall. As for the Giffard crests, while there is no obvious explanation for the panther's head, it seems probable that it formed the original crest of the family,[401] and it does not seem unreasonable to suppose that Sir John Giffard chose the crest of a bowman and the motto 'take breath, pull strong' to commemorate Richard fitz Gilbert, Earl of Clare, popularly known as Strongbow, the conqueror of Ireland in 1169, who was connected with the Giffards and gave various estates in Ireland, including Tachmelin, to Peter Giffard, the first Giffard of Chillington, the Grant still existing. It is perhaps significant that the motto was created in two stages. The first part, 'preigns alaine', was granted in 1513 with the panther's head, and the second part was added when the archer crest was granted in 1523.

The available evidence suggests that the story of the panther was probably invented in the early nineteenth century, when there was an Elizabethan revival and romantic and fanciful tales were not uncommonly woven around landmarks, one example being the legend of Gelert's grave at Beddgelert. In the case of Giffards Cross, it would have taken no great imagination to create a story linking the crests of the Giffard family with the family motto and the weathered cross. The story seems to be first recorded in the 1840's,[402] when it was even then noted that it "variegated according to the ideality of the fire-side informant",[403] and over subsequent years slowly takes the form of historical fact, given added authenticity by the popular Victorian historical novelist W. Harrison Ainsworth, who mentions the story in his 'Boscobel, or The Royal Oak, A Tale of the year 1651', published in 1872. The book led to an upsurge of interest in Boscobel, the Royal Oak, and indeed anything associated with the romanticised escape of Charles II. Harrison-Ainsworth almost certainly heard the story from his friend William Parke, the Brewood-born bookseller who had a long interest in the history of the village – Parke is mentioned by name in the preface to Ainsworth's book – or from James Hicks Smith, the Brewood historian who was at school with Ainsworth and who is known to have supplied him with a considerable amount of local information.

The theory that the legend is little older than the Victorian period may be strengthened by an observation made by the architectural historian Sir Nikolaus Pevsner who, in his description of Chillington Hall, says: "The chimneypiece is very puzzling," and adds, intriguingly, "and the style seems a rustic 1830 trying to look ancient".[404] Furthermore, the archer and panther painting recorded in 1663 shows the archer on the left facing left, with the panther to his right. The carvings on the chimney-piece have been reversed, so that the bowman appears to be aiming at the panther.

But perhaps the most persuasive opinion, which should resolve any uncertainty about the veracity of the legend, is that expressed by the Somerset Herald, J.R. Planché, who in the last century "dedicated a considerable portion of the leisure of nearly thirty years" to researching the Giffard family, and in 1873 described the legend of the panther rescue as a "preposterous sensational story invented to account for the two [crests] born by the Giffards of Chillington since the time of Henry VIII . . . Had they been assumed in commemoration of such an event, tiger and man would have formed one crest . . . No allusion is made to [the legend] in either grant, nor is there any record of any circumstance which could have been exaggerated into such a story to be found among the Giffard muniments. The panther's head is borne alone as the crest in the sixteenth and seventeenth centuries and never the archer, and the tradition is evidently one of the many which have had their origin in an attempt to account for remarkable and unexplained heraldic insignia."[405]

Rather sadly, there can be little doubt that the story of the shooting of the Chillington panther is nothing more than an entertaining but relatively modern fiction.

23. Blackladies

The Priory of the Black Ladies of Brewood of the Order of St Benedict [popularly known as Blackladies from the habit worn by the Order] seems to have been founded by, or soon after, 1150,406 when the foundation movement was spreading throughout Europe, and was dedicated to St Mary. A Charter exists which can only be loosely dated to between 1150 and 1160, but which refers to a then established community. The Bishop's Charter of Foundation is now lost, but his identity can be inferred with some certainty. The manor of Brewood, in which parish lies Blackladies, has been held by the Bishops from at least the Conquest, and they had 'woods' there before the disafforestation of the royal Forest in 1204. Blackladies lies within the Bishop's wood, within which King John permitted a park to be formed by an enclosure two leagues in circumference in 1200.[407] It is highly probable therefore that the site of the house was granted to the nuns, called dominae or moniales, by the Bishop of the diocese.

One Bishop in particular is known to have favoured the creation of establishments of this nature at about this period: Roger de Clinton, who was consecrated Bishop in 1128 and was founder of Buildwas Abbey and Farewell Nunnery near Lichfield, and who confirmed the monastic foundations at Blithbury and Canwell. If this assumption is correct, then the probable foundation date of Blackladies is no later than 1147, when the Bishop left England for the Crusades and never returned, reputedly dying at Antioch the following year.

From a very early date the priory was connected with the nuns of Blithbury [in Mavesyn Ridware], as shown by an agreement of about 1170 between the two houses and William de Ridware, and the eventual merger of Blithbury into Blackladies in the fourteenth century. The amalgamation explains why the largest item in the revenues of Blackladies in the 1530's was income from land at Blithbury. Additional evidence of the close links between the two houses is that Gailey, granted to Blithbury in about 1160, had passed to Blackladies before 1189. It was subsequently seized by Henry II, and as compensation the nuns were granted land at Brom near Clent by King John in a Charter dated at Haywood on 15th November 1200.[408] The Charter describes the nuns as "of the Church of St Mary at Brewood", [the dedication of the parish church, which in the thirteenth century was of St Mary and St Cedde, or Chad], and the distinctive description 'Black' does not occur before the thirteenth century. It has been suggested that the description indicates that they were first established near the church in Brewood before they settled on their permanent site, but apart from that description and references to 'the Nuns of Brewood', there seems to be no other evidence to support that view. Indeed, the description 'Nuns of Brewood' was applied to both

Blackladies and Whiteladies, the word Brewood meaning the Forest of Brewood, within which lay both houses.

Although the Bishop may have contributed to the creation of the house, his generosity was not unbounded, for the foundation seems always to have remained poor, and poverty is the probable explanation for its modest taxation over the years.

In 1204 Blackladies and Blithbury were among several nunneries each given two marks by the King. At some date between 1211 and 1216 the nuns exchanged land they held in Pattingham for an assart in Chillington, and also paid the owner, Isabel [Bassett] de Pattingham, twenty shillings. It has been suggested that Isabel could have been the daughter of the first Peter Giffard of Chillington, from which house the priory may have derived support.

In about 1225 Sibil de Broc granted Chetton Mill, south-east of Bridgnorth, worth two marks yearly, to the Nuns of Brewood. The taxation of 1291 shows that this grant was to the Black Nuns, and gives its value at that date at 16s per annum. In response to a petition from the priory, Pope Gregory IX [1227-41] took Blackladies under his protection, confirming its ownership of all present and future property, particularly the site of its house and appurtenances. The newly cultivated lands which the nuns worked themselves, together with their livestock, were declared free of tithes. The nuns' right to elect their

Thirteenth century seal of the Priory of Blackladies. Prioress was recognised by the Pope, and benediction was to be conferred on the nuns by the Bishop and ordination on their chaplain. In addition, the usual rights such as burial of outsiders in the priory graveyard, and free admission of females wishing to withdraw from the world – none of whom was permitted to leave, except to take stricter vows, without the consent of the Prioress – were granted. In 1241 the Sheriff was ordered to allow the Black Nuns of 'Brewud' one mark to pay for their chalice which was in pledge, an indication of the poverty of the priory.[409]

There are three grants ordered by Close Letters in the time of Henry III to the 'Nuns of Brewode', which, if they relate to the 'Black' nuns, probably indicate building activity during that period. One of them, addressed in 1241 to John Biset [a Justiciar of the Forest], orders him to allow the nuns of Brewood ["monialibus de Brewud"] to assart, or take into cultivation, three acres, presumably near their land, since it had been found not to be to the hurt of the Forest. The other Mandates were to the Keeper of Kinver Forest to give to the Prioress of Brewood as a gift from the King three oaks in 1256 and ten oaks in 1267 for use as timber. The gift was a royal favour of a type common during the period.

In 1276, while the King's huntsmen were hunting in Cannock Forest – which stretched as far west as the Penk at Brewood – a stag escaped and was chased into the fishpond of the nuns of Brewood: presumably the Black nuns. They connived at the appropriation of half the carcass – a serious offence – while John Giffard and John de la Wytemore took the other half. For the crime, Giffard and his companion were imprisoned and fined, the nuns "as they are poor they are pardoned for the good of the King's soul".[410]

In 1291 Blackladies was assessed at 2s. in Pope Nicholas's Taxation,[411] a particularly low figure, and in the same year an indulgence of one year and forty days was granted by the Pope to all who visited the priory on each of the four feasts of the Virgin Mary and the anniversary of the dedication of the church there, which meant that the nuns could expect to benefit from donations left by such visitors.

An important Assize was held in January 1293 before five Itinerant Justices in Staffordshire, at which enquiries were made into rights and privileges claimed by the religious houses and of questionable methods of obtaining property. The Prioress of Brewood is included amongst those listed in connection with such enquiries.[412]

In 1318 the Vicar of Brewood sued 'the Prioress and Convent of the Monastery of the Blessed Mary of Brewood' for tithes of wool and lamb from sheep belonging to the monastery pastured within Brewood parish. The case was settled when the Vicar agreed to waive the tithes then due, and in return the Prioress undertook to pay all future tithes.

A visitation to Blackladies by Bishop Northburgh in about 1323 produced a critical audit report, as a result of which obligatory [but not voluntary] payments by those wishing to join the community were forbidden. Because of its poverty, enlargement of the community was not permitted, and the Prioress and other office holders were ordered to present accounts to the whole house or senior members. Anabel de Hervil [the cellaress] and Robert de Herst [the keeper of the temporalities] were dismissed, and an annual rental received by one of the nuns was ordered to be used for the community. The Prioress was instructed to dine in the refectory and sleep in the dormitory, and a 'damsel' of the Prioress was to be removed from the house. The nuns were forbidden to speak to any secular persons, who were not permitted to live in the priory. Nuns not holding office, particularly Emma of Bromsgrove, were not to leave the cloister without permission, and a Franciscan was appointed to take confessions from the Prioress and nuns.

In the subsidy of 1327 Blackladies was assessed at 2s, one of the lowest assessments in Brewood, but by 1333 the fortunes of the house may have revived, for the assessment was 3s, one of the highest in the area. Between 1360 and 1367 five nuns were ordained at the convent.

Small occasional additions to the endowed land, probably donated by new members, had ended in 1279, when the Statute of Mortmain discouraged the practice of gifts of land, and there was apparently no royal licence [as there was in the case of Whiteladies] authorising future grants. Money gifts were permitted, however, and the substantial donation of £100 made in 1394 to secure prayers for Thomas de Brinton, Lord of Church Eaton [who died in 1384] must have been of considerable benefit, and was probably used for new buildings, which at the time of the Dissolution were extensive: the Dissolution inventory mentions a church with steeple [which meant a tower at that period, although a late seventeenth century sketch of the buildings shows a tower in the north range with a squat spire surmounted by a cross], vestry and chapter house, and a hall and extensive domestic accomodation. From references in early deeds, it is evident that the chapter house was existing at the end of the thirteenth century.

A scandal in 1413 involved John de Tutbury, of Gresley Priory, who was accused of abducting a nun of Brewood – presumably Blackladies. The full details remain unclear, but he was acquitted.[413]

As a result of long vacancies, the Bishop acquired the right to appoint new Prioresses, and exercised such right in 1442, 1452 and 1485, on the last occasion at the request of the underprioress.

A visitation of 1521 recorded a community of four, and all in order, although one of the nuns stated that young girls were sleeping with the nuns in the dormitory. The annual income was then £20 13s 4d, and there were no debts.[414]

In 1535 a list, almost certainly incomplete, recorded land and rents in Brewood parish, including Chillington and Horsebrook; Albrighton; Dawley; Tong; Bradley; and Bromyard, Kidderminster, valued at £11 1s 6d.

In 1535 the Valor Ecclesiasticus, or 'First Fruits' survey, was carried out, recording details of the assets of all monastic houses. The Commissioners who carried out the valuation of Blackladies were Sir John Talbot, Sir John Giffard, Walter Wrottesley and John Grosvenour. The survey provides evidence of the contents of the Nunnery immediately prior to the dissolution, and it is apparent that it was far from wealthy. Indeed, there is evidence that the nuns themselves laboured in the fields. It is also of interest that the Bishop wrote to the nuns in English, which may mean that they knew no Latin. If that was the case, they would seemingly have performed divine office with some difficulty and perhaps less understanding.[415]

The Dissolution of the monasteries was carried out by Henry VIII ostensibly to reform a corrupt monastic system, but in reality to reap the riches of the religious houses and because of the hatred of the monastic orders, who, as the special protégés of the papacy, were the most obstinate opponents of his ecclesiastical policy. Their widespread influence over the mass of the people rendered them dangerous enemies to a ruler of whose conduct they disapproved. At the beginning of 1536 there were more than 800 monastries, nunneries, friaries and other religious establishments in England and Wales. Four years later, by the middle of 1540, there were none.

In March 1536 an Act was passed transferring to Henry VIII all religious houses of an annual value of less than £200 a year, 376 in number, including Brewood Nunnery. Shortly before the Act, six small religious houses in the region were allowed to purchase exemption from the Act by payment of sums ranging from £20 to £122 6s, but the exemption only lasted until the autumn of 1538.[416]

Dr Thomas Legh was appointed as Thomas Cromwell's agent to deal with the surrender of the various foundations in the region, with the help of an assistant, Thomas Cavendish. In earlier cases, the co-operation of the local gentry had been secured by forming Commissions to which they were appointed for consultations about the surrenders, but by the time Legh arrived at Blackladies in 1538 the arrangement had been abandoned, not only because it was time-consuming, but also because difficulties arose when the Commissioners praised and supported religious establishments about which Cromwell's agents had previously been very critical.

On 11th October, Legh received a letter from Sir Thomas Hennege telling him the house of Blackladies was to be given by the King's orders to Sir Thomas Giffard of Stretton, a Gentleman Usher of the Chamber and eldest son of Sir John Giffard of Chillington, who had been anxious to acquire it for over a year, and instructing him: "At your now being there you shall put him into possession, and he may at leisure apply to the Chancellor of Augmentations for the lease." However, when Legh arrived at the house, he learned that there was another claimant. Prudently, Legh referred the matter to Cromwell, enclosing Hennege's letter, and reporting: "There was Mr Littleton[417] also who said the King was pleased he should have it, as he perceived by your Lordship when he was last in London." Legh was most anxious to avoid offending anyone, as becomes clear from his imaginative solution to his dilemma: "Wherefore I and Mr Candisshe have put them both in possession, and sold the stuff to them both till they may know the King's pleasure."

Having finished his business in Brewood, Legh had travelled the same day to Lilleshall – Blackladies may have been too poor even to afford him accommodation – and concluded his letter: "Now being at Lilleshall, I intend to put Mr Candisshe in possession of the farm of the house [Blackladies] who prays you that in his absence he be not in this behalf supplanted." In the event, it was Sir Thomas Giffard who won the tussle for the house.

The Deed of Surrender – which was signed by none of the nuns – is dated 16th October 1538, and the Inventory of items sold to Sir Thomas Giffard still exists, showing that the nunnery possessed a hall, parlour, kitchen, buttery and larder, with a large bedroom [in which all slept on two bedsteads] and a bailiff's chamber. Outhouses included a brewhouse and cooling house, bolting house for kneading bread, cheeseloft, and a 'Kylhouse', used for baking, all of which were more or less adequately furnished, with hangings of painted cloth in the parlour, and two tables in the hall – but only one bench. The nun's bedroom contained a feather bed and one tester of white linen, two coverlets and a blanket, described as old, one bolster, two pillows, and four pairs of sheets. The bailiff slept on a mattress on the floor, with a coverlet and a blanket. His axe remained in his bedroom when the house was sold. A tablecloth and two latten candlesticks, a bushel and a half of salt, four pewter porringers, four platters and two saucers, which are all mentioned, give some indication of the standard of living. Of grain there was a quarter of wheat [6s 2d], a quarter of oats [1s 8d], a quarter of 'munke-corn' – mongcorn – wheat and rye sown together [8s], and a quarter of peas [2s 8d] The one horse was sold for 4s, the wain and dung-cart for 16d. Ten loads of hay raised 15s. The silver, consisting of a chalice and three spoons, weighing a total of eight ounces, was sold to George Warren for 26s 8d. The total sum raised on the sale, including 26s 8d for an old debt repaid to the priory, was £7 6s 1d. The seemingly low prices were probably a realistic market value at the time.

Thomas Giffard also purchased the nunnery site and buildings, as well as the church, water mill and pasture under rent, by a Grant dated 8th February 1539 for the price of £7 6s 1d, while his father John, courtier and Member of Parliament, obtained the monastic properties of Sheen, Ronton, Tutbury and Stone.[418]

The Prioress, Isabella Launder, was given a 'reward', or compensation, of 40 shillings, and the three nuns, Cristabell Smith, Alice Beche and Felicia Bagshaw, 20 shillings each. Felicia Bagshawe had come to Blackladies from Farewell Priory at the time of its suppression in April 1527. The poverty of the Nunnery can be judged by the fact that the three nuns were awarded pensions of 33s 4d each, the lowest of any of the 200 individuals granted pensions in Staffordshire and Warwickshire.[419] On 1st February 1539 the Prioress was given a pension of 66s 8d, and eight servants – William Parker [chaplain], Robert Baker [perhaps the bailiff], Margarett Burre, Thomas Bolde, William Morre, Thomas Sith, Kateryn Alate and Phillip Duffelde – received 78s 2d between them. The Deed of Surrender shows that rents of £4 3s 4d were in hand [and confiscated], with 34s 9½d outstanding. Legh and Cavendish claimed expenses of no less than 60s for their efforts.

An interesting footnote to the surrender of Blackladies is the investigation of William Cavendish which began soon afterwards for allegedly granting higher 'rewards and wages' to the dispossessed members than had been declared. These 'bonuses' may have been bribes, for it is recorded that while riding back from Merivale in Warwickshire, Legh and Cavendish learned that the Abbot had not sold some plate as he had claimed. A messenger was despatched to collect it, and the Abbot surrendered it as an inducement to Legh and Cavendish 'to be good masters unto him and his brethren'. When questioned, both Cavendish and Legh admitted the facts, but whether they were disciplined or punished is not recorded. What is known is that as Legh and Cavendish went about their work they lived well and spent large sums on their own entertainment, even in Brewood spending on themselves nearly as much as they gave in rewards to the Prioress and nuns,[420] although it is difficult to conceive what may have justified a large expenditure at a small house like Blackladies. It is not inconceivable that part of their expenses was given as 'rewards and wages' to make their unpalatable task easier.

Prioresses of Blackladies included:

Isabella [after 1257]
Mabel/Amabilia [c.1272-73]
Alice [c.1283]
Emma [c.1301]
Alice de Swynnerton [occurs 1324, resigned 1332]
Helewysia of Leicester [elected 1332, occurs 1373]
Parnel Petronilla [c.1395-1412]
Margaret Chilterne [appointed 1442, resigned by 1452]
Elizabeth Botery [appointed 1452, died 1485]
Margaret Cawardyn [appointed 1485]
Isabella Launder [1521 – pensioned 1538, died 1551]

Blackladies passed down through the Giffard family. There is no evidence that the house played any part in the Civil War,[421] but during that period it was sequestrated from John Giffard, with part of the rent paid in 1646 to the Vicar of Brewood. The property was subsequently redeemed, but in 1655 it was again sequestrated and sold by the Treason Trustees to a Thomas Gookin – the sale has an air of nepotism, for in 1653/4 Samuell Gookyn was one of the Treason Trustees – who re-sold the following year to Francis Page of London. John Giffard, great grandson of Sir Thomas, the original purchaser, apparently had the property settled on him on his marriage, and by 1661 had redeemed it and was living there.

In March 1710, John's widow, Catherine, leased most of the house, retaining for her own use only: "the chapel and all rooms, paths and passages thereto belonging, the necessary house [privy} at the end of the gallery, the writing house, the use of one of the fireplaces in the kitchen, the water there and free passage through the same", the use of the various domestic offices and outbuildings, the "fishpool or pond lately made . . . the canals and stews at the bottom of the garden, the pond between the court and barns, half the pigeons in the dovecot . . . also the best court and the best garden".

From at least 1680 a Catholic burial ground existed at Blackladies, although worshippers at Blackladies Chapel were often buried at Whiteladies.[422]

It has been suggested that the grange, or home, farm of Blackladies was Hubbal [or Hobbal] Grange,[423] supposedly visited by Charles II after his flight from Worcester.

Blackladies – The house

The plan of the present substantial building on the site is T-shaped, the principal range facing east with a long rear wing extending to the west.[424]

The construction is of brick with stone dressings, two storeys high with attics. The architectural evidence suggests that it was built early in the seventeenth century, possibly utilising materials from the original Nunnery, and the continuous stone plinth of the buildings suggests that they are of the same period. The main range, with stepped dormers and end stepped gables – a feature more commonly found in East Anglia – contains the central entrance porch [probably a later addition], with a three-storey five-sided bay on each side incorporating mullioned and transomed windows. The left-hand bay is on a plinth which seems more recent than the rest of the house, and it is clear that the house has been much altered internally since it was first built. A panelled room on the ground floor has an arcaded oak overmantel and stone fireplace, and the oak staircase is of late Jacobean style although there is some evidence that it may not be in its original position. The forecourt is walled, and the decorative iron gates may be original. The west wing contains mullioned windows and moulded brick round-headed doorways, and a diagonally-shafted chimney which may be original.

Blackladies, a dignified and enigmatic building on the site of a former Benedictine nunnery established in about 1150. The present buildings, of mellow brick with stone dressings, probably date from the late sixteenth or early seventeenth century. The photograph was taken shortly before the house was sold in 1919, after wh'ch date much internal alteration and restoration work was undertaken.

A visitor to the house in 1846 mentions that it was then undergoing repair, and Mr Fisher, who occupied the house in the 1880's, built the window in the southern gable wall of the main house.[425] After its sale in 1919 the house was heavily restored. Whilst the foundations were undisturbed, the old beams were apparently 'stripped and adzed' and the old beams from the farm were burnt. A curious stone carving, said to represent a nun's veiled face, formely set in the chimney stack in a room in the roof of the west wing and by tradition marking the 50 year incarceration of a mad nun long ago, was then destroyed.[426] Many of the doors, windows, dormers and chimneys may date from the 1919 restoration. The main house and the west wing were divided into separate houses in 1976, but rejoined as one in 1992. From about 1920 water was supplied to the house by a hydraulic ram to the north [which still exists], which pumped water piped from Coldham into two large tanks in the attics of the west range. The pressure from the tanks was sufficient to supply a fountain which at one time stood in front of the main house.[427]

The age of the existing buildings has been the subject of much speculation. Although no illustration is known to exist, the original monastic buildings must have been of stone, the architectural style probably very similar to that of Whiteladies and Buildwas. If the present brick buildings are part of the old convent, they must have been built at some period prior to the dissolution, i.e. pre-1538. Although some brick buildings in the area were constructed at an early date – Pillaton Hall, near Penkridge, for example at the end of the fifteenth century and the now-demolished mansions of Tong and Pepperhill [Albrighton] well before 1540[428] – the poverty of the convent is well recorded, and there is nothing in the pre-dissolution survey to suggest a rebuilding. Indeed, the great majority of monastic buildings dated from before the boom in brick building in the second half of the fifteenth century, and the typical monastic structure was almost always stone, the few exceptions being in the east and south-east of England, where brick has been used since the twelfth century if one ignores earlier widespread use by the Romans. Neither does the price achieved on the sale of Blackladies reflect a new building. But the most conclusive evidence that the present buildings are of post-dissolution date is the alignment of the house, for the Benedictine builders were normally scrupulous in ensuring that the chapel faced due east – Buildwas, Wenlock and Lilleshall are aligned due east, and Whiteladies slightly south of east – and the other priory buildings would have been based on the same alignment. Blackladies is quite obviously not so aligned. Furthermore, the intention behind the dissolution must not be overlooked. Henry VIII was determined to break for all time the power of the Roman Church, and that meant the physical destruction of monastic property to prevent its re-occupation – "destroying the nest for fear the birds should build again", as it was put by Gilbert Thacker, the son of Thomas Cromwell's steward – the removal of the roof representing the minimum level of demolition. It is interesting that the convent was suppressed on 16th October 1538 and the sale of the site took place on 8th February 1539. The delay in the sale may be explained by the time required to remove the roof but there is also a tantalising record which suggests that the church at least may have been left intact: "Brewood Priory Co. Stafford A° 1540 in ye steeple [i.e. tower], 3 bells."[429]

The destruction of the monastic buildings raises another interesting question, namely the disposal of the stone. There is an almost complete absence of moulded or ecclesiastical stonework fragments normally found in the vicinity of monastic property, although two badly weathered pinnacles with carved diagonal moulding and scrolls were found to the west of the house some years ago, and the house and garden walls stand on plinths of sandstone blocks. Is it possible that the stone was acquired by Sir John Giffard, Thomas's father, as ready-cut masonry for the rebuilding of his house at Chillington, less than two miles away, which he is thought to have started some time after his mother's death in 1537?

The evidence, architectural and otherwise, suggests that the present much-altered buildings at Blackladies are of no earlier date than the 1540's, Thomas Giffard complying with the 1534 Act dissolving the smaller monastries, which required purchasers to keep "an honest conventional house and household in the same site and precinct", and are unlikely to predate the seventeenth century.

A large stable block to the north of the house has been converted into a house, in front of which is a pond, recorded in 1710, with a causeway with blind arcading on the south, divided from the forecourt of the main house by a tall wall. The causeway is traditionally known as The Nun's Walk. A track from Blackladies running north-east to Lapley Priory, a Benedictine house belonging to the Abbey of Rheims,[430] was known as the Monks Walk. The pond was dredged and enlarged in 1986.

Traces of interconnected rectangular fish ponds, or stews, lie to the west of the house. They are shown as water-filled in the Tithe Map of 1838.[431] Field names in early maps suggest that the mill known to have existed at Blackladies was to the north of the house, but had seemingly ceased to exist by the late seventeenth century.

Blackladies chapel

A small timber-framed chapel, probably dating from the seventeenth century, formerly stood on the north side of Blackladies, connected by ground floor and gallery passages to the north end of the west wing. It seems to have been close-studded on the upper part, and early illustrations indicate diagonal timbering in the connecting passage. A wooden bell turret was demolished in 1789. According to the Staffordshire historian Stebbing-Shaw, who seems to have visited Blackladies in the latter part of the eighteenth century: "the inside, which is small and neat, seems to be almost in the same state as the Nuns left it, some of their ancient relicks being still in use . . . on the floor are several coats of arms, inlaid in brick." The chapel is illustrated in a birds-eye sketch of the buildings, which include what is supposed to have been a hospitum, in a survey made towards the end of the seventeenth century, and is shown surmounted by a cross with trefoil arms, not unlike Giffard's Cross, in a drawing dated 1837.

Blackladies house and chapel, from Stebbing Shaw's 'History and Antiquities of Staffordshire', published between 1798 and 1801.

The interior of the chapel contained south and west galleries, the latter supported on twisted pillars, formerly painted and gilded, with a tessellated floor. Until about 1844 the curious wooden statue known as The Madonna of Brewood or Our Lady of Brewood stood before the altar, but is now in St Mary's Church, Brewood.

Blackladies chapel drawn in 1837.

The ground floor incorporated a long passage, the ceiling of which was painted 'cerlean blue, studded with golden stars', presumably very like the decorations discovered in recent years under old limewash in the former chapel at Moseley Old Hall.

Worship was transferred from Blackladies when St Mary's Roman Catholic church was opened in Brewood in 1844, but a Roman Catholic school in the chapel[432] which had existed since at least 1834, run at the expense of Mr Evans of Boscobel, continued until at least 1851, when the cost was met by Miss Evans of Boscobel. A drawing dating from 1846 suggests that a number of thin lancet windows may have been inserted by that date, but it seems more likely that the drawing is inaccurate, and resulted perhaps from the artist working from a field sketch and mistakenly interpreting the vertical timbering.[433] There is evidence that the chapel was dilapidated in 1851 but still standing in 1867, and demolished in about 1872, the site being used for pig-sties.[434]

The location of Blackladies chapel is now marked by a cross in a garden wall, the footings of which incorporate a small stone with chevron moulding which may be medieval.

Stebbing-Shaw records that in about 1790 a number of human bones were unearthed in a piece of ground to the west end of the chapel, and during restoration work in 1919, a skeleton was discovered 'in the foldyard' about 100 yards east of the stables.[435] The bones were probably connected with the old Catholic burial ground.

Claim to extraparochiality

Towards the end of the seventeenth century, a dispute about the extraparochiality of Blackladies resulted in a long series of protracted court cases.[436]

In 1680, Samuel Wightwick, who was entitled to collect the tithes of Brewood, began an action against John Giffard of Blackladies for unpaid tithes. Giffard's defence was that Blackladies had never paid tithes, and such monastic privilege had been confirmed after the dissolution by statute. Wightwick's case was dismissed. Undaunted, he began another action to establish whether Blackladies was part of Brewood parish. Again he lost, and yet again in another case, but during this time he 'drew in the parish to his quarrel', and managed to have Blackladies assessed for the Brewood poor rate. Peter Giffard, having succeeded John, appealed, but the rate was confirmed by the court. When he refused to pay, a warrant was issued against his property, and he therefore began his own action against the Overseers of the Poor for Brewood. The action failed, and he was eventually forced to satisfy the judgment made against him.

During these various actions some curious evidence was put forward. In 1680 a witness, John Jones, strained credulity by swearing that he had been Headborough of Brewood 63 years earlier, and had levied no rates on Blackladies. For Wightwick, it was claimed that a son of Peter Giffard had been buried at Brewood, although he had died at Blackladies. John Giffard admitted that this was so, but explained that the burial at Brewood only took place because his father also possessed Chillington, which had a vault in Brewood church. John Giffard added that there was a large church and spacious burial ground belonging to him at Blackladies. Furthermore, Blackladies had been confiscated, with Chillington, during the Civil War, but that he had been able to redeem it by payment of a fine which was inflated to compensate for the freedom of Blackladies from tithes and parish rates.

The principal grounds upon which the Giffards based their claim were:

(i)   Blackladies maintained its own poor independently from Brewood, and that families named Yates and Onions were maintained at the sole cost of Peter

Giffard at Blackladies

(ii) the church at Blackladies was maintained by Peter Giffard

(iii) the prominent families of Brewood had their own pews in the parish church, but there were none belonging to Blackladies or its inhabitants

(iv) during traditional perambulations of the boundaries of Brewood, Blackladies had never been included

(v) when payments were to be collected or warrants executed at Blackladies, the Justices always addressed the High Constable of the Hundred of Cuttlestone, and not officers at Brewood

(vi) during the Civil War, Peter Giffard's ancestor was sequestrated, his house plundered and garrisoned, and family papers burned by soldiers, which is why no ancient deeds could be produced to support the claim for extraparochiality

(vii) Blackladies was ordered to pay taxes with Church Eaton parish.

For Wightwick, the strongest evidence was perhaps the Agreement of 1318 between the Vicar of Brewood and the Black Nuns on the subject of tithes, but the defence was that the lands subject to tithes, whilst possessed by Blackladies, were not actually part of Blackladies. Ample evidence was produced to show that from the dissolution, no demands had ever been made for tithes or rates due to Brewood, and a lease existed dated 18th March 1661 of the tithes of 'The Kerrimores, Kerrimore Green and Bishopswood' to Sir John Giffard of Blackladies, in which no claim was made to tithes from Blackladies.

After nearly twenty years of litigation, the matter eventually reached the House of Lords, and judgment was finally – and surprisingly, in view of the weight of evidence in its favour – given against Blackladies.[437]

Blackladies and the relics of St Chad

The ancient parish church in Brewood is dedicated to St Mary and St Chad, and by tradition – though unsupported by evidence – Chad visited Brewood in about 670. According to the historian Bede, the body of St Chad [c.620-672] was first buried in St Mary's church, Lichfield, and moved to St Peter's, Lichfield, when that church was built. Thereafter, it was removed to the rebuilt cathedral dedicated to St Mary and St Chad. The fabric of the shrine was demolished at the Dissolution, but the Catholics had already removed some of the bones to ensure their safety, and they were taken by Arthur Dudley, Prebendary of Colwich 1531-77, and entrusted to 'two noble kinswomen of his own', who lived at Russell House, near Worcester. On the death of Dudley, the women divided the relics between two neighbours, Henry and William Hodshead. On 8th September 1651, Father Peter Turner, a Jesuit, heard a deathbed confession from Henry Hodshead of Woodsetton, near Sedgley, and was given one part of the relics, which passed on Turner's death in 1655 to Father John Leveson.

The box in which the relics were kept was broken open by soldiers and others during the Interregnum in 1658, some of the relics were taken, and one bone thrown to the ground and broken. On 2nd March 1644, a William Atkins, who was a witness to Father Turner's written statement as to the origin of the bones and who was later arrested in connection with the Titus Oates plot and died in his cell in Stafford prison, was in possession more of the relics. In 1667 all of the relics seem to have been held at Blackladies in the hands of Father Robert Collingwood,[438] who appears to have lived at Boscobel and was chaplain to the Fitzherberts of Swynnerton, near Stafford, who owned Boscobel and Blackladies. After the death of Collingwood, the relics were taken to Swynnerton.

Shortly before the opening of the Catholic cathedral in Birmingham, a key was found at Swynnerton Hall with a label attached stating that the key would open a chest in which the relics had been placed, and that the chest had for security reasons been removed to Aston Hall, near Stone. A search was made, the chest was discovered, and the relics found. From Aston they were taken to St Chad's at Birmingham in June 1841, where they still remain.[439]

24. Buildings

The centre of Brewood is Market Place, popularly known as The Square, with five roads radiating from it: Bargate Street, Sandy Lane, Newport Street, Church Road and Stafford Street, with Dean Street leading south-west from the parish church. The general architectural impression of the

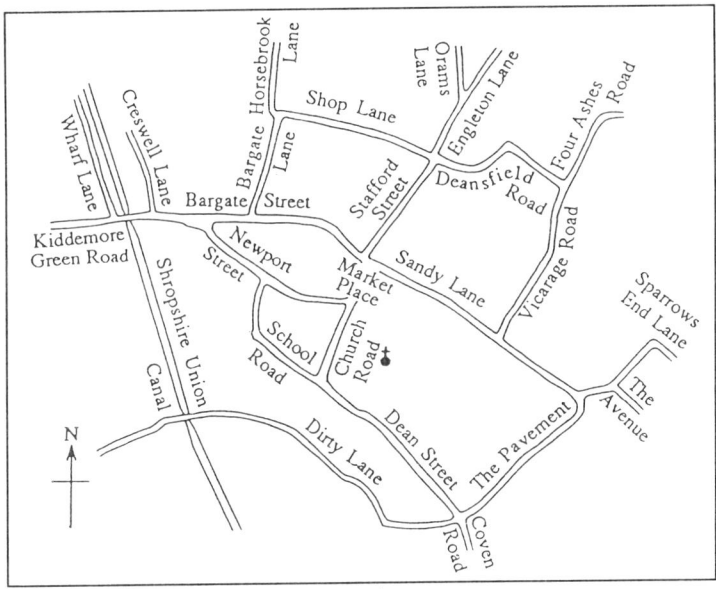

Brewood village. Scale approximately 1" to 500 feet.

village is Georgian, and most of the older houses are of red-brown brick, probably manufactured locally. Before the sixteenth century timber framing was used for all but the largest secular buildings, stone being used almost solely for plinths, and the poorest cottages may have been of mud.[440] From the late sixteenth to the eighteenth century timber framing became displaced by brick construction,[441] first replacing timber framing in the larger houses, and in the lesser buildings replacing stone as the plinth. By the early years of the 1700's it was being used for the exterior of most houses, but internal walls remained timber framed well into the century. However, brick did not completely displace timber framing in the farm buildings in the area until about 1760, nor from their interiors for another 20 years or so.

The fabled ships timbers said to be found in some houses are imaginary: Brewood is well removed from any major waterways, and except in early medieval times, when the King would often make gifts of oak from his Forests, timber was rarely transported over great distances to places with abundant woodland. It was however common practice for age-hardened timbers to be re-used several times in buildings of all types, and most of the older houses in Brewood incorporate much older timbering.

Although all the churches and the main bridges within the parish are of sandstone quarried nearby, and many of the roads and lanes are lined with unmortared sandstone blocks, there are few domestic buildings of stone. Handmade sand-faced tiles of local dark red clay, which turned dark blue during firing, but soon acquired a mossy green patination, are the usual roofing material.[442] Until perhaps a century ago thatch was not unusual,[443] and several buildings have steeply-pitched roofs, suggesting that they were originally thatched or roofed with shingles, but is likely that the opportunity was taken to replace thatch with tiles after the disastrous fire in Wheaton Aston which destroyed much of that village on 9th April 1777. Most of the oldest buildings in Brewood are in or near Dean Street and Market Place, but many other houses contain internal structures some centuries earlier than their façades.

Until fairly recent times several buildings in the village showed traces of large painted signs and advertisements on gable walls but, except for traces on Chequer House, all have now disappeared, either by weathering or under colourwash.

At the north end of Market Place, which was cobbled until some date between 1860 and 1866, is a cast-iron pump and brown marble horse-trough, a memorial to Major J.E. Monckton who died in 1891. The trough stands over an old well, and was fed originally by a squat cylindrical cast-iron pump, operated by cranked handles at each side assisted by a heavy iron

Market Place, c.1898. The post office on the left moved to its present location in 1901, when a shop was created from a private house.

188

fly-wheel, and surmounted until c.1902 by a lighting globe on a short column. The pump, originally surrounded by blue brick paving, was removed and taken to Somerford Hall in 1924, the trough being repositioned in front of the former Malt Shovel public house on the corner of Stafford Street and Deansfield Road, since early motor traffic had difficulty in negotiating around it. A small traffic island occupied the former site of the pump for some years in the 1950's and 1960's, and the trough was replaced in its present position in about 1980.

The old Brewood market pump was probably over this same well, and was possibly covered by some sort of roofed structure or clad in wood, for it is recorded that the pump was burned to the ground by an over-enthusiastic crowd, probably accidentally, during bonfire night celebrations on 5th November 1837.[444]

The north end of the Market Place sloped markedly to the east until about 1955, when it was levelled off and a low wall and railings erected at the north-east end.

On the south side of Market Place is The Dreadnought, a house and shop of smooth red brick built at some date after April 1908 and presumably named after the battleship launched in 1906. The distinctive bricks of the building are found in a number of houses scattered throughout the area,[445] which may be the work of the same builder. A large room on the first floor was used as a tea-room in the 1920's, run by Mrs 'Pansy' Powell, and a glazed panel in the double garage doors served villagers as a notice board displaying small advertisements for over 40 years until 1989. The building stands on the site of two old timber-framed cottages, described as 'unsightly and insecure' in 1896 when they were demolished, and is traditionally on the site of the Bishop's residence. An early photograph of Market Place suggests that the cottages were in line with the present building, and marks on the gable wall of the adjoining building to the south before The Dreadnought was built show that they were low with their ridge-line parallel with the road. Adjoining The Dreadnought

Broadgate House, 1903.

to the south is Broadgate House [traditionally named after the gate at which tolls were collected from those attending the market or fair], used since at least 1908 as a chemists, with a three-storey eighteenth century frontage and interior features of about 1680. In 1908 the house had two entrances, the smaller, probably non-original, on the south. The southern ground floor window was a narrow square bay, and that on the north was a sash matching the others. The house was the birthplace in 1828 of the Victorian civil engineer Thomas Andrew Walker.[446]

Glenhouse [formerly called, incorrectly, The Manor House], farther south, is a very severe stuccoed house of about 1800, with square windows and Egyptian pillared portico, and rear wings of the late sixteenth century and c.1700.

189

On the opposite side of Market Place are timber-framed houses of about 1600 with frontages dating from the early eighteenth century and later shop fronts. Four dormer windows in the roofline of one of the houses were inserted in about 1983, and for some years until c.1902 the shop served as the post office, before it moved to the house next to The Lion which was then converted into a shop. A number of well-finished upper cruck trusses

The Swan Hotel, c.1912, with weighing machine on the right, is a timber-framed former open-hall house now clad in brickwork, and said to be the oldest public house in Brewood. The bell high on the gable above the hotel signboard has a rope leading to a glass-fronted box on the right of the carriage entrance, and was used to summon firemen in emergencies.

are in the building adjoining to the north, which also has evidence of extensions to the west. Three upper-cruck roof trusses, perhaps as early as the fifteenth century, are incorporated in The Swan public house, a former timber-framed open hall house, remodelled in the second half of the last century, which stands at the north end of Market Place and said to be the oldest public house in the village. The Swan was the emblem of the Stafford family. On the opposite corner is Brewood House, a two-storey stucco building with shop front on the site of the former Fleur-de-Lis public house. Sadly, the records provide no information about the structure of the public house, known in the eighteenth century as the Fleur-de-Luce, which was demolished in about 1845.

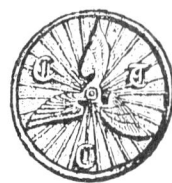

The Lion Hotel [until the mid-nineteenth century known as The Red Lion or The Lion and Giffard Arms], at the corner of Market Place and Stafford Street, is of late eighteeth century date[447] with keystones over the windows decorated with bunches of grapes. A Cyclists Touring Club roundel dates from at least 1902.[448] In

Victorian times the building was used as the local magistrates' court until the hearings were transferred to Penkridge.[449] The adjoining brick post office was converted in 1902 from a house of about 1780 which formerly had a pedimented frontage, and was [together with another detached building to the east, now demolished] known originally as The Malthouse and later as The Poplars. A private day and boarding school existed there in 1892. In the later eighteenth century a large house called The Malthouse adjoined The Lion, and is said to have then been 'the best in town'. It is unclear whether this house was the existing post office.

On the corner of Market Place, facing Stafford Street, is the architectural gem of the village, a tall, narrow, and delightfully eccentric brick house with elaborate Gothic frontage incorporating two canted bays, known as Speedwell Castle, formerly called The Lantern House or Folly House.

Market Place c.1895. Speedwell Castle was then occupied by W.H. Davies, grocer, and S. Bone & Co., grocers, according to the signs over the door. The shop on the right may then have been the post and telegraph office, run by Miss Bratt, who posted bulletins on the Boer War on the post office wall. The narrow chimney on the left is part of the former brewhouse which stood at the rear of the Swan Hotel and was built by Arthur Lowder, the licencee. Unfortunately the brewhouse was built adjoining the Swan, whereas the law required that the buildings be separated by a yard and wall. As a result the licence fee was increased so much that Lowder was forced to abandon brewing.

The building was reputedly constructed by William Rock, a local apothecary [a doctor who ran a shop] who is said to have won a substantial wager on a racehorse called Speedwell at some date before 1740, but there seems to be a complete absence of historical evidence to support the story, which may well be apocryphal.[450] The building, having two three-storey bays, with acorn-finials to the windows, flanking a central ogee entrance with a crocketed porch carried on columns of clustered shafts, was almost certainly created from designs produced by Batty Langley,[451] and incorporates details remarkably similar to the Gothic

Speedwell Castle, also called The Lantern House, photographed in about 1903. The building was at that time used as a store by David Brown, a provision merchant with a shop nearby in Stafford Street. The right hand window was then deeper – it has since been restored – and the building was in need of some repair to judge from the state of the pentice roof inserted over the ornate doorway. The building is held by tradition – probably wrongly – to have been built on the proceeds of a large win on a racecourse called Speedwell by a local apothecary, William Rock.

House at the bottom of the Stourbridge High Street and to those found at Shenstone Hall, near Lichfield. In the 1860's the building was rented by

192

the classics master at the Grammar School, and in 1875 a reading room was established there. From about 1890 to 1910 the building was used as a store for William Brown, provision merchant, with the west bay window lowered and a pentice roof between the bays, but the pentice roof has now been removed [although the line can still be traced], the window has been restored, and the house is split into flats. A jovial polychrome gnome

clasping a barrel or beerglass stood on the pinnacle of the porch from about the late 1940's until January 1991.[452] The house has been much altered inside, but retains an elaborate plaster ceiling and a 'Chinese Chippendale' staircase with fretted balustrade. Extensive renovation work was carried out in 1992.

Opposite Speedwell Castle formerly stood the Angel Hotel, dating from about 1800, the corner part of which was demolished in about 1935. The Jubilee Hall

The Speedwell gnome. in Bargate Street was created out of the clubroom at the western end of the de-licensed Angel[453] that year, to commemorate the jubilee of King George V.[454] Two K6 telephone kiosks in the space formerly occupied by the Angel were replaced by two new 'glass' kiosks in 1989.

The Angel Hotel, demolished in 1935, which stood on the corner of Stafford Street and Bargate Street, opposite Speedwell Castle. The clubroom to the west, in Bargate Street, was incorporated into the Jubilee Hall. The photograph dates from c.1915.

The majority of the houses in Bargate Street [also called Salop Street in the early nineteenth century], including Dawscroft House [after the Daws family], a large red brick building of irregular plan, of two distinct periods and with Ionic pillars at the entrance, and its former coach-house, Dawscroft Cottage, are late eighteenth century or later. The sandstone walling on the south side of Shop Lane marks the boundary of the garden of The Dawscroft. The walling was formerly topped with tall iron railings. The White House is of three storeys with a colour washed stucco frontage, but is constructed in yellowish bricks, seemingly not local. It dates from the early eighteenth century, but incorporates later alterations, and has a revival doorway. One truss in the back roof is a re-used king-post truss, perhaps from Sutherland House, and an early eighteenth century staircase leads from the first floor. A Victorian brick porch was removed in the 1960's.

Behind the unprepossessing frontage of Sutherland House [numbers 5-7] is a remarkable fragment of early vernacular architecture, essentially a fifteenth-century timber-framed open hall house. The architectural evidence suggests that when first built, the house was probably four bays in length – a two-bay hall with a single two-storey bay at either end of the hall. A single-bay timber-framed wing was added to the rear of the building in the seventeenth century, and at some date – perhaps the mid

Behind the simple façade of 5-7 Bargate Street lies the timberwork of a fifteenth century open-hall house. The photograph dates from about 1910. The Gamson family were well-known carriers in the village.

eighteenth century when the adjoining White House was built – the lower bay of the hall and the presumed service bay were demolished. The house contains an open-hall truss and spere truss, the former carried on richly moulded wall posts and joined crucks, the latter supported by substantial curved braces and with a crown post having down-swinging braces. All the roof-timbers are smoke-blackened. The house was rebuilt in brick in the last century, and at the turn of the century was a shop serving teas. It was rebuilt in 1986.[455]

The Beeches [formerly The Laurels, and popularly known as New Hall in Victorian times, but now named after several very large beech trees in the garden], a large brick house with plaster lined as ashlar, colour washed in recent years, was built on the site of two old cottages in 1836 as a doctor's house. The house was used as a surgery in more recent times, with the waiting room at the side. In 1874 it was recorded that a large half-timbered house called The Rookery stood opposite the back gates of The Laurels, "the stables and barns belonging to which, known as The Foldyard, are a square opposite . . . [together with] Bargate House they extended from the School land to Bargate Street, in the form of a Y intersected at its branch by Newport Street". A new house was built in the garden to the west of The Beeches in 1988.

Number 23 Bargate Street, formerly known as The Bargates, was rebuilt, together with the adjoining cottages on the west, in the 1970's. The bar gate after which the street took its name was presumably close by.

At the eastern corner of Bargate Street and Bargate Lane is Chequer House, until about 1895 The Chequered Ball public house. The brickwork of the gable wall still bears traces of painted lettering advertising 'Good Stabling'. Adjoining it on the east is a small single-storey timber-framed building with two blocked windows on a sandstone plinth which may be sixteenth century. Sandstone plinths extending east may be connected with the old manor barn which is said to have stood in the area. Forge Cottage dates from about 1750. Bargate House, formerly a malthouse, dates mainly from the early eighteenth century, but with older parts. A gabled stair turret at the rear houses an early eighteenth century dog-leg staircase. The blank wall facing Bargate Street is relieved by four trompe l'oeil tall sash windows. On the south corner of Bargate Lane and the east entrance to the former Dominican Convent [known in the nineteenth century as Stepping Stone Lane] are the former Bargate Stables, with the name incised on a sandstone plaque. Opposite is a row of cottages set end-on to the road with a sandstone block in the roadside wall incised 'Dawscroft Foreign'. Adjoining the cottages on the north is the single-storey, flat-roofed fire station, opened in March 1961 and built at a cost of £1000.[456]

The earliest part of the former Dominican convent, a long two-storey brick building with projecting wings[457] and five-sided porch, was originally the parish workhouse, built at some date before 1795, replacing the original workhouse which was in Kiddemore Green Road between Hockerhill and Churchfields. It is now St Dominic's School, a private school for girls, and was extended at the rear in 1956. Near the north west corner of the building is a small circular colour-washed building with a conical roof which may have been a summerhouse, although similar buildings elsewhere were constructed as privies, with one for males and one for females: a second such building seems however not to have existed. A large detached sports complex was built to the north of the school in 1987.

The former Lloyd's Bank, a single storey red brick building on the north side of Bargate Street, built in 1855 by the Trustees of the Brewood Savings Bank, which ceased in 1867, was taken over by Lloyd's the following year, and in 1872 was open from 12 noon to 3 pm on Thursdays [later changed to Tuesdays]. In 1987 it was converted into an annexe to St Dominic's School and a new entrance to the school from Bargate Street was created in August the following year, with the walling realigned. The uniform row of cottages to the west, which include an arched stable entrance, date from the mid nineteenth century. All have semi-circular door heads with prominent plain keystones. The immediate area was known as Bank Square in Victorian times, and in 1866 there existed some low timber-framed houses which could have been the remains of a larger building. At the junction of Bargate Street and Newport Street is an early K6 telephone box, designed by Sir Walter Giles Scott and introduced in 1936. The box is now protected by listing as a building of special architectural interest. The brick wall behind was built in 1935. The variegated concrete slab and blue brick paving in Bargate Street was laid in 1991, and the 'period' lamp standards were installed at the same date.

View west along Bargate Street, 1960. The house on the left was demolished c.1962.

The pinfold or pound, a small rectangular open structure in which stray cattle were kept, formerly stood at High Green on the south side of the road east of the canal bridge until at least 1907, when it was then said to be "full of rubbish . . . in a neglected condition . . . long an eyesore."[458] It was probably demolished soon after, and seems to have been replaced by a single-storey wooden building projecting into the road which was for many years a cycle shop run by Moses Evans. It was demolished in about 1960.

196

Immediately in front of what is now the garage stood an L-shaped brick house with bay window, pulled down in about 1962. The village stocks stood nearby until at least 1864.[459] A small brick cottage known as Pinfold Cottage on the south side of the road was demolished in about 1983. The south-eastern corner incorporated sandstone blocks. The site is now occupied by a house. The Bridge public house dates from between 1851 and 1872. In the space between the public house and the canal bridge formerly stood a two-storey building with narrow gabled end facing the road built from heavy squared sandstone blocks with an arched window at first-floor level and single-storey extension with pent roof to the east. The rear part of the house was brick built. The house may have dated from the building of the canal, and seems to have been demolished in the early 1960's.

The name High Green presumably distinguished it from another green [perhaps a 'low green', possibly in the meadows opposite The Pavement], and was almost certainly in the triangular area bounded by Bargate Street, Market Place and Newport Street.

St. Mary's Row, 1960.

A short distance to the west of the Catholic church formerly stood a terrace of six brick cottages, dating from at least 1808,[460] with another cottage on the north side of the east end of the row which may have served as the original workhouse. The cottages, known as St Mary's Row, were demolished in about 1960. At the north end of the lane to Brewood Wharf is the site of the old gasworks, which lay in the garden to the north of the house now named The Anchorhold, but still known to older villagers as The Gas House. Shafbury [sic] Cottage nearby has a plaque dated 1894, and very pronounced ridge-and-furrow in the garden to the north.

At the east end of Newport Street, in the early nineteeth century known as Back Street, and later Shiffnal Street, is a timber-framed building faced with brickwork in the early eighteenth century with a small open shop of the same date under a pentice roof with early glass in the central window of the first floor. The former fire station was at one time located in an adjoining outbuilding with stabling which has now been demolished. Opposite, on the north side of Newport Street, is a row of three houses, numbers 4 to 8, each of three storeys, dating from the later eighteenth century. The middle house has an elaborate glazed fanlight over the door and a blocked first-floor window with a plaque reading 'Providenti Locus', and the houses on each side have been pebbledashed. The rear of the buildings reveals evidence of much alteration, and it is possible that extensions once existed on the north: at various levels sandstone blocks are set into the brickwork to form irregular horizontal rows. The wall is broken by a narrow vertical staircase window to eaves level. On the west side of the houses is a short length of brick wall on which are scratched various initials and dates suggesting that the spot – opposite the site of the Fire Station – was a gathering point for village youths around the time of the First World War. Further north along Newport Street is the library, a single-storey sand-faced brick building with pyramid roof, wood-lined to the apex internally, opened on 27th March 1972. The library stands on the site of a terrace of brick cottages built between 1808 and 1834 which followed the curve of the road. One cottage on the north end of the row had two wide pointed-arched windows to the first floor. A stable adjoining collapsed into the road in the 1960's.

Newport House and the adjoining Barn House appear to have been built at the same time, possibly the late eighteenth century. The latter was converted from a barn c.1935. There is a small lancet attic window in the east gable of the latter. The buildings may be connected with the stables and barn known as The Foldyard, mentioned previously. Numbers 17 and 19 Newport Street [in the 1860's known as The Rookery and later as Deans End] are a complicated accumulation of buildings which seem to be of E-plan, perhaps dating from the seventeenth century, with an extension made on the east in 1991. In the early nineteenth century other buildings extended further south along School Road.

Two square black and white timber-framed houses divided by a small brick courtyard housing a pump lie on the west side of the junction of Newport Street and School Road and date from about 1600. The larger is a small house of two storeys and attics built around the central chimney. The

198

south-east corner post on the first floor internally displays elaborate roll moulding, and may have originated as a late fifteenth or early sixteenth century bressumer or ceiling beam from a grander building. Many of the other timbers are clearly re-used. The smaller of the two houses was substantially rebuilt using 20 year old oak in 1985. It was formerly part of a range of timbered cottages that extended further west, incorporating a house and locksmith's workshop, but that section was demolished in 1965, despite attempts to save it.[461] The demolished cottage was the birthplace in 1827 of John B. Haynes, a prominent Victorian missionary and theologian.[462] On the opposite side of the road was a double-pile red brick house of late eighteenth century date latterly known as Orchard Cottage, demolished in the 1970's and replaced with a new house. The colour-washed Methodist Church in School Road was built in 1868 as a Wesleyan Chapel.

West end of Newport Street, c.1965, showing Orchard Cottage (centre).

Numbers 1[463] to 7 Stafford Street are a unified terrace of six tall two-storey houses with attics dating from the late eighteenth or early nineteenth century. Number 11 Stafford Street has a nineteenth century stuccoed frontage on a seventeenth century structure. Gunstone House is a large house with internal timber framing dating from the early seventeenth century and a central Italianate doorway dating from about 1800. Opposite is Stafford House, a large three-storey building of about 1800 with shops on the ground floor, possibly two houses originally, with one doorway surviving. The shops were created in about 1955. The car park to the rear and the adjoining flat-roofed telephone exchange are on the former gardens of the house. The high walls of the garden survive, together with an old pear tree and weeping ash within the car park. Number 15 Stafford Street is a small early nineteenth century house with symmetrical frontage and Italianate doorway with projecting canopy. Loreto and Iona are two colour-washed houses created from a single house of about 1700, with evidence of a former wide stable entrance. A line of four cottages formerly extended south from Iona, and were demolished in about 1960. The colour-washed cottages now adjoining Iona were built in about 1980.

Opposite: a group of cottages at the junction of Newport Street and School Road photographed in about 1950. The main building, known as The Mansion House, dates from c.1600, but incorporates earlier timbers. The row of low cottages on the right was from at least early Victorian times the home of the Hayes family, and the birthplace of John Bayley Hayes, an eminent nineteenth century theologian. Other members of the family made locks in the cottages, which were demolished in 1965 with the exception of the part nearest the camera which was rebuilt in 1985. The lantern is typical of those found throughout the central village area from the later 1860's.

On the opposite side of the road two connected low timber-framed cottages adjoined 15 Stafford Street, divided by a passage from a three-storey brick house. All three were pulled down in about 1956. Number 28 Stafford Street is a small brick house with revival doorway, dating from about 1710.

The ladies fashions in the view south along Stafford Street suggest that it dates from about 1905. The tall building on the right and low cottages behind were demolished in 1956.

Maidens the Butchers is a red brick shop and house with two projecting ground floor bays and an arched yard entrance on the south. There is a plaque: 'AW 1896'.[464]

 Number 32 Stafford Street is a colour-washed low brick building with a painted sandstone plaque, now eroded, but which formerly read 'SIG 1715'. The house incorporates a re-used medieval tie beam. On the corner of Stafford Street and Deansfield Road is a large building, now two houses, dating from about 1800.

On the opposite corner of Stafford Street are the Parish Council offices,[465] a single-storey red brick building opened on 28th March 1932 [when it included a 'Fire Equipment Station'] and built on land acquired by the County Council for road widening after the demolition of old buildings to replace a wooden meeting room,[466] which had previously been used for council meetings, the Red Cross, as a doctor's surgery, and [on Wednesdays after school hours] as a library. On the north side of the building is an oak tree bearing a plaque recording that it was planted on 6th May 1935 to mark the jubilee of King George V.

Facing Stafford Street on the corner of Deansfield Road is the former Malt Shovel public house and malthouse, a complex building with many old beams, dating mainly from the seventeenth century, the west part of which in Engleton Lane was for many years until January 1991 used as a fish and chip shop. Some old cottages which formed part of the group were demolished in the early 1970's.

Looking north along Stafford Street to the Old Malt Shovel public house in about 1875. The proprietor was then Whitmore Aston, brewer and maltster. Window shutters were once common throughout the village, not only for security and privacy, but to protect vulnerable windows from damage by cattle driven through the streets to and from the market. Stafford Street is first recorded by name in 1493, but was probably ancient at that date. In 1845 and 1874 plans were published for a railway branch line from Bushbury Junction to the north end of Stafford Street, but the schemes did not proceed.

The Three Stirrups public house [named after the arms of the Giffards] is Victorian, built some time before 1851 on an earlier site. The red brick building was colourwashed in 1991. A short distance to the east in Deansfield Road stood Home Farm, a tall red brick three-storey former farmhouse, built in the late eighteenth century. It was demolished in about 1975.

A number of small houses and cottages in Shop Lane, several with datestones, are mainly from the second half of the nineteenth century, including 14 and 16, a semi-detached villa with an ornate central alcove containing a plaque reading DVFAL BARA/LLE/1873, and a later porch on the west side incorporating a stone trefoil head; Peel Cottage, dated 1865; South View Cottage [1878]; and Ivy Cottage [1892]. At the eastern end is a low cottage range of early eighteenth century date. The Gables has a late nineteenth century façade on a seventeeth century core. A small chapel was built in 1858 on the west side of the junction of Shop Lane and Pendryll Avenue. It was demolished c.1950, having been used as a carpenters shop for many years.

The short length of road from Market Place to the first National School was known as Church Street or Churchyard until, in 1864, a new road, Church Road, was made joining Dean Street, then known as Dean's End, with Market Place.

In Church Road, opposite the church, is a much altered three-storey brick house with symmetrical wings with semi-circular Italianate doorways and later shop front which was identified as the post office by the Ordnance Survey in 1884, and which was later used as the police station for many years until 1950. The cells still exist in the cellars. The house on the corner of Church Road and School Road was a sweet shop for many years until 1988. A thatched house near the church gate which was destroyed by fire in about 1870 was the birthplace of William Parke, the Brewood historian who ran a successful bookselling business in Wolverhampton and whose financial generosity lead to the Victorian restoration of Brewood church.

To the north of Church Road near Market Place formerly stood the original National School, built in 1818, a single-storey building replaced by a larger school and schoolhouse in 1859. The latter still exists, but the Victorian school and original school were demolished in 1966, a year after the present single-storey school was built to the west. The Victorian school faced Church Road, and was of red brick with stone dressings, with a wooden bell-tower capped by a squat four-sided spire, tall gables each side of a central porch, and decoratively-pierced bargeboards. The site of the original school is marked by a paved area with benches surrounded by a wall, with its former gables marked on the wall of the house which stands on the corner of Church Road and Newport Street. The site of the Victorian school has been incorporated into the playground of the present school, the low school wall still existing along Church Road. The iron railings which originally surmounted the wall were removed in the 1960's.

Dean Street contains a particularly impressive variety of vernacular architecture in its short length.

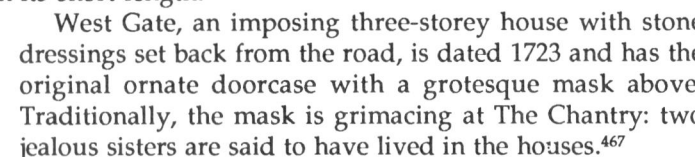 West Gate, an imposing three-storey house with stone dressings set back from the road, is dated 1723 and has the original ornate doorcase with a grotesque mask above. Traditionally, the mask is grimacing at The Chantry: two jealous sisters are said to have lived in the houses.[467]

Similar large houses are The Old Deanery [c.1810] and The Chantry [1712], the former having an older core and heavy provincial Baroque style façade with Tuscan half-columns around the central door-way, and the latter having a non-original Victorian pillared doorway [to replace a large square brick porch], added in the early 1960's from a demolished Victorian building in St John's Square, Wolverhampton, and 'triglyph' keystones to the tall sash windows. Chantry Cottage was formerly the stable to The Chantry, and incorporates a large bricked-in arch. The cottage on the west side of the footpath passage [known as 'the narrow entry' at the turn of the century and having a metal turnstile at the Dean Street end for many years thereafter] was a tea room run by Miss Rosa Fox from about 1906 until c.1920. The end cottage adjoining is timber-framed under pebble-dashed render.

Cottages at the north end of Dean Street in about 1905. The one on the left, Dean Cottage, became a tea room run by Rose Fox in the early decades of the century.

Dean House [formerly The Den], in 2" handmade bricks, on the north side of the street, has a symmetrical facade of about 1800. Unusually, much of the internal woodwork is in pine rather than oak. The four blocked spaces [the bottom left-hand space is a twentieth-century copy] never had windows, an indication of the severity of the Window Tax between 1782 and 1823. A vault within the churchyard is said to lie beyond the west wall of the cellar. Numbers 23 and 25 [Georgia Villa and Dean's Croft], a pair of red brick semi-detached houses with a frontage of c.1916, are on the site of an old malthouse, formerly known as Mullards. On the opposite side of the road is a low timber-framed sixteenth century house known at the end of the last century as The Sweep's House, with a projecting gabled wing to the north, used as a saddlers shop from about 1870 until the early 1900's. The house was virtually derelict by the 1970's, but has now been restored.

The Sweep's House, Dean Street, c.1890, so-called because for many years it was the home of Enoch Plant, chimney sweep, who is said to have employed several boys to climb up inside chimneys. The house, evidently in need of urgent repair, carries a board reading

E PLANT, WHO DOES LIVE HERE
SWEEPS CHIMNEYS NOT TOO DEAR
IF YOUR CHIMNEY SHOULD TAKE FIRE
HE WILL PUT IT OUT AT YOUR DESIRE

The sign remained in place until about 1920, and is well remembered by older residents.

The Admiral Rodney public house, much altered, and recently renovated, is late nineteenth century, and stands on the site of a much older public house of the same name, presumably dating from the early 1780's when the admiral achieved fame for important naval victories over the Spanish, Dutch and French. The colour washed building on the west side of the entrance to the car-park is a converted stable. For many years in the 1930's and 1940's petrol pumps existed on the west side of the public house, which then offered garage facilities. The Garth[468] is a large stucco-faced house of c.1820, with three blocked windows. The lower cottage of the pair adjoining on the east was for many years after the turn of the century a hardware shop run by David Brown, after he moved from Bargate Street, next to Speedwell Castle. 33-35 Dean Street, c.1780-1800, were formerly the police house before it was moved to Church Road in about 1920. A police station seems to have existed since at least 1849. To the east of 35 Dean Street is a bungalow built in 1930 in what was the garden of Dean

Street House opposite. In the garden to the rear of the bungalow are the ruins of a substantial rendered brick summerhouse of uncertain age, but certainly pre-1906, which was damaged by a falling tree c.1986.

On the south-west side of Dean Street are several timber-framed houses of about 1600, many of which retain original central chimneys and exposed timbering in side and rear elevations. They include Dean Street House, Deans End and Wood End [both originally one house] incorporating a Gothic bay window, and Old Smithy House, a large much-renovated house with an eighteenth century frontage, and steps leading to an entrance at the south.[469]

An early view of Dean Street, possibly dating from the end of the last century. The steps in the centre of the picture may be those of Mullard's malt house which formerly stood on the west side of The Garth.

The elaborate doorhead of Dean Street House, a large colour washed house with symmetrical façade and projecting wing to the east, bears the date 1791. The first-floor windows are in clusters of three with segmental heads of a type which seem to have been fashionable in the village at this period, each side of a central blind arch. The house is said to have been used as a girl's school in the nineteenth century. Other houses in the street date from the late eighteenth and early nineteenth century, with some of very recent date.

At the bottom of Dean Street, opposite The Pavement, is the most venerable house in the village, a timber-framed building, formerly a row of three cottages, known as Old Smithy Cottage,[470] which was originally a single-storey hall-house of about 1350. The hall, formed of two of the cottages, was of two bays totalling 28 feet by 18 feet. The roof, still at the original pitch, has a trussed rafter roof, with king-post and four-way struts, and internal smoke-blackened timbers. The wall plates have double-stopped chamfers and a later partition between the cottages has been formed from the cambered tie-beam of the open truss. There is evidence in the northern end of the hall roof that there may originally have been a further bay beyond it. The present structure in this position is an early seventeenth century timber-framed replacement. At the end of the sixteenth century a brick extension was built against the south-east wall of the former hall, and a spliced purlin near this end of the roof might be evidence of another bay there, although the timbering in the gable end is heavily weathered, suggesting that it has been exposed to the elements as an external wall. The house contains a seventeenth century staircase. The property, derelict by the early 1970's – a large section of roof tiles fell into Dean Street in January 1970 – was extensively renovated in 1988-9.[471]

Some 50 yards to the south was a cottage which stood derelict for a number of years until demolished in about 1950. Exposed in one gable-end was the timberwork of a medieval hall with cruck principals below collar-beam level, of a type associated with two-bay halls of about 1400.[472] The two hall-houses were clearly buildings of some importance in the fourteenth century, and may have been associated with the original residence of the Dean.

On the south side of Sandy Lane, close to Market Place is a single-storey red-brick mid-Victorian building with central arched doorway and three tall windows on each side, all with Italianate arches. The building was built by Mr Swann in 1857, mainly at the cost of Mr T.W. Giffard, as a reading room. It was still in use as a library in 1896, but in the early years of the present century was used by the Band of Hope as a meeting room, and

later as a clinic and institute.[473] The first meeting of the Parish Council was held in the building on 1st January 1895. It has recently been renovated for use as a shop. To the east were two short rows of low brick cottages, demolished between 1951 and 1957. Remains of the back walls, built into the high bank to the rear, have recently become exposed to view.

Grain Ridge in Sandy Lane was once a granary and malthouse built over a well on the north side, and formed part of the adjoining late eighteenth century house known as the Old House, formerly Sunnyside. Grain Ridge was converted into a house in 1935.

The Surgery is a flat-roofed complex in 'international' style, built in 1954 by Dr A.H. Cheshire and Dr H.S. Ayre on infilled quarry land at a cost of £4000. At the time it was the only privately-built health centre in Staffordshire. It was extended in 1990.

The Old Smithy, a nineteenth century brick house, incorporates a former smithy [which was worked until the 1930's] and old timbers built around the chimney of a much earlier structure. A beam in the east part of the house is reputedly from old cottages pulled down in Market Place in 1896, traditionally connected with the medieval Bishop's residence. A garage on the west side of the house – the former smith's shop – is built over an old well, with one on the east built into the hillside.

The Old Vicarage in Vicarage Road was built in 1860 in red brick with a slated roof to a complicated plan, with arched doorways and stone dressings. Deansfield, a large square brick building of two storeys with a low-pitched slate roof, was built in 1833 by the Rev A.B. Haden for his own occupation. It was used as a school in the earlier part of this century, and from 1960 as a home for the elderly. It was demolished despite opposition in November 1989 to be replaced by a purpose-built home for the elderly, of contemporary design, which was opened on 18th May 1991. The Lodge, a single-storey building with low pitched slate roof to match the former Deansfield House, dates from about 1835, and was restored in 1989.

A Nonconformist Chapel formerly stood on the south side of Sandy Lane, between Vicarage Road and The Pavement. It was a substantial red brick building with round-headed windows, a tall front gable having stepped sides and segmental head. It was demolished in August 1963 after falling into disrepair. The Manse, at the lower end of Sandy Lane, is a small three bay eighteenth century house of colourwashed stucco with later porch.

Barnfield, in The Pavement, is a former barn converted into a house in the 1930's. The police station and police houses in The Pavement were built in 1950.

Opposite: Sandy Lane from Market Place in about 1905. The buildings have changed little, although the pediment over the post office has now gone. The shop on the right is on the site of the former Fleur-de-Lis public house, demolished in about 1845. The footpath running down the hill fronted two short rows of cottages demolished in the early 1950's, the back walls of which can still be seen.

Along the west side of The Pavement formerly stood a number of low brick cottages with gabled rooflines, with a long timber-framed row of cottages at the southern end. Two cottages at the north end of the timber-framed row were formed out of a three-bay house probably dating from the early 1500's, with the end cottage containing a cross passage and original doorhead. The second cottage was formed from a single-bay hall and solar, with a large chimney inserted in about 1600. The southern half of the range was a two-bay cottage with smaller framing attached to the earlier building in the early seventeenth century, probably using earlier timbers.

Cottages at The Pavement, redrawn from a photograph in the 'Wolverhampton Journal', August 1907.

The range was built up to a uniform height in about 1700 and was thatched until about 1900. The cottages, much neglected, were demolished in 1962. Opposite the cottages was a well set in a recess in a red brick wall bordering the road on the corner opposite Dean Street. Another cottage of later date further north along The Pavement, demolished many years ago, contained a roof truss with cambered tie beam, collar beam and principals embedded in a gable end.

Opposite: the magnificent range of timber-framed cottages which formerly stood at the southern end of The Pavement, near the junction with Dean Street. The right-hand half of the building was a three-bay house of the early 1500's, and the end cottage on the right contained the old cross-passage with the original doorhead. The central cottage marks the position of the single-bay hall, the end walls of which were heavily smoke-blackened, and the solar, or upper-floor apartment. The large chimney was inserted in about 1600. The cottage on the left, with the smaller panels, was added in the early seventeenth century, using older timbers. The cottages fell into disrepair and were demolished in 1962, a much-lamented loss to the village.

The photograph above, taken in 1893, shows the range thatched as it would have been when first built, and the lower photograph, dating from about 1905, illustrates how the height of the cottages was increased in about 1900, with tiled roof incorporating new dormers capped by turned embellishments.

Brewood Hall, on the east of the village, is traditionally the site of King John's hunting lodge,[474] and before the fourteenth century the semi-official residence of the bailiff of the Bishop's manor, and is said to have been the seat of William, son of Roger Fowke, in the later fifteenth century, descending through the Fowke family until 1930. The two-storied brick mansion with attics dates principally from about 1640, apparently on an earlier, probably medieval, plan of a central hall block with symmetrical gabled cross-wings projecting to the east. In the Hearth Tax Assessment of 1666 the house was assessed at 10 hearths.

Dr Plot evidently visited the old house, for he mentions in 1686[475] that in the whitethorn hedge, between the garden and court before the house, were the figures of several animals, castles, etc., formed in topiary, and that in the orchard there was the whitethorn figure of a wren's nest, big enough to hold a man. In the garden was a yew tree, which formed an arbor, measuring five yards square outside and three and a half inside, "cut on the top with loop and crest, like the battlements of a town, adorn'd at each corner with a pinnacle, over which is wrought a canopy . . . two yards in diameter, which is carryed up" gradually to a small pinnacle. Near the pale of the orchard was a "fine yew tree, cut up gradually from greater to lesser rounds, to the number of twenty".

The building has timber-framed parts to the much altered rear, where blocked lunette windows can be made out. The east wall has two decorated lead rainwater heads. One shows two complete cherub figures, the other a cherub's head. A stone plaque below a first-floor window on the north wing of the east front has arms of the Fowke-Hussey family, with a tablet on the north-east wall dated 1700. Internally the house retains many oak floors, doors and door frames, a bolection moulded late seventeenth century fireplace and linenfold panels in a room in the north wing, and barleytwist balusters and square newels in the main staircase, but the building was considerably altered in the nineteenth century, with plate glass windows and cement quoins inserted around the windows and on the corners of the north and south wings, and a conservatory built between the front wings in 1858. The topiary work in the garden admired by Plot was also removed at this time. The front porch is modern. The garden walls and gate pillars date from the late seventeenth century, as do some of the outbuildings. A substantial timber-framed barn with long straight braces to the lower panels [similar to that at Barn Cottages] was demolished in 1968. Stone fleurs-de-lis,[476] about two feet high, which formerly surmounted each of the gate piers, are said to have been the origin of the mark used by John Turner, the famous Staffordshire potter, whose father once lived at the Hall. During the nineteenth century restoration the fleurs-de-lis were removed to the back garden, and replaced by two large stone balls. On the north-east side of the Hall is a large early eighteenth century red brick farm building with king-post roof and exposed first floor beams. The building seems to have been used as a malthouse in the last century. The sandstone gateposts and steps of the former path to the rear of Brewood

Hall still stand in Vicarage Road, a short distance from Sandy Lane.

Brewood Hall at about the turn of the century. The building is of mid-seventeenth century date, but was disfigured in Victorian times by the insertion of new windows with cement quoins and central verandah. The dovecote demolished c.1968 is on the right.

The houses of Hall Farm Close stand on the site of a large pond which was filled in in about 1960. The pond may have marked the site of Brewood Hall quarry, said to have been very deep, which was full of water before 1869.[477]

For the sake of completeness it must be added that local traditions of secret tunnels from Brewood Hall to the parish church – and, indeed, between various other unlikely points, including Blackladies and Whiteladies – are entirely without foundation, but are similarly found [and almost invariably unsubstantiated] in almost every parish in Britain. There are, however, a number of houses with extensive rock-cut cellars in the village area, which might help to explain the local folklore.

Brook House is a farmhouse and former beerhouse [known as The Vauxhall in about 1850] dating mainly from the eighteenth century,[478] with outbuildings containing earlier timbering. The garage opposite dates from about 1920, and is on the site of an old shed. Dean's Hall Farm, formerly 'Dean's Hill in Dean's End' noted in Gregory King's Notebook c.1680, is of L-plan and dates mainly from about 1700. The building is on two levels, the block of c.1700 facing north-east having an older but much-altered service wing at the rear. A large pilastered chimney serves both wings, and two rooms contain seventeenth century panelling, that in one room clearly re-used. A tall garden wall and derelict dovecote date from about

211

1700. A five-bay fifteenth century barn in the farmyard has three medieval cruck-trusses, and there is evidence that others once existed. The remaining trusses have tie beams, collar beams with curved braces, and upper collars. Although the side walls have been rebuilt in brick, short spur ties, which once connected the principals with the side framing, remain in situ. A two-storeyed timber-framed extension at the north-west corner of the barn is seventeenth century. Between the house and the nearby canal bridge is a low mound in which a skeleton was reputedly found some years ago. It is also said that fragments of gravestones were many years ago dug up near the pond to the south-east of the house. Various mounds and earthworks lie to the east of the house between the canal, Coven Road and Port Lane, and probably date from the construction of the canal in the late 1820's. They may however repay more detailed investigation. At least two buildings, perhaps houses, lay near the road into Brewood close to the Port Lane crossroads in the early part of the last century.[479]

Two or three cottages, at least one of which was thatched,[480] formerly stood on the east side of Hyde Mill Lane between Dean's Hall Farm and the Woolley. The Mount, in Hyde Mill Lane, was built on the site of a small cottage in about 1920.

Woodlands, a large pebble-dashed house near the south-east corner of Coven Road and Port Lane bears a large terracotta plaque inscribed '19.F.09'. To the east formerly stood a plain brick early nineteenth century house known as Lloyd's Nurseries and Tea Gardens. The house is said to have been converted from a single-storey building which contained heavy timbering, possibly crucks, and was demolished in the early 1950's. Hillcrest, at Hilltop, is one of the few stone cottages to survive in Brewood. Constructed of random sandstone blocks, it dates from the eighteenth century, and was much altered and enlarged in the 1980's. Park Cottage, latterly called The White House, on the eastern edge of the village, incorporates heavy timber framing and probably dates from the early seventeenth century.

The present brick farmhouse at The Hyde, with symmetrical north front rendered and lined to simulate ashlar, was built in the mid eighteenth century on a very ancient site. A ground floor room contains re-used mid sixteenth century panelling, incorporating carved medallion heads and shields bearing the arms of Lane and of Lane impaling Bagot. The original house lay a short distance to the east and was formerly surrounded by a substantial moat,[481] not necessarily for defence, for moats were also created as a status symbol and as fishponds. Since few moated sites appear to have possessed a well, moats seem also to have provided a source of drinking water and protection against fire in adjoining woodland or scrub, as well as the means of extinguishing fires which must have been all too common when timber and thatch were the usual building materials. This type of small-scale moat is associated in the region with areas of forest clearance.

The western arm of the moat still contains water, and a ditch remains on the south, but the north and east sides have been filled in. A sketch on an estate map of 1704 suggests that the earlier house was timber-framed, on an L-plan of two storeys with central chimney stack and central arched doorway. It appears to have stood to the east of the existing house. The moat was seemingly crossed by a bridge at the north-west corner. There is evidence that the old house existed well into the last century.

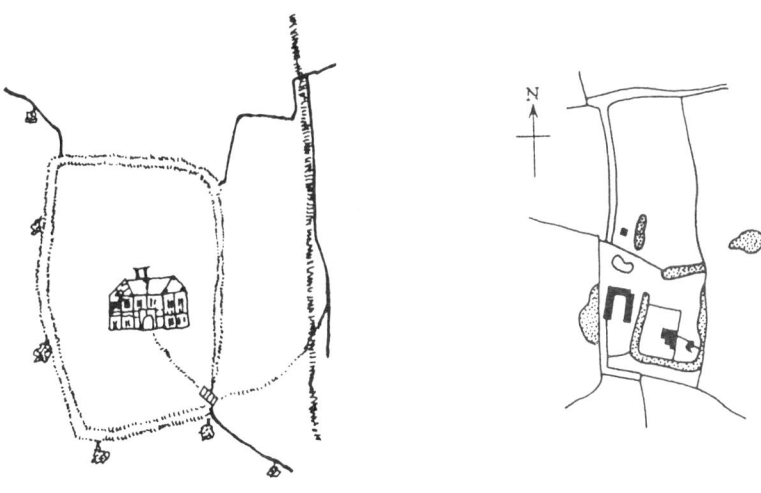

Left: redrawn extract from a Hyde estate plan of 1749, showing the old house and moat. There is what appears to be a bridge over the north-west corner of the moat [north is at the bottom]. Right: redrawn extract from Josiah Robins and James Sherriff's map of 1808 showing the moated old house at the Hyde, and the present house built to the west. With acknowledgements to Staffordshire Record Office D590/361 and D590/375.

The Woolley farmhouse has a north block with a large central chimney dating from the late seventeenth century, and a south block dated 1824 with the initials T.L.

In Chillington Street, a bridlepath off Port Lane, now much overgrown at the eastern end but formerly 'a paved causeway, much given to flooding', and one of the main approaches to Chillington Hall before the early eighteenth century, are several small thatched timber-framed cottages dating from about 1600, the last surviving remnants of Chillington village, formerly known as Chillington Town. The lodge at Giffard's Cross was built in the early nineteenth century. To the south of Giffard's Cross is the last surviving cottage of several which stood hereabouts. The small cottage, parts of which are stone-built, dates from the early eighteenth century. A fragment of a second cottage is incorporated in a nearby outbuilding on the south.

213

At the junction of Chillington Street and Port Lane is a pair of cottages, known as Barn Cottages, created from a seventeenth century timber-framed threshing barn with tall opposed entrances.[482] The building has what is by tradition a water-filled moat on the north-east, but ridge-and-furrow running into the pool suggests that the water probably fills old marl pits.[483] An otherwise detailed Chillington estate plan of about 1727 does not show the building or a moat, while a plan of 1808 shows the building with a circular pond to the north.

Depressions at Chillington Farm may be the remains of a former moated site.[484] A narrow rectangular area of water is shown on the west of the farmhouse on a map of 1808, and a wide rectangular depression lay to the east of the house in recent years. It is marked as an old sand pit on early Ordnance Survey maps.

The medieval village of Chillington was concentrated on the south of Chillington Hall,[485] and the majority of the houses were swept away during the early 1760's when the park was extended.

Bath Farm dates from the mid-eighteenth century and was named after a cold bath fed from a spring, which existed from at least 1727 and is said to have been used for bathing by local people. The stream from the spring, with other water drained from the area, now runs into an artificial channel, possibly constructed as early as the eighteenth century, but certainly before 1808, which runs into Chillington Pool. The farmhouse and nearby cottages date from the second half of the eighteenth century. A great oak, famed for its size, is said to have stood near the farm. Mounds and depressions in the south-east corner of a field to the south of the house appear to be a moated site,[486] on which a house stood c.1727. The building had disappeared by 1761.

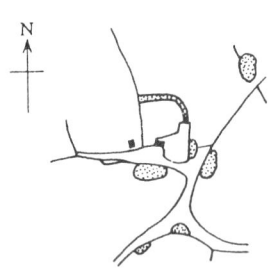

Redrawn extract from Josiah Robins and James Sherriff's map of 1808 showing moat at The Whitemoor. SRO D590/375.

On all sides of The Whitemoor are depressions which are almost certainly the remnants of another moat.[487] The present house dates from the nineteenth century, but the site may be much older. John de la Wytemore was arrested with John Giffard in about 1276 for killing the king's deer. He was evidently a person of some standing, and his residence may have been on or near the site of the existing house.

On the south side of the lane to Harvington Birch Farm, at its junction with the Coldham-Chillington lane, formerly stood a pair of semi-detached half-timbered black and white thatched cottages known as Bridgecroft. The cottages became dilapidated and were demolished c.1950. On the north side of the junction of the Coldham-

Chillington lane and the track to Hungry Hill, at the side of the large pit, were a pair of semi-detached cottages which became derelict and collapsed in about 1910. They were known as Sandhole Cottages.

Cottages at Bridgecroft, redrawn from a newspaper photograph c.1938. William Salt Library 148/2/72.

Pearse Hay farmhouse dates from the early seventeenth century, with exposed timber framing to the south, a vaulted cellar, and a three-storey extension of about 1835.

Long Birch farmhouse dates from 1878, but the garden walls to the east date from the early seventeenth century. Ornate wrought-iron entrance gates removed in 1990 had been installed from elsewhere about ten years

Long Birch, from Stebbing Shaw's 'History and Antiquities of Staffordshire', published between 1798 and 1801.

earlier. A much older house nearby[488] collapsed when restoration was attempted in 1874. The ruins were demolished and the foundations blown up. The old house seems to have been of three distinct periods. To the rear was a timber-framed jettied building with gabled wings, possibly medieval, in front of which was a tall block, apparently dating from the late sixteenth century, with mullioned windows and massive chimneys. At the front was an entrance range of two storeys with attics, of mid seventeenth century style. The symmetrical front had three curvilinear gables and mullioned and transomed windows. A central two-storey porch had an arched entrance with marble steps and hipped roof. An oak

Left: the old house at Long Birch from the south, redrawn from an old photograph, showing clearly the three periods of building, and, right, the house from the west, redrawn from a sketch by 'T.P.W.' made in 1838.

staircase and stone mantelpiece in the present house are said to have been taken from the old house. An L-shaped piece of water to the south west of the house which appears on a map of 1808[489] may have been the remains of a moat. A large pool to the south of the house which has been incorporated into ornamental gardens is said to be part cut out of sandstone in the form of a trench. A well at the farm is said to be 90' deep, cut in stone from 15' to the bottom. The farm was acquired in 1990 by Severn Trent Water Limited.

White House Farm, also known as The Sham House and in 1775 Pool Farm, south of Chillington, has a long painted brick north elevation, with a tall central pedimented block connected by colonnades to pedimented side pavilions, all with ball finials. The imposing façade, resembling a triumphal arch with its openings blocked, was designed[490] to screen the older farmhouse from Chillington. Extensive renovation work was carried out in 1988-9. A brick granary stands on the west of the farmyard. A large timber barn at the farm, reputedly removed from Long Birch in the nineteenth century, was demolished in 1988.

Leper House Farm is an early seventeenth century close-studded timber-framed building with eighteenth century rebuilding, incorporating a central chimney and a dormer window in a gable dated 1716. Near the farm to the east is a partly timber-framed barn with irregular framing on a sandstone plinth. A field name in a plan c.1727 suggests that a moat or fishpond may have existed immediately west of the farmhouse.[491] The farm is named after a house or hospital which is said to have existed for lepers visiting the nearby Leper Well.[492]

There is now no trace of old Gunstone Hall which existed until at least

216

1680, and must have been a substantial property, for it was assessed for 9 hearths in the Hearth Tax Assessment of 1666. The present Gunstone Hall is a gabled stucco farmhouse of about 1840 on the site of an earlier house.[493] Pools to the south-east of the house were created in about 1970. Gunstone Farm is a T-shaped house mainly of late seventeenth century date. In 1990 faint traces of wall paintings were noted in a ground floor room. One may have represented sailing ships. To the east of the house is a range of outbuildings and barns which includes three buildings of sandstone. Nearby to the south is a large disused stone quarry.

The oldest of the three farmhouses at The Hattons is the most northerly. Confusingly, the most southerly, described in 1841 as Lower Hattons, is now called Upper Hattons. It is an eighteenth century brick house with later additions at the east.

The middle house was built before 1775, and is now called The Hattons.

The Old Hattons, called The Hattons until at least 1841, dates mainly from the late seventeenth century. There is evidence that it was once larger. The present building is of L-plan, and below the east wing a cellar cut into the rock has windows in the stone plinth. A large chimney-stack which may have formed part of the older house is concealed by later additions against the east wall. Heavily-moulded ceiling beams also appear to be older than the rest of the house. The house was acquired by Severn Trent Water Limited in 1990 and modernised.

A deserted medieval village is believed to have existed in the area, the name Hatton being listed in the Subsidy Roll of 1327. Although the site is said to be lost,[494] a field named Town Leasow is shown adjoining the east of The Old Hattons on a Chillington estate map c.1727. It seems likely that the site has been destroyed by the construction of the nearby canal. The same map also shows a small field on the same side of the house called Vinyard.

To the east of Lower Hatton canal bridge, a small brick house known as Brook Cottages has been ruinous for many years. A fishing pool was created to the east on the site of a small wood on the west bank of the River Penk in 1990. Pendeford Cottages to the east of the Penk were demolished in the 1960's.

During the Second World War a mock factory is said to have been constructed on the east side of the canal to confuse enemy bombers seeking the Boulton Paul works at Pendeford.[495] No traces remain. Between the road and the River Penk at Coven Lawn is a disused Territorial Army centre which covers some five acres and contains concrete gun emplacements on which American guns were sited during the Second World War to protect Pendeford aerodrome and the nearby Boulton Paul aircraft factory.

Park Cottage lies in a remote position to the east of Chillington Wharf, its name perpetuating the Bishop's park. It dates from about 1600. The red brick cottage at the southern end of Chillington Lower Avenue dates from about 1780.[496]

A hall is recorded at Coven some time after 1331, occupied by the Coven family, and a hall-house, perhaps the same, is mentioned in 1666, taxable for 5 hearths, but no house called Coven Hall now exists, and its precise location is unknown.

A group of buildings between Coven and Standeford, variously known as Leetech, Leerach, Leerach Green and recorded in 1739 as Leet Each in the parish register, was destroyed by the construction of Stafford Road in 1936. The name survives in Lightash Lane.

Grange House Farm to the north of Coven incorporates a sixteenth century timber-framed crosswing jettied on three sides, supported on bull-nosed joists and with a heavy dragon beam at the south-west corner. There is a Tudor doorhead in heavy framing on the ground floor, and panelling of about 1600 in a first floor room. The building has a brick and plaster façade painted in imitation square panel timber framing. Local tradition says that Charles II called at the house during his journey to Moseley, and travelled along Cow Lane.

Grange Farm, Coven, c.1910.

Coven Farm is a T-plan, late sixteenth century timber-framed building. The upper storey was originally open to the ridge, revealing queen-post trusses.

A large colour washed brick building with blind arcading on the north elevation at the corner of Brewood Road and Lawn Lane, Coven, was built by John Smith, the Coven engineer, as a machine shop in about 1860, and was later used as a brewery. Adjoining it to the south formerly stood a sixteenth-century house largely rebuilt in brick, the gable end facing the

218

Coven c.1935. The roadside cottage right of centre was demolished in the 1960's.

road having stone walling and a projecting chimney stack, probably an alteration made in the seventeenth century. The house, which was the home of John Smith for some years, was demolished in the 1970's. Croft House is an L-shaped house with symmetrical frontage and central Tuscan pillared portico of about 1800. Coven House, a much-altered eighteenth century brick house, was demolished in the early 1960's.

The Homage, Coven.

In the centre of Coven is The Homage, a colour-washed brick house of rectangular plan, with two storeys, attics and cellars. A porch wing projects at the front, with a plaque bearing the date 1679, and the large central chimney incorporates a cellar fireplace.

The gable parapets, eaves cornice and cellar windows are of stone. The house is one of the earliest dated brick houses in the west of the county.[497] The extension on the north is of later date: in the early years of this century it was a red brick draper's shop. At the junction of Brewood Road and Poplars Farm Way is a colourwashed shop and house with flat-topped Regency façade to the west.

The Beeches, a substantial three-storey brick house at Coven formerly standing in a large garden, part of which was developed for housing in 1988, dates from the late eighteenth century.

In what is now the front garden of the vicarage formerly stood a

219

building known as the Iron Room, or Red Room, used from about 1897 for various village functions. Clad in red-painted corrugated iron and lined with wood, it was destroyed by arson in about 1969. Its origins may be connected with John Smith, the Victorian ironfounder and engineer who is known to have had a boiler workshop near the church.

Coven village hall was built in 1955. The Memorial Hall was opened in October 1975.

At Chambley Green[498] fourteen terraced council houses on three sides of a grassed square were built in 1955. Brook Cottage, on the western edge of the village, has several cast iron window frames, each containing several narrow angular lancets, in the older part to the south. The immediate area was a hamlet known as Gregory's Green in the early part of the last century.

Brewood Road, Coven, c.1910. The cottages on the left still stand. The others have long since been demolished.

A hall existed at Aspley by the early sixteenth century, and is probably incorporated within Aspley Farmhouse. The existing house is of H-plan with cross-wings at each end of the central block. Two storeys were created in the earlier hall by the insertion of heavy ceiling beams towards the end of the sixteenth century when a large chimney was built against the through-passage which formerly existed at the north end. The timber framed walls were rebuilt in brick in the eighteenth and nineteenth centuries. The house was surrounded by a moat on three sides in 1808,[499] but

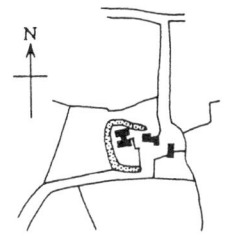

the only remaining trace is a depression on the west, through which runs a small stream. Another moated site lies just over the parish boundary to the east.

On 17th November 1976 H.M. Prison, Featherstone, a Category C Training Establishment covering 197 acres was opened on the site of a disused munitions depot at Brinsford. Originally housing 499 inmates, a new wing was opened in January 1991 to accomodate a further 100 prisoners. The parish boundary runs through the prison.

Redrawn extract from Josiah Robins and James Sherriff's map of 1808 showing moat at Aspley. SRO 590/375.

At Clay Gates [formerly Hell Gates], opposite the drive to Engleton Hall, is a single-storey brick cottage, with pyramid roof and central diagonally-set chimney, the remaining one of a pair known locally as The Pepperpots, dating from the 1850's. They were built as estate cottages by the Monckton family, apparently based on a Scottish design. The other cottage on the opposite corner has been replaced by a modern house. On the north side of the drive to Engleton Hall is an ancient yew.

The present Engleton Hall,[500] now a farmhouse, was built in 1810, but ponds and depressions to the south-east suggest a moat which may have surrounded an earlier house: medieval ridge-and-furrow runs into the southern part of the depression. Part of the northern section is wet. In the garden to the south of the house is a sundial made from a sandstone pillar recovered during the excavation of the nearby Roman villa.

At Broom Hall, reputedly the birthplace of Colonel Carless of Boscobel fame, a thatched half-timbered house, apparently dating from the seventeenth century, was substantially rebuilt in about 1884.[501] A timber-framed barn also dates from the seventeenth century. Pools to the north and west of the house filled in in the 1950's and formerly thought to be part of a moat are now believed to have been sand and marl pits.[502]

Yew Tree Cottage in Horsebrook is a small, well-preserved L-plan house of late seventeenth century date, with brick string course, stone eaves cornice, and leaded-lights set in wood-framed windows. Horsebrook Hall, a large square stuccoed building, may date from 1861,[503] when a house was erected to replace The Tanhouse, which was demolished in that year. A hollow-way marking an ancient disused lane runs from the east side of the Hall to Watling Street. A tall seventeenth century threshing barn at Horsebrook Farm was converted into houses in 1989. The farmhouse dates from the late seventeenth century. Horsebrook Manor Farm has a seventeenth century timber-framed barn, and Lea Fields Farm at Shutt Green is built around a late sixteenth century timber-framed house with central chimney. An outbuilding contains two upper-cruck trusses of about 1700.

Rose Hill [formerly known as Rose Cottage] adjoining Watling Street dates from about 1780. The Homestead at Shutt Green has been converted from a small cottage of about 1800, which was known as Ash Tree Cottage until the 1920's. Birks Barn Farm was built in 1835 to replace a farmhouse of the same name some 400 yards to the east which was demolished when Belvide Reservoir was created. The Hawkshutts [formerly Hogshead or Hawksyard], a farmhouse incorporating early brickwork, perhaps Tudor, but mainly of late eighteenth century date on an older site, was demolished in 1990, a new house having been created from an adjacent outbuilding. A building known as Coffins Barn lay a short distance to the south east in the last century.[504]

The present Somerford Hall[505] was built by Robert Barbor in the second quarter of the eighteenth century,[506] and it has been suggested that Somerford and Speedwell Castle may have shared the same architect. The Hall stands in Somerford Park,[507] and is a tall three-storied block of seven bays, flanked by single-storey pavilions. On the entrance front the pavilions have Venetian windows in arched recessed panels, set under pedimented gables with ball finials. The building was much altered in the late eighteenth century, damaged by fire early this century, unoccupied by the 1930s, in 1945 converted into flats, and is now being carefully restored to its former glory.

Somerford Hall, from unpublished sheets of Stebbing Shaws's 'History and Antiquities of Staffordshire', 1798-1801.

In the mid nineteenth century the house was "supplied by a large reservoir at the top of the house . . . filled by a waterwork invented and erected at great expense by Mr Monckton on the river at some distance", and surplus water from the house was carried along brick channels to irrigate the gardens.

Adjoining the west side of the house are extensive stables and outbuildings, including a square eighteenth century dovecote and early nineteenth century brick seven-bay Dutch barn with arcaded sides.

Somerford Grange is a tall farmhouse in Somerford Park dating from the 1760s, with a window [now internal] bearing an incised signature and the date 1771. The southern elevation is in Gothic style, designed to be viewed from the Park, with castellated parapet, circular windows and two projecting bays. The design of the building suggests that it may be by the architect responsible for Speedwell Castle, or the equally tall Gothic house at Coleshill [Warwickshire]. Somerford Farm has a seventeenth century timber-framed barn, and there is a small timber-framed cottage in the hamlet. At Catchems End, on the north side of the lane to Somerford Mill Farm, is a curious small flat-roofed cottage with stepped rear elevation known as The Castle. It probably dates from the late eighteenth century, and was presumably designed as a folly lodge to be viewed from Somerford Hall. The top of the building may once have been crenellated.

Gadshaw Cottage, which stood on the west side of the lane mid-way between the White House and Somerford Stone House was demolished in about 1965.

Hockerhill farmhouse dates from the eighteenth century, with later alterations. A large marlpit lay opposite the farm drive in Kiddemore Green Road. It was filled in the 1960's and bungalows built on the site. The Oakley is a large early Victorian[508] farmhouse which has for many years been used as a country club. Ponds to the east [since the last century a landscaped fishpond] and south are probably old marl pits. Yew Trees is a square farmhouse, now extended, with a plaque: 'J I [in a cross] 1844'. The yew trees by the roadside were cut down in 1983. Kiddemore Green Farm is an early nineteenth century red brick farmhouse with central doorway, symmetrical façade and central chimney stack.

Along the south side of Kiddemore Green Road are scattered small timber-framed cottages dating from the seventeenth century, including Yew Tree Cottage, enlarged in recent years, and The Thatched Cottage, which was the Plough Inn in 1808. It was modernised c.1965[509] and enlarged and rethatched in about 1980. Greenoaks, with much heavy square framing, was thatched until about 1930. Kiddemore Cottage was converted from a terrace of three late eighteenth century cottages incorporating earlier timbering in 1979, an adjoining barn to the west [formerly used to house steam engines used on local farms] having been demolished to provide a site for a new house for the Chillington estate in about 1960. A pair of half timbered cottages formerly stood to the south of Chambersfield in Shutt Green Lane. They were demolished c.1925 and the ground incorporated in the adjoining field. The Old Smithy in Kiddemore Green Road was extended in about 1880 and modernised in recent years. Villa Farmhouse dates from the early nineteenth century. The former Crown public house is now Greystoke Cottage. A small two roomed cottage opposite was demolished in about 1960. Honeysuckle Cottage is built on the site of another small cottage. A half-timbered thatched cottage in

Old Weston Road, Bishops Wood, housing a post-office, was demolished in the 1960's for new housing.

Except for small developments of housing along the roads to Kiddemore Green and Coven, little residential development took place in Brewood village in the late nineteenth and early twentieth centuries, an indication of the declining population, but since 1945 many new houses have been built, both council and private, primarily in the area to the north-east of the village centre. Crestwood Park, an open-plan estate of houses and bungalows within gated cul-de-sacs leading off a spine road was built in the late 1950's and the early 1960's. Hall Farm estate followed soon afterwards, with further developments in St Chad's Close and Horsebrook Lane. A new estate was commenced on the west side of Bishop's Wood in the 1960's, and Moors Farm estate on the south west of Coven in the late 1980's.

Just across the parish and county boundary in Offoxey Road, Bishop's Wood, is Acorn Cottage, otherwise known as White Oak Cottage. The parish perambulations suggest that in 1838 and 1861 it was a beerhouse known as The Royal Oak. It bears a wooden plaque with the date 1818, and until about 1970 had a large stone acorn on the apex of the roof. The acorn was then removed to Weston Hall. In the garden of the cottage is a tall pyramid-shaped sandstone hen-house with the inscription 'To please the pigs'. Close by is a much altered small sandstone building with stepped gables. The door and window heads are triangular and on the south wall is a plaque reading 'Ranz-des-vaches'. The building and hen-house were put up by the eccentric George Durant the younger of Tong Castle in about 1842.[510] A small sandstone milepost, which also serves as a bench mark, stands on the county boundary on the east side of the cottage. On the opposite side of the road is the tip of a glacial boulder, now almost completely buried, recorded in the nineteenth-century perambulations as the Shire Stone.

25. The Grammar School

It is possible that Brewood Grammar School [now Brewood Middle School] had its origins as a chantry school founded by the Bishop of Lichfield, perhaps as early as the thirteenth century, for there are several references to chaplains of Brewood in early records,[511] and a chaplain was then usually a chantry priest. Proof of the early origin of the school is said to be the existence until 1827 of a carved chancel stall in Brewood Church for the headmaster, since the right to such a stall supposedly predates the Reformation. Chantry schools were so-called because they existed to supply choristers for daily sung or chanted mass for both the living and the dead. They were closely associated with the parish church and run by the parish priest who, in pre-reformation times, was expected to teach reading and writing.

From about the thirteenth century until the Reformation, chantries were founded in most towns and villages, usually by benefactors who made an endowment for a daily mass for the welfare of the benefactor during his life and for his soul after his death. It is known that in about 1300 Robert Papagy endowed two selions of land in 'Whete Croft' for a Sunday mass in Brewood church for the repose of his soul. The 'Priest's Service' mentioned in about 1551, which was endowed with land and cottages in Brewood producing £5 or £6, may be this same mass.

Further evidence that a chantry school existed in Brewood is a reference to the village in connection with the Act of Dissolution of Chantries in 1547, when such endowments were appropriated by the Crown, and by the two stalls which existed in the chancel of the parish church until 1879, traditionally assigned to the headmaster and usher of the Grammar School. Other evidence may be the name Chantry House for the large house opposite the church in Dean Street. On the other hand, in 1554 Sir John Giffard stated that he had known Codsall church since the 1480's, when he went to school there: presumably the curate kept a school or took private pupils. The inference may be that there was no such school at Brewood.

Indignation at the suppression of the chantries may have been the reason why Matthew Knightley and Sir Thomas Giffard founded – or refounded – the school, recorded in a Chancery action which occurred some time after 1560 – possibly 1575[512] – when Thomas Lane and John Moreton, for themselves and the parishioners of Brewood, brought proceedings against John Giffard and John Lane. The plaintiffs' claimed that

> Matthew Knyghtley, clerk, D.D., and John Gyffard and Thomas Gyffard . . .
> of their godly and virtuous disposition which they had and bare towards the
> virtuous education and bringing up of tender youth in learning . . . within
> the parish of Brewood . . . by sundry consequences gifts and assurances . . .

granted to one John Lane and certain other . . . inhabitants of the said parish and to their heirs, diverse messuages, lands, rents, etc., in Brewood, Chillington, Gunston, Wylnall, Wheton Aston, Lapley, Busshebery, Gaton and Covyn. All these grants were made to the intent that the said John Lane and others and their heirs . . . should appoint, with the profits thereof paid yearly, for ever, one honest discreet man, sufficiently learned in grammar, to keep a Free Grammar School in Brewood, there to instruct all manner of children and young men as well of the said parish as elsewhere, in Grammar and in such other learning, as was convenient and necessary to be taught . . . without taking or demanding anything for the same . . .

The nature of the action was set out in general terms, essentially that John Giffard tried to appropriate for his own benefit the freehold interest in the school estates. John Giffard conceded in his response that the freehold belonged to the school, claimed the action had been commenced as a result of ill-feeling between John Moreton and himself and did not have the support of the villagers of Brewood, and that Thomas Lane did not even live in the parish. The plaintiffs denied these allegations, but apparently took no further action. John Giffard later appointed a bailiff to administer the school property.[513]

Dr Matthew Knightley was a grandson of Richard Knightley of Fawsley [a direct descendant of the Knightleys of Staffordshire] and his great grandmother was a Giffard of Chillington. He was also a nephew of Robert Knightley of Engleton, whose daughter Isabella by her marriage brought Engleton to the Moretons [later the Ducies]. Few details are known about Dr Knightley's early life, but he may have been born and raised at his uncle's house at Engleton and educated at Brewood Grammar School.[514] Although most of the Knightleys were puritans after the Reformation, Matthew was a Catholic in 1547, but seems to have avoided the religious persecutions of the period by adopting Catholic or Puritan guise, as necessary. He is thought to have been rector of Foulmere, in Cambridgeshire, from 1517, and parson of Cossington, near Loughborough, until his death in 1561. He is commemorated by an inscribed slab bearing his portrait [not in its original position] in the chancel of Cossington parish church, where he was buried.

The benevolence of Dr Knightley towards the villagers of Brewood is further shown by his Will, dated 21st June 1560, which includes a bequest "to the poor people of the town and parish of Bruyde where I was born, £4 . . . to the vicar of Bruyde, 6s 8d. . . to the schoolmaster there, 6s 8d," and instructions for his books to be sold and the money given to poor scholars, and for other Godly uses.

The most renowned headmaster in the early history of the School was the Reverend William Budworth, who came to Brewood from Rugeley school in 1731. He was headmaster until 1735, and in 1737 became Vicar of Brewood. He is remembered as a strict disciplinarian. An usher, the Rev George Bromley, who was also curate of Brewood, left the area as a result of Budworth's 'imperious temper', and did not return until after Budworth's death in 1745.

In 1736 Dr Samuel Johnson, then aged 25, newly married and impecunious, applied for the post of usher at the school, having previously met Budworth at a school in Market Bosworth, but was not appointed.[515] It would seem that the earlier meeting persuaded Budworth that Johnson's eccentric appearance and mannerisms would serve him ill as a teacher. Brewood's loss was posterity's gain, for Johnson opened his own school at Lichfield, and when that failed, moved to London and eventual fame.

Brewood Grammar School, redrawn from an undated watercolour, probably late eighteenth or early nineteenth century. Reproduced by kind permission of the Trustees of the William Salt Library, WSL 121/68.

In 1820 there were 35 pupils in the upper school, and 25 in the lower school, more than half of them boarders. The classics were taught free, but for English reading, writing and arithmetic "regular quarterages" were charged, even for poor parishioners. In 1860 there were only 26 pupils, of whom only one was a boarder. In 1874 it was claimed that the school had "practically ceased to be of any advantage to the inhabitants of the neighbourhood," and the Charity Commissioners were requested to conduct inquiries, as a result of which the Commissioners published a report two years later.

The old school and schoolhouse, the former a long single-storey building in which both the master's and the usher's classes were taught, and the latter a building apparently of late seventeenth century date, with mullioned and transomed windows and central curvilinear gable, stood by the roadside. After the acquisition in 1799 of the two houses on the opposite side of the road by the joint gift of Richard Hurd, Bishop of

227

Brewood Grammar School by R. Paddy, from Stebbing Shaw's 'History and Antiquities of Staffordshire', 1798-1801.

Worcester, and Sir Edward Littleton, both former pupils,[516] the road was diverted behind the two houses, which were then converted into a single house and schoolroom for the usher, and these buildings, considerably altered and said to bear a bricklayer's date of 1778, represent the oldest part of the present school buildings. The master's house was enlarged, and the garden front rebuilt by Hamlett Harrison, the vicar and headmaster, but little of the original school or schoolhouse now remains, the former having been rebuilt between 1850 and 1860,[517] and the schoolhouse during the 1840's. Extensions to the school were made in 1898, 1926, 1935 and 1952. The buildings are of red brick with yellow brick quoins, and incorporate many gables and tall rectangular chimneys with a slim, open bell tower with a small spire. The schoolroom in the usher's house, now known as Rushall House, was, with the dormitories above, reconstructed in 1856, and the building has within the last few years been converted to office use. The old swimming pool on the west side of the canal may have been constructed by the school in the second half of the last century. In 1896 the school was said to be 'in declining condition', and to remedy the situation a School of Agriculture was created two years later, funded by the County Council, which over the years gained a considerable reputation. In the 1920's the school had 24 acres of land under cultivation. A sports field was created in about 1912. The County Council now operate a school farm to the north of the school buildings. Since 1973 it has been used as a farm centre for visiting children from urban primary and special schools.

Brewood Grammar School was transferred to the local education authority, Staffordshire County Council, in about 1930 and ceased to exist as such in July 1975. It is now occupied by Brewood Middle School.

26. Schools

The parish register records Abraham Barwicke as schoolmaster in Brewood in 1641,[518] but we have no information about where he may have taught. From a number of entries in and after 1745 in the Overseer's Accounts it is evident that the Governor of the workhouse received periodic payments for teaching children to read, and there is also an entry in the same Accounts for 1756/7: "Paid old Povey for teaching school", but no further details are known. The earliest reference to a charity school dates from 1724, and may refer to the establishment in the Liberty of Somerford at which 13 poor girls were educated and clothed at the expense of the Misses Monckton in 1834. In 1851, 18 girls attended the school, which was still in existence in 1854.

From at least the early years of the nineteenth century the genteel atmosphere of Brewood led to the creation of a number of boarding and day schools in Brewood, including a 'gent's boarding school near the church' in 1818 run by the Rev. Henry Kempston [who later became headmaster of the Grammar School, while retaining his own school], and a 'ladies and gent's boarding and day school' run by Mrs Bridgen[519] and Miss Fowke 'near the church' in 1829, and a 'gent's boarding and day school' run by Ladbury Waldron in Dean's End in the same year. In 1834 Miss Bennett was running an 'Academy' at Deans Hall, and there were two others in Dean Street: Maria Boyden's and Brigden & Fowkes Ladies Boarding Academy. Another establishment in Stafford Street was run by Mary Cales. At the same date there were also schools run by Anne Hazeldine at Kiddemore Green and Elizabeth Male at Somerford, with a day school at Coven run by John Hughes.[520]

In 1851 there were three private schools in Dean Street, and one in Market Place, all taking boarders, and a workhouse school, and the number of school teachers in the village had then increased from 2 in 1793 to 13. A boarding and day school existed at Broadgate House in 1859,[521] and 'Dean Street Academy' was advertising the same year, claiming to have been established in 1837. This may have been the boarding and day school run by Mrs Pearson in Dean Street who advertised

> Board and Instruction, including Writing and Arithmetic, Reading, Geography, Grammar, History (both Ancient and Modern) with useful and ornamental Needlework at £14 per annum for pupils under 12 years of age, £16 for pupils over 12, £10 per annum for weekly boarders, 10/6d per quarter for daily pupils, £1 per annum each for music and dancing, and 30s. per annum for laundry. Each pupil to be provided with a pair of sheets, two towels, and a knife, fork and spoon.

At about the same period a boys school existed in Dean Street run by Mr Cholditch, and a school is said to have existed in Dean Street, with a boys' school at Smithy House. The Misses Telford ran a "preparatory boarding school (Catholic) for young gentlemen" at The Poplars in 1864, and a school still existed there in 1892; the Misses Mellow were running another boarding school in 1864, and William Pearson had a "commerical, day and boarding school" in Dean Street in the same year. A ladies school in Church Road, is recorded in 1892, and a ladies school existed in Horsebrook Lane in 1912. At about the same date Mrs Docker was running a girls school at The Deanery.

The Old School House adjoining the Lion Inn in Stafford Street is a pair of semi-detached cottages. For many years in the early part of this century the northern half was a private school for girls run by Miss Hollis.

A scheme for a National School in the village appears to have been started in 1816, and two years later subscriptions enabled a building to be erected to accommodate 350 children. The school, on the north-west side of the road linking Market Place and Dean Street, was a long single storey brick building, and the first master was John Wootton. By 1834 some 140 children were being taught there by subscription. In 1851 a master and mistress taught 60 boys and 50 girls. From 1858 the school was awarded an annual parliamentary grant, and two years later a larger single-storey red brick school was built to the south-west of the old school. The architect was E. Banks, who designed Coven Church. A local subscription had raised all the funds before building work started. The foundation stone was laid in July 1859, and the school opened on 21st January 1860. It faced east close to Church Road, and had sandstone quoins, a central main gable and two side gables, all with decoratively-pierced bargeboards, with a central wooden bell-tower capped by a short four-sided spire. A separate schoolhouse was built at the same time to the south-west of the school, the Monckton family contributing half the cost of all the building work. The older school building was in use as a Working Men's Institute from November 1862 until at least 1874, but subsequently reverted to use by the adjoining school, latterly as an office for the headmaster. The average school attendance in the 1880s was 140 juniors and 60 infants, and in 1894 and 1910 averaged about 155. In 1955 the school became aided, with an average attendance of 292, and the Victorian school buildings and original school adjoining [but not the schoolhouse, which still stands] were demolished some twelve months after a new single-storey flat-roofed replacement had been built a short distance to the west.

The new school was opened on 7th September 1965, and is known as St Mary and St Chad First School. The site of the original school is now a walled and paved area with benches, and the site of the second school has been incorporated into the playground of the present school. Log books from 1863 survive, and the old school bell is still preserved at the new school.[522]

By 1834, 33 children were being taught at a Roman Catholic school attached to the old chapel at Blackladies, the expense being met by Mr Evans of Boscobel. Although the chapel ceased to be used for religious purposes on the opening of the new Catholic church in Brewood in 1844, the school seems to have continued, for in 1851 Miss Evans of Boscobel was meeting the cost.

A Roman Catholic school was built to the north of St Mary's Roman Catholic church in 1844 and was run by a lay mistress from that date until 1916, although in 1860 and 1868 it was described as being under the superintendence of a Sister of St Paul. In 1884 the average attendance was 72, and averaged between 60 and 70 until 1916. In 1920 a Dominican Sister took over as headmistress, and until recent times there was at least one nun, and often more, at the school, which is now housed in single-storey flat-roofed buildings built in the 1970's and known as St Mary's Roman Catholic Primary School.

A school for Protestant children is said to have been run in the first half of the last century by the philanthropic Miss Evans of Boscobel in a cottage at Park Pales, Bishop's Wood, and in 1855 a National School to take 71 children was built to the east of the church in Bishop's Wood. The attendances were 50 or so from 1884 to 1910, and although it was enlarged in 1912 to take 100 children, it had fallen into serious disrepair by 1933. In 1951 it came under the control of the County Council, and when the present school was built in 1969 on the south-west edge of the village, the old brick building with tall lancet windows was converted into a house.

The old school in Coven is said to have been built in School Road in 1839 [although a school is shown on Teesdale's map of Staffordshire of 1832] and was used as a chapel prior to the consecration of St Paul's church in 1857. In September 1858 the building was first used as a church school, a condition of admission being that the children should attend Sunday School and pay a weekly fee. The dining room was added in 1883. The school had an average attendance of 110 in 1884 and 1900, which had risen to 150 by 1910. In 1937 the figure was about 130. The school came under the control of the County Council in 1951, and has been disused since the present school was built.

Now used as a girl's private school, the long two-storey brick building with projecting side wings and porch in Bargate Street, Brewood, began life as the parish workhouse and dates from some time before 1795. In 1837 the building became the workhouse for the area covered by the Penkridge Union, and was extended between 1838 and 1842 to provide accommodation for 200, until in 1872 a new Union Workhouse was opened at Cannock. The building and gardens were sold in 1878, and used as a private residence by Miss Monckton, and from 1919 were used as a Dominican convent with about 30 boarding pupils. By 1939 it was evident that taking boarders was uneconomic and the school gradually became a day school. The large white statue of the Virgin over the porch presumably dates from this period, and hides an illegible weathered sandstone plaque on the building. Large extensions were made to the rear in 1956, and in recent years several new buildings have been added, including a large red-brick sports complex to the north-west, with a new entrance road created from Bargate Street in August 1988.

BREWOOD NATIONAL SCHOOL.

RULES FOR PARENTS.

VISITORS FOR THE YEAR.

GIRLS,   BOYS,

I.—SEND your Children to the School with their faces and hands clean, their hair combed, and their cloaths mended.

II.—Never let them miss the School or the Church, unless they be ill, or hindered by some cause which the Visitor may think sufficient. In those cases give notice at the time to the Master or Mistress by some of the other Children.

III.—If Children do wrong, they must be punished. If you think your Children ill-used, make no complaint to the School, or in their hearing, but speak privately to the Visitor.

IV.—As often as you can, hear your Children repeat the Church Catechism, and read the Holy Bible, that they may learn their Duty to God and Man; and see them pray to God constantly Morning and Evening, that they may, through Jesus Christ, obtain daily Grace to perform it.

V.—Teach them to be humble before God, respectful to their Superiors and to those who are older than themselves, obedient to their Master and Mistress, kind and obliging to all, especially to their School-fellows. Never let them be idle and wandering about the streets and fields, particularly on the Lord's Day; and punish them strictly if they should ever be guilty of stealing, lying, quarrelling, tale-bearing, or using bad words.

VI.—When your Children quit the National School, if they remain in the parish, take care they attend the Sunday School, or they will forget what they have learned.

VII.—Above all, endeavour to set before them a Christian Example in your own words and actions.

Remember, God sees and will judge both you and them.

School Hours, Nine o'Clock in the Morning, and Two in the Afternoon.

J. SMART, PRINTER, WOLVERHAMPTON.

c. 1850

27. Inns and Ale Houses

Beer and ale have been since the earliest times important beverages, for unboiled water was often unfit to drink as a result of contamination from animals and humans. Malted barley was used for making ale, a beverage which did not involve the use of hops and tasted like sour water. It was drunk at all times, taking the place not only of tea, coffee, etc., but also of water, being cheap and plentiful. A thirteenth century writer, describing the extreme poverty of the Franciscans when they settled in London in 1224 wrote: "I have seen the brothers drink ales so sour that some would have preferred to drink water." Records exist of the appointment of ale-tasters, responsible for ensuring the quality of ale, at the monthly Brewood manor court from 1338, and the twice yearly View of Frankpledge included assize of bread and ale, at which bakers and brewers were called to account for supplies which failed to meet the appropriate standard. In 1473 each brewer in Bewood and Horsebrook paid 1d toll to the Bishop as lord of the manor every time ale was brewed or gave the value in ale.[523] Names of alehouse keepers from the late sixteenth century onwards exist, often in Recognisances taken by the Quarter sessions. Sadly, the details of the alehouses themselves, including names if any, are lacking, but in 1604 there were fifteen licensed alehouses in Brewood parish,[524] and in 1702 fourteen.[525]

One of the earliest inns to be mentioned in the parish is the Bleu Bell recorded in a parliamentary survey of the parish in 1646, and again in the Constables' Accounts of 1669. The building is known to have stood on Watling Street, and was almost certainly a predecessor of the present Bell public house, which dates from the late eighteenth or early nineteenth century. It was called the Bell from at least 1775. Opposite stood the Royal Oak Inn, now Road Farm. From at least 1808 to 1831 a public house known as The Red Lion stood on the north-east [sic] side of the junction of Watling Street and Ivy House Lane. At some date after 1831 the lane to Congreve was diverted to the east side of the building to align with the lane to Brewood.

The Bradford Arms dates from about 1700 and is mentioned by Dr Stukeley in a letter of 1713 as "an inn called 'Ivetsey Bank'." In 1754 it was called The Sun. In 1798 it was described by Stebbing Shaw as "a noted old inn on the Watling Street-way". Watling Street alongside was lowered and widened in the late 1970's. The Spread Eagle at Gailey was in existence by 1775. The Red Dog, on the south side of Watling Street, shown on Yates map of 1775, was close to or at what is now Bell Field Farm. References in the parish registers show that it was in existence from at least 1742. In 1808 the Thatched Cottage at Kiddemore Green was a public house known as The Plough, and Catchems End was known as Catchems Inn.[526] The Ball at Coven – demolished in 1981 and sometimes known as The Golden Ball – existed in 1808 and the Three Hammers is recorded in 1767.

In 1829 there were 13 inns or public houses listed in the parish:[527]

Admiral Rodney, Dean's End [Dean Street, existed before 1818]
Anchor, Cross Green [existed in 1792, original building demolished in the 1960's]
Angel, Stafford Street [recorded in 1796]
Black Lion,[528] Slade Heath [now Black Lion Farmhouse]
Chequered Ball, Bargate Street [existed before 1818, operated until c.1895. Now Chequer House]
Crown, Kiddemore Green [now Greystoke Cottage]
Fleur-de-Lis, Market Place [existed before 1814, possibly in 1755;[529] demolished c.1845]
Four Ashes
Harrow, Standeford
Rainbow, Coven
Red Lion, Stafford Street
Swan, Market Place [existed before 1818]

The Giffards Arms and Red Lion are recorded as separate but apparently adjoining establishments, with different proprietors until about 1850, when The Giffards Arms and Lion is shown under a single name and proprietor, presumably having been combined into one establishment. The name seems to have been shortened to The Lion by 1867. It was at the Red Lion that the Hon. John Byng was 'put into a white-washed room, and got a miserable, neither hot-nor-cold dinner' in 1792.[530]

Copper token ⁷/₈" diameter found near Dean's Hall Farm. The back is plain. c.1800.

The Three Stirrups does not seem to be mentioned before 1850, and The Bridge public house is first recorded in 1872. A Boat public house existed in Bargate Street from at least 1851 until about 1895. The Chequered Ball, now Chequer House, in Bargate Street, was a public house until about 1895, and traces of the words 'Good Stabling' can still be made out on the west wall. The chequer pattern was one of the earliest signs for a public house. Both the Chequered Ball and the Boat were popular with Irishmen, presumably from the canal boats, who are said to have entertained themselves by fighting in large groups in the area on Sunday afternoons. The Malt Shovel, at the corner of Engleton Lane and Deansfield Road, was for many years a malthouse in the last century, and a public house from about 1870 to c.1930. In about 1850 there was a beerhouse in Bargate Street known as The Royal Oak, and another in Stafford Street, the name of which is now lost. Brook House, opposite Hyde Mill Lane, was a beerhouse known as The Vauxhall at about the same period. In 1868 there was a Crown Inn in Shop Lane.[531]

The Chequered Ball public house on the corner of Bargate Lane and Bargate Street, photographed in about 1882. The couple in the doorway are almost certainly the proprietors, Joseph Ward and his Irish-born wife Johannah. In 1880 Joseph is recorded as the proprietor of the Boat Inn in Bargate Street, and in the 1881 census returns is described as 'publican and Chelsea Pensioner', although aged only 42. The Chequered Ball ceased to be a public house in about 1895, but is little changed to this day: traces of the words 'Good Stabling' can still be made out on the gable wall. Photograph reproduced by kind permission of Mr. L. Wakelam.

In the middle of the last century an alehouse known as The Vine existed in Dean Street, and 'The Old Workhouse' is said to have been a public house under the sign of the White Horse. It may have been the original workhouse in Kiddemore Green Road which is said to have been between Churchfields and Hockerhill [perhaps the house at the eastern end of the cottages was known as St Mary's Row], but around the turn of the century the so-called Mansion House, the old half-timbered house at the junction of School Road and Newport Street, is said to have been known locally as the old workhouse. Again, it is possible – though unlikely – that the public house was located in part of what is now St Dominic's School, which was for many years the workhouse in the last century. Wherever it was located, The White Horse is reputed to have been very popular with poachers, perhaps suggesting that the building near Hockerhill, which was more isolated, was the actual location.[532]

The Rainbow public house, Coven, demolished in 1968. The photograph dates from about 1908.

A New Inn is mentioned in Coven between 1860 and 1892. The old Rainbow at Coven was demolished in 1968. The New Inns at Kiddemore Green is an old beerhouse, dating from at least 1881. The Royal Oak at Bishops Wood is a former cottage: an earlier beerhouse of the same name was in what is now Old Weston Road. It is now a house known as Old Inn Cottage. In 1838 Acorn Cottage, just across the county boundary in Offoxey Road, was a beerhouse known as The Royal Oak.[533] Aquaduct House, built in 1835 at the north west junction of the Watling Street and Shropshire Union Canal, was a public house for many years.

28. Libraries

During the reign of Queen Anne [1702-14] a library of 72 theological volumes was formed at Brewood by the Institution of Parochial and Lending Libraries. The library was housed in the vicarage in 1864.[534]

A reading room with a small library, built at the expense of Mr T.W. Giffard in 1857 by Mr Swann at the top end of Sandy Lane, was still in existence in 1896. The building was used around the turn of the century by the Band of Hope, and has recently been converted into a shop. In about 1842 a library of about 600 volumes was created 'under the auspices of the clergy', and in 1874 was housed in the old school in Church Road, then occupied by the Working Men's Institute. This may be the 'parochial library' recorded in 1860 and 1868, with members paying an annual subscription of 4s, and the 'church library of divinity', with some 70 books, recorded between 1884 and 1896. Many of the books were said to be dilapidated in 1890. A 'reading room' was opened by Mr Smith of Coven Ironworks in 1857[535] and may have been the reading room in Dean Street recorded in 1883.[536] A reading room was also opened at Speedwell Castle in January 1875, with 48 members each subscribing 1s. per month.[537] A confectionery and tobacconist's shop in Market Place opposite Newport Street ran a small lending library for some years during the 1930's.

The present library, on the north side of Newport Street, is a single-storey red brick building with shallow wood lined pyramid roof open internally to the apex. It was opened on 27th March 1972, and replaced the library in the wooden huts now known as The Scout Huts in Deansfield Road, which in turn replaced an arrangement whereby books stored in cardboard boxes in a wooden meeting room where the parish council offices now stand in Stafford Street were made available every Wednesday after school hours. The same building was also used for meetings of the parish council, the Red Cross, and as the doctor's surgery.

29. Water Mills and Windmills

In the medieval period, mills [and bread ovens] were the perquisite of the lord of the manor, who charged for their use, and no tenant was permitted to use any others.

In 1086 and 1291 the Bishop of Lichfield is recorded as holding two mills in Brewood,[538] indicating a significant area of arable land producing corn, and one of these was probably at Engleton, of which various leases exist from 1467 until the mill, a flour mill in 1882, became disused towards the end of the nineteenth century. The building at that time was of brick, and dated from the late seventeenth century, incorporating earlier timbers, the east wall against the former mill wheel site having dressed sandstone in its lower courses. The building is now converted into a house, stone having been brought from the former Teddesley Hall for the restoration in 1956, and the site of the mill leat, which was used as a rubbish tip in 1906, is occupied by gardens.

The second of the mills held by the Bishop at Domesday was probably at either Somerford, or what is now known as Brewood Forge. In 1120 Richard de Somerford obtained licence for a mill, and a mill rebuilt by the Bishop before 1288 seems to have been on the same site at Somerford. In 1337 John de Aldenham and his son were accused by the Bishop of diverting the Saredon Brook by a trench to Coven mill, reducing the water available for the Bishop's mill at Brewood, probably the one at Somerford. It was alleged that the lack of water meant that working night and day, only 6 quarters of "each kind of corn" could be produced, instead of the usual 30. Somerford mill was leased to the Bishop as a fulling mill, in which cloth was fulled or milled by pressing between rollers and cleansed with soap or Fuller's Earth, before 1473, and was being used as a corn mill by 1620. In 1623 there were complaints that its operation was restricted, possibly by the diversion of water to the new forge a short distance upstream. The mill was in use as a corn mill until at least 1884, and the former mill building is incorporated in the northern half of Somerford Mill Farm at Catchem's End. The working floor of the mill was built on a brick arcade, and the wheel, which was removed many years ago, was housed in the kitchen block. The side walls contain eighteenth century leaded lights, and older beams have been re-used in the roof. The mill leat [which carried the main flow of the Penk in the last century] now serves only as a drainage channel, and the mill pool on the south side of the building was filled in c.1960 and is now part of the garden. The living accomodation adjacent to the mill dates from the early eighteenth century, with stairs of that date, but the large size of the principal beams suggests the rebuilding of an earlier structure. A large square sandstone trough in the yard is fed by a natural spring. A turbine mill at Somerford was used as a sawmill and for grinding feed in 1956.

Near the eastern end of Chillington Lower Avenue, at the point where the Penk runs close to the Brewood to Coven road, is the site of a pond bay and forge, and possibly one of the mills mentioned in Domesday.[539]

The sale of Blackladies after the Dissolution in 1539 included a water mill, the site of which is now uncertain, but from the field name Mill Meadow probably lay to the north of the house, where sandstone blocks lying near the stream may be associated with the mill buildings.

Water mills at La Hyde and at Chillington are mentioned in 1297. The former is again recorded in 1477, and an early nineteenth century three-storey brick-built mill with two millstones and overshot iron mill-wheel [now removed] was in use until 1939. Adjoining the mill, and now incorporated with it, is a house of L-shaped plan of the same date as the mill. The mill at Chillington is again mentioned in 1556 and 1727, and appears to have been a short distance south of the site of Paine's bridge at the south-east corner of Chillington Pool.

The Coven mill mentioned by the Bishop of Lichfield in his complaint of 1337 may have been the one shown on Yates map of 1775 lying to the west of Coven Heath, called Old Mill Farm on the First Edition 1" Ordnance Survey map, just within the parish boundary, or it may have occupied the site of the water mill attached to Aspley by 1704, described in 1757 as located on a 'brook running . . . to Somerford Mill', which is probably the same as the Standeford Mill on the Saredon Brook mentioned in 1760. That mill was used as a corn-mill until about 1912, and for grinding horse-feed until 1939. The building has eighteenth century origins with additions of about 1840 to the mill-house. The house was partly rebuilt after a fire in 1933, but the buildings were unoccupied in 1956. The house has now been restored, but the mill pool was filled in many years ago. The core of Coven Mill House [Old Mill Farm], which was mentioned in a perambulation of 1588 and may have been the mill to which Charles II was taken on his journey from Boscobel to Moseley, was part stone built and may have dated from the seventeenth century. The small brick mill, of eighteenth century date [in use until the last century] and the mill house were demolished in the 1970's, having been derelict from at least 1956, by which date the mill pool had been filled. The remains of the sluice gate which fed the mill were still visible in 1985, but all traces of both mill and sluice gate have now disappeared.

Windmills were introduced into Staffordshire in about 1300 – perhaps by returning crusaders – and until tower mills became common from the seventeenth century took the form of post mills with the body of the mill turning on an upright post set into cross-timbers sunk into the ground. A windmill – probably a post mill – existed between Hyde mill and the Kiddemore Green road, probably to the north-west of Hockerhill farmhouse, in or before 1775 until at least 1798 [the field south of Oak Cottage is shown as Windmill Hill on the 1838 Tithe map] but no trace of the mill mound remains. Field names in a Chillington estate map of about

1727 suggest that a windmill once lay on or near the pine-topped hill known locally as Windy [windmill?] Clump, or Spion Kop, a reminder of the Boer War, south-east of Chillington Hall, opposite Long Birch, but had by that date disappeared. The hill has low earthworks on the summit of unknown date but which may be connected with a post mill.

In the latter part of the eighteenth century a windmill existed at Coven Heath. At that time the area was not within the parish, but it was included under the boundary reorganisation of 1934. Both the Brewood and Coven Heath windmills appear as post mills on William Yates map published in 1775,[540] but although different symbols were used for tower mills, the map may be inaccurate: Codsall is shown with a post mill, but had in fact a tower mill, which still exists.[541]

30. Roads

Concentrated in the Brewood area was a network of Roman and possibly pre-Roman roads. Even at that early period roads were not simply rough trackways suitable only for packhorses and pedlars, since the design of roads, bridges and urban streets all have their origin in the iron-shod wheel developed in the Iron Age. The sophistication of the Roman network and construction is well known, and demonstrated locally by the many wagon-loads of stone which were hauled from a considerable distance, perhaps from Ludlow and Wem, for the construction of the villa at Engleton. Pottery, wine and oil were regularly imported from the Continent into the most remote areas of Roman Britain, and samian pottery from Gaul or Colchester is found on the various Roman sites in the area. But it must not be forgotten that the Romans used not only their characteristic straight alignments, perhaps properly called military or post roads, but also utilised the existing myriad of tracks and paths established long before the Roman conquest.

Of the various Roman roads in the Brewood area [discussed in more detail in Chapter 4], it seems that Watling Street, the Roman name for which is unknown, was kept in good repair, for it was known by name throughout its length in Anglo-Saxon times, and the Old English word straet was used only for the most important highways, probably suitable for wheeled traffic. In the eleventh century Watling Street was one of the four 'chimini regales', or royal roads. These were required to be wide enough for two wagons to pass or for 16 armed knights to ride abreast. Any assault committed upon one of these roads was considered a breach of the King's peace and punishable by a fine of 100 shillings, at a time when a cow was worth 2 or 3 shillings. The importance of Watling Street to the people of Brewood is indicated by the triplicated name used in fairly recent times: Streetway Road.

Strangely, the word 'road' was unknown in the Anglo-Saxon period, and indeed is rarely found before the seventeenth century. The word lane was used in Anglo-Saxon times, and may have meant a minor road between hedges, and a 'portstraet' meant a road to a market town. Port Lane, running from Codsall to the east of Brewood, has the same derivation, the earliest reference to its name dating from 1569,[542] but it was unquestionably ancient even at that time. The depth of the road across Hilltop and, before it was destroyed by the construction of the M54 motorway, the deep cutting up the short steep hill just north of Gunstone crossroads, attest to its long use. Its curious alignment, which seems intended to by-pass the village, is explained by its origin: the present road as far as Giffard's Cross follows more or less the alignment of the Roman road from Pennocrucium, and may well have been used continuously since that period. It is less easy to explain why the later road turns south at Giffard's Cross [the Roman road seems to have forked with both roads continuing slightly to the west] and takes a line which passes between Codsall and Bilbrook, both Domesday settlements, and forks near Oaken, with one road leading towards Wrottesley, itself very ancient, the other continuing south through Perton to join the Wolverhampton to Bridgnorth road. King John's various visits to Brewood are known to have been made during his travels between Lichfield and Kinver, where there was another royal Forest, and the road south leads in the general direction of Kinver, passing near Oaken, which had connections with Brewood Forest. In the early medieval period roads connecting the royal Forests may have acquired a special status and been maintained accordingly.

Another road of early date is the road from Brewood to Bishop's Wood, recorded as 'Kyrrymorelane' in 1406,[543] and presumably [but not necessarily] the road now known as Kiddemore Green Road, which was called Brewood Lane in the 1841 census returns. From Roman finds near Blackladies, Boscobel and Whiteladies, and from the monastic sites at both Blackladies and Whiteladies, it is apparent that it was a route of importance in early times. Possible Mesolithic or Neolithic finds from Kiddemore Green suggest that a ridgeway route following the same line may have been in use from prehistoric times. Within living memory the road was used as a drove road for cattle bought and sold at Wolverhampton and Penkridge Markets.

There is evidence that a ridgeway road – perhaps a saltway – ran from Penkridge to Wolverhampton in Saxon times, crossing through the east of the parish following roughly the line of Old Stafford Road. A road is also identified in a Saxon charter giving the boundaries of Hilton and Featherstone in 994AD as a 'straet' at 'brenesforde' [Brinsford] – perhaps "the way called Greenway" in an undated medieval deed. It seemingly crossed Bushbury Hill, and a possible link with the road is noted in Stebbing-Shaw's 'History of Staffordshire':

> Tradition says, that a great road ran from Chester to London had its course formerly over Byshbury-hill, and from thence towards Wednesfield. However that might be, certain it is that evident traces of a road yet remain in a field about half a mile North West of the church, and which are still distinguished by the name of London Road.

At the time of the Norman Conquest the road network in England was probably as sophisticated as it was seven hundred years later, as graphically illustrated by the events of 1066. King Harold covered 200 miles to York in 4½ days, gathering an army on the way, defeated Harold Hardrada, and in a week had marched back to London. Eight days later, Harold's army had reached Hastings, 250 miles from York, for its ill-fated battle with William of Normandy.

In the Middle Ages the road system in Brewood parish was undoubtedly more dense than in modern times. Every wood, meadow, field, house and barn was accessible by cart or wagon, and footpaths and tracks must have criss-crossed fields and heaths, connecting hamlets, mills and farmsteads.

Unidentified roads or lanes within the parish in medieval times, and the dates they are recorded, include Byll Lane [1567]; Bromehalelane [1417]; Chirchefeld lane [1462]; le brodelane [1372]; le bullone [1406]; le grene lane [1576]; le hethlane [1401]; Hiklefordlone [1487]; le leelone [1453]; Morelone [1441]; Notehustelone [1417]; Penkrichelone [1400]; Ratonestrete [1406]; Syche lane [1569]; Wilmermoreslone [1390]; and Wythiebedlone [1452].[544]

One type of business which consumed much time in the manor court in medieval times was the encroachment of common land. With occasional exceptions, highways were part of the common land of the manor, and were generally considerably wider than modern roads to allow carts and wagons to steer a course through the quagmire in bad sections, which must have been all too common in wet weather. They were bounded by hedges or ditches, and did not belong to adjacent landowners. Any encroachments of common land were known as purprestures, and most cases concerned the narrowing of a road, either by a neighbouring farmer moving forward his frontage, or by a trespasser creating a dwelling within the road itself. Such encroachments were often regularised by the manor court on payment of an annual fine to the lord of the manor. Examples of purprestures in Brewood are on the southern side of Kiddemore Green Road between Brewood and Blackladies [allotments east of Oak Cottage have been created on the site of the sunken lane], and immediately south of Giffard's Cross on both sides of Port Lane. In each case existing hedge lines show the

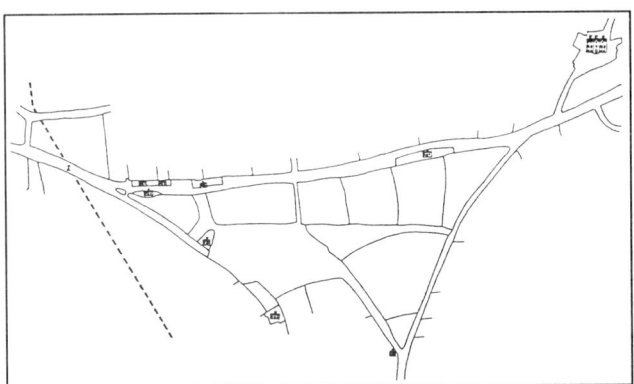

Redrawn extract from a Chillington estate map c.1727 of Port Lane from Giffard's Cross (left) to Long Birch (right), showing cottages built on encroachments made into the wide roadway. The Upper Avenue had not then been created: its line is indicated by a superimposed dotted line. The road running down from Giffard's Cross is to Ackbury. Thieves Lane and Chillington Street are shown, but not the building which now forms Barn Cottages. The straight line running horizontally across the centre is a hedge, which still exists, marking a lost Roman road. With acknowlegements to Staffordshire Record Office D590/363.

earlier width of the road, with squatters cottages built on encroachments. Early maps[545] show that other dwellings were built within these encroachments, known locally as slangs, but have now vanished. In 1864 Port Lane was described as "a level and retired highway, skirted by wide arable, and garnished with a few mean cottages . . ." The foundations of one such cottage can still be identified after ploughing in the edge of a field to the west of the road between Barn Cottages and Long Birch, the hedge-line having long-since been brought forward to increase the area of cultivation, and thus narrow the road. To the north, the former hedge-line was marked by remnants of ancient hedges until they were destroyed by works connected with the M54 motorway in the late 1970's.

The church had always been involved in the maintenance of the road network for the benefit of its own substantial commercial interests, but with the dissolution of the monastries in the 1530's, the medieval principle of road and bridge maintenance as an obligation of land tenure was soon forgotten by new landowners more interested in the rights of ownership than corresponding duties, and the network of major highways began to fall into disrepair. It is clear that the poor road system was due largely to an inefficient administration of the road network. Whereas in France the main arterial highways were constructed by the state, in England the legal responsibility and expense for maintaining roads lay with the parish through which the roads passed, which was a very heavy burden for many parishes. From the mid sixteenth century belated attempts were made to reconstitute arrangements for maintaining roads, and various statutes enabled parish authorities to conscript labour to carry out such repairs, every villager being required to carry out six days unpaid work on the roads each year. Some idea of the relative deterioration in the road system in the sixteenth and seventeenth centuries can be gained from the scarcity of bridges of the period which remain today. There are very many bridges from earlier centuries, and many from later, but very few in the region which date from between 1540 and 1740.

The state of the roads in Staffordshire varied from place to place: when Sir Amias Paulet wrote to Secretary Walsingham on 3rd October 1585 about the possibility of housing Mary Queen of Scots at Chillington House, he noted that between Chillington and Tutbury "the wayes be alreadye as deepe and as fowle as ys possible", but Plot remarks a century later that "the highways, owing to the gravelly nature of much of the soil, are universally good." James I is reputed to have said during one of his royal progresses of Staffordshire that it was fit only to be cut into thongs, to make highways for the rest of the Kingdom.[546]

From at least the end of the sixteenth century until the second half of the nineteenth century, Watling Street served as a drove road for cattle and sheep from North Wales, which used a route from Wrexham to Newport, via Whitchurch, and from central Wales via Shrewsbury and Wellington and then on to the south of England via Northampton. However, the Chancery and Exchequer proceedings for the early seventeenth century suggest that of the large numbers of cattle driven from Wales to England, the majority were sold in the Midlands, with only small numbers infiltrating to the southern counties. The road was used to transport coal from the Shropshire coalfields by packhorse train in the sixteenth and seventeenth centuries, and there is evidence that it was in good condition in the eighteenth century.[547]

In 1654 the Commonwealth parliament passed 'An Ordinance for better amending and keeping in repair, the common highwaies within this nation'. This provided for a rate, not exceeding 1s in the pound, for the repair of roads, levied on all those in the parish who paid poor rates. In about 1656 the Overseers of Highways for Brewood made an assessment "according to the late Ordinance", but they had to appeal to the Quarter Sessions for "an order to enforce the payment of several moneys assessed, which they now refuse to pay, which money the said surveyors have disbursed out of their own money".[548] From 1834 the parish was divided into eight 'liberties', each of which maintained its roads separately.

From the late seventeenth century, parliament spent much time passing legislation for making or improving particular roads, with the creation of turnpike trusts which covered many of the main roads. The trusts were local trustees with powers to acquire land for new roads and to charge a toll on traffic to pay for the upkeep of the roads. Watling Street, which was used as the alternative London to Chester route, was one of the first roads in the area to be turnpiked in 1759, with tollgates installed at Ivetsey Bank and Gailey, which helps to explain why the journey by passenger coach from London to Shrewsbury took four days in 1753, and only two days in 1764. In 1790 a journey from London to Birmingham took two days in summer but four in winter, and cost £2 – about two months wages for a labourer. The burden of maintaining the section of Watling Street that formed the parish boundary was removed from Brewood in 1879, when the road was declared a main road, with the upkeep the responsibility of the county, Staffordshire being one of the last counties to lift maintenance obligations from the parish.

What may be evidence of an early traffic accident or even highway robbery on Watling Street is found in the Brewood parish register for 1713. On 23rd November were buried in Brewood churchyard "Robert Browne and another passenger who dyed att James Willoughbye's house att the Streetway att the same time, whose name we know not."

The main Stafford to Wolverhampton road was made after 1747, the section through Brewood parish following the line of a pre-Conquest routeway – possibly a Saltway, from a pre-Conquest place-name in a charter of Kinvaston – which passed through Penkridge in the north and Wednesfield in the south, and turnpiked in 1761 under an Act of 1760. The preamble to the 1760 Act recited that ". . . the road leading from the road called the Streetway [Watling Street] through the town called Wolverhampton . . . is in a ruinous condition and in many parts very narrow and incommodious for travellers and carriages, and cannot be effectually

amended, widened and kept in good repair by ordinary course of law . . ."
The straight sections of the road from Four Ashes to Somerford Bridge date
from this period, constructed some time before 1781. Until that time, the
approach to Brewood from the east was along roads that ran from Four
Ashes and Standeford and joined to turn north near Somerford Hall
through what was formerly Somerford village, meeting the existing road
at Somerford Grange Farm, but in about 1781 the Hon. Edward Monckton
built the present road running further north to Four Ashes and closed the
section by the Hall after his proposal that the road from Brewood should
cross the Penk at Somerford Mill to the Stone House at Catchems End was
rejected by a vestry meeting held on 17th December 1781, on the grounds
that the footbridge at the mill, apparently the responsibility of the lord
of Somerford, would require replacing by a carriage bridge, and the
maintenance costs would have fallen on the parish. The present Stafford
to Wolverhampton road was realigned and converted into a dual
carriageway in 1936-39, Old Stafford Road through Slade Heath marking
the former route. In 1990 workmen laying gas pipes uncovered a milestone,
in the form of a rectangular sandstone pillar bearing a cast-iron plate, on
the north side of the bend in the road to the west of Black Lion Farm. The

words "To W-hampton 5 Mile To Stafford 11 Miles" were
clearly discernible. The stone almost certainly dates
from 1773, when an Act was passed requiring all turnpike
trusts to provide guide posts and milestones on their
roads. It was found some 500 yards south of the position
in which it is shown on Yates map of Staffordshire,
1775, based on earlier surveys, but is correctly shown on
later maps.

Gailey roundabout dates from 1937.[549] The two roundabouts in the
Wolverhampton to Stafford road at Coven were created in 1984. The
junction was until then notorious for accidents.

An Act of 1794 proposed to turnpike the road from Wolverhampton to
Ivetsey Bank. From the Wergs it was to fork northwards through Codsall
Wood to Watling Street. There is no evidence that the road was actually
turnpiked or that any tollgates were erected along the route.[550] The road
was called Shire Lane in the last century, since it lies in part along the
Staffordshire-Shropshire border, suggesting that it may be well over 1000
years old in those sections, for the boundary is likely to have followed the
road. In 1846 a reference to a journey between Codsall and Boscobel
describes ". . . a toilsome march through the deep dust and sand of an
unfrequented lane . . ."

If we can rely on the generally accurate map of Staffordshire surveyed
by William Yates and published in 1775, until some time between 1769 and
1808 the only route from Coven and the south-east into Brewood was the
lane which runs from The White House, at Somerford Park, to Sparrows
End Lane.[551] Dean Street [known as Dean's End until the last century] did
not continue beyond the lane to Hyde Mill. [Yates map of 1775 and Pitt's

map of 1796 suggest, improbably, that it stopped at The Pavement.] The Coven road from the east turned south west near Park Cottage [now called The White House] and joined Park Lane. It did not continue to Brewood. In 1792, the Hon. John Byng, travelling from Giffard's Cross to the Anchor public house and the navigation [canal] passed the 'forge houses' [the Forge], and was diverted into a road 'by no means good, but passable,' until he reached his destination.[552] The present road is shown on Robins and Sherriff's map of the parish made in 1808.

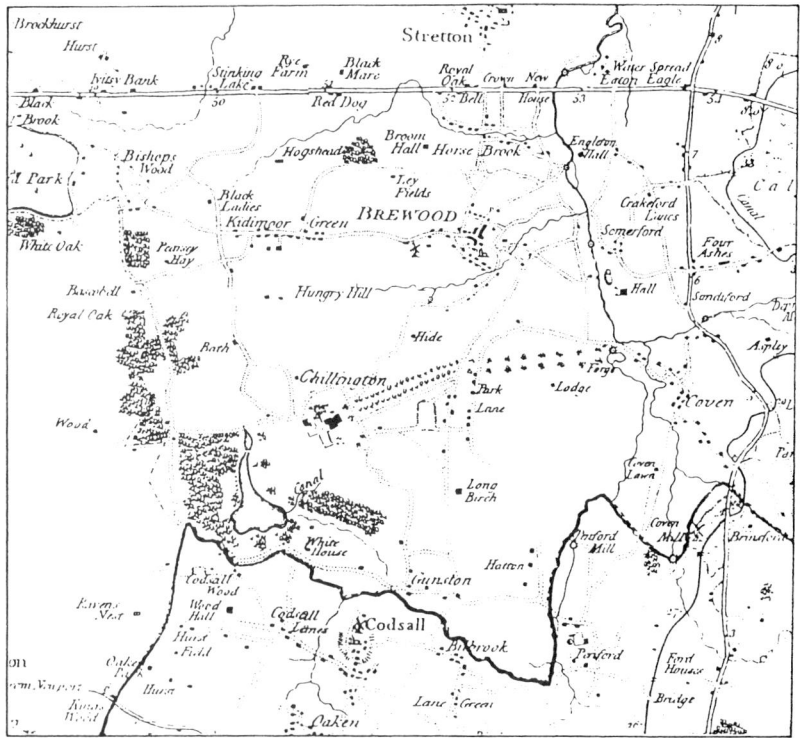

Extract from William Yates map of Staffordshire, published in November 1775 from surveys begun in 1769 and based on the first triangulation survey of the county. The windmill on the west side of the village and the approach roads on the east are of particular interest.

The direct route through Coven avoiding the sharp bends was opened in April 1988. The earlier route past The Beeches had been in use for a least 200 years.[553]

Offoxey Road was constructed between 1805 and 1815 by George Durant of Tong Castle. Before that date the road connecting Brewood to Tong was Hubbal Lane, which is now in part so wet and overgrown as to be almost impassable. The straight road from Bishop's Wood to The Bradford Arms probably dates from the same period. The lanes to the west mark the earlier route. Until the early nineteenth century a lane called Tripe or Trice Lane, latterly Sling Lane, meandered north-east from Blackladies to Stinking Lake on Watling Street.[554]

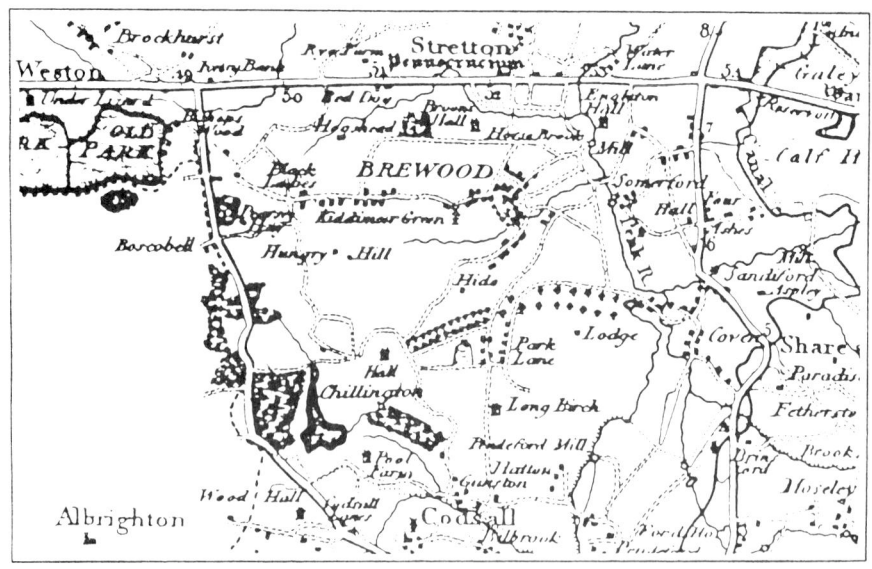

Extract from William Yates revised map of Staffordshire, 1798.

The road from Gunstone to The Hattons is narrow, with sharp turns and undulations, resulting from its route through the 'Monie Pits' – the Many Pits, now a small plantation – which were probably created by gravel extraction.

A road connecting Old Stafford Road at Cross Green with Featherstone was constructed in 1942 to serve a new armaments factory built in fields to the north of Moseley Old Hall.

One interesting topographical description is the word 'lawn', found in Langley Lawn and Coven Lawn – now Lawn Lane. As might be expected the word means a wide grass ride: both lawns were formerly glades passing through wooded areas, Langley between Boscobel and Codsall Wood, and Coven between Coven village and Pendeford. Coven Lawn may have been "the road to Pendeford" from Coven which formed the boundary of Cannock Forest in 1286.

Cobblers Bank [recorded in 1884] and Tinkers Lane may have derived their names from itinerant tradesmen who periodically visited the village and camped in these areas, although a family by the name of Tinker is recorded in the village in the eighteenth century. The track opposite Elm Cottage in Kiddemore Green Road was known as Spirit Lane in the last century and was reputed to be haunted. It was a cul-de-sac by 1838, but now continues in a sweeping arc to emerge in Wharf Lane between the Wharf and the Catholic church.[555] Thieves Lane was the name given to the lane between Port Lane and Park Lane, recorded in 1401 as Theveslone,[556] and the name Chillington Street for the overgrown lane between Thieves Lane and Chillington attests to its former status as the main approach to Chillington House. The lane from Coldham running east

248

then north to Kiddemore Green was known as Foxes Lane from at least 1900.

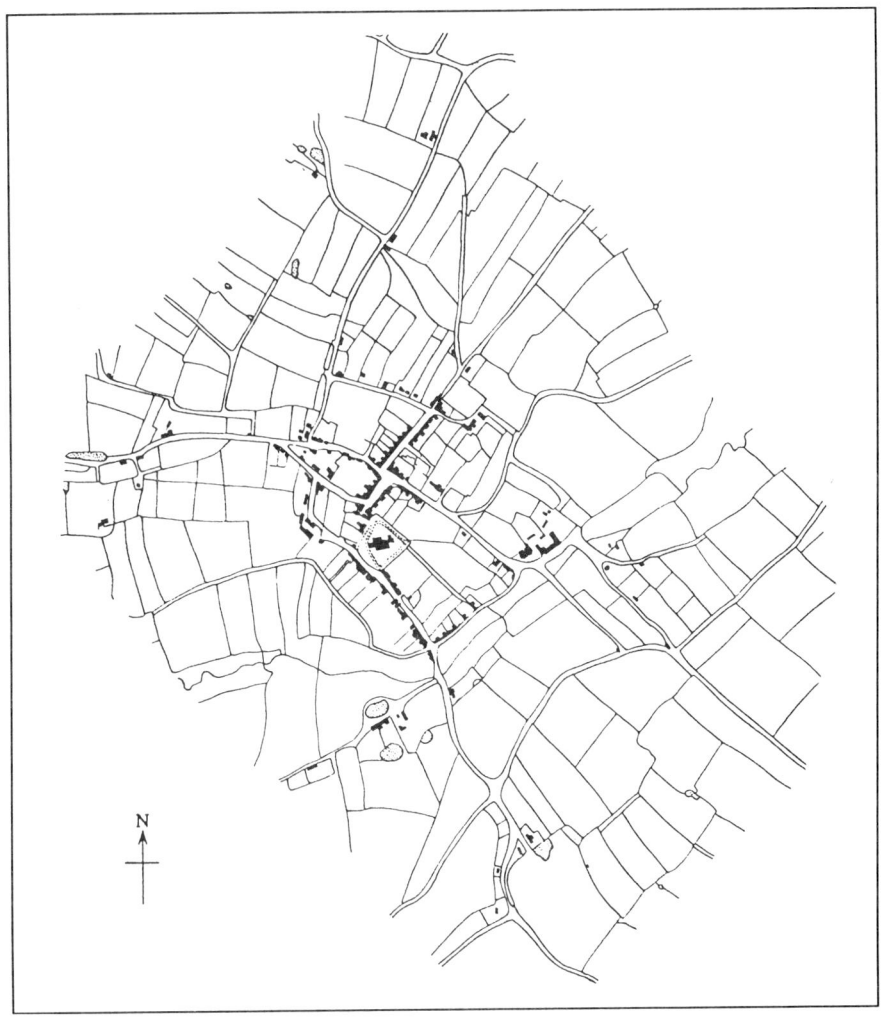

Redrawn extract from the earliest-known large-scale map of Brewood parish, surveyed by Josiah Robins and James Sherriff in 1808. With acknowledgements to Staffordshire Record Office 590/375.

Within the village, the alignments of The Swan public house, Sutherland House in Bargate Street, Old Smithy Cottage, the demolished Pavement cottages, and other early buildings attest to the early date of most of the roads in the central and southern part of the village. The road which formerly ran through what is now the yard of the Grammar School was diverted in 1799 to its present line to the east of Rushall House. Church Road was created in 1864 [the variation in stonework in the churchyard

249

wall in Dean Street can clearly be detected, with larger blocks in the earlier section] after the demolition of buildings at the south-west end of Market Place, but a pathway existed before that date, and there is some slight evidence[557] that an earlier road may at one time have run south-west from Market Place, but turned south-east after a short distance to run past the north end of the church, continuing parallel with Dean Street down the hill to The Pavement. The north-east gate to the churchyard marks the top end of such road and the former limit of Church Road, then known as Churchyard. There is also evidence that until the middle of the last century Newport Street was variously known as Back Street and Shiffnal Street, and Bargate Street was also known as Salop Street.

Redrawn extract from the Tithe Map of Brewood parish made in 1838. A comparison with the 1808 plan on page 249 shows how the village expanded in the thirty years during which the canal was constructed. With acknowledgements to Staffordshire Record Office D88/5/5.

Although the word 'gate' – in Bargate, Broadgate, Westgate – is found in the central village area, it carries its modern meaning, and does not seem to be connected with the Scandinavian 'gata', meaning road. The first two gates at least are traditionally places where gates existed for market tolls to be collected, and Westgate may have taken its name from another gate in Dean Street or from the west gate of the churchyard. Stepping Stone Lane ran westwards from a point mid-way along Bargate Lane, before turning north-west on the west side of what is now the Catholic school. The road, now broken by the Shropshire Union Canal, led to the fields, and is now barely traceable at its western end. The location of the stepping stones is unclear, and it is not inconceivable that the name is rooted in the old English word 'stybbing', meaning a clearing, hence 'meadow of the clearing with the stone'.

Until 1855 Vicarage Road joined Sandy Lane at an angle, running west across the front of buildings on the site of what is now the Old Vicarage and joining Sandy Lane almost opposite the churchyard steps. The curving sandstone wall on the north side of the entrance to the Old Vicarage probably indicates where the road turned. Vicarage Road between Sandy Lane and Deansfield Road was known as Watery Lane in 1855 and the road from Stafford Street to Vicarage Road was called Green's Lane in 1905. Coneybere Gardens, known as such from at least 1905, marks the site of the former coney burrows, or rabbit warren. Icke's Lane [named after a local family],[558] recorded between 1818 and 1912, was an alternative name for Shop Lane, and was spelt in various ways, including Eakes and Eyckes. The name Shop Lane does not seem to have been recorded before 1834,[559] and is said to take its name from a former locksmiths' shop. The location of Peak Lane, mentioned in 1829, is now uncertain, although it may be a misprint for Park Lane. Dirty Lane was known as such in 1900, and Bridge Lane, mentioned at the same date, was the lane, now called Cresswell's Lane, which runs alongside the Bridge public house.

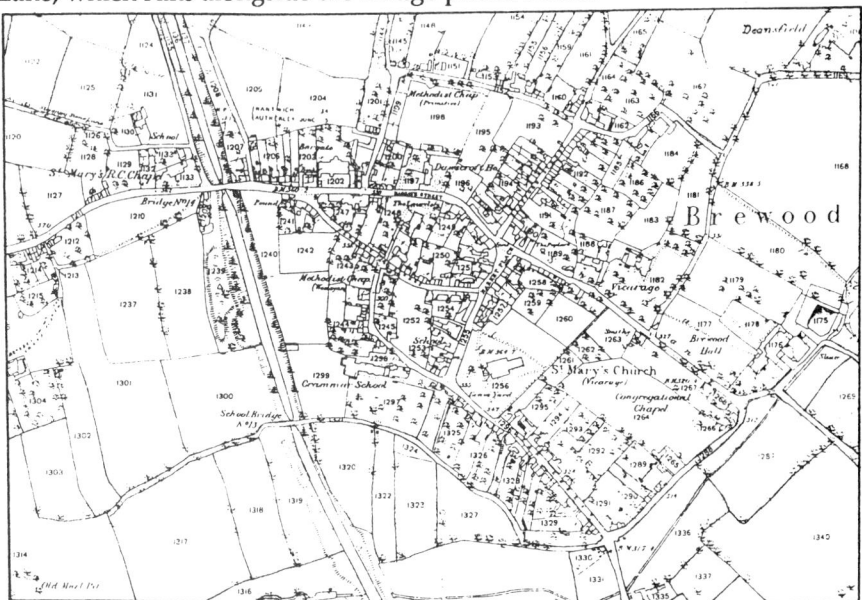

Extract from the Ordnance Survey 25" map published in 1884.

251

The Pavement was probably so named because it was – untypically – stone paved. It is tempting to associate the name – and the short length of road past Brewood Hall – with the Roman road from Pennocrucium, with which both roads are aligned [as are Hyde Mill Lane and a length of lane east of The Woolley], particularly since there is a pronounced river terrace in the fields to the north east which would have served as an obvious line for a road, raised above the flood level of the stream. The name predates the nineteenth century, but its precise age is uncertain. In other places the name has been applied where Roman mosaic floors have been found. The 1841 Census Returns mention Court Lane, listed between The Pavement and Sandy Lane. It was presumably close to what is now St Chad's Close. The southern end of Dirty Lane is clearly a continuation of The Pavement, and aerial photographs suggest that it continued west for some distance roughly parallel with the stream, although it was evidently disused by the eighteenth century, for it is not marked on a map of The Hyde estate made in 1704.

Sparrow's End may take its name from Sparrow's Cottage, mentioned in 1829. The name was originally attached to the area immediately east of Dean's Hall Farm. The junction of Sparrows End Lane and Tinkers Lane was known as Hill Top – recorded as such in the parish register in 1769 – until at least the 1920's. The name is now attached to the area east of the Port Lane and Coven Road crossroads.

The depth of the sunken lane – now a bridlepath – formerly called The Avenue, from Brewood Hall to Tinker's Lane, attests to its ancient origins, and indeed Baugh's map of Shropshire, 1808, suggests that it may have been the route into the village from the east at that date. The straight alignment of Orams Lane [named after the Oram family] is of particular interest, and may mark a very early route into the village, although boundaries of adjoining fields appear to be medieval, and to pre-date the road. Horsebrook Lane formerly turned west into Shutt Green Lane and north after a short distance to join the present road: the existing route cutting off that corner was created between 1808 and 1838. Until about the 1960's the lane from Shutt Green continued eastwards across Horsebrook Lane to join Engleton Lane. That disused and overgrown lane, and the present lane which runs north west from Somerford Bridge, almost certainly mark the headlands of old open field strips, and were probably lanes used to reach the strips. The western end of Shutt Green Lane was known in the early years of this century as Colley's Lane, after Mr Colley who lived at the cottage which formerly stood near what is now the house called Chambersfield.

The village was described in 1860 as paved,[560] and Market Place at least was macadamed before 1866.[561] Wharf Lane near its junction with Kiddemore Green Road may display one of the last traces of cobbled road surface in Brewood. Old cobbles still remain in many areas beneath the present road surface and fragments of squared sandstone slabs were uncovered during repaving on the east side of High Green in 1991. Older villagers and early photographs confirm that until well into the present century most roads were unmade or surfaced with compacted blue stone, dusty in summer and muddy in winter.

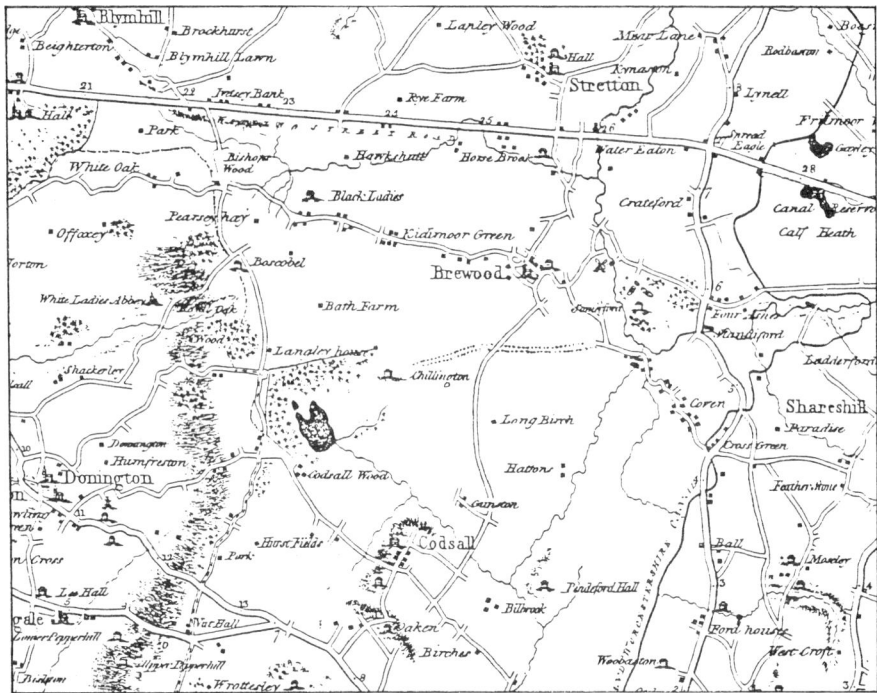

Extract from Baugh's map of Shropshire, published on 1st August 1808. Baugh was a map engraver and draughtsman who acquired surveying skills and worked for Thomas Telford on the Holyhead road. His map of Shropshire has been surprisingly little used by Staffordshire historians, although it covers a considerable part of Staffordshire. It was apparently based on an entirely new survey, noted for its accuracy. The route into Brewood from the east along the sunken lane opposite Brewood Hall is of partiuclar interest. The windmill north-west of Somerford is almost certainly intended to represent Somerford watermill: no windmill is known to have existed.

In the eighteenth century the postal services developed rapidly, and mails were conveyed between Birmingham and the Lancashire districts by horseback from 1721 until 1760, when a mail cart was introduced.[562] The mail coach between Birmingham and Liverpool, which first operated in 1785, passed through Four Ashes at night,[563] and the Manchester to London coach at about one or two pm on Mondays, Wednesdays and Fridays in 1793. The Chester Wagon left parcels at the Crown Inn on Watling Street every Thursday and the Shrewsbury Wagon every Friday in the same year.[564] The Bristol to Manchester mail coach, which started running in 1810, passed through Four Ashes during the day. By 1818 the Post Office was at 'The Giffard Arms' [or 'Jeffords Arms'] in Stafford Street.[565] When the Grand Junction Railway from Birmingham to the Liverpool and

253

Manchester Railway at Newton-le-Willows began operating on 1st July 1837, only one of several horse-drawn coaches which had previously called at Four Ashes was retained: the Red Rover, known as 'the Potteries Coach', running from Manchester to Birmingham during the day, connecting with the Greyhound, a night coach from Birmingham to London until 1846. By 1834, the Emerald, the London to Chester and Liverpool coach, was passing through Brewood daily in each direction, stopping at the Lion Inn, northwards at 10.30 am and southbound at 4.00 pm, and for many years taking on two additional horses with postillion riders to assist it on the bad Kiddemore Green road past 'the marlpits' – probably those opposite Hockerhill Farm – and through Bishop's Wood to Ivetsey Bank. The road via Gailey was apparently in better condition, for a rival coach, the Albion, needed only four horses on that route. The Emerald stopped running in 1837. In 1834 a coach call The Dispatch left the Lion for Wolverhampton every Wednesday at 10am, returning at 6pm.

By 1811, a coach was running to Brewood daily from the Golden Ball at High Green, Wolverhampton, operated by John Bentley, and for many years after 1837 a two horse coach ran through Brewood, in about 1850 running between Wolverhampton and Kiddemore Green, probably turning at a loop in the road forming a roundabout at the junction of Kiddemore Green Road and the lane to Coldham opposite Blackladies. For some years after 1855 a horse-drawn omnibus ran to Wolverhampton and back twice a week, and many carriers were employed on the same route. In November 1902 Alcock Bros. were running a horsedrawn bus to Wolverhampton on Wednesdays and Saturdays, leaving Market Place at 9.00am and returning from Mitre Yard, North Street, at 3.15pm.[566] The first motor bus service to Wolverhampton started in about 1922.[567]

An incomplete series of accounts from the Supervisors of Highways exists for 1730 to 1750, but the entries are of a routine nature and contain little of note. They do confirm, however, that there were two separate Supervisors for the township of Brewood: one for 'High Town', and one for The Deanery, the latter probably covering Dean Street, The Pavement and Sandy Lane.

One of the greatest physical changes within the parish in recorded history – comparable with the major landscaping of Chillington Park in the eighteenth century and the building of the canals – was undoubtedly the construction between 1980 and 1983, after a fruitless campaign to save the southern part of Chillington Park from mutilation, of the M54 motorway and associated bridges, approach and drainage works. As well as huge volumes of earth moved to create the four-lane highway and necessary landscaping, including an earthen embankment serving to mask noise to the south of Chillington, the lanes crossing the line of the motorway were 'improved' in various ways. The sharp Z-bend at Boscobel was reduced to a gentle S-bend. Ancient hedgerows and trees were ripped out along Port Lane, and the road straightened and widened, with wide verges created to the north of Giffard's Cross and to the south of the motorway itself. The gradient of the short steep hill to the north of Gunstone crossroads was reduced. The lane from Coven to Pendeford was realigned to the south of the motorway, and a new short length of road created to join with Gunstone Hall Lane. Junction 2 of the motorway on the Wolverhampton to Stafford road is just within the parish boundary,[568] and the proposed Western Orbital Route seems destined to link with the motorway near Pendeford and pass through the south-east corner of the parish.

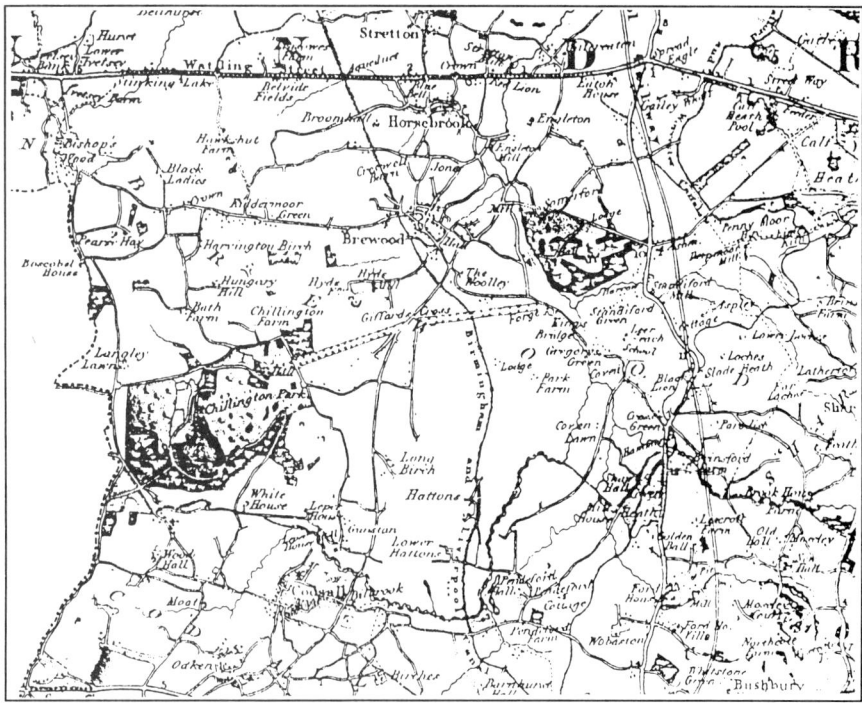

Extract from Teesdale's map of Staffordshire 1831-2. The map is not free from errors: The Woolley is inexplicably mis-located.

31. Rivers

The principal rivers in the parish, which stands at a watershed between the Severn to the west and the Trent and Humber to the east, are the Penk, which rises in the area between Yew Tree Lane and Wrottesley Road, formerly occupied by meadows called Penkridge Well,[569] and its tributaries, Saredon Brook [recorded as Sarebrook River in 1679] which joins the Penk to the west of Coven, and the Moat Brook, which forms [or more properly formed, for the brook has over the years changed its course, leaving a meandering boundary on the map as a legacy of its former position] the southern limits of the parish. Moat Brook was so-called from at least 1638 – as 'Mot Brook' in the Codsall parish register – and may derive its name from a moated medieval site[570] at Moor Hall, Codsall, where Strawmoor Lane crosses the brook, or a moat or fishpond which field names in an early Chillington estate map suggest may have existed at or close to the Leper House, near Gunstone.[571] It is perhaps surprising that the brook is not called Bilbrook, for the village of that name is said to take its name from 'brook in which billers or watercress grew',[572] and Moat Brook is the nearest stream to Bilbrook. The name of the River Penk is probably taken from the settlement name Penchrich – technically known as a 'back formation', since settlements are invariably named after a river rather than vice versa. The place where Watling Street crosses the Penk was known in 1286 as Stretwyle.

There are references in the thirteenth and fourteenth century documents to 'Prestford broke'[573] – Priestford Brook – and though its identity is uncertain, it may have been at or near Pearse Hay, which was at one time called Priests Hay.

Leats to divert water to the mills were created at Engleton and Somerford. Engleton, where a fishery in the mill-pond is mentioned in a lease of the mill by the Bishop in 1467,[574] is now filled in and forms part of the garden of the mill, but Somerford still exists, although it now carries only drainage water. Both the Penk and the Moat Brook were once famous for their trout, which began to disappear in the 1870's.[575]

An ambitious scheme was put forward by Thomas Congreve in 1717 for linking the river Severn with the Trent by means of weirs to 'canalise' the Penk and the Smestow, linking them at Wolverhampton. One version of the scheme envisaged a dam at Pendeford 24' high and another at Tettenhall, with the construction of 32 locks, each 15' high over a length of 70 miles, but the proposals were found to be impracticable, and the scheme came to nothing, although it is of interest that the proposed route bears a general similarity to that later adopted by the Staffordshire and Worcestershire canal.[576]

Rather surprisingly, the stream which runs through Brewood village seems to have had no fixed name, although the field opposite The

Pavement is shown as Pickens Brook Meadow on the Tithe map of 1838 and in Victorian times the stream was marked by the Ordnance Survey as Chillington Brook, and was also known as Brewood Water.[577] Its source is south of Coldham, although a tributary with the name Chillington Brook runs into it from the Hyde, and it joins the Penk on the west side of the Somerford Bridge. Pronounced river terraces between Brewood village and the Penk indicate that the stream was once much wider. Until drainage works in recent years the meadows alongside the stream were often flooded after heavy rainfall. A rectangular earth-banked pool between Brook House and the canal was created in about 1984.

A stream from Lady Isabella's Well, to the south of Bishops Wood on the Shropshire side of the road to Boscobel which forms the county boundary, formerly crossed the road and was known as the Ladies Brook. It passed through Pearsehay and to the west of Blackladies to The Hawkshutts. From there it ran east to feed Belvide Reservoir, and left the reservoir by a culvert under the canal. After running in a deep cutting alongside Watling Street it merges with the stream from Lapley, which crosses under Watling Street, and forms the Horsebrook, receiving water from the Leabrook, which has its source at a spring near Oakley House.[578]

Bath Farm, north of Chillington, takes its name from a former spring-fed cold bath dating from at least 1727, said to have been used for bathing by local people. A slate bath reputed to have come from the site is in the stable yard at Chillington Hall, and the spring, now piped, feeds what was described in 1874 as 'an artificial canal', which has existed since at least 1808 and drains water from the southern slopes of Boscobel and Pearse Hay into Chillington Pool.

A curious prognosticating pool at Pendeford, seemingly fed by an underground spring, is mentioned by Plot, but appears to have been just outside Brewood parish.

One puzzling survival just outside the village is the so called 'swimming pool' on the west side of the Shropshire Union Canal, between Dean's Hall Bridge and School Bridge. The stream from the west, which passes under the canal in a large tunnel, has been lined with sandstone blocks and slabs to form a rectangular cistern or pool some 95' long and about 30' wide, with a narrow sluice gate at the east end to regulate the water level. Although Elizabethan, Georgian and Victorian coins have been found nearby[579] and the construction is typical of a medieval stew or fishpond, other evidence suggests that it was built or rebuilt by the Grammar School at some date after 1838 and before 1884 – it appears on the Ordnance Survey map of the later date, but not on the Tithe Map of the earlier, and is not mentioned in an admittedly brief description of the school facilities published in 1860. It seems to have been used for swimming by children of the village for many years until at least the Second World War, when a small wooden changing hut which existed in 1884 lay on the north bank. The pool and sluice remain, although much decayed and overgrown. In 1321 one of the customs in Brewood was the payment by "the tenants of the irrigated land" on the Feast of St Michael of 'stuck', which may have been rent for the use and upkeep of sluice-gates which controlled the supply of water to the fields. It is possible, however, that the payment was that of 'stoc-gabulum', or market due, a form of tax imposed elsewhere in the fourteenth century.

32. Bridges

The largest bridge in the parish is Somerford Bridge, formerly known as Stone Bridge, which stands at or close to the point where the Romano-British road from Pennocrucium to Ackbury Heath crossed the river, either by a ford or a bridge. The existing bridge is of sandstone with four arches, splayed breakwaters, and pedestrian refuges on both sides. It was repaired at the expense of the parish in 1605, as evidenced by one of the earliest surviving entries from the Constables' Accounts for Brewood:

> A half lewne [a levy or rate] layed the 24th day of June, Anno Domini 1605, for repayring of the Stonbridge, by the consent of those whose names are underwritten:

Imprimis				
	Brewood		xxs	[20s]
	Chillington	xiijs	ivd	[13s 4d]
	Horsebrook	xs	vjd	[10s 6d]
	Gunstone		vjs	[6s]
	Somerford	vijs	ijd	[7s 2d]
	Engleton		iijs	[3s]

Amongst the "names underwritten" are Thomas Bickford, William Smyth, of Woolley, John Mott, Jacob Yate, Edward Eccleshall, and John Harper. The assessment is of particular interest as it provides an indication of the relative affluence of the various parts of the parish at that time.

The bridge was again repaired, with Streetway Bridge [carrying Watling Street over the Penk], in 1711, this time at the expense of the county. The total cost for both bridges was £127.[580] In 1796 the bridge was completely rebuilt, and the present structure dates from that time. With an original width of 11 feet, the bridge was widened on the west side of 25 feet in 1930, when the earlier stonework was found to be in perfect condition.[581] At about the same date the course of the river on the east side of the bridge was realigned having formerly flowed north-east alongside the bridge before turning south-east.[582]

In 1695 Camden's 'Britannia' mentioned a stone bridge where the Watling Street crossed the Penk "at Pennocrucium", presumably on the site of the present Stretton Bridge, and this same Streetway Bridge[583] was rebuilt in 1658, an entry in the Constables' Accounts for that year recording:

> May 23rd: Paid Mr Launder the money for the new bridge
> in the Streetway   £2 1 8d

The present bridge, of three segmental arches in rusticated ashlar, dates from the early nineteenth century, probably 1809.

Two bridges over Dean's Hall Brook and Brewood Hall Brook were repaired by the parish in 1663 as appears from the Constables' Accounts:

For mending the bridge at Dean's Hall Brook	4d
For mending the bridge at Brewood Hall Brook	8d

The wooden bridge at Gunstone was repaired in 1663 and replaced by a stone bridge in 1682:

1663 for timber and sundry repairs to Gunston Bridge	£1 5 4d
1682 For making a new Stone Bridge at Gunston	£2 10 0d
[from the same Accounts]	

Further repairs were made in 1678 to Brewood Hall Bridge and to a bridge at Engleton, as appears from the following entry:

Payd to John Roberts for planks and mending the bridges at Engleton and at Brewood Hall and the Cowclose Bridge	12s

Standeford Bridge, which carries the Stafford to Wolverhampton road over the Saredon Brook before it joins the Penk, is mentioned in 1630, and the Constables' Accounts contain an entry for 1682: 'To Mr William Mansell, for his charges in seeking to make Standeford Bridge a hundred bridge – £1 2 0d'. The bridge was rebuilt in ashlar as a cart bridge in about 1757, and was widened at the expense of the county in 1823.

Jackson's Bridge [formerly known as King's Bridge, perhaps after the escape of Charles II], which carries the Brewood to Coven road over the Penk, may well be 'the bridge of Coven, near the Park of Brewood', mentioned in the boundaries of Cannock Forest determined by a jury in 1286. In 1823 it was described as a "very ancient stone bridge of two arches, now very much out of repair . . . very dangerous . . . several accidents have happened there . . . heretofore call'd Kings Bridge, Coven Bridge, and latterly Jackson's Bridge from a man of that name having been drowned there". The following year the bridge was rebuilt in ashlar by the county on the south of the old bridge. A short length of the old lane still exists on the north-west side of the 'new' bridge.

At least two bridges across the Penk at Engleton seems to have existed from at least 1745, for the Constables' Accounts record a payment of 5s 10d in that year "for repairing Engleton bridges [sic]".

A narrow concrete bridge of two spans was built over the Penk at Somerford in 1931. The old brick footbridge, of surprisingly delicate design, between the concrete bridge and Somerford Mill, is known locally as The Devil's Bridge. It probably dates from the mid-eighteenth century. Until the early twentieth century the main flow of the Penk ran under the bridge and mill. The bridge over Brantley Pool at Somerford dates from the eighteenth century, the two arches flanked by fluted pilasters. It is built of ashlar, and has twentieth century alterations, including a parapet of concrete pillars and metal rails.

Low's Bridge over the Penk near the Lower Forge is mentioned in 1724.

There are thirteen bridges in the parish over the Shropshire Union Canal, and five over the Staffordshire and Worcestershire Canal. Each bridge originally had an oval cast iron plate on each side with the number of the bridge, but few now remain. Of particular interest is Telford's cast iron aquaduct, which carries the Shropshire Union Canal on circular stone piers over Watling Street at Stretton, with the inscription: 'Thomas Telford F.R.S. L&E [Fellow of the Royal Society, London and Edinburgh]'. Local information suggests that when the road beneath was lowered to increase the headroom for modern traffic earlier this century, a large number of horse-shoes and ox-shoes were unearthed. The blue brick plinth was installed at that time. The ornamental stone bridge with flanking balustraded wings carrying Chillington Lower Avenue over the canal was built in about 1830 to a design by Telford. In Victorian times it was known to boatmen as the Fancy Bridge.

The parapet of the bridge over the Shropshire Union Canal at High Green, Brewood, was increased in height to improve safety in 1896, the southern parapet was replaced with vertical steel railing in the 1960's, and in 1986 a detached steel-framed footway was constructed on the northern side.

33. Canals

In 1772 James Brindley's 46-mile Staffordshire and Worcestershire Canal was completed, having been commenced in a field at Compton on 1st September 1766.[584] One version of Brindley's original proposals for the Duke of Bridgewater in 1769 was a route passing between Brewood and Somerford, but the chosen line took the canal in a meandering line following the contours across the eastern edge of the parish, by-passing Coven and over two miles from Brewood township. The principal landowner in Brewood was probably indirectly responsible for the route of the canal, for at the time the Giffard family fortunes were at a low ebb. Thomas Joseph Giffard was in debt – in 1790 he placed his lands in commission and entrusted his affairs to Lord Loughborough – and showed little interest in the project. The positioning of the canal away from Brewood was the principal reason for the economic decline of the village, but to balance that the village was spared the expansion and 'improvements' of the period that have despoiled many other places.

In 1830 work commenced on the Birmingham and Liverpool Junction Canal – since 1846 known as the Shropshire Union Canal – under the supervision of Thomas Telford, the excavation work being undertaken entirely by hand with horses used for haulage. The local section of the canal opened in January 1834, and the first boat passed through the 39 miles of the new canal on Monday 2nd March 1835. Just as the Giffards were probably the main reason why the earlier canal bypassed Brewood, they are certainly the reason why the Shropshire Union Canal took a route close to the village centre, for Mr T.W. Giffard of Chillington helped to promote the canal, selling 38 acres of land to the canal company in 1830, and in the same year the trustees of Brewood Grammar School sold 2¾ acres of land to the canal company at £200 per acre, on the understanding that the company would build a wall, which still exists, between the canal and 'the Croft', the grassed area behind the school on which modern buildings now stand. As a bonus, the school sold sand from the excavations, in the 1840's selling 497 boatloads at 10s per load.[585] It was intended that a lane made to connect Bargate Lane and Cresswell Lane to the east of the canal north of Brewood bridge would have a path down the embankment, but by 1874 it had been blocked off. Overgrown traces of a wall built of finely-squared sandstone blocks still exist running north-west at the point where Cresswell Lane turns north-east.

Belvide Reservoir, built as a 208-acre feeder for the Shropshire Union Canal was constructed in 1834 on 202 acres of land sold by Mr Giffard in 1832 for £16,710, when an easterly flowing stream was dammed with two huge earthern embankments, on which work began by the whole of the canal labour force in July 1833, one alongside Watling Street, the other at right angles at the east end faced internally with near-vertical brickwork. Work on the reservoir had been delayed as a result of problems in obtaining possession of the site, and to meet its needs for water until it was completed the canal company obtained 4000 'locks' of water from the Wyrley and Essington Canal, which was conveyed in a stream along the Hatherton valley with the consent of local landowners to Autherley Junction. The water might more easily have been obtained from the Staffordshire and Worcestershire Canal, but that company adopted a hostile attitude towards the newcomers, and refused to supply a drop. To overcome possible supply problems in the future, it was decided to increase the proposed capacity of Belvide, and in 1838 Mr Giffard sold a further 7 acres of land for £901 so that the resevoir could be extended. In Victorian times the reservoir was noted for the size of its pike.[586] The reservoir and its surroundings were protected as a Site of Special Scientific Interest in 1951, a status confirmed under the Wildlife and Countryside Act 1981. In 1951 West Midland Bird Club negotiated an access agreement, and formally established a bird reserve in 1977. Since that date the south-western perimeter has been artificially landscaped and small islands created to attract wildlife.

Until the construction of the reservoir [named after Belvide Fields, the flooded area], the lane to the present Birk's Barn Farm continued eastwards, roughly parallel with Shutt Green Lane, to the south of Bell View Farm, and the eastern edge of the lane is still marked by double hedgerows. The original Birk's Barn Farm was some 400 yards east of the present farmhouse, and was demolished when the reservoir was constructed. The foundations are occasionally exposed in the south-east bay of the reservoir when the water level is exceptionally low. The agreement for the sale of the land for the reservoir provided for the canal company to rebuild on the south bank of the reservoir Birks Barn farmhouse and other buildings which would be engulfed.

The engineering work involved in the construction of the canal and ancillary projects is quite remarkable, with the canal running along the crest of high embankments in some places in the parish, and elsewhere through canyon-like cuttings. It marked the end of major canal development in Britain, and was the last major work undertaken by its originator and engineer, Thomas Telford.

The construction of the canals, or 'navigations', brought a large influx of 'navvies' and other workers into the area. The 1831 census returns show that no less than 278 men in the parish were then engaged in the building of the canal.[587] Gravestones in Brewood churchyard suggest that at least some of the 'engineers' and workforce came from 'North England' [ie. Scotland], particularly Sutherland.[588] Local businesses, particularly the hostelries and beerhouses, enjoyed a short period of prosperity after the Shropshire Union Canal was opened, but neither of the two canals played a significant rôle in the history of Brewood.

In 1836, iron represented 36% of the volume of freight carried on the Shropshire Union Canal, general merchandise 32.5%, iron and coke 13%, building materials 6%, lime and limestone 12%, and road materials, manure etc., the balance. In later years, under strong competition from the railways, the canal managed to hold some of this trade, primarily iron and coal from Wolverhampton to Liverpool. By 1851 there were 'commodious wharves and warehouses' in Brewood town and Chillington, which ensured that much of the bulky material formerly transported by wagon or cart, particularly coal, could be shipped easily by water. A wharf also existed on the west side of the canal immediately south of Dean's Hall Bridge. The opening of the canals was not however an unmixed blessing, as was noted in 1874: 'notwithstanding [the] convenience, Canal traffic has never been popular in Brewood . . . the Boatmen have ever been dreaded as depredators', and the following rhyme from 'The Wolverhampton Civic Saturnalia' of 1855 perhaps explains the reason:

> Chorus of boatmen:
> Gaily the fire in our caboose is crackling,
> Where many a rabbit and hare has been stewed,
> And many a hen has stopt short in her cackling,
> That wakened the echoes at Coven and Brewood[599]

The commercial life of the canal went into rapid decline after the First World War, and was virtually at an end by the 1930's, superceded by the motor lorry. Pleasure craft have been part of canal life from an early date – in 1904 small sailing trews were in use on the canal at Brewood, and in 1905 Arthur Beech's passenger steamers 'Compton Queen', 'Margaret' and 'Victoria' made afternoon trips from Compton to Brewood, Coven and Calf Heath at return fares of 1s. for adults and 6d. for children – and have, in recent years brought renewed life to the canal system, many visitors to the village now arriving by water. In 1968 the canal was declared a 'Cruising Waterway', which ensures its maintenance by British Waterways Board to standards prescribed in the 1968 Transport Act, and the whole course through Brewood parish, including all the bridges, is now protected as a linear Conservation Area.

34. Railways

Under an Act of 1834 the Grand Junction Railway was authorised, linking Birmingham with Newton-le-Willows on the Liverpool and Manchester Railway, and the Birmingham to Stafford section, constructed by Locke, runs through the east of Brewood parish. The line cost £1,500,000 and was called the Grand Junction because it linked the three greatest towns in England outside London: Birmingham, Liverpool and Manchester. Local excavations for the line cut through hard sandstone which was used for the bridges. Stone blocks were also used on this stretch of line in place of wooden sleepers. The largest embankment on the line was at Standeford, which took two years to build, not being finished until shortly before the inauguration. Nearby the contractor, Thomas Townsend, struck a spring of clear water, and a water station was erected on the spot. The line was opened on 4th July 1837 with the inaugural trip from Manchester to London taking 4½ hours, an average of 22mph for the 97-mile trip. The station at Four Ashes was opened in the same year, with two trains running daily to both Stafford and Wolverhampton in 1838, and six trains a day in each direction by 1851. A station south east of Gailey, known as Spread Eagle, was rarely used by the people of Brewood, being half a mile further from

The closest railway station to Brewood was at Four Ashes, pictured here c.1920. It opened in 1837 and was demolished in 1951. Pedestrians from Brewood reached the station by a footpath from Sparrow's End Lane which passed Brewood Hall Farm and Somerford Mill. Photograph reproduced by permission from the Alec Chatwin collection.

the village. Four Ashes and Spread Eagle were intermediate or second-class stations: first-class trains stopped at first-class stations only, such as Wolverhampton and Stafford. The railway from Wolverhampton to Shrewsbury was opened in 1849, and Codsall Station was opened in 1851.[590] In 1845 the Shropshire Union Railway and Canal Company published

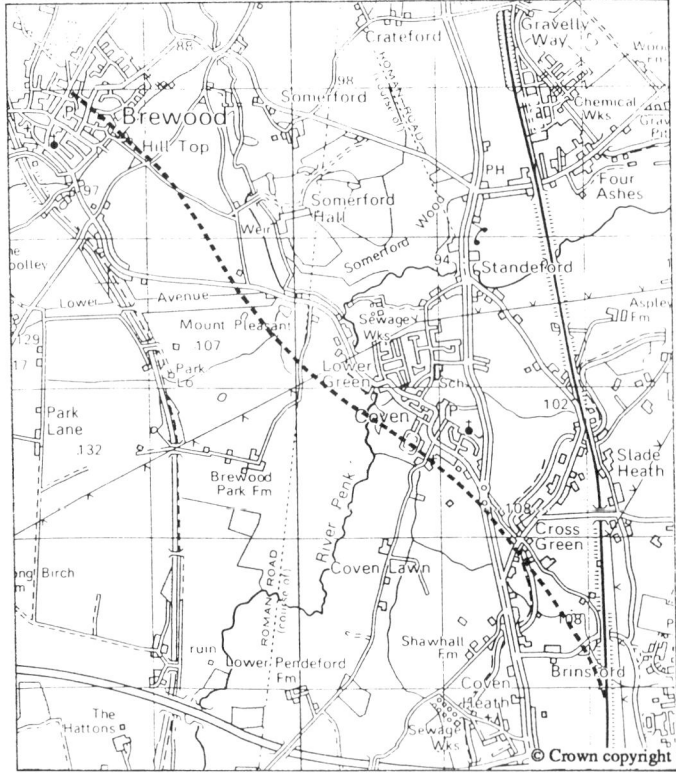

Line of proposed railway, 1845.

proposals for a new line[591] running through the west of Brewood. Plans advanced to the stage where the secretary to the trustees of the Grammar School wrote to each trustee asking for views about selling school land for the purpose. Every trustee objected, and the proposal came to nothing. In 1874 plans were revealed for a branch line of the London and North Western Railway from Bushbury Junction to the end of Stafford Street in Brewood, to be known as the Wolverhampton and Brewood Railway, with a station at Fordhouses. There was every indication that the line would be constructed, but again the scheme did not proceed. In 1896 the Parish Council, apparently concerned about the declining prosperity of the village, discussed the possibility of the London and North Western Railway extending its line to Brewood, but the matter was not pursued. As late as 1922 plans were laid for a Newport and Four Ashes Light Railway via Wheaton Aston and Brewood, but as on previous occasions the scheme progressed no further than the planning stage. Spread Eagle station survived until 1951 under the name Gailey, and in the same year the station at Four Ashes was demolished.

35. Agriculture

In general terms the area around Brewood was perhaps more closely related to the agricultural practices of the border counties to the west than to the Midland shires: historically, both before and after the Roman conquest it was linked to a Celtic kingdom centered further west, and the landscape is notable for the numerous early farmsteads in relatively isolated positions, whereas in the Midland shires comparatively few such farmsteads existed before enclosure.

In various parts of the parish, and particularly west of Horsebrook and north-east of Somerford Bridge, is evidence of medieval cultivation in the form of 'ridge and furrow'. The ridges, or 'selions', were formed over a period of time by the cultivation of narrow strips, whereby the action of the mould-board of the plough turned the sod inwards towards the centre. Over many seasons, marked ridges would develop which assisted the drainage of low-lying ground, while furrows developed between the ridges. A medieval plough team[592] was a lengthy affair, with up to four pairs of oxen on heavy ground. The conventional theory is that it was therefore necessary for the ploughman to commence his turn before the leading beast had reached each end of the plough ridge. The leading pair would be swung to the left, and the turn completed at the 'headland'. Thus most ridges are not straight, but in the shape of a reversed 'S' or aratral curve. Recent investigation has thrown some doubt on this widely accepted explanation, for it is suggested that oxen do not need a long turning space, but whatever the origin, a number of reversed-S hedgelines were until recent years discernible on both sides of Engleton Lane on the edge of the village, and older maps show numerous fields with such boundaries in many other parts of the parish. A bundle of strips, all running in one direction, made up a 'furlong', commonly known as a flatt in Brewood, or sometimes a shot or shut, and a number of furlongs made up one of the huge 'open fields'.

Although much has been written about the inappropriately named two-field and three-field system, which is now thought to have developed in the late tenth century,[593] the furlong seems to have been more important than the field, and the basic unit on which rotations were practised. Brewood township had three open fields in 1302-3, and Chillington farmed open fields at about the same date, but eventually up to nine fields at Brewood were grouped and subject to rotation.[594] The term open field refers to the fact that the strips were unhedged, although hedgerows will have existed along some of the headlands or 'butts'.

From an early date assarts – licenced clearances for cultivation – were granted in Brewood: the nuns of Brewood were taking assarts in 1211-14; in 1129-30 the inhabitants of Chillington paid a one mark fine for assarting;

in 1155 Henry II made a grant to the Bishop of an assart of 80 acres created after 1135; and in the mid-twelfth century assarts at Broomhall to Siward the Cobbler, Ailric Berley, Leofric and Ravekel are recorded in Brewood.[595] The 'birch' names in Brewood parish – Strangleford Birch, Harvington Birch, and Long Birch – provide evidence of clearances of land for cultivation, for the word derives from the Middle English 'breche' meaning newly-broken land.

The arable land received an unchanging three-yearly succession of wheat or rye; of spring crops such as barley, oats, beans or peas; and fallow. There is evidence that oats predominated on the Bishop's manor of Brewood and in 1242 they were the only crop sown.[596] In 1298 the Bishop had 406 acres of arable demense on his Brewood estate, and in 1307 and 1308 wheat, rye and peas were grown, the latter probably benefitting soils cropped repeatedly with cereals. Peas were also grown as food for farm servants and stock, and as small scale cash crop. After sowing, the arable fields were fenced off with hurdles against livestock until after the harvest, and the strips cultivated by individual tenants, with the same compulsory rotation as applied to the fields, which ensured that good land and poor land in the open fields was shared fairly amongst all. Everyone had strips in each of the arable fields, but one third were always fallow in rotation. On Lammas Day [1st August, the old Celtic festival of Lugnasid] separate use ended and common rights began. After harvest, the hayward removed the hurdles and the village livestock grazed the fields. Holdings in the open fields were not always distributed evenly, and modern research in Scandinavia has suggested that 'solskifte' or sun-division may be the reason: the sequence of strips held by each individual was based on the course of the sun across the sky, so that some were in shadow and others in the sun – there is an early reference to a field in the parish called Sun Fallow.[597]

From at least 1696, open fields named Eachells or Nechells Field[598] [later called Home Croft and Brick Kiln Croft], Shurgreave Hill Field [at least 41 acres], Hargreave Field [at least 28 acres, and apparently near Somerford Bridge] and Burgage Field [apparently shared by the Bishop's manor and the Deanery manor], and Cross Field, Mill Field, Street Field and Butts Field in the vill of Horsebrook within the Bishop's manor were being enclosed, and by 1800 there seem to have been no open arable fields in the manor. In the Deanery manor, Churchfield, Shuttfield and Quarryfield [at least 20 acres and shared with the Bishop's manor] were open in 1700 but had been enclosed piecemeal before 1800.[599] The straight alignments of fields to the north-west and east of Brewood village almost certainly date from the period of enclosure: it is inconceivable that they could be remnants of 'centuriation' dating from the Roman period. The manor of Coven had three open fields in 1596: Broadmeadow Field [still an open field in 1657], Fulmore Field, and "Ryecrofte".

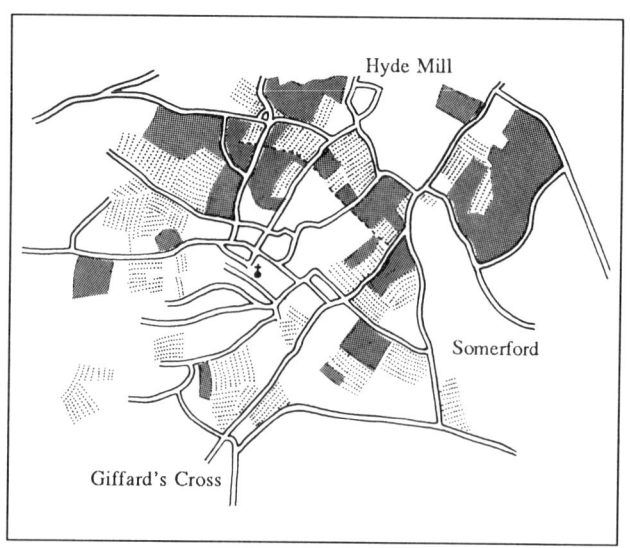

Hyde Mill

Somerford

Giffard's Cross

Conjectural plan, based on field surveys and aerial photographs, showing Brewood roads and lanes in the Middle Ages, and the strip fields [certain = dotted lines; probable = shaded]. Much of the remaining land will have been included in the vast open fields.

During the early medieval period it seems that in the Bishop's manor at Brewood one-fifth of the harvest was retained for feed, one fifth sold, and the rest consumed by the tenants, their animals, and the Bishop's household. The crops grown by the villagers were similar to those grown on the land of the Bishop. On their arable fields they grew wheat rye, barley and oats, often mixing wheat and rye as maslin, and barley and oats as drage. One-tenth of the produce was taken as tithes by the church, and tithe barns existed at Dean's Hall Farm, Brewood Hall, and, by tradition, on the north side of Bargate Lane at or close to what is now the site of Forge Cottage.

In southern counties barley and oats seem to have been harvested loose, but in lowland Staffordshire, as recorded by Plot, it was customary to bind the corn, which meant that local barns would have been smaller than those in the south. The arable land of Brewood was improved by the use of local marl from an early date,[600] and old marl pits are scattered in large numbers throughout the parish. The marl helped to bind together particles of light soil and also added calcium in the form of lime which was contained in the marl, and pits were located at the higher end of virtually every field. The practice of marling was virtually abandoned in Staffordshire by 1850.

On the outskirts of the arable nearest the village lay one or more 'hams', or pastures, in which a limited number of privileged livestock might graze. Coldham, to the west of Brewood, may be one such 'ham', or the name may derive from the word for home, and mean cold dwelling.

In the lowest part of the village to the east of The Pavement alongside the brook, which has at some time in the past been conducted into an artificially straight channel, lay the meadows, annually divided into lots or doles, which provided the hay for winter feed. The meadows would be sown at about midsummer, and from then until spring would provide common pasture. Sometimes the doles, of varying sizes, were tied to the arable holding, so that each man received the same dole each year, and sometimes they were drawn annually by lots.

Besides the arable fields, the hams and the meadows there were the common pastures, bordered by the uncultivated wastes providing fern and heather for litter, bedding or thatching; underwood for hurdles; furze and turves for fuel; timber for building; and beech mast and acorns for feeding the swine. Most of these rights were subject to fixed annual payments to the lord of the manor. The wastes were often taken into cultivation to increase the arable,[601] and the scale of assarting in the area is demonstrated by field names which incorporate the words 'stocks', 'stubs', 'stubbings', 'ridding', 'brant', and 'hag', which all denote land cleared for cultivation.

In 1086 the Bishop of Chester held woodland at Brewood one and a half leagues long and a league broad, that is, about three quarters of a mile long and half a mile across. There is the intriguing possibility that the Roughs, to the west of the village,[602] are remnants of this woodland. In 1139 and 1144 the Bishop's possession of his 'hay and forest' was the subject of a Papal Confirmation,[603] and in about 1155 Henry II granted the Bishop 80 acres of assarted land at Brewood, taken after 1135 from the royal Forest.[604] In a Charter of Confirmation granted by Roger, son of Alan la Szouche, to Buildwas Abbey, 'pannage in his wood of Brewode' is specified – a sty or piggery owned by the Abbey in Brewood Wood is recorded in 1247 – and among fines received in 1199 by Hugo de Nevill, Justice of the Forest, is one of 12 marks [£8] from Hugh de Pichford to assart 40 acres of his own land at Pichford and 20 acres in his wood of Bruwude. In 1314 an area of woodland known as 'Stryfwode' [that is, 'strife-wood', wood which was the subject of a dispute] was bought by the Bishop from Sir Fulk Pembrugge, lord of Tong. This was the wood which subsequently gave its name to the village of Bishop's Wood. The underwood was valued in 1321 at 50 marks [£33. 6s 8d.], although only 12s. had been raised that year. Roger Fowke of Brewood was granted rights by the Bishop to take timber from 'the common wood of Brewood called Bishop's Wood at Kerrimore' for 40 years in 1538, and the grant was confirmed by the Dean and Chapter.

The word 'green' in Kiddemore Green indicates that the place was formerly an open area surrounded by woodland, but traces of ridge and furrow throughout the parish attest to widespread cultivation from at least medieval times, and suggest that apart from the area straddling the Staffordshire-Shropshire border and the deer parks at Brewood and Chillington, the parish may have been relatively free from woodland by

271

the early Middle Ages. Although the ironworks between Brewood and Coven would have required vast quantities of charcoal, and seventeenth-century documents confirm that substantial quantities of charcoal were available locally to feed both forges and furnace, the source would have been renewable underwood, not mature trees, and the forges and furnaces may have helped to ensure the survival of nearby woodland. Probably by the fifteenth century, and certainly by the end of the eighteenth century, the Brewood landscape contained no more woodland than it does today. One indication of the early clearance of woodland is the names Gunstone, Hatton, Chillington and Engleton, for the 'tun' element was not normally applied to settlements in forested areas.

In Staffordshire, holly trees were deliberately planted from at least the sixteenth century as winter feed for cattle, sheep and deer,[605] which may explain the numbers which exist in hedgerows within Brewood Parish, most noticeably between Bishop's Wood and Blackladies. It is of interest that Stebbing Shaw mentions that holly was conspicuous on most of the high land in Bushbury parish c.1798.

To the villager, the most important right was the use of the common pasture, which was often the only source of feed for the livestock of arable farmers. Strangers had no rights on these pastures, and commoners who turned out more stock than their allotted share could be fined in the manorial court. Every morning the cattle were driven to the common by the village herdsman and each evening driven back to the owner's shelter. Likewise the sheep were driven to the common by day and folded by night. At the end of the thirteenth century there were substantial dairy herds on the Bishop's manors, one of the largest being 45 head at Brewood and a flock of a few hundred sheep. In the early fourteenth century there were 2300 sheep in Longdon, Haywood, Baswich and Brewood. Sheep were as much prized for their manure as their fleeces, and until winter were penned in the common field on the stubble, but during the winter each commoner was obliged to supply his own hay. Enough wool was produced in Brewood to clothe the population, with additional fleeces from the Bishop's sheep collected from his manors in Shropshire and Staffordshire and taken to Haywood for sale to merchants. The importance of sheep is shown by a record in 1341 that the men of Stafford claimed that their livelihood depended on sheep farming.[606] Wolverhampton may have been one of the few English wool staples through which the export of wool was compulsorily directed in 1354, and was a classic wool town in the fifteenth century – in 1493 Edward Giffard was a Bailiff of the Staple of Wolverhampton – with merchants dealing in wool from a large area to the west and into Wales,[607] and it seems reasonable to assume from the existence of at least one fulling mill [at Somerford] in the second half of the fifteenth century that Brewood relied, to a large extent, on sheep farming, which perhaps explains the relatively early enclosure of the open fields, and was almost certainly the source of the wealth which led to the various alterations and improvements to the parish church.

In 1361 it was recorded that one-third [70 acres] of the Bishop's land had been sown with corn and fine wheat before his death, and that 60 acres of meadows in Parkmoor were much reduced in value by a flood at mowing time.[608]

Hemp and flax were also cultivated from at least Tudor times.[609] A statute of Henry VIII decreed that a certain amount of flax and hemp should be grown on every farm over 60 acres, and production increased in Staffordshire in the late seventeenth and early eighteenth centuries in order to supply local weavers. The Chillington Catholic registers record the death in 1722 of Francis Howell, 'hatcheller' [flax-dresser], as well as Walter Deal, weaver, in the previous year. In 1741 David Martin, tenant of a farm on the Chillington estate, was given notice to quit for abuse of the land because he had sown many acres with flax seed, which was thought to impoverish the land. During the Napoleonic Wars the government granted bounties to encourage the cultivation of flax and hemp. Both crops died out after 1815 as a result of foreign competition. Barley provided grain for food and brewing, and wheat, rye, oats, peas and beans were eaten by both the villagers and their animals. Even nettles were utilised, the fibres being made into cloth. Every farmhouse and many cottages kept poultry, and many also kept pigs and bees and maintained herb gardens and orchards, providing meat, eggs, cheese, butter, milk, honey, fruit and herbs of all kinds.

Bishop's Wood was noted in former times for the quantity of damsons produced by cottagers in the area, which were used for dyeing as well as eating, particularly during the First World War, when a square wicker basket, known as a pot, containing 90lbs of fruit, would sell for 2/6d. A mature tree could give as many as 400lbs of damsons annually. The fruit was taken to Penkridge station and sent to Liverpool. After the juice had been removed for dyeing, the pulp was processed as jam. The demand for dyeing dropped when synthetic dyes were introduced after the First World War, but picked up in 1933 when the fruit was in demand for canning. Many old trees still remain. A more exotic fruit may be commemorated by the field name The Vinyard on the east side of The Old Hattons, recorded in a 1727 estate map. Grape vines may have been grown on the site: vinyards are mentioned in Domesday Book and it is known that grapes were regularly cultivated in England until the seventeenth century, but in some areas house-closes were sometimes called vinyards. The name Codlen is attached to several fields to the north of The Hyde on an estate map 1704, suggesting the existence of fruit orchards: a codling was a type of cooking apple.

Fish ponds provided fresh fish, [including bream, perch, pike, roach, crayfish, eels, and, from the fifteenth century, carp], an important part of the diet in Catholic medieval England: in theory at least it was the prescribed diet on all Fridays and Saturdays, the eves of major feasts, and the whole of lent. Several fish ponds are recorded in the parish, including Blackladies from 1286, Coven in 1307, Brewood manor in 1321 [although no rent was charged since there were no fish], Engleton in 1346, and Hatton in 1571. Field names at the south-east side of Chillington Pool containing the word 'stewers' indicate the existence of medieval fish stews.

Dovecotes providing eggs and fresh meat year-long existed at Blackladies [now vanished], Dean's Hall [rectangular; derelict], Somerford [still standing], Brewood Hall [octagonal with cupola, sixteenth century, demolished c.1968], and Chillington [c.1730, octagonal, with cupola, well preserved]. By law, only the lord of the manor was permitted to maintain a dovecote, and since the pigeons ate vast quantities of corn, they were very unpopular with the lord's tenants. Deer and rabbits were also available to the privileged few from Brewood Park and Chillington Park, and a wildfowl decoy on the east side of Chillington Pool in the form of a narrow arm of water covered with net over metal hoops provided duck in the eighteenth and nineteenth centuries.

By 1724, 'waste ground called Bishop's Wood' within the Bishop's manor of Brewood was common pasture for tenants of the manor, and in 1834 was still an open common of some 44 acres with several cottages built on encroachments. In 1844 it was formally enclosed by an agreement between the Bishop as lord and Mr T.W. Giffard as lessee. Enclosure in the area does not seem to have been widespread before 1517, by which date only 118 acres had been enclosed in Cuttlestone hundred, of which only 85 acres were for pasture, and none had occurred before 1502. Indeed, virtually all the enclosures seem to have occurred without the need for parliamentary intervention – which explains the absence of straight roads and regular fields from the period of parliamentary enclosure found elsewhere – although by an Act of 1850, 55 acres of Slade Heath and Coven Heath were enclosed in 1855. Calf Heath had been enclosed by Lord Hatherton in 1658.

In 1796 Mr Lockley, farming at Boscobel, wrote: "the land of this neighbourhood . . . is marl and not well adapted to ox teams: partially it may; and where the turnip or sandy land will admit their use, there cannot exist a doubt of their utility: they must work easy, or they cannot get on at all. And they appear to me best adapted to carting out manure. Six oxen are necessary upon the marl or wheat-land . . . nor will that sort of land always admit of a wheel-plough, attended only by one servant. Six oxen would work a two-furrow plough in the light turnip land: that alone is the soil to which they are adapted . . ."[610] Oxen were still used within the parish well into the nineteenth century: a painting of c.1838 shows a team of oxen and herdsman near Chillington Hall.[611]

Earlier writers[612] have suggested that references to 'bull beef' which appear in the Overseers' Accounts in the eighteenth century may refer to a trophy of beef awarded at the bull-baiting at the September Wake, but it is evident that Brewood was amongst those parishes which purchased and maintained a parish bull, an animal frequently encountered in old accounts.[613] Meat would seem to have formed a regular part of the bull's diet, and there is little doubt that the 'bull beef' was meat fed to the parish bull.

William Pitt, a writer on agricultural matters, says in 1796: "I have acquainted myself a good deal with the manner of life in this neighbourhood [Brewood], and find poor labouring men often dine out of a potatoe-pudding, or early cabbage, washing the same down with some of their home-brewed beer: now, if such men could be prevailed on to partake of milk, they would find their meal equally wholesome and cheaper, as the beer would not be necessary,"[614] but local farmers would not sell their milk, preferring to convert it to cheese and butter. The writer went on to compare the children in the north "who eat their bread and milk with the greatest satisfaction, are more healthy in general, strong, hardy and well-looking." It seems the children of Brewood at that date were both under-fed and under-sized.

Stebbing-Shaw, writing of the locality [Pendeford] at about the same period, mentions that the "staple articles of grain are wheat, barley and oats, a few peas, fewer beans, sometimes a small quantity of buck-wheat; also hemp and flax, and clover and rye-grass plentifully; turnips on a considerable scale, and cabbages and potatoes in a smaller quantity. The main farming is cultivation, dairying and fattening stock from elsewhere. The horses are mostly black and brown; cows chiefly of long horned sort, and sheep of various sorts. Many cows brought in to fatten from Shropshire, Cannock Heath, Wiltshire, Dorsetshire and Leicestershire. They are fed with grass, or clover in Summer, and with turnips in Winter, and with a little hay in bad weather."

Under the Tithe Commutation Act of 1836, the Tithe Commissioners surveyed the landholdings in Brewood parish in great detail, listing owners, occupiers, field names, nature of use, etc., accompanied by a large-scale plan.[615] The tithe awards were made in 1842, replacing the tithes by annual rent charges amounting to £2597 17s 1d [of which £670 was payable to the Vicar and £1827 8s 1d to the Dean of Lichfield] which were themselves extinguished under an Act of 1936.

In Victorian times, wheat was the principal crop in the north and west of the parish, with barley and turnips predominating on the lighter soils of the south and east. Guano was imported in large quantities from South America for use as a fertiliser in the 1840's and used widely in the area, particularly at Chillington.[616]

During the early years of the present century several young men from Brewood emigrated to farms in the Dominions, particularly Canada.

Brewood and District Agricultural Society was formed in 1901, and in 1914 eight farmers met in Brewood and founded the Wolverhampton and District Farmers Co-operative, which grew rapidly, having 108 members by 1916 and sufficient assets to purchase a grinding mill in 1917 and a milk factory the following year. By 1919 it had become Staffordshire Farmers.[617]

In 1940 there were eleven farms over 150 acres. Since the Second World War the previous dominance of permanent pasture in the parish has given way to intensive arable production, often after improvements in land drainage and the grubbing out of old hedgerows. Recent years have seen the widespread cultivation of oilseed rape, but it is not the crop known as rape grown in earlier centuries, which was the plant Brassica naps, usually grown as food for sheep. William Pitt records in 1796 that whilst he had never known it cultivated for seed, and many leases contained restrictions to prevent it,[618] it was sometimes grown on an early stubble for spring feed for sheep, upon land intended to be sown with turnips the following summer. After the second world war many poplars were planted in a copse to the south of Somerford Mill farmhouse to provide wood for the match industry, but demand declined and the trees still stand.

36. Trade, Industry and Utilities

Until very recent times Brewood was virtually self-sufficient, producing all its own food, clothing, light, heat and building materials out of resources to be found within the parish. Timber and sandstone provided natural saleable assets, and the land, after much toil, was capable of producing good crops and raising livestock. Timber and stone were used for its church, houses and barns and, in more recent times, bricks were made from local clay fired in local brick-kilns. Wheat straw or reeds provided thatching for buildings and ricks, and the parish had its own sand and gravel pits, the gravel especially valuable when the turnpiking of the eighteenth century made better road surfaces necessary.

The underwood provided wattles for the framework of hurdles for folding livestock and for wattle-and-daub, still used for internal partitions in the eighteenth century and to be found in many Brewood houses to this day. Charcoal was produced from renewable underwood in large quantities and used for domestic, commercial and industrial purposes, and furze and kindling were burnt in the beerhouses, brewhouses and kitchens in the parish. Osier beds to the north of Chillington Park; south of Somerford Mill; on the north bank of the Penk south of Brewood Park Farm; south of Kiddemore Green Farm and on the southern boundary of the parish at Pendeford provided material for basket-making.

Power was generated from the streams by water wheels from at least the eleventh century, and the sites of two windmills are known within the parish. There were almost certainly others of which we have no knowledge. Reeds dipped in tallow provided lighting, and the only essential commodities which could not be obtained locally were iron [a survey made in 1646/7 suggests that ironstone was available within two miles of Brewood Park, but the location is unknown] and salt, but the latter was available at no great distance from Stafford or Shirleywich.

During the course of its history, Brewood has seen almost every type of rural industry, and indeed some considerable industrial activity, and as early as the thirteenth century the Bishop of Lichfield had created burgage tenure in an attempt to promote the commercial expansion of the village.

The Poll Tax Assessment of 1380-1 identifying the 249 taxable individuals [that is, over 14 years old] by name and occupation includes 50 husbandmen [male and female], 31 labourers [ditto], 6 tailors, 4 salters, 4 carpenters, 3 tanners, 3 gristmillers, 2 blacksmiths, 2 wheelwrights, 2 corn millers, 2 thatchers, 2 pedlars, 2 roofers and a cowman, weaver, baker, draper, cooper, shoemaker, fuller, corn-dealer, barker, thresher, blanket-maker, fuller, rope-maker, a butcher, and 15 serfs.

Frequently found after ploughing in many parts of the parish are small lead disks or jettons with various simple raised patterns of dots and lines on one side. These are believed to have been used as trade tokens from at least medieval times, and have been found in large numbers in many areas of England.

Perhaps one of the more intriguing occupations to come to light from Elizabethan Brewood is that of Edward Northall, who is described in a Recognisance dated 30th September 1593[619] as a goldsmith of Brewood. The parish registers show that he was a local man baptised in the village church on 7th June 1565, and it seems reasonable to assume that he carried on his craft in the village.

At one time the village was the centre of a substantial timber trade, which in the eighteenth century was mainly in the hands of the Emery family. [Emerys occupied Brewood Hall for a few years in the nineteenth century, and a field adjoining the north of the Hall was still known as The Timberyard in the 1930's.] During the same period a large tannery was run by the Sansom family,[620] possibly at The Poplars, which was then to the east of what is now the post office. Much timber from the Chillington estate was sold in the 1790's, probably to meet the debts of the Giffard family. In 1842 John Cartwright was operating a timber yard at Bargate Stables in Bargate Lane. It seems that by 1874 both the timber business and tannery had closed. Another tannery existed at Horsebrook: Horsebrook Hall replaced the Tanhouse, demolished in 1861. Thomas Vaughton was the tanner in 1765. The timber and tanning businesses were complimentary, for tanning was achieved by steeping hides in pits containing water in which oak bark had been soaked to extract the tannin. Both activities probably have a long history in the village. In 1380 John Mannselle is recorded as a tanner and Thomas Barker and William Barnville are listed as barkers, and Henry Northale is listed as a barker in a 1426 court action. In 1649 Peter Giffard is known to have sold to Francis Spooner, tanner, of Brewood, bark for £5 10s from Brewood Park.

The list of jurors [eligible by income] for Staffordshire in 1784 includes 28 named individuals in Brewood, with the occupations of most of those listed: ten farmers, and a miller, maltster, glazer, grocer, barber, butcher, breeches maker, schoolmaster, carpenter, and baker, together with two 'gentlemen'. A number of old houses in Brewood are said to contain ornate mantelpieces and fireplaces by a man named Marigold, about whom nothing is known, although there is a gravestone on the north side of Brewood churchyard recording the death of William Marigold on 11th November 1796 at the age of 48. He was licensee of the Angel public house.

The first reference to lockmaking in the parish can be traced back to 1706, when Catholic Returns record William Fawkner of Chillington, locksmith. In the same Returns, Thomas Partridge of Kiddemore Green and Francis Gervase of Billheath are both shown as nailers. By the mid-eighteenth century Wolverhampton was recognised as a centre of the lockmaking industry, and by 1767 at least 3 locksmiths and 2 screwmakers existed in Brewood parish. In 1796 William Pitt recorded[621] that

"Wolverhampton, and its neighbouring populous villages, produce locks of every kind, and of the very best quality," and a contributor to 'The Gentleman's Magazine' in 1797 reported that "in several hamlets in [Brewood] considerable quantities of locks and other articles are made,[622] but most of the inhabitants are employed in agriculture". The firm of J. Wallors and Son, locksmiths, is known to have existed in Brewood in the following year.[623]

In 1801 Brewood parish had a population of 2867, of whom 343 were employed in agriculture, 337 in 'trade, manufacture or handicrafts', and 2167 'others'. By 1811 Brewood township had a population of 991, made up of 212 families, with 69 employed in agriculture, 87 in 'trade, manufacture or handicraft', and 56 not engaged in any business.

POST-OFFICE, at the Jeffords Arms.

Bye Mail to Wolverhampton every day except Sunday, departs at half-past nine in the morning, returns at half-past four in the afternoon.

ANSLOW Moses, gentleman, Deans end
—— Isaac, stone mason, Stafford street
—— Sarah, victualler, Rodney, Deans end
Baker Charles, victualler and butcher, Red Lion, Stafford street
—— Joseph, butcher, Bargate street
Bill John, gentleman, Stafford street
—— John, butcher and maltster, Stafford street
Bird William, stone mason, Sandy lane
Boyden Zachariah, clerk of the parish, near the Church
Bradbent William, carrier, Market place
Bratch John, plate lock manufacturer, Bargate street
Bratt William, druggist, grocer, and mercer, Stafford street
Brewster Joseph, thrashing machine maker and corn miller, Market place
—— James, saddler and harness maker, Stafford street
Bridgin Hannah, schoolmistress, Deans end
Bullock William, boot and shoe maker, Stafford street
Careless Rebecca, gentlewoman, Bargate street
Cook Sarah, shopkeeper, Stafford street
Crossley John, butcher, Back street
Dawe James, blacksmith, Bargate street
Dawe William, joiner, near the Church
Day James, gentleman, Back street
Edwards Thomas, shoemaker, Stafford street
Ellis Thomas, excise officer, Dean end
Etheridge Jeremiah, shoemaker, Deans end
—— Elizabeth, shopkeeper, Stafford street
Graham John, shopkeeper and gardener, Deans end
Green William, butcher, farmer, and maltster, Stafford street
—— Thomas, gentleman, Stafford street
Greene John, surgeon, Church street
—— Robert, stock lock manufacturer, Bargate street
Grinsell James, shoemaker, Deans end
Grundy Mary, gentlewoman, Bargate street
Hawes George, saddler and collar maker, near the Church
Higgins Benjamin, wheelwright, Peak lane
Howell Thomas, blacksmith, Deans end
Hurd M. and D. gentlewomen, Bargate street
Hutton Rev. John, vicarage
Keep John, grocer and flour dealer, Deans end
Kempson Rev. Henry, boarding and day school, nr the church
Kemsey Rev. Matthew, near the Church
Kenyon Robert, free grammar and boarding school, Market pl.
Layton Thomas, bricklayer, Deans end
Look Thomas, gardener and seedsman, Bargate street
Machin Francis, blacksmith, near the Church

Meredith Thomas, plumber and glazier, Stafford street
Mills Sarah, baker and flour dealer, Market place
Moreton Elizabeth, victualler, Chequered Ball, Bargate street
—— William, shoemaker, Bargate street
Morris James, joiner and builder, Sandy lane
Mullard Thomas, maltster and farmer, Deans end
Pardoe Thomas, butcher, Stafford street
Parke Robert, governor of the house of industry, Bargate street
—— James, hair dresser, Stafford street
Parkes James, victualler, veterinary surgeon, and blacksmith, Angel, Stafford street
Pearson William, victualler, Swan, Market place
Perry Heber, victualler, Jeffords Arms, Stafford street
—— William, (Cow Leeches kept,) near the Church
Pitt James, blacksmith, Bargate street
Price Thomas, joiner and builder, Back street
Ray John, baker, flour dealer, and butcher, Market place
Robinson J. J. surgeon Stafford street
Ransome Thomas, carrier, Sandy lane
Shaw John, wheelwright, Bargate street
Shenston William, corn factor and miller, Standiford mill
Shotten Thomas, tailor, Deans end
Simister Hugh, victualler, Fleur de Lis, Market place
Simmon Bridget, gentlewoman, Stafford street
Simmons John, shoemaker, Market place
Simpson J. H. grocer, draper, and dealer in glass and earthenware, Market place
Smith Joseph, plate and bambury lock manufacturer, Stafford st
Stoker Joseph, wheelwright, Bargate street
—— Joseph, wheelwright, Sandy lane
Till John, saddler, harness and collar maker, Market place
Turner John, Esq. Deans end
Vaughton A. and B. grocers and drapers, Market place
—— John, gentleman, Deans end
Wakelein Richard, cooper, Bargate street
Waldron Ladbury, boarding school, Deans end
Walford John, boot and shoe maker, Stafford street
Wallors William, gardener and seedsman, Bargate street
Wibley Anne, widow, near the Church
Winsper Joseph, brick manufacturer, Bargate street
Wood Richard, stone mason, Deans end
—— Peter, cooper, Bargate street
Woolfe C. & N. grocers and drapers, Market place
Wooton John, master of the national school, Deans end
—— Jane, widow, Stafford street

CARRIERS.

WILLIAM BRADBENT to Wolverhampton, every Monday, Wednesday, Friday, and Saturday, from the Market place.
THOMAS SANSOME to Wolverhampton, every Monday, Wednesday, and Saturday, from Sandy lane.

Early local directories provide much information of interest to historians, but only list the more prominent inhabitants – farmworkers, servants and labourers, for example, are never mentioned. The earliest directory to mention Brewood is dated 1793. The entry shown above, the second earliest, is from 'The Staffordshire General and Commercial Directory' of 1818.

By 1817 the principal industry in the village was the manufacture of agricultural machinery. For some years such machinery was manufactured in a building now demolished near Market Place called first The Malthouse and later The Poplars, and in 1818, Joseph Brewster of Market

279

Place was described as a thrashing machine maker and corn miller and was hiring thrashing machines to farmers throughout Staffordshire. By 1829 there were at least three lockmakers in Brewood and one at King's Bridge, Coven, and it is interesting that although Joseph Brewster of Market Place was then described as a 'thrashing and winnowing machine manufacturer', the village is described at that date as 'a place of no manufactures'. The Brewood lockmakers were outworkers manufacturing the ironwork for fine-plate locks [otherwise known as stock locks], which were mounted in wood cases and used mainly for yard and stable doors. Metal components were taken to Wolverhampton for assembly into the wooden cases. The cheapest of these locks were sold for as little as 6s per dozen.[624] In 1850 four lockmakers are listed in Brewood – three at The Pavement – with two at Coven, but by about 1865 there were said to have been no less than 30 employers in Brewood parish involved in the manufacture of components for fine plate locks, with 150 workmen earning an average of 18s–28s weekly.[625] By 1870 there were at least nine lockmakers in the parish, but the trade was apparently in decline by 1874, and in Coven, where it had flourished more strongly than Brewood – doubtless due to its proximity to Wolverhampton – had been replaced by the manufacture of steam engines, manufactured by John Smith the engineer, who created the Village Foundry, Coven,[626] which continued in business well into the present century.[627]

In the last century watchmaking and clockmaking were carried out in Brewood, and several early nineteenth century white dial longcase clocks bearing the name Nickolds survive in the village.[628] Locksmithing did not die out completely in the village, for a locksmith is recorded in 1940.

Amongst the more unusual occupations, rope-making, probably for the canal trade, was carried out at The Black Lion at Slade Heath from at least 1838 – the field on the north-east side was called The Rope Walk – and in 1835 Mary Willetts and in 1872 Mrs Harriet Price gave their occupations as 'straw bonnet maker'. Early photographs suggest that boaters and bonnets were very popular in the last century.

Between 1834 and 1874 the malting industry employed many local workers. Malting is the process of partially germinating grain, usually barley. Malt was used in the manufacture of beer, with between 30 and 50 lbs required for each barrel of beer. The usual method of preparation was to spread the grain, several months after harvesting, some two feet deep, and water it liberally until roots began to appear after about two days. The grain would then be dried over a heated floor with frequent turning with wooden shovels to prevent overheating. In 1844 there were 10 working malthouses, namely The Angel, Brewood Hall, The Fleur-de-Lis, Grundy's [otherwise Wakelam's, in a building to the rear of Grain Ridge], Mullard's in Dean Street [on the west side of The Garth], Bill's [later Green's], Deans's Hall, The Malt Shovel, The Admiral Rodney, and Webb's [or Jenson's] in Sandy Lane. The last five of these were still operating in 1874, in addition to the malthouse in Bargate House [Lees], which commenced activities after 1844. In 1874 there were also malthouses at Somerford Farm, Somerford Hall [for private use], two at Coven [Hughes'], one at Standeford Mill, and one not working at Long Birch.

PRIVATE RESIDENTS.

Acton Rev. Edwd. Chas. D.D. [Roman Catholic], St. Mary's Presbytery
Aston Miss
Cholditch Samuel Stephens
Crane Misses
Crean Thomas, M.D
Crump Charles, M.A
Davenport James, Brook house
Docker Charles, Dean street
Giffard Walter Peter, Chillington hall
Giffard Walter Thomas Courtenay, J.P. Chillington hall
Heath Mrs. Dean street
Ladbury Misses, Dean street
Molineux Charles Edward, J.P
Monckton Major John Edmonston
Monckton Misses, Brewood hall
Niedermann M. Joseph, Hargate street
Owen Rev. David A. Spreadwell house
Powner Thomas, Dean street
Purchase John, Sparrow's end
Rushton Rev. Wm. M.A. Grammar schl
Rushton Edward
Simpson Mrs. Bellfield house
Smith James Hicks, Daw's croft; & 9 Serjeants' Inn, Fleet st. London e.c
Smith Miss, The Laurels
Smith Mrs. Horsebrook hall
Smyth Henry J
Sparham John Jeffes
Thurstans John, Stafford street
Vernon A. Leveson, J.P. Deansfield
Wall Rev. Richard, M.A. Grammar schl
Way Rev. Benjamin [Independent]
Webb Mrs. Bargate street
Wilson-Patten Capt. Eustace John, J.P. Somerford hall
Wrottesley Rev. Edward John, M.A. [vicar]

COMMERCIAL.

Alcock William, beer retailer, Bargate
Aston James, cowkeeper, Gravelly way
Atkins William, farmer, The Huttons
Beach Sarah Mrs.), farmer, The Hattons
Beckett Mary Ann (Mrs.) & Sons, leather sellers, Horsebrook; & at Wolverhampton
Benton Owen, farmer, Lea fields
Bill Henry, cowkeeper, Sparrow's end
Bill Thomas, brewer & miller, Hyde mill
Birch James, farmer, Harvington birch
Blakemore William, boot maker, Kiddemore green
Boyden Thomas, boot maker, Stafford st
Boyden William, boot maker, School la
Biart Elizabeth & Fanny (Misses), Post office

Smyth Henry J. surgeon
Sparham John Jeffes, surgeon
Storrr Thos. cowkeeper, Shutt green
Storrr William, collector of taxes & assistant overseer, Shutt green
Strongitharm Geo. wharfinger & lime dlr
Swann Benjamin, carpenter
Tart Francis, tailor, Stafford street
Taylor Edwin, stone mason & engraver
Taylor Henry, builder, brick, tile & pipe maker, quarry worker & stone mason, Sparrow's end
Taylor Jas. tinman & brazier, Church gt

Bratt Henry, druggist, grocer & ironmonger
Buckley John, farmer & maltster, Somerford
Burrows Joseph, saddle & harness maker
Burslem Henry Henn. draper & tailor; & at Penkridge & Brewhill
Bushy Jas. farmer, Kiddemoore green
Cartwright John, wheelwright & shopkpr
Chester James, locksmith
Cluett James, hair dresser & shopkeeper, School lane
Cook Henry, beer retailer
Cox William, Bridge inn
Crean Thomas, physician
Cullwick Mary (Mrs.), farmer, Somerford
Daw James, blacksmith
Daw Julia (Mrs.), carpenter & brick maker, Newport street
District Gas Light Co. Limited (Firmstone Heath, lessee)
Docker Charles, artist, Dean street
Docker E. Sarah (Mrs.), ladies' boarding school, Dean street
Ellis John, market gardener & seedsman, Churchlane
Everall Philip, cowkeeper & carrier, Ickes lane
Faulkner Peter, painter, plumber &c. Ickes lane
Fletcher Mary (Mrs.), carrier, Bridge croft, Kidemoore green
Fox John Gilbert, farmer, & licensed to let horses, Hockerill
Fox Joseph, saddler & harness maker
Gamson Joseph, haulier, Shop lane
Green Charles, chemist & druggist
Green Japh. jun. grocer & provision dlr
Green Joseph Thos. farmer & maltster
Green William, farmer, Rose hill
Gwilliam Thomas, leather seller & boot & shoe dealer
Hadley James, boot maker
Hales Edward, farmer, Long birch
Hall Henry, wheelwright, Kiddemoore green
Hall John, blacksmith, Kiddemoore grn
Hall Thos. blacksmith, Kiddemoore grn
Hancox Isaac, farmer, Kiddemoore grn
Harris George, butcher & cattle dealer
Harvey John, shopkeeper, Horse Hook
Heuse William, grocer, baker & provision dealer, Market place
Heatley Jas. Henry, farmer, Engleton hall
Higgs John Birch, steam thrashing machine proprietor, Kiddemoore grn
Hine Joseph, baker & shopkeeper
Hodgetts Samuel, farmer, Broomhall

Taylor James, wheelwright, Kiddemoore green
Thorne Sarah (Miss), ladies' boarding school, Dean street
Till Thomas, saddle & harness maker, Stafford street
Toledroo John, farmer, Gunstone, Codsall
Wakelam William, licensed to let post horses, & carrier
Walker Robert Hay, land agent to Walter Peter Gifford, esq. Chillington
Walker Thomas George, stationer, bookseller & bookbinder

Holford George & William, hauliers
Holford Wm. beer retailer, Bargate st
Holland William, baker & shopkeeper
Holles Henry, farmer, Horsebrook
Ingram Thos. farmer, Park la. Chillington
Johnson William, registrar of births, deaths, & marriages. vaccination officer, & poor's rate collector
Jones Esther (Miss), dress ma. Stafford st
Jones Hugh, farmer, Horsebrook lane
Keeling Frederick Joseph, farmer & miller, Somerford
Lea James, farmer, The Huttons
Lees Edward John, stationer & insurance agent
Lees William John, maltster & seedsman, Bargate street
Lloyd Joseph, florist
Lloyd Joseph, locksmith
Lloyd's Banking Company Limited (attendance, thursday from 12 till 3 p.m. Richd. John Wilshaw, manager)
Machin Michael, blacksmith, School la
Manning Thos. stationer & news agent
Meekin Charles, coal dealer, Newport st
Meln William, land agent
Mellow Elizabeth & Sarah Ann (Misses), boarding school
Mellow Mary (Mrs.), miller, Engleton ml
Miller Matilda (Mrs.), farmer, Deans hall
Morton Wm. Crown, kiddemoore green
Nickolds Edward, watch & clock maker
Openshaw Geo. farmer, Cratefordmarsh
Oldfield Joseph, nursery & seeds man
Pardoe Thos. stone mason Sparrow's end
Parker Mary (Mrs.), shopkeeper
Pears Edward, inland revenue officer
Picken Elizabeth (Mrs.), laundress
Pitt Henry, painter, Hargate street
Plant Mary Ann & Frances (Misses), grocers, & china & glass dealers &c
Plant Wm. & Caroline (Miss), Lion inn
Plant Enoch, chimney sweeper
Plant John, farmer, Kiddemoore green
Price Harriet (Mrs.), straw bonnet makr
Rav John, Swan
Richards George, Admiral Rodney, & maltster
Roch ll Joseph, cowkeeper, Crateford
Shelfield Thomas, farmer, The Hyde farm
Sheratt William, farmer, Bath farm
Smith George, blacksmith, Somerford
Smith George Lee, farmer, Langley lawn
Smith Thomas, Angel inn, & brick, tile & pipe maker
Smith Thos. boot & shoe maker, Dean st
Smith William, farmer, White house, Chillington

Whitehurst Thomas, beer retailer, Kiddemoore green
Willetts Robert, farm bailiff to Charles John Elwell, esq. Kiddemoore green
Williams James, farmer, Park cottage
Wilson Thomas, farmer, The Westley
Wood Charles, cooper, Bargate
Wood John, boot maker, Horsebrook
Wootton Benjamin, boot maker, Dean street
Wright John, confectioner
Yates William, farmer, The Lodge
Yeomans Moses, butcher, Mount Pleasant

COVEN

PRIVATE RESIDENTS.

Barrett Rev. Thomas, B.A. [curate]
Brock John, Stanneford cottage
Chambley William, The Beeches
Cox William, Stanneford cottage
Heller Mrs
Heaxton Rev. Inglis George, M.A. [vicar], Vicarage
Oakley James, Slade heath
Rodgers Mrs. Standeford lodge
Smith John
Smith John, jun

COMMERCIAL.

Bickford George, farmer & maltster, Paradise
Bickford William, farmer, Paradise
Bickham William, farmer, Park farm
Bowdler Richard, farmer, Four Ashes
Broadbent George, locksmith, Mount Pleasant

Buckley William, Harrow, Standeford
Chambley Brooke, farmer
Clift Thomas, farmer
Farmer Joseph, coal dealer
Fletcher Hy. station master, Four Ashes
Groves Wm. coal merchant, Four Ashes
Hadley Wm. market gardener, Standeford
Hall William, shopkeeper, Four Ashes
Hammersley Thomas, Anchor
Horton Elijah, boot maker, Standeford
Howell Joseph, cowkeeper, Standeford
Hughes James, butcher & farmer
Hughes William, farmer
James Joseph, shopkeeper
Kirk Samuel Martin, Four Ashes inn, & farmer, Four Ashes
Lloyd John, locksmith
Lovatt Thomas, farmer, Four Ashes
Oakley Richard, farmer, Laches
Piggott William, tailor & postmaster

Reynolds Leonard, boot ma. Light Ash
Riley Thomas, shopkeeper
Roberts Edward, farmer, Four Ashes
Smith John, jun. locomotive & stationary engineer & boiler manufacturer, iron & brass founder, & agent for John Fowler's, jun. patent steam ploughs, Village foundry
Smith John, sen. farmer
Smith Joseph, boot maker, Standeford
Smith Joseph, farmer, Hammers farm
Thompson George, farmer, Aspley farm
Wade Joseph, blacksmith
Waring Richard Bourne, farmer, Standeford farm
Wedge Richard, farmer, maltster & miller, Standeford
Williams Thos. wheelwright & carpenter
Wright Ann (Mrs.), New inn, & shopkeeper

Part of the entry relating to Brewood from 'The Post Office Directory of Staffordshire', 1872.

The pale pink local sandstone which lies close to the surface in various parts of the parish is easy to cut when quarried, but the surface hardens and darkens when exposed to the air and weathers reasonably well. Fifteen cubic feet are said to weigh one ton. The stone is known to have been quarried in Brewood from at least the mid-fifteenth century, for in 1466 5s 1d was spent "in costs for the stone at Brewood" during work on Walsall parish church.[629] By 1834, Stradsfield Quarry on the south side of the junction of Coven Road and Somerford Road, between the east end of Lower Avenue and Coven Road [almost certainly the quarry in Brewood Park mentioned by Pitt in 1796][630] was providing freestone for building, and was eventually worked over an area of four acres to a depth of about twenty feet. The stone was used in the new churches at Bishop's Wood and Coven, the Catholic church in Brewood, and for the restoration of Lapley church. Many of the high-banked lanes near the quarry are faced with overgrown drystone walling of sandstone blocks. The quarry, owned by the Giffards and worked by Charles Taylor of Brewood in the last century, and before that by W. Godfrey of Birmingham, has long been disused. In 1915 it was recorded that "most of the quarry is in the Keuper Marl; but in holes in the floor the junction of the Marl and Sandstone is visible. Here under 16' of Keuper Marl comes red sandstone, in beds about a foot thick and seen to a depth of 5 feet. The junction is sharp, and there are none of the transitional strata known as Waterstones. The dip is westward at 3°".[631] The quarry has now been filled in, but a small section remains to the west of the lodge at the east end of the Lower Avenue, and the western edge can be detected alongside a hedge opposite the lane to Somerford. A brick and sandstone house known as The Stone House which formerly stood by the quarry on the north-east side of the junction of the Coven road and the road to Somerford was demolished in about 1950. The site is now occupied by a small triangular copse.

Another quarry on the opposite side of Coven Road seems to have been worked until about 1910 by the Monckton family, with the stone used for buildings on the Somerford Estate. In the early years of the century the quarry was occupied by buildings used as brickworks. It has now been filled in, but the edges are evident around Stradsfield House, built on the site c.1955. Sandstone was also obtained from a quarry, said to be very deep, on the north side of Brewood Hall. It was said to have been full of water before 1869.[632] Its site was marked by a pond until the houses of Hall Farm Close were built over it in the 1960's. It seems likely that some of the fossil footprints from Brewood recorded in the last century came from this quarry. Another quarry lay a quarter of a mile north-east of the junction of Tinkers Lane and Sparrows End Lane. It was disused in 1915. A large quarry, overgrown in 1915, half a mile west of Brewood Park Farm, provided brown sandstone, and is said to have produced the stone for the bridge carrying Chillington Lower Avenue.[633] Sandstone is also said to have been extracted from a small quarry below the dam on the east side of Chillington Pool, some of which was used in the construction of Bishops

Wood church. Small quarries also existed in many other parts of the parish. One such quarry was just to the north of Giffard's Cross, on the opposite side of the road. Within Brewood village, the area between the Church and The Pavement, known as Deacon's Sand Hole, was quarried for sand from c.1920 until about 1950, which accounts for the low-lying ground. The entrance was what is now St Chad's Close.

Sand and gravel have been extracted since the 1930's from a very large pit to the south-east of Boscobel which is now used for commercial tipping. Barnfield sand and gravel beds on the outskirts of the village between Horsebrook Lane and Orams Lane have been in use since about the end of the last century, and a small quarry lay to the north of Bishop's Wood, in the angle formed by the Ivetsey Bank Road and the track to Blackladies. In 1915 ten feet of red and buff coloured sand could be seen, well bedded, with 3 to 4 inches of gravel composed of small pebbles of quartzite and quartz.[634] Another sand quarry lay to the west of Port Lane, near Long Birch. A new road was built through it when the M54 motorway was constructed, the quarry having been abandoned in about 1965. A large pit to the south of Gunstone Farm is a former stone quarry. Gravel was formerly extracted from quarry workings on the east bank of the Penk at Engleton; from large workings at Four Ashes; from a small quarry 200 yards north east of Park Lodge; and from shallow pits 500 yards north of Somerford Bridge and at Bath Farm. On the outskirts of the parish Dr Plot mentions a remarkable stone quarry at Pendeford some 14 or 15 yards deep, with whitish stone at the top, reddish stone at 10 yards, and whiter stone at the bottom.[635]

Brick kilns existed to the north of Chillington Park;[636] mid-way between Coven and Standeford Mill; near the north-east corner of the junction of Port Lane and Coven Road; mid-way between that crossroads and Stradsfield; and a short distance north of Pearse Hay Farm, between the house and the road. A brickworks also operated around the turn of the century in the quarry to the west of The Stone House on Coven Road. Three old limekilns, disused in 1882, lay immediately north of The Wharf, alongside the Shropshire Union Canal. One of the first things William Pitt did when he took the 230-acre New House Farm at Pendeford in 1780 was build a limekiln by the Shropshire and Worcestershire canal where it ran through the farm. During the next three years he burnt 1200 quarters of lime to dress his arable. Stone from quarries in the Dudley area was burnt there and sold to local farmers.

A municipal gas supply was connected to the village by Stafford Corporation in 1916. Before then the District Gas Light Company Limited had operated a private gas works from the spring of 1864,[637] immediately north of the house called The Anchorhold, near Brewood Wharf. The house is still known locally as The Gas House. The gas was produced by heating coal – delivered by canal to the adjoining wharf – in a retort, producing gas, tar and amonia liquor and turning the coal into coke. Up to 10,000 cubic feet of gas could be extracted from each ton of coal. The processing plant was housed in a large two-storey brick building some 60′ north of and parallel to The Anchorhold. The building had tall round-headed windows at mid-height, and the roof ridge was raised to form a longitudinal vent. At the west end of the building was a tapering square

A poor but possibly unique photograph of Brewood gas works c.1903. The houses to the left and right, and the cart shed in the centre, still remain, but all traces of the works have disappeared.

section chimney approximately 40′ high and a single circular gasholder. No trace now remains of the production buildings or retorts, which in 1874 were described as 'a perennial nuisance both to air and water', but the water-filled circular brick gasholder base still existed c.1950, when all the pipework and remaining apparatus was removed. The smell of gas was still very strong. The first gas lighting was installed in the parish church and independent chapel in October 1864, and street and domestic lighting soon followed. Lighting in the village was effected by means of large four-sided lanterns, usually wall-mounted, some of which remained in the village until recent times. In 1922 the West Staffs Gas Company was awarded a contract by the Parish Council to light eleven gas lights around the village centre from dusk until 10.30pm, between 1st October and 20th April at a cost of £46. The gaslighter was Mr Daniels. Electricity arrived in Brewood from Wolverhampton by 1928, in which year 19 electric street lights were set up within half a mile radius of the village centre, and by

1940 almost the whole of the parish was served, the sub-station lying in a small brick building on the east side of the bend in School Road. The last part of the parish to be connected may have been Ringhills in 1948. Soon after electricity poles were installed in the village, a serious accident occured when a vehicle collided in the dark with a pole in Sandy Lane. As a result, white bands were painted on all poles, and often appear in early photographs.

Market Place c.1910. Traces of cobbles can be detected in the foreground, but for some reason the pump has been painted out. The gas lantern is typical of those found throughout the village from the mid-1860's.

The local geology has ensured a readily accessible water supply via springs and wells, and from about 1870 ingenious self-operating hydraulic rams were introduced to pump water uphill in various parts of the parish for agricultural, commercial and domestic purposes, one example [c.1920] remaining at Blackladies, another near the southern end of Shutt Green Lane, and a third [c.1880] incorporating a derelict 10' diameter iron waterwheel, some 300 yards north of Brewood Hall Farm, each housed in a small brick pumphouse. In 1882 a 'pumping engine' existed to the north-west of Chillington Hall, and c.1906 a hydraulic ram in a field at the rear of Kiddemore Green Farm pumped water to Oakley House.

In September 1900 the Medical Officer of Health for Cannock Rural District Council observed that

> ... most of the well water at Brewood is impure. The wells are shallow, the soil is porous, and in the course of years few can be the wells that escape contamination. One of the most urgent requirements in Brewood is a pure public water supply. To dig fresh wells, or to clean out old ones is adopting a makeshift policy.

The quality of water at that date is demonstrated by a report from the Wolverhampton Borough Analyst who tested ten samples, seven of which were contaminated by sewage, and two "not satisfactory in some respects, but not considered unsafe for drinking [sic]." Twelve samples taken from springs and wells in Brewood township on 24th March 1915 were tested by the Wolverhampton Public Analyst: eleven were found to be unfit for drinking due to 'sewage or animal contamination'.[638] In the same year a parliamentary Bill was passed, despite heavy opposition from local landowners who feared the local water table would be affected, empowering Wolverhampton Corporation to sink a borehole at Hurst Farm, Ivetsey Bank, a quarter of a mile north of The Bradford Arms, and pump water to an embanked and covered service reservoir 250 yards south-east of Boscobel House, with water piped from there to existing mains to the south of Tettenhall Rock. Boscobel was chosen for the reservoir because of its commanding height. The work was interrupted by the First World War, and when it recommenced in 1920, the Ivetsey borehole hit a monoclinal fault at 1,186', and the project was abandoned. In 1922 pumping stations were built by South Staffordshire Waterworks Company Limited north of Somerford Bridge and at Slade Heath, bringing the first piped water to Brewood and Coven. The supply was extended from Elm Cottage in Kiddemore Green road to Bishop's Wood between 1936 and 1948, interrupted by the war years. The Somerford waterworks, extended in 1937, draw water from a depth of about 275', and are housed in a large red-brick building with windows set in blind arcading which runs to the eaves. The roof is surmounted by a matching pair of square turrets, each with a weathervane. A large rectangular iron water tower supported on lattice framework and camouflaged by a coppice of Scot's pines on the southern edge of Bishop's Wood was demolished in about 1978, and a house built on the site.

In about 1907 a sewage works was constructed to the north of Brewood Hall Farm, and it was necessary for an Inspector from the Board of Trade to hold a Court of Enquiry on the application of the Rural District Council for an Order to dissolve the Drainage District of the Town of Brewood made in 1875, but even today most outlying parts of the parish rely on septic tanks or cess pits. A large sewerage pipe was laid from the Brewood works to the Coven works in 1987. The pipe runs east through Somerford Park and passes under the Penk north of Brewood Park Farm. A small treatment works lies to the north of Bishops Wood, and a small

Allen W. V. The Yew Trees, Oakley
Archer Richard H., White house
Beetlestone Miss Stafford house
Bennett Simeon, The Gables
Brown Miss Ida, Coneybere gardens
Bryans Alfred William, Deansfield
Dunkley Rev.Preb.Chas.,The Chantry
Evans William, The Bungalow
Fellows Mrs. Caroline, Stafford house
Fisher Miss, Somerford
Gannan Ernest John B.Sc. (head master), Grammar school
Giffard Thomas Arthur Walter M.B.E. Chillington hall (letters through Wolverhampton)
Gosling Vincent Samuel, The Mount
Hampton C. G. W. Woodlands
James Henry S., Oakley
Kirkaldy William Brond M.D. Bargate close
Lees Charles Herbert, Hill Top house, Coven road
Lloyd-Davies Mrs. Stafford street
Moore Mrs. G. M Bargate house
Morris William Henry, Shutt green
Owen Rev. William (Congregational), The Manse
Pearce Mrs. West Gate
Saunders Robert, Shop lane
Smith Rev. Leslie Knights (vicar, & surrogate), Vicarage
Sawley Miss, Oak villa
Steube Rev. Percival Joseph (Roman Catholic), St. Mary's
Taylor Mrs., The Deanery
Tinders Jn. Ludford,Horsebrook hall
Veall Miss, Sunnyside
Vincent Thomas, Horsebrook
Wheavell Miss, Dean street
Worsey Mrs. Brook house
Wynn Arthur Romer J.P.(Merioneth), Dawscroft house

COMMERCIAL.

Early closing day, Wednesday.

Astbury Albt. Alfd. farmer, Park la
Barker Jn. charabanc propr. T N 33
Beach Jn. farmer, Crateford
Bennett Hy. Holland, chimney sweep, Pavement
Bennett Norman, shoe repr
Bickford George, farmer, Somerford grange
Biddle Albt. rat catcher, Park lodge
Bill Arth. carpntr. Southview
Bill John, joiner, Shop lane
Birtles Sidney, farmer, Horsebrook
Bishop Geo. farmer, Cresswell Barn
Blake Jas. Major, farmer, Bath farm.
Codsall Wood (letters through Wolverhampton)
Blowitt Frank Richard, shopkeeper, High Green
Bourne Anne (Mrs.), Giffard Arms & Lion hotel
Brewood Club & Institute (Vincent Holt, hon. sec.), Sandy lane

Broughton Wm. blacksmith,Summerford
Brown William, grocer, Stafford st
Cartwright Geo. Hy. farmer, The Hattons
Condlyffe Arth. Jas. farmer, The Sham ho
Condlyffe Frank, farmer,Leper House farm (letters through Codsall, Wolverhampton)
Convent of the Order of St. Dominic & Boarding School for Girls(Mother Superior)
Cutliwick H. Ronald L.D.S.R.C.S. dental surgn
Daw Jas. & Edwin, blksmths.Sandy la
Daw Geo. plumber
Doughty Arthur Sidney, Three Stirrups P.H. Stafford street
Edwards Thomas, draper, Market sq
Ellisson James Bradley, chemist
Evans Lewis, tailor, Newport street
Evans Moses, cycle agt High Green. T N 21
Fox Ross (Miss), refreshment rooms, Dean street
†Gamson Jsph. shopkpr. Streetway rd
†Gamson J. & Sons, motor engnrs. Stretton garage
Gamson Thos. antique dlr. Market pl
Gibbs Wltr (Mrs.), butcher
Gillows H. Angel hotel
Grammar School(Ernest John Gamson B Sc. head master)
†Green Raymond, farmer, Rose hill
Hadley Sl. (Mrs.), shpkpr. Church rd
Hull Thomas, plumber & painter, Newport street
Harding Ernest Edward, farmer, Gunstone house (letters through Codsall, Wolverhampton)
Hawkins Bert, lock mkr. Stafford st
Heath William, farmer, Cottage farm
Hollos Ann Smith (Miss), ladies school, Stafford street
Holt E. butcher, Stafford st
Holt Vincent, poultry farmer, Ingleton la
Holt Wm. Jsph. frmr. Hackbury Hth
Jenkinson Wm.coal dlr.Brewood whrf
Jephcott Alfd. Coke, grocer, Bargate
Kirkaldy William Broad M.D., C.M. Edin. physician & surgeon, & medical officer & public vaccinator Brewood district, Cannock Area Guardians Committee, Bargate close
Lawson Thos. farmer
Lewis Harry, bricklayer, The Pavement
Line Mijamin Jn. Admiral Rodney inn, Dean st. T N 21
Lloyd Joseph, florist. Coven road
Lloyd Thos. greengro. Dean st
Lloyds Bank Ltd. (sub-branch) (attendance tues. & fri. from 10:15 a.m. till 1.15 p.m.); head office, 71 Lombard st. London E C 3
Mansfield Geo. insur. agt. Oulton, Kiddermore Green rd

Marshall Lewis Vincent, coal dlr. High grn
†Marson W. H. milk dlr. Shutt grn
†Moreton Samuel, frmr. Broom-hall
Newey Leonard, registrar of births & deaths & deputy registrar of marriages, Brewood sub-district, Cannock Registration District; & relieving & vaccination officer & collector to the Cannock Area Guardians Committee
†Nolan Gertrude (Miss), Blue Bell inn Streetway rd
Payne H. B. & Sons,butchers,Bargate
Pearson Wm. saddler, Stafford st
Perkin Rowland, baker, Market pl
Perkin Wm. baker, Market pl. T N 7
Perry Jn. rating officer & clerk to the Parish Council, The Lowlands
Perry John. painter, Hill top
Picken Fredk. Chas. farmer, Uplands, Kiddermore green
Ravenscroft Jn. W. greengro
Roberts Alethea Theresa (Mrs.), butcher, School road
Roberts Mary (Mrs.), greengrocer & draper
Robinson Stanley, farm bailiff to T. Perry esq. Chillington farm, Cotsall Wood (letters through Wolverhampton)
Robinson Wm. Saml. frmr. Hockerill
Saunders Geo. baker, Stafford st
Smith Jan. teacher of dancing, The Bungalow, Stafford st
South Staffordshire Waterworks Co. (Fred J. Dixon M.Inst.C.E. engineer), Somerford pumping station
†Stokes Arthur, farmer, Leafields
†Stokes James, farmer, Bellfields
Stonehouse Jas. shopkpr. sq
Swift Benj. farmer, Horsebrook
Swift Joseph Jn. farmer, Dean's hall
Thornley Thos.Hy.frmr.Gravelly way
Tolefree John, farmer, Gunstone (letters through Codsall,Wolverhamptn)
Wadsworth Francis Osborne, farmer, Brewood Hall farm
Wakefield John, confectioner, Post office, Market place
Wakelam Fras. Heath, The Bridge inn, beer retlr. High Green
Wakelam Norman Leonard, motor car propr. T N 41
Walford Wm. wheelwright,Bargate st
Walker William Henry, farmer, Somerford mill
Wall Joseph, boot maker, Pavement
‡Walley Minshall, farmer, Engleton hall. T N 8
Wassall Sarah Jane (Mrs.), confectnr
White Bros. farmers, Woolley farm
White Edwin, farmer, The Hide
‡White George, farmer, Somerford
Wilkes Jarvis, confectnr
Wilson Herbt. Hy. farmr. Somerford
Winterton Abraham Edwd.Swan hotel
Woodhouse Thos. farmer, Marsh frm
Wright Arth. Edwd. collector of poor rates

COVEN.

(Marked thus * receive their letters direct from Wolverhampton.)

PRIVATE RESIDENTS.

Blower Henry, Light Ash
Cooper William Ewart, The Beeches
Edwards Rev. Hy. (vicar), Vicarage
*Kenn Thomas George, Northfields, Four Ashes
*Millington Reginald Gilbert James, The Bungalow, Four Ashes
*Powell Joseph Albert, The Grey Gables, Four Ashes
Smith Joseph H. The Woodlands
*Stephens George, Four Ashes
Walker Rt.Ward, The Croft bungalow

COMMERCIAL.

Beddard Anne (Mrs.),frmr.Slade Hth
Bickford William Charles, farmer, The Manor house, Paradise
Bird Chas. market gardnr. Slade Hth

Cooke Thos. Arblaster, farmer, The Croft. T N Standeford 17
Elkington Alfred, boot maker
*Four Ashes Manufacturing Co. Ltd carbon manufacturers, Four Ashes T N Standeford 5
Grey Jsph. Rainbow P.H
Hand Alfd. grocer
Hartshorne Jn. poultry farmer, Church ho
Holt William, farmer, Slade Heath
Horton Edward Harrison, farmer, The Grange
Kench Charles, farmer
McLean John, building contractor. T N Standeford 2
*Maline Francis, farmer, Four Ashes
Oakes Frank, farmer, Paradise
Owen Jn. Fredk. fruit. Low. Laches
Porsehouse Richard, market gardener, The Lawn
Roberts Samuel, farmer, Coven farm
Spend Alfred, farm bailiff to Lady Joan M. Legge, The Hammers farm, Coven Heath
Taylor L. Vincent, Anchor inn

*Walley Thos. Minshall,farmer,Aspley farm (postal address, Four Ashes)
Williams Jn. farmer

STANDEFORD.

PRIVATE RESIDENT.

Parker William, White lodge

COMMERCIAL.

Bickford Henry, jun. farmer
Cowern Ernest Thomas, miller (water), Standeford mill
*Hall Joseph, farmer, Four Ashes
Kirk Annie Elizabeth (Mrs.), Four Ashes inn, Four Ashes
Kirk Stephen, butcher
Latham John Robert, Barrows inn
Liller John, shopkeeper
South Staffordshire Water Works Co. (Fred J. Dixon M.Inst.C.E. engineer), Slade Heath pumping station. T N Standeford 3
Wassell John, farmer, Mt. Pleasant
Whatton Gertrude (Mrs.), grocer
Wright Maud Mary (Mrs.), confctnr. & post office. T N Standeford 1

Extract from Kelly's Directory of Staffordshire 1937.

287

pumphouse in the angle of the river Penk and Deepmore Brook at Coven. A treatment works which included two large and two small circular settlement beds which lay a short distance to the north-east was levelled in recent years. Only a flat grassed mound remains on the eastern edge.

A telegraph office opened in Brewood post office in 1870,[639] and telephones had reached the village by 1920 – Mr T.A.W. Giffard of Chillington Hall seems to have been one of the first subscribers. Brewood telephone exchange was originally located in The Dreadnought in Market Place, run by Mr Stonehouse. A new single-storey brick exchange on the south side of Stafford House in Stafford Street, was opened on 20th December 1943, with 100 subscribers. After the construction of the present exchange to the north of Stafford Street car park in the 1960's, the redundant exchange was converted into a shop in about 1981, and into offices in 1988. An ancient walnut tree adjoining the building was destroyed by a severe storm in November 1989, but was replaced by a walnut sapling.

From c.1884 until c.1969, Brewood had its own weekly newspaper, 'The Brewood Courier', published in Cannock, from where a reporter [Mr Gill senior, and later his son] would visit the area by bicycle in the early part of the century to meet regular contacts for the latest news. A weekly newspaper called 'The Brewood Advertiser' existed from 15th October 1898 until 17th October 1900.[640]

From Victorian times, and perhaps earlier, tourism was an important source of income for many villagers, and visitors enjoyed the facilities of the various public houses and tea rooms. In the early years of the century the latter included Rose Fox's tearoom at Dean Cottage, at the top of Dean Street; The Perry's of The Uplands in Sparrow's End Lane; and 'Pansy' Powell's in Bargate Street near Speedwell Castle and later at The Dreadnought in Market Place. ['Pansy' was so-called after a dog she kept with the same name]. John Wakefield who ran the post office, and Mr E. Roberts, a professional photographer, published many postcards of local views after the turn of the century.

The eastern edge of the parish to the south and east of Four Ashes houses a variety of industrial complexes, including a carbon factory which commenced production in 1922, and a tar distillery built nearby in about 1950.

37. Ironworks in Brewood

During its history, the parish has not always escaped the noisier and more spectacular industrial processes, for Brewood is known to have had iron-works from at least the fifteenth century, although surprisingly few physical traces now remain.

Iron is produced from iron ore, which does not occur in any quantity in the Brewood area [a survey made in 1646-7 suggests that iron was then available within two miles of Brewood Park but this source – which must have been within the parish – has not been traced] and is mined as an oxide mixed with other material. To extract the iron, the ore must be heated to a very high temperature. Until about 1500 the process was carried out in a basin-shaped depression lined with fire-clay. The ore, probably obtained from the Walsall, Wednesbury or Darlaston area, was mixed with limestone – mined at Benthall Edge, west of Ironbridge, or near Dudley – as a flux, and with the abundant local charcoal [wood or coal providing insufficient heat], and the mixture ignited. The heat was increased by bellows driven by a water wheel until molten iron and waste slag formed in the bottom of the basin.[641] The mixture was called bloom, and the furnace known as a bloomery. When hammered, the slag and iron would separate and the resulting wrought iron could be worked by re-heating.

The introduction of blast furnaces in about 1500 enabled larger quantities of iron to be produced. Hollow towers were loaded with ore and charcoal. Water driven bellows forced air into the fired mixture, and the molten iron led into channels to form pigs of brittle cast iron, which were converted into wrought iron by burning off the excess carbon in a charcoal hearth called a finery. The wrought iron was re-heated in another hearth, called a chafery, and beaten by tilt hammer into the required shape.

Ironmaking consumed vast areas of woodland: an acre of forest would furnish 10 tons or so of charcoal, which would produce only about 7 tons of iron. The depletion of woodland resulted in an Act of 1558 prohibiting the production of charcoal for ironmaking, except in Kent. The Act was widely ignored, although it caused the seventeenth century ironmasters to develop the use of sea-coal and pit-coal for smelting. It is clear that ironmaking in Brewood developed as a result of the ready availability of charcoal and a suitable supply of water to power the water wheels, with ironstone available at no great distance.

At least five water wheels were usually required: one each for the blast furnace bellows, the finery bellows, the finery hammer, the chafery bellows and the chafery hammer. The introduction of the steam engine, which could be installed close to the source of the iron ore, marked the end of waterside iron making, by which time coke had long replaced charcoal as fuel.

From the fifteenth to the eighteenth centuries the South Staffordshire ironworks, including Brewood, were of considerable importance, and latterly consumed a large proportion of English iron, especially that processed in the Forest of Dean, Shropshire, North Staffordshire and Cheshire.[642]

There have been a number of ironworks and forges in Brewood parish, which lay at the centre of a region of ironworks lying in the Penk and Stour valleys and was on the main traffic route of bar and rod iron produced at Consall and Oakamoor, east of Stoke-on-Trent, to the finishing works and nailmakers in south Staffordshire, but it is difficult to piece together a coherent chronological sequence with any certainty from the occasional documentary references.

There was certainly a forge in Brewood in or before 1485, leased by the lord of the manor to Thomas Smith at a rent of 4d; there were hammer mills, fineries and chaferies producing bar iron during Elizabethan times; and there are references to Gilbert Robertes, George Rowe and Nicholas Willey, 'hombermen' or hammermen [iron-workers] of Brewood Park in 1603.[643] A Chancery Writ of 1559 refers to the purchase of 400 scythes by William Ball of Brewood from Nicholas Johnson, scythesmith,[644] but Johnson was almost certainly not a Brewood man, for finished goods were normally made elsewhere.

It has been suggested that one of the two ironmills on Cannock Chase operated by Sir William Paget in 1563 may have been the first blast furnace in the Midlands, but a furnace is recorded at Shifnal a year earlier, and Brewood may have had a furnace from about the same date – or even earlier – for the surname Furnace/Furnis/Furnese appears in the Brewood parish registers from 1572 – Annis Furnace was baptised on 30th November 1572 – though it is unclear whether the word had the same meaning at that time.

In about 1620 a forge was built on the Penk less than a quarter of a mile south of Somerford Hall by Thomas Chetwynd of Rugeley and Walter Coleman of Cannock, and the enterprise seems to have been marked by shift-working, for in 1623 Francis Somerford was complaining that his meadowland was being flooded and his water-mill starved of water, presumably by a coffer dam erected at the forge, and that he and his family were disturbed 'by the usual knocking thereof at several times of the night', by 'unwholesome smoke, sparks and air . . . and by the ill neighbourhood of disordered and ill-disposed persons usually employed in and repairing unto such iron-works'.[645] The Somerfords were probably no more pleased by the proximity of the furnace which lay a quarter of a mile from the forge adjoining Brewood Park in the 1640's, by which date there were at least 28 furnaces in the Midlands,[646] square structures about 20 feet high usually built of local brick or stone on streams, with a bridge or ramp constructed to the top of the structure to enable ore and charcoal to be loaded in the furnace.

The origins of Brewood Park Forge, otherwise known as Brewood Upper Forge, at the southern end of Chillington Lower Avenue, are unknown, but in 1645, during the Civil War, it was being supplied with charcoal by Peter Giffard of Chillington. From at least 1650 the forge was operated by Philip Foley, a member of the great ironworking family which had profited from the opportunites of the Civil War and ran at least 24 other ironworks, and much information about the Brewood ironworks is contained in the voluminous Foley papers held in Worcestershire Record Office.[647] Of particular interest are the 'sale particulars' produced by Philip Foley in 1674 in connection with negotiations with Sir Clement Clerke and John Foorth for the sale to them of "the Brewood and Grange Works". The Brewood works consisted of Brewood Upper Forge, Brewood Lower Forge, and Coven Furnace. The 'sale particulars' included a statistical table of raw materials consumed and iron produced by Brewood Upper Forge 1650-73, Brewood Lower Forge 1656-66 and 1671-3, and Coven Furnace 1650-73, although it was apparently inactive – "stood" – in 1663-6, 1668, 1671 and 1673. This can be explained by fluctuating demand for bar iron, which led to the occasional shutdown of some furnaces, for pig-iron deteriorates if kept too long, and could not be stockpiled. It was claimed in the 'particulars' that Brewood Upper Forge could produce 140 tons annually and Brewood Lower Forge 120 tons, with the added observation:

> These forges are very advantagious, having 2 fineryes at Upper works, and lye just at Coven furnace for cariage of pigs [iron ingots], and Lower worke new built and workmen's houses new built. They lye near to abundance of woods, and make colsher iron, where Hampton is the place of sale in bars, or Stourbridge in rods. Coles and all materialls come in here as cheap as at any workes whatsoever and note that these workes . . . are and may be managed with as small a stock as any workes in all the country the iron being still sent away as it was made and the debts owing by few men and those punctuall paymasters.

Coven furnace was shown with a potential output of 500 tons per annum, with Foley's note:

> This is a small rent (the clarks house not included) and lyes very neer the forges for cariage, and to Wirly where the ironstone is gott. There is a bargain [contract] for 17s 3d per ton to supply it with ironstone which is cheap, and when that bargain is out I have stone in my own land at Wirly to furnish you or at least to prevent rising the price. Here may be 700 tons cast at a blast and in every respect very comodious.

The prospective buyers were also assured that amongst "woods to supply these works with charcoles" were those of Sir Thomas Wilbraham [of Weston Park], Sir Edward Littleton [of Pillaton], Mr Pierpoint at Tong, Mr Leveson, Mr Gifford at Chillington, and "divers about Albrighton . . . which lye all convenient". Further woods of Sir Theo Biddulph of Lapley

"May bee above 1500 cords within 3 miles of Brewood", and "near Coven furnace within a mile and a halfe great quantyties beside". These encouraging observations were of course intended to induce potential purchasers to acquire the works, and should not be treated as objective assessments, but they appear to have achieved their desired effect, for the sale took place. However at some date after 1675 in circumstances which are unclear Philip Foley had recovered possession of the works.

The reference to woods of Sir Thomas Wilbraham is of interest, for in about 1970, during the renovation of the roof of the greengrocer's shop on the west side of Market Place, a letter was discovered lodged behind a purlin. The letter, from Sir Thomas to William Mansell of Coven, is dated 12th September 1684 and quotes rates for cutting and cording wood at Ivetshey. William Mansell was the clerk employed by Foley to cover a group of three ironworks: Brewood Upper Forge, Coven Furnace, and Wombridge Furnace, near Telford, and it is possible that he lived at Market Place.

The output of Brewood Upper Forge in 1667 was 109 tons, making it the most efficient of the Foley forges, with a gain of £2 3s 1½d per ton, and the same year Coven Furnace produced over 587 tons. In 1668 Brewood Upper Forge made 161 tons of bar iron, with 132 tons delivered to Bustleholme slitting mill, near West Bromwich, which Thomas Foley had leased for 21 years in 1650 with Gerard Fowke of Gunstone. Slitting was the process whereby bar iron was converted into rods by water-powered rollers and circular cutting plates. Coven furnace processed 114 tons of iron from Gornal, and there is a record of a mortar being cast for 6d, in addition to some "potts". The following year the output was almost 123 tons of bar iron from Brewood Forge, half of which was taken to Bustleholme, and 464 tons of sow iron was cast at Coven. In 1670 there were two pairs of finery bellows and one pair of chafery bellows at Brewood Upper Forge. A schedule of stock taken the same year mentions a "frame and gates in the Brewood river", evidently to regulate the flow to the works. In 1674 Brewood Upper Forge produced only 118 tons of bar iron, to the displeasure of Philip Foley who endorsed the yield accounts: "There is a sad waste of coles here, there will be great loss by that account".

The reference in the 'particulars' of 1674 to "the Lower worke new built and workmen's houses new built" is puzzling, for when the lease of Upper Forge was renewed for 17 years in 1673 at a rent of £20, a reference to Lower Forge suggests that it may then have been disused.

Brewood Park Forge was still operating in 1682. In 1696 there is a reference to the New Forge near Shurgreave Field in the manor of Brewood, worked by George and Thomas Rock of Horsebrook, and from 1698 bar iron from Brewood produced from pig iron brought in from Elmbridge via the Severn, Bewdley and Hampton Lode was carried to Stourton slitting mill for slitting. In 1709, Thomas Rock was processing pig iron from Vale Royal in Cheshire for the makers of ironwork such as nails and saws in the south of the county, and appreciable quantities of pig iron from

Lawton Furnace in north Staffordshire were also being utilised by the Brewood forges. In 1717 two forges were listed in the parish, the Upper Forge in Coven and the Lower Forge in Brewood [perhaps the same as New Forge], which together produced 100 tons per annum. A Chillington estate map c.1727 mentions [but unfortunately does not show] 'Coven Furness'. The Lower Forge was disused by 1753, and part had been demolished. Upper Forge was disused by about 1841.[648] The buildings were used as a corn-mill until destroyed by fire in about 1869, but the ruins existed until well into the present century. Low brick footings and the remains of a mill-race between Coven Road and part of the former mill pool now mark the site. In

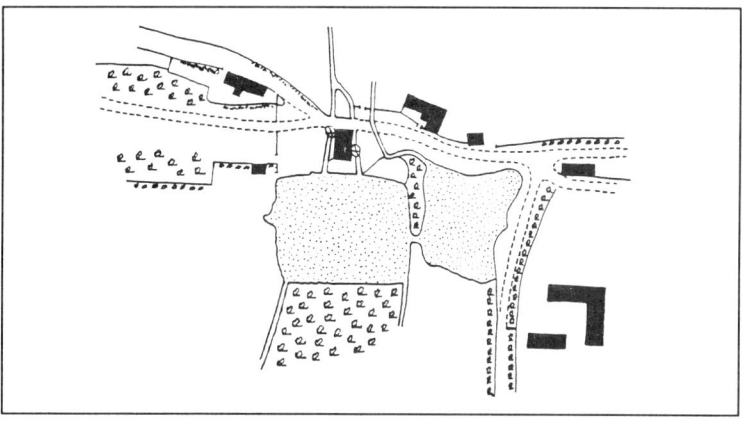

Redrawn plan of Brewood Forge. The original is pasted to the inside cover of a volume of nineteenth-century estate maps, but seems to date from the late eighteenth century. Two pools then existed, with two waterwheels and two spillways, as well as what appears to be an overflow ford. The lane south to Brewood Park Farm follows the line of a Roman road. With acknowledgements to Staffordshire Record Office D594/374.

1808 the forge pool extended east to the lane to Brewood Park Farm, and measured about 650' by 250', divided by a causeway which now marks the east bank of the present pool. To help feed the pools, a meandering leat or watercourse was created from the Penk due east of Brewood Park Farm, the S-shape line still marked by ditches and field boundaries. A long earthen dam runs along the western side of the remaining pool. This was the Pond Bay which held back the water to provide the necessary head of water for the water wheels, with two spill-ways taking water from the mill-race north to the Penk. The pool had been reduced to its present size by 1838. Forge House, on the opposite side of the road, dates from the early eighteenth and late nineteenth centuries, built around a large, late sixteenth century brick chimney, and was modernised in the mid 1980's. In 1941 it was the home of 75-year old Edwin 'Mole' Evans, one of the few remaining professional molecatchers in Staffordshire

Traces of black soil, cinder and slag around Cinder Hill estate at Coven are evidence of the eighteenth century Coven furnace or iron-bloomery.[649] The forge dam is said to have been in existence c.1925. Cinderhill Meadow on the south bank of the stream to Standeford to the north-east of Coven sewage works may be the site of the furnace. Aerial photographs suggest that the stream formerly ran a little to the south of the existing course, and a small rectangular waterlogged enclosure of sandstone blocks which may have been connected with the furnace lies on this line, with slag, cinders and black earth to the east. The ground appears to be much disturbed, and the watercourse has been culverted.

Between Kiddemore Green Farm and the stream to the south is a spring-fed small square embanked pool, restored as a swimming pool in recent years, which is recorded in 1838 and may have originated as a hammer pond, for just beneath the surface of a small rough area on the south bank of the stream, through which runs a footpath to The Whitemoor, are cinders, limestone and clinker which suggest the existence of an early bloomery – a blast furnace produces slag. The field is named The Devil's Horn in the 1838 Tithe Map: the word devil was often applied to infertile or difficult ground. Areas of black soil on the north side of the stream in the fields adjoining the footpath are typical evidence of iron-working. A piece of Roman samian pottery has been found in this black earth, but the site is probably medieval. Since it does not appear to be mentioned in later records, it was presumably disused by the seventeenth century.

It should be emphasised that the ironworking industry in Brewood is unlikely to have been responsible, as sometimes claimed, for the destruction of the local woodland for fuel. On the contrary, it was almost certainly the ironworks which saved the woodland from becoming farmland: the furnaces and forges used only the renewable underwood, not the timber trees.

It seems that the iron works and forges of Brewood could only extract a small quantity of the iron in the ore, and during the First World War the spoil [in addition to quantities said to have been removed from east of Standeford] was retrieved, taken away and resmelted to extract the remaining iron:[650] in earlier times it was unprofitable to process ore with an iron content of less than 40%, but ore with a minimum iron content of 25% can be processed economically by modern methods.

Of particular interest is a link between Brewood and one of the earliest ironworks in America. In 1715 Joseph Farmer left England and went to Maryland, followed soon after by Stephen Onion from Brewood and William and Thomas Russell, to search for high quality iron ore for English furnaces. These pioneers established Principio Furnace in what is now Cecil County, Maryland, near the point where the Susquehannah River empties into Chesapeake Bay. Principio Furnace has a place in American history, for it produced guns for both the American Revolution and the war in 1812, and was sacked and burned by the British in both wars. Stephen Onion and one of the Russells returned to England in 1724, sharing a cabin with Benjamin Franklin. Stephen Onion married Deborah Russell in 1725 at Edgbaston church. A commemorative marble plaque to the Onion family is on the wall of what is now the vestry of Brewood parish church,[651] and descendants of the family still live in the parish.

38. Market, Fair and Wake

Markets have been of vital importance throughout history, and the early Plantaganet kings sold charters for weekly or bi-weekly markets to finance their military campaigns. For the proprietor – the owner of the land on which it took place – a market provided a rich income from the tolls and taxes levied on the traders for the goods they sold or even diplayed and fees for the use of stalls. Originally held on Sundays, the artisans' free day, markets were transferred to weekdays after pressure from the Pope.

The earliest recorded reference to a fair or market in Brewood dates from 28th July 1221, when the Bishop of Coventry and Lichfield, William de Cornhull, was granted a market each Friday until the full age of Henry III, with a further grant to the King's cousin, Roger, Bishop of Coventry and Lichfield, on 2nd June 1259 for a market to be held in the manor each Monday, but there is some evidence that Brewood may have possessed two markets before the King's reign, i.e. before 1216, although the Quo Warranto Pleas of 1293 state that Brewood possessed no market before that date.[652] In all, Henry granted no less than 20 towns and villages in Staffordshire the right to hold a weekly market and a yearly fair. The grants would have enabled the Bishop as lord of the manor to stimulate trade and industry in his rural holding, thereby as landlord increasing his revenues. Until 1285, when church authorities forbade the practice, markets were frequently held in churchyards, but it is probable that Market Place in Brewood has always been the site of the local market. Markets and fairs were held under the jurisdiction of the steward of the lord of the manor, and were opened by proclamation and perhaps a local ceremony. Any merchant found selling after the end of the market was liable to forfeit twice the value of all that he had sold.[653] In 1321 there is reference to the payment of 'stuck' to the Bishop by his tenants of irrigated land at Brewood.[654] The payment probably related to the maintenance of the 'stokgates' which controlled the flow of water to such land, or, less likely, stuck may have been 'stoc-gobulum', a form of market due.[655]

In 1382 a royal commission found that Sunday markets had been held without licence for the previous 20 years at Rugeley, Stone, Penkridge and Brewood, to the prejudice of the Saturday market at Stafford. These Sunday markets were presumably additional markets, since there is no evidence that the licenced weekday markets ceased to exist. At some date between 1387 and 1390 the King confirmed the Bishop's right to his Monday and Friday markets in Lichfield, Haywood, Longdon, Rugeley, Cannock, Eccleshall and 'Berewich' [Bradley].

Often the right to hold a fair or market was the first stage in a long evolutionary process which ended in urban status, and while many villages did prosper and later became important towns or cities, Brewood is among those places which failed to develop, and indeed fell into decline in later centuries. In many cases it is difficult to ascribe specific reasons for the lack of growth, but in the case of Brewood the location of the village must have been a major factor. It is not placed on a river crossing or cross roads, or even on a principal highway, and those surrounding markets which had a geographical advantage slowly began to attract trade and business at the expense of Brewood.

The nearest markets to Brewood in the medieval period were Wheaton Aston, Penkridge, Church Eaton and Pattingham,[656] and whilst by the early seventeenth century Penkridge horse fair attracted buyers from all over England, Brewood had only local trade, which by 1646 seems to have been discontinued, for a parliamentary survey records that 'there hath been a weekly market but that is now [blank]'.[657] The presumed lapse was doubtless due to the Civil War, but an attempt appears to have been made to revive the market, although it is said to have been insignificant in 1650, and twenty years later was described as 'almost discontinued'. A Tuesday market seems to have existed in the seventeenth century, but was said to be 'of no great concernment, being almost discontinued' in 1673,[658] although subsequently it may have revived, for a Tuesday market is again recorded in 1747. In 1796 the Friday market is described as very trifling.

It is said that the market house, popularly called the Market Cross, or Butter Cross, collapsed in 1810.[659] The Market Cross, which appears to have stood on the north or east side of Market Place,[660] was almost certainly so-called because it was surmounted, as was the custom throughout the country, by a cross, supposedly to remind traders to exercise the Christian duties of honesty and fair dealing. The Market Cross was also traditionally the place where public whippings of offenders and vagabonds were carried out.

Even females were not exempt from whipping, and an entry from the Constables' Accounts for Brewood for 1688 reads: 'For whipping Mary Hollygreen 1s 0d'. It was presumably at a whipping post attached to the Market Cross or at the stocks in High Green that the poor creature, [perhaps a vagabond, although the name Hollygreen appears very frequently in the Overseers' Accounts in the eighteenth century] suffered her punishment. The Constable was the officer responsible for administering the whipping, but the charge seems excessive: 4d was the standard charge in Wolverhampton in the early eighteenth century.[661]

Brewood Market Cross seems to have been built towards the end of the seventeenth century, but it evidently replaced a much older structure, for the church registers record the burial on 5th March 1618 of a 'certaine poor man dyinge in the cross', and on 23rd March 1619 of 'Margaret, a poore wandering wench, dying in the crosse'.[662]

Until its collapse, the Market Cross, a covered market area supported on stone or wooden pillars, possibly with a room above, was used by the lord of the manor for the court leet[663] [manor court] at the annual fair in September, but with the loss of the building, the court was transferred to the Swan Inn. The Friday market seems to have ceased at some date after 1818.[664] In November 1833 it was revived, but by 1840 it was again discontinued owing to the rapidly increasing influence of Wolverhampton, although butter and eggs were still being sold on Fridays at the site of the Cross, marked until 1860 by a blank space in the surrounding cobbles.[665]

The origins of fairs can be traced back to Roman times, the word fair deriving from the Latin for holiday – 'feria'. The earliest fairs were an extension of the market, and primarily for trade, usually the sale of livestock. The right to hold a three-day fair each year at the manor of Brewood on 'the vigil, feast and morrow of the Nativity of the Virgin' [7th, 8th and 9th September] was granted by Henry III to Roger, Bishop of Coventry and Lichfield, in 1259 and confirmed by Richard II in or about 1388.

An insight into disorderly behaviour at fair time some two centuries later is obtained from the Quarter Sessions Rolls for 1600, where an undated Examination is recorded of John Duncalfe, Constable of Brewood, in the following curious terms:

> He seieth that vppon occesion of quarelling words wch fell forth betwene this examinant & oon Clement Clarke they appoynted a place to fight at long laye launde [Langley Lawn] in chillnington on the 9th of september last betymes in the morning wch was the morrowe after Brewood fayre, but seieth that the said Clement came not to the place at the time appo[inted] & further yt he did not appoynt to meet t[he] seid Clement at any other place nor at any other tyme.
> Signed: Jo. Duncalfe   Ro. Fowkes[666]

The report suggests that the fair had by that date been reduced to one day. In 1646 the fair is recorded as being held on 8th September only, and the tolls and profits – presumably hit by the turmoil of the Civil War – were assessed at only ten shillings per annum. The main trade in 1662, when the fair was held over two days, 8th and 9th September, evidence of increasing trade after the Restoration, was in horses, and the toll books show that buyers and sellers were mainly local, and rarely bought, sold or exchanged more than one animal each. Horse fairs were more strictly regulated than others: horses were costly animals and dealers were well-versed in the arts of deception. Names and occupations of sellers were listed in the toll books and all horses minutely described. In the library at Chillington Hall is a parchment-bound manuscript court book for Brewood fair, recording horses sold and details of the buyers and sellers from 1716 to 1739. The book provides an interesting insight into the greater distances then travelled by some buyers and sellers. It is possible that the fair had again reduced to one day by 1741, and when the Gregorian calendar replaced the Julian calendar in 1752 – 2nd September was followed the next day by 14th September, and tradition says that crowds formed demanding 'give us back our 11 days' – the fair was moved to 19th

September. Fairs fixed by feasts were, by implication, exempted from the Act which corrected the calendar: the change was very unpopular in the rural areas, and the villagers of Brewood seem to have exercised their right not to change the day of their fair, and continued to adopt what was known as the old-style calendar.[667]

The names of The Bargates [now 23 Bargate Street], Bargate House and Broadgate House mark the site of the barred gates where the lord of the manor took his tolls at the fairs moved to 19th September and, from at least 1834, the second Tuesday in May, but it seems evident that there must have been other gates to prevent access from other directions. Manor court books still exist from the eighteenth and nineteenth centuries containing details of the officers responsible for regulating the conduct of fairs. The entries show the names of the constables and headboroughs of the various townships; the pinder, responsible for stray animals; the beadle, who would assist with the inspection of weights and measures and act as market crier; and several 'warders', each covering a specific area, such as Stafford Street, Sandy Lane, Bar Gate, Sheep Fair and Horse Fair. From 1753 until the 1830's there is regular reference to 'Bull Ring'. The precise location is uncertain, but in one entry it is linked to Stafford Street, and it may have been near the Three Stirrups public house, where bull baitings are by tradition said to have been held.

The fair was very much a livestock market, with cows and sheep penned in Market Place: substantial iron staples were attached to the wall of the Swan Inn for attaching sheep hurdles. In the early years of the present century a weighing machine stood against the wall between Speedwell Castle and The Swan Inn for weighing loads of hay. It was some 7' tall and took the form of an ornate rectangular waisted iron frame with a circular dial in a square frame at the top, and vertical rails at each side of the weighing platform. Sheep and pigs were penned in Bargate Street, and in the nineteenth century an adjoining field was known as Horse Fair, since horses were bought and sold there. The former pinfold, used for confining stray cattle and sheep, stood on the south side of High Green, east of the canal bridge, until at least 1907, when it was then said to be dilapidated, full of rubbish and an eyesore.

Until 1852 the September fair closed at noon, and the court leet was opened by a procession, which included the display of ceremonial poles which were at one time kept at the Swan Inn. The court was concluded by a dinner for the copyholders. The May fair had been discontinued by 1860, and the September fair came to an end after the First World War.

It seems to have been customary for a wake [that is, a pleasure fair as opposed to a market] to have been held on the Sunday following the September livestock fair [unless the 19th fell on a Saturday, when the wake would be held on 27th September], at which bull-baiting was one of the 'entertainments', replaced when made illegal in 1835 by horse racing at Hockerhill. The date of the wake originally coincided with the feast day of the patron saint of the church, St Mary the Virgin, on 8th September. The eve of this day was the occasion of 'waking' or keeping vigil at the church on the night before the great day, and the word was later applied to the games, feasts and other festivities that took place at this time. A decree of 1536 ordered that every parish must hold its wake on the first day in October, regardless of the date of the patronal festival, but the enactment seems to have been ignored in most places, including Brewood: it probably suited the villagers to keep their feast during the slack post-harvest month of September, the date having moved to the Sunday following the 19th September when the Gregorian calendar was adopted.[668]

Brewood Wake was seen as the highspot of the year in the centuries before Christmas achieved that position mainly as a result of festivities and customs introduced in the Victorian period, and Wake Sunday – which developed into Wakes Week from the second half of the last century – was the day when the harvest festival was customarily held and the time when villagers and children working away flocked home, long-lost friends and relatives appeared on visits, and neighbouring communities poured in to see the sports and perhaps attend the 'feast dinner' in the evening.

The day was celebrated by feasting and the consumption of large quantities of ". . . a queer kind of gingerbread. It was made in flat pieces and cut on the top so as to look like finger biscuits. This made it easy to break." According to older villagers who remember the Brewood Wakes held in the early years of this century, this so-called 'gingerbread' was at that time formed into hollow finger shapes or curls seemingly in all respects identical to what are now called brandysnaps, and were cooked on a steel plate over a brazier and served in newspaper cones called 'pokes'. In 1834 Elizabeth Parkes, daughter of James and Mary Parkes, licencees of the Angel Hotel, started a manuscript notebook of recipes and remedies. Included in the book are five recipes for gingerbread, all based on varying quantities of butter, flour, sugar, treacle and ginger, one with the addition of five drops of lemon essence, another with an egg, and a third with candied lemon, orange peel, nutmeg, mace and cloves [for "best" gingerbread]. The recipe for "transparent gingerbread – Mrs Smith's recipe – very nice" required 2oz butter, ¼lb flour, ¼lb treacle, 2oz sugar and a spoonful of ginger, spread thinly on a buttered tin and baked for a few minutes. This may well have been the traditional Brewood recipe.

Many places served their own special feast dish, like the famous Eccles cakes of Eccles in Lancashire or the baked warden pears of Bedford, and gingerbread may have been the local regional tradition, for in the seventeenth century the traveller Celia Fiennes noted in her diary that she had seen gingerbread being sold in the market place at Lichfield during the 'Green Bower Feast', an ancient flower festival which took place at Whitsun.

Some idea of the type of behaviour seen locally at wakes is given in a petition sent by John Jackson, the Puritan Vicar of Lapley, to the county justices in October 1655 appealing for them to suppress wakes weeks, claiming

> ...that at all or most of the townes in the said county there are annually still observed and kept the wakes on the Sabboth dayes by feasting friends and farrainers. Out-butchers, resorting thither on the wake-eve only, utter much meate for the wake-provision. And a great parte of the weeke after are the wakes continued and upheld by loose people, especially by ale houses, licensed and unlicensed, without restraint for that tyme, and by multitude of vaine people that can give no good account of their concourse, besides a great rable of common beggars. Great part of the wake-weekes is spent in promiscuous dancing, maurice-dancing, tipling, gameing, quarrelling, wantᵒnnesse. Hereby God is highly dishonoured, superstition fostered by dedicateing dayes and tymes to saints departed, the name of God torne in pieces, sabboth prophaned, peace endangered, brawleing occasioned, wantonnesse furthered, tyme and money misspended, the good names of others traduced, other men's wives, children, servants and goods coveted ...[669]

It would appear that many of the individuals guilty of 'maurice-dancing' were papists from Lapley, with other dancers and musicians coming from Stretton and Church Eaton.

From at least the eighteenth century, the main attraction at the wake was the bull baiting. The 'entertainment' took the form of a tethered bull, which was whipped, taunted, and set upon by bulldogs. The dogs were induced to attack the bull, one at a time, and trained to seize it by the nose, which when accomplished was called 'pinning the bull'. Bets were placed on which dogs would survive the longest or die first. Baitings are said to have been carried out at three places in the village: at High Green; at the corner of Stafford Street and Engleton Lane – probably the site of the Bull Ring recorded between 1753 and the 1830's – but mainly in Market Place,[670] where a ring and staple to which the bulls were said to have been tethered could apparently still be seen until at least 1890, but are now covered by road metalling. The baitings were viewed with considerable apprehension by the villagers, for the wake would attract the roughest elements from the mining districts around Cannock who would bring with them an army of Staffordshire bulldogs. It was said that 'they did not even wait for daylight on Monday morning to commence the disgusting and brutalising sport'. The baitings probably attracted a greater audience after 1777, when the Town Act prohibited baitings in Wolverhampton, and spectators moved beyond the town boundary to other attractions, including Tettenhall Michaelmas Wake and Brewood Wake. Bull baiting seems to have continued in Brewood until it was made illegal in 1835.[671]

On 27th September 1858 Brewood Wake included a variety of games and competitions, including bag-racing, 'goose gingling' [where one person, blindfolded, attempted to catch another ringing a handbell, the prize being a goose], pole swarming [greasy pole], wheelbarrow and donkey races, preceded by a fat pig show for local cottagers, with 12 prizes awarded. The highlight of the day was a prize draw from a large wagon drawn by four horses which was laden with 150 parcels, such as sacks of flour, cheeses, bacon, blankets etc., valued at between 3s. and 15s., the ticket holders being limited to the poor of the parish. Sadly, but not unusually, the day's events were marred by a good deal of fighting, doubtless resulting from the liberal consumption of alcohol, between locals and men from Wolverhampton, although no serious injuries were reported.[672]

By 1864 the wake had declined to the point where it consisted merely of 'two cake stalls and two public house balls'.[673] After Market Place was macadamed at some date between 1860 and 1866,[674] the District Surveyor objected to stakes for the stalls being driven into the road surface, and the wake moved to the outskirts of the village, probably Churchfields, opposite the Catholic church. By 1874 the wake seems to have revived, since there were then 'shows and sports', and in 1878 it included a shooting gallery, merry-go-rounds, 'goose-gingling', pole-swarming and dancing, with a football match at Churchfields against a visiting team from St Luke's club, Wolverhampton – the visitors won. In the evening there was dancing in the Angel, Malt Shovel and Chequer Ball, some of which may have stayed open all night. In 1890 it was reported that the "festival started on Sunday and about 600 people came into the town from all the district. Some of the visitors became rather boisterous. On the Monday the fair started in the Market Place and a brisk business was done." In the early years of this century the wake was held in a field behind the Three Stirrups public house, and included maypole dancing. The wake seems to have lapsed after the First World War, probably eclipsed by Brewood and District Agricultural Show, subsequently known as Brewood Show.

On the 24th September 1989 the Market Place was closed to traffic and the wake revived, with great success, to mark the twentieth anniversary of Brewood Civic Society. Attractions included maypole dancing, clog dancing, sideshows, stalls, a brass band, a play [Maria Marten and the Red Barn], and singers, with many attending the bunting-decorated market place wearing period costume.

39. Recreations, Clubs and Societies.

The name Games Crofte attached to the southern slopes of Broom Hall on an estate map of 1704 and recorded as early as 1584 suggests a site on which games and sports were held; Sport Leasow, shown on the 1838 Tithe Map, lay on the north side of Kiddemore Green Road at Bishop's Wood, opposite the lane to Pearse Hay; and references in 1774 and 1791 to Bowling Alley Piece on the north side of Grange Farm at Coven and Bowling Green on the west side of Bell Field Farm on Watling Street may indicate that bowling, very popular at that time, took place there.[675]

When bull-baiting was made illegal in 1835, it was replaced in Brewood by horse-racing.[676] A race track – known as Brewood Racecourse – and a wooden grandstand were created at Hockerhill Farm, although a newspaper report in 1861 refers unflatteringly to the latter as "something like a hay crib run to seed". The stand may have been constructed on the 'grandstand mound', some 200 yards to the north-west of the farmhouse, with the racecourse laid out in a roughly oval shape between the grandstand and the stream to the south. The mound is no longer detectable on the ground, presumably having been ploughed out, but it may have been of very ancient origin, for the name Hockerhill [formerly Hockerill] is believed to mean 'hill with a [burial?] mound'.[677] It is known that a windmill – probably a post mill – stood in the area, and it may have utilized the same mound. The races seem to have taken place until at least 1859,[678] and were apparently unconnected with the steeplechasing from Brewood Racecourse started by three prominent foxhunters from Albrighton Hunt: John Mytton, Captain J. White and Mr T.W. Giffard of Chillington. Those races, over distances of 3 and 3½ miles, were supported by the Hunt until they lapsed in the 1860's.[679]

In 1864 a new court of The Ancient Order of Foresters was formed at Brewood as a friendly society, and took the name Royal Oak.[680] Its meetings were held at The Angel. Another society, The Odd Fellowship, a lodge of the Manchester Unity of Oddfellows, seems to have been in existence by 1844.[681] For many years around the turn of the century the procession of The Brewood Independent Order of Oddfellows was an annual event, with members wearing aprons and sashes marching around the village displaying ceremonial staves and regalia with banners carried aloft, accompanied by a brass band and decorated floats. A juvenile branch of the Order existed with its own banners. The Oddfellows meeting place was the Three Stirrups public house.

In the last century concerts, recitals and readings were regular features of village life. By 1851 Brewood Cottage Garden Society was organising several shows of fruit, vegetables and flowers each year, but it seems to have lapsed due to the lack of support soon afterwards. In 1884 a reading room was established by Mr A. Monckton of Stretton Hall at a house in

Dean Street, and members decided to re-form the Garden Society, the first show being organised on 5th August 1884 at Somerford Park. Prize money exceeding £20 was awarded and, in addition to various horticultural exhibits, sporting activities took place and music was provided by The Staffordshire Volunteer Band. Prizes were presented by Lady Boughty, who lived with her husband Thomas Boughty at Brewood Hall. The event may have been the precursor of the annual Brewood Flower Show, which proved very popular and from at least the turn of the century was held in the grounds of the Dawscroft on the first Thursday in August, changed to the first Tuesday in 1903. In 1911 the Flower Show included a cycle parade, maypole dancing, and entertainment by 'Wilder's Troupe of Performers.'[682]

For many years around the turn of the century the Band of Hope, which met in The Institute at the top of Sandy Lane, held weekly meetings and arranged trips from the village.

Brewood Bank of Hope leaving for a day trip to Milford in 1909, photographed by John Wakefield, postmaster and photographer, from an upper window of the post office. The single storey building in the background is the original school. In the foreground is the old pump with its cranked handle.

The origins of Brewood Show, held for over half a century, lie in Brewood and District Agricultural Show, organised originally for farmers within a 10-mile radius of Brewood church by John England Hart and W.J. Devereux of Cheslyn Hay, held from 1899, first on Mr Swann's field at Oram's Lane, and subsequently at various venues, including the field opposite the Catholic Church, on at least one occasion a field next to the marl pits [opposite Hockerhill?] in Kiddemore Green Road, and at another time at the back of Brewood Hall.

The festivities commonly started with a procession led by a uniformed brass band which assembled in Market Place and paraded around the village, usually anti-clockwise, down Dean Street and up Sandy Lane. Villagers would don fancy dress, and the procession would include decorated horse-drawn floats, including 24 girl maypole dancers dressed in white tunics, red, white and blue sashes and white knee socks on a float bedecked in ribbons. The cavalcade would make its way to the show field, where marquees were erected for the display of produce in the flower and vegetable competitions. Only horses were displayed in earlier years, with judging taking place in morning and afternoon, but most of the events took place after lunch, started by maypole dancing which began at 2 o'clock. The dances included the single plait, double plait, gypsies tent and spiders web, perfected after many hours of practice around a pole erected in the school playground. It is said that an attempt one year to include boys in the maypole dancing proved to be disastrous and was quickly abandoned. The maypole repetoire lasted for over an hour, and was repeated at six o'clock.

The dancing was followed by children's sports, including egg-and-spoon races, three-legged races and sack races, and light hearted events for horsemen, which included riding to one side of the arena, dismounting to thread a needle, and remounting to ride to the other side to sew on a button before returning to the start. Other popular games were musical chairs on horseback, and a competition which involved two teams of three riders who attempted to manœvre a huge push-ball into the opposing goal.[683]

When the show moved to Somerford Park, visitors attended from a very wide area. In 1911 one of the attractions was aeroplane flights, and in 1925 those attending were entertained by "a demonstration of man-tracking by Mr R. Clark's bloodhounds". Covered wooden grandstands were later erected for spectators, but the show was suspended for six years during the Second World War. In the 1950's Brewood Show was advertised as 'the best one-day show in England.' On 7th August 1950 almost 29,000 people attended, causing considerable congestion on local roads and lanes, and there were over 600 livestock entries. The last show was held on 6th August 1953.

Travelling fairs are known to have temporarily occupied the field immediately west of the Bell Inn on Watling Street up to the early years of this century. In the nineteenth century the field was the venue for Stretton Wake, held on the second Sunday in September, with sports, games and dancing on the following day. Coins and other artifacts turned up after ploughing suggest that the field may have been the site of fairs or wakes since early medieval times.

Brewood football team, the origins of which are now lost, was known as Brewood Exchange in 1905.

The Brewood, Stretton and Lapley Cricket Club was formed in April 1910, and played on a field on the north side of Somerford Park. Brewood

Cricket Club is believed to have played originally at its present ground between Engleton Lane and Four Ashes Road, then known as Deansfield, but the date of its formation is unknown. At the turn of the century the only cricket was apparently played at Somerford, but the Club had returned to Deansfield before the First World War. Activities were suspended from 1914 to 1921, when the Club was re-formed, playing on a temporary ground at Brewood Hall. The following year the Club was based at 'the marl-pit ground' [at Hockerhill Farm, between the farmhouse and the stream] which had been laid out as a running track by the local Oddfellows Lodge, but the field proved to be unsuitable for cricket and there were several accidents. As a result the Club moved back to Deansfield in 1923, and has not moved since.

A recreation ground lay at Cowclose Meadow on the west side of the stream east of Dean's Hall Farm in the early decades of this century, and a recreation field in Sandy Lane, behind what is now the surgery, was created in 1933. A rifle range was created in the sandpits in the same area in the 1950's. In 1914 a tennis court was created a short distance west of Hockerhill farmhouse. The court was abandoned during the First World War, but after the war, two courts were made and a wooden pavilion erected. A ladies cricket club existed in Brewood in 1919, run by the wife of the headmaster of the grammar school. A golf course and driving range were created at The Three Hammers in about 1960.

1st Brewood Scout Troop, c.1911.

A scout troop was formed in the village in 1911, associated with the 5th Wolverhampton group. It began with 50 members and its first leader was Arthur Lloyd, who was soon replaced by an older man, L.H. West, in accordance with scout policy. A guide troop has existed in Brewood since at least 1921, when it met in outbuildings in the cobbled yard of the old vicarage. The first meeting in Brewood cubs was held on 1st May 1961.

29th May, Restoration Day and birthday of Charles II, was formerly a day of celebration in the Brewood area, so closely associated with the escape of the King. From at least 1663 the church bells would be rung, and in the later Stuart period the people of the district would start early and travel to Chillington or Boscobel, where they "adorned themselves in oak leaves and spent the day in outdoor sport". The day was also known as 'Oak Ball Day' to the children of Brewood, and celebrated as a holiday. Children who did not wear sprigs of oakleaves ran the risk of being 'nettled.' A local children's rhyme ran: 'Oak-ball day, the twenty-ninth of May, if you don't give us a holiday, we'll all run away'. In the presence of the schoolmaster and parents, the boys of the village gathered on the green at High Green and divided into two teams. The royalists fixed oak-balls in their caps, the other team represented roundheads. Each team formed into horses and riders, one boy on the back of another, armed with a wooden lance or sword, and battle commenced. The last rider remaining mounted was proclaimed 'King Charlie', and crowned with oak leaves.

November 5th was formerly celebrated in Brewood with a huge bonfire in Market Place, and the old wooden market pump fell victim to the fire on 'Gunpowder Day', 1837.

40. Population

Apart from the four centuries or so of Roman occupation, when the population may have reached several thousand for short periods, the population of Brewood from the earliest times to the present century has been spread more regularly around the parish, demonstrated by the division of the parish in 1834 into eight Liberties or Constablewicks, namely Brewood town, Chillington, Coven, Engleton, Gunstone and the Hattons, Horsebrook, Kiddemore, and Somerford, which maintained their poor jointly but their roads separately.

In the Domesday survey it is possible to arrive at tentative estimates for the population of Brewood, Chillington and Coven as 280, 155 and 45 respectively, giving a total of 490, one of the highest figures in the county. Using actual Domesday figures, it is possible that over 3% of the population of Staffordshire lived in Brewood parish, with 1.8% in Brewood village alone.

In 1298 there were about 30 free tenants and tenants of new land, 29 tenants of burgages, 62 neifs and 36 cottars on the Bishop's manor.[684] In 1327 a subsidy was granted by Parliament to Edward III to meet the expenses of the war with the Scots. The Subsidy Roll[685] records 19 taxpayers in Brewood-cum-membris, including Jordano le Botiler de Nigris Monialibus [Keeper of the Cellar of the Black Nuns], 20 in Chillington, 9 in Horsebrook, 4 in Engleton, 6 in Somerford, 5 in Hatton and 9 in Gunstone, altogether producing £9 8s 5d. Thirteen taxpayers were separately listed in Coven, giving a figure of 85 for the parish, almost 2% of the total of 4,400 for the whole of Staffordshire.

In the Subsidy Roll of 1332-3,[686] 19 people were assessed for tax in Brewood, 18 in Chillington, 9 in Horsebrook, 7 in Somerford, 4 in Engleton and 12 in Hatton and Gunstone combined, producing a total of £8 12s 11d. Coven was listed separately with 11 taxpayers giving a total for the parish of 80. The figures provide some indication of the relative population density, even if population figures cannot be extrapolated precisely, and can be compared with the number of taxpayers recorded elsewhere: 56 at Stafford, 57 at Lichfield, 30 at Wolverhampton [plus 80 cum membris], 62 at Tamworth, 38 at Abbots Bromley and 41 at Rugeley.

The 1377 Poll Tax return for Brewood indicates that there were then 280 inhabitants over the age of 14, although that figure should be taken as a minimum: it seems that in some places up to 20% of taxpayers managed to avoid the tax by disappearing when the tax collectors visited the area. The population of Staffordshire at this date has been estimated at 35,000.

In the Poll Tax assessment of 1380-81,[687] 249 people over the age of 14 are listed in "Brewode, Chilynton, Horsebroke, Engletone, Hatton, Dunston [Gunstone]," and 29 in Coven. The same assessment identifies 15,993 people in the county and the population of England was then probably rather less than three million.

A curious incomplete survey made in 1532-3[688] gives the following population figures: Brewood 94; Chillington 49; Coven 38; Somerford 61; Horsebrook 35; Gunstone 24 – a total of 301.

The Muster Roll of 1538[689] shows 129 men and youths in the parish at that date, with 46 in Brewood, 29 in Chillington, 21 in Coven, 13 in Somerford, 12 in Horsebrook, 6 in Gunstone and 2 in Engleton. A multiplier of 6 or 7 is often used to arrive at a tentative figure for parish population: in the case of Brewood parish a multiplier of 6.5 produces a figure of 840.

Using W.G. Hoskins' formula for assessing population figures [average annual number of births over 10 years x 30] gives figures for Brewood parish of 711 for 1570-9; 949 for 1580-9; and 896 for 1590-9. The parish registers are incomplete for other years, but for 1610-9 produce a figure of 657, and for 1621-9 888. The figures must be taken as a very rough guide only for, apart from any other distorting factors, the registers for the years quoted may be unreliable, but an 'average of the averages' provides a figure for the period 1570-1620 of 820.

In 1666 there were 305 households recorded in the parish with 71 individuals not chargeable, and the Hearth Tax assessment – every fire-hearth and stove within each property was taxed at two shillings per year – of the same year for Brewood Constablewick[690] can be broken down as follows:

Number of hearths		entries	
1	–	131	
2	–	30	
3	–	6	
4	–	6	
5	–	1	
6	–	1	
7	–	0	
8	–	1	
9	–	2	
10	–	1	[Brewood Hall]
15	–	1	[Chillington]
total:		180	households

As a rough guide to population figures, the total entry of hearths is often multiplied by 4.5. Hence Brewood's figure of 297 hearths and 71 individuals indicates a population of about 1400. The Hearth Tax of 1660 had recorded 242 hearths, producing a possible population figure of 1089, but it would be wrong to assume a population increase of some 25% over six years. It would perhaps be safer to take the population of Brewood c.1663 as 1250 or so.

In 1666 Coven had 30 households assessed for Hearth Tax [including the unidentifiable hall house], with 26 individuals not chargeable.

Number of hearths		entries	
1	–	15	
2	–	7	
3	–	4	
4	–	2	
5	–	2	[including one for the hall house]
	total:	30	households.

In about 1680[691] Brewood township had some 60 houses, Coven had 40, Engleton 5 or 6, Gunstone 10, Horsebrook 30, Kiddemore Green 30, with 'a good farm' [Hawkshead or Hogshead House – now The Hawkshutts], and Bishop's Wood was described as 'a little vill beyond Kiddemore Green'. Somerford had 30 houses, and Standeford was described as a vill in Somerford.

In 1691 the Pendeford agronomist William Pitt estimated that locally there were an average of 6 inhabitants per house, and that many of the farmhouses had double that number or more. The situation was almost certainly the same in Brewood.

In 1801, there were 557 inhabited houses in the parish, with 592 families, 24 uninhabited houses, and a population of 2867: 1405 males and 1462 females. 343 people were employed in agriculture, 337 in 'trade, manufacture or handicrafts', and 2167 'others'.

By 1811 Brewood township had 210 inhabited houses with a population of 919. The figures can be broken down further, for 212 families are recorded, 69 employed in agriculture, 87 in 'trade, manufactures, or handicraft', and 56 not engaged in any business. There were 475 males and 516 females. At the same date there were also 578 people living in the liberty of Somerford, 283 males and 295 females.

In 1834, after division into the eight Liberties, Brewood town was described as 'a small but well-built market town, with several good streets and a spacious market place'.

Taking population figures for each of the Liberties and other areas, it is possible to see how movement has occurred over the last three centuries:

Chillington, with 30 houses in c.1680, and a population of perhaps 130, had only five farms in addition to the Hall in 1834, explained by the clearance of Chillington village when the landscaping of the park was carried out in the early 1760's.

Coven, with 40 houses c.1680 and a population of perhaps 180, had a population of 499 in 1831, and by 1851 was 'a large Liberty, with a considerable village', and a population of 650. Its proximity to the Wolverhampton-Stafford road undoubtedly explains its dramatic growth, seemingly at the expense of Brewood.

Engleton, with a handful of houses c.1680, was only 'a small estate' in 1834, and has seen little growth since that date.

310

Gunstone and the Hattons were described in 1834 as adjoining hamlets with four farms and a few cottages, and remain much the same.

Horsebrook was described as 'a small hamlet' in 1834, and the description still holds good.

Kiddemore Green, with 30 houses in c.1680, and described as "a hamlet of scattered houses" in 1834, remains unchanged.

Bishop's Wood, which was in 1724 all waste ground except for a rabbit warren, was described in 1834 as an open common with a few cottages, many of only one storey, built on encroachments upon the waste, but in 1841 had a widely scattered population of 700, in 1844 was enclosed, and is now a sizeable commuter village, with a population of several hundred or more.

Somerford seems to be an example of spectacular growth and rapid decline, undoubtedly associated with the use of Somerford Hall as the main residence of the Monckton family:[692] from a population of some 61 in 1532, perhaps 135 in c.1680, 578 in 1811 [283 males and 295 females], to a small fraction of that number now.

From census returns made every ten years since 1801 [except 1941] it is possible to show the population movement in the parish:

1801	–	2867	1901	–	2535
1811	–	2860	1911	–	2567
1821	–	2762	1921	–	2578
1831	–	3799	1931	–	2960
1841	–	3641	1941	–	[no census]
1851	–	3565	1951	–	3576
1861	–	3399	1961	–	5751
1871	–	3237	1971	–	7239
1881	–	2948	1981	–	7135
1891	–	2667			

The figures show the upsurge in population during the canal-building period of the 1820's – the population figure for 1831 includes 278 men engaged in such work – and the gradual decline towards the end of the century coinciding with the agricultural depression, the removal of the Union Workhouse to Cannock in 1872, and the introduction of mechanization into farming. The transfer of the workhouse poor to Cannock in 1872 is reflected in the figures and the effects of the 1914-1918 war and the terrible influenza epidemic of the same period are also evident. The steep increase between 1951 and 1971, when the population more than doubled, is attributable to the post-war building boom and the rapid growth in the 1960's of large-scale housing development concentrated in Brewood, Coven and Bishop's Wood.

It is interesting to reflect that only in the second half of the twentieth century has the population of Brewood parish reached the probable population level of the various Roman sites to the north of Brewood at their peak.

Population of Brewood Parish 1801-1981

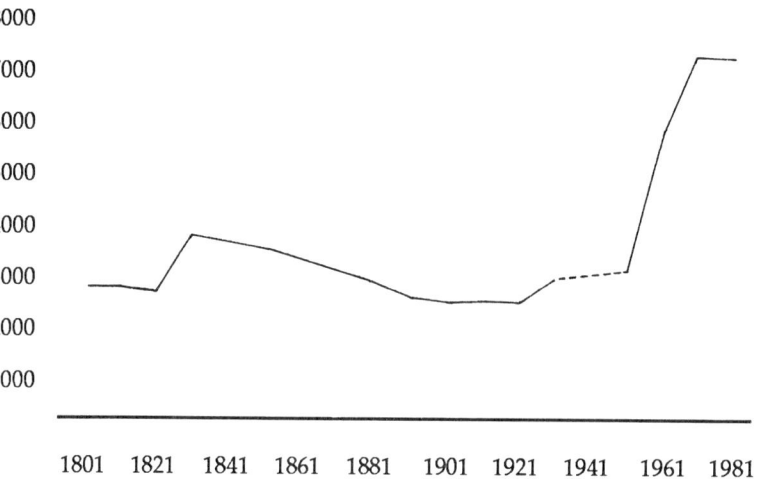

41. Public Accounts

In the sixteenth century the parish or township was made responsible by parliament for the discharge of two aspects of local administration: the relief of the poor and the repair of the roads. Unpaid officials were appointed annually in each parish as Overseers of the Poor, Overseers of the Highways, Churchwardens, and Constables.

Each of these four sets of officers was authorised to levy a rate to finance their work, and all were obliged to keep accounts. For a non-corporate parish like Brewood, the accounts are of particular value, for they are the only official records which give an insight, however fragmentary, into day-to-day affairs within the parish. Between at least 1730 and 1750 Brewood town had two Overseers of the Highways, one for 'High Town' and one for the Deanery. Most of the matters dealt with in the various accounts are of a routine nature, but the more interesting entries from the Constables', Churchwardens' and Overseers' Accounts are given below.[693]

Constables' Accounts:

The Constables were responsible not only for keeping the peace, but for the collection of government tax. Records exist of the election of Constable at the View of Frankpledge held twice-yearly in the manor of Brewood from 1441. The Constables' Accounts for Brewood exist in fragmentary form from 1600, and more completely from 1656 to 1752.

1656	April 14th	Given to John Ponder and Francis Build; their wives; and one childe; who came from Barbadus; having a pass to travel to Warrington[694]	0	0	6
		For carrying them away and discharging the parrish of them	0	0	6
	June 24th	Paid for setting up a pair of shooting butts in Horsebrook		1	4
		Paid for lodging a cripple one night whose name was Anne Harborow and her child and for her dyet	0	1	0
		Paid to the high Constable for the keeping of a childe whose name was Anne Chaseborough		{	8
		whose parents were executed at the Assizes.		{	10

[The offence is not known, but in the eighteenth century there were no less than 975 capital offences.]

| | Sept 2nd | Paid for my presentment of all the Papists | | 1 | 0 |
| | | And for my oaths thereto | | | 4 |

313

			£	s	d
	Sept 14th	Paid for 80 summonses to Papists to appear at Quarter Sessions		6	8

[This entry illustrates both the severity of the penal laws under the Commonwealth, and the low scale of fees for magisterial business, the "summonses" being one penny each.]

			£	s	d
	Sept 18th	Given to Thomas Powers; his wife and 7 children; who came from Sorndwell, with a testimoniall of the loss of all their goods by fire.	0	1	4
		Returning the names of all the Ale Sellers in Brewood to the Excise Office at Penkridge. . . .		1	0
1657	June 12th	For carrying clods and setting up a pair of shooting butts in Brewood		5	0
		My charges to Hilton and Heathill to look for a miller that had got Jane Bursley[695] with child		1	0
		My charges & those that went with me & horse hire to Walshall with Jane Bursley to the house of correction.		3	4
1658	Feb 25th	My charges and presentments at Cannock about the Recusants		1	4
	May 23rd	Paid Mr Launder the money for the new bridge in the Streetway	2	1	8
1659		Given to two companies of Egyptians [gypsies] that had passes[696]		2	0
		Given to a trumpeter, with three others who were maimed, and had a pass under the Lord Protector's seal		1	0
	May 17th	To the High Constable at Penkridge, for charges in defending two suits in law commenced against the Hundred of Cuttlestone, for two robberies done in the same hundred		12	6
1663		For going to Stafford about the books		1	6
		For writing the list of the books to fetch them by		1	0
	April 30th	For going to Stafford to pay for the books, being called God and the King's		1	6
		[These entries remain a mystery]			
		For repairing Brewood shooting butts		1	0
1665	June 12th	Bestowed on them that were charged, and others, to help about the fire in the Dean's End: and on the morrow to carry water with carts		2	0

	Given to a gentleman which had a pass to go from Ireland to London, being sent to me by Mr Walter Giffard, of Chillington	1	0
1665	To the High Constable, for infected persons that were in Cheslin Hay	12	6
1666	To Francis Tisdale, his wife and seven children, who had a pass and the Privy Seal		8
	Payd to Justice Congreve's Clarke for a warrant for ye apprehending and punishing of Thomas Mathews and John Dyther who were apprehended at Kerrimore Green and taken before Justice Congreve.		4
	My charges that day upon ye headburrow [Headborough] of Kerrimore Greene and others to assist me to ye Justices with ye said persons.	1	0
June 24th	Bestowed in Ale upon some neighbours, that were raised in the night to goe to Chillington to meet A company of Strange horsemen which went to White Ladys with A funerall, not then knowing their occasion[697]	1	0
July 27th	For releeving and carrieing 7 cripples to Coven.	2	7
Sept 16th	Given to John Mawburn, with his maid and five children, who had the King's Broad Seal		6
	Payd for writinge an assessment and duplicate and books for ye collection for ye window Tax money	5	6
	Payd ye chargyes for ye assessors of ye window Tax.	4	0
1667	To Katherine Jones coming with a pass from London to travel to Winifred's Well[698] . . .	8	
	To George Whithridge, for going to Stafford to Certify the coroner of the Manner of the death of Nicholas Roe's man	3	0
	To the same, for the sack which he gave to the Coroner	2	0

[presumably Whithridge and the Coroner settled the matter over two shilling's worth of sack, as no inquest appears to have been held over "Nicholas Roe's man."]

| 1668 | [There are many references to expenses arising out of a charge against Thomas Richards for the murder of Humphrey Wood. The outcome of the affair is not known.] | | | |

| 1673 | Given to a seaman having a pass, having but one arm and one eye .... | | | 4 |

| 1674 | Given to Captain Timothy Crow, having an Order to travel under His Majesty's own hand and Privy Seal .... | | 4 | 0 |

1678	My charges and Peter Leadbetter's going to Stafford, the 25th of December, with a papish priest to the goal		6	0
	To the turnkey, for receiving the priest			4
	For hire of a horse to carry the priest			8

[The entry shows that Christmas Day was treated as an ordinary business day. There are many entries for this year, when the Popish Plot caused widespread alarm, relating to "Papishes" and "Papishes' estates", and for "going by command to search for priests". The identity of the priest taken to Stafford is not known.]

1682	For dining with the Bayley of the Hundred		2	6
	For making a new stone bridge at Gunstone	2	10	6
	To Mr. William Mansell, for his charges in seeking to make Standeford Bridge a Hundred bridge	1	2	0

[There are many references to the raising of a hue-and-cry, sadly without details. For example:]

c.1686	For carrying a hueancry to Watereton	0	0	2
	For carrying a hueancry to Coven	0	0	2
	For carrying a hueancry to Horsebrooke	0	0	3
	For carrying another hueancry to Watereton	0	0	2
	For another to Coven	0	0	2

1688	To a leter of request sent to me from Vicar Tomkis, to redeem several slaves out of Turkey		4	6
	For whipping Mary Hollygreen		1	0
	For taking Will Haulle to goal upon suspicion of stealing several horses		6	0
	Allowed John Yates for lodging and relieving 14 passengers one night having with them one horse coming from Ireland with a pass to travel from London.		3	6

1693	To Mr Gudwin, for the man that cutt his		
	throat......................................	14	6
	For fetching Mr Gudwin.....................	1	0
	To John Sayer, for maintaining the man	4	6
	[This alarming incident remains unexplained]		
August 14th	For takeing John Biddle before Mr Vernon. . .	1	0
	For takeing John to ye house of correction. . . .	1	0
1721	For attending and takeing a Tinker to		
	Bridewell [ie gaol].............	5	0

Churchwardens' Accounts

Two Churchwardens were appointed who, with the Vicar, were responsible for the maintenance of the fabric of the church and other incidental matters. The office of Churchwarden would seem to have been suspended during the interregnum, the officers having ceased to be elected in Brewood in 1646 at the end of the incumbency of the Reverend William Chaundler, and the duties were apparently exercised by the 'Constable of the Constablewick of Brewood,' to whom 'lewnes' or levies were granted. The minutes of 4th March 1643 record of Thomas Smith and John Tranter, the outgoing Churchwardens, "that there remains due unto them laid out of their purse over and above the summe of £2 3s., which sum they are contented to get by law or otherwise, of such parties in ye Parish as are behind of their lewnes and other payments." It seems that payments made by Churchwardens before the money had been received were discouraged, and indeed Smith and Tranter may have been acting unlawfully. Further problems seen to have arisen in the early eighteenth century: in 1727 many parishioners signed an objection to the Churchwardens' Accounts for 1725.

1653 The sheet for this year is torn and partly illegible, but references can be deciphered to "maimed soldiers"; to John Carles, for mending chimes and making the dial work; and to a poor minister that preached.

1656 [The following details relate to repairs to the church roof. Similar charges appear at intervals in the accounts until 1759]

To Godman Hosbourne, of Codsall Wood,			
for a thousand of Shingles for the			
Church....................................	2	0	0
To Wm Shorte, of Somerford, for			
carrying them from the farther side			
of Chillington Parke to Brewood		3	0
To Rauph Gaslinge for a piece of timber			
to make a pole for ye laying of ye			
Shingles..................................			8
Beer for those who fetched the ladders and			
helped to rear them			2

To Mr Carter, for nails to the Shinglers		3	8
To the Shinglers	1	3	0
For 400 Shingles more	1	0	0
M Orton for nails for ye shingles		3	8
For two pieces of timber to make spars			
for the south porch		1	4
For a wall-plate for the same		1	0
For work done about the same			8
To the Shinglers more	1	0	0
Bestowed on them when they had			
finished their work			6
To Ralph Gaslynge, for a board to make			
one side of a crest for the south porch		1	0
For great nails for the upper end of the			
spares on the south porch			2
To Christopher Hall, for 10 strikes of lime			
for the repair of the north porch, and for			
pointing the leads and other places about			
the church		3	8
For 300 tiles for the north porch		6	0
To George Swan, for nailing and pointing			
the leads, and for tiling the north porch			
and other work		9	9
For tenpenny nails for the leads, and			
lath nails for the north porch			8
To the Sexton, for sweeping and carrying			
dust forth of ye church, after the			
Shinglers and Masons had finished			
their work			6
To John Harris for amending ye clapper			
of ye third bell		1	0
For a bell rope		2	8
For ye Oyle for Bells			8
Payd to John Warrington for a new Wheele			
for ye second bell.		15	0
Charges bestowed of him in bargaining with			
him to make ye said wheele, and also when he			
brought it, and those that helped up with it.			8

[In this year and many successive years there are regular quarterly payments of £1 3s 4d for maimed soldiers.]

Given to John Warner, of little Saredon, who			
had his home and goods burnt by fire		5	0
For bread and wine for a Sacrament	1	4	6
To Francis Newball, for looking to the			
chimes		10	0

318

Payd to Francis Nowhall, for 2 journeys one to bring part of the clock to be amended at Tonge, and ye other to Penkridge to fetch wine for ye sacrament........................		1	0
To John Baddeley, of Tonge, for amending ye clock and three journeys coming..............		8	10
Payd Jane Wilkes for two journeys to Penkridge one to helpe her father carry the wine, and ye other to bring home ye wine bottles...................................			8
For wine for a private Sacrament, at Brewood Hall..................................		1	0
For the minister's dinners that preached one lecture day...............................		2	0
To Jane Wilkes, for ridding the graves........			4

1663	To ye ringers on May ye 29th for ringing in honour of his blessed Majesty's most gracious restoration..........................		3	0
1667	To Jane Bursley, for watering ye yew trees in ye churchyard........................			2

[this would indicate recent planting, and suggests the possible age of the existing trees.]

For 12 quarts of wine at the Cock, at Wolverhampton...........................	1	4	0
For going to Hampton[699] to exchange the flagon.......................................		1	0
In exchange of the flagon...................		1	6

[In this and succeeding years there are occasional payments of 1s each for foxes heads, and very frequent payments of 2d each for hedgehog heads. In 1556 Churchwardens were made responsible by law for the destruction of vermin, and with the assistance of six local men were required to raise a parish rate to reward parishioners according to a fixed scale. Animals "locally classed as vermin" might be included – hedgehogs, polecats, foxes and so on – the heads of which "shall be . . . in the presence of the Churchwardens . . . burned, consumed or cut asunder." In 1667 nearly 100 hedgehogs are paid for, and in 1671 the number is 210]

1677	Paid for stopping out the jackdaws..........		3	4
	To the Plummer for mending the leads.....	1	15	0
	My charges at Lichfield, seeing for a minister to give the Sacrament..............		3	6
1698	Paid W. Pendrell for 3 foxheads.............		3	0
	Paid Richard Lloyd for a foxhead............		1	0
	Paid John Jones for 5 hedgehogs.............			10

| | | Paid Richard Yates for 3 hedgehogs . . . . | | 6 |
| | | Paid Elizabeth Wilkes for washing ye surplis, and ye other things and scouring ye plate for ye whole year . . . . | 3 | 6 |

In 1698 is the first charge for "processioning", or walking the bounds of the parish. A considerable amount of alcohol seems to have been consumed. Similar charges for processioning occur at irregular intervals.

| 1716 | Feb 12th | Ringing for news . . . . | 4 | 0 |
| | Mar 8th | For ringing again . . . . | 2 | 6 |

[It has been suggested that "the news" was the final suppression of the Jacobite Rebellion]

1720		For a form of prayer about the plague	2	6
		For the old clark's debts	11	0
1727		For wine for communicants in the sickness. . .	13	9
		To a man, with two wooden legs and a pass		6
1728	June 20th	Paid to the ringers for the King's birthday	5	0
1738		For killing two owls [presumably within the church]		6
		To the Rev Mr Budworth	1 0	0
		To the same, for copying the Register	10	0
1739		For four owls	2	0

[Foxes and owls are frequently recorded for many subsequent years. Owls nesting within the church were a constant nuisance in early times, and their connection with the church in Brewood has a permanent record: the first of the parish registers, dating from 1562 but recopied in 1603, commences with an ornamental capital letter, on one of the scrolls of which is drawn a small owl.]

| 1742 | | Payd two men one night to watch ye churchyard bye ye parson's door. . . . . | 2 | 0 |

[one would like to know more about this cryptic entry.]

| 1795 | Nov 5th | Payd ye ringers for Gunpowder Treason . . . . | 9 | 2 |

Overseers' Accounts

For the parish of Brewood four Overseers of the Poor were annually elected in vestry, one for each of the 'four quarters', or Liberties, of Coven, Brewood town, Chillington and Somerford, and separate accounts were kept for each, until a uniform rate was adopted for the whole parish in the nineteenth century. The Overseers Accounts relating to Brewood commence in 1662, cover the period until 1756, and are almost complete.

The entries are generally of a routine nature of no great interest, but include:

Year	Description	£	s	d
1662	For going to Wrottesley with Mr Fowke, of Gunston, in the behalf of the parish		1	0
	Spent at Codsall to make Mr Fowke to drink			4
1675	To the minister for burying Jackson's child			6
	To the clark			6
	To the gravemaker			4
	For ale		1	0
1688	George Sansom paid to three passengers for lodgings and victuals, going with a pass from London to Ireland		1	6
1717	My charges for going to Basscobell [sic] to Mr Pendrill's		1	0
1724	Given Widd. Duffeilde in Sicknes.	0	3	1
	Widd. Duffeild now in need.	0	3	0
	pd for her Shroud.	0	2	6
	pd for attending Widd. Duffeild	0	4	0
	pd to the Minister for her funerall	0	0	10
	pd to the Clerke	0	0	10
	pd to the Sexton	0	0	6
	given to the Neighbours for carrying her	0	1	0
1729	[The following are a physician's charges:]			
	For curing Old Duncalf's leg		10	0
	For curing Hipwood's rib, and physic for his fever	1	0	10
	For dressing Lyon's girl's back. [after whipping?]		5	0
	For curing old Davis's daughter of a dropsy		6	6
	For physic for Pott's wife in her illness		3	0

[The following entries relate to an appeal tried at Stafford. The nature of the subject is not known.]

Year	Description	£	s	d
1734	Expended at Michaelmas Session, in defence of the parish against William Harla's appeal:			
	At Brewood on the witnesses		1	0
	And at Penkridge		1	0
	At Stafford before dinner, 16 persons, at 4d each		5	4

			£	s	d
		Paid Counsellor Littleton's fee	1	1	0
		And Mr Swingfield Jarvice	1	1	0
		For 16 persons' dinner, 1s 6d each	1	4	0
		Expenses after dinner, 6d each		8	0
		For 3 Subpoenas - the rest of the witnesses coming without		3	0
		Meat and drink at supper, sixpence each		8	0
		The same for each at breakfast		8	0
		Sixteen dinners for the second day		16	0
		Expenses after dinner		8	0
		Paid the Court fees		4	4
		For a sheet of stamped paper to take the security upon		1	7
		Paid for horsehire, 7 horses, 2 days each, at 1s a day		14	0
		For their hay and corn		8	6
		Given to the servants at the inn		2	0
		The Solicitor's charges during the Sessions, ordinary and extraordinary		1	10
1745	May 18th	Paid the Governour [of the workhouse] and monthly bills	1	15	3¼
		paid for hemp and provisions for the work	1	3	5
		A load of Coals to the workhouse	0	14	0
		pd for repairing Engleton bridges	0	5	10
		pd towards the Governours Sallary and for teaching the Children to read	0	4	0
	Dec 28th	pd for 2 pair of second hand shoes to the Workhouse		1	4
1748	October	Pd to Mr Mayo for bringing the Madwoman Down		11	6

[The following entries give an indication of prices:]

			£	s	d
1746		3 strike of pease[700]		8	0
		3 strike of corn		6	9
		3 strike of blend corn		8	11
		6 new cheeses		5	0
		144 lbs of bacon, at 3½d	2	2	0
		72 lbs of beef, at 1d		6	0
		3 horse loads of coals		4	0
1747		136 lbs of beef		11	0
		60 lbs of cheese		10	6
1756		31 lbs of beef, at 1¾d		4	6
		2 lbs of butter, at 4¾d			9½

a calf's race			10
a pint of ale and a loaf			2½
a leg of beef			10
126 lbs of beef, at 1¼d		13	0½
3 strike of potatoes		6	0
10 strike of corn	3	6	8
a sheep		3	8
a bushel of salt		4	0
a bushel of oatmeal		7	0

[A few entries from 1756 and 1757:]

Paid the tailor, a day's work		6
Paid old Povey for teaching school		1½
For ale for old Phebe		2
For a pair of spectacles for Dan Harley		5
For half a pint of wine for old Phebe		3½
Paid Jerry Etheridge, for two pairs of shoes	9	6
For a clog for Richard Leek		8
For 25 cwt of coals	12	6
For 2 lbs of tobacco	2	0

42. Wells and Well Dressing

In 1686, Dr Plot records:

> They have a custom in this county, which I have observed on Holy [i.e.
> Maundy] Thursday, at Brewood and Bilbrook, of adorning their wells with
> boughs and flowers. This, it seems, they do, too, at all the Gospel places,
> whether wells, trees or hills; which being now observed only for decency
> and custom's sake is innocent enough. Heretofore, too, it was usual to pay
> their respects to such wells as were eminent for curing distempers, on the
> saint's day whose name the well bore, diverting themselves with cakes and
> ale, and a little music and dancing; which, whilst within these bounds, was
> also an innocent recreation. [701]

It is readily apparent that Plot was writing under noticeably Puritan
influences. In 1728 it was recorded that in former times "the people, and
those not of the meaner sort only, placed a sanctity in [the wells], bought
Alms and offerings to them, and made vows at them. . ." A writer to 'The
Gentleman's Magazine' in 1794 mentions well-dressing at Brewood and
Bilbrook at that date, and there is evidence that the custom was still
being observed as late as 1882.[702]

Worship of wells and springs is known to have existed in the Celtic
period, and formed a major aspect of Iron Age religion. The famous temple
complex around the hot springs at Bath owes its origins not to the Romans,
but to the Iron Age, as shown by Celtic finds. In Saxon times well-worship
was known as 'Weill-weorthung', and although attempts were made by
the early Anglican church to curb the practice, it continued in many places
until fairly recent times, and well-dressing is carried out even to this day,
particularly in Derbyshire. It is uncertain which wells in Brewood were
decorated, or the precise nature of their decoration. There is no evidence
that the dressings took the form of flower petals pressed into damp clay to
form pictures or designs, as in Derbyshire, and the decorations at Brewood
would almost certainly have been the more usual flowers and green
branches, as observed by Plot.

Curious attractions in Brewood parish were the two sulphur wells, one
[formerly eight feet deep] on the south side of the dam of the Great Pool in
Chillington Park and the other, known as the Leper Well, in a field at
Gunstone near Leper House Farm. A third well may have existed at
Stinking Lake, near Watling Street, north of Blackladies: the evidence is
not strong, but the very name suggests a sulphurous spring.[703] The Leper
Well, now protected as a scheduled monument, lies at the junction of Lower
Keuper sandstone and Keuper marl, and takes the form of a shallow
eliptical brick-lined pool some 7' 2" wide, 6' 2" broad and four or five feet
deep, with sandstone benches set internally around the perimeter some 3

feet from the upper edge. Six sandstone steps lead into the water on the east side, and an oak sump or drain appears to have been built into the north wall. The brickwork suggests that the present structure probably dates from the eighteenth century. A decaying alder tree grows out of the western side of the well.

The Leper Well, photographed during cleaning c.1982

From these wells [another existed at Codsall Wood],[704] which are more properly springs, was drawn the sulphurous water traditionally taken as a remedy for leprosy, and a lazarhouse, or house for lepers, is thought to have existed on or near the site of Leper House Farm. The extent of leprosy in the Middle Ages is difficult to calculate, for diagnosis was uncertain and it was doubtless confused with other diseases such as impetigo, scrofula, lepra, lupus, tuberculosis, erysipelas, or even veneral disease. Leprosy is caused by an organism found in nasal secretions and saliva, and transmitted by close contact. In medieval times the long-term consumption of rotten and putrid meat and fish was a likely predisposing factor. The drastic but unhelpful treatments included bleeding and branding with a hot iron. The earliest leper hospitals date from the eleventh century, and by the thirteenth century some 200 existed in England, usually sited well away from residential centres: a field known as Lazarus between Ivetsey Road and Bellhurst Farm at Wheaton Aston may have been the site of one such house. At the height of its spread as many as one person in 200 may have been a leper, and under the statute De Leproso Amovendo those affected were treated as outcasts, but by the end of the fifteenth century leprosy had virtually disappeared except in the extreme north and west.

Typically, a chapel was located near a leper hospital, but there is no evidence, either documentary, physical or in early field names, to show the existence of such a building near the Brewood Leper Well. The name Leper House Close for the field to the west of Leper Well may suggest that any leper house stood to the south of the lane. The first known reference to lepers in Brewood is in the name 'the lepre house,' recorded in 1597.[705] Plot records[706] the use of the water for the treatment of scabs and itch in both humans and animals: "They commonly drink about 3 quarts at a time", lesser quantities apparently proving inneffective. It was also said to have been used by the local inhabitants for brewing and boiling meat. Although Plot mentions in particular a well at Codsall Wood, a close reading of his report and a later reference to the nearby Leper-house suggests that the well he describes may in fact be the Leper Well. He records that the water was comparatively clear, and that in about 1650 some intrigued investigators dug nearby and uncovered "a sort of mineral Earth that crash't in the boaring [as some described it] like rotten wood; which being carried to London was found to be sulphurous . . ." It seems that the superstitious country people attributed the well to the devil, who was believed to supply the sulphur from his subterranean kingdom. A villager who lived at the Leper House c.1880 stated that the well was used for bathing, with men and women using it on different days.[707] Earlier in the last century the water is said to have been bottled and sent to London and other places. The water has no evidence of being sulphurous today.

In 1871 Mr Daniel Jones read a paper to a meeting of the Midland Institute of Mining, Mechanical and Civil Engineers in which he suggested that the sulphur springs at Codsall and Chillington had their source at the surface about four miles to the east, near the junction of the coal deposits with the permian, with the water sinking beneath the permian and percolating through coal and pyrites to become charged with sulphur, then rising in a fault between the permian and the surface. That the sulphurous water did not come from the alluvium or drift at the higher levels seemed to him evident from the fact that nearby wells supplied pure water. Evidence that the sulphur did not originate from the sandstone beneath the surface was the artesian well which penetrated 265' into the sandstone at Cosford which was free from sulphur. Conclusive proof, he suggested, was provided by two springs at Adbaston in Shropshire: one was saline, the other sulphurous.[708] Sulphur deposits are formed by the chemical reaction of the two gases hydrogen sulphide and sulphur dioxide released as a result of volcanic processes deep within the Earth, and the theory may well be correct.

It is doubtless no more than coincidence that the Roman roads from Pennocrucium changes direction slightly at Ackbury Heath, one on an alignment which would take it close to the Leper Well, and it would be mere speculation to suggest a link between the well and the religious significance of wells and water to the Celtic natives, although it is of interest that the well lies between two ancient villages – Bilbrook and Brewood – both of which have Celtic elements in their names and are known to have practised well-dressing, but are well away from other well-dressing areas – indeed, they are the only places connected with well-dressing mentioned by Plot in the whole of Staffordshire – and that the Leper House itself is called The Corch on a Chillington estate map of 1761, cors being the Welsh word for bog or marsh.

It should be added that there was another spring of some fame on the parish and county boundary on the west side of the road from Boscobel to Bishops Wood, some 150 yards south of Offoxey crossroads, the site formerly marked by an ancient weeping ash.[709] The spring was formerly known as Lunt's Well or Lady Isabella's Well, but called the Wishing Well by local people, and fed a stream called the Ladies Brook which flowed through Pearse Hay to The Hawkshutts. Its history and the reasons for its name are lost in antiquity, although there may be a connection with Isabella, the first recorded prioress of Blackladies, or Dame Isabella Launder, prioress of Blackladies at the time of the dissolution.[710] The spring was capped in brickwork in about 1982.

From at least 1727, before Bath Farm was built, a 'cold bath' lay close to the road south of Coldham, but nothing further is known about it.

Until the 1950's a public well existed in Brewood at the east side of the junction of The Pavement and Dean Street, set into a brick wall. The well, with a hinged iron lid and iron bucket, was repaired at the expense of Mr W.T.C. Giffard in 1896. No trace now remains. Another well in the grass triangle to the south of Rambler Cottage in Sparrow's End Lane was said to be disused and dangerous in 1907, and was filled in soon afterwards.

Water in Bishops Wood was difficult to obtain because of its height, but in addition to the above supply villagers used a well at Acorn Cottage, a spring at the southern end of the bridle path off Old Weston Road, and a spring on the east side of the field gate adjoining the Old School. Two steps led down to it, but having become neglected and overgrown it was covered over in recent years. The semi-detatched cottages to the east are known as Springfield Cottages. A well at Hawkshutts is said to be 95' deep.

Two springs on the east side of Park Lane supplied water in that area.

43. Bells and Bellringing

From the earliest times church bells were used by way of warning or celebration, and life in the medieval period was regulated by the ringing of the church bells, the only means by which villagers could know the time. A fine was payable if the parish authorities failed to ring the church bells when the reigning monarch passed through the parish, although it is not known whether the Brewood bells were rung when Elizabeth I visited Chillington in 1575. Three shillings was paid to the bellringers of Brewood in 1663 and 2s 6d in 1677 to mark the restoration of Charles II on 29th May, and in 1698 2s 6d for "ringing upon ye King's birthday." In 1715 and other years payments were made for "ringing Queen Anne's birthday." The ringers were paid 2s 6d to celebrate St George's Day in 1677.

The great bell was rung from about 1625 between 8 am and 9 am on Good Friday and the feast of St James [25th July], the days when doles were distributed to the poor.[711]

The parish accounts for 1735 contain an entry: "Paid Harlow for ringing ye corfeu bells, 6s." The custom of ringing the Curfew Bell at dusk was honoured in a number of Staffordshire parishes, but the origin is obscure. Traditionally, it was first imposed by William the Conqueror upon the Saxons to prevent seditious meetings under cover of darkness by the disaffected people. The word curfew itself is Norman in origin, deriving from 'couvre-feu', meaning to cover up the fire and put out the lights. The custom may well pre-date even the Normans, for there was a practice in King Alfred's reign to ring a bell for regulating the hours of labour, not unlike the Angelus bell, and it seems probable that the bell was no more than a reminder that all fires and lights should be extinguished to avoid disastrous accidents. At Brewood, the evening curfew bell was tolled in the winter months from Allhallowmas [November 1st] to Candlemas [February 2nd] for about 15 minutes, commencing at 8 pm each evening, and the great bell was then tolled the number of the day of the month. The amount paid to the bellringer was long considered a parish expense, and the custom was only stopped in 1872 because the then Vicar is reported to have felt that the charge could not be justified for 'a stupid old relic of English feudalism', Mary Daw being one of the last ringers.

In medieval times, all churches rang bells on Shrove Tuesday morning to remind parishioners to to come to confession ['shriving'] before Lent began. Confession went out with the Reformation, but the pre-Lenten carnival atmosphere of the day continued, as did the custom of eating pancakes and, in many places, Brewood included, bellringing. The ringing of the 'Pudding Bell' for a quarter of an hour before 11 am on Shrove Tuesday had been discontinued in Brewood by 1874.

From at least November 1902 the bells chimed for ten minutes before service on Sundays, and again for ten minutes after a break of five minutes, then the first bell was rung for five minutes.[712]

The festivities on 5th November included the inevitable ringing of the church bells, for the parish accounts regularly record that in the eighteenth century, 9s 2d was: 'Payd ye ringers for Gunpowder Treason', and similar payments were made on the same date for many years after.

When the commissioners of Edward VI visited Brewood church in 1553 there were four bells: a sanctus bell and three sacring bells. In 1638 "3 whole lewnes [levies] were laid out and levied for and towards the payment of a new Bell lately provided by the said Churchwardens for the use and service of the Church." This was probably the existing great bell.

In 1889 there was a ring of seven bells [which did not include a bell added in 1638], and there are now nine, eight recast from the metal of the old bells [none seemingly original] in 1896 by J. Taylor & Co., of Loughborough [the bequest of Charles Docker of The Deanery] with the marks reproduced, including:

Mr Richd. Fowler Vicer. Jas Barber & Thos Hickin, Ch:wardens. Lester & Packe, of London, fecit. 1761. [29" diameter]

Henry Bagley made mee 1692. [31" diameter]

AMBROUS [three bells and a coronet in a shield]

M.M.T. [2 hounds passant]. [33" diameter. A further indecipherable inscription also appears on this bell. It would seem that the lettering is the mirrored image of JOHN + GIFFARD. The shield has been identified as that of the Norfolk Bell Founders.]

Mr John Moss Vicar, Mr Richard Jordan & Thomas Handcocks Churchwardens 1734. [36½" diameter]

"TE DUEM LAUDAMUS 1585. [with initialls H.O., now identified as Henry Oldfield, who helped to cast "Great Tom" in Lincoln Cathedral]. [39" diameter]

VENI CREATOR SPIRITUS. MENTES TUORUM VISITO. [43" diameter]

A small bell long disused weighing about ¼cwt and dated 1767 was rehung in 1930.

In the belfry is a board on which are painted the following rules:

THE RINGERS RULES
Ye gentlemen ringers both far and near
That are disposed to ring here
To mark this law and keep it well
The man that overthrows his Bell
Sixpence forfeit he must pay
Before he goes hence away.

329

He that ring with Glove, Spur, or Hat
Sixpence he must pay for that
If he either curse or swear
Sixpence must pay while you are here
Tis not a place to quarrel in
To curse and swear it is a sin.
J. BREWSTER.   W. ICKE.
Churchwardens 1846

Bellringers will be interested to know that on 21st April 1901 a peal of Stedman triples, 1260 changes was rung in 47 minutes on the occasion of the incumbancy of the Rev C. Dunkley. On 27th May 1901 a peal of Stedman triples, 5040 Thurstans, was rung in 3 hours 3 minutes, and on 23rd April 1921 Thurstans one part peal of Stedman triples, 5040 changes, was rung to commemorate the twentieth anniversary of the Vicar's institution.

A remarkable hand-bell peal took place on 24th February 1912, when 5040 changes of doubles in ten methods was accomplished by John Perry, 1-2-3; Thomas Perry, 4-5-6. Two sets of handbells are still held within the church, one with the maker's mark JT.

44. Nonconformity

As early as 1736 Joseph Mountford had obtained a licence for his house at Crateford to be used by Protestant Dissenters. George Whitefield's preachers were in Brewood in 1745, and a convert was George Burder, the first recorded nonconformist preacher in the village. He later became a prominent congregational minister, and it is said that on one occasion while preaching in a barn in Brewood in 1777, a noisy crowd outside disrupted the service by banging on the doors and thowing stones through the window. It seems likely that local nonconformity was boosted by John Wesley, who preached at Wolverhampton and Bilbrook in 1761, 1764, 1770 and 1772, when his audiences doubtless included many from Brewood and the surrounding area. Until 1800 preaching in Brewood was conducted by casual preachers, but in that year John Simpson, verger and clerk to the parish church, obtained a certificate to preach at a cottage, having left the established church after a disagreement with the absentee Vicar, Thomas Muchall. Muchall lived at Longdon, near Rugeley, where he was also curate, driving by carriage to Brewood for Sunday services and residing at the Swan Inn. Simpson held services at the cottage with the assistance of two preachers from Wolverhampton, and on 3rd May 1803 a Congregational chapel[713] built in Sandy Lane at the expense of Simpson's brother-in-law, James Neale of St Paul's Churchyard, London, was opened.[714]

From about 1806 Brewood became a centre for mission work by students from Hackney College, who, during the summer vacation, conducted open air services in the neighbourhood. Gospel Meadow in Coven which lay on the north bank of the Penk on the west of the village, adjoining the Brewood road, may have been connected with such services.[715] The Sandy Lane chapel was enlarged in 1825, and rebuilt in 1842, but a planned small graveyard behind came to nothing, although it is said that the housekeeper of one minister was buried there, in the garden of The Manse. The chapel seated 275, with accomodation for 120 others. Services at the chapel had ceased by 1940, and the building, which had fallen into disrepair, was demolished in August 1963 and the site used for housing. The chapel was a substantial red-brick building with round-headed windows and tall front gable with stepped sides and a segmental head, and had fitted galleries internally. The central entrance was approached up steps on the east and west.

A number of houses in Brewood were licensed for dissenters' meetings, probably Methodist, including in 1800 that of Joseph Underhill [Congregationalist], 1822 Humphrey Webb, 1824 Thomas Leek, 1826 John Beaumont, 1840 Richard Wakelain, and 1851 John Thomas and Edward Blakemore.

The Wesleyan chapel in School Road, Brewood, a small brick building, now colour-washed, has a date stone showing that it was built in 1868, and in the 1940's seated 120 worshippers.

A house of William and George Holland certified as a meeting house in March 1831 was probably used by Primitive Methodists, since William, a plate lock maker in the village, was manager of the Primitive Methodists twenty years later, when small meetings were held in a house in Shop Lane. A chapel to accomodate 80 worshippers was built on the west corner of Shop Lane and Pendryl Avenue in 1858, but had closed before the turn of the century. The brick building was single storey, with the gable facing Shop Lane having a flat canopy on scrolled supports over a central doorway flanked by two round-headed windows. It was later used as a carpenter's shop and coffin makers, and by 1956 had been demolished. Pendryll Avenue was created at some date after 1884.

A branch of the Salvation Army was founded in Brewood in Victorian times, but had ceased to exist by 1895, after which date a Band of Hope which met in the Institute in Sandy Lane seems to have been well attended for many years.

In 1826 a chapel for Protestant Dissenters at Coven was registered by John Bell. This was the Weslyan Methodist chapel, which was rebuilt in 1839 at a cost of £340. There is a local tradition that Methodist meetings were also held on the upper floor of John Smith's iron foundry. The building of a Sunday School was started in 1914, but due to the war it was not completed until 1925. It cost £1503.

45. The Devil

Several places in Brewood are [or were] connected by name with the devil: Clay Gates,[716] at Engleton, on the course of the Roman road which crosses the Penk at Somerford Bridge, was also known as Hell Gates, and Hell Floor [where local tradition says ghosts have been seen[717]] lies between The Hyde and Chillington Upper Avenue – a short distance from the same Roman road, which is aligned close to the Leper Well. The two names are of interest, for the Old English word 'heall' means rock or stone, and the word 'gate' can mean an opening or a road – often a Roman   road – hence 'paved Roman road'; and the word 'floor' was often applied to places where Roman tesselated pavements have been discovered: 'the mosaic floor.' On the other hand, the antiquity of the names is uncertain [although Hell Floor is recorded in 1867] and the former may have been simply a contemptuous fairly recent nickname for the two cottages opposite the drive to Engleton Hall Farm, which were also known as The Pepperpots. The eighteenth century high-arched brick footbridge on the east side of Somerford Mill was known locally as Devil's Bridge. A field name Hell Moor has been recorded, and a field adjoining the south side of the stream between Kiddemore Green and The Whitemoor was called The Devil's Horn,[718] probably from its poor soil and shape.[719] There is also evidence that some cottages in Brewood were formerly known as Hell Cottages:[720] their location is now uncertain, but they may have been the cottages on the corner of Ivy House Lane and the lane running west to Horsebrook which have been known locally for .many years as the Boot and Shoe, doubtless because they lie at Cobblers Bank.

The names may be associated with a traditional but unexplained rhyme from Brewood:

Blymhill Lawn where the devil was born
Wheaton Aston where he was Christened
Weston where he learned his lesson
Church Eaton where he was beaten
Watling Street Road where he took up his abode
Ivetsey Bank where he drank
Bishops Wood where he stood
Boscobell where he fell
Gailey Pool where he was called a fool
Langley where he was angry
Pearce Hay where he was sent away
Kiddemore Green where he was seen
Hungry Hill where he took a pill
Bargate where he ate
Brewood where he was shoed

Giffard's Cross where he lost his horse
Horsebrook where he lost his pluck
Tong where he was hung
Coven where he was put in the oven
Stretton where he was eaten
Chillington Hall where he was finished off bones and all
Boscobell where he was sent to hell.[721]

46. The Parish Boundary

We do not know how the English parish originated. The word comes from the pagan Roman Empire, where it meant a large region or province, and in England came to mean the area marked out to provide support to, and be served by, the parish church. The boundary of Brewood parish is of uncertain age, but in the main is certainly pre-Domesday, and probably much older still: it is now recognised that in many cases parish boundaries perpetuate land units which are pre-Roman, or even pre-Celtic, giving formal ecclesiastical, and thus legal, recognition to boundaries of great antiquity. When originally established, parish boundaries invariably utilised physical features of the landscape, although such features are not always apparent today.

It is significant that Roman roads generally appear to have been adopted as parish boundaries in areas where there was little pre-Roman settlement, and the use of Watling Street as the northern boundary of Brewood parish suggests that the Roman road may have been the first significant feature in the development of the local landscape: such roads seem to have been ignored in areas where settlement can be shown to pre-date the Roman era. No nearby parishes to the east or west take Watling Street as their boundary. The inference may be that Brewood was one of the later estates, probably created at some date in the Saxon period, although it is not inconceivable that it is based on the estate of the Roman villa at Engleton, which may in turn have had Iron Age origins.

Boundaries of early parishes tend to run uninterruptedly between one landmark and another, suggesting that they were fixed when there was still uncultivated areas and boundaries could be laid out without the need to take account of existing rights to particular patches of arable. Jagged boundaries, such as that on the west of the parish which is also the county border, suggest that the bounds had to accomodate pre-existing cultivated land, and it is possible that the pronounced right-angle to the west of Chillington is connected with the nearby Roman site at Wigmore Wood.

The earliest reference to the parish boundary is in a Saxon Charter of 994[722] containing boundary clauses for the estates of Hilton and Featherstone, the latter adjoining Brewood, which enables a fragment of the Brewood boundary to be identified: ". . . from Brenes ford along the road to Lece brook . . ." Brenesford survives in the name Brinsford, within Brewood parish, and the road mentioned is almost certainly an Anglo-Saxon road which ran from Standeford to Wednesfield along the approximate line of the Roman road which ran south east from Pennocrucium. Lece brook, or boggy brook, is the origin of the place name The Laches, and is followed by the parish boundary for over a mile. The Featherstone boundary then leaves the Brewood boundary and turns south-east. The Brewood boundary to the south takes an erratic course until it meets the river Penk north of Pendeford, where the river and its tributary, Moat Brook, mark the greater part of the southern boundary.

Weston-under-Lizard, called in early records Weston-under-Brewood, [and later Weston Hugh's, or Weston Hewes, after an early occupier,[723] to distinguish it from other 'west towns' in the area] was seemingly part of the parish until the thirteenth century, but is now a separate parish. The north-western corner of the parish boundary follows for a short distance a stream which rises at Bishop's Wood and joins Whiston Brook at Longnor Hall. Coven Heath and Brinsford were incorporated after boundary reorganisations in 1934, transferred from Bushbury in Seisdon hundred, increasing the area of Brewood parish from 12,152 acres to 12,517 acres.

The earliest recorded description of the complete parish boundary is found in a parliamentary survey of Brewood made during the Civil War in 1646:

> From the Bleu Bell in Watling Street and so eastward to New Bridge, then to Smalbroke Meer, a House called the Heath, and so upwards by that water to a way leading to Wolverhampton, and so thro' a piece of land of Mr Morton's called little moor and so downwards to Hoghay. Southward, then to a brook called Saybrook, and so down that water to Stainford Bridge, So to a meadow called Kimble, where a Brook meets Saybrook pinke, so to Church bridge and so a cross the water parting to Acton's Mill, then westward to Roodford, so up that water near unto Gunston to a footbridge leading towards Codsall called Gunston Bridge: from thence up to the Water side to a Leasowe called Wood Leasowing in the holding of John Smith, then to a lane that leads towards Codsall Woods and so compassing all the lawn called Langley Lane and so to Spicer House, and from thence unto Baskable Gate, and then to Pearce Hayside to Bishops Wood then to Charters Mires, the bounds upon the west being Shropshire; by Charters Mires by a little smal water that leads to Stinking Lake in Watling Street, from thence to the Bleu Bell, being the First Stage, allowing half the street way to the Bounds of the said Manor.[724]

The custom of beating the bounds on Ascension Day evolved during the reign of Elizabeth I from the older ceremonies of Rogationtide, known as 'Gang Days', i.e. 'going' or 'walking' days, which had been banned since the Reformation after becoming disorderly. Primarily a religious ceremony, beating the bounds was also used to preserve the limits of the parish boundary into the minds of children and illiterate villagers in the days when maps were inaccurate and rare, and the parish boundaries were of importance in the adminstration of the Poor Laws. 'Bumping' children at particular points was customary, and will be seen to have taken place during the perambulations of Brewood.

The next specific reference to the perambulation of Brewood parish would seem to date from 1698, when the Churchwardens' Accounts include a charge for 'Processioning', presumably to cover the cost of alcoholic refreshment, of which a considerable quantity seems to have been consumed, although the claim to extra-parochiality by Blackladies included references in about 1680 to earlier traditional perambulations of the boundaries of Brewood. Similar charges appear in the Accounts at irregular intervals, but the earliest detailed report of a perambulation dates from 1838. On 25th and 26th May, William Icke and Robert Walker, churchwardens, and Thomas Mills and Hugh Mellor, Overseers, accompanied by Mr Birk of Horsebrook and perhaps others, walked the bounds. The following is taken from a manuscript account of the perambulation:

Started from the Blue Bell [now The Bell, on Watling Street], on Friday morning, at ten o'clock, along the road for Stinking Lake; where it becomes the boundary between Lapley and Brewood, and then up the said brook, between Blymhill and Brewood, to road from Bishop's Wood to Ivetsey Bank; the bridge there belongs to Brewood; followed the brook to the road leading from Bishop's Wood to Blymhill: the bridge here belongs to Blymhill; along the bottom of the gardens joining Lord Bradford's and Mr Stubbs's land to the commencement of Tong, near the beer-shop known by the name of the Royal Oak; thence through the croft belonging to Mr Vaughton [sic] to Lady Isabella's Well, where the road is the boundary, the road belonging to Brewood; up to Boscobel, and then along the garden fence of Boscobel House through the Old Coppice to Donnington, and along the Donnington Lane to the road leading from Boscobel to Codsall Wood, walking the garden held by William Wright, and all the road and trees into Brewood parish, and along the fence between Donnington and Brewood to Salter's Cottage; then walked the fence adjoining Lord Shrewsbury's land, and so into the road; walked along the Deer's Leap (16 feet), Chillington Park Wall, through Johnstone's gardens, Matthewson's and Lawrence's Leasowes along Cockshutts into the lane leading from Codsall Wood to Gunstone; then across the fields of Mr Wilk's farm, as marked out by stones put down in the fences, and at the bend of the fences again into the lane, and along the outside of the lane to the fence between Mr Giffard's land and the field belonging to Mr Morris, along which to the brook, which brook is the boundary to the foot-bridge at Gunstone, where a piece, beyond the present brook, belongs to Brewood; the brook continues the boundary until near the bridge, on the road leading from Brewood to Bilbrook, where a piece of land, lying in Mr Jone's field, belongs to Codsall parish; the brook is the boundary from the place down to the land belonging to Edward Monckton, Esq., at Coven Lawn.[725]

Unfortunately, the manuscript is incomplete, and the account of the second day's walk is now lost.

The earliest complete account of a perambulation dates from 1861:

This ceremony commenced, agreably to notice, from the Bell Inn, in the Streetway Road, westward, on the morning of 16th September. Mr Birks of

Horsebrook, who, as a grown man, had walked the boundaries 23 years ago, acted as chief guide. As the clergy of the parish took no part in the perambulation, the old custom revived in many parishes of late years, to connect religious services with municipal ceremony, was not observed. The Order of the Vestry for the Perambulation of the Parish having been read, the procession [which consisted of nine adults, including Francis McCasko, policeman, and 14 youths or children] started along the Watling Street or Streetway Road, the brook which divides Brewood from Blymhill, and to the Shire Stone, at a lodge called the Royal Oake,[726] where those who had not previously made the perambulation were bumped: on to Lady Isabella's Well, up the road to Boscobel, outside Boscobel fence through Spring Coppice to Renshaw Wood Lane – at this part of the route not only was the Royal Oak distinctly visible, but a magnificent view over the valley of the Severn, commanding the Wrekin and the Clee Hills: along the Renshaw Wood Lane to the road leading from Boscobel to Codsall Wood, where the road runs parallel with Chillington Park wall, and on through lanes and fields to Gunstone; here Pendeford Brook is the boundary to Coven Lawn, at which place, it being half-past five, the procession returned to Brewood and dined at the Swan Inn.

On Tuesday morning, starting from Coven Lawn, across the fields to the Three Hammers Bridge, and along the brook to Brinsford, the Shropshire Union Canal had to be crossed once, the Staffordshire and Worcestershire Canal twice, and the Grand Junction [L & N W Railway] twice: on through Paradise, Aspley, the Four Ashes and Crateford, leaving Eaton House to the right, into Streetway Road and back to the Bell Inn, where the perambulators dined. Parish authorities from Codsall, Saredon and Shareshill met the perambulators on their respective boundaries. The farmers on several points accompanied the procession through their grounds, and the inhabitants generally [!] showed the greatest courtesy, though surprise was expressed that it was so long since a perambulation had passed before.

The parishioner's churchwarden accompanied the perambulation on foot throughout, took the chair at both dinners, and was amongst the first to wade knee-deep through the culverts under the canals and railways. The actual time passed in walking was 7½ hours on Monday and 6½ hours on Tuesday. The boys and others engaged in the procession showed the utmost endurance and good humour, and at Deepmore Brook, the boundary to Shareshill, the broadest and deepest stream to be crossed, the young men shouted, as lifting Mr Birks upon their shoulders, they plunged into the water.[727]

One of the party, Edward Haynes, the sexton, has left his own account of the perambulation in small, neat handwriting with unexpectedly archaic spellings. The account, which varies to a surprising extent from the 'official' report, is strikingly reminiscent of the form taken by Anglo-Saxon boundary charters:

The Boundery of the parish of Brewood Sept 16-17-1861

I Edward Haynes went with others from Bell Inn Street Road to stinking lake brook and commenced to walk the brook to the road leading to Ivesy and round the lower end of Bishops Wood through some gardens and field up to the house called the acorn or Royal oak Inn then cross the road into a small couft called Vaughtons croft to Isabela well with a weeping ash hinging over it from thence to boscobill garden headge down the side of the field into the wood through the wood by brook and then cross the road into the field the side of the other wood till the gate then through into the field leading to donington the field belong to langly and at the top of it is a tryangle posted and railed and planted then up the side of another field belong to Mr Yeates round the pit and then down the side of a new planted

edge quick which was mooved into donington lane keep the edge side till the gate and then we clamed the whole of the road hear we all pertook of lunch and then to Willian Wright garden now through into the field and a long the edge side of the fields to a cottage and just miss the cottage take the road up to mark and then keep alonge the old park wall to Johnson garden edge and through the garden to lodge gate from thence through the next the middle of several gardens into a meadow to Giffords garden arms over the brew house to cotshull garden from there through some fields with land marks deviding it from Codsall & Brewood to pit from there through the joinyng fields to the bend of lane then take the whole of the lane by White house to leaper house then cross the road over the stile down the side of the edge to brook leading to gunston the brook is sig sag to brook bilbrook to a perpendicular edge which gose from the brook up to bilbrook deviding Tettanall and codsall but continue the brook on to penford mill under the canall to brook sigsag Hedttens on left hand to

339

brook for some time farther then penford mill cottages till we come to a land mark stone with T & B on Tettenall and Brewood then up the fields by marks to the coven lawn lane the mark of stone continue on across the fields 75 yards distances from the wood on your right the stone mark continue across the fields the the Showhill and on till you come to the three hammers brook

Second day we continued the brook which is sigsag to the old canall we crossed it on a boat a boatman stopped and steered all of us across and then we all jumped down the precipes a long the side of the brook across the fields leaving brinford to the right into brinsford lane cross the lane into the field to railway called london and north western under the culvelt by brook into field called doll ground across another lane and then across several fields by land marks till you come to paradice across fields by land marks to stone mark deviding Brewood and sharehill the proceeding on by marks deviding Sardon & Brewood field after feild till we come the old canall near gailey warf 2 men waded through to the other side to mark there is stone mark too path side then down the side of the edge till we turned by land mark to right hand straight a cross several fields till we came to the deep moore mill across the dam and there the garden corner about three or four roods are in Brewood parish then proceed along the brook in the long narrow meadow to a small triangler pice of meadow land opposite side of the brook then through the brook up 2 feild to groves garden into the farm building over it into the lane called calf health lane here we pretook of lunch bread chees and beer from here we went cross the lane straight along the edge side of several field till we come to the rail way again called london and northwestern railway here we all run across rails into an old lane which came out against a small cottage were peter Perry lives commonly known by the name of peter bussle here we crossed the lane all got over the edge into a turnip field belongong to marsh farm to a oak tree in the middle then from it to the corner of the fieldn to brook down the side of the marsh farm house by brook which gose through several fields leaving Mr Robinson of eaton house on our right hand and Mrs Brewster of Engleton on our left hand with the above named brook till we came into street road or watling street road keeping the left side of the road till we come to the Bell Inn again the place we all started from about half past 5 Oclock and there waited a short time and then pertook of a good supper beef and mutton and plump pudding

The first day we came back from coven lawn to the swan Inn and there we pertook of a semelor meal beef mutton and plump pudding

On 9th January 1851 the ecclesiastical parish of Bishop's Wood was formally created within the civil parish, and in July 1858 the ecclesiastical parish of Coven was formed.

47. Boscobel House and the Royal Oak

Although just across the county and parish border, the story of the escape of Charles II and his stay at Boscobel is closely linked with Brewood.

By 1632, a cousin of the Giffards of Chillington, John Giffard of Whiteladies, a Roman Catholic, had converted buildings on his estate into a three-storey lodge to provide temporary accomodation for hunting parties. The lodge, called Boscobel from the Italian 'Bosco bello', meaning 'fine wood' [traditionally named by Sir Basil Brooke of Madeley Hall, a guest of John Giffard at the housewarming[728]], seems to have been designed to impress, set in a particularly elevated position to give a commanding panorama in a wide arc from the south west to the north east – including the Clee Hills, the Wrekin, Caer Caradoc and the Lawley, between 20 and 25 miles distant – and with elaborate timber framing and gables. It seems that the house may have been designed originally with secret hiding places for the possible concealment of priests or others in times of persecution, of which the Giffards had painful personal experience, although the evidence suggests that the hiding places were relatively unsophisticated and may have been installed after the house had been built.

At the outbreak of the Civil War in 1642, the Catholics identified with the royal cause, and Boscobel appears to have been the site of a skirmish, for there is a record in 1646 of a royalist who 'served the King in the war and had been in Boscobel House at its surrender'. There is also evidence that after Sir George Booth's royalist forces were routed in Cheshire in August 1659, Lord Brereton, who was in Booth's party, sought sanctuary at Boscobel and remained undetected.

Although John Giffard died in Ireland in 1651, Boscobel remained a refuge for royalist fugitives, and after fleeing from Worcester, Charles II was persuaded to stay at the house, after first going to Whiteladies and making an unsuccessful attempt to flee into Wales. With the Restoration in 1660 the story of the King's escape became well-known, and many versions, most of them fanciful, were published. The romantic story of the oak tree captured the public imagination, and by 1662 Boscobel and the Royal Oak were a popular attraction, but the tree had even then been the target of souvenir hunters, for in 1660 all the young branches had been taken by visitors,[729] and in about 1677 the owners of Boscobel, Basil and Jane Fitzherbert, were forced to protect it with a high round wall. Over a doorway in the wall was an inscription on a plate, the work of the Rv. G. Plaxton, recording the story of the King's escape. The London Post newspaper of 19th August 1700 announced that according to advice lately received from Staffordshire, the tree called the Royal Oak had been blown down in a storm. In 1704 the diarist and arboriculturist John Evelyn recorded[730] that he had heard that the 'Famous Oak near White Ladys' had been killed by people hacking off parts of the tree, and in 1712

William Stukeley described the tree as 'almost cut away by travellers', adding that a young thriving plant from one of its acorns was growing close by. This is the first known reference to a second tree, but there are several later accounts of a young tree. For example Justice William Fortesque, afterwards Master of the Rolls, entered in his Circuit Diary in April 1738:

> "Ivetsey Bank . . . we can see within 40 or 50 yards where ye Royal Oak was out at ye Window, tis about a little mile from this Place direct on ye right Hand, but ye Way to it is from ye 1st House. The old & True Tree is not standing tho' they pretend at ye Inn to give you some of it. There is a Young Tree stands in ye Place where ye old one did; tis walled round & in the middle of a Field wh. was formerly all wood & coppice by ye name of Boscobel Wood that is now grub'd up."

In 1784 a detailed account of the ruinous wall mentions 'a tree of middling size, growing within the wall but not in the centre', and adds that 'the old tree has been carried away piece-meal by curious visitors . . . many snuff boxes and other toys have been made from the wood'. In 1791 a single tree 'about four score years old' is recorded. Stebbing Shaw, writing in 1798, says that "the place where the famous tree once flourished is yet to be discovered by a Square wall built about it, where is another tree from one of its acorns . . ." In 1809 there is a reference to a visit two years earlier to see a tree 'said to have originated from an acorn of the Old Oak'.

Local evidence of the destruction of the old tree comes from the Rev Joseph Dale, curate of Donington from 1811 to 1849, who recorded that he was told at the beginning of the nineteenth century that the last remains of the tree had been rooted up many years before, and the position of the younger tree in the corner of the enclosure had made it possible to take out 'the whole of the stock and the thickest portion of the roots' of the old oak. In the early nineteenth century a seat formed from 'a large block with an inscription' is recorded as having been cut from a root of the Royal Oak, and at a meeting of the Salopian Archæological Association in 1878, the Rev W.A. Leighton stated that an aunt of his, born near Boscobel in 1756, remembered as a child the old stump of the Royal Oak, with the younger tree growing beside it.[731]

The dilapidated wall around the new tree was replaced in 1787, and that wall replaced by the existing iron fencing in 1817. Within the fencing are three inscribed brass plates, two in Latin and one in English. The smallest was installed in 1787 when Basil and Eliza Fitzherbert rebuilt the brick wall erected by their predecessors. The two larger plates date from 1875 and give a history of the tree, describing how the wall was replaced by railings in 1817. The inscription also refers to the tree as the original Royal Oak. Both plates replace another made in 1845 which described the tree as descended from the Royal Oak. It is clear that by 1875 the second tree had grown to considerable size, and the Victorian appetite for romantic drama persuaded the owner to remove the words suggesting that the tree was not the one which had sheltered the King.

The account left by Charles indicates that the tree in which he hid was then of considerable age, and had been pollarded. The size of the present tree – genus Quercus Robur Pedunculata – indicates that it is perhaps 300 years old, which dispels any doubt that it cannot be the original Royal Oak.

It is of interest that the oak was a symbol of state and monarchy before the escape of the King from Worcester. The diarist John Evelyn records a medal struck in 1638 to commemorate the investiture of Charles as Prince of Wales which showed an oak towering above surrounding saplings as a symbol of royal supremacy, and in 1649 an allegorical sketch was published showing Cromwell's soldiers pulling down a tree representing the British state, and entitled 'The Royall Oake of Brittayne'.

Boscobel House was formerly part of a working farm – although there is evidence that in 1687 Richard Penderel had a beerhouse at Boscobel called The Royal Oak, which was almost certainly at Boscobel House – and over the years has been very extensively altered. The present staircase dates from the late eighteenth or early nineteenth century, and both the hiding place on the first floor and the attic are probably non-original. In the first floor room is a small closet to the left of the fireplace, originally a garderobe or stool-room, and the hiding place in the floor was probably constructed in the nineteenth century. The hiding place at the top of the attic stairs has certainly existed for very many years, but again its

Boscobel House, from Thomas Blount's 'Boscobel', published in 1660. Since the illustration of Whiteladies in the same engraving is known to be a faithful representation, it is likely that this is one of the earliest and most accurate illustration of Boscobel House as it would have been in 1651.

authenticity is uncertain.[732] In the nineteenth century the popular and prolific historical writer William Harrison Ainsworth wrote a

343

fictionalised version of the King's escape: 'Boscobel, or the Royal Oak', which first appeared in 1872 and, although based on fact, his invented additions to the story soon became adopted as historically accurate, to the extent that an oratory which had never existed was created on the ground floor to satisfy the fictionalised version of the events. The book revived interest in the house, and in the years before the First World War it became 'a sort of Mecca for Black Country trippers', and visitors from all parts of the world now arrive to view the humble lodge which sheltered a fugitive King.

Five trompe l'oeil windows in the form of quincunx on the upper part of the south facing chimney [thought to allude the five wounds of Christ] served as a sign to strangers that the house was owned by Catholic sympathisers. Five stone tablets in similar formation can be seen above the door in the west wall at Benthall Hall, near Ironbridge, which dates mainly from the late sixteenth century.

The white-pebble legend inlaid in the garden path which reads "Sext. id Sept. 1651, in hac domo Carolus Secundas tutela quinque fratrum de stirpe Penderel pôtitus est eorum demque ope incolumis evasit" ["on 7th September 1651, Charles II in this house obtained the protection of five brothers of the Penderel family, and by means of their help safely escaped"] has existed from at least 1860.[733] The mound on which the summerhouse stands may be the original.[734]

The house, together with its contents and historic relics, was sold by auction on 17th June 1913 by the Rev Canon Carr, and was placed in the guardianship of the Ministry of Works in 1954 by the owner, Lord Bradford. Much renovation and reconstruction has since taken place, particularly in recent years, on the complex of buildings which forms the house and farm, and a ticket office and shop created from an outbuilding were opened by the present owners, English Heritage, in 1988, but visitors may be surprised to find the house now furnished in Victorian, rather than Carolean, style.

The Mount

Half a mile to the south-west of Boscobel on the crest of the hill of the west side of the lane to Whiteladies formerly lay 'The Mount', a flat-topped circular mound with a diameter of about 50 feet and a maximum height of 3 feet, which seems first to have been recorded on a map of Whiteladies estate c.1753.[735] The perimeter of the mound was well defined in 1790, although there was no evidence of a surrounding ditch. In 1937 the mound was covered in trees. It was levelled by ploughing in 1968, but nothing of significance was noted, and its origin is uncertain, although it is most likely to have been a tumulus. Fragments of Roman pottery and coins dating from the first to the fourth century and a late Saxon key have been found nearby.[736] The mound is said to have been the site of an anti-aircraft battery during the second world war.

48. Whiteladies

The convent of the White Nuns of St Leonard of Brewood, of the Order of St Augustine, was fully established towards the end of the twelfth century, although nothing is known of its foundation. It was deliberately sited in accordance with Augustinian policy in an isolated and secluded position. The attractions of the site had been noted long before, however, for Roman pottery fragments found nearby attest to occupation during that period.

Since the time of Leland, Antiquary to Henry VIiI, who visited the house soon after it was dissolved, it has often been wrongly ascribed to the Cistercian Order, apparently because of the similarity of dress of the Cistercian and Augustinian nuns. The convent was small, with between five and nine nuns during the middle ages. It was under the supervision of the Bishop of Lichfield, and no lay lord claimed patron's rights. Its endowment was modest, consisting of the priory property and scattered pieces of land in a triangular area now bounded by Shifnal, Wolverhampton and Bridgnorth, although it also held some property in west Shropshire and in Nottinghamshire. The few records that exist suggest an uneventful history, with only minor complaints, such as the suggestion in 1338 that money had been spent on luxeries, and that hounds were kept. In 1535 the house, reported to be "in great decay", was valued at only £17 10s 8d. The priory was suppressed with the smaller houses in 1536 and the prioress received a pension of £5. At the Dissolution Lord Stafford was anxious to acquire it, but the asking price was too high, and it was not until May 1538 that the dispersal was completed and the site leased for 21 years to William Skevington of Wolverhampton [who seems to have lived at Whiteladies until his death in 1550], with the ownership passing in 1540 to William Whorwood, Solicitor-General to

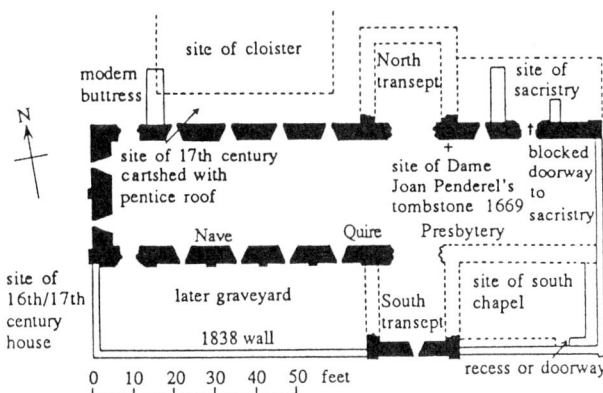

Plan of Whiteladies Priory ruins. Scale approximately 40' to one inch.

Henry VIII. Skevington may have been responsible for building the substantial timber-framed house with a large hall, probably open to the roof, a range of chambers to the west of the hall, and a two-storeyed entrance porch in a wing projecting from the west range of the ruins. In front of the house was a walled courtyard with a small timber-framed gatehouse opposite the entrance porch. Around the house are said to have been scattered cottages known as the town, all now vanished.

In 1595 the property passed from Thomas Throckmorton to Edward Giffard, and the sale included 80 acres of woodland, including Boscobel Wood. The estate remained in the Giffard family, and in 1651, when Charles II sought refuge after the battle of Worcester, was owned by Dorothy Giffard, although the house had then been sequestrated and was awaiting purchase.

Whiteladies, redrawn from watercolours made on 9th August 1791 by Edward Williams. The upper view shows the gatehouse to the north of the priory ruins, the lower view is of a surviving fragment of the range of buildings which adjoined the west end of the priory. The watercolours appear to be accurate in detail. Reproduced by kind permission of Shropshire Record Office.

The monastic buildings and sixteenth century house in which Charles was given shelter have long since vanished, although a part of the two-storey gatehouse, converted into a shepherd's house, was still standing in 1791,[737] and two small cottages attached to the west side of the ruin [apparently on the site of the half-timbered house which sheltered Charles] were pulled down in 1815,[738] apparently to allow the new owner to avoid liability for the payment of poor rates. All that remain today are the ruins of the priory church and the nineteenth century boundary wall which encloses a small Catholic graveyard formed in and to the south of the ruins.

Whiteladies, from Thomas Blount's 'Boscobel' of 1660. The engraving is probably a faithful representation.

The ruins, approached along a short rough track – on a map of Whiteladies estate c.1753 the junction of the track and the lane to Boscobel is labelled "4 Ashes" – which runs through a small wood, stand in an open site of about an acre sloping down to a small stream to the west. In the 1930's excavations showed where the stream had been widened and dammed to form a fishpond, but that evidence has now gone. On the higher ground to the east lie the buried foundations of an isolated building, to the west of which burials have been found. Evidence of extensive buildings on the south side of the ruins was visible until fairly recent times, and it is possible that considerable remains existed until 1838, when they were utilised to build a wall at the destroyed east end of the building and to enclose the enlarged burial ground on the south. In 1866 there were said to be some enormous yew trees on the site.

The ruins of the priory church indicate a small building 114' long, with a total width of 70', little altered since the end of the twelfth century, consisting of a square-ended aisleless presbytery of three bays, a crossing with single north and south transepts apparently without eastern chapels, and a five bay aisleless nave. A fine round-headed Romanesque arch with scalloped and foliage-carved capitals leading into the north transept survives intact, with a plain round-headed window to each bay of the nave and chancel. There is a continuous projecting label course in the north wall between the transept and the west end, showing where a lean-to roof once existed. This roof seems to have been used as a cart shed in the early nineteenth century. Below the easternmost window of this wall are traces of a doorway, with chamfered jambs and pointed arch, probably of the thirteenth century. The stonework of the blocked arch contains a curious splayed opening. In the later Middle Ages a sacristry was added north of the chancel, and a corresponding building, probably a chapel, was built at the same time. At least part of the convent was evidently floored with thick square red tiles embossed with geometric patterns with green or yellow lead glaze, and some of the buildings seem to have been roofed with lozenge-shaped roofing tiles of friable stone composed entirely of fossil shells. Fragments of both tiles and roofing stone have been exposed after ploughing around the site.

Here lyeth
The bodie of a Friende
The King did CaLl.
Dame Joane.
But Now Shee is
Deceast and Gone.
Interred Anno Do
1669.

The tombstone of Jane Penderel – 'Dame Joane' – from an engraving in 'The Gentleman's Magazine' of 1807.

Sadly, most of the gravestones have been defaced or damaged, but formerly included an ogee-headed slab[739] with the inscription under an incised cross: "Here lyeth/The bodie of a Friende/The King did CaLL/ Dame Joane. /But Now Shee is/Deceast and Gone. /Interred Anno: Do/ 1669".[740] The slab was replaced in about 1800 when the original was destroyed, traditionally by Mary Stockton or Stocking, a servant at nearby Meashill Farm who used the pieces as scouring stones. The replacement slab was vandalised and destroyed in 1975. There is evidence that this slab was a replacement of the replacement, i.e. the third slab.[741] Several coffin-shaped sandstone slabs also lie within the ruins. These were originally found outside the walls near the east end, along with other gravestones, including one of the fourteenth century with an engraved foliated cross and chalice and other fragments of the same date with inscribed crosses in various styles.

From the end of the seventeenth century the property followed the descent of Boscobel until 1819, but when Boscobel and most of the Whiteladies estate was sold in that year, the site of the priory was retained by the Fitzherbert family. Until the 1930's the ruins were covered with a heavy growth of ivy, which had caused considerable damage to the stonework, exacerbated by vandalism, and the interior of the ruins was overgrown and the ground uneven. In 1938, the site was passed into the guardianship of the Ministry of Works – now English Heritage – by the then owner, Lord Bradford.

In 1897 it was said that the site of Humphrey Penderel's windmill at Whiteladies was distinguishable by a large hole in which had stood the post in the corner of the meadow, and the millstone had then been moved to Whiteladies Farm.[742] There is no trace of the stone now. Indeed, the land is relatively low-lying, and hardly suitable for a windmill. It has been suggested that Shackerley water mill was Penderel's mill,[743] but a map of Whiteladies made c.1753 shows Whiteladies mill 400 yards south-west of the priory, near the junction of two streams, and one of a series of paintings of the escape commissioned by Charles II after the Restoration clearly shows a water mill near Whiteladies.[744]

49. Local place-names and early references[745]

Ackbury Heath – the *bury* element means *wood, grove* [Herkebarowe, c.1200]

Albrighton – *Æthelbeorht's tun* [Albricstone 1086]

Aspley – *the aspen wood* [Espele Wode c.1275][746]

Bargate – *tollgate*

Barn Spring – *barn copse*

Bath [Farm] – *pool*

Belvide [Reservoir] – *fine view*

Bilbrook – *brook in which billers or watercress grew* [Bilrebroch 1086] The word billers is said to be of Celtic origin.

Bilheath – *heath on a headland*

Birk's Barn – *the barn of Mr Birk* [18th century]

Blackladies – *convent of the Nuns of the Black Ladies* [Blakledys 1362]

Boscobel – *beautiful wood* from Italian bosco bello.

Brantley [Pool] – *the wood or glade cleared by fire*

Brinsford – *Bruns ford* [Brenesford, Brunesford 996]

Broadgate – *tollgate* [site of]

Broom Hall – *the corner of land where broom grew* [Brom(e)hale 1150]

Bushbury – *the Bishop's Manor* [Byscopesbyri 996]

Calf Heath – *the enclosure of the calves* [calfre heie 994]

Catchem's End – a derogatory name, 19th century [Catchems Inn 1838]

Chillington – *the settlement by the spring* or, more likely, *the farmstead associated with Cilla* [Cillentone 1086]

Clay Gate – possibly *clay road* [on Roman road]

Codsall – *the small valley or corner of land of Cod* [Codeshale 1086]

Coldham – *the cold house or the cold clearing* [Coldhome 1581]

Congreve – *the grove or copse in a valley* [Comgrave 1086]

Coven – possibly *[place] at the coves or bays* [Cove 1086][747]

Crateford – *the ford of the water crakes* [Crakeford 1327]

Cream Pot – A Victorian whimsy

Cross Green – *open space with a cross*

Dale Flat – *valley furlong*

Deans End– [le Denesend 1430]

Deepmore [Brook] – *the deep marsh*

Eaton – *farmstead by the river*

Engleton – *the farmstead of the Angles* [c.1206]

Featherstone – *the tetralith* [Feother(e)stan 996]

Ford Houses – *houses at the ford*

Four Ashes – *the four ash trees* [1577 – Saxton's map of Staffordshire]

Gailey – *woodland glade overgrown with bog-myrtle* [Gageleage c.1002]

Giffard's Cross [Gyffardes crosse 1569]

Gunstone – *the farmstead of Gunni* [Gunniston c.1260][748]

Hag Hay – *the enclosure with haws or coppiced wood enclosure*
Hatton – *the farmstead on the heath* [Hadton 1227]
Hawkshutts – corruption of Hogshead
Hocker[h]ill – *hill with a [burial?] mound*
Holbrook [Pool] – *brook in a hollow*
Horsebrook – *the brook used by horses* [Horsebroc 1262]
Hungry Hill [Farm] – *hill with poor soil or possibly hill with wood on side.*
Hyde – *hide of land* [la Hide, Hyde 1199]
Ivetsey – *Ufegeat's enclosure* [Quy(e)ot(t)eshay 1310]
Kiddemore Green – *the marshland with brushwood* [Kyrremore 1383]. The word Green implies surrounding woodland.
Kinvaston – *the farmstead of Cynewald* [Kinwaldestun, Kinevoldestun 996]
The Laches – *swampy pool* [lece broc 994]
Langley [Lane & Lawn] – *Long wood or glade* [Longeley land 1569]
Lapley – *the woodland glade at the end of the estate or parish* [Lappeley 1061]
Leafields [Farm] – *fallow fields* [leefylde(s) 1535]
Longbirch – *the long newly-cultivated strip of land* [Le Longebruch 1425]
The Monie Pits – *the many pits*
Moseley – *Moll's wood* [Moleslei 1086]
Oaken – *place of the oaks* [Ache 1086]
Oakley – *oak wood*
Oram's Lane – 18th century, after the Oram family.
Paradise – *perfect place* – [le olde paradis 1338]
Pearse Hay – *the enclosure of Piers or Pearce*
Pendeford – *Penda's ford* [Pendeford 1086][749]
Penkridge – *mound on a hill* [Pencric 958]
Perton – *peartree farm or orchard*
Port Lane – *the lane of the town* [1569]
Renshaw Wood – *Reyner's wood* [Reynershawing 1300]
Ring Hill – *hill with a circle* [with possible prehistoric connotations]
Rock Bank – *bank of the rats*
Rodbaston – *Redbald's farmstead* [Redbaldestone 1086]
Saredon – *Searu's hill or withered hill* [Sardone, Seresedone 1086]
Shackerley – *Robbers wood*
Shareshill – *hill with a shelf* [Servesed 1086]
Shifnal – *Scuffa's halh or valley* [Schuffanhalch 675]
Shutt Green – *open space with channel of fast water* [le shutegrene 1320][750] or *furlong green*[751]
Slade Heath – *heath in the valley*
Somerford – *the ford usable only in summer*, perhaps implying the existence of another ford. [Sumerford 1204]
Spring Coppice – *young plantation*
Stafford – *ford by the landing place* [Stæfford 913]

Strangleford Birch [Farm] – *the overgrown ford* [Strangleford 1327]

Standeford – *the stony ford* [on the Roman road] [Staunford 1245]

Stretton – *the farmstead on the Roman road* [Estretone 1086]

Tettenhall – *Teotta's or Teota's valley* [Teotanheale 910 – Anglo-Saxon Chronicle]

Tong – *tongs, fork of a river* [Twongan 1002]

Water Eaton – *farmstead by the river* [Eatun 994]

Watling Street – *the road to St Albans* [Wætlingstræt 926]

Wergs – *willows* [Withegas 1202]

Weston under Lizard – *the west farmstead* [Guestona 1081]

Wet Hay – *the wet enclosure*

Wheaton Aston – *the farmstead to the east where wheat grows* [Estona 1167]

Wolverhampton – *Wulfrun's high tun* [Heantune]

Woolley – *wood or glade of the wolves* [Wolveley 1199]

Wrottesley – *Wrott's wood* [Wrotteslea in Saxon Charter]

Wyrley Lane Plantation – *plantation of the Lanes of Wyrley*

As noted elsewhere, early county maps show the names Cotton to the east of Brewood and Hilton to the south-west. Cotton is evidently a perpetuated mistake for Coven. Hilton may be the former moated site between Bath Farm and Chillington, or it may be connected with Hilltop at Coldham.

References and Notes

NB: Many extracts quoted in the text are from secondary sources, and unverified. They should be treated with appropriate caution.

Abbreviations: LJRO: Lichfield Joint Records Office.

NSJFS: North Staffs Journal of Field Studies.

SHC: Staffordshire Historical Collections, formerly the Transactions of the William Salt Archæological Society, from 1936 The Staffordshire Record Society.

SRO: Staffordshire Record Office.

TSSAHS: Transactions of the South Staffordshire Archæological and Historical Society.

VCH: Victoria County History of Staffordshire.

WSL: William Salt Library.

1.   The Staffordshire hundreds – pre-Conquest administrative units – date from at least the tenth century: Rowlands 5. In about 1604 Cuttlestone Hundred was divided into eastern and western parts. Brewood lies in East Cuttlestone, and in the administrative area of South Staffordshire District Council [until 1st April 1974 Cannock Rural District Council].

2.   Noted landmarks in the last century were 'the double oaks', two oaks growing inches apart leaning towards the road on the north side of the bend in Kiddemore Green Road between Elm Cottage and The Oakley. The trees still exist. Dutch elm disease, which changed the face of the English countryside in the early 1970's, killed a number of trees in the parish, perhaps most noticeably along Ivetsey Road in Bishop's Wood, but the area escaped relatively unscathed from the most severe storm of modern times on 16th October 1987. A large number of trees in Chillington Park were however lost in gale-force winds on 7th and 26th/27th February 1990.

3.   T.H. Whitehead and others, "The Country between Wolverhampton and Oakengates", [Memoirs of the Geological Survey; Explanation of Sheet 153], 1928. A local tradition is that there is no higher land to the east of Bishop's Wood and Brewood until the Ural mountains. However, the land to the west of Oakham reaches a height of 754'.

4.   Found just under the surface of the field nearby and dragged out by Mr A. Tipton of Hockerhill Farm in the 1960's.

5.   There is a large erratic boulder at Boscobel House. The distribution of erratics in the area has been investigated in detail: see D. Mackintosh, "Quarterly Journal of the Geological Society", Vol. xxxv 1879 245; also F.W. Martin, "Proceedings of the Birmingham Philosophical Society", Vol. vi 1888 93-117 and Vol. vii 1889 85-112.

6.   It was reported in the "Stafford Advertiser" of 23rd November 1867 that the imprints of two large human feet had been found, the impression of the left foot measuring 15" in length [sic]. See also VCH I 34; Wakefield 1959, 10; H.C. Beasley, "Notes on

examples of footprints, etc., from the Trias in some Principal Museums", Proceedings of Liverpool Geological Society, Vol. viii 1898 233-7, and Plate XI.

7. p.143.

8. Stebbing Shaw II 199; "Staffs Advertiser", 21st November 1795.

9. The sound was likened to a carriage driving through a window, and the sensation described as a double swaying motion on the surface of the ground: Hicks Smith 1864, 5.

10. *ibid.*

11. Parish Magazine, April 1903.

12. Measuring 5.1 on the Richter scale.

13. Measuring 5.2 on the Richter scale, with its epicentre at Church Stretton. The tremor lasted several seconds, with buildings trembling and swaying. Damage was caused to Chillington Hall, where a weakened main beam over the staircase collapsed, necessitating extensive emergency repairs.

14. TSSAHS XIV, 1-5.

15. Greenslade & Stuart 9.

16. Trans. Shrop. Arch. Soc. LIX 10. Also VCH I 193.

17. SJ 80218094. On display in the Countryside Museum at Weston Park. Two stone axes are also reported to have been found at Tong: Tong Archæological Group.

18. SJ 742066. Trans. Shrop. Arch. Soc. LIX 10, and SJ934050, the latter Class VI of polished epidotised intermediate tuff, and with strong side facets, from Great Langdale or Scafell Pike: Sites and Monuments Record, Staffs County Council, record 6/08/01915.

19. Held by the author. Identified by Mr M. Stokes, Shrewsbury Museum, and Dr. L. Barfield of the Department of Archæology, Birmingham University. Some of the flints are almost certainly Mesolithic. Field walking has failed to locate any flints on the west side of the river.

20. SJ 848068. Sites and Monuments Record, Staffs County Council, record 6/03/02185. Held by Mr K. Shropshire, Wood Hall Farm, Codsall Wood. Flints and fragments of Neolithic pottery have been found at Acton Trussell church: Habberley 1986.

21. Held by author. [A perfectly spherical fine-grained stone ball 2" in diameter, tentatively identified as a sling stone, and a plain spindle whorl in fine grained dark sandstone have been found nearby: both held by author.] A fine-grained stone pebble-hammer with abraded sides and hour-glass perforation was found south-east of Rowley Hill Farm, Stretton in 1989; held by the author: Sites and Monuments Record, Staffs County Council, record PRM/4417. Another kidney-shaped pebble-hammer in red stone was found nearby some years earlier at SJ89851225: information from Mr J. Jameson, Rowley Hill Farm. A similar macehead is recorded in NSJFS 2 1962 29. A stone macehead was also found when Bull Bridge over the river Penk was reconstructed in 1963, and another has been recorded from Whiston Cross, Albrighton: Antony Gunstone, "Some Prehistoric Implements from South Staffordshire Reported to the Birmingham City Museum", TSSAHS 13 46-7. See also TSSAHS Vol 77 1959 3; Bulletin of Board of Celtic Studies 1927 4 74-91; Trans. Shropshire Arch. Soc. 1947 129-138, 1949 24-36; and Vine 1982, which provides a full gazetteer and detailed analysis of perforated stone implements – and much other prehistoric material – from Staffordshire. Perforated stone implements have been broadly categorised as

maceheads or pebble hammers, the former defined as shaped and perforated stone implements without a cutting edge, the latter as artificially perforated natural pebbles. Stone maceheads are believed to have derived from Neolithic antler maceheads, and pebble hammers are associated with finds from the Mesolithic to the Bronze Age. An 'hour-glass' or waisted perforation would suggest an early date, and a cylindrical perforation is characteristic of the late Neolithic or early Bronze Age: see Reginald A. Smith, 'The Perforated Axe Hammers in Britain,' in "Archæologia" Vol 75 1926.

22. p.403.

23. Presented by John Huntbach [a local antiquarian who lived at Featherstone, and later at Seawall, a moated house which formerly stood at what is now the junction of Showell Road and Guy Avenue, Bushbury], to his uncle Sir William Dugdale: Sir John Evans, "Ancient Bronze Implements, etc", 86. The name Seawall survives in Showell [Circus], Bushbury. Stebbing Shaw writes of Seawall: "This old seat of the Huntbaches has been many years dilapidated, and a neat farm-house erected on its site surrounded by a moat": Vol. II 187.

24. Stebbing Shaw I 31; "Archæologia" V 113; although the latter palstave may be the same as the one found at Beacon Hill, the result of confused reporting. A socketed axe-head is said to have been found in spoil during the construction of the M54 motorway at Tong Castle in 1972: Tong Archæological Group. Vine 1982 gives details of other Bronze Age finds at Wednesfield, Finchfield, Wrottesley and Wolverhampton Grammar School.

25. SJ907051, SJ91200845 and SJ906114: P.J. Watson, "Some new Middle and Late Bronze Age axes from South Staffordshire and the West Midlands," Transactions of the Birmingham and Warwickshire Archæological Society Vol 93 1983-4 1-7. The Four Ashes palstave is unrecorded: local information. In 1991 a 1" fragment of the narrow end of a flanged palstave was found to the west of The Stubbers wood, Stretton, SJ87201165: local information.

26. Held by the headmistress, St Dominic's School. It may have been deposited in spoil from the construction of the nearby canal.

27. Information from Mr K. Fellows, 136 Ward Grove, Lanesfield, Wolverhampton. A small white unworked flint flake, found south-east of Avenue Bridge near the highest point of Brewood Park [SJ89350730] may be of the same period, but could also be of natural origin: held by author. A Bronze Age flint scraper was found at White Cottage [?], Codsall, c.1942. No other information is known: NSJFS 4 1964 20.

28. Information from Mr K. Fellows *supra*.

29. In November 1796 Mr Dickenson "discovered a remarkable eminence called Roley Hill, with a gentle declivity to the meadows adjacent to the river Penk, which has the convenience of a ford in this part. This eminence occupies about five acres, and is crowned with a tumulus, which appears to have served for an exploratory mount . . ." Dickenson later revisited Rowley Hill, and also examined Beacon Hill: "No vestige of ruins or ramparts remains on either . . .": Stebbing Shaw I 31. See also VCH I 192-3; 376. The mound at Rowley Hill is still identifiable, but the only traces of a ditch are on the east, where it is up to one-foot deep and, so far as it is possible to determine its boundaries, appears to have been c.62' diameter. The mound has a maximum height of about 3'. The field in which it lies has not been ploughed within living memory.

30. Stebbing Shaw Vol II, Appendix p.19; 181; 187.

31. p.403. Another low is also mentioned in enclosed ground to the east of Great Saredon.

32. SHC 1938 297. For a slightly different version of the diary entry see Chatwin 1991 83.

33. SJ 91860815. Sites and Monuments Record, Staffs County Council, record 6/03/01077; SHC 1938 297; NSJFS 5196535. The site was in Field 894a on the Tithe Map.

34. Information from Mr S. Wright, Standeford Nurseries, Coven.

35. Hooke & Slater 39; Hooke 16. Tuters Hill on the outskirts of Pattingham may derive from the Old English, 'tot-ærn' meaning 'look-out place house', and mark the site of a lost hill-fort: Gelling 1988 146-7; Foxall 54.

36. Greenslade & Stuart 19-20. TSSAHS 21 1979-80 1-14.

37. Wakefield 9.

38. Oakden 47.

39. VCH I 180.

40. Oakden 44. Two fields named Church Yard are recorded in Alveley and Coreley in Shropshire, both remote from their parish churches. Skeletons were found in the first: Foxall 58.

41. Mentioned at some date between 1225 and 1259 as "pons de Cuthulvestan" and again in 1291. The present bridge dates from the 17th and 18th centuries with later alterations: VCH V 104-105. The original location of Cuttlestone is intriguing. The other four Staffordshire hundreds are all named after hills or mounds: Totmonslow [Tatemaneslav 1086 – 'the tumulus of Tatmonn']; Offlow ['the tumulus of Offa']; Seisdon [Saisdene, Seisdone 1086 – 'the hill of the Saxons']; Pirehill ['look-out hill']. It does not seem unreasonable to suppose that Cuttlestone was connected in some way with the 'chief mound' which gave its name to the district, a name inherited by the Roman settlement of Pennocrucio and perhaps by the Anglo-Saxon Pencersaetan people. That chief mound may have been at Rowley Hill [317'], on which a tumulus is known to have existed, or, perhaps less likely, on the higher Beacon Hill [389'] to the north-west. No tumuli are known to have existed on Beacon Hill, but a palstave was found there and, notwithstanding eighteenth century observations that no artificial features remain – see footnote 29 *supra* – the D-shaped summit plateau, some six or seven acres in extent, is very clearly defined, dropping down several feet on the east, north-west, west and, in a broken way, on the south. There are various ground features, including on the south-east what resembles a simple double-banked earthwork entrance, obviously man-made, which may repay further investigation, but which may be simply the remains of the banks of a cartway associated with the numerous quarries scattered around the north side of the hill. The hill has far-reaching views in every direction, and would have made an obvious moot site. It is said that there were formerly many rocks on the summit. Could 'Cuthwulf's Stone' have stood on the hill, which changed its name when its earlier status as a meeting place ceased and it became one of a series of signal stations? A fanciful theory that the meeting place was the 'Gorsedd' or Judgement Seat at Penkridge appears in NSJFS XLII 1907-8 116. See also W.B. Smith, "Staffordshire", Cambridge University Press 1915 103. Could that stone have been removed from Beacon Hill? That would explain how nearby Cuttlestone Bridge aquired its name. Stebbing Shaw states "Tradition says, that at or near Cuddleston Bridge was once a town or settlement of considerable magnitude and note": Vol II 291. The 'remarkable stone cross' standing in the road at Penkridge recorded by Stukeley in the early eighteenth century was probably destroyed soon after, since it is not mentioned by later writers.

42. SHC 1916 139. Rowlands 1987 5 suggests without explanation that the name may be associated with the area at the junction of the rivers Sow and Penk [east of Stafford]. This is clearly an error. Cuttlestone Bridge is near the junction of the river Penk and Church Eaton Brook. It has been suggested the name derives from Cuthwulf, who fell in the battle of Fethan leag in 587. The site of the battle has not been satisfactorily identified [see Olof S. Anderson, "The English Hundred Names", Lund 1934 145-6; Gelling 1988 14], although Bedford seems the most likely place [see M.J. Whitlock, "The Origins of England", Croom & Henn, 1986.]

43. At a height of 431'.

44. Oakden 42. Featherstone, nearby to the east, [Feotherstan in a charter of 996] is believed to derive from "the tetralith", or 4-stone monument. [Oakden 122-3]. Could the stones have been a burial chamber of 3 uprights and capstone? No trace of a tetralith survives.

45. Held by the author. A rectangular enclosure of unknown date is said to have been identified on aerial photographs on the highest part of the southern slope – see Sites and Monuments Record, Staffs County Council, record 6/03/4019 – but the evidence is not entirely convincing.

46. At a height of 461'.

47. Held by the author. The site is a typical one for a tumulus, the brow of a shoulder of land from which the ground falls steeply to the south.

48. p.401.

49. pp.30-31.

50. p.3.

51. The Roughs may be medieval woods, surrounded by wood banks with the usual ditch on the unwooded side. In fairness to Hicks Smith, it must be added that a piece of Roman samian pottery has been found on the north bank of the stream some 300 yards west of Big Hyde Rough.

52. SHC 1938; Webster 88-9.

53. Habberley 1986.

54. Cambridge University Collection CBC 78 taken 27th August.

55. "The Independent", 4th August 1987.

56. By Dr J.K. St. Joseph FSA.

57. By members of Birmingham Archæological Society.

58. By the Department of Classics of the University of North Staffordshire in July 1953 and 1954, and during road-widening works in 1959. See also Trans. of Birmingham & Warwickshire Archæological Society Vol 86 1974 57. A note exists from W.F.E. Mansell apparently dating from the 1930's: "There is an old wall situated on the left hand side of the old lane leading off the Watling Street just below the Stretton bridges and in the field behind is a lot of stone masonry." [Wakefield notebook 148/2/72 WSL]. Fragments of the wall remain to the north of the double bend, overgrown by the roadside hedge.

59. Parke 2.

60. Gelling 1984 243. Wakefield noted that there was an apparent ford in the Penk south of Rowley Hill where the water was only 3" deep: letter to Mr J.S. Horne of Rowley Park, Stafford, dated 17th October 1932. This may be the ford mentioned in Stebbing Shaw I 31.

61. Stebbing Shaw states "Tradition says, that at or near Cuddleston bridge was once a town or settlement of considerable magnitude and note": footnote, Vol II 291

62. Dr J.K. St Joseph, "Roman Forts on Watling Street", Birmingham Archæological Society, 1953; G. Webster, "Further Excavations at the Roman Fort, Kinvaston, Staffordshire", TSSAHS Vol 73 1955 100-8; "West Midlands Archæological News Sheet" No 16 Council for British Archæology Group 8 1973. Kinvaston may have been discovered much earlier:. Emmanuel Bowen's map of Staffordshire, 1749, shows "Kinnerston" as having "ancient fortifications".

63. Dr J.K. St. Joseph, *ibid*.

64. SJ 90501050. "Journal of Roman Studies" 55 1965 76-7.

65. "West Midlands Archæology" issue 24 1981 94-6. To the west of the group of buildings at Water Eaton is a moat: VCH V 123.

66. Margery 1957 28-9; "The Independent," 11th June 1991. The road from Blythe Bridge via Fulford, Hilderstone, Weston and Stafford to Pennocrucium was said to form part of a lost road running 200 miles from Doncaster to Avonmouth, probably built between 47 and 57AD. Could a section have joined Ackbury Heath with Watling Street at the Ivy House, to complete the alignment, running through Brewood? No traces have been found on the ground.

67. C.S. Smith's map of Staffordshire 1801; Pitt's Topographical History of Staffordshire 1817.

68. Information from Mr S. Wright *supra*. The finds almost certainly mark a settlement site.

69. The name Clay Gates is interesting for 'gata' is the old Norse word for a road, and is often used to mean a Roman road. Hence the possible meaning 'Roman road of clay'. [cf. Claregate, on or near the line of the Roman road from Pennocrucium to Pendeford. The name Clare is recorded in the 1260 Staffordshire Tallage Assessment: SHC 4th Series 13 6-7.].

70. Yates map of Staffordshire 1775 suggests that a section of the road was in use at that date, leading from Pendeford Hall to Pendeford Mill, which may have been the mill of the same name visited by Charles II after his escape from Worcester, although Old Mill Farm at Coven Heath is the most likely site. Until the construction of the M54 motorway, the southern part of the section was marked by a lane and a line of trees, the northern part by the eastern edge of Ash Coppice. In the 1950's the line of the road to the south is said to have been marked by a hedgeline through Barnhurst Farm, and a section was excavated by G.J. Barnsby with pupils from Etheridge Secondary Modern School, Bilston: G.J. Barnsby, "The Origins of Wolverhampton to 1085", Wolverhampton Borough Council 1985 4. The excavations revealed nothing of interest: information from Mr Barnsby.

71. Information from Mr D. Morgan, 3 Hall Farm Close, Brewood. Sites and Monuments Record, Staffs County Council, record 01616. There is the intriguing possibility that Chillington Lower Avenue marks the line of a Roman road connecting Giffard's Cross to the Roman river crossing to the east of Forge House.

72. Sites and Monuments Record, Staffs County Council, record 6/03/01897.

73. Information from Mr K. Fellows *supra*. Crop marks of two straight lines, intersecting at right angles at a pond half a mile east of Westbeech Farm, are visible on RAF air photographs CPE/UK/2469/4288-9 at SJ834001. No traces are visible on the ground: letter to author dated 22nd February 1977 from Ordnance Survey, Archæology

Division. See also VCH XX 3. A bronze palstave from Wrottesley [SO 855986] is recorded in Vine 257.

74. Stebbing Shaw mentions "some remains of old entrenchments, or moated site, at the Corner of [Patshull] park under the Peper hill . . ." Vol. II 286.

75. Information from Mr K. Fellows *supra*.

76. Both held by author.

77. All information from Mr K. Fellows *supra*.

78. – ditto –

79. – ditto – A Roman gold coin is said to have been found near Boscobel in 1843: see "Documents concerning the parish of Boscobel", Section U, Local Studies Dept, Shrewsbury Library.

80. Information from Tong Archæological Group. Is it possible that the parish of Brewood with its hybrid Celto-Saxon name may preserve in its boundaries the outline of a Roman-British estate which preceeded it? The supposed villa site at Wigmore Wood might give some clues, for although much further research is necessary to determine the earliest forms, the name Wigmore may derive from the Old English 'wic', and before it the Latin 'vicu', the smallest unit of local government in the Roman world: Gelling 1988 67-74, 247. Is it conceivable that the regional administrative centre for a group of villas – including Engleton and others now lost or destroyed – was at Wigmore, and that the county/parish boundary follows the boundary between the estates, the element 'more' deriving from 'gamære', meaning boundary? Or does the name mean simply 'quaking marsh'?

81. Information from Tong Archæological Group.

82. Information from Mr. D. Morgan *supra*. There are various cropmarks including a rectangular ditched enclosure to the south-west of Meashill Farm near Whiteladies, and what may be a Roman building has been identified at Lizard Grange north of Tong: "Documents relating to the Parish of Tong", section U, Shrewsbury Local Studies Library. On the south side of Watling Street, opposite Burlington Pool, two Roman forts of 43 and 6½ acres were located on aerial photographs in the late 1960's: Robinson 24. In September 1989 a hoard of about 400 second century bronze coins is said to have been found near Wheaton Aston, and another hoard of some 1500 coins on the line of the Roman road to Chester north of Wheaton Aston in May 1990. It is said that 'some years ago' a tesselated pavement was uncovered by workmen at Whiston Mill near Penkridge.

83. In the south-east corner of the angle formed by the road at Shutt Green passing over the Shropshire Union Canal are two fields called Great Castle Croft and Little Castle Croft: Tithe Apportionment D932/6 SRO. Great Castle Croft adjoins a huge spoil bank on the east side of the canal, and the fields might be thought to have taken their name from such mound. However, the name is recorded as early as 1493 [Oakden 44], and the field boundaries run across and therefore clearly pre-date the canal. The word 'castle' in place-names is often linked to Roman camps, or to a castle, or is derived from the Old English 'ceastel' or 'cestel', meaning 'a heap'. There are no obvious ground features in either field. The area, which is flat and adjoins a stream, may be the site of a Roman fort. Or is it possible that beneath the spoil bank lies an artificial mound after which the fields were named? No mound or other feature is marked on Robins & Sherriff's map of 1808 590/375 SRO. The name Hell Floor on the north side of Chillington Upper Avenue may also be significant. The word floor was

often applied in early times to Roman tesselated pavements. The age of the name is uncertain, but it is mentioned in Hicks Smith 1867 34. The line of a conjectured Roman road runs nearby to the east. A more prosaic explanation is that the name derives from the Old English 'helde', meaning a slope. The old brick and sandstone cottages in Offoxey Road to the west of White Oak Farm were formerly known as Little Oak Farm or Floors Farm, and fields to the west include the word Floor in their names.

84. Oakden 44. Its location is not known. Could it have been the 'ring' of Ringhills?

85. F.M. Stenton, "Anglo-Saxon England", 1971 40; Palliser 1976. The 13 are Brewood, Cannock, Cheadle, Eccleshall, Hints, Kinver, Leamonsley, Lichfield, Morfe, Penkhull, Penkridge, Penn and Pensnett.

86. Hooke 12; Hooke & Slater 9; Margaret Gelling, 'The Early history of West Mercia', in "The Origins of Anglo-Saxon Kingdoms", Ed. Steven Bassett, Leicester University Press 1989 185-201. This interpretation is based on a study of the bounds set out in a Worcester Charter [CS 455] dated 849. It is tempting to speculate on a connection between the tribal territory of the Pencersæten and the 'terretoria' of the Roman villas at Acton Trussell, Engleton and Wigmore Wood, which might collectively have covered the northern part of the tribal area.

87. C.C. Taylor, "The Origins of Lichfield, Staffs", TSSAHS X 1968-1969 43-52.

88. Wilkes claims that Offa made his capital for three years at Brewood during his campaigns against the Welsh: p.28. No source is given for this surprising claim.

89. Palliser 63.

90. It has been suggested that the name Pendeford, thought to be connected with the Mercian King – 'Penda's ford' – may commemorate a particular and early phase of Saxon colonisation: Penda was campaigning c.628.

91. By Bishop Richard Peche, who was consecrated in 1162 and became a monk in St Thomas's Priory, Stafford. See also TSSAHS Vol.II 1960-1. It is of interest that the rounded hill north of Bath Farm was formerly known as St Thomas Hill: see Chillington estate map c.1727 D590/363 WSL.

92. Known as The Clark's Pillar in 1818: Parson CXC.

93. Mander 1960. See also Hooke & Slater 20.

94. It is possible that Gunni may have been a thegn of King Canute, and was granted the estate in the early eleventh century. The name Steynesmoor is recorded in 1364, and derives from the Old Norse personal name Steinn: Oakden 49. The field name 'Danatre Yort' recorded in 1493 may mean 'tree of the Danes': Oakden 47.

95. Stebbing Shaw states that a great battle is said to have been fought at Bushbury in 907: Vol. II 181.

96. The first recorded reference to Staffordshire is as "Stæffordscir" in the Anglo-Saxon Chronicle of 1016.

97. Information from Mr K Fellows *supra*.

98. Hicks Smith; Wakefield 12; article by 'Mara' in "Express & Star", 29th November 1927.

99. Oakden 37.

100. Oakden 35.

101. Other hybrid names in the area with both Celtic and English elements include Penkridge, Walton [3 times: near Stafford; near Eccleshall; and near Newport – from

"tun of the Wealas", or Welsh], Penn, Morfe, Pensnett, Barr, Walsall and Lichfield: Gelling 1978 91. See also Gelling 1981 1-20.

102. The Domesday entry for Stafford records 179 houses, but 51 of those were deserted, perhaps the result of destruction by William's army. It was the only borough rendering less to the King in 1086 than 1066.

103. Anglo-Saxon Chronicle E.

104. Listed in Domesday under Warwickshire, either in error or because Corbucion held most of his estates in that county.

105. Robert de Stafford was, after the King, the most important landowner in Staffordshire.

106. Nut collecting is one service known to have occurred at Brewood. In Eccleshall tenants were required, inter alia, to carry corn, malt and oats to Brewood, and in Longdon services included driving cattle to various places, including Brewood: VCH VI 28. [The lord of the manor of Brewood was the Bishop of Lichfield, who had his palace at Eccleshall and manor houses at Longdon and Brewood.]

107. Rowlands 1987 15.

108. Rackham XV.

109. Eyton 1881 takes the league as 1½ miles, but recent research suggests that a Domesday league was ½ mile: Slade 21. Hooke & Slater prefer a league of 1½ miles: p.15. If the larger figure is correct, Brewood had 2,160 acres of woodland, Coven 60 acres, and Chillington 1,440 acres.

110. Robins & Sherriff's map of 1808.

111. A Churchfield is shown in the south-east angle formed by Dirty Lane and the Shropshire Union Canal on the Tithe Map of 1838. The name is sometimes found attached to fields where masonry remains have been discovered.

112. Harleian MSS 1085, fo. 240. Eyton Vol. 9 130 gives a date between 1163 and 1166.

113. VCH 21. It is said that salted bream and pike were supplied to King John when at Brewood from the King's Pool at Stafford: J.L Cherry [edited by], "Stafford in Olden Times", J. & C. Mort 1890 31.

114. Rotulis Literarum Clausarum.

115. There was a de Brewode family in the thirteenth century, but little is known of them: see Stebbing Shaw II 292.

116. Hicks Smith 1864 13.

117. Eccl. Comm. 124088 SRO.

118. Vol. II 292. Shaw had acquired the topographical collection of the Rev. T. Feilde, vicar of Brewood, which perhaps adds some weight to the statement. The Census Returns of 1841 record Court Lane, between the entries for Sandy Lane and The Pavement, presumably in or near to what is now St Chad's Close.

119. Wakefield 18.

120. Hicks Smith 1864 15. When the short road from Church Road behind the houses at the south-east end of Market Place was created in February 1989 no foundations were located during the shallow excavations, but the churchyard wall appeared to be constructed on huge carefully squared sandstone blocks, about 5' long and 2' deep. These proved to be only 4" thick and set on sand.

121. Parish Magazine contribution by C[harles] D[unkley], c.1925.

122. 590/375 SRO.

123. The Crown still held property in Brewood in 1546, for by a Deed dated 23rd January of that year, Sir William Paget, one of two Chief Secretaries to Henry VIII, exchanged his manor of Kepyer, County Durham, for various lands, manors and estates of the King, including all his lands at Brewood. The Great Seal of England is affixed to the Deed: SHC 1937 187-9.

124. Information from Mr D. Morgan *supra*. It is possible, however, that the bulla is of Innocent IV, written IIII, with the last digit obliterated.

125. SHC 1939 14; DNB LX 298. For deeds signed at Brewde by the Bishop on 28th December 1255 see SHC 1937 52. Eyton [Vol. 10 152] also mentions a letter dated at Brewood 25th November 1256.

126. Roger de Clinton is reputed to have purchased the see of Lichfield for 3000 marks: VCH III 23.

127. Palliser 148.

128. VCH VI 6.

129. See M. Beresford & H.P.R. Finberg, "English Medieval Boroughs – A Handlist", David & Charles 1973 161.

130. Palliser 1979 148.

131. Until the early 1950's it was possible to detect signs of extensions to these tofts to the south of Dirty Lane on a north-south alignment. Such toft extensions commonly date from the sixteenth and seventeenth centuries, and are known as 'garthends' or 'garrends'.

132. SHC VI Pt.II f. 190.

133. VCH V 21; Cal of Close Rolls p.478. The King had left Gloucester on 4th October and arrived in Storton/Tourton on 11th October. This may have been Stourton: from 12th to 14th the King was at Worcester: "Collectanea Archæologica", Vol II Pt I, Longman, Green Longman & Roberts, 1863 120-1. It is possible that the King passed through Brewood in July 1277 – on 9th July he was in Wolverhampton, and from 10th to 13th at Eccleshall: *ibid*. 120.

134. "Select Cases in the Court of King's Bench, Edward II", Vol. IV, Selden Society Vol. 74 1955 lii.

135. View of frankpledge dealt with misdemeanours of tenants, being the 'view' or supervision of the policing system called 'frankpledge', whereby every free man was required to join a 'tithing' of ten or a dozen people, who were collectively responsible for each others' good conduct. This local 'police court' business was a prerogative of the lord of the manor's jurisdiction over petty criminal matters, and in Brewood was conducted at the twice-yearly court leet. The word 'leet' derives from the Old French 'eslite' (elected), probably so-called because it also elected a jury and chose the manorial officials, including the bailiff, the constable, the pinder or hayward who dealt with grazing animals, and sometimes the ale-tasters and bread-weighers, an early form of consumer protection. An incomplete series of rolls of court leet and baron from 1338 to 1786 is held at SRO: VCH V 27.

136. SHC 1939 74. The claim was evidently to maintain the immunity of the Bishop's estates from the increasing jurisdiction of the Sheriff: VCH III 17.

137. Rowlands 1987 20. VCH VI 6.

138. Harleian MSS Cod. 3868. Walter Langton is the last Bishop known to have resided at Brewood.

139. Stebbing Shaw xxxi-xxxii. The three commissioners appointed to make this levy in Staffordshire included John Giffard of Chillington: VCH I 232.

140. R.E. Glassock, "The Lay Subsidy of 1334", The British Academy/O.U.P 1975 282.

141. A wara was a measure of land which may have equalled a virgate or ¼ of a caracute, ie., 20-30 acres.

142. No. 159 in PRO. SHC 1912 216.

143. The "Marlpit of Methplekes against the road which passes from Tong towards the Wood [Bishop's Wood]" was mentioned in an action in 1260: Griffiths 145.

144. Mander 1940 2.

145. SHC.

146. SHC XVII 188-191. See also R.H. Hilton, "The English Peasantry", Clarendon Press, 1975.

147. Cannock Chase was granted to the Bishop by the King in 1290 out of the much larger royal Forest of Cannock: VCH V 59.

148. VCH II 335.

149. VCH Shropshire I 484. The inhabitants of Tong and Tong Norton were fined in 1167 for offences against the Forest laws: Griffiths 144. See also C.H. Cox, "The Royal Forests of England," Methuen 1908 132-3, 222; Jean Burrell, 'The Forest and the Chase in Medieval Staffordshire' in "Staffordshire Studies," University of Keele Vol III 1990-1 23-50.

150. SHC 1923 300-1.

151. Cantor 39.

152. In 1129-30 the people of Chillington paid one mark by way of fine for assarting, and in the mid twelfth century there are records of assarts made by Siward the Cobbler, Ailric Berley, Leofric and Ravekel on the manor of Brewood: VCH II 34; VI 6.

153. Oakden 43.

154. They were still found in Cannock Forest in the 1280's: Greenslade & Stuart 30.

155. Trevor Rowley, "The Landscape of the Welsh Marches", Michael Joseph 1986 154.

156. VCH II 336; VCH Shropshire I 484.

157. A place called 'Dersprynge' is mentioned in the bounds of Wrottesley in 1088: VCH XX 11. Norman Forest law prohibited the creation of fences and hedges which would restrict the movement of deer, so villagers built 'corn ditches', earthen banks faced in stone and fronted by ditches, to protect their crops from the deer. Mere Oak nearby almost certainly takes its name from the Anglo-Saxon 'mær', meaning limit or boundary – of Wrottesley and Pattingham, and also perhaps the Forest.

158. Hawkswell, near Patshull, on the Staffordshire-Shropshire border, was in Brewood Forest: Wrottesley 1902 49. Kingswood may also have been within the royal Forest: VCH XX 80; II 336. Stebbing Shaw suggests that Brewood Forest extended to Kingswood and Westbeech, but that after disafforestation Kingswood was given to the men of Tettenhall: Vol II 303. Perton, Wrottesley and Bilbrook may have been within the Forest in the late 1160's: VCH XX 29.

159. Eyton 2 181.

160. SHC 1923 294, 300-1. Cannock Chase was created in 1290, the former royal Forest officials being replaced by those of the Bishop: VCH V 59. See also Stebbing Shaw II 312.

161. VCH II 237.

162. Charter Rolls I John.

163. There is a celebrated entry on a Fine Roll which records that "the wife of Hugo de Nevill gives the Lord King 200 chickens that she may lie with her husband for one night". The exact meaning of this cryptic entry has baffled historians: M. Ashley, "The Life and Times of King John", Weidenfield & Nicholson, 1972, 149.

164. Cal. Rot. Chart (Rec. Com.) i 122.

165. Close Rolls 7 John.

166. "Select Pleas of the Forest", Selden Society xiii 9-10.

167. Trevor Rowley *ibid*. 152.

168. It is unclear whether the fishpond was at Blackladies or Whiteladies: both places were in Brewood Forest, and nuns from both were described as Nuns of Brewood, but since Blackladies is much closer to Brewood Park, it has always been accepted that the fishpond was at Blackladies.

169. Transactions of Staffs. Arch. Soc. V 163.

170. The word hay, a term found only in the Marcher counties, literally means hedge, but the medieval hays seem to have been enclosures used for the control of deer. The hays were constructed for the purpose of either capturing game, usually roebuck, or in some cases for rearing game. At a later date the term was used in the region to mean larger enclosures, particularly in connection with debased Forests.

171. Mentioned in Abstract of Title dated 1862 with Giffard papers in Staffs. Record Office. The Moors adjoins the former lane between Villa Farm and Greystoke Cottage leading north to the Hawkshutts.

172. In the late 1600's at least part of the Dean of Wolverhampton's property at Codsall Wood was a park: VCH XX 85.

173. SHC vi 1885 182; M. Cantor, "The Deer Parks of South Staffordshire", pamphlet in Wolverhampton Reference Library.

174. Lichfield Charter F1426. The Bishop also had parks at Wyrley, Packington, Heywood and elsewhere. See also Cal. L R Henry III 1240-5 319; SHC 1924 330. Frost 1973 suggests that a park existed at The Hyde in 1372 [p.90], but the evidence is doubtful.

175. Eccl. Comm. 124088 LJRO.

176. E.P. Shirley, "English Deerparks", 1867 179-80.

177. Oakden 42.

178. See Tithe Map 1838.

179. A crude representation of Brewood Park appears in Joseph Browne's map of Staffordshire, 1682, in Plot's "The Natural History of Staffordshire".

180. The link with Dublin is Penkridge, the Deanery of which was connected with the Archbishopric. In 1259 Fulk de Sandford [who two years earlier had officiated at the burial of the late Bishop of Lichfield, Roger de Weseham, who had died at Brewood] persuaded Pope Alexander to permanently annexe the Deanery of Penkridge to the see of Dublin, and in 1260 to augment its revenues by conferring on the Archbishop in

perpetuity the prebends of swords in Dublin Cathedral: DNB Vol. L 272.

181. SHC 1911 12.

182. J.P. Jones, "A History of the Parish of Tettenhall in the County of Stafford", John Steen and Co. Ltd., 1894 94.

183. TSSAHS VII 37.

184. VCH V 26

185. TSSAHS VIII 37.

186. SHC 1930 363.

187. Information from Mr P.R. de L. Giffard, Chillington Hall.

188. VCH III 56.

189. A cord was a pile of wood 8' x 4' x 4'.

190. Stebbing Shaw II 292.

191. Perhaps dating from the grant of free warren in 1319.

192. The name dates from at least 1905, when it was meadow. A market garden later occupied the site.

193. The description 'Black Death' was invented by a Mrs Penrose in 1823. During the fourteenth century it was known as 'the Great Pestilence'. Contrary to popular belief, bubonic plague is neither contagious nor infectious, and can only be spread by the agency of certain fleas.

194. Alice de Harlegh, Prioress of Whiteladies, who died in 1349, may have been a victim of the plague. Richard Morys, Vicar of the White Nuns, is said to have died of the plague in 1394: Griffiths 209.

195. Hicks Smith 1864 13-14. The present location of the Return is unknown. See also VCH VI 37-8.

196. VCH III 56. In the Subsidy Roll of 1327 85 inhabitants are recorded [including 13 in Coven recorded separately] and in the Roll for 1332-3 80 people are listed [including 11 in Coven, shown separately], but since the basis of the taxation is uncertain, it is not possible to extrapolate estimated population figures.

197. VCH IV 6; Rowlands 1987 20.

198. The population of Staffordshire at this date has been estimated at 35,000: Palliser 80.

199. Vol II 163.

200. "Stafford Advertiser", 22nd September 1849. 605 people died in Bilston and 281 in Willenhall: VCH I 307.

201. On 29th November 1352 Sir Hugh de Wrottesley waylaid the Sheriff of Staffordshire on the road between Dunston and Penkridge and killed him and several of his party. Sir Hugh was imprisoned and his property confiscated, but he was later pardoned by the King: J.P. Jones *op. cit.*

202. VCH I 240.

203. Coroner's Rolls 1-13, H. IV, No. 167; SHC XVI 82.

204. Coram Rege Hillary 2 H. V.

205. Staffordshire Indictments I H. V.

206. – ditto –

207. This malefactor was seemingly involved in other such incidents: see VCH I 240.

208. It is of interest that one of the few places where ghosts have reputedly been seen is Hell Floor, close to Ackbury. [Hicks Smith 1867 34]. Is it conceivable that folk memory could perpetuate the incident for over 500 years?

209. De Banco, Trinity 1 and 4 H. VI.

210. SHC 1927 171.

211. SHC 1927 168.

212. SHC 1927 168-9.

213. SHC 1929 I 265.

214. SHC 1935 338.

215. SHC 1935 408.

216. The Codsall registers begin in 1587 and record the burial of 12 vagrants up to 1621, most before 1600.

217. Rowlands 1987 109.

218. Tithe Map 1838 D880/5/5 and Apportionment D932/6 SRO.

219. Oakden 48. The name Dead Woman's Grave is also found in Codsall, at the junction of County Lane and Husphins Lane. It is mentioned in the Codsall parish register in 1676 [p.78] and 1689 [p.91]. The spot is marked by a glacial erratic. See also VCH XX 79; "Black Country Bugle Annual," Mercia Publicity 1989 17-19.

220. Extracted from "Poor Relief in Staffordshire 1662-1840", Staffs. County Council 1968, 11.

221. Hicks Smith 1867 6. From September 1719 there are many entries in the parish registers relating to 'paupers'. The original workhouse may have dated from the 1730's, when the Workhouse Test Act encouraged such developments. The overseer's accounts make frequent reference to the workhouse from 1745, including many payments for hemp.

222. "Stafford Advertiser," 13th May 1865. Lord Hatherton became first chairman of the Board of Guardians, a post he held for 26 years. His son and grandson held the same position for 26 and 32 years respectively. The first chairman found work for many workhouse inmates reclaiming land on Cannock Chase. No official records are available for the first four years of the Penkridge Board, but Lord Hatherton kept a journal which throws much light on the early days of the new Poor Law administration.

223. For details of Brewood charities see Griffith 129-30; VCH V 47-8.

224. Hicks Smith 1874 11.

225. For contemporary letters and documents relating to recusancy in Elizabethan and Jacobean Staffordshire see SHC 4th Series 9.

226. While Elizabeth I may have occasionally travelled in a litter, she normally went on horseback, sometimes riding pillion.

227. By a statute of 33 Eliz. all except maiden ladies and nobles, lords, knights and gentlemen possessing land worth 20 marks a year were required on Sundays and holidays to wear woollen caps, on penalty of a fine of 3s 4d per day. When Elizabeth was at Stafford, Mary Queen of Scots was confined at Buxton: it was the moment in their lives when the two Queens were geographically closest to each other: VCH I 249.

228. The official guide to Chillington gives the date as 11th August: James Smith, "Chillington Hall", Hourdsprint 1973 1. The Queen had intended to travel from Stafford to Worcester, but changed her plans because Worcester was suffering from an outbreak of smallpox: 7/29 WSL.

229. In the WSL is a copy of Hicks Smith 1864 with an illuminating note in the author's handwriting: "The Compiler has been most careful not to do anything that should hurt the amour propre of the Squire of Chillington, disclose the recent rise of the Moncktons of Somerford, or shock the protestant prejudices of the Vicar."

230. "Mara".

231. Information from Mr P. R. de L Giffard *supra*.

232. This was during a progress through East Angia when a number of recusant gentry were exposed, some of whom spent the next 20 years in and out of prison. Rookwood's son Ambrose was executed for his part in the Gunpowder Plot of 1605.

233. In 1584 Thomas Gresley, the High Sheriff, was ordered by Queen Elizabeth to seize household goods from the attainted Lord Paget's mansion at Beaudesert and convey it to Tutbury for the use of Mary Queen of Scots: Dudley Wilks, "Fragments of Stafford's Past", R.W. Hourd & Son, 1932 47. See also VCH I 251.

234. SHC 1929 I 49.

235. On 28th November: Cal. State Papers Domestic 1581-90 561. But not before his armour had been confiscated: SHC 4th Series 9 16. His name is notably absent from a list of those who contributed funds to a subscription begun early in 1588 to help defray the cost of the force assembled to resist the Spanish invasion. An early subscriber in March was Roger Fowke of Brewood. Giffard's equivocal attitude was almost certainly the reason for the confiscation in 1588 of land he held at Broomhall, inherited from his grandfather who had held it since at least 1556. It is not widely known that there were English and Irish volunteers with the Armada fleet. At least 20 disaffected Catholic nobles sailed with the Armada, many the younger sons of English aristocrats who hoped that a Spanish conquest of England would secure for them land and power. One – Richard Burley from Weymouth – was hanged as a double-agent on his return to Spain. The Spanish army in the Netherlands had an entire English regiment, and 900 of them were to take part in the invasion of England.

236. VCH I 249.

237. SHC 1930 II 336-7.

238. For a contrary view, and interesting information about the hiding places at Boscobel, see Granville Squires, "Secret Hiding Places", Stanley Paul & Co., Ltd, 1934.

239. Mander 1960 65-6.

240. "A list of Staffordshire Recusants 1641", Staffordshire Catholic History Society 5 1964 5-7. VCH V 44 would appear to be incorrect.

241. Hicks Smith 1867 24.

242. SHC 4th series II 80-82.

243. "Staffordshire Catholic History" 5 5-7.

244. Stebbing Shaw I 384.

245. Fea, 1908 309-11. At the outbreak of the French Revolution in 1789, the Catholic College at Douai secretly buried its valuables beneath the hearth at St Edmunds College, Douai. A witness to the burial, Father Thompson, revealed the secret of the treasure in about 1840 to the Prior, but it was not until 1863 that a request was made to

Napolean III for permission to search for the treasure. Permission having been granted, a search began on May 10th. The following day a rotting wooden chest was uncovered at a depth of 8' containing several table services and about a dozen goblets, most of which were inscribed, including two with the arms of the Giffard family. One was engraved "1747 ex dono Nob: D: Detri Giffard de Chillington. Phiam. Defdts sub. R: D: Tho. Worswich, C.A.", the other "C.A. Ex dono Nob: D: Thomae Giffard de Chillington, Anno 1755". Both were clearly gifts from the Giffards, and are now held by Oscott College, Birmingham. [From a note in the catalogue of an Exhibition of Catholic Art and Antiques held at Oscott College on 8th-27th July 1929.]

246. M.W. Greenslade, "The 1767 Return of the Staffordshire Papists", Staffordshire Catholic History 17 5.

247. Wrottesley 1902.

248. SHC V NS 264-66.

249. Arms.

250. Body armour.

251. Strips of overlapping armour, especially for protecting arms and elbows.

252. An ornamental jerkin or jacket.

253. A globular helmet with outcurved back.

254. SHC 1935 299.

255. SHC 1935 402.

256. D 932/5 WSL.

257. SHC XV. Bound up with the 1640 Muster is the Muster Roll for 1634: *"A list of the Trayned horse for the County of Stafford, taken at Stafford the fifth day of June and at Lichfield the second day of October in the yeare of our Lord God 1635*

Cuttlestone Hundred		
Curasiers [inter alia]	*Peter Gyffard Esqr*	2
	Thomas Foulke of Brewood }	
	& Mr Wareinge }	1
Light Horse [inter alia]	*Mathew Moreton* }	
	Thomas Moreton }Esqrs	1
	John Foulke of Gunston	1"*

258. Andrew Giffard, the fifth son of Peter Giffard, was killed near Wolverhampton at an early stage of the conflict fighting for the royalist cause: Parke 1860 109.

259. Rowlands 1987 160.

260. Mander 1960 83.

261. Stebbing Shaw II 145.

262. "From a MS entitled "Providence Improved" of 42 extremely closely written ¼ to pages but which is partly copied p.106 et seq. of Vol. 50 of Coles MSS. Add MSS 5851 P1. CLXXXII". – manuscript note in handwriting of C.H. Bayley in "Notes & Collections Relating to Brewood", p.8 in Brewood Library, to which is added: "[this diary contains much curious information as to the Civil War in Staffs. He was a violent Parliamentarian]". See also VCH III 105; SCH 1927 138-9.

263. Wrottesley 322. See also HCS 1941 139.

264. SCH 1941 140. Mander 1960 87.

265. Mary Weate, "The Parish of Lapley-with-Wheaton Aston", Lapley Parish Council 1982 22. No source is given for this incident, about which there must be some doubt, for Tong Castle seems not to have been taken for parliament until 28th December, by a force from Eccleshall. On the other hand an Order of the Stafford Committee made on 25th January 1644 records that "captaine leiftenant Sergeant shall have the benefit of the discharge of captaine Creswall towards his great losses that he sustened when hee was taken prisoner at Chillington for the preservinge of Sir William Brereton his corne at Weston Lizeard". Brereton was then living at Weston. Much interesting information about Tong Castle during the Civil War is contained in Transactions of Shropshire Archæological Society, 4th Series Vol II 1-21.

266. D.R. Guttery, "The Great Civil War", Cornish Brothers Ltd., 1950.

267. From "Mercurius Aulicus", 26th December 1643, "A Diurnal communicating the intelligence and affairs of the court to the rest of the kingdom", a royalist news-sheet.

268. Taken from a translation of the Grant of Arms in Brewood church.

269. Minion lived until 1680: his burial is recorded in Brewood parish register on 22nd November.

270. Stebbing Shaw II 4.

271. Stebbing Shaw II 305.

272. SHC 4th Series I xiv.

273. Mander 1960 84.

274. At about this time royalist troops quartered in Penkridge were defeated in a skirmish with parliamentary forces: VCH V 106. Wilkes records [p.186] that many cannon balls have been found near Pillaton.

275. G. Wrottesley, "History of Wrottesley", Harrison & Sons 1903 322. Eccleshall and Rushall churches may also have been garrisoned: Mander 1960 87-8. See also "Captain Symmond's Diary", The Camden Society 74 1859.

276. D.R. Guttery op. cit.

277. State Papers Domestic SP29/58/73 in PRO. Also SHC 4th Series II 75.

278. The Scottish Army camped at Tong Heath on the same day.

279. Amongst the royalist officers was Captain Roger Fowke whose father, also Roger, was from Brewood Hall. Colonel George Mason of Gunstone fled to America in 1651, followed by his family and the younger Fowke, settling in Virginia, where Mason's son married Fowke's daughter. The Masons built a grand residence, Gunstone House, on their plantation overlooking the Potomac River, and their son George assisted George Washington to draft the Virginia Declaration of Rights in 1776. The first 10 amendments to the United States constitution were supposedly based on Mason's Bill of Rights. One of Mason's descendants who became U.S. ambassador to Britain visited Brewood and Gunstone in 1865: Hicks Smith 1867 54; Wakefield 26. Gunstone House in Virginia is preserved as a historic building: see National Geographic Magazine Vol LV No.4, April 1969.

280. Fea; Hughes; Kingston; Matthews.

281. Kingston. Fea refers to a narrow lane near Merton [? Nurton] Hill, p.16, quoting Tettenhall Antiquarian Society Proceedings, May 1882. Wrottesley indicates that the lane was County Lane: p.181.

282. The jewel was buried by Blague near the house at Blore Heath where he was

subsequently captured and sent to the Tower of London. It was recovered from its hiding place by Izaac Walton and taken to Blague in the Tower. Blague eventually escaped and managed to deliver the jewel to Charles in France.

283.   Under the command of Col. Ashenhurst.

284.   So-called either because the coppice was young, or from the springs in the area, which still flourish. In 1651 Spring coppice was what is now marked by the Ordnance Survey as Royal Oak Wood.

285.   Hubbal Grange may have been originally the grange, or home farm, of Blackladies – perhaps the virgate of land granted by the nuns of Blackladies to the abbot and convent of Buildwas at some date before 1247, when it was exchanged by Alan la Zouch, then lord of Tong, for benefits elsewhere [Mander 1940 28] – and in the eighteenth century was the largest farm in Tong parish. Between 1780 and 1797, during the minority of the second George Durant of Tong Castle, Hubbal and its outbuildings were apparently demolished by John Bishton, the agent at Tong Castle: Robinson 61. A small half-timbered cottage known as Hubbal Grange or Pendrill's Cot was built on the site and has often incorrectly been identified as the house visited by Charles. The cottage was occupied until at least 1953 ["Shropshire Magazine", July 1953 21], but having become derelict over many years [see drawing at Robinson 61 and photograph in R. Leek & E. Jones, "A Guide to the Midlands Way", 1979 131] it eventually collapsed in 1979. Some old timbers, brickwork and stonework, much overgrown, mark the site. Nearby to the west is a low gable in random sandstone blocks and a long length of sandstone wall some five feet high running south from the gable. The walling is all that remains of the building illustrated in Fea 1897 28. A quarter of a mile south of Hubbal are some curious earthworks on the west bank of the stream, almost certainly man-made. Their age and purpose are unknown. Hubballs Mill Forge, recorded in 1669 [VCH II 115], has no connection with the site: it was near Bridgnorth [SO 692916]. See also Trans. Shropshire Archæological Society, Vol XLIX 1937-8 14-15.

A stone and timber outbuilding (right) which formed part of Hubbal Grange, and (left) the half-timbered brick cottage known (erroneously) as Hubbal Grange, otherwise Penderel's Cot, as illustrated in Allan Fea's 'The Flight of the King', 1897. The cottage has virtually disappeared, but fragments of the outbuilding survive.

286.   Not to be confused with Joane [or Jane] Penderel, the wife of William Penderel, who was buried at Whiteladies in 1669, and called by Charles II "Dame Joane".

370

287. Sir Basil Brooke, who by tradition named Boscobel House, came from Madeley Court.

288. Information supplied by The Royal Observatory, Herstmonceux.

289. Carless is said to have been the second son of John Carless of Broomhall, although the parish registers do not record his birth and a correspondent to "Notes and Queries", 1st series X 344, suggested, somewhat improbably, that he was the son of Anthony Careless, Warden of the Clothiers Company in Worcester in 1665, who died there on 5th January 1670. A family of the surname Carlos at Stratford-upon-Avon is mentioned in the Visitation of Warwickshire [Harleian Soc. xii 23]. The surname Carles however occurs frequently in the area around Tong from at least early medieval times. A translation of the Grant of Arms to Carless dated 21st May 1658 at Brussels is in Brewood church. He is referred to as "William Carlose, son of John Carlose of Bromwal [sic]", and is recorded as having mustered a troop, then a regiment of cavalry, then undertaken the management of Lapley House and Tong Castle. He was captured and kept in custody for a year, then went to Ireland and to Spain, where he served in the army for 3 years before returning to England to fight for the royalist cause. The Grant records that ". . . he hid us for many Days and Nights in the shelter of a poor cottage and in the top of a shady oak". Fea 1908 states that he was a major in Lord Talbot's troop in 1651. He is also said to have given Mary, the Princess of Orange, the first news of her brothers escape [p.327].

290. Perhaps to support an alias, for with his local knowledge he would have needed no guide.

291. Formerly a heelmaker.

292. This incident is open to doubt, since although a reward of £1000 was offered, it was not announced until 10th September in London.

293. Transactions of Shropshire Archæological Society, 4th Series Vol. II 12. Also 2nd Series Vol. VIII 290.

294. Traditionally it was on this journey that Charles observed that his horse was "the heaviest dull jade he ever rode on", to which Humphrey Penderel replied: "My liege, can you blame the horse so heavily, when he has the weight of three Kingdoms on his back?"

295. From Charles' own account: "I could never get my Lord Wilmot to put on any disguise, he saying that he should look frightfully in it; and therefore did never put on any." There is some evidence that Wilmot was even accompanied throughout by his servant, Robert Swan.

296. Whitemoor lane is recorded in 1305: Oakden 43.

297. Some accounts suggest that Walker may have been living at Whiteladies at the time of the escape.

298. In 1622 about 10 Jesuits in Staffordshire were based at a house in the county big enough for 8-10 of them and fitted with priest holes under the protection of a powerful patron: Thomas McCoog, "The Establishment of the English Province of the Society of Jesus", Recusant History XVII 1984-5 136-7. The house has not been identified – Boscobel has been suggested – but Chillington House seems much more likely. For interesting observations on this and Charles II's escape see Michael Hodgett, "Worcestershire Recusant", No. 48 Dec 1966.

299. The latter mill was in existence from at least the 1650's. Between then and the nineteenth century it was known variously as Barnhurst, Pendeford or New Mill, the last name suggesting the existence of another, older mill. The mill was demolished in

1961. Yates map of Staffordshire, 1775, shows two water mills at Pendeford. The northern one, although labelled Pendeford Mill, has not been documented, but the field to the west [sic] side of the Penk at that point is shown in the Tithe Map of 1838 as Mill Meadow. See also VCH XX 33. Fea 1897 64 suggests that the mill to which Charles was taken was Old Mill Farm at Coven Heath, marked as Old Mill on the First Edition 1" Ordnance Survey map of 1834. That mill is en route to Moseley. It is mentioned in a perambulation of 1588 [in Bushbury manor papers in the Foxley Collection, copy in Wolverhampton Public Library], was in operation until the last century, and was demolished in the 1970's. In 1991 the remains of a sluice gate in the stream which fed it could still be seen a few yards from the west bank of the Staffs and Worcs canal: Chatwin 63. According to Lord Clarendon's later version of events, the King was forced by blistered feet to spend the night in a cottage, where he stayed overnight, with an adjustment in the dates of subsequent events. That version is not supported by the weight of evidence.

300. By accident or design it was Huddlestone who heard Charles' deathbed confession and administered the last sacraments in 1698 at the age of 90.

301. There has been considerable confusion between Francis Yates who accompanied the King from Worcester to Whiteladies and the Francis Yates who accompanied Charles from Boscobel to Moseley. Possible clarification is contained in Fea 1904 xxiv-xxv.

302. Fea 1904 xv. Several people named Blount appear to have assisted the King before the battle of Worcester, including Sir Walter Blount, Robert Blount of Keswick, Peter Blount and Edward Blount. The author of "Boscobel" may have been related to one of these 'loyal subjects': see "The Boscobel Tracts", bound with "Memoirs of the Court of Count Grammont", edited by Sir Walter Scott, George Bell & Sons 1891 444. Another possibility, based on evident local knowledge of Staffordshire and Shropshire, is that the author was a member of the old Staffordshire family of Blount of Blount Hall, which became extinct in the middle of the eighteenth century: Fea 1904 xv.

303. Seemingly with the help of a pass from the parliamentarians in a false name obtained by William Penderel from Humphry Ironmonger, an old friend of Carless who lived in Wolverhampton: Fea 1904 111.

304. A translation of the Grant hangs within Brewood Church. William Carless son of William Carless, Governor of Tong Castle, is said to have been admitted to the Jesuit College in Rome in 1654: Trans. of Shrop. Arch. Society, New Series Vol I.

305. John Penderel is said to have lived at Beamish Hall, Albrighton, after the Restoration: Fea 1904 59.

306. Fea 1904 59. His grandson was a godson of the Queen, Catherine of Braganza, and was sent to Rome to be educated at the Jesuit College, but was later released from his vows to become a secret agent of the Stuarts, then once more in exile, and became a Sardinian Marquis with the title Penderel di Boscobello. [Matthews states, without quoting sources, that Richard Penderel died in 1672, William in 1706, and Humphrey in 1710: p.173. But see Transactions of Shropshire Archæological Society, 3rd Series Vol. VII 1907 190-2 and Journals of The Pendrill Family History Society.]

307. The derivation of the name is unknown, though various imaginative suggestions have been put forward: see Archæologia 1873 58-9. The consensus of opinion is that the name means 'fat cheeks'.

308. It is said that he furnished 30 vessels and 100 men for the conquest, and himself headed this contingent at Hastings. Other accounts say that he was the Conqueror's standard bearer in Normandy, but begged to be excused at Hastings on the ground of

old age, and that two of his sons fought with William, one returning to Normandy and one remaining in England to found the Giffard family. It is said that only four families in England can claim direct descent from a Norman who fought at Hastings: the Mallets, the Gresleys, the Marrisses, and the Giffards. However, J.R. Planché, who spent many years researching the family, stated "I have hitherto searched in vain for any charter or contemporary document which throws light one way or the other on the question, and neither I nor any other geneaologist I am aware of can produce a pedigree of the Giffards of Chillington which can be authenticated to a generation earlier than of Peter, the son of William, and nephew by marriage of Peter Corbucion of Chillington." [Archæologia 1873 64].

309. Some accounts suggest that this was Walter's eldest son, also called Walter, but see Archæologia 1873 61.

310. Possibly from a manor in Nottinghamshire variously spelt Styrap, Stirop and Sturrop, which may have been connected with the Giffards: Archæologia 1873 65-6.

311. John Mytton [1796-1834], sportsman and eccentric, who inherited a fortune at an early age. He was MP for Shrewsbury for a short time, High Sheriff of Shropshire and Merionethshire, and a member of the Albrighton Hunt. He lost his entire fortune by reckless living, at one time consuming an average of 5 bottles of port daily. He died of alcoholism in the King's Bench prison aged 37: DNB XL 15.

312. Rowlands 1987 29.

313. VCH V 27. Amongst Staffordshire charters in the possession of the Marquis of Anglesey is a vellum court roll of Brewood manor dated 1468: SHC 1939 153.

314. D1766/35 SRO.

315. 'Halh' names are common in Staffordshire. Most sites fit the definition 'small valley' or 'dry ground in a marsh'. The halh element in the names Codsall, Tettenhall and Broom Hall probably means 'small valley' or 'hollow': Gelling 1984 105. The statement by Parke [5, 100-1] that Broom Hall is mentioned in Domesday Book is incorrect.

316. A knight's fee was the endowment of a mounted warrior.

317. 590/436/1-2 WSL.

318. A court of record held periodically in the hundred, lordship or manor before the lord or his steward, and attended by residents of the district. It was of considerable importance before the passing of the Constabulary Act, when constables, headboroughs and other officers were appointed.

319. An assembly of the freehold tenants of the manor under the presidency of the lord or his steward.

320. TSSAHS XII 1970-1 35.

321. – ditto –

322. – ditto –

323. There are Hydes at Coppenhall and Kinver.

324. Inquisitions 23 Ed. I 176. The court would have been the court leet, traditionally held at Easter and Michaelmas.

325. William Smith's manuscript map of Staffordshire, made in 1599, shows in addition to Hilton Park, north-east of Wolverhampton, held by the Vernons, another Hilton a short distance north-west of Chillington, also marked as held by the Vernons, presumably in error, for the Vernons are not known to have held property in Brewood.

John Hilton of Brewood, gentleman, is recorded in 1640 [Thorpe 366 WSL], and the parish registers record the burial on 9th September 1729 of Elizabeth, wife of Bartholemew Jones of Hilton.

326   On the west side of the churchyard is a gravestone to Jeremiah Smith, "Joiner and Borderman of the Deanery Manor", who died on 29th March 1767. 24 acres were released in 1904, and 8 acres conveyed to the Grammar School for a sports field in 1911.

327.   Rowlands 1987 44.

328.   VCH III 141; TSSAHS Vol. II 1960-1.

329.   For drawings illustrating the possible development of the nave, see VCH V 42.

330.   SHC VI II 92. In medieval times the church porch was a place of importance, for not only were penitent sinners given absolution for their sins before entering the church, but the baptism service began there and part of the marriage service was held there.

331.   A previous organ was installed and opened on Wake Sunday, 24th September 1815: Parson ccxvii.

332.   Parke 13.

333.   The Briscoes were shop-owners who lived at Old Fallings Hall and subsequently rented Somerford. Walter Giffard married Constance Briscoe. They lived at Pendrell Hall, Codsall Wood, and their son Richard moved to Chillington Hall.

334.   Transactions of Birmingham Archæological Society Vol. 68 22.

335.   The first and second tombs are thought to be by the Royleys of Burton. There is no trace of earlier monuments to the Giffards mentioned in Ashmole MSS No. 853f. 28.

336.   "Stafford Advertiser", 23rd March 1878.

337.   VCH V 43 says shortly before 1851 by the Earl of Ducie.

338.   Hicks Smith 1864 30. The father of the first stationmaster was churchwarden when the church was altered.

339.   Unveiled by the Rev. E.J. Carlos of St Georges, New Thundersley, Essex, in May 1960.

340.   Approximately 9" x 5" x 1", and believed to be 13th century: VCH V. In Wakefield's notebook [p.60] is the entry: "An old red tile with red markings on is said by the British Museum to be 14th Century, as was also an Etruscan tile with ancient figure on found whilst digging a grave": 148/1/72 WSL. It is unclear whether the latter is the Judas tile.

341.   VCH V 40.

342.   See Parke; SHC 1915 37-40. Also introduction to "Brewood Parish Register", Vol I Stafford Parish Register Society 1906. There are references to Richard de Brewode, chaplain, in the mid-fourteenth century [1347 – Calendar of Close Rolls p.246; 1350 – Inquisitions Ed. III Vol IX 215], but he may not have been connected with the church of Brewood.

343.   Domesday Book.

344.   Doc. 25 Magnum Registrum Album; SHC 1924 94.

345.   SHC 1924 192.

346.   SCH 1921 4-5. For reference to Philip le Clerk see Cal. of Close Rolls p.478.

347.   SCH X NSII 110.

348.   SCH X NSII 144.

349. – ditto –

350. After his death, his servant was accused of robbing him of money and jewels: VCH V 40.

351. Buried at Brewood 12th May 1587: parish register.

352. Said to have been "no preacher, a notable swearer and drunkard": VCH V 40.

353. Buried at Brewood 20 November 1629: parish register.

354. Also appointed vicar of Bushbury on 7th August 1641. Buried at Bushbury on 26th May 1684.

355. He was the son of Thomas Dolman of Seisdon, who was a member of the Stafford Parliamentary Committee during the Civil War: SHC 4th Series I 349. His wife Margaret was the daughter of William Bendy, a member of the same Committee.

356. Buried at Brewood 3rd October 1715: parish register. In 1668 an unlicensed schoolmaster of the same name seems to have been teaching at Codsall: VCH XX 143.

357. Buried 12th October 1760 at St Mary's Church, Stafford.

358. Died 23rd March 1762 aged 30: Parke 28.

359. Known for his fondness for antiquarian and topographical research. He made considerable progress in collecting materials for a general history of Staffordshire which he intended to publish. He purchased Dr Wilkes' collection of antiquarian papers on Wilkes' death, and seems to have lived in Brewood from 1762 to 1769 when he ran into financial difficulties and emigrated to Gloucester County, Virginia, where he died in about 1775. His papers were eventually acquired by Stebbing Shaw.

360. Fea 1897 57. However, a list of the more noteworthy tombstones and monuments in the churchyard recorded in 1860 [Parke 26-30] does not include any reference to a Careless memorial. Since no illustration of, or reference to, any contemporary gravestone or monument is known, it seems probable that any such memorial – if indeed one ever existed – was lost or destroyed long ago. [Ashmolean MS 853 gives details of gravestones in Brewood churchyard in 1680].

361. SHC VI Pt.II.

362. VCH V 40.

363. A large stone built into the brickwork of the end house in School Road was said to mark the boundary of the old Vicarage Croft: 148/1/72 p.60 WSL. The block – and another round the corner in Church Road – still exists.

364. Hicks Smith 1874 13.

365. Postcard c.1933, ref. 443/32 in WSL. Mr P.R. de L. Giffard *supra* suggests that the statue came originally from Chillington. It is said to have been kept in a chest in the schoolhouse until shown to Father Groom who arranged for it to be displayed in the church. In the earlier years of this century it is said to have been carried round the village to the houses of the sick, and to have had a reputation for curing eye ailments: Wakefield [148/1/72 WSL] 37.

366. Gelling 1978 176-7. In Old English the letter c was pronounced ch when it appeared before i. On reliable evidence the common use of the element 'tun' has been dated to the two centuries between 750 and 950 AD. It is also of interest that the word would not have been used for a village or farm lying in a forest area, indicating that the area around Chillington was clear of heavy woodland from an early date: see Gelling 1981 4.

367. There is a reference in 1266 to the taking of deer from Cannock Forest without warrant by six people including Robert Chenney. The venison was carried to Chillington "which was then in the hands of the said Robert [sic]": J.P. Jones *supra*. 112. This was during the period of Simon de Montfort's rebellion when the Giffards were ejected from their estates at Chillington and Walton.

368. Information from Mr P.R. de L. Giffard *supra*.

369. SHC vi 1885 182.

370. SHC 1931 65.

371. Stebbing Shaw II 302.

372. This construction was exposed during renovation work in the saloon, which also revealed a Tudor fireplace two yards to the left of the present fireplace. Information from Mr P.R. de L. Giffard supra.

373. Recorded on 23rd September 1663: Feilde Notebook 7 [SMS 426] WSL.

374. SHC V NS. The undated map of the old house is SRO 590/571d.

375. When imprisoned in Castle Bolton, Wensleydale, for six months, Mary had a retinue of 51 servants, and at Wingfield 48, plus 210 guards, etc.

376. Of Pillaton.

377. DNB XXIII 302-3. Wilkes, p.121, suggests that Mary was allowed freedom of movement, though under strict surveillance while at Tutbury, and that by tradition she visited the Giffards at Chillington and stayed at Pepper Hill near Albrighton in 1569 and 1570. No sources are given for this information. See also Wrottesley 143-159; A.G. Smith, "The Babington Plot", Macmillan & Co., Ltd., 1936.

378. p.360.

379. See Byng 142-4. During the eighteenth century William Pitt described Chillington as one of the two finest timbered estates in the county. Profits from timber felled in 1760 amounted to £978.19s, and there were further heavy fellings in the 1790's, when the poet Cowper was celebrating the sowing of groves of oaks in the Park: VCH VI 68.

380. 590/635 SRO.

381. 590/645 SRO.

382. VCH V 29 suggests that the building dates from 1787 and was perhaps the work of Soane.

383. It is referred to in the Will of Peter Giffard made in 1739. At the time of the Babington conspiracy Richard Giffard, the second son of John Giffard, was arrested, probably as a result of his association with the conspirators, but was soon released in the absence of evidence against him.

384. Eccl. Comm. 124088 LJRO. The Avenue may have continued eastwards, over what is now Coven Road, the line marked by a hedge on the east side of Forge House.

385. Sycamores, not a native tree, were introduced in the seventeenth century: Palliser 108.

386. Byng 142-4. The fortunes of the Giffard family at this date were at a low ebb.

387. The formal gardens of the mid-1700's, swept away later in the century, were also restored in a simplified form to a design by Inigo Triggs.

388. Mr P.R. de L. Giffard has planted a small copse to the north of the Hall in memory of Airey Neave, his brother-in-law, who was married in Brewood Church in 1942. Two grey firs represent two guards at Colditz prison camp, from which Neave escaped in

January 1942. He was killed by a terrorist car bomb in 1969.

389. In 1858, for example, the Stourbridge and East Warwickshire District of Ancient Order of Foresters held a giant picnic for the benefit of the widows and orphans fund. Several bands provided entertainment, and special trains were laid on from Birmingham and Shrewsbury. The visitors from Birmingam alone numbered 1,900: "Stafford Advertiser", 7th August 1858. Trips to Chillington were regularly organised from Birmingham. It was said that a one-legged Peninsular War veteran was employed as a boatbuilder to construct and maintain the boats on the lake. The rhododendron-lined canal was navigable almost as far as the Hall: Walter White, "All around the Wrekin", Chapman and Hall 1860 12. In 1859 an anonymous correspondent was complaining that entry to the park could only be obtained by ticket from the Giffard's Arms, the proprietor advertising that he had recently added a large assembly room: see "The Wolverhampton Spirit of the Times", 9th and 27th July 1859.

390. An indication of the problems at this period is the formation of the Chillington Association for the Protection of Property and Prosecution of Felons, which existed between 1828 and 1859 [590/741 SRO] and which in June 1851 at a dinner held at The Lion presented PC Batkin of Brewood with a sabre and belt for his valuable services: "Stafford Advertiser", 14th June 1851.

391. For comments on the effect on Chillington Park, see "Country Life", 13th September 1973 727-8, and Roy Strong and others, "The Destruction of the Country House, 1875-1974", 1974 129-30.

392. Further north, a cross stood on the Wolverhampton-Stafford road at the junction of the lane to Lower Drayton in 1754: VCH V 104.

393. Oakden 49.

394. *ibid.* 47.

395. *ibid.* 48.

396. SCH 1931 8.

397. Byng 142-4. Giffard's Cross was the site of an open-air service on Rogation Sunday for many years until the 1960's. The service normally started at 3.00pm. If the weather was wet, the church bells would ring at 2.45 to tell villagers that the service was transferred to the church. A small portable organ was often taken to the outdoor service.

398. The cross is now 5' 8" tall, the bottom two feet or so having been cut off as the wood had rotted. Nearby stands a modern sculpture in Ancaster stone carved by Mr J.A. Twentyman which is said to represent the legendary panther, and a small bronze cannon mounted on a gun trolley. The barrel bears the inscription "W. & F. Kinman fecere 1786", with the Giffard crest and arms.

399. Oakden 41.

400. Including Parke 68; "Farbairns Book of Crests", 4th Edition, Vol I, T.C. & E.C. Jack, 1905 225; "Banners Standards and Badges from a Tudor manuscript in the College of Arms with an Introduction by Lord Howard de Walden", The de Walden Library, 1804 201, 244.

401. Wrottesley 210. Mr P.R. de L. Giffard *supra* suggests that as the panther is rarely found in heraldry, the crest may have been a personal gift of the King to mark the esteem in which he held John Giffard. Wrottesley suggests [p.111-12] that the grant of the standard of a demi-archer and the Giffard motto may reflect the favour with

377

which John Giffard was regarded by the King, who was himself a skilled archer. From the same source [p.205-6] we learn of an undated deed of the reign of Edward I [1272-1307] in which Sir Robert Giffard, the rector of the church of Clovelly, granted to Gervase Giffard, son of Walter Giffard of Clifford, all his lands at Westerabouwood [West Bowood] within the manor of Abbotsham. The seal shows a man kneeling on one knee taking aim with a bow and arrow. This device is a pun on the name of Bowood, but it is surely a remarkable coincidence that the Herald's added this device to the standard of Sir John Giffard of Chillington in 1523.

402. John Timbs & Alexander Gunn, "Abbeys, Castles & Ancient Halls of England & Wales. Their Legendary Lore and Popular History", F. Warner & Co., 2nd edition, Vol II, 554. Also Palmer 1846, and "St James Magazine" September 1849. Mr P. R. de L. Giffard *supra* believes the story goes back to at least 1800, for he remembers his father telling him how he was told the story by his grandfather, who was told it as a child.

403. Palmer 53.

404. Pevsner visited the Hall for 15 minutes, promising to call back. He never did: Mr P.R. de L. Giffard *supra*.

405. Archæologia 1873 66-7.

406. See VCH III 220-222. An Inquisition was held at Cannock into, inter alia, the Monastry of Black Nuns at Brewode on 29th April 1527: "The jury are ignorant of who the patrons or founders of the Nunnery were": SHC 1939 82.

407. Magnum Registrum Album No. 221; SHC 1924.

408. Charter Rolls 2 John.

409. Cal. Liberate R. 1240-45 71.

410. The Prioress found herself embroiled in another dispute in 1283, when a Papal Bull was addressed to the Bishop to the Black Nuns of Brewood, in which Clement de Wolverhampton, clerk, sued Alice, Prioress, Robert de Stafford and Robert atte Hyrst for taking by force two oxen belonging to him at Horsebrok, worth 40s., and in a separate action Clement sued Alice and Robert and another for forcibly breaking into his house at Horsebrok and taking his goods and chattels worth 100s. The defendants failed to appear, and the Sheriff was ordered to distrain. He managed to recover only 10s from goods taken from Alice, and the defendants were therefore ordered to re-appear before the court. The outcome of the case is not recorded: Griffiths 205-6.

411. Tax Eccl. P. Nich. 162.

412. Close Rolls 1237-42, 473; 1254-56, 334; 1264-68, 331.

413. SHC XIX 176.

414. SHC 4th Series VII has details in Latin [p82-83] of Bishop Blythe's visitations, c.1515-1525, which include Whiteladies and Blackladies.

415. Rowlands 1987 98.

416. *ibid*. 99.

417. Edward Littleton of Pillaton.

418. Rowlands 1987 99.

419. – ditto –

420. F.A. Hibbert, "The Dissolution of the Monasteries", Sir Isaac Pitman & Sons Ltd., 1910.

421. In the William Salt Library is a portfolio said to contain "Captain Eyre's Journal", with drawings by Eyre and Hollar, among which is a sketch of Blackladies inscribed: "1644. The Old Benedictine Nunnery at Brewood, which was held against the Royalists under Lord Wilmot for six days when they left to attempt the raising of Dudley Castle, where was blocked in Sir Thomas Levison for the King. This house is large, and was founded in the time of King Richard ye first, but when valued at the visitation the value was small." This portfolio, including the sketch of Blackladies, is an elaborate forgery, produced in the Victorian period, but may have misled other historians – e.g. Rowlands 1959.

422. See claim to extraparochiality. Brewood parish registers record the burial at Blackladies of Joseph Lloyd on 13th August 1719. The register of burials at Whiteladies runs only from 1828. Until then the burials were entered in Donington register under an Order of Sessions dated 15th January 1694.

423. Robinson 61. See also SHC 1939 204.

424. A detailed description of the house was compiled by the Royal Commission on Historical Monuments (England) in 1983. See also VCH V 37. The engraving [Plate 8] in Stebbing Shaw Vol II which purports to show Blackladies is a view of the old house at Long Birch.

425. Niven 13.

426. Mander 1940 44.

427. Information from Mr D.L.H. Bywater, Blackladies.

428. The gatehouse at Upton Cressett, Shropshire, is dated 1580 and is said to be the earliest dated brick house in the county. See also E. Mercer and P. Stamper, "Plaish Hall and Early Brickwork in Shropshire," Transactions of Shropshire Archæological & Historical Society Vol LXVI 1989 90-96.

429. Vol. 27 p.89 Coles MSS British Museum. However, it is possible that the reference relates to Brewood church. It is of interest that the Inquisition held on the death of Sir Thomas Giffard, who died in 1560, refers to "the site" of Blackladies, whereas all other holdings are described as "manors" or "lands and tenements" [Wrottesley 124.] The same description is used in the Inquisition on the death of John Giffard in 1613 and Walter Giffard in 1632 [ibid. 140, 162].

430. Granted by Earl Aelfgar to the church of St Remigius, Rheims in about 1061. It was dissolved in 1415 and all its possessions granted to the recently founded college at Tong. No remains are now visible. The Monk's Walk may be part of the path between Lapley and Tong.

431. They may have been the fishponds into which the stag was chased in 1276.

432. There is some evidence that the school was in another building at a later date which was being used for stabling in 1882: Niven 13. Griffiths visited Blackladies in 1881 and says: "The chapel between the pool and the stockyard is now used as stabling; in one wall is a stone cross, perpendicular, let into the wall": [207-8]. It seems that he confused the stable with the then demolished chapel.

433. Palmer 48. There are other errors in the drawing and in other illustrations in the book. The chapel and part of the house are illustrated in Stebbing Shaw Vol.II.

434. Niven 13. The pewter chalices from the five Catholic chapels at Boscobel, Blackladies, Chillington, Long Birch and Whiteladies are now held at Oscott College, Birmingham: Wakefield 75.

435. Mander 1940 43.

436. Parke 1860 99-101. Whiteladies was both extraparochial and extramanorial: Gelling 1990 53.

437. All extraparochial places automatically became civil parishes in 1894.

438. There is a tradition that he was buried at Blackladies: Hicks Smith 1867 26.

439. "The Catholicon", Vol. i April 1818; Henry Foley, "Records of the English Province of the Society of Jesus 1875-1884", Vol. III 795-7; Cherry 56. [Both Foley and Cherry misdate Hodshead's confession as 1615]. See also SHC Vol VI Part II 1886 214.

440. Some mud cottages still existed at Chebsey in 1819: Peters 213.

441. Brick making seems to have started in the area in the sixteenth century, and by the early eighteenth century brick had effectively replaced timber-framing in new buildings, particularly after the second Great Rebuilding c1670-1720. There was a considerable expansion of brick-making in the area, encouraged by the ready availability of suitable clay, and by 1831 Staffordshire was the main brick-producing county. The imposition of the Brick Tax in 1784 encouraged the trend towards larger bricks, with 2¼" bricks appearing in 1762, mixed with 3" by 1762, and 3" alone by 1815. A decline in brick production in the early 1840's was probably due to a further tax in 1839, as was the appearance of 3¼" bricks. The use of these declined after the tax was removed in 1850: Peters 3-5.

442. The tiles, with integral nibs, measure 10½" by 6¼", a size fixed by statute in1477.

443. The Overseers' accounts contain a number of references to payments made for thatching houses of the poor, and Pitt mentions thatched cottages, farmhouses and farmbuildings in 1796, although he states that tiles and slates were to be preferred, and mentions the loss of almost all of Wheaton Aston by fire: p.22.

444. It is unclear whether there was a pump between 1837 and 1892: no pump is shown on the 25" Ordnance Survey map of 1884. Indeed, there is some slight evidence that the spot may have been the site of the old market house until it collapsed in 1810: see Q S Epiphany 1799 SRO. In SRO [D014/6/1] is an Account Book 1776-1781 of Francis Madin, Blacksmith, which contains a loose manuscript sheet:

"The account of Repairs done at the Town Pump by me Thos Arckin

May 7 me and 2 men taking the pump and putting down		0	7	6
Tallow flanell and Resin and nails			1	10
Letther			0	4
August 5 Man half day going to ye wood			1	0
Bouring a tree		0	12	0
a new spout		0	1	3
Letther and nails		0	1	1
cement and flanell		0	0	7
me and men a day and half putting the pump down and completing it		0	7	0
		1	12	7"

445. Including Parker's Place and Meadow View in Brewood Road, Coven, dated 1896 and 1906 respectively; Oak Villa in Engleton Lane; Maidens Butchers in Stafford Street with a plaque "AW 1896"; and Hawthorns, in Coven Road, Brewood.

446. Thomas Andrew Walker was born on 15th October 1828. His father, agent to the Chillington estate, subsequently moved to Villa Farm at Kiddemore Green, and later to The Whitemoor. Thomas was educated at Brewood Gramar School, followed by a brief period at Kings College studying engineering. His studies were cut short by the

need to earn a living, and before he was 17 he had gained experience working as a railway engineer. In 1845 and 1846 he was involved in parliamentrary surveys, and in 1847 was working on the North Staffordshire Railway, based at Stafford, where he remained for 5 years, before sailing for Canada to assist in the building of the Grand Trunk Railway. Two years later he was building railways in the Canadian Lower Provinces, returning to Britain in 1861. In 1863 he was surveying for railways in Russia, and in the following two years engaged in similar work in Egypt and The Sudan. In 1865 he returned to England to supervise the construction of the Metropolitan and District Railways, completed in 1871. Soon after, in partnership with his brother Charles, he undertook the contract for the extension of the East London Railway from the end of Brunel's Thames Tunnel, under the London Docks and through Wapping, Shadwell and Whitechapel. Walker so impressed the supervising engineer, Sir John Hawkshaw, that he was awarded the contract for the Severn Tunnel. While engaged in this work, Walker was also building docks at Barry, Preston and Buenos Aires, and was also constructing the Manchester Ship Canal. He died aged 61 at Mount Ballan, Chepstow, on 25th November 1889. Walker was a particularly philanthropic and humane employer, showing great concern for the physical and spiritual welfare of his workforce, often providing hospitals, coffee houses, concert halls, schools and mission halls, as well as comfortable cottages. When he died, 24,000 workers were employed by his company, and he left a fortune of £750,000: Wakefield 67-8.

447.   Presumably on the site of an earlier building: on Sunday 1st July 1792 the Hon John Byng, travelling from Blackladies, wrote: "I began to feel myself quite perish for dinner and hurried along to Brewood, whose tall spire was in sight. In this mean market town the Red Lion ale house received me; and being put into a white-washed room, got a miserable, neither hot-nor-cold dinner. . ." Byng 142-4.

448.   Until at least 1930 a matching roundel existed to the right of the door reading "Official Quarters: National Cyclists Union".

449.   Wakefield 27. The old court building at Penkridge now houses the library.

450.   It is generally held that Speedwell Castle was built by William Rock, apothecary, who married Mary How of Boscobel and died in 1753 – see VCH V 23, which relies on Hicks Smith 1874 34. Stephen Bayley ["Carpenter's Gothic", NSJFS Vol.16 1976 42-6] explores the matter in more detail, stating "what evidence there is tells us quite incontrovertibly that Speedwell was built by a local apothecary, William Rock . . ." What seems to have been overlooked is that Hicks Smith, by no means a meticulous historian, had earlier stated equally categorically [1867 16] that it was built by Thomas Pendrell Rock, [stated by Hicks Smith 1874 to be the son of William and Mary Rock, a suggestion not evidenced by the Chillington Catholic register, which records the baptism of other children of William and Mary] who is said to have owned the racehorse 'Speedwell'. In fact the horse was owned by the Duke of Bolton [see John Cherry, "Portraiture of Horses", 1740]. Hicks Smith's earlier statement appears to be based on a footnote in Parke 1860 40, where it is stated that Thomas Pendrell Rock, who is said to have inherited the name Pendrell as a descendant of Humphrey Penderel of Boscobel fame and practised as a surgeon, and was buried on 28th November 1815 aged 87, "was the builder of a singular-looking house at Brewood which he named Speedwell Hall [sic] after a race horse, the winner of some valuable stakes," the first published reference to the builder of Speedwell Castle: the footnote does not apppear in the first edition of Parke, 1858. There is no evidence to show why Hicks Smith altered his earlier attribution, but the relatively early date ascribed to

Speedwell by Bayley is perhaps based in weak evidence. The matter is complicated by the fact that William Rock, apothecary, who was living in Brewood from at least 1701 [Chillington Catholic Registers] had a son, William, baptised on 5th June 1728, [the year of the birth of Thomas Pendrell Rock] who also became an apothecary. William senior was buried at Brewood on 27th August 1752, William junior on 9th December 1753, but any attempt to compile a pedigree becomes confused by the existence of other Rocks in Brewood at the same period, including those connected with the operation of the ironworks. The wills of William senior and William junior are in LJRO, but throw no light on the origins of Speedwell Castle. The attribution of Speedwell to Thomas Pendrell Rock would seem more likely, particular since John Hay, responsible for the greater part of Parke 1860 has proved to be a reliable historian. The stylistic evidence of Speedwell, both internally and externally, which suggests a date in the early 1760's, may be the most reliable guide to its age. Even the name is of little assistance, for evidence that it pre-dates the nineteenth century is lacking, although the word castle – which the footnote in Parke 1860 implies might be a relatively recent appellation – might suggest that the building was formerly crenellated. However, restoration work on the parapet in 1992 indicated otherwise. It is possible that the house was built to reflect the styling of Tong Castle, remodelled for George Durant by Thomas Farnolds Pritchard [or 'Capability' Brown, who also worked at Chillington – see Robinson 57], c.1765. Is it possible that whilst employed at Chillington and Tong, Brown found time to design a miniscule town-house on the most conspicuous, albeit compact, site available in Brewood? To add to the mystery, against the traditional story of the origins of Speedwell Castle in Wakefield's notebook [148/1/72 WSL] is the single word 'wrong' in her handwriting.

451. Batty Langley, born the son of a Twickenham gardener in 1696, became in turn a landscape gardener, drawing master, surveyor, hydraulic engineer, manufacturer of artificial stone ornaments, journalist, prolific author, and architect. At one time one of the most fashionable landscape gardeners of the period, Batty wrote a number of illustrated practical handbooks on almost every aspect of building, garden layout and plant cultivation from 1726 onwards, and set up a school of architecture in Soho with his brother Thomas, an engraver. But what brought Langley fame in the last decade of his life was his series of Gothic designs, first issued in 1741 and 1742 as 64 plates engraved by his brother, which were reissued in 1747 as a single volume called "Gothic Architecture, Improved by Rules and Proportions". In particular, the plates depicted five 'Gothic orders' of Langley's own invention, for which he was widely ridiculed, but the 'Batty Langley Manner', characterised by an exhuberant style incorporating the ogee or S-curve, proved nevertheless to be very popular. From 1742 onwards his designs were widely adopted by builders and architects, and even spread across the Atlantic, inspiring houses in towns such as Providence, Rhode Island. The Gothic Pavilion at Painshill was built to Langley's designs. He died in poverty in Soho in 1751.

452. An earlier ornament in the same position was in the form of a large flat fleur-de-lis, an unlikely ornament which may have come from the Fleur-de-Lis public house on the opposite corner of Market Place, demolished c.1845. Batty's design books suggest that the original finial may have been a decorative acorn.

453. The licence was transferred to a Tettenhall inn on 9th April 1932: Wakefield notebook 48/1/72 p.73 WSL.

454. The land was bought from Butlers Brewery of Wolverhampton for £300. The sale

included the old stables and an old cottage in the yard. The hall was built by F.G. Kirk of Four Ashes to designs by Lavender and Twentyman at a cost of £2700, and opened in January 1936. At the time there were proposals to built a cinema in Brewood, and in the meantime to use the hall for that purpose once or twice a week. There is no evidence that it was ever so used.

455.   Royal Commission on the Historical Monuments of England, HBMC19 RCHM (1T) 1084.

456.   A fire engine has existed since at least 1851, when the 'Fire Engine Superintendent' was Thomas Layton, the parish clerk. At the turn of the century the fire-engine was a four-wheeled horse-drawn apparatus with the words BREWOOD PARISH COUNCIL on the sides, and Arthur Lowder, proprietor of the Swan, was captain of the fire brigade. He was called out when the old 'Red White & Blue' public house on Cannock Road burnt down, and also when Somerford Hall caught fire: 'Black Country Bugle', April 1983. The engine was also in attendance at a fire at Park Farm in 1905 and, together with those from Somerford and Penkridge, when a serious fire destroyed the rickyard, but no buildings, at The Woolley on 6th November 1910. The pump was hand operated. [Parish Magazine, December 1910]. The appliance was moved to Home Farm until 1911, when it was kept in an old coach house owned by Mr Wakelam, captain of the brigade. Mr W.H. Carter subsequently ran the brigade. A new machine, named Marjorie after a fire officer's daughter, was obtained from Penkridge in 1938 and housed in a wooden shed opposite what is now the library. See also J.R. Power, "A Duty Done – the History of Fire Fighting in Staffordshire," Staffordshire County Council 1987 22, 88. For fire brigade records commencing in 1895 see D880/7/3 SRO. [There is a reference to an engine at Chillington in 1860: see "The Wolverhampton Spirit of the Times", 4th February 1860.]

457.   An elaborate cast-iron pump is on the front of the west wing, and there are a number of other wells at the rear, in addition to one in the floor of the old kitchen. The façade of the building is constructed from very hard but blemished [i.e. cheaper] bricks. By local tradition, the workhouse dead were buried in quicklime in front of the building. There is no evidence to support the tradition.

458.   Parish Council Minutes, February and October 1907. The Ordnance Survey 25" map of 1884 shows the pound, which seems to have been located where the garage now stands. 'le pynfold' is recorded in 1484 [Oakden 45] but was not necessarily in the same position. The pinfold in Coven seems to have been on the east side of the village: cf. 'Pinfold Croft', Tithe Map 1838.

459.   Hicks Smith 1864 14. Stocks were known to the Anglo-Saxons, as shown by drawings of the period. The second Statute of Labourers of 1351 ordered stocks to be erected in every town for the punishment of unruly artisans, and in 1376 the Commons urged Edward III to set up stocks in every village. Punishment in the stocks began to die out in the early nineteenth century.

460.   They appear on Robins & Sherriff's map of 1808.

461.   Wolverhampton "Express & Star", 9th March 1980. The cast iron range and some locksmith's tools are said to have been removed to Stafford County Museum at Shugborough at the time of demolition.

462.   John Bailey Haynes was the 6th son of Benjamin Haynes and brother of Edward ('Old Ned') Haynes, the eccentric verger, who customarily wore a uniform of cast-off frock-coat and top-hat when wheeling his barrow around the village. John Haynes attended Brewood Grammar School, and at 14 became a Sunday school teacher, then a

lay reader at Bilston, where he assisted the Rev. J.B. Owen during the dreadful cholera outbreak of 1848-9. He later moved to Wellington, Shropshire, and subsequently settled in North Brighton. A prominent theologian, he became well-acquainted with the leading churchmen of his day, but decided not to become ordained. He travelled widely in Europe, formed a society to assist those wishing to emigrate to Canada, and published many tracts and articles. He worked until shortly before his death aged 76 in 1903, and left a collection of 25,000 books and 150,000 pamphlets: Wakefield 70-72.

463. The cellars are extensive, incorporating those of the demolished Angel Inn to the south, and extend to the Jubilee Hall.

464. For Albert Whitehouse, who had the shop built as a butcher's shop.

465. The Parish Council was created in 1894. It held its first meeting on 1st January 1895 at the Institute in Sandy Lane.

466. This may be the Parish Council Room mentioned in the Parish Magazine for November 1902.

467. Title deeds show that an earlier house on the site was known in 1691 as 'The Family House'. [Deeds in WSL: information from Dr R.C.H. Taylor, Westgate].

468. A garth is a close or piece of land beside a building. The house was apparently so-named because it was built in the garden land of a building adjoining or opposite.

469. The canopy on Old Smithy House was added after 1905 and the shutters after 1925.

470. A smithy is shown on the Ordnance Survey 1" map of 1935-6.

471. For a drawing of the timberwork in Old Smithy Cottage, see VCH V 22.

472. A measured drawing of the timberwork is given in Hannah, 225-6.

473. Ordnance Survey 1/2500 map, 1924.

474. Although there is no evidence of any kind, documentary or otherwise, to support that tradition, such lodges were often located whenever there were large areas of royal Forest. Richard I built a hunting lodge at Kinver which may have been typical of the smaller royal houses: seemingly a hall with adjoining buttery and pantry, a kitchen, a chamber and a gaol for Forest offenders. It was surrounded by a palisade and entered through a gateway defended by a wooden tower. A fishpond adjoined the site. At Writtle in Essex the layout of King John's hunting lodge has been revealed by excavation. The main buildings were a range of chapel, hall and kitchen built of timber, cob and thatch. Together with a courtyard, the range was defended by an enclosing wet ditch crossed by two bridges. The ditches were fed by an adjacent stream, which also supplied a nearby fishpond.

475. pp.380-1.

476. The emblem of the Fowke family. The former public house of the same name in Market Place may have been connected with the family, who held land there from at least 1618: Eccl. Comm. 124088 SRO.

477. "Memoirs of the Geological Survey: Explanation of Sheet 153", 1928 133.

478. It is mentioned in 1783: Oakden 40. In about 1848 it was a beerhouse called Vauxhall: "Brewood Courier", 1st January 1898.

479. Robins & Sherriff's map of 1808; Tithe Map 1838.

480. It stood on the east side of the lane between Dean's Hall Farm and The Woolley. It was the home in the last century of Amos Jenks, who died in 1893 aged 103. At the age

of 100 he walked to Hednesford and back: "Midland Counties Express", 7th October 1893.

481. In 1808 all sides were wet. In 1907 "260' & 290', 250' x 100', fragmentary, part wet": VCH I 358. See also "Moated Sites in South Staffordshire", P.J. Larkham, TSSAHS XXIV 1982-3 8.

482. The barn, now demolished, at Brewood Hall was of similar construction.

483. Sites and Monuments Record, Staffs. County Council, record 6/03/02184.

484. Sites and Monuments Record, Staffs. County Council, record 6/03/01065. The Tithe Map shows a field north [sic] of the farmhouse as Moat Meadow. See also Larkham *op. cit.* 37.

485. Sites and Monuments Record, Staffs. County Council, record 6/03/01898.

486. SJ073853. A principal wide ditch aligned north-south on the west side of a roughly square platform is some 120' long, with other ditches running east from each end. The field contains heavy ridge and furrow. Is it possible that this is the site of "Hilton", shown north of Chillington on early maps, but never identified? A John Hilton of Brewood, gentleman, is recorded in 1640: Thorpe 366 WSL. Topographically Hilton is more likely to be Coldham. Other clues to the lost name of the moated site may be found in Stebbing Shaw II 292, where an undated thirteenth century deed of land at Brewood is mentioned, with various witnesses named, most associated with identifiable manors. Two cannot be identified: John of the Sych and Thomas of the Lee. Sych or sic was a stream, and lee was a meadow, so it is not possible to link either name to the site. The Lay Subsidy of 1327 also gives place-names which remain unidentified, including Nore, Walle and Penynton. The name Boreshanky or Boreshanks appears in the parish register in 1643 and 1685, but has not been identified. Between 1731 and 1738 the parish registers record the name "Nittelown", which has not be identified. It may however be a corruption of Little Onn.

487. Robins & Sherriff's map of 1808 shows depressions which tend to confirm this possibility.

488. The old house is illustrated in Stebbing Shaw II [Plate 8], misdescribed as a view of Blackladies. When Thomas Giffard died in 1718, his widow moved to Long Birch and lived there until her death aged 95 in 1754. She took her chaplain, the Rev. I Johnson, who died in 1739 and was succeeded by the Rev. John Horniold, who became Bishop of Philomelia in 1753, and died in 1778. His slab tombstone is in Brewood church, together with that of Bishop Berington, who succeeded him. After 'Good Madam' Giffard's death, the Hon. Catherine Collingwood lived at Longbirch. Her husband had been executed in 1715, having joined the Jacobite Rebellion under the Earl of Bridgwater. Her tomb is also in Brewood church. Long Birch was at one time the residence of the Roman Catholic Vicars Apostolic of the Midland District from about 1756 until 1804, when Bishop Milner left to live at Gifford House, Wolverhampton: Wakefield 44-5. Both Horniold and his successor Thomas Talbot enlarged the farm attached to the house, the latter in particular having the wealth and expertise to run it successfully. His successors found the expense too much: Bishop Milner recorded "the expense of keeping the gentleman's farm (as is unavoidable in the situation of a bishop) and entertaining all visitors and horses must make it a loosing [sic] concern to any bishop who has not a plentiful future of his own, not to speak of the remoteness of the situation and the difficulty of procurring letters, victuals, etc": VCH III 110. Horniold built a house at Oscott in case the Vicars Apostolic should ever be forced to leave Longbirch. The house became the first Oscott College in 1794: VCH III 111.

489. Robins & Sherriff's map of 1808.

490. Perhaps by 'Capability' Brown. VCH V 24 suggests James Paine or Sir John Soane.

491. Wakefield records [148/1/172 WSL] that the father of a woman who lived there c.1880 spoke of a moat having been round the house.

492. The original Leper House may have been on the south side of the lane and west of the well, where a Chillington estate map c.1727 [WSL] gives the name of the field as Leper House Close. A close was usually, but not always, a piece of land adjoining a house. The 'lepre house' is mentioned in a court paper of 1652 [Oakden 41], and the Codsall parish register records the baptism on 16th March 1597 of "Joyce, d[aughter] of Richard Carrington (born at ye Lepre House)". It is of interest that the present Leper House is shown on a 1761 Chillington estate map as The Corch. The meaning of the word is uncertain, but it may be derived from the Middle Welsh 'cors', meaning 'reed', which would fit the topography.

493. See "Staffordshire Life", March 1952 21, 27.

494. TSSAHS 12 1971 35; SHC 7 1886 237; Sites and Monuments Record, Staffs. County Council, record 6/03/01900.

495. Boulton Paul Aircraft Limited began at Pendeford in 1936, and became famous for the production of the Boulton Paul Defiant warplane. In addition it manufactured large numbers of 4-gun power-driven turrets. Anti-aircraft guns were located on the north side of Kiddemore Green Road, to the east of The Oakley. A stray bomb is said to have caused a huge crater in a field near Crateford Lane. Many Italian prisoners-of-war, based in Penkridge, assisted on local farms.

496. Other cottages formerly stood nearby, but in November 1849 three were destroyed by fire caused by children playing with fire in an adjoining shed. The occupiers were not insured: "The Stafford Advertiser", 8th December 1849.

497. Palliser 100.

498. Members of the Chambley family farmed at Coven from at least 1834, and various Chambley graves lie near the north-west side of Brewood Church.

499. On the north, west and east: Robins & Sherriff's map of 1808.

500. According to Stebbing Shaw [Vol II 305], the original Engleton Hall was "a substantial stone residence built on an eminence close to the Penk". A quarter of a mile south-west of the present farmhouse are the remains of walling built of large rectangular sandstone blocks which runs on a north-south alignment from the south-west corner of a nineteenth century brick shippon. The walling is some 125' long and 6' wide, and the two or three visible courses are surmounted by a hawthorn hedge. The remains incorporate odd fragments of hexagonal sandstone pillars. The First Edition 1" Ordnance Survey map shows the lane from Crateford turning south past the remains before crossing the Penk to the north of Engleton Mill. Wakefield 1968 81 suggests that the old hall was alongside the old lane. For the moat at Engleton see TSSAHS 12 1971 35; Sites and Monuments Record, Staffs. County Council, record 6/03/01906.

501. Fea 49.

502. Sites and Monuments Record, Staffs. County Council, record 6/03/02132.

503. The Tithe Map of 1838 shows a building of narrow irregular shape.

504. Mr Coffin, agent to the Giffard family, lived at Blackladies in the first half of the eighteenth century.

505. A hall existed at an earlier date, for the Brewood parish register records the burial on 12th August 1612 of Thomas Cartwright of Somerford Hall. Somerford passed down through the Somerford family until William Somerford sold to Walter Wrottesley in the time of George III, and in 1734 it was sold to Robert Barbor, a London lawyer and Member of Parliament. His son sold Somerford to the Hon. Edward Monckton, who also purchased Brewood Hall, Stretton Hall [in 1790] and other property at Coven and Aspley. The Monckton family originally came from Yorkshire, where three successive generations are said to have been knighted on the field of battle for bravery. Robert Monckton was second-in-command to General Wolfe when he stormed the Heights of Abraham in Quebec. The Hon. Edward Monckton was the first colonel of the Queen's Own Regiment in Staffordshire, holding the rank until his death at the age of 98. He had amassed a large fortune with the East India Company, and married the daughter of Lord Pyrt. They had nine sons and five daughters. He greatly improved Somerford, and was a Member of Parliament for 32 years, although he never made a speech. His family was very benevolent, and his daughters started a free school for local children, who wore scarlet uniforms. One pupil, Miss Daw, became a cook to Queen Caroline. Mary, Countess of Cork and Orrery, the sister of Edward Monckton, was well acquainted with many eminent writers of the period. She often visited Somerford, and is buried in Brewood church, which contains a commemorative plaque to her memory: Wakefield 68-70. In 1912 Col C.E. Gouldbourn D.S.O. lived at Somerford, and was the commanding officer of a Territorial Force of Divisional Troops based at Brewood, which consisted of the 1st North Midland Brigade, Royal Field Artillery, Wolverhampton; the 4th North Midlands Brigade, Royal Field Artillery, Derby; and the North Midlands Royal Garrison (Heavy) Artillery, Hartshill, Stoke-on-Trent. Colonel Gouldbourn reputedly drove the first car to be seen in Brewood: Photographic Collection, Staffordshire County Museum, Shugborough.

506. ". . . the large drawing room on the left side of the old part erected by Mr Barbour": Stebbing Shaw II 306.

507. Attibuted to Humphrey Repton [1752-1818] by Mr P.R. de L. Giffard *supra*. An avenue of trees from Four Ashes to the Hall is shown on Robins & Sherriff's Map of 1808. The pool is said to be haunted: Wakefield 85.

508. Robins & Sherriff's map of 1808. The name does not appear on the Tithe Map of 1838.

509. A large chimney was removed in the modernisation, and a panel of wattle-and-daub is said to have been removed to Bakewell Museum.

510. Griffiths 140.

511. Henry, chaplain of Brewood [before 1242]: Doc. 25 Magnum Registrum Album; SHC 1924 94; Sir Robert de Twyford, chaplain, appointed 1275: SHC 1924 92.

512. Parke 42. Much information about the school is contained in VCH VI 149-152.

513. Parke 42. See also Griffith 127 and SHC 1931 188-193.

514. Dunkley 14. Knightley's Will confirms that he was born in Brewood: SCH 1931 192.

515. There is no evidence that Johnson ever visited Brewood.

516. Thompson 15. One of the most prominent pupils to have received his early education at Brewood, probably the Grammar School, was William Huskisson, MP [1770-1830], of Oxley Manor, Bushbury, who became Colonial Secretary, but achieved the greater, if tragic, distinction of being the first person killed by a train in Britain [George Stephenson's 'Rocket'], at the opening of the Liverpool-Manchester railway on 15th

September 1830. However, there were several accidental deaths on railways earlier than this. On 5th December 1821 David Brooke was knocked down and killed by an engine while walking along the Middleton Railway at Leeds. The parish registers of Egglescliffe, Durham, record the death of an unnamed woman who was "killed by a steam machine" on the Stockton and Darlington Railway on 15th March 1827. Mr Brooke appears to have been the first person killed by a locomotive, but even his was not the first accident on a railway. The parish registers of Mitcham record three deaths on the horse-drawn Surrey Iron Railway, the first public railway in the world, opened on 26th July 1803. The first of these accidents occurred on 23rd August 1807, when Thomas Strattin was "run over by a Cart on the Iron Railway". The other deaths occurred on 20th June 1808 and 22nd July 1810.

517. Bayley suggests that the school was destroyed by fire in the 19th century. There appears to be no evidence to support that statement. For details of the school in 1860, together with acrimonious correspondence relating to the sale of school land in Willenhall in 1853, see Griffith 1860 126-166.

518. The parish registers contain an entry for 15th July 1641 for the burial of Jane, wife of Abraham Barwicke, schoolmaster. At Lichfield [document DD1] is a licence dated 1684 from Dean Addison to William Cooke as schoolmaster of the Free School at Brewood: SHC VI pt II 60.

519. Described as a schoolmistress of Dean's End in 1818 in Parson & Bradshaw.

520. "White's Directory of Staffordshire", 1834.

521. "Stafford Advertiser", 1st January 1859.

522. In the south-east corner of Brewood churchyard is the gravestone of Sarah Parke, who died on 2nd February 1875 aged 83 years, "upwards of sixty [sic] years schoolmistress in Brewood".

523. VCH V 27.

524. For details of alehouse keepers in Brewood in the late sixteenth and early seventeenth century, see SHC 1929 I 265; 1940 184-5, 305.

525. D1798/153 WSL.

526. Local folk memory records the name 'The Green Man'.

527. "Pigot & Co's Directory of Stafford".

528. Shown on Robins & Sherriff's map of 1808. In the last century James Glover had his licence removed because he accepted from passing waggoners their master's produce in exchange for drink.

529. 590/20/1-14; 590/304/1 SRO. The fleur-de-lis was the emblem of the Fowke family, which held land called The Court east of the church in 1618.

530. The service seems to have been little better 50 years later: "Inquiring for food, we found that neither beef, pork, nor mutton, fish, or fowl could be obtained" – Palmer 53.

531. "Stafford Advertiser", 15th February 1868.

532. Much information about public houses in the last century appeared in "The Brewood Courier", 1st January 1898 and 2nd February 1901. Both pieces were written by T. Cluett.

533. Mentioned in the perambulation of the parish boundary in 1838. In about 1687 a Wolverhampton priest, Father Gavan, was on trial at Stafford Assizes. Gavan and a Jesuit named Ireland had been staying at Tixall Hall at the discovery of the Popish Plot. Ireland was caught and executed. Gavan reached London, but was arrested.

Richard Penderel, a witness at his trial, was cross-examined about Ireland's visit to Boscobel House. During his evidence, Penderel stated that he [Penderel] kept the Royal Oak at Boscobel: Wakefield notebook 148/1/72 143 WSL; James Broughton, "Staffordshire collections", PN4246 WSL. This may have been the first public house of the name in the country.

534. Hicks Smith 1864 25.

535. "Stafford Advertiser", 14th November 1857.

536. "Stafford Advertiser", 20th January 1883.

537. Brewood Parish Magazine, April 1875.

538. Since fulling mills did not appear until the end of the twelfth century, the early references must be to corn mills.

539. SHC 1919 240-2.

540. The mill at Coven Heath does not appear on Yates revised map of 1799.

541. A windmill lay just across the parish boundary between Bilbrook and Pendeford, on the west side of the canal, in the last century: 1st Edition Ordnance Survey 1" map; VCH XX 34.

542. Oakden 42.

543. *ibid.* 41.

544. *ibid.* 46-9.

545. Giffard Papers D590/363 a & b, SRO.

546. Plot 110. Plot himself suggests that generally the roads were good.

547. Gough's edition of Campden's "Britannia", 1806 ii 496, 505. In 1717 the raised causeway was so clearly visible that Dr William Stukeley, the antiquarian, described it as "laid very broad and deep with gravel not yet worn out, where it goes over commons and moors", and in 1727 would not allow any of his companions to ride upon it "to save it as much as possible from being worn out": VCH II 275; "Itinerarium Curiosum" 1776 Vol. I p.60.

548. SHC 1934 40.

549. The old Spread Eagle Inn at Gailey was demolished during road widening in 1929: VCH V 104.

550. 34 Geo. III c.133; SHC 4th Series 13 113.

551. Baugh's map of Shropshire, 1808, suggests The Avenue opposite Brewood Hall.

552. Byng 142-4.

553. Yates Map of Staffordshire, 1775. The name is recorded in 1571: Oakden 43.

554. It is not shown on Robins & Sherriff's map of 1808, but is marked on the Tithe Map of 1838.

555. Wakefield [p.15] seems to misplace it, connecting it to the Roman site at Pennocrucium.

556. Oakden 46.

557. Hicks Smith "1680 Brewood Map". The Tithe Map shows a short length of road existing in 1838.

558. William Ick [sic] is listed as a farmer at "Wooley" in White's Gazetteer, 1834.

559. But was recorded on Yates map of 1775.

560. Lewis 311.

561. Hicks Smith 1867 9. Macadamed roads were those constructed to the design of John Macadam in graded layers with a surface of crushed stone, not to be confused with tarmacadam. Although tar was available as a by-product from the gas works from 1864 and tarred road surfaces were introduced as early as 1832 and became widespread from 1845, roads in Brewood appear not to have been tarred until the early years of the present century. The Road Improvements Association, formed by the two national cycling clubs in 1886, encouraged experiments to eliminate dust from rural roads and to create a smooth waterproof surface for bicycles and cars. In 1901 E.P. Hooley, Nottinghamsire County Surveyor, noticed that a burst barrel of tar near Derby ironworks had bonded furnace slag to produce a hard smooth surface: modern tarmac had been discovered

562. Hicks Smith 1874 53.

563. Samuel Ward of the Four Ashes, who died in 1859 aged 85, is said to have recalled the first coach to pass his public house and witnessed the last: Hicks Smith 1867 31.

564. "Universal British Directory", 1793.

565. In 1829 a one-horse car took mail and passengers to Wolverhampton every morning [except Sunday] at 9 a.m., returning to Brewood by 7 p.m. The date and location of the first post office in Brewood is not known, but various trade directories show that in 1818 it was at the Giffard Arms, and eleven years later "near the Church" and run by Heber Perry. In 1834 and 1841 the postman and carrier is listed as Heber Perry of School Lane. By 1848 the post office was at The Lion, run by Henry Wright: "Brewood Courier" 1st January 1898. From at least 1861 to about 1900 the postmistress seems to have been Elizabeth Bratt, who is first listed in Stafford Street [perhaps the Giffard Arms] and who in 1899 was in Bargate Street – perhaps the shop next to Speedwell Castle – when posters were displayed giving the latest news of the Boer War. The 25" ordnance Survey map of 1884 shows the post office at the old police station in Church

Road. In 1900 the post office was run by John Wakefield from what is now a greengrocers shop on the west side of Market Place, and the following year it moved to its present site next to The Lion after a shop was created from a private house. Later Ordnance Survey maps suggest that for a short time in the 1920's the post office may have been at the Dreadnought, but older residents throw doubt on such evidence. From at least 1872 there was a wall letter box at Kiddemore Green, in the wall of the glass-house at Oakley Farm, and another at Horsebrook, near the bridge. Both were removed in the mid 1980's. The box from Horsebrook has been preserved by the Parish Council at the Council Offices. In the early years of this century the village postman is said to have been Jackie Tart, who walked 22 miles a day for a wage of nineteen shilling a week.

The Brewood postman, c.1900.

566. Brewood Parish Magazine, November 1902.

567. Thornton 122.

568. Modifications to the Stafford Road included the demolition in 1981 of The Ball

[formerly The Golden Ball] public house at Coven Heath.

569.   VCH XX 1. It is of interest that much of the Staffordshire/Shropshire boundary follows the narrow ridge separating the headstreams of the Penk from those of the Stour, which is the watershed between the feeders of the Trent and Severn

570.   It was occupied in 1690. The house had been demolished by 1796, but the moat still existed in 1849: VCH XX 79.

571.   Another possibility is that the word moat is associated with motte, or mound, and means 'stream where there was an embankment': Oakden 14.

572.   Ekwall 42. The word 'billers' may be Celtic in origin.

573.   Stebbing Shaw II 292-3.

574.   VCH V 32. In the early decades of the present century the leat south of Engleton Mill was used as the local rubbish dump.

575.   It is said that in 1857-8 the Moncktons, as riparian owners, dredged the Penk for 10 miles between Wolverhampton and Congreve. The river was supposedly the 4th best trout stream in England in 1896, and a salmon is said to have been caught at Stretton Mill in 1915: Vivian Bird, "Staffordshire", B.T. Batsford Limited 1974 77-9.

576.   Wilkes 153; VCH II 285.

577.   Brewood Brook and Dean's Hall Brook are both mentioned in the Constables' Accounts for 1663: Oakden 39-40.

578.   Hicks Smith 1867 33.

579.   Information from Mr D. Morgan supra.

580.   SHC 1934 82.

581.   The narrowness of the old bridge was criticised at the inquest held on June 1871 on Anthony Spicer, a waggoner aged 41 employed on the Chillington estate, who was crushed between a wagon and the parapet. He left a widow and eight children: "Stafford Advertiser", 17th June 1871.

582.   A cast-iron plaque near the north-west of the bridge reads: "THIS BRIDGE (which is a County bridge) is insufficient to carry weights beyond the ordinary traffic of the district, and owners, drivers or persons in charge of LOCOMOTIVE TRACTION ENGINES, or other ponderous carriages of unusual weight, are hereby warned not to pass, and are desired to take notice they will be held liable for any damage that may be caused by such Engines or Carriages passing over, or attempting to pass over, the same. Walter Cheadle. County Surveyor". [W.H. Cheadle was County Surveyor 1888-1910.] An identical plaque from the south-east side of the bridge is held in the Parish Council Room.

583.   The place was known in 1286 as Stretwyle: SHC 1916. The bridge may be the "Eton" bridge mentioned c.1283 and c.1344: VCH IV 163.

584.   Stebbing Shaw II 200. In 1796 the canal boats were carrying 20 to 24 tons at 2½d to 3d per ton: *ibid*.

585.   Thompson 30.

586.   Skating parties were often held on the resevoir at night, with food laid on tea chests for tables, and illumination provided by hurricane lamps: Thornton 58.

587.   VCH I 320.

588.   On the north-east side of the graveyard, near the wall, is the tombstone of "HUGH ROSE Engineer late of Crich Bonar Bridge in the County of Sutherland, North

Britain, departed this life at Brewood August 26th 1832 aged 60 years".

589. In 1865 the "more influential" inhabitants of Coven sent a petition to the Chief Constable asking for a policeman to be stationed in the village, claiming that robberies, especially of foul, game and other property exposed at night, were often committed, and that the nearest police officer was in Brewood: "Stafford Advertiser", 28th February 1865.

590. VCH XX 80.

591. 590/303 SRO.

592. There were 3 in the Bishop's manor in 1086, 4 in 1307-8: VCH VI 8.

593. Gelling 1984 236.

594. SHC 1941 4; Rowlands 1987 24.

595. VCH II 347; VCH II 337; VCH VI 6.

596. Rowlands 1987 25; VCH VI 20. For details of peasant holdings, status and rents in Brewood, see VCH VI 26, 28.

597. 590/494 SRO. Details of fields and areas appear in deeds held at Wombourne Wodehouse. See also Griffiths 1860 131.

598. Each Hill Meadow lay on the north side of Kiddemore Green Road, between The Oakley and Brewood: Tithe Map 1838. For field names in Brewood see Griffith 131; Oakden 43-9; Frost 121.

599. SHC 1931 80. 600 acres at Gailey Common were enclosed in 1773: Rowlands 1987 24. 40 acres of 'waste land' at Codsall Wood were enclosed in 1820: SCH 1931 96.

600. Rowlands 1987 26. In 1260 the Marlpit of Methplekes was referred to in an action "against the road which passes from Tong towards the wood [Bishop's Wood]": Griffiths 145.

601. SHC 1941 5; VCH II 34; VI 6. Small-scale moated sites, of the type found in Brewood parish, are believed to be associated with areas of forest clearance.

602. Which are recorded in 1704: D590/361 SRO. Big Hyde Rough was then known as The Hyde Rough, and Little Hyde Rough as The Coppy [coppice].

603. Magnum Registrum Album No. 452 [SHC 1924]. The Confirmation suggests that the Bishop may have taken advantage of the unrest during the reign of Stephen to annexe part at least of the Forest area: VCH II 337.

604. When the land mentioned in this grant was made over to the Bishop, its boundaries were delineated by the royal Forest officials: VCH III 15.

605. Palliser 86.

606. Rowlands 1987 26. See however G.P. Mander, "The Wolverhampton Antiquary" Vol. I No 6 pp.169-172.

607. Palliser 86. It has been suggested that the name Mercers Meadow in a late seventeenth century map of Blackladies is connected with the Mercer family, and does not necessarily suggest that clothmaking was carried out there at one time: Oakden 48. But the Tithe Map of 1838 gives the name Weavers Field for the same land.

608. Hicks Smith 1864 12.

609. Dye made from purple hemp is mentioned in accounts of Brewood manor in the early fourteenth century: Hicks Smith 1864 10. Flax leaves would have provided fodder,

with linen thread produced from its stalks, while its seeds contain an oil which was used in cooking or for lighting. The Valor Ecclesiasticus of 1535 records tithes to the value of 13s 4d for hemp and flax paid to the vicar: Parke, 99. The tutoring or dressing of hemp may be suggested by the name Tutorhouse leasow for a field immediately south of the Hattons, marked on an estate map c.1727 [D590/363 SRO].

610. Pitt 149.

611. 'The Chillington Oxen' by Lucas Beattie, dedicated to T.G. Giffard.

612. e.g. Parke 95.

613. W.E. Tate, "The Parish Chest", Phillimore & Co. Ltd., 1983 118, 186, 247, 260. However, there is also reference to "a huge piece of beef", evidently to be consumed by visitors to a Black Country Wake, in J. Timbs, "Nooks and Corners of English Life", Griffith and Farran 1867 261.

614. p.237.

615. D880/5/5; D932/6 WSL.

616. Rowlands 1987 264.

617. Staffordshire Farmers was put into receivership in June 1990.

618. In 1741 Daniel Martin of Blackladies, tenant of a farm at Gunstone, gave a bond to Peter Giffard that he would not again sow more than one acre of flax, hemp, rape or other impoverishing seed, without licence: 590/560 SRO.

619. SHC 1930 II 352.

620. George Sansom senior was buried at Brewood on 14th May 1719 in linen, and notice of it was given to the churchwardens. Under the Burial in Woollen Acts of 1666 and 1678 "no corpse of any person (except those that shall die of the plague) shall be buried in any shirt, sheet or shroud or anything whatsoever . . . or in any stuff or thing, other than what is made of sheep's wool only . . ." Penalties were imposed on those in breach of the legislation, which provided that within eight days of the funeral an affidavit was to be made that the law had been complied with. The penalties were £5 against the estate of every person not buried in wool, on the householder in whose house he or she died, on the persons connected with the funeral, on the minister neglecting to certify the non-receipt of the affidavit, and on overseers neglecting to levy the penalty. Half the penalty went to the poor and half to the informer, so when the Acts were defied, it was usual for a member of the deceased's family to act as informers, and so in effect reduce the penalty. The legislation was not repealed until 1814. For many years after 3rd May 1689 all burial entries in the Brewood parish registers are followed by the words: "and an affidavit made thereupon".

621. p.169.

622. The introduction of Mason's fly-press in 1794 enabled cottage locksmiths to cut out the parts very quickly. Various forms of oliver, a foot operated spring hammer introduced in the early 1800's, enabled locksmiths to work single-handed, and well into the nineteenth century the typical domestic workshop consisted of no more than a hearth, oliver-hammer, anvil and bellows. Locksmiths at Codsall were recorded during the eighteenth century, and one at Bilbrook in the 1780's. There was a locksmith at Codsall Wood in 1841, one at Codsall in 1861, and one at Oaken in 1871: VCH XX 86.

623. Hicks Smith 1864 25-6.

624. S. Timmins, "Birmingham and the Midland Hardware District", Robert Hardwicke 1866 87.

625. Ironwork for locks was also made at Pendeford: VCH II 253.

626. John Smith was born at Coven in 1827. His father, also John, was a tenant farmer at Hammers Farm. As a youth, John Smith junior may have worked with John Fowler of Leeds, steam plough manufacturer, and possibly with Clayton & Shuttleworth, engineers of Lincoln. Certainly he was friendly with Nathaniel Clayton, after whom he named his son, Clayton Smith, and was an early purchaser of a Fowlers steam plough. By 1850 John Smith senior was listed as a farmer and manufacturer of Rivington's Patent Mills, and his son as an engineer and general machinist [Kelly's "Staffordshire Directory"]. In the early days father and son probably carried on business at Hammers Farm, producing locks, stationery horizontal engines and portable engines, and undertaking specialist repair work and hiring out plant for colliery owners throughout the Black Country. In 1857 he built a partly self-propelled 6hp engine which required a horse only to steer it and assist it up gradients. Later that year Smith exhibited three steam engines, ploughing tackle and a threshing machine at Bushbury Agricultural Society Show. In August 1858 he patented two inventions relating to steam engines, and in September his 12hp steam ploughing engine was awarded a silver medal at Staffordshire Agricultural Show at Lichfield. Regular demonstrations thereafter took place at local farms, and in about 1860 an expansion of business led to the erection of the Village Foundry, a large 5-bay machine shop. It is said that the building was near Coven church, but it is that which still stands on the corner of Lawn Lane and Brewood Road – near Coven Methodist church. At least two, and possibly all, of the bays had sliding doors and above the machine shop was a pattern shop, which was also used as a meeting place for the Sunday school, in which John Smith senior was interested. Nearby was the blacksmith's shop, linked to the main building by a foundry. Smith's house was near the opposite end of the machine shop. It is said that boilers were made in a separate building near Coven church [the Iron Room?]. On 13th October 1860 Smith was fortunate to escape uninjured when the boiler of a traction engine – not one of his own – which he was delivering after repair exploded. Another man on the engine was scalded: "Wolverhampton Spirit of the Times", 20th October 1860. In 1861 John Birch Higgs from Kiddemore Green, his brother-in-law, joined Smith as his partner, and the same year they patented two improvements to threshing machines and exhibited a traction engine and threshing machine at the Royal Agricultural Society of England's Show at Leeds. The following year a steam engine was displayed at the R.A.S.E. Show at Battersea, but by then the business was turning from agriculture and concentrating on the manufacture of industrial plant, presumably in greater demand and more profitable. In 1862 the Village Foundry, then employing up to 50 men, built a small narrow-gauge railway locomotive for a colliery in Willenhall. It was delivered in January 1863, a larger one was built in July, and in September an even larger one was made. Various other 0-4-0 and 0-6-0 narrow gauge engines were supplied to local railways and collieries, at least one of which, weighing some 22 tons, was delivered by road, fitted with temporary road wheels and horse-drawn from Coven. By 1874 the foundry's fortunes were declining, probably as a result of Smith's failing health. A retirement sale of the contents of the ironworks was held on 30th March, and included machinery, tools, equipment, patterns, boilers, locomotives and engines in progress. The foundry buildings were retained, and the firm of Smith & Higgs continued as threshing and ploughing contractors. In about 1878, his health deteriorating further, Smith moved to Saredon Mill, Shareshill, and died from a diabetic coma on 2nd February 1879. He is buried at Coven church. VCH II 144. See also D.H. Tew, "John Smith of Coven, Engineer, 1827-79", Newcomen Society xxvi 161;

"Stafford Advertiser", 2nd February 1935.

627. The Village Foundry existed until at least 1912, when Miss Edith Mary Higgs, presumably related to Smith's brother-in-law, is listed as a "machinist": Kelly's "Staffordshire Directory".

628. Thomas Nickolds is listed as a clock and watch maker in 1834, Edward Nickolds as a watch and clockmaker between 1851 and 1872, and Isaac Lyons King of Dean Street as a watchmaker in 1892.

629. VCH II 190.

630. p.13.

631. "Memoirs of the Geological Survey: Explanation of Sheet 153" 1928 133. In November 1858 Richard Pritchard, aged 43, died from burns after an explosion caused by foul gas in the quarry. It seems that he had not waited for the 'doggy' [supervisor] to test the area with a safety lamp before he started work, and on entering the place with a candle an explosion occurred, an event previously unknown at the quarry: "Stafford Advertiser", 4th December 1858.

632. Edward Hull, "Rocks of the Midland Counties of England", 1869.

633. "Memoirs of the Geological Survey . . ." op. cit. 134.

634. ibid. 188.

635. 167-8. The quarry seems to have been worked until about 1800: VCH II 191.

636. For the rebuilding of Chillington Hall in the 1720's, bricks were also obtained from Brewood, Penkridge and Tettenhall: VCH II 255.

637. "Stafford Advertiser", 15th October 1864.

638. Information extracted from archives of Severn Trent Water Authority, Tettenhall.

639. "Stafford Advertiser", 9th July 1870.

640. The Newspapers Library at Collingdale Avenue, North London, holds copies of the "Cannock Chase Courier", 1884-1969 [but not the "Brewood Courier"], and Nos. 1-105 [1898-1900] of the "Brewood Advertiser". See "Tercentenary Handlist of English & Welsh Newspapers, Magazines & Reviews", The Times 1920 301.

641. Two irregular basin-shaped lumps of cast iron some 8" across and 5" deep, found at Hilltop, Coven Road, Brewood in 1988 [held by the author] may be relics of the Brewood bloomeries.

642. An iron foundry existed at Penkridge by 1635: VCH V 106. There was a forge at Congreve by 1717 producing 120 tons per annum which remained in use until at least 1832. Families such as Rock of Brewood each controlled a number of ironworks for several generations: Rowlands 1987 22.

643. SHC 1940 33.

644. SHC 1931 156.

645. VCH V 20.

646. Rowlands 1987 146.

647. VCH II 117; NSJFS LXXXVIII 1953-4 33-4. For details of the Foley accounts, see Worcestershire Historical Society, New Series 1978 and 1990. The Brewood and Coven ironworks became part of a conglomerate of ironworks in the West Midlands, Shropshire and the Forest of Dean called 'The Ironworks in Partnership'.

648. The iron foundry recorded in Brewood in 1851 [White's Directory], when John Dent

was foundry manager, is the Village Foundry in Coven.

649. Sites and Monuments Record, Staffs County Council, record 6/03/01079

650. Wakefield 62. During the First World War 'Old Dan' of The Pavement is said to have collected 20 tons of ore which was sold for £21 a ton.

651. See Earl Chapin May, "Principio to Wheeling 1715-1945", Harper & Brothers, New York. The present author records his appreciation to Mr F.P. Hudson of Atlanta, Georgia, for drawing his attention to the connection between Brewood, Principio and the Onion family.

652. VCH I 283.

653. John Ray senior, licensee of the Swan Inn in the early part of the last century, butcher and baker, was responsible for touring the village 'crying the fair', or formally closing it: "Brewood Courier", 1st January 1898.

654. Hicks Smith 1864 10, 13-14.

655. See R.E. Latham, "Revised Medieval Latin Word List", O.U.P./British Academy 1965 453. For a reference to a 'Stokgate' in a brook at Batchacre in 1806, see D.H. Robinson, "The Sleepy Meese", Waine Research Publications, 1988 54. The Old English 'stocc' meant 'stock, trunk of tree': Ekwall 443.

656. Rowlands 1987 40. There may also have been a Tuesday Market at Lapley: Parson ccxxxiv. Penkridge Market was discontinued by 1584 and not revived until 1617: VCH 5 129.

657. Eccl. Comm. 124088 LJRO.

658. Richard Blome, "Britannia", 1673 206. Also Pitt *op. cit.* 3; Rowlands 1987 187.

659. Manuscript note in Parke, Brewood Library copy: "The Market Cross . . . fell down in 1810 just as preparations were making for celebrating the majority of the late Mr Giffard." However, Mr T.W. Giffard came of age on 28th March 1811. VCH V 25 implies that there was a market cross and a market house. This is not supported by the evidence: Hicks Smith 1864 8 refers to ". . . the Market House (or the Cross, as it was called) . . ." It does not appear on Robins and Sherriff's map of 1808, which suggests that it may well have disappeared by that date.

660. Hicks Smith "1680 Brewood Map". In the Quarter Sessions records for Epiphany 1799 SRO is an order relating to the diversion of a footpath from Hockerhill to Market Place. A crude sketch plan suggests that the market cross may have filled the northern part of Market Place. This would explain the irregular shape of Market Place.

661. J. Roper, "Wolverhampton Town Constables' Accounts 1688-1750", 1966. As late as January 1814 a man convicted at Stafford Quarter Sessions of stealing a large cheese was sentenced to be publicly whipped at Wolverhampton: Mander 1960 154.

662. Wolverhampton market cross was built in 1532: Mander 1960 46.

663. An incomplete series of rolls of court leet and baron from 1338 to 1786 is held at SRO: VCH V 27.

664. Pitt *op. cit.* ccxxvii.

665. Hicks Smith 1864 8.

666. SHC 1935 287.

667. Wheaton Aston had two fair days: 20th April and 2nd November.

668. Wheaton Aston Wake was held on Trinity Sunday in June. Lapley Wake was held on

the first Sunday in May, and was known as the 'Falfillary' Wake, after the Snakes Head Fritillary flowers which grew in considerable quantities: VCH IV 144. [The flower still grows in Motty Meadow, which was made a National Nature Reserve in 1982 to protect it. This is the farthest north it grows in the British Isles.] Stretton Wake was fixed in 1761 at the Sunday after 8th September [VCH IV 164], with sports and games the following day, on the field adjoining the west side of the Bell Inn, ie. within Brewood parish. Codsall Wake was held on 6th May in 1821 and on the 5th-6th May in 1823. Bull baiting and bear baiting were among the entertainments: VCH XX 80.

669. Q/SR M1655 f9 SRO.

670. It is said that on one occasion a mild-looking bull from Stretton tossed one dog over the Fleur-de-Lis Inn, and another dog through a window of the same building: Wakefield 56.

671. VCH II 367. See also "Stafford Advertiser", 4th October 1834 and 30th September 1848. The contempt for those keeping bulldogs is shown by the Bilston Fund for Relief in the cholera epidemic of 1849, when those with bulldogs were excluded from benefits: 43 WSL. It is said that the Brewood bull was kept by Old Tom Lloyd, who lived at Hill Top and dressed both himself and the bull in ribbons before parading through the streets. It is recorded that on one occasion the ring and iron stake to which it was affixed were taken up by gypsies, but they were apprehended and the ring replaced.

672. "Stafford Advertiser", 9th October 1858. In the 1860's it was said of Black Country Wakes "forty years ago it was dangerous to pass through a town during the Wakes. The inhabitants who took active part in these sports were so infuriated with drink and excitement and their feelings were so hardened by scenes of torture, that they regarded neither the limb nor life of any who happened to offend them. There was no amusement provided either for young or old but the most vicious and degrading, and the Wakes seldom passed without some other blood than that of the bulls being spilt – the blood of comrades, and too frequently of wives and children who dared to remonstrate with a furious husband and father . . . Happily modern Wakes have been divested of nearly all the characteristics of the olden festivals. The only vestiges which distinguish them are the booths, clowns and drinking bouts; and these amusements are only indulged in by children and the lowest class population. Among the features recently introduced in connection with district Wakes may be enumerated out-door fêtes, flower shows, bazaars, and excursions . . . The cultivation of cottage window flowers, now happily so general throughout the same district, is another refining agency, which has helped in no small degree to root out the love for the grosser sports among the people . . . But, perhaps the most powerful agent improving the character of modern Wakes is the influence of popular excursions . . . [to] Enville, Hagley, Shugborough, and Teddesley . . . Nevertheless, the Wakes are still disgraced by sad scenes of intoxication and other excesses . . ." From John Timbs, "Nooks and Corners of English Life", Griffith and Farran 1867 pp.261-3, quoting a correspondent to the "Birmingham Daily Post".

673. "Wolverhampton Chronicle", 28th September 1864.

674. Hicks Smith 1866 9.

675. From a reference to Bowling Alley Piece in the Will of William Woolrich dated 1774. The land lay on the north-east side of Grange Farm: Tithe Map 1838. It is possible however that the name merely reflected the shape or flatness, rather than

the use, of the land. Another piece of land with the same name lying west of Standeford Mill and north of Coven is also marked on the Tithe Map. For the Bowling Green at Bell Field see D487 SRO. Moat Leasow and an L-shaped piece of water to the south-west of the house are shown on the same plan, and may indicate a former moat.

676. VCH I 367. See also "Stafford Advertiser", 4th October 1834.

677. Ekwall 243.

678. See "Stafford Advertiser", 30th September 1848; "The Wolverhampton Spirit of the Times", 26th September 1859 pp.264, 270.

679. VCH II 361. See also "The Wolverhampton Spirit of the Times", 26th March 1860.

680. "Stafford Advertiser", 30th April 1864.

681. *ibid.* 5th June 1871.

682. Parish Magazine, July 1911.

683. Thornton 82-3.

684. VCH VI 6.

685. SHC VII 236.

686. SHC X 121.

687. SHC XVII 188-91.

688. SHC 4th Series 8 84-6.

689. SHC NS 264-6.

690. SHC 1927 55-60.

691. Gregory King's Notebook, SHC 1919 240-2.

692. Who moved from Somerford to Stretton Hall in 1845.

693. Many taken from secondary sources [Parke; Wakefield] and unverified.

694. It is of interest that a sixth Penderel brother, Thomas, was once thought to have died fighting for the King at Donnington, 2 miles from Stow-on-the-Wold, on 22nd March 1645. It is unclear whether he actually fought at Donnington, but 8 years later he was living in Barbados. He married there in 1653, had a son in 1658 who died the following year, and died in 1659. It is possible that he knew Ponder and Build, who perhaps broke their journey at Brewood to bring news to his family and friends. See Kingston 1933 14. [Is the similarity between the name Ponder and Penderel mere coincidence?]

695. Jane Bursley's name appears several times in the accounts. She was buried in Codsall on 18th October 1705 by the vicar of Brewood.

696. In 1530 an Act was passed "Concerning Outlandish People calling themselves Egyptians . . . using no craft or merchandize, but deceiving people that they by Palmistry . . . can tell . . . fortunes and so cheat people of their money, and commit many heinous felonies and robberies". All such persons were banned from the realm within 16 days, or their goods would be forfeited. In 1554 another Act made it a felony [i.e. a capital offence] for "Egyptians" to remain in the realm after 20 days from proclamation of the Act, except for those "as shall leave that naughty, idle and ungodly life", and serve some honest householder, and in 1563 it was made a capital offence to consort with gypsies. The parish register of St Nicholas Church, Durham, records that in 1592 "Simson, Avington, Fetherstone, Fenwicke, and Lancaster, were

hanged for being Egyptians": J.S. Burn, "The History of Parish Registers in England", E.P. Publishing Limited 1976 193. The 1563 Act was not repealed until 1783 as a law of 'excessive severity'.

697. Night burial probably dated from Cromwellian times, when the Puritans made it an offence for Catholics to bury their dead during the day with their customary religious services. Some families are said to have continued the practice of night burial long after it ceased to be necessary: Hackwood 77. Donington parish register records the burial on 15th May 1623 of Thomas Harrington of Byshton "in the night by command of the Bishop". It is possible that his death was suicide.

698. This may have been St Winifred's Well near West Felton in Shropshire, which was noted for its curative properties, or St Winefride's Well at Holywell in Flintshire. In the last century there was a tombstone at Whiteladies which read: "Tobias chap. 12 v 7. Here lies Winefred White late of Wolverhampton, who was instantaneously cured of Hemiplegia by bathing in St Winifred's well, Flintshire. June 28 1815. Died of consumption, January 13, 1825, aged 45 years": manuscript addition to Parke 55, Brewood Library copy. See also Palmer 45-6.

699. Wolverhampton was commonly known as Hampton in early times.

700. A strike was a unit of dry measure, usually a bushel, but in some places half a bushel and in other places 2 or more bushels.

701. p.101.

702. Niven 13. Erdeswicke suggests that well dressing was also carried out at Wolverhampton and Lichfield in the eighteenth century. The practice is also said to have taken place at Blymhill and according to Hackwood [p.140] Codsall and Seawall [Showell].

703. Plot refers to ". . . that stinking water which crosses Watlingstreet Way, not far from Horsebrook . . ." [p.104].

704. In the corner of the courtyard of an Inn known as 'The Crow in the Wood', popularly known as The Brimstone Alehouse: Plot 102. The water from the well came bubbling up through a wooden pipe and left a yellowish dust on the grass: Palmer 37; Wakefield 48; "Black Country Bugle Annual", Mercia Publicity 1989 17-19. The site lies within the grounds of what is now Pendrell Hall. Ochre-coloured deposits around a land drain which discharges on the west bank of the stream between the Leper Well and the motorway are the result of iron in the water. An analysis of the water in 1992 revealed no trace of sulphur.

705. "16 March 1597 bapt. Joyce, d[aughter] of Richard Carrington (born at ye Lepre house)": Codsall parish register.

706. p.101.

707. Wakefield notebook 148/1/72 139 WSL.

708. "Stafford Advertiser", 7th January 1871.

709. The tree is mentioned in Edward Haynes' account of the parish perambulation in 1861. In good health, it was cut down in 1990.

710. Griffiths suggests [p.210] a connection with Lady Ysabel of Pattingham. No explanation is given.

711. VCH VI 48-9.

712. Parish Magazine, November 1902. Full details of the bells, including drawings of the

marks made before the bells were re-cast, appear in C. Lynam, "The Church Bells of the County of Stafford", [no publisher] 1889, copy in LJRO.

713. For details of nineteenth century nonconformist chapels in Brewood see SHC 4th series III.

714. Simpson died on 3rd October 1819 aged 82. A gravestone to Simpson and his wife on the east side of Brewood church relates that "This pious couple endured much for the cause of Christ being amongst the earliest friends of the gospel in this Town they were blessed in life and death and will be had [sic] in everlasting remembrance".

715. It has been suggested that there is a connection with Rogationtide beating of the bounds [Oakden 45], but no such events have been recorded.

716. Recorded on the Tithe Map 1838.

717. Hicks Smith 1867 34. The name does not appear on an estate map of 1704: D591/361 SRO.

718. Recorded on the Tithe Map 1838.

719. Quantities of clinker and cinders lie under the surface: an ironworking bloomery appears to have occupied the site.

720. Oakden 41. Wakefield also recorded: ". . . three innocent-looking cottages in the heart of Brewood should be called 'Hell Bank' . . . though one inhabitant tells me the cottages were near the old fair ground, and the place got its name from its noisy characters": "Express & Star", 29th November 1927. The location of the cottages is unknown.

721. Mary Wakefield, "Ancient Brewood", 1932 65. Similar ditties are said to have been recovered from Milwich and Dilhorne: Wakefield notebook 148/1/72 WSL.

722. Hooke 1983 83.

723. Sir Hugh de Weston, who died in 1305: Oakden 180-1.

724. Eccl. Comm. 124088 SJRO.

725. Hicks Smith 1867 43.

726. Hicks Smith suggests that the reference to the Royal Oak is an error for White Oak Lodge: 1867 44. This is not so: the Royal Oak was a beerhouse at what is now Acorn Cottage, opposite the Shire Stone. "The 'White Oak' tree, now standing, is by the farm house of that name . . . between Tong and Blackladies on the way to Brewood, it formerly used to be white-washed. The reason for this being to render it a more conspicuous signpost, marking the way through the forest by a bridle path to White Ladies Abbey; now the shortest cut to Albrighton Station": G.H. Boden, "The History of Tong Church, College & Castle", Whitehead Bros. (Wolverhampton) Ltd., c.1935 81.

727. "Wolverhampton Chronicle"; Hicks Smith 1874 72.

728. Gelling 1990 53. There is a reference to Stephani de Boschomele – Stephen of Boscobel – in Shropshire in 1256: Selden Society Vol. 96 1980 232. Dr Margaret Gelling has suggested in correspondence with the author that the name may be continental, and sees no reason to doubt the traditional story of the derivation of the place-name.

729. Fea 1908 51-2. Much interesting information about the early history of the Royal Oak is contained in Henry G. de Bunsen, "Boscobel", Simpkin and Marshall 1878.

730. "Silva; or Discourse on Forest Trees, etc", 1664.

731. Shropshire Archæological Society Transactions, August 1878 Vol i. The best available evidence is that the present tree was planted c.1691: see paper read to North Staffs. Field Club by Robert T. Collins on 21st November 1890.

732. See Granville Squires *supra* 166, 175.

733. Walter White, "All Around the Wrekin", Chapman & Hall 1860 13.

734. From its location it is not inconceivable that it originated as a tumulus: see "The Gentleman's Magazine", 1790 Part I 36-7.

735. D64115/Boscobel SRO; copy in Shropshire Record Office 4128/1. The mound is shown surmounted by several tall trees in a field called Mount Piece. See also "Gentleman's Magazine", 1790 Part I 37; VCH Shropshire Vol. I 1908 411; Transactions of Shropshire Archæological Society XLIX 1937-8 16.

736. Information from Mr K. Fellows *supra*.

737. "The Gentleman's Magazine", Vol. lx 1790 36. The official guide says the building was still standing in 1809.

738. Fea 1908 19. The timber-framed house in which Charles II took refuge was built in the later 16th century and is said to have been of 18 bays in 1587. Isaac Fuller's painting, commissioned by Charles II c.1670, suggests that it may have incorporated part of the prioress's lodgings if, as has been suggested, it stood west of the former cloister, a favoured position for such lodging: VCH Shropshire II 84. A seventeenth century painting by Robert Streater in the Royal Collection shows a walled garden south of the priory church with a doorway in the south wall and minor buildings along its west side. This may have been the outer court.

739. On the north side of the ruins, within the chancel of the chapel near the door.

740. This commemorates Joan [or Jane] Penderel, the wife of William Penderel, sometimes confused with Joan [or Jane] Penderel, mother of the Penderel brothers – see Fea 1904 94.

741. H.G. de Bunsen, in "Boscobel, An Account of The Royal Oak, Boscobel House and The Whiteladies", [Simkin & Marshall, 1878] states that the stone was broken by "Molly Streking, a servant at Meese Hill, in about 1807": p.52-3. It appears that the Rev. Dale, then rector of Albrighton, [or David Parkes, Roman Catholic priest of Brewood, who raised a subscription, c.1852 according to "The Gentleman's Magazine", 1853 504.] renewed the stone. The second stone was destroyed in about 1901, and replaced by Mr Daniel Jones of Kilsall Hall: letter in "Birmingham Daily Post", September 1903. From Bunsen is a note that the last burial at Whiteladies was of Mary Walker, aged 81, for 34 years housekeeper at Boscobel House to Miss Frances Evans. She died on 6th September 1865: p.46.

742. Robinson 62; Fea 1908 19-20, who also states that Whiteladies Farm was built c.1815 from materials salvaged from demolished cottages at Whiteladies.

743. Robinson 62.

744. By Isaac Fuller, now in the Banqueting Hall at Whitehall: see E. Croft Murray, "Isaac Fuller's Paintings of Charles II's Escape after the Battle of Worcester", Archæologia 103 1971, 199-212, Plate C. The paintings include the only known portraits of Colonel Carless, showing him to be of stocky build with plump face and light coloured wavy hair. The c.1753 map is D64115/Boscobel SRO, with a

copy in Shropshire Record Office: 4128/2. The mill was at SJ 82300740. No traces remain.

745. See particularly Oakden; Ekwall; Foxall; Gelling.

746. The Domesday reference mentioned in Oakden 36 is evidently an error, and relates to Aspley near Eccleshall: see Slade 42.

747. It has been suggested that the name means 'the valley or recess that runs in among steep hills' from the Old English 'cofa' meaning 'cave', 'cove' – Runcorn, Rumcofa in the Anglo-Saxon Chronicle 915, said to mean 'wide bay', shares the same root. [Ekwall 115, 126, 396; Oakden 37], but the local topography makes this seem unlikely. Intriguingly, Foxall states "another mysterious [field] name found on the Welsh border and mainly in Clun, is Covia, with its variants Croviats, Croviard, Covey and Coviath": p.11. It does not seem inconceivable that the name Coven may have derived from a lost Celtic word, but it is of interest that Cowley, in Gnosall, was recorded as Covelau in Domesday. The name is believed to mean 'Cufa's woodland glade': Ekwall 126-7; Oakden 156. Coven may derive from the same name. Gelling suggests that the name may refer to a now obscured feature of the river Penk [1984 215], perhaps "[place] at the coves", and it is of interest that aerial photographs show that the river may at one time have formed a wide loop to the east of its present course to the south of the present village. There were also several loops in the former course of Deepmore Brook to the north. For completeness it should be added that there was a British goddess Coventina, a water-spirit. Dr Margaret Gelling feels that there can be no link between this name and the place-name Coven.

748. The name is of a type known to philologists as a 'grimston-hybrid', ie a name in which Old English 'tun' is combined with an Old Norse personal name which is thought may represent the taking over of established English settlements by the victorious Danes of the great army of 865AD: Gelling 1988 232-4.

749. Ekwall 361. The name may be connected with the Mercian King – although it is probable that other Mercians bore the same name – and commemorate a particular and early phase of Saxon colonisation: Penda was campaigning c.628. The topography – a steep hill by a river crossing – might suggest that the later spelling Penford is particularly apposite, the Welsh word 'pen' meaning 'hill', but the earliest forms put the derivation beyond doubt.

750. Oakden 42.

751. Foxall 3; J. Field, "English Field Names", David & Charles 1972 203. The narrow strips of the open fields were arranged in furlongs, also called shots or shuts in the Staffordshire and Shropshire region [from Old English 'sceat'], but more commonly known as flatts in Brewood.

*"How these curiosities would be quite forgott, did
not such idle fellowes as I am putte them downe!"*
– John Aubrey, 1626-1695

Select bibliography

Diana Ashcroft, "Report on the Roman Villa at Engleton, near Brewood", Staffordshire Record Society, 1938.

Steven Bassett [edited by], "Origins of Anglo-Saxon Kingdoms", Leicester University Press, 1989.

Brewood Parish Magazine.

Brewood Parish Register, Vol 1, Staffordshire Parish Register Society, 1906.

Stephen Bayley, "The Buildings of Brewood", Brewood Civic Society, 1973.

A.M. Broadley, "The Royal Miracle," Stanley Paul & Co., 1912.

J. Byng, "The Torrington Diaries", Eyre & Spottiswood (Publisher) Ltd., 1936.

L.M. Cantor, "The Medieval Forests and Chases of Staffordshire," North Staffs Journal of Field Studies, Keele University, 8 1968.

A.H. Chatwin, "Bushbury Parish and People 1550-1950", 2nd edition, Metropolitan Borough of Wolverhampton, 1991.

J.L. & K. Cherry, "Historical Studies Relating Chiefly to Staffordshire", J.C. Mort Ltd., 1908.

"Collections for a History of Staffordshire" [otherwise Staffordshire Historical Collections], Staffordshire Record Society, various volumes.

A.F. Denholm, "The Impact of the Canal System on three Staffordshire Market Towns, 1760-1850", Midland History XIII 1988, 55-76.

P.J. Doyle, "The Giffards of Chillington: a Catholic landed family 1642-1861", unpublished M.A. thesis, W.S.L.

W.H. Duigan, "Notes on Staffordshire Place Names", Henry Froude, 1902.

Charles Dunkley, "Brewood Grammar School and The Old Grammar Schools", Staffordshire Courier, 1936.

Eilert Ekwall, "The Concise Oxford Dictionary of English Place Names," Oxford University Press, 4th edition, 1960.

W.D. Eynan-Williams, "The Priory Church of All Saints, Lapley", n d

Rev R.W. Eyton, "Antiquities of Shropshire", 1854.

Rev R.W. Eyton, "Domesday Studies: An Analysis and Digest of the Staffordshire Survey", Trubner & Co., 1881.

Allan Fea, "After Worcester Fight", John Lane, 1904.

Allan Fea, "The Flight of the King", 2nd ed., Methuen & Co., 1908.

H.D.G. Foxall, "Shropshire Field Names," Shropshire Archæological Society, 1980.

Pauline M. Frost, "The Growth and Localisation of Rural Industry in South Staffordshire 1560-1720", unpublished Ph.D. thesis, University of Birmingham, 1973.

Margaret Gelling, "Some thoughts on Staffordshire Place Names," North Staffs Journal of Field Studies 21 1981.

Margaret Gelling, "Place Names in The Landscape", J.M. Dent & Sons Ltd., 1984.

Margaret Gelling, "Signposts to the Past", 2nd edition J.M. Dent & Sons Ltd., 1988.

Margaret Gelling, "The Place Names of Shropshire", Part I, English Place-Name Society, 1990.

R. Glover, "Visitation of Staffordshire, 1583," Mitchell & Hughes, 1883.

J. Gould, "Romano-British Farming near Letocetum", Transactions of South Staffordshire Archæological and Historical Society, XII, 1971-1972.

M.W. Greenslade & L.M. Midgley, "A History of Brewood", Victoria History of the County of Stafford, 1959.

Greenslade & Stuart, "A History of Staffordshire", Phillimore, 2nd edition, 1984.

George Griffith, "The Free Schools and Endowments of Staffordshire, and their Fulfilment", Whittaker & Co., and Hill & Halden, 1860.

George Griffiths, "A History of Tong", [2nd ed., with additions], Simpkin, Marshall, Hamilton, Kent & Co. Ltd., 1894.

D.R. Guttery, "The Great Civil War", Cornish Brothers Ltd., 1950.

T. Habberley, "Excavation of Probable Roman Villa, Acton Trussell, Staffordshire", Tong Archæological Group, 1986.

F.W. Hackwood, "Staffordshire Customs, Superstitions and Folklore", E.P. Publishing Limited, 1974.

I.C. Hannah, "Medieval Timber Houses in Sedgley, Brewood, Walsall & Willenhall", Staffordshire Record Society, 1940.

Harrison, Harrod & Co's Directory of Staffordshire & Shropshire, Thomas Danks, 1861.

F.A. Hibbert, "Monasticism in Staffordshire", J. & C. Mort Ltd., 1909.

J. Hicks Smith, "Additions and Emendations to Notes and Collections relating to Brewood", W. Parke, 1864.

J. Hicks Smith, "Brewood: A Resumé Historical and Topographical," W. Parke, 1867.

J. Hicks Smith, "Brewood: A Resumé Historical and Topographical: Supplement," John Steen & Co., 1881.

Della Hooke, "The Landscape of Anglo-Saxon Staffordshire: The Charter Evidence," Keele University, 1983.

D. Hooke and T.R. Slater, "Anglo-Saxon Wolverhampton: The Town and its Monastery", Wolverhampton Borough Council, 1986.

J. Hughes [edited by], "The Boscobel Tracts", William Blackwood, 1831.

D.A. Johnson & D.G. Vaisey, "Staffordshire and the Great Rebellion," Staffordshire County Council, 1964.

Kelly's Directory of Staffordshire, various editions.

H.P. Kingston, "The Wanderings of Charles II in Staffordshire and Shropshire after Worcester Fight, September 3rd 1651", Cornish Brothers Ltd. 1933.

Samuel Lewis, "Topographical Dictionary of England", S. Lewis & Co, 1840.

G.P. Mander, "The Priory of the Black Ladies of Brewood, Co. Stafford", Staffordshire Record Society, 1940.

G.P. Mander, "The History of Wolverhampton", Wolverhampton Corporation, 1960.

"Mara" [M.E. Wakefield], "Brewood", [private printing], 1959.

Ivan D. Margery, "Roman Roads in Britain", Phoenix, 1957.

William Matthews [edited by], "Charles II's Escape from Worcester", G. Bell & Sons Ltd. 1967.

J.A. Morris, "White Ladies," Shropshire Archæological Society, no date, [c.1934].

W. Niven "Illustrations of Old Staffordshire Houses", Chiswick Press, 1882.

J.P. Oakden, "The Place Names of Staffordshire (Part I, Cuttlestone Hundred)", English Place-Name Society, 1984.

D.J. Oldfield, "Pennocrucium, Staffordshire", an article in "West Midlands Archæology", No 24, edited by M.O.H. Carver, Council for British Archæology Group 8, 1981.

Richard Ollard, "The Escape of Charles II", Hodder and Stoughton, 1966.

Arthur Oswald, "Country Life", February 1948.

D.M. Palliser, "The Staffordshire Landscape", Hodder and Stoughton, 1976.

D.M. Palliser, "Dearth and Disease in Staffordshire, 1540-1670", an essay from "Rural Change and Urban Growth, 1500-1800", edited by C.W. Chalkin & M.A. Hariden, 1974.

D.M. Palliser & A.C. Pinnock, "The Markets of Medieval Staffordshire," North Staffs Journal of Field Studies, II 1971.

F.P. Palmer, "Wanderings with a Pen and Pencil", Jeremiah How, 1846.

W. Parke, [but written by John Hay] "Notes and Collections relating to Brewood, with a Supplement", [private printing] second edition, 1860.

W. Parson and T. Bradshaw, "Staffordshire General & Commercial Directory", J. Leigh, 1818.

J.E.C. Peters, "The Development of Farm Buildings in Western Lowland Staffordshire up to 1800", Manchester University Press, 1969.

Pigot & Co's Directory of Staffordshire, 1829.

W. Pitt, "General View of the Agriculture of the County of Stafford", G. Nicol, 1796.

R. Plot, "The Natural History of Staffordshire", 1686.

Oliver Rackham, "The History of the Countryside", Dent, 1986.

A.L.F. Rivet & Colin Smith, "The Place Names of Roman Britain", B.T. Batsford Limited, 1981.

D.A. Robinson, "The Wandering Worfe", Waine Research Publications, 1980.

M.B. Rowlands, "Catholic Registers at Chillington", Staffordshire Parish Register Society, 1959.

M.B. Rowlands, "The West Midlands from A.D. 1000", Longman, 1987.

D.J. Simkin [edited by], "A Guide to some Staffordshire Churches", Staffordshire Historic Churches Trust, no date [c.1983].

G.F. Slade "The Staffordshire Domesday", reprinted by Staffordshire County Library, 1985.

Stebbing Shaw, "The History and Antiquities of Staffordshire", J. Nicholls and Son, 1798-1801, with unpublished revised proofs on Brewood parish, printed in facsimile by EP

Publishing Ltd., 1976.

J.K. St Joseph, "Roman Forts on Watling Street", Birmingham Archæological Society, 1953.

Christopher Taylor, "The Origins of Lichfield", Transactions of South Staffordshire Archæological and Historical Society, 1968-9.

D. Thompson, "A History of Brewood Grammar School, 1553-1953", 1953.

H. Thornton, "My Childhood," A.C. Thornton [private printing], 1988.

Transactions of Shropshire Archæological Society, Vol LIX.

J.R. Veall, "Old Houses in Wolverhampton and its Neighbourhood", 1889.

Philip M. Vine, "The Neolithic and Bronze Age Cultures of the Middle and Upper Trent Basin," British Archæological Reports Series 105 1982.

M.E. Wakefield, "Ancient Brewood", [private printing], 1932 and various later editions.

M.E. Wakefield, "Brewood", [private printing], 1968.

Graham Webster, "The Cornovii", Gerald Duckworth & Co. Ltd., 1975.

J.J. West, "Boscobel House", H.M.S.O., 1981.

White's History, Gazeteer & Directory of Staffordshire, 1834; 1851.

Adrienne Whitehouse, "Brewood and Penkridge in old photographs," Alan Sutton Publishing Ltd., 1988.

R.C. Wilkes, "The Story of Penkridge", Penkridge Parish Council, 1985.

G. Wrottesley, "Giffards from the Conquest to the Present Day", SHC 1902.

G. Wrottesley, "History of Wrottesley", Harrison & Sons, 1903.

G. Wrottesley, "Staffordshire During the Civil War", Transactions of the North Staffs. Field Club, Vol. XIV.

Index

410

412